Canada
at the
Millennium
A TransCultural Society

Charles J. Humber
Editor-in-Chief

Published in conjunction with the Multicultural History Society of Ontario
HEIRLOOM PUBLISHING INC.
Mississauga, Ontario, Canada

CANADA HEIRLOOM SERIES

Volume I	CANADA: From Sea Unto Sea
Volume II	CANADA's Native Peoples
Volume III	ALLEGIANCE: The Ontario Story
Volume IV	PATHFINDERS: Canadian Tributes
Volume V	WAYFARERS: Canadian Achievers
Volume VI	VISIONARIES: Canadian Triumphs
Volume VII	CANADA at the Millennium: A TransCultural Society

Heirloom Publishing Inc.
6509B Mississauga Road North
Mississauga ON L5N 1A6

Tel: (905) 821-1152
Fax: (905) 821-1158
E-mail: heirloompublish@sympatico.ca
Websites: Heirloom-pub.com
                 http://collections.ic.gc.ca/heirloom_series

Chairman	William Melbourne
Publisher/Editor-in-Chief	Charles J. Humber
Project Manager	Helen de Verteuil
Office Manager	Karyn Humber
Consultant/Staff Writer	Melbourne James
Production Consultant	Angela Dea Clark
Copy Editor	Christine Hebscher
Index	Gayle Humber

Cover Design	Hart Broudy
Book Design	Amstier Graphics: Peter Reitsma
Film	DPI Graphics Group Inc.
Printing	Batten Graphics
Binding	Beck Bindery

CANADA *at the Millennium: A TransCultural Society*
Printed and bound in Canada

Copyright 1998 by Heirloom Publishing Inc.
Published 2000 by Heirloom Publishing Inc.
All Rights Reserved

Canadian Cataloguing in Publication Data

Main entry under title:
CANADA *at the Millennium: A TransCultural Society*

(Canada heirloom series ; 7)
Includes bibliographical references and index.
ISBN 0-9694247-5-2

I. Canada–Population–Ethnic groups. 2. Canada–
Civilization–1945- I. Humber, Charles J. II. Series.

FC105.M8C325 2000   971'.004   C98-900519-4
F1035.A1C325 2000

This book was typeset in Goudy and printed on Mead Matte,
80lb text.

Contents

Preface

CANADA at the Millennium salutes and honours 50 ethnocultural groups who have journeyed to Canada, primarily this past century, from 50 political jurisdictions worldwide. Enhanced by images of nearly 500 personalities, this seventh volume of the ongoing CANADA Heirloom Series showcases the achievements of Canada's diverse peoples, how they have invigorated and energized Canada, both culturally and economically, and effectively built a progressive society.

Ethnic centres and cultural associations and various consulates and embassies, as well, were unselfishly instrumental in guiding the publisher to individuals from across Canada who now highlight this millennium production.

And although the goal of this publication was to focus on contemporary people, some individuals no longer with us are posthumously profiled because their contributions were too significant to overlook.

Since the majority of Canada's polyethnic population trace their roots to Europe, half the diverse groups celebrated in this publication are European in origin. The other half trace their cultural roots to the Near East and Asia, to South and Central America, and to the Caribbean as well as to Africa.

Co-venturer with Heirloom in this production is the Multicultural History Society of Ontario, a non-profit organization based on the campus of the University of Toronto. Led by Carl Thorpe, Associate Director, Dora Nipp, CEO, Carolyn Braunlich, Administrator, Lillian Petroff, Co-ordinator, Educational Programs, and Nick Harney, this 25-year-old organization, chaired by Dr. Milton Israel, provided Heirloom with 80 percent of the 50 editorials published in CANADA at the Millennium. And although Lillian Petroff's work constitutes the great percentage of the editorials, still others have contributed timely chapters, including Toronto librarian Diane Dragasevich, Historian Andrew Gregorovich, Susan Papp-Aykler, Görsev Pristine, Professors Milda Danys, Isabella Kaprielian-Churchill, Emmanuel Seko, D.McCormack Smyth and Carlos Teixeira.

Many kindred spirits have contributed their time voluntarily. These include Onnig Cavoukian, Richard Cumbo, John Chu, Mike Dang, the Hon. Bill Dickinson, Rifaat Fares, Rick Kollins, Laas Leivat, Professor Varpu Lindström, John Nazareth, Bruno Rubess, Fernando Sinn, Fr. Jonas Staškevičius, Dr. Chris Stefanovich, and Professor Suwanda Sugunasiri. Not to be forgotten are Zulema de Souza, Keder Hyppolite, Monica Crisan, Naseem Javed, V. Rev. Nicholas Boldireff, Professor Oiva Saarinin, Fareed Ismail, Jim and Dena Nicoloff, Dr.

Samuel Noh, Elémer Bogyay, Didi Kaneff, Guillermo Devoto, and photographer Struan Campbell-Smith for his picture of Nelson Mandela on page 376.

A list of Heirloom's corporate sponsors is found on page 333. Without their generous support, CANADA at the Millennium would not be! The timely contributions of Power Corporation of Canada, moreover, and the financial support of the Margaret Breckner Foundation and the Wappel, Shahinian, and Kololian families, have all contributed financially to making this "cultural ambassador" a reality. Others whose unselfish interests have helped make CANADA at the Millennium possible include Dr. Shayne Tracy and Fred D'Silva, Director, Canadian Race Relations Foundation, and Doug Hull and Nora Hockin of Industry Canada.

The publisher personally contacted most of the nearly 500 individuals whose biographical profiles visually enhance this publication. Their cooperation in supplying material and photographs has resulted in a very striking portfolio of Canadians at work. To my colleagues at Heirloom, including Helen de Verteuil, my right hand, Mel James, who, as a consultant, assisted me in soliciting illustrations and preparing captions, and Dea Clark, production consultant, I extend heartfelt thanks. To Peter Reitsma who has designed each of the seven volumes of CANADA at the Millennium, Heirloom extends gratitude and appreciation. To Gay, my wife, and Karyn, my youngest daughter, many thanks for putting up with me over the past 30 months. Your generous and great support has meant a lot. Every publisher, moreover, should have a business associate like Bill Melbourne whose careful guidance over the last 15 years has resulted in Heirloom's overall mandate to make a meaningful contribution to society. We only wish that Phyllis Melbourne was still with us to see the fruits of our endeavours. Heirloom also extends very warm and heartfelt thanks to President Vaira Vike-Freiberga, President of Latvia, the Hon. Sheila Copps and the Hon. John Manley for their respective introductions as published in CANADA at the Millennium. Their timely remarks have given much prestige to an ambitious visionary project. Lastly, Heirloom Publishing recognizes the Millennium Bureau of Canada for its endorsement of a publication that salutes and honours a remarkable country transcending nationalism and embracing transculturalism.

Charles J. Humber
Publisher/Editor-in-Chief

CANADA at the Millennium: A TransCultural Society

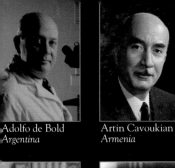
Adolfo de Bold
Argentina

Artin Cavoukian
Armenia

Josef Penninger
Austria

Andy Knight
Barbados

Anne Whitten
Belgium

Anna Maria de Sou[...]
Brazil

gnat Kaneff
Bulgaria

Amelia Jiménez
Chile

Lap-Chee Tsui
China

Joe Mavrinac
Croatia

Peter Newman
Czech Republic

Rifaat Fares
Egypt

Urjo Kareda
Estonia

Yemisrach Hailemeskel
Ethiopia

Peter Nygård
Finland

Margrit Eichler
Germany

Colin Saldanha
Goa

Eleni Bakopanos
Greece

Chandra Madramootoo
Guyana

Maryse Alcindor
Haiti

Emma Perlaky
Hungary

Anila Sitaram
India

"We are all immigrants to this land"

Lotfollah Shafai
Iran

Lino Saputo
Italy

Donovan Bailey
Jamaica

Juhn Wada
Japan

Hyung-sun Paik
Korea

Modris Eksteins
Latvia

Biruté Galdikas
Lithuania

Lillian Petroff
Macedonia

Valerie Buhagiar
Malta

Maria Abalos
Mexico

John de Visser
the Netherlands

Zia Chishti
Pakistan

Ma-Anne Dionisio
Philippines

Tamara Jaworska
Poland

Published by HEIRLOOM PUBLISHING INC.

In Conjunction with the Multicultural History Society of Ontario

Arlindo Vieira
Portugal

Monica Crisan
Romania

George Ignatieff
Russia

Nik Manojlovich
Serbia

George Gross
Slovak Republic

Lorraine Klaasen
South Africa

osé Evangelista

Michael Ondaatje

Eva Svensson

Wandee Young

June Marion James

Aysan Sev'er

Sylvia Olga Fedoruk

Kim Phuc

Foreword

wonderful family, and I was able to advance and excel in my profession. I am grateful for the numerous occasions I have had to serve Canada in various capacities during my long academic career. I am grateful to the colleagues in Canada who elected or appointed me to various positions of leadership. The skills I have learned while occupying these are now very useful in my new office.

In June 1999, when my native country, Latvia, entrusted me with the high office of President of the Republic, I was happy and proud at this opportunity to serve my native land. Nevertheless, it was with sadness that I fulfilled the precondition of renouncing my Canadian citizenship as a presidential candidate, for I had worked hard for that citizenship, and I valued it highly.

Canada is a vast and glorious land that will always remain in my heart for the beauty of its diverse and majestic landscapes, the warmth and humanity of its people, the justice and fairness of its social system and the equal opportunities that it offers to all. In Canada, a citizen can count on so many things that are only dreamt of in other countries. It is a wonderful land of opportunity where, with sufficient personal dedication and effort, each new citizen can realize his or her personal dreams.

To Canada's new citizens I can say: be proud of your newly adopted country. Respect Canadian institutions, because they respect you as a human being. Cherish what Canada offers, and remember how fortunate you are to live in such a civilized place. Give this country your work, your dedication, your love, and you will not be disappointed, but will reap great rewards. I wish you luck and success as persons and as citizens. May you find fulfillment in what you do, and may you contribute to the good of the society you live in.

A new Millennium is upon us. It will only be as good as we make it. Let us all work together to make it better than any century before!

FOR well over a century, Canada has been a land of opportunity for the hopeful, and a haven for the persecuted and the downtrodden. It has provided refuge for millions of people from all parts of the globe, including myself, and allowed them to build or rebuild their lives in a climate of peace, stability, freedom and affluence.

My parents fled Latvia as war refugees just before the Soviet invasion and occupation of Latvia in 1945. I grew up in refugee camps in Germany, went to school in French Morocco, and arrived in Toronto in 1954. My early years in Canada were extremely difficult ones. So difficult, in fact, that I would not wish them on anyone. At the age of 16, not speaking any English, I had to leave school and take a job as a bank teller, so as to help pay back the loan for our travel to Canada. I had to work my own way through university; I spent six years of my youth without taking any holidays. What sustained me throughout was the hope that, some day, my efforts would be rewarded, and I would have a better life. That is exactly what happened. I eventually had a very full and satisfying career, throughout which I was never held back by prejudice of any kind. I truly can testify to the fact that Canada is a land of equal opportunities for anyone who is willing to work hard.

I am grateful for this occasion to express my gratitude to the country I had adopted as my own for 45 years of my lifetime. In Canada, I was able to grow and develop freely as an individual, I was able to raise a

Viara Vike-Freiberga, Ph.D.
President, Republic of Latvia

Introduction

The Honourable Sheila Copps, P.C, M.P.
Minister of Canadian Heritage
Ministre du Patrimoine canadien

Canada has made its mark in history as a champion of peace and democracy. We owe our secure and prosperous place in the world in large measure to the energetic and hard-working peoples who have chosen to make Canada their home. Originating from countries the world over – from Argentina to Vietnam – they have brought a wealth of knowledge, talent, and skills that have been devoted to the building of our country.

CANADA at the Millennium: A TransCultural Society is a fitting tribute to our country and its people, poised to enter the new era with a confidence that is supported by our strong democratic foundation and that has been shaped by the values that have guided our journey to the new millennium. The 50 nations celebrated in this illustrious volume testify to the richness of our cultural diversity and our openness to the world.

As Minister of Canadian Heritage, I congratulate Heirloom Publishing and the Multicultural History Society of Ontario, for their commitment to our Canadian history and heritage. This issue of the Canada Heirloom Series adds enormously to our understanding of Canadian society and will be certain to stir our pride in our past and our hope for the future.

Le Canada est reconnu comme un ardent défenseur de la paix et de la démocratie. C'est en grânde partie grâce au dévouement et au travail d'hommes et de femmes qui ont fait du Canada leur terre d'accueil que nous vivons dans un lieu prospère et pacifique du monde. Originaires des quatre coins de la planète, de l'Argentine au Viêt-Nam, ces personnes ont mis leur talent, leurs connaissances et leur savoir-faire au service de la société et ont contribué à bâtir notre pays.

CANADA at the Millennium: A TransCultural Society est un hommage éloquent à notre pays et à notre population qui s'apprêtent à entrer dans le nouveau millénaire avec confiance, forts de la tradition et des valeurs démocratiques qui les ont guidés jusqu'ici. Les 50 peuples que célèbre cet ouvrage d'envergure sont des symboles de la richesse de notre diversité culturelle et de notre ouverture sur le monde.

À titre de ministre du Patrimoine canadien, je félicite la maison d'édition Heirloom Publishing et la Multicultural History Society of Ontario de leur engagement à l'égard de l'histoire et du patrimoine du Canada. Cet ouvrage des Canada Heirloom Series se veut un outil indispensable pour faciliter notre compréhension de la société canadienne. Il permettra sans aucun doute d'aviver la fierté que nous inspire la grandeur de notre passé et de raffermir notre espoir en un avenir meilleur.

Sheila Copps
Minister of Canadian Heritage/Ministre du Patrimoine canadien

Hungarian Canadians, dressed in the traditional costumes of their ancestors for Toronto's annual Caravan festivities, 1997, celebrate their cultural heritage on stage at the beautiful Árpád Room at the Hungarian Canadian Cultural Centre, Toronto. The backdrop to the stage is an impressive mural depicting eastern Europe's most famous river, the Danube, passing under Lánc Hid, the first bridge to span the Danube and the bridge linking the ancient cities of Buda and Pest, known today as Budapest, the capital of Hungary. [Photo, courtesy the Hungarian House]

from **Hungary**

The First Hungarians in North America

ONE of the first Hungarians to travel to North America was Stephen Parmenius, chief chronicler and historian for the expedition of Sir Humphrey Gilbert. Parmenius landed on the shores of Newfoundland in 1583. The young Hungarian humanist wrote one of the earliest accounts of the land that would become Canada.

Some three centuries later, in the 1880s, Hungarian immigration to Canada began in earnest. Pal Oscar Esterházy brought Hungarian immigrants from the coal-mining region of Pennsylvania in the United States to settle in what is now Saskatchewan. They lived in tents until family houses were built. Esterházy's dream was to establish a "New Hungary" on the Canadian prairies. Today the town of Esterhazy bears his name while such other Hungarian villages as Otthon, Békevár, Pinkefalva, Mátyásföld and Székelyföld have virtually faded into memory.

According to official statistical sources, in 1901 there were approximately 1,500 Hungarians in Canada; by 1914 their numbers had substantially increased to 15,000.

Although, at the turn of the century, Hungarian immigrants lived mostly in the Canadian countryside, it was shortly thereafter that Hungarian associations and churches were being established in many cities including Winnipeg (Manitoba), Sydney (Nova Scotia), and Niagara Falls, Welland, Hamilton, Windsor, and Brantford, in Ontario.

Early Hungarian Organizations and Associations

The majority of Hungarian immigrants who arrived in Canada during the interwar years left their homeland primarily because of economical and political upheaval. Many of them came from areas detached from Hungary after the First World War. They came from the county of Bácska-Bánát in Yugoslavia; from Transylvania in Romania; and from the southern part of the newly-created Czechoslovakia. The majority were skilled tradesmen, such as butchers, carpenters, shoemakers, and blacksmiths who found work in Ontario at such centres as Brantford, Kitchener, Oshawa, St. Catharines, Niagara Falls, and Port Colborne. At this time, Hamilton's steel mills and iron foundries attracted the largest Hungarian population in Canada.

Pal Esterházy founded a colony of Hungarians on the Canadian Prairies in 1896. His dream was to establish a "new Hungary" in Canada's far west. The town of Esterhazy, Saskatchewan, which bears his name today, is geographically located near the largest potash mine in the world. This view of Count Pal Esterházy was taken, circa, 1890. He died in New York City in 1912. [Photo, courtesy The Hungarian Canadian Cultural Centre]

Hungarians who arrived during the interwar period faced economic hardships, sometimes living in dire circumstances. It was the time of the Great Depression and unemployment was high. All unemployed immigrants were required to report to work camps established by the government. Those who didn't report to the camps were deported. Many Hungarians lived in such camps, working in lumber camps and road and railway construction for 20 cents a day, plus room and board. These harsh conditions only changed with the onset of World War II.

Immigration to Canada virtually ceased during World War II. From 1947, the flow of Hungarians to Canada regained momentum, the largest number arriving between 1948 and 1952 at which time 10,151 Hungarians were admitted. These immigrants had all left their homes during and after the Second World War. Following the war, many of them lived in isolated camps for years; for this reason they were called "Displaced Persons."

Located in the heart of Toronto where a majority of Hungarian-born Canadians reside is the beautiful Hungarian Canadian Cultural Centre. [Photo, courtesy the Hungarian House]

From letters in the Canadian National Archives, we learn that displaced persons in Europe following World War II were devastated and traumatized by the psychological effects of waiting, of not knowing when their "lives in limbo" would end. Prospective immigrants, as a result, were willing to accept any kind of work. There were instances of doctors volunteering for a year of gardening or farm labour in order to enter Canada. Many new immigrants were sponsored by Hungarian farmers who had earlier settled in Canada during the interwar years. After fulfilling the terms of the one- or two-year contract signed prior to immigration, they usually moved to larger urban centres, where in time, most succeeded in obtaining white collar work, albeit not always in their former professions.

Many Hungarian organizations were founded by the post-Second World War immigrants. These included the World Federation of Hungarian Veterans (W.F.H.V.) and the Royal Hungarian Gendarmerie Veterans' Benevolent Association, each trying to maintain the culture and traditions undermined in Hungary after 1945.

The Széchenyi Society, a Calgary-based group, was created to establish Hungarian credit courses. The Society, through the Hungarian Cultural Studies Appeal, in 1978, endowed a Chair of Hungarian Studies at the

University of Toronto. The first project of the Rákóczi Foundation was the publication of a Hungarian Heritage Handbook, an English-language reference text highlighting Hungarian history, geography, literature, art, and music. The Hungarian Helicon Society was founded in 1952 "to preserve, explain, and promote the thousand-year-old cultural and historical heritage of the Hungarian nation." The existing Hungarian Canadian community not only injected new blood but was rejuvenated by the substantial contributions of the post-war emigrants. The differences between this wave and the one to follow eleven years later, following the Revolution in 1956, are both striking and profound.

The 56ers

The Hungarian Revolution in October of 1956 caught the world by surprise. The reaction of Hungarian Canadians, as well as Canada's general public, was spontaneous and vigorous. With the establishment of the Hungarian Canadian Relief Fund in Toronto to administer the collection of money and creation of a blood bank, the public response was tremendous. By November 1, 1956, in order to attain nationwide support and increased efficiency, the Relief Fund was turned over to the Canadian Red Cross.

Landing as refugees in Montreal, Quebec, aboard a Maritime Central Airways DC-4, this November 1956 night view depicts some 70 Hungarians fleeing the revolution which had ravaged their European homeland in 1956. [Photo, courtesy Dwight E. Dolan/National Archives of Canada/PA 125700]

The Legion for Freedom was formed in response to hundreds of telegrams, phone calls and letters received by relief organizers requesting the formation of an international brigade to aid Hungary. Within two weeks, 3,000 individuals had indicated willingness to participate in such a brigade, half of these volunteers being non-Hungarians.

Early in November 1956, the Hungarian Revolution was crushed. Some 200,000 Hungarians fled their homeland following the Revolution. Canadian officials immediately began eliminating immigration red tape by giving priority to applications from Hungarian refugees. Medical requirements were minimized. Towards the end of November, the Canadian government elected to pay all costs in connection with the movement of Hungarian refugees to Canada. Immigrants no longer had to repay their passage.

Those fleeing the Revolution represented the brightest and best of Hungary's urban population. In total, approximately 37,000 Hungarian refugees were admitted to Canada following the 1956 Revolution.

Each province set up special programs to accommodate the refugees. Saskatchewan offered to accept 2,000 Hungarians. Two government ministers were named to coordinate the relief work in Manitoba. In Alberta, near-

Below: Gergely Pongratz, left, the living legend of the 1956 Hungarian Revolution, as the guest of Toronto's Hungarian House, visits Canada in 1998. Here, he greets, far right, Csaba Gaal, editor, Kanadai Magyarság, the largest Hungarian weekly newspaper in the western world, Elemer Bogyay, President, Hungarian Canadian Cultural Centre, Toronto, Mr. Karoly Borbas, Museum Curator of the W.F.H.V., and Mrs. Borbas. All fled the 1956 Hungarian Revolution and came to Canada as refugees. [Photo, courtesy the Hungarian House]

Right: Founded after the 1956 diaspora, and published in Toronto, the Kanadai Magyarság is, today, the largest Hungarian weekly in the western world. By the 1980s, it had absorbed several papers in the United States and had split into both Canadian and American editions.

ly 70 civic groups participated in resettlement programs. British Columbia offered accommodation and jobs to 1,000 Hungarian refugees. The University of British Columbia was first to offer haven to the 285 students and 29 professors from the Faculty of Forestry at the University of Sopron. Members of the faculty emigrated together and U.B.C. offered them university affiliation and facilities so that the Hungarian students could complete their studies without interruption.

Nearly 20,000 Hungarian refugees settled in Ontario. Ontario was a popular destination because all refugees were accepted – there were no requirements or recommendations. Moreover, Ontario provided a wide variety of opportunities and resettlement programs. The Ontario Federation of Agriculture conducted a province-wide appeal to provide homes for 700 refugees. The City of Timmins offered to accommodate the refugees from the Budapest Mining School, 27 professors and 177 students in all. The University of Toronto offered to take 250 engineering students and staff from the University of Sopron. Finally, the numerous Hungarian Canadian communities of Southern Ontario, where the immigrants found welcome and countrymen ready to

Left: Michael Poczo, entrepreneurial immigrant of the 1956 Hungarian Revolution, arrived in Canada with only a suitcase full of dreams and ambitions. During the next 43 years, with the hard work ethic typical of Hungarians, he built one of the most widely respected custom machine shops in North America, Poczo Manufacturing Company Limited, located in Brampton, Ontario. Poczo Manufacturing is a first rate, internationally respected customer centric company, with ongoing aggressive growth plans for the future. Always young at heart, Mike enjoyed working with the younger generation to encourage them to build their futures. He was a devoted family man whose second love was flying his own plane. Michael's life is representative of what immigrants can and do achieve upon their arrival in Canada. [Photo, courtesy Magyar Haz]

Right: Before immigrating to Canada from Budapest, Hungary, Emma Perlaky, had completed two graduate degrees, one in applied mathematics and another in computer science, from Eotvos Lorand Tudomanyegyetem. Emma settled north of Toronto and began working for IBM in 1982. Four years later, she co-founded The Integral Group Inc., a family-run business establishment specializing in Electronic Data Interchange (EDI). Today, The Integral Group is a much respected hi-tech company satisfying the needs of clients across Canada. [Photo, courtesy The Integral Group]

assist them, constituted another important incentive to settle in the province.

Many of these political refugees were single. Not surprisingly, St. Elizabeth of Hungary Roman Catholic Church and the First Hungarian Presbyterian Church, both in Toronto, were flooded with requests to perform marriages for newly arrived refugee couples. Mass refugee weddings took place, with as many as twelve couples getting married at once.

In 1966, the tenth anniversary of the Hungarian Revolution was commemorated by Hungarian communities across Canada and a monument was erected in Toronto. The Freedom Monument is in Wells Hill Park on the shores of Lake Ontario, renamed Budapest Park at the time of its dedication.

Undoubtedly, the great impact these newer Canadians had on the earlier established Hungarian Canadian communities was immense. Churches had to be modernized and enlarged to accommodate the increase in parishioners, and new congregations were formed. Hungarian community/cultural centres were rejuvenated. The Hungarian House of Toronto became the Hungarian Canadian Cultural Centre – the largest such cultural centre in the Hungarian diaspora. The *Krónika* (Chronicle), the official monthly of the centre, was a cultural magazine distributed in some 30 countries worldwide, until 1993. The János Halász Library, housed within the Centre, was named after the Hungarian-born medical doctor whose collection of some 24,000 books laid the foundation of this important library.

Universities in Hungary suffered great intellectual loss following the Hungarian Revolution of 1956. Many professors who fled their homeland came directly to Canada. The Forestry Faculty, University of Sopron, immigrated en masse to Canada. This view depicts Dean Dr. Kalman Roller, centre, and other refugee colleagues from Hungary, visiting the University of New Brunswick campus in January 1957, en route to Powell River, British Columbia, where a transitional school affiliated with the University of British Columbia had been established, enabling students and professors, alike, to learn English so that they could start life anew at the University of British Columbia campus in Vancouver the following September. Professor Kalman Roller received from the University of British Columbia an Honorary Doctorate of Science degree in June 1999. [Photo, courtesy Metro Toronto Reference Library]

In Canadian urban centres, Hungarian restaurants became famous for their splendid cooking and special dishes. In the field of medicine, Dr. Paul Rékai and Dr. John Rékai founded Central Hospital, the first multilingual hospital in Toronto. Dr. Hans Selye in Montreal pioneered the study of the effects of stress upon our health and well-being. Other Hungarian-Canadians who have become prominent in their fields of endeavour include Dora de Pedery-Hunt, well-known designer of Canadian medals and coins; Robert Lantos, founder of Alliance Communications Corporation; Andrew Sarlós, financial guru; Peter Munk, resource executive; and Anna Porter, writer and publisher of note, to name a few.

In 1867, Antal Wappel was elected to the Hungarian Regional Parliament in Sopron to help administer the newly established Austro-Hungarian Empire. In 1998, three generations and a half a world away, his great-grand-

In this view, Margaret Wappel is seen with the Order of Hungary Medal *presented to her in 1998 by Arpad Göncz, President of Hungary, in recognition of her great work in establishing and perpetuating Hungarian culture in Canada. She is flanked by her two sons, Robert D.J. Wappel (left), a well-known Toronto lawyer, and Thomas Wappel, M.P. (right), Member of Parliament for Scarborough SouthWest.* [Photo, courtesy Wappel family]

son, Thomas Wappel, was elected to the Canadian Parliament. He was the first person of Hungarian origin to be elected to that body and in his maiden speech, he spoke the first words of Hungarian ever officially recorded in Parliament in Canadian history. Tom's grandmother, Margaret Breckner (née Kadar), immigrated to Canada from her native Erdely in 1931. Her family settled in Montreal where Margaret, whose great passion was the theatre, immediately began producing and directing plays in the Hungarian language. The family moved to Toronto in 1935 where Margaret Breckner created an Hungarian theatre ensemble which performed extensively throughout Canada and the United States. Her daughter, Margaret Wappel, starred in many of these productions which showcased the rich tradition of the Hungarian theatre and its many famous operettas. The Wappel-Breckner family helped to found many of the Canadian-Hungarian cultural institutions that continue vitally today, such as the Hungarian-Canadian Cultural Centre, The Hungarian House of Montreal, The St. Elizabeth of Hungary Roman Catholic Parish and the Helicon Society. The Margaret Breckner Foundation was created by the family to continue to foster, develop, and advance Hungarian cultural expressions in Canada. To integrate successfully into Canadian society without losing touch with their cultural heritage is what is important to the Wappel family, indeed, to all Hungarians who immigrate to Canada.

It has now been more than 100 years since the first Hungarians settled on the Canadian prairies – a century of struggle and perseverance on the part of Hungarian immigrants. From the early beginnings on the harsh Canadian prairies, to the desperate conditions during the Depression, Hungarian immigrants fortuitously succeeded in establishing viable communities. Each wave of immigrants came with their own particular set of talents, cultural traditions and values, and through their hard work, they have collectively contributed significantly to the Canadian way of life. ♥

Susan Papp-Aykler

from **Chĭle**

CHILE is a unique and beautiful country in South America. Unfortunately, Chileans have been divided across deeply rooted political lines. Political polarization came to a crisis in 1969 as the country democratically elected a Marxist government led by Salvador Allende, and furthermore with the military coup that overthrew the Allende regime in 1973. A group of generals led by Augusto Pinochet took the government in 1973 and was in power until 1990. These two major events triggered the immigration of Chileans into Canada.

The first group of Chileans left their country during the Allende regime due to the socialistic policies being implemented, methodical loss of private property and ultimately the economic chaos that followed. Those first settlers left Chile on their own, unable to claim refugee status because the crimes they suffered during the Marxist government were never reported by the media.

The second, much larger group, came to Canada after the coup. While many Chileans were forced by the military to leave their country, others left of their free will because they felt far from safe under the imposition of military rule. Arrests, disappearances and political repression marked a new reign of terror as the regime of the military junta was unwilling to tolerate any political opposition or to forgive those that had either participated in paramilitary operations or worked with the ousted Allende government.

Reacting to human rights abuses in Chile, several countries opened their borders to fleeing Chileans. Many political refugees went to neighboring Latin American countries, and also made their way to Cuba, to Eastern European countries and to Soviet bloc member states. Initially, desperate Chilean refugees came to Canada in two small groups that had sought political asylum in the Canadian embassy in Santiago; they were the first victims of the military war on communism. Responding to a vocal lobby led by Canadian church groups and many non-governmental organizations, Ottawa implemented a special immigration program for the significant number of Chileans who faced humanitarian abuses. This program would later help to recognize refugees as a distinct class of immigrants entitled to Canadian asylum in a new Immigration Act that came into effect in 1978. In the end, almost 7,000 Chileans finally made their way into Canada.

[Right] Chilean-born Dr. Pablo Sanhueza and his family came to Canada in the late 1970s. Graduating in Psychiatry from the University of Toronto in 1984, Dr. Sanhueza now works in various hospitals caring for immigrants and helping them to adapt to their new country. His knowledge of Spanish, Italian, Portuguese, French, and German has made this newer Canadian a valuable asset to all immigrants choosing Canada as their new homeland.
[Photo, courtesy Dr. Pablo Sanhueza-Luco]

OPPOSITE: Osvaldo Nuñez was born in Curico, Chile, in 1938. He obtained a law degree from the University of Chile, Santiago, in 1964, and received a Master's Degree in Industrial Relations from the Catholic University of Louvain, Belgium, in 1969. In the early 1970s, he was Executive Director of the Labour Education Institute, a department of the Minister of Labour under the Chilean government of Salvador Allende. Mr. Nuñez fled his native land, arriving in Montreal in 1974 with his wife and two sons. Before being elected to the Federal Parliament of Canada for the Bourassa Riding (Montreal North) as a candidate of the Bloc Québéçois party, Mr. Nuñez was a well-known member of various Quebec Labour unions for nearly 20 years. This view of Mr. Nuñez was taken in the House of Commons in March 1997 when he was the Official Opposition Critic for Citizenship and Immigration. A hard worker for immigrant and refugees rights, Mr. Nuñez has made a significant contribution to Canada and Quebec in the field of international cooperation. [Photo, courtesy Osvaldo Nuñez]

[Left] Claudio and Marcela Durán arrived in Montreal on October 7, 1973. They were from Santiago and were among the first group of refugees to flee their homeland. Four days later, they arrived in Toronto with their daughter Francisca, age six, and son, Andrés, age one. Claudio has been a Professor of Philosophy at Toronto's York University since 1974, receiving in 1993 the "Canadian Professor of the Year" award by the Council for the Advancement and Support of Education. Marcela, who completed an M.A. in History and Philosophy at the Ontario Institute for Studies in Education in 1975, is today an Equity Consultant for the Toronto District School Board. [Photo, courtesy Claudio Durán]

[Right] Victor Saldivia, was born in Valdivia, Chile, and Juan San Martin was born in Santiago. Victor, viewed here, back row, middle, and Juan, far right, back row, are the co-founders of Grupo Taller. Formed in Toronto, Ontario, in 1978, this band's music is Latin American in origin offering a variety of fused rhythms from the Afro-Cuban tradition and native sounds from the Andes. Taller uses a variety of instruments, including guitar, Colombian tiple, and Venezuelan cuatro, incorporating a wide variety of the folklore roots of South America. The band participates in a wide cross-section of internationally sponsored cultural events, especially within the Latin American communities of both Canada and the United States, all in an effort to maintain their cultural heritage and introduce it within the Canadian context. [Photo, courtesy Rodrigo Moreno]

After General Pinochet relinquished power to a new democratically elected government in 1990, three subsequent democratic governments have been formed by a coalition of centre-left parties including Christian Democrats and Socialists. Since the eighties Chile has reached a leading economic position in South America. With GDP per capita at US$ 5,000, the Chilean economy has generated more than twice the wealth that existed in the early seventies.

[Left] Fernando Sinn, born in Santiago, obtained an industrial-mechanical engineering degree at the Catholic University of Chile. Fernando and his wife Cecilia left Chile with their first-born daughter in 1971. Fernando, who followed a manufacturing management career in the appliance business, and then with a Toronto-based engineering company, developed automotive operations in South America, is currently an international marketing executive with Magna International Inc. Viewed in this 1998 photo Fernando and Cecilia are proud Canadians whose three children are all graduates of the University of Western Ontario. [Photo, courtesy Magna International]

[Right] Shortly after the conclusion of World War II, when he was eight years old, Adam Policzer left Hungary, his place of birth, and immigrated with his family to Chile. Graduating in architecture from the University of Chile, Santiago, in 1964, Adam was employed to work for the Ministry of Housing during the Allende regime. In 1975, he arrived in British Columbia with his wife and three young children. Obtaining membership in the Architectural Institute of B.C., he formed a partnership with another Chilean exile, Julio Gomberoff, and launched into developing social housing projects, his firm winning many awards for design and heritage. He is viewed here, left, in 1998, with former British Columbia Premier, Glen Clark, at the new site of an apartment building for the Lions Paraplegic Lodge Society, East Vancouver. [Photo, courtesy Adam Policzer]

From 1980, Chileans have continued to immigrate to Canada, even though some have in fact returned to their country to rebuild their lives in their homeland. Many have emigrated because of severe economic adjustment that has resulted from the return of the companies previously confiscated from a massive free market transformation of the Chilean economy and the privatization of most public services. These are the new economic immigrants in search of good employment opportunities and a better future for their families. According to the 1996 census data, a total of 33,835 Canadians claim Chilean ancestry. The same census indicates that a total of 11690 Chilean immigrants reside in Quebec; 10875 in Ontario; 5315 and 3860, respectively in Alberta and British Columbia.

Chilean settlers have moved between Ontario and the West depending on economic conditions. A booming western economy attracted many to Alberta and Manitoba in the seventies whereas, in the late eighties economic opportunity in Ontario and British Columbia made these provinces favorite targets of Chilean migration. The urban and industrial centres of Canada have attracted most of the immigrants: Chileans are concentrated in Montreal, Toronto, Calgary, Edmonton and Vancouver.

Many immigrants who came from the middle and upper class have high levels of skills and education. Chileans in the field of the natural sciences, engineering, teaching, and health care have had their Chilean professional degrees and work experience accepted, or have returned to university to obtain new degrees and secure jobs in their areas of expertise. Many have made contributions in the engineering, manufacturing, construction and transportation sectors, as well as in health care, arts and sports. Others have successfully entered the clerical and service related sectors in Canada. They have successfully established their families and focused on rebuilding their lives as Canadians, leaving their past behind.

Born in Talcahuano, a fishing port in Southern Chile, Hernán Humaña attended the University of Chile in Santiago where he earned a degree in Physical Education and was an honoured volleyball player with the Chilean national team. Coming to Canada in 1973, Hernán began coaching volleyball and eventually earned his Master's Degree at York University, Toronto. Voted the best volleyball player in Chile prior to his coming to Canada, this celebrated York University coach was voted Ontario University Association Coach of the Year, 1997, '98, '99, and was Canada's coach of the Men's Indoor Volleyball Team at the 1992 Barcelona Olympics, and was coach, as viewed here, right, of the Men's Beach Volleyball Team which won a Bronze Medal at the Atlanta Olympics in 1996. [Photo, courtesy Hernán Humaña]

Emerging Chilean entrepreneurs have opened their own businesses and stores, created consulting firms, and published a number of Spanish language magazines and newspapers. Chileans also have made important contributions to the Canadian Hispanic community at large. Canadians of Chilean origin have created a variety of organizations for women, politics and culture as well as finance and social welfare. Like most refugees, Chileans began working towards the welfare of their homeland. In the seventies some sent money and food to help support their relatives. Later, many worked for the democratization of Chile until the end of the military regime in the late eighties.

The community also has an increasing involvement and commitment to life in Canada. Members of the group are active at different levels in the political process. Over the last few years there have been political candidates of Chilean origin in national, provincial and municipal elections. Most notably, Osvaldo Nunez of the Bloc Quebecois was elected to the House of Commons in 1993. ✠

Amelia Jiménez immigrated to Canada from Chile in 1977 after completing her studies in printmaking at the Catholic University of Chile. She quickly learned English, enrolling at the Ontario College of Art in 1980. By 1982, she was studying at Studio Camnitzer, near Luca, Italy. Invited to Bogota, Colombia, in 1984, Amelia was part of an international team of artists paying homage to Chilean poet and Nobel Prize winner, Pablo Neruda. Today, this multi-media expressionist, as viewed here, whose acclaimed works have been exhibited in Chile, Canada, Germany, Ecuador, Mexico, Colombia, and Puerto Rico, is an education officer with the Art Gallery of Ontario and works with young people to encourage their creative expression.
[Photo, courtesy Amelia Jiménez]

Adrift for five days on the South China Sea in a Vietnamese refugee boat in 1980, Ninh Văn Vu and his six-year-old son Quôc Thuân and 211 other Vietnamese boat people were rescued by a West German merchant ship, Cap Anamur, and taken to a refugee camp at Singapore where they stayed for nearly five months before immigrating to Canada as refugees. Eighteen years later, Canadian Quôc Thuân, as viewed here, graduated from the University of Waterloo in Electrical Engineering in the presence of his proud family. [Photo, courtesy John D. Chu via Ninh Vu]

VIETNAMESE IMMIGRATION to Canada began after the Second World War. Then, between 1950 and 1975, a small number of students enrolled at the University of Toronto while others, drawing upon a French colonial past and secondary language skills, entered a number of francophone universities in Quebec, Ottawa, and Moncton, New Brunswick.

Many of these students soon found themselves making the psychological shift from migrant to immigrant: they no longer worked towards a return home but accepted a commitment to life in Canada. The early settlers answered the human resource demands and staffing requirements of Canadian postsecondary institutions, business, and industry as professors, scientists, engineers, and administrators, and so set the stage for growth of the immigrant community.

from Vietnam

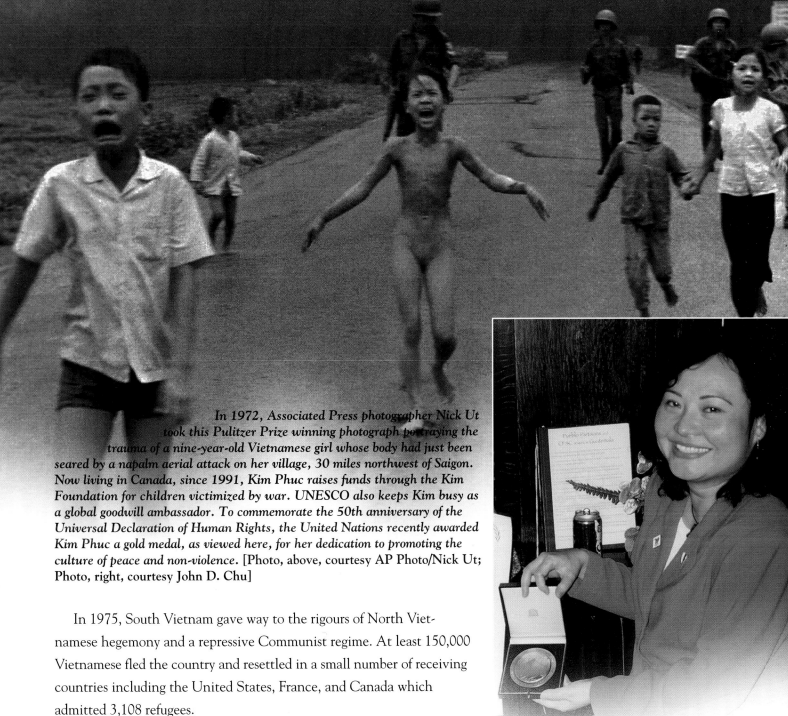

In 1972, Associated Press photographer Nick Ut took this Pulitzer Prize winning photograph portraying the trauma of a nine-year-old Vietnamese girl whose body had just been seared by a napalm aerial attack on her village, 30 miles northwest of Saigon. Now living in Canada, since 1991, Kim Phuc raises funds through the Kim Foundation for children victimized by war. UNESCO also keeps Kim busy as a global goodwill ambassador. To commemorate the 50th anniversary of the Universal Declaration of Human Rights, the United Nations recently awarded Kim Phuc a gold medal, as viewed here, for her dedication to promoting the culture of peace and non-violence. [Photo, above, courtesy AP Photo/Nick Ut; Photo, right, courtesy John D. Chu]

In 1975, South Vietnam gave way to the rigours of North Vietnamese hegemony and a repressive Communist regime. At least 150,000 Vietnamese fled the country and resettled in a small number of receiving countries including the United States, France, and Canada which admitted 3,108 refugees.

Between 1978 and 1981, several hundred thousand Vietnamese of all origins escaped from their homeland by boat in a desperate search for freedom and safety. In response, thousands of individual Canadians took immediate steps to create a chain of support for the "boat people." Banding together in small groups, they applied under refugee sponsorship provisions of the new Immigration Act to bring refugees to Canada.

By the end of 1980, the Government of Canada had joined with church groups and private refugee sponsorship programs to admit over 60,000 Vietnamese, Cambodians, Laotians, and ethnic Chinese – most likely the highest per capita resettlement effort of any receiving country. Vietnamese immigration to Canada continues today and consists of refugees sponsored by relatives and family members, private groups, and government.

The 1996 Canadian census records that 136,810 people declared themselves to be of Vietnamese ethnic origin (single and multiple responses). Newcomers gravitated to Canada's major city centres including Toronto, Montreal, Vancouver, Calgary, Edmonton, Ottawa, and Winnipeg. There are also lesser concentrations of Vietnamese in Quebec City, Regina, Halifax, Sherbrooke, Lethbridge, London and Windsor.

Thanh Lê grew up in Da Nang, the first city in Vietnam where American forces landed in 1965. A navy recruit, Thanh Lê escaped by himself from Da Nang, drifting in a boat in the South China Sea to the Hainan Island, thence to Hong Kong where he stayed in a refugee camp for nearly 18 months. In 1979, he arrived in Canada as a refugee. Now married to a Vietnamese-born refugee and living in Canada, Thanh Lê is a mould maker in Rexdale, Ontario, where he works for Glendan Mould Inc. [Photo, courtesy Charles J. Humber]

Born in the north Vietnam village of Bach Sam, John Do Trong Chu studied Law at Indochinese University in Hanoi, then International Relations in the United States at both the University of Minnesota and Georgetown University before returning to Vietnam in 1954 to enter government services. Having served his government with diplomatic postings in India, Indonesia, Cambodia, Australia, and Thailand, John Chu (with his wife Thérèse Trân Thi Mâu, formerly a member of the first Vietnamese Parliament), in 1975, was on a leave of absence from government services for three months when Saigon fell to Viet Cong communist forces. They are seen, in this view, standing in front of a painting in their Toronto home depicting one of Vietnam's national landmarks, located in Gia-Dinh Province, called Lăng Ông, a shrine commemorating Marshall Lê Văn Duyêt, a famous general of the first Nguyen Emperor. [Photo, courtesy Charles J. Humber]

Vietnamese Canadians can be found in all sectors of the economy including agriculture. Most of the early immigrants and refugees who came before 1979 found a variety of professional, managerial, or other skilled jobs. The new arrivals created economic opportunity for themselves and other Canadians by establishing a variety of immigrant enterprises. Vietnamese restaurants specializing in Cha-gio (Imperial egg rolls) and Pho (beef noodle soup), grocery stores, dressmaking ventures, and food processing companies have helped to increase the volume and variety of foodstuffs and cuisine in Canadian cities and towns. Additionally, there are Vietnamese Canadian hairdressers, herbalists, and acupuncture specialists. Also, Vietnamese-owned franchises of popular milk and convenience stores dot the urban retail landscape.

The Vietnamese in Canada undertook the daunting task of creating a comprehensive group support system and voluntary social and cultural institutions. University student and mutual aid societies, professional, religious, political and human rights organizations nurtured a national culture and community-in-exile. After 1978, new types of organizations were formed for women, senior citizens, children, traditional and popular music groups,

In the early 1980s, Dr. Lê Ba Tôn Nu and her husband Châu Võ co-founded the Hong Lac Music and Dance Ensemble in Ontario to perpetuate the legacy of traditional Vietnamese music. One of the two central instruments of music in Vietnam is the Dan Tranh or 16-string sitar as viewed here played by Anne Châu-Phô Võ. This amateur group has performed throughout Ontario and Quebec, the French Pyrénées, Belgium, as well as Washington, D.C. [Photo, courtesy John D. Chu]

athletic clubs, and literary societies. Vietnamese journals, magazines, newspapers, radio and television programs came into existence and flourished.

The celebration of Têt, the lunar New Year, in late January or early February, centres around the ritual worship of ancestors and war dead. Têt celebrations include firecrackers – to ward off evil spirits – the distribution of little gifts of money to children, and performances of dance, song, poetry, humourous or satirical skits. The ritual, cultural, and political components of this celebration serve to make Canadians of all ethnic backgrounds more aware of the vibrant presence of the Vietnamese-Canadian community.

A number of religious institutions also shape Vietnamese group life in Canada. Buddhism and Christianity are the two major religions of the community. Buddhists, in fact, practise tam giáo (the Three Teachings), a blend of Taoism, Confucianism, and Buddhism. Vietnamese-Canadian Buddhist temples are the centres for much of the community's ceremonial and cultural life. More than just providing weekly prayer gatherings, wedding celebrations, and funeral rites, the temples also organize religious retreats, Sunday school and heritage-language classes for children, and a wide range of social gatherings.

Catholic and Protestant Christian members of the community, in turn, are ably served by Vietnamese or Vietnamese-speaking clergy and nuns.

The Vietnamese-Canadian community accepted challenge and hardship as the consequence of the acts of flight and migration but assumed that prosperity and safety for its children could also be a consequence of those acts. The community has succeeded in proving that its arrival in Canada has made good sense for all Canadians. ☺

On the sixth day of the second lunar month of each year (March in the Roman calendar), Vietnamese worldwide commemorate the Two Trung Sisters who liberated Vietnam from Chinese domination in 40 A.D. This national holiday, sometimes referred to as "Women's Day," is celebrated yearly in lavish ceremonies similar to this one held in Toronto in 1999. [Photo, courtesy John D. Chu]

from **Armenia**

The photographic eye of Onnig Cavoukian captures a precious moment in the life of his Armenian-born grandmother. A devout Christian her entire life, Mayreni Cavoukian sojourned in Jerusalem, Cyprus, and Egypt before permanently settling in Canada in 1958. [Photo, courtesy Cavouk Portraits]

CANADA'S ARMENIAN population has immigrated from many parts of the world. In the 1890s, a handful of Armenian merchant families from Constantinople (Istanbul) and a pioneer group of factory recruits came to Canada from the Ottoman Empire, primarily from Keghi and other districts in eastern Turkey. By 1915 approximately 2,000 Armenians had settled in Canada, essentially in southern Ontario. Small groups of Armenians also settled in Montreal. Migrants from the Caucasus region of the Russian empire also established temporary staging areas in the prairie provinces before moving on to California.

Classification of the Armenians as Asiatics by the Canadian government in 1909 served to slow the pace of the group's arrival for the next five decades. From 1919 until World War II, Canada admitted only about 1,500, all survivors of the genocide of 1915-1923 that saw 1.5 million Armenians fall prey to massacre, disease, starvation, and exposure.

Among these 1,500 newcomers were 109 unaccompanied young boys, brought in by the Armenian Relief Association of Canada, who settled at Georgetown, Ontario. Called the " Georgetown Boys," they eventually were dispersed as farm labourers in southwestern Ontario.

After major changes were made to Canada's immigration programs during the 1960s, thousands of Armenians entered the country. Admitted under the manufacturing, mechanical, professional, or clerical immigration classifications, they came largely from Turkey, Egypt, Syria, Lebanon, and Iran, and a smaller number from Europe. Most recently, Armenians have been emigrating to Canada from the former Soviet Union.

The 1996 Canadian census records the presence of 37,500 Armenians in Canada, the sum total of individuals making single-or multiple-group responses. Community spokespersons and scholars argue that this group has not been properly enumerated and believe there are actually 50,000-70,000 Armenians in Canada since landed immigrants are traditionally recorded in Canada by former citizenship and *not* by nationality or historic roots.

Before 1914, Armenians were recruited to come to Canada as unskilled labourers in the expanding foundries and growing industrial base of southern Ontario. From the first decade of the twentieth century until the 1940s, Brantford, Galt, Guelph, Hamilton, and St. Catharines in Ontario were the largest and most active Armenian communities in Canada.

Cairo-born, Canadian-raised, and of Armenian descent, Atom Egoyan is one of the most celebrated contemporary filmmakers on the international scene today. His works have received both critical acclaim and commercial success around the world. Saluted and honoured at Cannes, Berlin, Moscow, Paris, London, New York, Taipei, Budapest, Greece, Switzerland, Sweden, and the United States as an immensely talented filmmaker, Atom Egoyan, viewed left on set with actor Ian Holm, galvanized international stature as a film artist when The Sweet Hereafter *(1997) became the most-honoured film of the 1997 Cannes Film Festival, winning the Grand Prize of the Jury, and was nominated the same year for a double Academy Award for both Best Director and Best Adapted Screenplay. In 1999, Mr. Egoyan was made an Officer of the Order of Canada and Brock University awarded him an honorary Doctor of Letters degree.* [Photo, courtesy Johnnie Eisen]

It is only in the last forty years that Toronto and Montreal have developed into major centres of Armenian settlement. Initially, Toronto was home to a small coterie of successful rug merchant families who lived in the city's affluent north end, some factory hands in the West Toronto Junction, and a growing number of refugees and nascent entrepreneurs in downtown and eastern Toronto. After World War II, newly arrived Armenians settled throughout the metropolitan area, establishing new and interesting community neighbourhoods in North York and Scarborough. They also fanned out to the satellite cities of Markham, Mississauga, and Thornhill.

Park Avenue was the early place of residence and commercial centre for the Armenians of Montreal. After 1960, members of the community made their way northward and began to inhabit Ville Saint-Laurent and Nouveau Bordeaux. By the late 1980s, Armenians had settled in new districts in the greater Montreal area including Cartierville and Laval, and along the Park Avenue Extension.

Today the Province of Quebec vies with Ontario as the province with the largest Armenian presence in Canada. Metropolitan Montreal ranks with Toronto as the two largest Armenian settlements.

The early Armenian settlers in southern Ontario helped to ensure its industrial takeoff. They performed the heavy, dangerous, and noxious work in the iron foundries. Armenians worked as shake-out men, stokers, core-makers, pattern makers, and moulders at General Motors in St. Catharines, at International Harvester in Hamilton, or at the Brantford foundries of Pratt and Letchworth, Massey-Harris, Cockshutt Plow, Buck Stove, Waterous Engine Works, and Verity Plow. During the interwar years, Armenians also obtained work at the foundries in Galt and Guelph, Ontario.

Born in Istanbul, Republic of Turkey, to Armenian parents who settled in British Columbia in 1979, Aline Kutan has studied music at both the University of British Columbia, where she majored in Opera at the Faculty of Music, and at Université Laval in Québec City where she studied under Louise André. After winning, in 1995, the New York Metropolitan Opera National Council Auditions, she made an impressive U.S. debut in October 1996 with the Arizona Opera, singing, as viewed here, the title role in Lakmé. A coloratura soprano, Ms. Kutan has been heard at New York's Lincoln Centre as Sylvie in Gounod's La Colombe. She has toured both Spain and France and has sung in over 600 performances of Andrew Lloyd Webber's The Phantom of the Opera while touring Canada. Today she lives in Montreal where she performs, among others, with the Montreal Symphony Orchestra. The winner of many awards, Aline Kutan, whose "shining new voice" is as well known abroad as it is in Canada, has a bright international future. [Photo, courtesy Arizona Opera]

Born in Nice, France, 1943, some 28 years after his parents had escaped Ottoman oppression, Gerard Paraghamian immigrated with his Armenian family to Canada in 1955. Graduating from the Ontario College of Art, 1967, this future mixed-media artist was a successful art director in advertising until the mid-1980s when he decided to paint full time. Official artist of Toronto's SkyDome, as well as Expo 86, Gerard Paraghamian is viewed in this scene, extreme left, October 1993, with future Prime Minister Jean Chrétien and Syrian-born Sarkis Assadourian, who, in 1993, became the first Armenian-Canadian to be elected to the House of Commons, representing the riding of Don Valley North. Re-elected in 1997, Mr. Assadourian, formerly Executive Director of the Armenian Community Centre, North York, now represents Brampton Centre in Ottawa. [Photo, courtesy Gerard Paraghamian]

Many soon found an opportunity to take up a trade or operate their own business. They chose to enter barbering, tailoring, shoe repairing or farming, or to run boardinghouses or coffeehouses. Armenians also established restaurants, hairdressing salons, ice-cream parlours, grocery stores, and confectionery shops.

The immigrant community's early entrepreneurial focus was the oriental carpet industry. Families such as the Courians, Babayans, Alexanians, Ounjians, Pasdermajians, Bedoukians, and Adourians imported and sold rugs. Others washed or repaired rugs. Many eventually used the community's dominant position and high standing in the carpet industry as a springboard into the rug merchant ranks.

In the early years, many Armenian refugee women worked in domestic service, often under contract for a two-year period. Armenian women later joined the industrial workforce during World War II, finding employment in canneries, textile mills, and tailoring establishments. Their children, in turn, during the 1950s and 1960s undertook a variety of commercial activities or entered the professions of medicine, nursing, and teaching.

The well-educated and highly skilled post-1950 immigrant arrivals expanded the world of Armenian enterprise, establishing auto sales and service, jewellery and watchmaking, printing, and photography businesses, food service and catering-related enterprises, as well as leather goods and precision tool manufacturing companies. They also entered the professional fields of pharmacy, law, accounting, and computer technology.

The Armenian pioneers, and more especially their children, have made a number of distinguished contributions to Canadian society. Prominent Armenian Canadians in the fields of science and education include physicist Armen Manoogian; Ara Mooradian, formerly senior vice-president of Atomic Energy of Canada; his sister, Dr. Anahid Mooradian-Kiernan, the first Armenian woman medical doctor in Canada; Edward Safarian, professor of economics and former Dean of Graduate Studies, University of Toronto; Alexander B. Davies, internationally recognized as a pioneer of naturopathic medicine; Dr. J. Basmajian; and engineer John Adjeleian who designed the retractable roof of Toronto's popular SkyDome.

Exemplifying Entrepreneurship

The Kololian and Shahinian families are good examples of the entrepreneurial spirit amongst Armenian-Canadians. Kevork Kololian and his wife Armenouhi (Armen), upon immigrating to Canada from Egypt with their two children, Vahan and Nairy, in 1962, established K.K. Precision Industries Inc. The enterprise began modestly, but with big dreams. One employee in a 600 square foot factory became an industrial concern, which today employs nearly 200 people and supplies highly sophisticated machine parts to the aerospace and machinery manufacturing industries. In 1984, 22 years after founding K.K. Precision Industries, Kev, third from

left, sought other entrepreneurial pursuits (he has since launched four other businesses) at which time Vahan, far left, and his brother-in-law Yervant (Eddy) Shahinian, second from left, proposed a buy-out by the second generation. "There is no question that the next generation has brought the discipline and structure to build the company. They have done a great job," says the father with pride. Vahan, who is not active on a day-to-day basis at K.K. Precision, having founded and built with his partners the venture capital firm, Polar Capital Corporation, says that "Baba (Armenian for Dad) did the risk taking and heavy lifting, with huge support from my mother, which laid the groundwork for Eddy, Rye (Eddy's brother), far right, and Nairy to take the company to the next level." The Kololians and Shahinians are not unique in Armenian circles. In fact, both Canada and the U.S. have seen many Armenian entrepreneurs establish similar successful businesses. Both Nairy, second right, and Armen have recently received community service awards which also speaks to the community orientation of Armenian families in general. Armen's award was from the Armenian Relief Society in recognition of her 25 years of service and Nairy's citation was from Prime Minister Jean Chrétien in recognition of her dedicated community work in both Armenian and other Canadian circles.   [Photo, courtesy Charles J. Humber]

Most Armenians immigrating to Canada this century tended to settle in either Ontario or Quebec. In 1979, nevertheless, they were active in creating the Armenian Cultural Association of the Atlantic Provinces. This view, taken circa 1990, in Halifax, Nova Scotia, depicts an Atlantic Association picnic. Gathering together as one big family, these are the descendents of those who faced genocide in Turkey early in the 20th century and eventually came to Canada via such countries as Syria, Jordan, Egypt, Palestine, and Lebanon. One of these descendents, Dr. Dickran Malatjalian, sitting, middle, had parents who were born in Turkish-occupied Armenia, were forced to flee their native homeland, met and married in Jerusalem, and eventually produced a son, who immigrated to Canada and settled in Halifax where, today, he is a practicing medical doctor. [Photo, courtesy Dr. Dickran Malatjalian]

Celebrating Armenian Heritage

One of the World's Premier Colour Portrait Photographers

It all began in Cairo when Artin Cavoukian (1915-1995) reached 16 years of age and entered the studio of his father Ohaness, a celebrated Armenian-born painter turned photographer. Little did young Artin know that his career as a portrait photographer would eventually take him in 1958 to Canada where he would become one of the world's premier colour portrait photographers. This portrait of Artin Cavoukian, left, was taken by son Onnig who perpetuates the Cavouk tradition synonymous with excellence. [Photo, courtesy Cavouk Portraits]

Celebrating 50 years of Portrait Photography

One of the best-known Armenian surnames in Canada is Cavoukian. Escaping Turkish oppression in 1915, the family with three-month-old Artin fled to Jerusalem then resettled in Cyprus, finally setting up a photographic studio in Cairo, Egypt, before immigrating to Canada in 1958. This family portrait was taken at the Cavouk Studio on Bloor Street, Toronto, in 1980, to celebrate the 50th anniversary of Artin Cavoukian, right, as a photographer. With hand on his mother Lucie's shoulder, Onnig represents the third generation to carry on with the family business. His brother Raffi is recognized internationally as a children's songwriter and popular performing artist while his sister, Dr. Anne Cavoukian, is the Information and Privacy Commissioner for the Province of Ontario. [Photo, courtesy Cavouk Portraits]

In 1999, Isabel Kaprielian-Churchill, far right, the Henry Kazan Professor in Modern Armenian Immigration History at California State University, Fresno, receives from Pena Tarzi (née Markarian), Chairperson of the Armenian Relief Society, Toronto, a special award recognizing her lifetime achievements in higher education and service for Canada's Armenian community, especially in documenting the history of Armenians in Canada. [Photo, courtesy Albert Kaprielian]

Born in Hamilton, Ontario, in 1924, Professor Edward Safarian is very much aware of his ancestral roots linking him to Armenia, the homeland of both his parents who were forced to flee their native land earlier this century. Formerly, President, Canadian Economics Association, and Dean, School of Graduate Studies, University of Toronto, this distinguished research scholar and much respected university professor of International Economics and Canadian Public Policy is, today, one of Canada's leading economists on international trade issues and matters vitally important to Canada's prominent role on the world's economic stage. [Photo, courtesy Edward Safarian]

Armenian Canadians Yousuf Karsh and his brother Malak of Ottawa established impossibly high standards in the fields of black and white portrait and colour landscape photography. Yousuf Karsh, whose career spanned six decades and whose legacy is a Canadian national treasure, was named by the publishers of *International Who's Who* as one of the most influential people of the twentieth century. Artin Cavoukian's portraits, on the other hand, brought international acclaim to this Armenian-born Canadian as the world's foremost colour portrait photographer of his time. Other members of the prominent Cavoukian family are notable performer, Raffi, a children's songwriter and popular performing artist and his sister, Anne, the Commissioner of the Information and Privacy Commission of Ontario. Onnig Cavoukian is the third generation to carry on the tradition of the world-renowned Cavouk Portraits. Richard Ouzounian made his mark in theatre and radio while the director Atom Egoyan and actress Arsinee Khanjian helped the Canadian film industry scale new heights.

Armenian Canadians have begun to distinguish themselves for their work in race relations on a number of multicultural organizations. In 1993, Sarkis Assadourian became the first Canadian of Armenian descent elected to the House of Commons.

Ara Mooradian (1922-1996) first joined the Chalk River Laboratories of Atomic Energy of Canada Limited in 1950 where he worked on plutonium separation and developed fuels for Canadian research and power reactors. Born in Hamilton, Ontario, to parents who had fled persecution in Asia Minor, this much respected Armenian-Canadian, a Fellow of the Royal Society of Canada and recipient of the W.B. Lewis Medal, retired in 1987 as Executive Vice President, Research and Development, AECL. [Photo, courtesy Chalk River Laboratories, AECL]

While contributing to Canadian society, Armenians have also been determined to preserve their heritage and assert the existence of a glorious national tradition. By the 1920s, Armenian Canadians had organized regional, cultural, political, and religious associations. Branches of the Armenian Revolutionary Federation, or Tashnag party, the Armenian Social Democratic party, or Hnchag party, and the Armenian Democratic Liberal Party, or the Ramgavar party, were also established.

The Armenian General Benevolent Union (AGBU), with its headquarters in the U.S., was established in Canada in 1923. With chapters in Montreal, Toronto, and Vancouver, the AGBU and its community centres have helped shape Armenian charitable, educational, and cultural life not only in Canada but throughout the world, including the Republic of Armenia and the Republic of Mountainous Karabagh. Another group, the Armenian Relief Society, founded in Canada in 1910, is primarily a women's charitable and educational association.

Religious loyalties to the Armenian Apostolic church, to the Armenian Catholic rite, and to a number of Armenian Evangelical churches have also contributed to the variety of Armenian-Canadian life.

Armenian organizational life of today has evolved to include a number of professional and business associations: the Armenian Bar Association, the Armenian Engineers and Scientists of America, the Armenian Medical Association of Ontario and of Quebec, the Canadian Armenian Dental Association, and the Canadian Armenian Business Council.

In order to provide for their religious, political, educational, athletic, and cultural needs, Armenians, particularly in Toronto and Montreal, have built large and beautiful complexes which incorporate their church, community centre, and elementary and secondary Armenian language full-day and supplementary schools.

With much hard work, Canada's Armenian immigrants have succeeded in building a new life for themselves and their children as well as cultivating a sense of belonging to Canada. ⍟

FOR GENERATIONS, the Maltese commuted to neighbouring North African states and the eastern Mediterranean to work as traders, craftspeople, and labourers. Only in the last decades of the nineteenth century did the people of Malta look beyond the limits of their traditional migratory orbit. Overpopulation, unemployment, underemployment intertwined with rising expectations, and the limited resources and small size of the country resulted in emigration. (The chief island of Malta and the islands belonging to it measure only 122 square miles in area.)

The first Maltese, few in number, are believed to have arrived in Canada in the middle of the nineteenth century. During this period, pioneer settler Louis Shickluna, who had come to St. Catharines, Ontario, in 1838, built a shipyard on the Welland Canal. Decades later, thousands of disillusioned naval tradespeople and dockyard workers who had suffered job layoffs after the completion of a major maritime construction project in 1907 and the Armistice in 1918 spearheaded the first major immigration to Canada of several hundred settlers of Maltese origin. Apart from these early arrivals, most of the Maltese population in Canada came as a result of the effects of the Second World War: limited work in the dockyards, the exodus of the British military presence (Malta had been headquarters of the British Mediterranean Fleet), and the closing down of military facilities.

The census statistics of 1996 recorded the presence of nearly 30,000 Maltese in Canada (single and multiple origins). Today, there are more people of Maltese origin in Ontario than in any other single province (26,250 in 1996). Most congregated in Toronto's west end, settling in "The Junction"– formerly the Town of West Toronto Junction. As well, several families chose to settle in a number of other Ontario centres including London, Oshawa, Whitby, Windsor,

A leader of the nuevo flamenco movement, a music that blends the passionate Gypsy roots of rumba and fandango with Afro-Cuban and jazz rhythms, Roger Scannura, in his late teens, immigrated to Canada from Malta. In Toronto, he discovered the godfather of Spanish flamenco, Pepe Habichuelas, and followed him to Spain where he studied under his tutelage for three years. Today, as an inspirational flamenco guitarist, Roger Scannura has thrilled sold-out audiences in both North America and Europe. His latest recording, Medina, with his band, Ritmo Flamenco, pays homage to flamenco's 800-year-old Moorish traditions. [Photo, courtesy Maltese-Canadian Society of Toronto via Richard Cumbo]

from **Malta**

Hamilton, St. Catharines, Ottawa-Hull, and Kitchener. They also settled widely across Canada in such cities as Halifax, Montreal, Winnipeg, Calgary, Edmonton, Vancouver, and Victoria.

Maltese work gangs were initially drawn into the labour-intensive meatpacking industry. Maltese mechanics and tradespeople who arrived later brought their skills to bear in car assembly plants, in the construction industry, or on the railway. Additionally, a variety of immigrant enterprises also emerged. The first successful businesses were grocery and variety stores. Maltese bakeries played an additional role as informal gathering places. The subsequent growth of Maltese urban settlements encouraged the proliferation of Maltese real estate firms and travel agencies. Today, Canadians of Maltese origin participate in the larger economy as lawyers, health care professionals, managers, bankers, public servants, and administrators.

Maltese-Canadians developed a number of self-help organizations and mutual benefit societies. The Maltese residents of Winnipeg established the Maltese Protective Society in 1913. The Maltese-Canadian Society of Toronto, founded in 1922, helped newcomers to understand Canadian society and to take care of one another. In 1931, it supported the building of the community's first church, St. Paul the Apostle, which organized social events and the celebration of such traditional Maltese holidays as Malta's National Day (September 8), the conversion of St. Paul (January 25), and the shipwreck of this Apostle (February 10) on the shores of Malta in 60 A.D. Other organizations in the city include the Grand Priory of Canada of the Sovereign Order of St. John of Jerusalem (Knights of Malta), the Maltese Veterans Association, and a number of sports and soccer clubs. A member of the Windsor community founded the Malta Service Bureau in 1951 to serve the new arrivals and act as a community information and cultural centre. In 1974, through the Maltese-Canadian Society of Toronto, these and other community organizations came together to create an important umbrella organization, the Federation of Maltese Organizations (now the Maltese-Canadian Federation).

These organizations, the mainstays of many multicultural celebrations and ethnic festivals, vigorously sought opportunities to promote Maltese traditions and culture to Canadian society at large. The Malta Band Club of Toronto, founded in 1971, sponsored the Valletta Pavilion as part of the city's popular International Caravan celebrations. Maltese residents of Windsor participate in that city's International Freedom Festival and the Carousel of Nations. Members and supporters of the Maltese-Canadian Club of London and the Maltese-Canadian Centre join in the celebrations of Cavalcade,

Born in Mosta, Malta, Valerie Buhagiar immigrated to Canada with her parents in 1964. Pursuing a theatrical career, by the time she was 18 years old, she had toured China, the United States and Canada as a puppeteer. Graduating from Toronto's George Brown College's Acting Programme in 1986, Valerie's writing, directing and producing debut was The Passion of Rita Camilleri, *a film winning several awards including the Silver Plaque at the Chicago Film Festival in 1993. Ms. Buhagiar has won several theatre awards including two separate Dora Mavor Moore Awards for* The Lorca Play *and* White Trash, Blue Eyes. *This view of Valerie Buhagiar, right, was recently taken at the Karlovy Vary Film Festival in the Czech Republic where a retrospective of her work as an actor and filmmaker was featured. She is currently the host of* The Showcase Revue.
[Photo, courtesy Valerie Buhagiar]

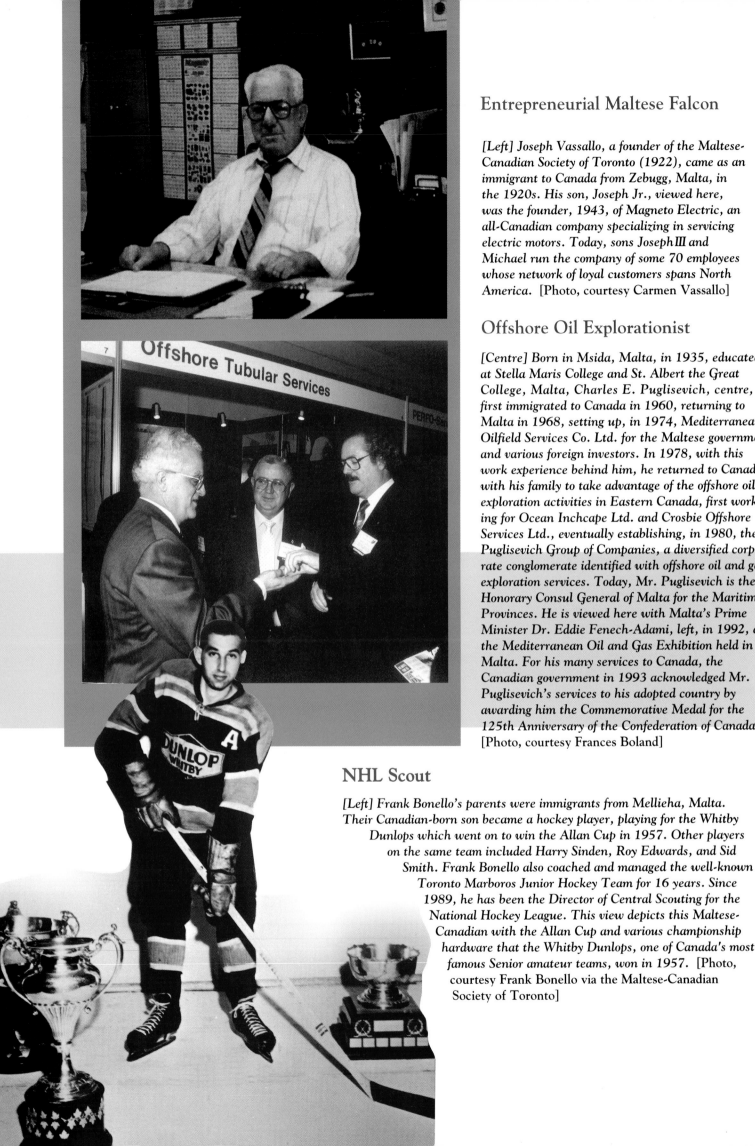

Entrepreneurial Maltese Falcon

[Left] Joseph Vassallo, a founder of the Maltese-Canadian Society of Toronto (1922), came as an immigrant to Canada from Zebugg, Malta, in the 1920s. His son, Joseph Jr., viewed here, was the founder, 1943, of Magneto Electric, an all-Canadian company specializing in servicing electric motors. Today, sons Joseph III and Michael run the company of some 70 employees whose network of loyal customers spans North America. [Photo, courtesy Carmen Vassallo]

Offshore Oil Explorationist

[Centre] Born in Msida, Malta, in 1935, educated at Stella Maris College and St. Albert the Great College, Malta, Charles E. Puglisevich, centre, first immigrated to Canada in 1960, returning to Malta in 1968, setting up, in 1974, Mediterranean Oilfield Services Co. Ltd. for the Maltese government and various foreign investors. In 1978, with this work experience behind him, he returned to Canada with his family to take advantage of the offshore oil exploration activities in Eastern Canada, first working for Ocean Inchcape Ltd. and Crosbie Offshore Services Ltd., eventually establishing, in 1980, the Puglisevich Group of Companies, a diversified corporate conglomerate identified with offshore oil and gas exploration services. Today, Mr. Puglisevich is the Honorary Consul General of Malta for the Maritime Provinces. He is viewed here with Malta's Prime Minister Dr. Eddie Fenech-Adami, left, in 1992, at the Mediterranean Oil and Gas Exhibition held in Malta. For his many services to Canada, the Canadian government in 1993 acknowledged Mr. Puglisevich's services to his adopted country by awarding him the Commemorative Medal for the 125th Anniversary of the Confederation of Canada. [Photo, courtesy Frances Boland]

NHL Scout

[Left] Frank Bonello's parents were immigrants from Mellieha, Malta. Their Canadian-born son became a hockey player, playing for the Whitby Dunlops which went on to win the Allan Cup in 1957. Other players on the same team included Harry Sinden, Roy Edwards, and Sid Smith. Frank Bonello also coached and managed the well-known Toronto Marboros Junior Hockey Team for 16 years. Since 1989, he has been the Director of Central Scouting for the National Hockey League. This view depicts this Maltese-Canadian with the Allan Cup and various championship hardware that the Whitby Dunlops, one of Canada's most famous Senior amateur teams, won in 1957. [Photo, courtesy Frank Bonello via the Maltese-Canadian Society of Toronto]

London's ethnic festival. Members of the Malta Social Club in Durham Region set up a Malta Pavilion featuring traditional foodstuffs, crafts, music, and dance as part of the city of Oshawa's Fiesta Week.

The Maltese-Canadian print and broadcast media play an important social and cultural role. A number of quarterly magazines and newspapers – past and present – keep readers informed of events in Malta and around the diaspora. The first Maltese-Canadian radio program began broadcasting in Leamington, Ontario, in 1954 and served a faithful audience in Windsor and Detroit. Today, members of the Toronto community enjoy a community television program.

Since the Roman Catholic Church was the state church of their homeland, most Maltese immigrants naturally celebrate that faith in Canada. The community church, St. Paul the Apostle, flourished and grew by tending to the spiritual needs of the group; it moved into a spacious new building in 1956 and then acquired a rectory and auditorium in 1960. Ever generous with their time and energy, Maltese-Canadian parishioners became active in a number of Catholic agencies and social service organizations including the St. Vincent de Paul Society, the Catholic Women's League, and the Holy Name Society. In many ways, the Maltese immigrants have made major contributions to Canadian life. ♥

Malta's Prime Minister Dr. Alfred Sant came to Canada and participated in ceremonies honouring the 75th anniversary of the founding of the Maltese-Canadian Society of Toronto. He is seen here, left, recognizing Maltese-Canadians Connie Dejak, née Galea, and Richard Cumbo, for their Maltese-Canadian volunteer service in Canada. [Photo, courtesy Maltese-Canadian Society of Toronto]

As a young man, Larry Attard immigrated to Canada in 1973 from B'Kara, Malta, and immediately took up horseracing. One of North America's leading jockeys until a tragic fall at Woodbine Racetrack in 1997 prevented him from ever riding again, Larry won the Queen's Plate in 1983 aboard Bompago. He also won two Prince of Wales trophies, one in 1992 aboard Benburb of Knob Hill Farms Stables and the other, as viewed here, aboard Kiridashi, in 1995, from Minshall Farms. [Photo, courtesy Maltese-Canadian Society of Toronto via Richard Cumbo]

LATVIANS in Canada can trace their heritage to a country in northern Europe that sits on the eastern shore of the Baltic Sea and is bordered by Estonia on the north and Lithuania on the south. There were few Latvians in Canada until the late 1940s. Small Latvian settlements in Manitoba were established near Dauphin and around Lac-du-Bonnet on the Bird River by groups of prewar immigrant farmers escaping Russian rule and Baltic-German baronial power. Like other Baltic-German groups, the great majority of Latvians arrived after 1946, making their way from displaced persons' camps in Germany. The new arrivals, many holding degrees in engineering, medicine, law, and other professions, initially made their way to the agricultural, forestry, and mining areas of Canada in order to fulfill the work contracts required by immigration authorities.

Sarmite Bulte was elected a Liberal Member of Parliament for the federal riding of Parkdale-High Park, Ontario, 1977. Following Soviet occupation of their homeland, her Latvian-born parents immigrated to Canada in the late 1940s. Born in Hamilton, Ontario, upon completing her undergraduate studies, 1975, at the University of Toronto, Ms. Bulte followed her career dreams, graduating in Law from the University of Windsor, 1978, being called to the Ontario Bar, 1980. An advocate for women's issues, Ms. Bulte has served as President, Canadian Association of Women Executives and Entrepreneurs, 1987-88. She is a Past Vice-President, International, Women Entrepreneurs of Canada. Currently, Director of the Council for Business and the Arts in Canada, she is Past President and Chairman of the Board of Directors, The Canadian Stage Company, one of the largest not-for-profit theatre companies in Canada. Active in the Latvian community with the Latvian Credit Union, she presently serves on the Governing Council of the Latvian National Federation in Canada. Married and the mother of three children, "Sam" Bulte, in this view, is addressing the Vietnamese Association of Toronto's celebration of the Year of the Cat at the Têt Festival, February 6, 1999. Ms. Bulte's father now resides in Latvia and is Chairman, Freeedom Monument Restoration Committee in Riga. [Photo, courtesy Sarmite Bulte, M.P.]

from **Latvia**

Within a few years of completing their contracts, the skilled workers, technicians, and professionals moved to the rapidly growing metropolitan areas.

In 1996, Statistics Canada tallied the presence of 24,120 persons of Latvian origin in Canada. Ontario was the biggest magnet with 15,535 Latvian Canadians. There were 4,470 Toronto residents of Latvian origin. Latvian communities were also found in other Ontario centres including St. Catharines, Hamilton, London, Kitchener, Waterloo, Guelph, and Oshawa. Outside of Ontario, Latvians were also found in Vancouver, Winnipeg, Montreal, and Halifax.

The postwar community was remarkable for its entrepreneurial spirit and for the creative energy of its professional class who founded a number of firms specializing in architecture, construction, landscaping, printing, auto retail sales and repairs, insurance, realty, financing, and retail sales. And out of these ranks, the Benjamin Film Laboratories, founded by George Benjamin, has attained considerable visibility and renown. It should also surprise no one that an increasing number of Latvians have quickly risen through the ranks to become senior

Talivaldis Kenins, composer, teacher, pianist, was born, 1919, in Liepaja, Latvia. Forced out of his native land by Soviet occupation following World War II, he continued his work as a musician at the Paris Conservatory until 1951, the year he immigrated to Canada to assume duties as organist-choirmaster for the Latvian congregation at St. Andrew's Lutheran Church, Toronto. His teaching career began in 1952 at the University of Toronto. When he retired in 1984, he was internationally known as an esteemed composer. Professor Kenins has composed eight symphonies, 12 concertos, major chamber music and choral works, and has performed abroad with international enthusiasm. In 1995, he was named Officer of the National Three-Star Order of the Republic of Latvia. In this 1988 view at Roy Thomson Hall, Toronto, the Honourable Lincoln Alexander, Lieutenant Governor of Ontario, congratulates Dr. Kenins at the première of Gloria by the Toronto Mendelssohn Choir. [Photo, courtesy Talivaldis Kenins]

executives and bone fide members of Canada's corporate elite. O. Allan Kupcis, former President, Ontario Hydro, E.N. Legzdins, Executive Vice President and Chief Operating Officer, First Canadian Funds Inc., wholly owned subsidiary of the Bank of Montreal, and Bruno Rubess, former President, Volkswagen Canada are good examples of this select group. Latvian women, in turn, have come into prominence, especially in the fields of teaching, medicine, health care, and politics. In the latter category, it would be difficult to exceed the achievement of Dr. Vaira Vike-Freiberga, Professor of Psychology at McGill University who came to Canada in 1954 as a

Born in Asune, Latvia, Alfred Stikuts left his homeland in 1944. By 1950, he and his Latvian-born wife, Lita, had settled in Toronto where for nearly 50 years he has been selling real estate, the last 40 years of which have been as an independent realtor. [Photo, courtesy Charles J. Humber]

A third generation pianist, Arthur Ozolins was born to Latvian parents in Lubeck, Germany, 1946. International attention focused on this musician in the early 1970s when The New Yorker heralded his emergence as "... one of the great virtuoso pianists of our time." He has also performed in such renowned halls as the Sydney Opera House, Australia; Sala Verdi, Milan; Teatro Colon, Buenos Aires; Theatre des Champs-Elysées, Paris; Schauspielhaus, Berlin; Shostakovich Hall, St. Petersburg, among others. He has toured with such orchestras as the Royal Philharmonic, St. Petersburg (Leningrad), Stockholm and Oslo, Barcelona, Ulster, and Taiwan. Recipient of the first Juno Award given in classical music, Arthur Ozolins, for more than 25 years, has been at the heart of music-making in Canada and his various celebrated recordings have made him popular worldwide as a master pianist. [Photo, courtesy Arthur Ozolins]

Plastic Surgeon Specialist

Born in Riga, Latvia, Arnis Freiberg lived in a displaced persons' camp in Mannheim, Germany, between 1944 and 1948. The family, unable to return to Latvia as the result of Communist occupation there, immigrated to Canada in 1948. Receiving his M.D. from the University of Toronto, 1961, Dr. Freiberg completed his residency in Plastic Surgery in 1967. Specializing in hand surgery, Dr. Freiberg has been a lecturer in the Dept. of Surgery at the University of Toronto since 1967 and full professor of Plastic Surgery since 1993. He has been clinically affiliated with a number of hospitals including Toronto's East General Hospital, St. Joseph's Health Centre, and the Toronto Hospital. Winner of numerous medical awards, Dr. Arnis Freiberg, in this view, stands with Biruta, his Latvian-born wife of 42 years. Dr. Freiberg has a Fellowship in the Royal College of Physicians and Surgeons, 1967 (Plastic Surgery). [Photo, courtesy Dr. A. Freiberg]

New President, World Association of Nuclear Operators

Born in Riga, Latvia, Allan Kupcis immigrated to Canada with his parents in 1952. Upon completing his B.A.Sc., M.A.Sc. and his Ph.D degrees from the University of Toronto, Dr. Kupcis went on to complete post doctoral training at Oxford University while on a NATO Scholarship. He launched his career as a Research Engineer at Ontario Hydro in 1973, serving as Chief Executive Officer from 1995-1997 and President and Chief Operating Officer from 1993-1995. Following his retirement from Ontario Hydro, Allan Kupcis was elected President, World Association of Nuclear Operators. This view of Allan Kupcis, right, with Andrew Sarlos, was taken at the Great Wall of China on a recent Team Canada Trade Mission to the far east. [Photo, courtesy Allan Kupcis]

Esteemed Historian and Author

Modris Eksteins fled Soviet occupation of Latvia, 1944, living in refugee camps in the British zone of occupation in Germany, 1945-1949. The family left Europe, 1949, migrating, first, to Winnipeg, when Modris was five years old, resettling in Toronto shortly thereafter. When Modris entered Trinity College, University of Toronto, 1961, he began a long and serious commitment to understanding the causes that profoundly destroyed so much of eastern Europe's rich culture and heritage by the end of World War II. A Rhodes Scholar, Professor Modris Eksteins graduated from Oxford University with a doctoral degree in History, 1970, and has taught at the University of Toronto ever since. One of his books, Rites of Spring: The Great War and the Birth of the Modern Age, won the Trillium Award, 1990, and has been translated into seven languages. His most recent book, Walking Since Daybreak: A Story of Eastern Europe, World War II, and the Heart of Our Century, is necessary reading for anyone interested in the cultural history of the 20th century. In this view Professor Eksteins, left, stands with Richard von Weizsäcker after the former President, Federal Republic of Germany, was granted the degree of Doctor of Laws, honoris causa, by the University of Toronto. [Photo, courtesy Frost Photography via Dr. Modris Eksteins]

Automotive Executive

Bruno Rubess was born in Riga, Latvia, and immigrated to Canada in 1953. As a life insurance underwriter, Mr. Rubess eventually entered the automobile industry as a salesman with Mercedes-Benz, 1955. By 1962, he had joined Volkswagen Canada as Sales Training Manager, becoming, within a decade, its President and Chief Executive Officer. Mr. Rubess and his Latvian-born wife, Biruta, as viewed here in traditional Latvian costumes, were married in 1953. Together they have been active in Latvian activities, helping organize the Canadian Latvian Cultural Centre in Toronto. They have also participated in a variety of youth seminars and numerous fundraising causes over many years of volunteerism. Retiring from Volkswagen's headquarters in Germany in 1992 as Chief of Corporate Strategy, that same year, Mr. Rubess became the only non-resident appointed for six years to the Board of the (Central) Bank of Latvia where he continues as management consultant to guide the Bank's numismatic coin program and major building activities. Mr. Rubess is also an Officer of the Three Star Order of Latvia. [Photo, courtesy Bruno Rubess]

Latvian immigrant from Germany. After 45 years in Canada, she returned to Latvia to become, in 1999, Latvia's first female President.

Latvians in Canada have founded several organizations to provide educational, social, cultural, and youth services and activities. The Latvian written literary tradition also continues. A plethora of weeklies and bulletins, journals and yearbooks are published by local Latvian societies, Lutheran church congregations, schools, and professional and special interest groups. Latvians in Canada also continue to publish a wealth of plays, poetry, short stories, and essays. Author and playwright Banuta Rubess, the second woman in Canada to win a Rhodes Scholarship (1978), is but one community talent. The community has also vigorously maintained its support of Latvian-Canadian choir and theatre groups, folkdance ensembles, and visual and performing artists. In turn, Latvian Canadians contribute much to the development of Canadian arts and culture: opera singer Maris Vetra, who came to Halifax in 1947, was a founder of the Nova Scotia Opera Association; Alfred Strombergs conducted the Atlantic Symphony Orchestra; composer Janis Kalnins, who conducts the New Brunswick Symphony Orchestra, founded the Fredericton Civic Orchestra; and Imant Raminsh of British Columbia, is a much respected composer/conductor for the Vancouver Symphony, the Vancouver Chamber Choir, and the Vancouver Bach Choir, among others. Finally, Toronto pianist Arthur Ozolins continues to delight audiences the world over with his mastery of the keyboard. ⚜

Before she was 10 years old, Latvian-born Vaira Vike-Freiberga had fled Red Army oppression, along with her parents in the mid 1940s, and lived with thousands of other Latvian displaced people in Germany before the family migrated to Canada, eventually settling in Toronto, 1954. After completing B.A. and M.A. degrees at the University of Toronto, this future President of Latvia moved on to McGill University in Montreal, completing her Ph.D. in Psychology in 1965. During her 45 years in Canada, Vaira Vike-Freiberga became a distinguished, much respected and internationally-known Psychologist who had been a full Professor of Psychology at Université de Montréal for 21 years before returning, 1998, to head up a newly created Think Tank in her native land. Shortly thereafter a group of leading intellectuals in Latvia urged her to run for President in the upcoming 1999 elections. Four days before her successful election as President of Latvia, she surrendered her Canadian citizenship so she could be a legitimate contender. As the first female President of any former Soviet Republic, Vaira Vike-Freiberga reminded fellow Latvians following her stunning election that Canada's policy of official multiculturalism is a model Latvia should follow if it is to resolve the differences that exist among the large ethnic groups left in Latvia after 50 years of Soviet rule. [Photo, courtesy The Toronto Star]

Originally from Taguig, Metro Manila, Philippines, Ma-Anne Dionisio immigrated with her family to Winnipeg, Manitoba, in 1990. Two years later, she was playing a lead role in Experience Canada: Spirit of a Nation, a musical which toured Canada and was written to commemorate Canada's 125th anniversary as a nation. The next year Ma-Anne was selected to play the lead role of Kim in Miss Saigon, a part she performed for the entire two-year run of the show in Toronto. Most recently, she starred in both Asia and South Africa in the international touring production of Les Miserables. For the 1999 season at Ontario's Stratford Festival, Ma-Anne played the lead role of Maria in Leonard Bernstein's West Side Story. [Photo, courtesy Butler Ruston Bell Talent Associates Inc.]

from the Philippines

COVERING nearly 2,000 kilometres of the Pacific Ocean between China and Indonesia, the islands of the Philippines are home to more than 78 million people speaking some 85 dialects including English, Tagalog, and Sugbuanon.

The Philippine islands were colonized first by Spain in 1521 and then controlled by the United States until after World War II. The population of these islands is diverse, with people of Indonesian-Malay, Negrito, Chinese, Spanish, American and other European heritage.

Migration has always been a tradition within the Philippines, with movement from the smaller islands to Manila and the southern island of Mindanao, yet Filipinos did not arrive in any significant numbers in Canada until the late 1960s. Between 1971 and 1992, Filipinos constituted between four and six percent of annual immigration to Canada. Today, these newer Canadians constitute one of the fastest-growing immigrant communities in Canada. By 1996, there were 243,000 people of Filipino heritage living in Canada with half of those in Ontario, 50,000 in British Columbia and 25,000 in Alberta.

Early Filipino immigrants were mostly single women who primarily worked as nurses, medical doctors, technologists, and secretaries, but in the late 1970s and '80s the gender imbalance had substantially decreased because family reunification became a priority of Canadian Immigration policy. Even today, roughly sixty percent of all Filipinos in Canada are female. Since the late '80s, Filipino women many with university degrees, have arrived to work initially as nannies and domestics in order to fit in with Canada's employment needs. Filipinos have tended to settle not in ethnic neighbourhoods but close to work and public transport. Nevertheless, Canada's major cities are home now to Filipino organizations, many of which are based on the region of the Philippines from which people emigrated, such as the Ang Bisaya Association sa Metro Toronto and the Circulo Ilongo in Vancouver. Special interest groups such as the Philippine Women's Sports Association of Montreal, the Fiesta Filipina Dance Troupe and Kabataan Theatre Group in Toronto, the Philippine Choral

Dr. Rey D. Pagtakhan, M.P. (Lib., Winnipeg North-St. Paul), was raised in Bacoor, Cavite, and graduated in Medicine from the University of the Philippines. A Professor of Pediatrics, medical author, community volunteer, and now a parliamentarian, he has received several awards in the Philippines, U.S.A. and Canada. He immigrated to Canada in 1968 and was first elected to the House of Commons 20 years later. Formerly the Parliamentary Secretary to the Prime Minister, he is currently Chair of the House of Commons Standing Committee on Citizenship and Immigration. In this recent view, Dr. Rey Pagtakhan is conferring with the Prime Minister of Canada, the Rt. Hon. Jean Chrétien. [Photo, courtesy Dr. Rey D. Pagtakhan]

Born and educated in the Philippines as a medical laboratory technician, Arturo Tapiador Viola, by 1967, had adopted Canada as his new homeland, rising to the ranks of Director of Laboratories for the Niagara-on-the-Lake General Hospital in Ontario before retiring in 1994. A tireless volunteer, Art is the only Lord Mayor in North America and the first Asian to be elected mayor of any Canadian municipality. Raising funds for such organizations as the Heart and Stroke Foundation, the Canadian Cancer Society, and the Red Cross, Art was honoured in 1992 with the 125th Anniversary of the Confederation of Canada Medal. After receiving the Most Outstanding Alumnus Award from Centro Escolar University while visiting Manila in 1999, Lord Mayor Art Viola, in this view, presents University President, Dr. Lourdez T. Echauz, with a commemorative plaque on behalf of all the residents of Niagara-on-the-Lake. [Photo, courtesy Art Viola]

Society in Mississauga, and the Philippine Charity Society in Vancouver provide social activities for many people of Filipino heritage. Professional organizations include the Manitoba Association of Filipino teachers, the Filipino Nurses Association, and the Filipino Canadian Medical Association of Toronto. The taste of Filipino immigrants for hometown delicacies is answered by the many Filipino grocery stores, which carry items such as frozen banana leaves used for wrapping rice cakes, canned and dried fish, sausages ("langgonisa") and cured

Dr. Anita Beltran Chen was born in the Philippines, receiving both her B.A. and M.A. degrees in Sociology at the University of the Philippines before completing her Ph.D. degree in Sociology at the University of Chicago, 1962. Founding Chairperson of Lakehead University's Department of Sociology in Thunder Bay, Ontario, Dr. Chen has been a faculty member at this institution since 1964. Throughout her long academic career at Lakehead, she has gained respect nationally and internationally as a distinguished scholar. Her latest book, From Sunbelt to Snowbelt: Filipinos in Canada, was published in 1998 by the Research Centre for Canadian Ethnic Studies, University of Calgary. She was an invited contributor to Encyclopedia of Canada's People published in 1999 by the University of Toronto Press. Dr. Chen's work was recognized in 1998 when she received, as viewed here, the Pamana ng Filipino Award from Philippine President Joseph Ejercito Estrada at a ceremony at Malacanang Palace in Manila. The citation of the awarded plaque sums up her contributions and achievements: "For her pioneering achievement within the academic community of Canada and her significant research undertaking which she has effectively used for the promotion of public awareness and understanding of the character of Filipino migration to Canada." [Photo, courtesy Dr. Anita Beltran Chen]

Fiesta Filipina Dance Troupe of Canada, when it toured eight major cities of the Philippines in 1997, was called the pride and joy of "Fil-Canadians." This internationally acclaimed Folk Arts Ensemble has received numerous awards and distinctions on tours to International Festivals in Portugal, France, Italy, Greece, Austria, Spain, the Pyrenees, as well as Disneyworld's Epcot Center. Dedicated to promoting international goodwill by sharing Philippine culture and traditions through music, story and dance, the Fiesta Filipina Dance Troupe was founded in 1966 by a party of Toronto resident Filipinos headed by Dr. José Teodoro and Eleanor Calbes. As cultural ambassadors, this celebrated ensemble has also performed at the Olympic Games staged in both Mexico City and Montreal. The Fiesta Filipina Dance Troupe continues to delight audiences with the vitality and rich colour of their performances, and has succeeded in bringing to the consciousness of international audiences the colour and enchantment of Filipino cultural heritage. [Photo, courtesy Fiesta Filipina Dance Troupe]

meats ("tapa" and "tocino"). Bakeries make cassava cakes, rice-based desserts (kakanin) and a butter and sugar-topped bun ("ensaymada"). In many of these establishments one can pick up Filipino community newspapers such as the *Philippine Reporter* in Toronto, the *Filipino Journal* in Winnipeg and the *Pahayagan* in Ottawa that provide community news, dates for folk song performances or various Catholic religious festivals. Performance skills are highly appreciated and many Filipino Canadians were pleased to see the success of Ma-Anne Dionisio as the lead in *Miss Saigon* in Toronto. ♦

Cynthia Goh was born on a remote island in the Philippines where there was no water or electricity. Selected to attend a special science high school when only 11 years old, by the time she was 18 she had graduated in Chemistry from the University of the Philippines and was heading for California. She earned a doctoral degree from the University of California by the time she was 23 years old. After teaching stints at UCLA, Cornell, and Columbia, she immigrated to Canada, settling at the University of Toronto where today she is Associate Professor and Associate Chair of the University's Chemistry Department. In addition to her teaching duties, Dr. Goh concentrates her research work, among other matters, on the molecular structure of protein filaments in Alzeimer's. In 1996, Philippine President Fidel V. Ramos presented her with the Philippine Heritage Award at the Malacanang Palace. [Photo, courtesy Dr. Cynthia Goh]

In 1989, Luis Luna came to Canada from Argentina to participate as a dancer in a show called A Rose for Mr. Tango. He fell in love with Canada and applied to stay in Canada as his newly adopted home. Today he is a well-known Tango teacher and owns the El Tango restaurant, specializing in Latin foods, in Mississauga, Ontario. [Photo, courtesy Consulate General of Argentina]

from **Argentina**

ARGENTINIAN migration to Canada began at the beginning of the twentieth century. An early group movement from Argentina to Canada that took place in 1901 involved the migration of Welsh colonists from Patagonia to Saskatchewan. Between 1946 and 1973, a second wave of immigration to Canada coincided with economic and political decline in Argentina. These developments provided a powerful impetus for many professionals, entrepreneurs, and skilled workers to move north. In the decade after 1973, as the result of political instability and oppression, the high level of inflation, and terrorist group activities, Argentinian immigration increased to more than 1,000 per year. There were a number of claims for refugee status. Many Argentinians arriving in Canada in the early 1970s declared their intention to work in manufacturing, assembly and repair work, engineering and construction. Still others sought employment in management, education, administration, and office services.

According to 1996 Canadian census data, 7,115 persons claimed Argentinian ancestry (single and multiple responses). Many Argentinians (3,535) settled in Ontario, and most of these chose Toronto and surrounding areas. Among the professionals, the largest numbers are physicians, dentists, architects, and engineers. Many who arrived in the 1970s became electricians, mechanics, carpenters, construction workers, hairdressers, small

Canada afforded Fernando Massalin and his wife Maria an opportunity to start over again in a new land which offered stability and adventure. The company he founded, Toronto International Farms Company, is now ranked as one of the top 500 companies in Canada. Since Argentina is famous for producing the world's finest polo players, it should be no surprise to learn that Fernando not only is active in two polo clubs but was also part of the Canadian polo team participating in the 1998 World Cup.
[Photo, courtesy Consulate General of Argentina]

APEC SME Business Lunch

de la PME **EC pour l'établis**

Present **or/Commanditaire pr**

BRIDGE

Canada's Ambassador to World Trade Organization

Probably the best-known Argentine-born Canadian is Sergio Marchi, Canada's Ambassador to the World Trade Organization. Formerly, Minister of International Trade during the second Chrétien government, other portfolios of this York University educated politician have included Immigration and Environment. In this view, the The Hon. Sergio Marchi is addressing an APEC SME business luncheon in Ottawa, September 18, 1997. [Photo, courtesy Office, the Minister for International Trade]

Pathologist Discovering New Hormone

Born in Parana, Argentina, Dr. Adolfo de Bold is a clinical biochemist trained at the National University in Cordoba. He has an M.Sc. and Ph.D. from Queen's University. His wife Mercedes, also Argentine-born, shares the same academic training and research interests. At present Dr. de Bold is Professor of Pathology and Laboratory Medicine at the University of Ottawa. His research has earned him international recognition for his discovery of a hormone named Atrial Natriuretic Factor (ANF) which has led to a better understanding of the function of the cardiovascular system in both health and disease. [Photo, courtesy Ottawa Civic Hospital]

retailers, or travel, insurance, and real estate agents. The Argentine community in Ottawa is characterized by a large number of professionals that includes university professors and civil servants.

The second-largest concentration of Argentinians in Canada (1,985) is found in Quebec with almost 50 percent having arrived between 1971 and 1980. Montreal is home to more than 90 percent of Quebec Argentinians. The occupational profile of this group indicates a preference for the social sciences, administration, manufacturing, construction, business, and the fine arts.

In the west, British Columbia is home to nearly 1,000 Argentinian immigrants, the majority being either first- or second-generation Argentinians of European descent. The Vancouver community is composed mainly of professionals and entrepreneurs of small and medium-sized businesses, scholars and teachers, artists, and social workers. There are also concentrations of Argentinians in the cities of Calgary and Edmonton. Many of these Alberta residents are employed in the oil industry, particularly with those companies that have interests in Argentina.

Because of small numbers and relatively recent arrival, ethnocommunity organizational and institutional life is still in the initial stages of development. The limited number of cultural organizations and activities among Argentinian Canadians can be attributed to the group's entrepreneurial mentality that drives many community members to seek integration into Canadian society first. Only after they have succeeded in their careers do these individuals organize associations to maintain and promote their cultural heritage.

Dr. Alberto Aguayo, presently Director of the Centre for Research in Neuroscience at McGill University, is concerned with the study of the effects of damage to the central nervous system and the capacity of nerve cells in the eye, brain, and spinal cord to recover from injury. Born in Bahia Blanca, Argentina, Dr. Aguayo is an internationally celebrated medical doctor. Many countries have recognized his work including Sweden, Japan, France, Germany, and the United States where he is a Fellow of the Institute of Medicine of the National Academy of Sciences. [Photo, courtesy Consulate General of Argentina]

Teresa Ottens, above left, was born in Argentina in 1953. After travelling the world, she settled in Canada in 1985 with her husband and two children. In 1987 she founded the International Women's Association of Toronto where she fostered friendship between women of different nationalities. A graduate of the Ontario College of Art and Design, she has exhibited her works in her native city, Buenos Aires, and participated in a variety of exhibits in Canada. Here she is seen with former Toronto Mayor Barbara Hall at Toronto's City Hall. [Photo, courtesy Consulate General of Argentina]

The high educational level and European roots of many members of the Argentinian-Canadian community have enabled a number of individuals to make exceptional contributions to Canadian culture and society. The novelist and editor, Alberto Manguel, won both the Harbourfront Literary Award in Toronto and the British McKitterick Prize for a first novel. He is well known for his contributions to literary programs of the Canadian Broadcasting Corporation and the CTV television network and for his articles in a host of Canadian and international print media. In architecture, Carlos Ventin is particularly noted for his conversion of courthouses, schools, town halls, jails, factories, and other obsolete structures. His firm also worked on the restoration of the Ontario legislative buildings at Queen's Park and the old city hall in Toronto. In the halls of *academe*, B. Carlos Vazan of the University of Ottawa is internationally known for his work on medieval

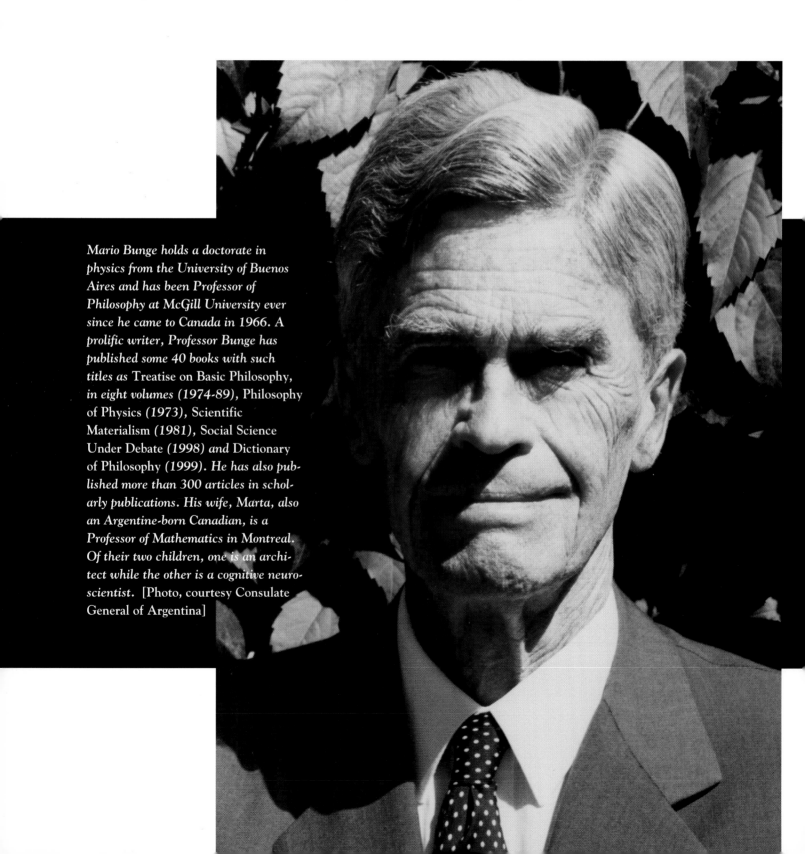

Mario Bunge holds a doctorate in physics from the University of Buenos Aires and has been Professor of Philosophy at McGill University ever since he came to Canada in 1966. A prolific writer, Professor Bunge has published some 40 books with such titles as Treatise on Basic Philosophy, *in eight volumes (1974-89),* Philosophy of Physics *(1973),* Scientific Materialism *(1981),* Social Science Under Debate *(1998) and* Dictionary of Philosophy *(1999). He has also published more than 300 articles in scholarly publications. His wife, Marta, also an Argentine-born Canadian, is a Professor of Mathematics in Montreal. Of their two children, one is an architect while the other is a cognitive neuroscientist.* [Photo, courtesy Consulate General of Argentina]

philosophy, history, and education. Professor Mario Bunge, based at McGill University, is the author of numerous books and publications on the philosophy of science. And in the medical sciences, Adolfo de Bold at the University of Ottawa Heart Institute won international recognition for his discovery of ANF, a hormone that has provided a major breakthrough in cardiac physiology.

That many Argentinians have ancestry in other countries has allowed them to establish meaningful relationships with other groups such as the Italian communities in Toronto and Ottawa and the Jewish community in Montreal. Argentinians have also collaborated with other Latin Americans in organizing soccer clubs, producing radio programs, and publishing Spanish-language newspapers that include *El Popular* and *El Correo* in Montreal.

And because many Argentinians came to Canada as a result of political unrest or economic decline, this experience motivated a number of them to enter public life. Sergio Marchi of Argentinian and Italian ancestry, who arrived in Canada from Argentina as a child in 1959, was first elected a member of parliament for the Toronto riding of York West in 1984. He served as opposition critic in several portfolios and as chair of the Ontario and national caucuses of the federal Liberal Party before becoming a cabinet minister in the government of Jean Chrétien in 1993. Leaving the government in 1999, he is today Canada's Ambassador to The World Trade Organization. Such achievements and accomplishments serve to demonstrate the pride of these individuals in being Argentinian Canadians. ♻

Presently professor of Cellular and Molecular Medicine and head of the Neurotransmission Research team at the University of Ottawa, Dr. José-María Trifaró was born and raised in Argentina, graduating in medicine with honours from the University of Buenos Aires in 1961. Internationally renowned as a biomedical researcher, Dr. Trifaró is recognized for demonstrating the presence and the function of different proteins in secretion and is in constant demand worldwide by major conferences as a guest speaker. His research has been supported by the Medical Research Council of Canada for more than 30 years. [Photo, courtesy Consulate General of Argentina]

Born in a smoke sauna (savusauna) in Karstula, Finland, 1944, Matti Ilmari Terho, left, after completing high school as well as compulsory army training in Finland, enrolled at Helsinki University, 1964, as an undergraduate theology student. While pursuing his studies, he took an all-paid, one-year scholarship to Waterloo Lutheran Seminary, Ontario, and remained at that Institution until he completed both his undergraduate and graduate degrees. On becoming an ordained minister in the Lutheran Church, Reverend Terho was made Pastor of St. Michael's Finnish Evangelical Lutheran Church, Montreal, 1969, and has lived in the Montreal area ever since. Rev. Terho was Chaplain to the 1976 Montreal Olympics and in 1980 was Director of Chaplaincy Services to the Winter Olympics, Lake Placid, New York. Before his retirement, 1999, Rev. Terho had been University Chaplain at Concordia University for 25 years. A deeply spiritual man who has contributed to the ever-growing ecumenical movement, in this 1996 view, the Reverend Matti Terho, left, stands with Anglican Priest Alan T. Perry and participates in an ecumenical eucharist service at St. James the Apostle Anglican Church, Montreal. The Roman Catholic parish of St. Jean Baptiste, Montreal, loaned the chalice, visible on the altar, for this ecumenical service. [Photo, courtesy Rev. Matti Terho]

PEOPLE OF FINNISH HERITAGE living in Canada today number just under 100,000 with over 65 percent living in Ontario. Emigrating from the cold, rugged Scandinavian landscape, Finns were well prepared for the harsh environment many chose in northern Ontario, the prairies, and British Columbia.

Over the last century, 90,000 Finns settled in Canada during three different periods of immigration. Between 1890 and 1914, Finns arrived, encouraged by Canadian Pacific Railway recruiters, from the western coastal regions of Ostrobothnia and the industrializing southern provinces of Finland mainly to pursue work opportunities. Later, after the civil war of 1919-1930, many left-wing Finns came to Canada to avoid the new right-wing regime. Among them was the former socialist Prime Minister, Oskari Tokoi. This phase ended with the introduction of new Canadian immigration laws and then World War II. Between 1947 and 1967, a third group of Finns from the southwestern region of Finland came to find work but they were now accompanied by eastern Finns who had been dislocated by the Soviet annexation of Karelia.

Finns who arrived in Canada before World War II were predominantly working class. Initially, it was mostly males who immigrated to work in the British Columbia forests, Thunder Bay, or Sault Ste. Marie in lumbering, mining, farming or construction. The gender imbalance gradually changed with the arrival of female domestics.

from Finland

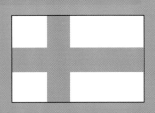

Dr. Veli Ylänkö, who graduated in medicine from the University of Turku, 1957, prior to immigrating to Canada from Helsinki, 1972, was Assistant Professor, Department of Family and Community Medicine, University of Toronto, before he retired, 1995. A private practitioner since 1987, Dr. Ylänkö, , President, Toronto Finnish Seniors' Centre, 1982-92, is active today in both Finland and Canada with Medical and Community Associations. Deputy Speaker of the worldwide Finnish Expatriate Parliament, Dr. Ylänkö, was honoured, 1992, with Canada's Commemorative Medal celebrating the 125th Anniversary of Confederation. Recognized by the Finnish Red Cross with the Medal of Merit, Dr. Ylänkö, , as viewed here, 1993, was made, for his many years of volunteer services to Finnish people worldwide, Knight, First Class, Order of the White Rose of Finland, by Finnish President Mauno Koivisto. [Photo, courtesy Dr. Veli Ylänkö,]

In 1972, Anneli Ylänkö, right, with her husband, came to Canada from Finland as a teacher, becoming Principal of the Toronto Finnish Language School in 1975. Founding President of the Finnish Language Teachers' Association of Canada since 1984, her Teacher's Handbook, supported by the Department of Multiculturalism and Citizenship, Government of Canada, is used extensively in Finnish schools worldwide. A member of the Finnish Expatriate Parliament, Anneli Ylänkö, for fostering appreciation of Finnish culture worldwide, was given Finland's Society Silver Medal in 1990, and was made, in 1995, Knight of the Order of the White Rose of Finland. In this view, she is holding her certificate signed by Finnish President Martti Ahtisaari. [Photo, courtesy Anneli Ylänkö]

Today, 53 percent of Finns in Canada are female as compared to 35 percent in 1911. Even today, Finns are employed in lumbering, mining, and construction, although the number of educated professional and business people is rapidly increasing.

Displaying a strong egalitarian conscience and historical linkages with the socialists in Finland, Finns have been active in such labour movements throughout the century as the Western Federation of Mine Workers, Lumber Workers Industrial Union of Canada, and the Women's Labour League. Numerous newspapers and social clubs encouraged mutual aid and cooperation. Social life also thrived around various Finnish Lutheran, Pentecostal, and United Church of Canada congregations. These early organizations influenced second generation Finns such as Paul Siren, Order of Canada recipient and influential leader of the UAW during World War II and later ACTRA (Alliance of Canadian Cinema, Television and Radio Artists) until the mid-1980s.

Finns have organized seniors' centres in Vancouver, Thunder Bay, Sault Ste. Marie, Timmins, Sudbury, and Toronto. These have become hubs of community activity. Finnish language instruction is now taught beyond Finnish summer camps and is available through Ontario's International Languages Program. Moreover, the University of Toronto offers a comprehensive Finnish Studies program and publishes an academic *Journal of Finnish Studies*. Finnish can also be studied at Lakehead University.

Several prominent Finnish Canadians have caught the attention of the broader Canadian society in the last several years. Peter Nygård, the clothing designer in Toronto and Winnipeg, has become a well-known businessman.

"Peter the Great"

Born in Helsinki, Finland, Peter Nygård, with his parents and family, immigrated to Deloraine, Manitoba, to escape the ever-impending post World War II threat of communism in his native land. Called "… the greatest designer [of fashion] in North America" by Ed Bodde, General Manager, Saks Fifth Avenue, this "Prince of Fashion" and "King of Polyester" is, today, Founder and Chairman of Nygård International, Canada's largest manufacturer of women's apparel. With manufacturing facilities in Winnipeg, research a[n]d design quarters in New York, Montreal, Europe, and Hong Kong, a production and distribution centre in L[os] Angeles, and world headquarters in Toronto, "Peter the Great," a member of the 1976 Canadian Olympic Yachting Team, was awarded Canada's 125th Anniversary Medal in 1992. [Photo, courtesy Lance Thomson/Manitoba Business]

Furthering Rights of Canadian Artists

Paul Siren traces his roots to Finnish-born parents who settled early in the 20th century near present-day Thunder Bay in northwestern Ontario. Born, 1917, in a two-room log house, Paul Siren was largely self-educated. Active in the labour movement, first, with the United Automobile Workers Union (1942-1960), then with ACTRA (Alliance of Canadian Cinema, Television and Radio Artists) when he was appointed General Secretary, 1965, with responsibility for its administration and the recognition of collective bargaining agreements. When he retired in 1986 the Hon. Pierre Juneau, right, President of the Canadian Broadcasting Corporation, congratulated Paul Siren, left, for his 21 years of service to further the rights of Canadian artists as both a mentor and as advisor. One of Paul Siren's most out-standing contributions was his instrumental work on the Status of the Artist. Co-Chair with Gratien Gélinas on the Federal Task Force on the Status of the Artist, 1986, and, until 1991, Co-Chair on the subsequent Canadian Advisory Committee on the Status of the Artist, this committee promoted and strengthened the position of professional artists in Canada. Paul Siren was appointed a Member of the Order of Canada, 1987, and received a "Nellie" from ACTRA, 1985, and Diplôme d'Honneur, 1992. [Photo, courtesy Paul Siren]

Finn Force

Judy Erola's Finnish roots in the Sudbury area of Northern Ontario go back to her grandfather, Thomas Jacobson (formerly Karppi), who came to the Sudbury district from Finland, via New York, in the late 19th century. Niilo, a son of Thomas and Susan (nee Franssi) Jacobson, married Laura Rauhala. Their daughter, Judy, burst on the public scene as a radio and television personality in the 1950s. By 1980, a going concern, Judy Erola was elected to the House of Commons as a Federal Member for Nickel Belt, and later was made Minister Responsible for the Status of Women and Minister of Consumer and Corporate Affairs. After her career in politics ended, she became President, 1987, Pharmaceutical Manufacturers' Association of Canada, a position she held until her retirement, 1998. Judy never neglected her Sudbury roots. She was the force behind the creation of Science North and the funding of Laurentian University's Centre for Mining and Mineral Exploration Research. For her service, Laurentian University awarded her an Honorary Doctorate of Laws, 1996, as portrayed in this view with Laurentian University Professor Oiva Saarinin, Ph.D., also of Finnish background, whose publication, Between a Rock and a Hard Place: An Historical Geography of the Finns in the Sudbury Area, was published in 1999. [Photo, courtesy Oiva Saarinin]

Varpu Lindström was born in Helsinki, Finland, and immigrated to Canada with her parents, 1963, as a young teenager, attending secondary school in Niagara Falls, Ontario, and obtaining university degrees at York University, including a Ph.D. in History, 1986. Currently Professor of History and Women's Studies and the Chair of the School of Women's Studies, York University, she has also served as Master, Atkinson College. Dr. Lindström is a specialist in Finnish Immigration History. She is recognized in Finland for informative radio programs on a variety of historical and current Canadian topics. Lindström is the founder of Canadian Friends of Finland, a volunteer organization promoting cultural programming and exchanges between Canada and Finland since 1982. She was recipient of Knight of the Order of the White Rose of Finland, First Class, 1991. Varpu's Husband, Börje Vähämäki, was born and raised in Vaasa, Finland, receiving his academic degrees at Abo Academy (Åbo Akademi) in Turku, Finland, including his Ph.D., 1984. After teaching Finnish Studies at the University of Minnesota, Minneapolis, he moved to his current professorship at the University of Toronto where he specializes in Finnish linguistics, Finnish literature, and Finnish folklore. Vähämäki is the author of several books on the Finnish language, including textbooks. He is also the founding editor of the Journal of Finnish Studies and an accomplished literary translator. He was awarded Knight of the Order of the White Rose of Finland, First Class, 1998. In this view, Börje celebrates his wife Varpu's 50th birthday at their home, Villa Harmony, Beaverton, Ontario. [Photo, courtesy Pauline Gustafsson]

Recently, the arrival of Jukka-Pekka Saraste as conductor of the Toronto Symphony Orchestra has caused excitement. In popular culture, Finnish hockey players such as Teemu Selänne formerly of Winnipeg Jets and Saku Koivu of Montreal Canadians have become celebrated icons within Canada's most popular of winter sports, hockey. ✛

His father was born in Finland, had changed his surname from Lakaniemi to Salo, migrated several times throughout northern Ontario, including Copper Cliff and Magpie, near Wawa, before settling in Sudbury, 1918. Four years later, the Salo family returned to Finland, leaving behind young Wilf, aged 15, to fend for himself. Over the next decade, Wilf Salo worked on the railway, for various mining companies, at lumber camps, even took up wrestling and driving taxi cabs, before marrying Nellie Pernu, of Sudbury, and settling down as floor manager for Silverman's Store, 1929-1965. Wilf is best known for serving as Sudbury's official Santa Claus. For over 50 years, his reputation grew far and wide. He not only served Silverman's as Santa but was Santa Claus for the Shriners, the Lions Club, the General and Memorial Hospitals, Police and Fire Departments, Retarded Children's Association, the CNIB and, of course, Sudbury's own Santa Claus Parade. His TV Santa started on CKSO-TV in 1952 and lasted 35 years. Knowing how to say "Merry Christmas" in 14 different languages separated this Finnish Canadian from all others who were Santa Claus pretenders. [Photo, courtesy Oiva Saarinin]

from **South Africa**

Living in Montreal since 1977, Lorraine Klaasen was born in Alberton, South Africa.
Like her famous mother, Thandi, who has performed in South Africa over the last 35 years,
Lorraine is a heatwave jazz singer. She was the recipient in 1997 of the honoured Martin
Luther King Award given to individuals who have successfully shared their heritage and whose
art works have generated unprecedented awareness of their culture. A regular performer at
Montreal's International Jazz Festival, Lorraine Klaasen is Montreal's hidden treasure – the
African Queen of Jazz whose infectious rhythms bring the spirit of Africa to North America.
[Photo, courtesy Lorraine Klaasen]

N O COUNTRY has had as checkered a history, solely predicated on race, as South Africa, at the southern tip of the African continent. The peoples of South Africa are traditionally grouped into four races: Bantu, white, coloured, and Asian. This hierarchial racial stratification became the bedrock of apartheid policy.

Seventy-seven percent of the South African population of some 42 million people is Bantu. This largest of

First settling in Saskatoon, Saskatchewan, Mike Mkangwana immigrated to Canada from Cape Province, South Africa, in 1984. Today, Mike lives in London, Ontario, where he is an assistant manager of a furniture manufacturing company. In this view, as Vice President of the Canadian Council of South Africans, Mike Mkangwana is standing with his wife, Vicki, and Prime Minister Jean Chrétien who, in 1998, hosted a gala dinner for Nelson Mandela when the former South African President made an impressive State Visit to Canada.
[Photo, courtesy Mike Mkangwana]

Dr. Alan Hudson, born in South Africa and educated at the Universities of Cape Town, Toronto, and Oxford, immigrated to Canada in the 1960s. A neuro-surgeon who served at Toronto's St. Michael's Hospital as Head of the Neurosurgical Division and at the University of Toronto as Chair of Neurosurgery, in addition to serv-ing as Honorary President, World Federation of Neurological Societies, is currently the President and CEO of The Toronto Hospital.
[Photo, courtesy The Toronto Hospital]

South African groups is made up of an extraordinary variety of tribal and cultural identities. The Nguni group is divided into Xhosa (former President Nelson Mandela's tribe), Zulu, Swati, Ndebele, and Xitsonga. The Sotho Group comprises Northern Sotho (Pedi), Southern Sotho (Sotho), and Western Sotho (Tswana). The Venda are closely related to the Shona of Zimbabwe. And then there is the unique Khoi-Khoi group made up of the Khoi, Nama, and San. Their languages are characterized by implosives (palatal, dental, and bilabial). Some of these extraordinary sounds, commonly known as clicks, have made their way into Xhosa, in particular, Zulu, and to a lesser extent Southern Sotho.

The second largest group of people living in South Africa today are whites, whose numbers have been steadily dwindling through emigration since the demise of apartheid. They now number 10.7 percent of the population. They include people of European origin such as the Afrikaaners (descendants of Dutch, German, and French Huguenots), by far the largest group, people of British stock (English, Scottish, Welsh, Irish), Portuguese, Jews, and East Europeans.

Born in the South African province formerly called the Transvaal, raised in the South African town of Heidelberg, and a graduate in medicine from the University of Witwatersrand, 1962, Dr. Cassam A. Bhabha immigrated to Canada in 1968, settling in Toronto where today he practices medicine. In faith, a devout Muslim, Dr. Bhabha over the past six years has served as President, International Development and Refugee Foundation (I.D.R.F.) assisting the less fortunate around the globe. This "people helping people" organization targets third world countries with the assistance of the Canadian International Development Agency. Dr. Bhabha's volunteer work with women in the remote areas of the South African republic generated much needed voter education prior to the historic First Election of 1993.
[Photo, courtesy Dr. C.A. Bhabha]

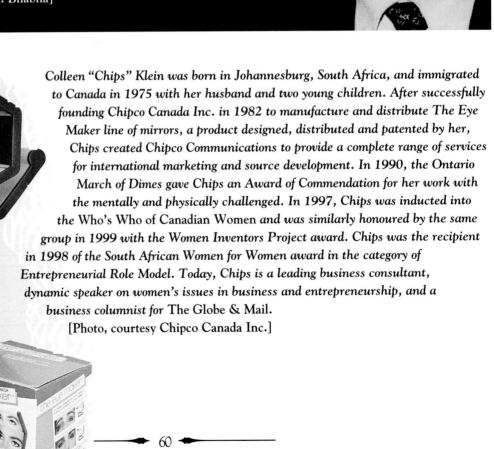

Colleen "Chips" Klein was born in Johannesburg, South Africa, and immigrated to Canada in 1975 with her husband and two young children. After successfully founding Chipco Canada Inc. in 1982 to manufacture and distribute The Eye Maker line of mirrors, a product designed, distributed and patented by her, Chips created Chipco Communications to provide a complete range of services for international marketing and source development. In 1990, the Ontario March of Dimes gave Chips an Award of Commendation for her work with the mentally and physically challenged. In 1997, Chips was inducted into the Who's Who of Canadian Women and was similarly honoured by the same group in 1999 with the Women Inventors Project award. Chips was the recipient in 1998 of the South African Women for Women award in the category of Entrepreneurial Role Model. Today, Chips is a leading business consultant, dynamic speaker on women's issues in business and entrepreneurship, and a business columnist for The Globe & Mail.
[Photo, courtesy Chipco Canada Inc.]

Gerald W. Son Kee, a second generation South African of Chinese descent, graduated from Rhodes University in the Eastern Cape, before immigrating to Canada with his family in 1990. Currently a successful financial consultant with Merrill Lynch, Gerry maintains cultural ties with the South African community serving as a director for the Canadian Council of South Africans, South African Business Association and the Canadian/South African Chamber of Commerce. Wearing a smile, Gerry Son Kee, right, in this view, with his family and presiding judge, October 1995, has just become a Canadian citizen. [Photo, courtesy Gerry Son Kee]

Dr. Phakamile Madikiza was born at Palmeton Methodist Mission at Lusikisiki, Transkei, South Africa. Today, in addition to his own private practice, he has been on staff since 1985 as consultant Paediatrician and Neonatologist at Centenary Health Centre, Scarborough, Ontario. Dr. Madikiza earned his medical degree (MB.ChB.) from the University of Natal, South Africa. Before completing Residency Training at British Columbia's Children's Hospital (1980-84), Dr. Madikiza also had Paediatric Residency Training at the University of Natal, Durban, South Africa, and the University of Ibadan, Nigeria. While a Neonatology Fellow at the University of Manitoba, he qualified as a Paediatric Specialist and was admitted to the Specialist Registrar of the Royal College of Physicians of Canada. A humanitarian whose service is tireless, Dr. Madikiza, among other matters, is currently involved in teaching medical students at the Centenary Health Centre which is one of the satellite teaching hospitals for University of Toronto medical undergraduate students. A former refugee himself, Dr. Madikiza has a broad understanding of the plight of displaced people. His work with paediatric patients with Sickle Cell Anemia has enabled him to contribute to the improvement of conditions and care and support for Sickle Cell patients and their families. As a volunteer mentor for the Advancement of Visible Minorities in Health Sciences (since 1995), he addresses students in high schools and has a high school student work with him at his office or hospital during the summer. Since 1991, Dr. Madikiza has been a Board Member of the Evergreen Hospice. This volunteer organization works with patients and their families to ease the distress that is so often associated with terminal illness and bereavement. His wife Dorcas, also from South Africa, is a teacher with the Toronto District School Board and is a Board Member of the Canadian Council of South Africans as well as South African Women for Women. [Photo, courtesy Dr. Phaks Madikiza]

Bringing Upbeat Township and South African Jazz Styles to the Western World

Themba Tana, born in Capetown, South Africa, in 1950, has been based in Vancouver, British Columbia, since 1980. His love for music was augmented by formal training at Cape Town University, Zimbabwe's Kwanogoma College, and ethnomusicological research throughout South Africa, Zimbabwe, Mozambique, and Malawi. Since his arrival in Canada, Themba has taught African cultural awareness through music and dance at Capilano College, Simon Fraser University, and the University of Calgary. Whether performing in British Columbia, Ontario, the Yukon, or in Australia and Japan, Themba, whose music compositions have been recognized at the Cannes Film Festival and been nominated for a Juno Award, incorporates traditional tribal, upbeat township, and South African jazz styles. For over 10 years, Themba Tana has performed and recorded in concerts, radio, and television in Japan, Canada, and Australia. For his 1998 CD, 11 Jungle Walk, Themba uses both traditional African instruments and Western ones to evoke not only the sounds of township life, but the greater world he now lives in. With guest artists, the result is genuine musical fusions – with Japanese shakuhachi (bamboo flute), aboriginal drums etc., all reflecting what he calls "the heartbeat of music." [Photo, courtesy Judy Lee]

Encouraging the Growth of a United South African Community in Canada

Mandisa Maduna immigrated with her mother to Canada in 1977. Graduating from high school, Mandisa attended Seneca College specializing in Early Childhood Education. Today, she is a Director of a childcare centre in Toronto and is President of the Canadian Council of South Africans whose purpose is to encourage the growth of a vibrant and united South African community in Canada and to strengthen the links between South Africa and Canada.
[Photo, courtesy Mandisa Maduna]

Asians, from the sub-continent of India (Indians and Pakistans), and Chinese make up 2.5 percent of the population and constitute a third, but nonetheless important, group living in South Africa today. Coloureds, a classification designated by previous South African governments for people of mixed ancestry – European, Khoi-Khoi, and slaves brought in from Malaysia – comprise 8.8 percent of the population and constitute the fourth and last of the major groups living in South Africa today. This percentage may dwindle in the future, as a number of coloureds now prefer to be classified as black. The remaining one percent of the population is made up of people described as other.

In Canada there are some 25,000 people who were born in the Republic of South Africa, but the total could be nearly 60,000, if descendants of South Africans are included. Fifty-six percent of these South African-born peoples live in Ontario; 25 percent live in British Columbia; and approximately 10 percent in Alberta. Although Toronto is home to 40 percent of South Africans in Canada, many live in the Greater Toronto area (GTA). Vancouver has approximately 15 percent of the South African population in Canada, and Montreal 5 percent. In contrast to the population distribution in South Africa, 73 percent of South Africans living in Canada are white. Twenty-five percent are of British descent, 20 percent are of Jewish origin, and 35 percent have multiple European origins. This immigration pattern reflects the restrictions imposed on movement by the South African government during the apartheid era. In the 1960s, Canada liberated its immigration laws to be less racially biased. Most South Africans of all backgrounds migrated after 1971. Although this position reflects the changed

The story of Dr. George Mbolekwa is one of resilience and determination. It is also inspirational. Born in Western Native Township, Johannesburg, he achieved so well in school that he was awarded a scholarship to attend high school in East London. Upon graduation, Dr. Mbolekwa was admitted on scholarship, in 1949, as a pre-med student at University College, Fort Hare, eventually graduating in medicine, 1955, from University of Witwatersrand, Johannesburg. Interning first at the Charles Johnson Memorial Hospital, Zululand, then at Baragwnath Hospital, Johannesburg, where he was one of the first of his race to be admitted as an intern, Dr. Mbolekwa, after working first in the Transkei, then Port Elizabeth, for nearly two years, escaped imminent arrest in 1962. Fleeing Port Elizabeth and his beloved South Africa by boat, Dr. Mbolekwa eventually arrived in England, practicing in the U.K. until he immigrated to Canada in 1971 with his wife, Doris, and their five children. An orthopaedic surgeon, Dr. Mbolekwa, in this 1970 view, is holding his honoured certificate following his admittance as a Fellow of the Royal College of Surgeons, Edinburgh. [Photo, courtesy Dr. George Mbolekwa]

circumstances in Canada, it was also mostly due to the mounting violence and instability in South Africa during that tumultuous decade at which time many liberal whites, blacks, and Asians left South Africa rather than face harassment by a rigid government for their opposition to apartheid. Some were put in jail or under house arrest. Many left the country because they could not stand seeing their children conscripted into an army whose main purpose was to oppress its fellow citizens rather than to defend the country against foreign aggression.

Since Canadian immigration policy traditionally favoured immigrants with high educational backgrounds and job skills, South Africans who live in Canada are generally well educated and many are professionals. According to the 1991 Canadian census, 31 percent of white, a similar percentage of Asians, and 25 percent of black South Africans in Canada have university degrees compared to 11 percent as a whole for Canada. The high education of black South African immigrants is impressive. Given the restrictions placed on them during the apartheid regime, it is a testament to the human spirit that no amount of oppression can completely quell its aspirations. Thus South Africa's brain drain has been a great boon to Canada, especially at a time when South Africa could ill afford to lose such a rare human resource.

The late Arthur Keppel-Jones was born at Rondebosch, Cape Province, South Africa, in 1909. Because of the racial-political situation in his homeland, Dr. Keppel-Jones, a Rhodes Scholar in 1929, left his native South Africa to immigrate with his family to Canada in 1959. When he wrote the influential When Smuts Goes *in 1947, Professor Keppel-Jones accurately predicted the political chaos that would engulf South Africa if the United South African Party, led by Jan Smuts, went down to defeat at the hands of the Afrikaaner Nationalist Party. When Smuts and his party were defeated, the racial discrimination policy known as apartheid quickly became law, drawing international condemnation, sanctions, and isolation. Dr. Keppel-Jones was a distinguished professor for many years at Queen's University, Kingston, Ontario. Before he died, in 1996, he was an avid boatman and cruised northern Ontario lakes. In this view he is on Buck Lake north of Kingston, Ontario, circa 1963. [Photo, courtesy Michael Keppel-Jones]*

Ebenezer Modeni Sikakane was born outside Estcourt, KwaZulu-Natal, in South Africa. His education started with schooling at the age of eight because he had to walk quite a distance to get to the nearest school. He then went on to obtain a teacher's diploma; a B.A. in Theology from the University of South Africa; a Th.M. from Fuller Theological Seminary, California; and a D.Min, from Trinity Divinity School, Deerfield, Illinois. Ebenezer married Emily Sibisi, a school teacher from Newcastle, South Africa, and they taught together for six years until he entered the ministry. After that he taught at the same college for eleven years and then went on to evangelism with African Enterprise for nine years. In 1978 they moved to Canada with their five children. Ebenezer taught at Tyndale College and Seminary for sixteen years, heading up the Intercultural Studies Department of the College. After retiring from lecturing in 1996, he is now part-time pastor of Churchill Community Church near Stouffville, Ontario. He is also honorary Canadian Director of African Ministries, an organization operating in South Africa. In this view, Rev. Sikakane congratulates recent graduates from Tyndale College. [Photo, courtesy Rev. Ebenezer Sikakane]

The apartheid regime has had a chilling effect on South Africans and their associations overseas. The "group areas act" under the old apartheid regime residentially segregated people by imposing arbitrary racial categories. At first, South African heritage organizations and institutions in Canada tended to be based on one racial group or another. Furthermore, the old South African regime was notorious for employing agents to infiltrate suspected anti-apartheid organizations overseas. The policy in turn discouraged too much mixing among South African expatriates, because nobody trusted anyone, especially since the apartheid regime was not too reluctant to exact retribution on someone's captive relatives back home in South Africa.

In recent years, however, as the apartheid regime was replaced by a democratic government in South Africa, expatriate organizations in Canada began to work together, regardless of racial or cultural differences. In 1997, the Canadian Council of South Africans (CANCOSA) was established to encourage the growth of a vibrant and united South African community in Canada and to strengthen the links between Canada and South Africa. And, in 1998, the Canadian Friends of the Nelson Mandela Children's Fund was launched by President Mandela before a crowd of 50,000, including 45,000 school children, at Toronto's famous SkyDome.

While South Africa, the nation, enters its place in the community of democratic societies for the twenty-first century, the South African presence in Canada as a collective group is only now showing signs of emerging. ❂

Emmanuel Seko

Born, Georgetown, Guyana, 1961, Mark McKoy was 12 years old when his family immigrated to Canada, 1973, settling, Toronto, Ontario. As a high school student, Mark showed early interest in track and field and was soon making a name for himself winning hurdle events wherever there was a track meet. At age 20, he represented Canada at the Commonwealth Games, Brisbane, Australia, 1982, and won the Gold Medal in the 110-metre hurdles. He repeated this achievement at the Commonwealth Games, Edinburgh, Scotland, 1986. Although disappointed with his performance at the 1988 Seoul Olympics, placing 7th in the hurdle finals, he spectacularly redeemed himself in the Summer Olympics, Barcelona, Spain, 1992, taking the Gold Medal in the 110m hurdles, the first Track and Field Gold Medal for Canada in 64 years. A five-time Olympian, Mark was a member of Canada's National Track and Field Team, 1980-94. He still holds the world record for the 50m hurdles and is the former world record holder in the 60m hurdles. Married to Yvette, a former East German middle distance runner, Mark, the proud father of two children, is President and CEO, United Family Martial Arts, Mississauga, Ontario, with 750 members, and is also Owner/Operator, Mississauga-based Gold Medal Enterprises which specializes in speed and power training for athletes. In this view, Mark McKoy is seen winning the Canadian 110-metre Championship, Montreal, 1990. [Photo, courtesy Ontario Track and Field Association]

from **Guyana**

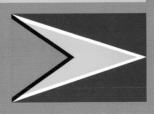

GUYANESE in Canada come from a country characterized by ethnic, linguistic, and religious diversity. Situated along the northeastern coast of South America and facing the Atlantic Ocean, the former colony of British Guiana shares a border with Venezuela on the east. Within its domain live nearly 800,000 people. Of these, half are people of Asian Indian descent, followed by those of African origin (30 percent), with the remainder consisting of "coloured" (mixed African and European origin), Amerindian, Portuguese, and Chinese peoples.

Dr. T. Vidhya (Vid) N. Persaud, born, 1940, Port Mourant, Guyana, earned his M.D., Rostock University, Germany, 1965, and Ph.D., University of the West Indies, 1970. After completing his internship in Berlin, Dr. Persaud served as Government Medical Officer, Guyana, 1966-67. He was appointed Lecturer/Senior Lecturer, 1967-72, University of West Indies. In 1972 Dr. Persaud joined the medical faculty, University of Manitoba, where he became Professor and Head of the Department of Human Anatomy and Cell Science, 1977-1993. Dr. Persaud is now Professor Emeritus, 1999, University of Manitoba; Associate Professor of Obstetrics, Gynecology and Reproductive Sciences, since 1979, and Professor, Pediatrics and Child Health, since 1989. Dr. Persaud is deeply involved in the study of embryology and birth defects, and since 1965, has published numerous research papers and 22 books in this area including Advances in the Study of Birth Defects (Vols. 1-7, 1979 to 1982), Environmental Causes of Human Birth Defects, 1990, and The Developing Human, with the University's former Head of Anatomy, Dr. Keith L. Moore (6th ed., 1998). Dr. Persaud has received several awards in recognition of his teaching and research including the Dr. and Mrs. Saunderson Award for Excellence in Teaching, University of Manitoba, 1985; Albert Einstein Centennial Medal, Academy of Sciences, Germany, 1981, Andreas Vesalius Medal, University of Pisa, 1986, and the J.C.B. Grant Award, Canadian Association of Anatomists, 1991. Dr. Persaud is considered one of the world's leading authorities in the field of teratology. [Photo, courtesy Dr. T.V.N. Persaud]

At 12 years, Andra Persaud Thakur, born on a sugar plantation where his grandfather had served as an indentured bonded labourer, was forced to quit school in his native Guyana to help his father, a peasant rice farmer. Apprenticed as a tailor in the off season, Andra became a journeyman at 13, and by 21, owned a small sewing business employing 12 journeymen and apprentices. He was 27 before the opportunity arose to return to school, enrolling at Alberta College, Edmonton, and after two semesters, went to the University of Alberta as a mature student. Eight years later, with a B.A., M.A., and Ph.D. in Anthropology, he taught in West Africa over the next six years, first, at the University of Ghana, then the University of Benin, Nigeria, before returning to the University of Alberta, 1984. Until 1987, he served briefly as executive director, Edmonton Immigrant Services Association, then moved to Nanaimo, B.C., to teach cultural anthropology and cross-cultural education at Malaspina University College. Professor Thakur has lectured in China, is affiliated with a university in India, has taught in Northern Thailand and more recently conducted Field Schools in India, Thailand, Malaysia, Bali, and the Caribbean. With reference to International Development, Professor Thakur, in his brief biography, cites the comment by Jerry Rawlings, President of Ghana: "Canada is the country that says the least and does the most." Andra adds in the same biography, "Had I not come to Canada, I might never have completed my primary or secondary education." In this view, Professor Thakur, right, while teaching in Ghana, visits, circa 1980, President Jerry Rawlings of Ghana. [Photo, courtesy Professor A.P. Thakur]

The first Guyanese came to Canada during the late nineteenth century. The early arrivals settled primarily in Nova Scotia, Ontario, and Quebec. By 1921, a community of over 200 Guyanese had settled in Toronto while others established themselves in smaller numbers elsewhere. The great majority found work as sleeping-car porters who provided remarkably efficient and discreet service to railway passengers. Guyanese immigration came to a virtual standstill after World War I as new Canadian immigration legislation expanded the list of those to be refused entry to include anyone belonging to a race or nationality simply deemed unsuitable. Guyanese immigrants only began arriving in Canada again after 1955 as part of a regularized scheme under which an annual quota of 100 unmarried female domestic servants could enter the country on temporary employment visas and obtain permanent residence after a few years of service. Economic instability, growing unemployment, pressure on the Asian Indian population by the government of Linden Forbes Burnham produced a surge in Guyanese emigration to Canada during the 1960s and 1970s. Canada emerged more fully as a major destination for Guyanese immigrants only when all the vestiges of racial and ethnic discrimination were officially expunged from Canadian immigration regulations and procedures and a point system instituted to measure an applicant's qualifications in a series of categories.

Those who came during peak years of Guyanese immigration made their way to the industrial heartland of Canada, with Ontario as the main destination. The logic of economics and chain migration catapulted Toronto and the urban centres of Mississauga, Brampton, Ottawa, Hamilton, and Windsor into the premier positions as Guyanese settlement areas. In the 1996 Canadian census, 40,520 individuals described themselves as being of Guyanese origin. Of these, 22,110 said Guyanese was their only ethnic origin, and 18,410 said it was one of their ethnic origins. A total of 35,055 Guyanese lived in Ontario, with Toronto home to 15,425. Outside central Canada, Guyanese were drawn to the metropolitan areas of Vancouver, Calgary, Edmonton, and Montreal. These Canadian urban centres provided the greatest scope for the linguistic skills and the professional talent in medicine, engineering, insurance, and banking as well as for merchants and entrepreneurs.

Guyanese have also shown a strong preference for areas of residential concentration, most notably in Toronto. Traditional arriving and staging areas in Toronto include Jameson Avenue and Queen Street West, Finch Avenue West and Weston Road, Lawrence Avenue East and Markham Road, Albion Road and Islington Avenue, and Lawrence Avenue West and Weston Road.

Dr. Chandra Madramootoo has made Water Resources his profession. Graduating B.Sc. (1977), M.Sc. (1981), and Ph.D. (1985), Agricultural and Biosystems Engineering, McGill University, Dr. Madramootoo has taught these subjects at his alma mater since 1984. Born, Georgetown, Guyana, 1954, after completing his B.Sc., he worked for three years on irrigation systems for banana farms at the Caribbean Agricultural Research Development Institute, St. Lucia, before returning to McGill to complete his graduate work. While taking his Ph.D., he was invited to be a lecturer, becoming full professor, 1995. A world-recognized expert in the field of irrigation, drainage, and flood control, Dr. Madramootoo was named Founding Director, McGill's Brace Centre for Water Resource Management, 1999. He has been a consultant on water projects in Eygpt, Pakistan, Sri Lanka, India, and St. Lucia, has been author or co-author of over 100 papers and has presented more than 50 papers at international conferences, seminars, and various symposia. Serving as adviser to CIDA, FAO, EU, and the World Bank on matters associated with water projects worldwide, Dr. Madramootoo, as a participant in a World Water Council project, has helped prepare Canada's world vision for water usage and the environment in the 21st century, and has helped develop Canada's regional vision for water, food, and rural development in the Americas. [Photo, courtesy Dr. Chandra Madramootoo]

Guyanese tend to establish sports, dancing, and recreational clubs rather than large, formal ethnocommunity organizations. The immigrants, in turn, have contributed to Canadian culture in the area of music as Canadians have enthusiastically embraced the sound of steel bands, calypso, and reggae.

It is reasonable to assume that the religious identity of the Guyanese in Canada resembles that of the homeland. Most Guyanese belong to one of three Christian denominations: Roman Catholic, Anglican, and Baptist. The Guyanese Asian Indian community in Canada, consisting of both Hindus and Muslims, has not yet established any major religious centres. Rather the group participates in the various churches, temples, and mosques serving Canada's diverse nationalities. ☘

After teaching elementary school for six years in her native Guyana, Eucline Claire Alleyne obtained a B.A., Albion College, 1970, M.A., Howard University, 1972, and planned to work in the United States. After Canadian friends encouraged her to immigrate to Canada, she was made Admissions Officer at the University of Toronto's Faculty of Nursing, 1973-76; then Registrar, Faculty of Applied Science and Engineering, 1976-81; Associate Registrar, Woodsworth College, University of Toronto, 1981-88, and Registrar, Faculty of Education, 1988-96, before her present appointment as Registrar, University of Toronto's Ontario Institute for Studies in Education. While carrying out these tasks, Claire Alleyne found time to earn a Doctorate in Education, 1987. In 1994, she was named winner, University of Toronto Chancellor Award of Excellence for her many contributions as an active member of numerous volunteer committee at the University. Daughter of a minister, her parents and a sister followed her to Canada where her father became minister of the United Church, Severn Bridge, Ontario. [Photo, courtesy Dr. Claire Alleyne]

Writer, teacher, and race relations expert, Cyril Dabydeen, a native of Guyana, worked his way through Lakehead University, Thunder Bay, Ontario, by planting trees in Quetico Provincial Park and Trapper Lake, northwestern Ontario, before graduating, B.A., 1973, and earning, M.A., 1974, and M.P.A., 1977, the same year he published his first poems. His poetry and fiction now comprise several volumes with many works also appearing in anthologies published in Canada, the U.S.A, and the U.K. He taught at both Ottawa's Algonquin College and University of Ottawa before serving as coordinator, Mayor's Race Relations Committee, Ottawa, 1984-89, and as Race Relations Manager for the Federal Government and the Federation of Canadian Municipalities between 1989 and 1999. The recipient of numerous literary prizes, Cyril has been actively involved in several literary societies, particularly those dealing with writers from the Caribbean, observing in a University of Oklahoma Press article, 1999, that "as West Indian-born writers inhabiting Canada, we will continue to fashion our own dreams in unique ways as we react to a complex Canadian social and cultural landscape." Poet Laureate of Ottawa, 1984-87, Cyril is also a member of PEN International. [Photo, courtesy Cyril Dabydeen]

SPANISH EXPLORERS led by Christopher Columbus initiated significant European contact with the island of Hispaniola in 1492. Situated in the Caribbean Sea between Cuba and Puerto Rico, the island became a Spanish colony, but in 1697 Spain ceded the western third of the island to France. Finally, in 1804 the French colony declared its right to self-government and became Haiti, the first independent Black republic.

At age seven, Bruny Surin, born, Cap-Haïtien, Haiti, 1967, came to Canada, joining both his mother and father who had preceded him and his sister to Montreal by one year. His first track and field events were the long and triple jumps but he switched to sprinting, 1989, the same year he won the first of six Canadian Championships in the 100 metres. A member of the 4x100m relay team which won a Gold Medal at the 1996 Atlanta Olympics, Bruny is a four-time World Champion (two outdoor – 4x100m Relay, two indoor – 60m), a Commonwealth Champion, and one of the World's fastest humans throughout the 1990s in both the 100 metres as well as the 50/60 metres. Bruny enjoyed the finest outdoor season of his career, 1999. At the World Championships, Seville, Spain, he clocked 9.84 seconds in the 100m, equalling Donovan Bailey's 1996 world record time for that event which, in the same race, was broken by U.S. sprinter Maurice Greene who won the Gold Medal in 9.79 seconds. Bruny's Silver Medal time was the third fastest 100 metres in history. Bruny's wife, Bianelle Legros-Surin, is his manager. Together they have two daughters and reside as a family in a Montreal suburb where he is coached by Michel Portmann, Professor of Kinanthropology, University of Quebec. In this view, Bruny Surin, at the World Championships, Seville, Spain, 1999, demonstrates his strength in a 100-metre quarter final. [Photo, courtesy Peter J. Thompson]

Born, 1935, Camp-Perrin, Haiti, Alphonse Boisrond completed his secondary education at the Philippe Guerrier School in nearby Cayes. Upon graduating in Medicine, University of Haiti, 1963, Dr. Boisrond began his practice by serving five villages on the outskirts of Port-à-Piment. He then learned that Canada needed doctors. Upon immigrating to Canada, 1965, fleeing political unrest in Haiti, he settled in Montreal where he enrolled at the University of Montreal, specializing in thoracic surgery. After completing 30 months training in anaesthesiology at Hôtel-Dieu and St. Justine hospitals, Dr. Boisrond established a family practice, 1973, in St-Léonard, faithfully serving Montreal's Haitian community until 1997, at which time he was forced into retirement due to impaired vision. In 1975, understanding that Haitian immigrants in Montreal needed help in adjusting to an adopted homeland, Dr. Boisrond co-founded Mouvement Fraternité Haiti-Québec (MFHQ). He also co-founded a Haitian community centre to meet the needs of a growing Haitian community. As well, 1980, Dr. Boisrond founded le Centre Haitian d'Archives et de documentation. Suffering from deteriorating vision, he founded the Haitian Association for the Blind and People Suffering from Amblyopia, 1992. In the 35 years he served Montreal's Haitian community, Dr. Boisrond gave one day a week of volunteer service to the Mouvement Fraternité Haiti-Québec, the equivalent of four years work without monetary gain. [Photo, courtesy Dr. Alphonse Boisrond]

from Haiti

By the end of the nineteenth century, political anarchy and economic instability had forced many Haitians to look beyond their home in search of work. At first, they ventured to the Dominican Republic, on the eastern part of the island, and then to Cuba. Between 1950 and 1970, artisans, domestics, and other workers gradually expanded the circle of Haitian labour outposts in the Caribbean to include the Bahamas, Puerto Rico, Jamaica, Curaçao, Aruba, Martinique, and Guadeloupe. During this period, Haitians also made their way to the United States where over 200,000 settled in New York City alone. Still others gravitated to Brazil, France, and Italy.

The 1970s witnessed the beginning of large-scale immigration of Haitians to Canada. Today, over 90 percent of all Haitian Canadians live in the province of Quebec, with Montreal being the home base to by far the largest Haitian community with a grand total exceeding 70,000 persons. The vast majority reside in the city's downtown core and the northeastern suburbs. Other Haitian communities in Canada include Ottawa-Hull and Toronto.

Haitian immigrants fulfilled many of Quebec's economic needs. The presence of Haitian doctors, nurses, teachers, and journalists coincided with the Quiet Revolution. The revolution against both American and English-speaking Canadian economic and cultural domination of Quebec was to be the stairway that led to success for these skilled, French-speaking immigrants.

Filling out the community's labour ranks, skilled Haitian tradespeople and service workers also contributed to the industrial and commercial development of urban Quebec. And since 1987, Haitian restaurants and travel

One of 16 siblings, Max Charleston was born, 1947, in Gonaïves, Haiti's third largest city where his father, Emmanuel Barbot, was a school superintendent and his mother, Oliane, a shopkeeper. After attending high school and Teacher's College, Max furthered his post-secondary school studies, University of Haiti, pursuing Law and Economic Sciences, 1971-75. La famille Barbot, as with so many Haitian families at this time, suffered under the abusive powers of the Duvalier regime. In order for Max to escape dictatorship, he changed his surname to Charleston, his mother's family name. Arriving in Canada, December 1975, Max chose to live in Toronto where job opportunities in the teaching profession were plentiful. Hired by the Metropolitan Toronto Separate School Board, 1976, Max began teaching Elementary School French, as a second language. He continues to teach high school French during the evenings for the Toronto District School Board. Max has joined various Haitian cultural groups in Toronto and has formerly served l'Association Haitienne de Toronto as both Secretary and Vice Chair. "Whenever the opportunity arises," he is "helping my fellow citizens in difficulty with the law, the immigration system, and the ones experiencing difficulties integrating into the Toronto milieu." [Photo, courtesy Max Charleston]

Like many before and after her, Gladys Guérin, born, Petion-Ville, Haiti, 1950, came to Canada to further her education, with intentions of returning home, but ended up working and getting married in Canada. Since 1987, the Treasurer of l'Outaouais Urban Community, the regional government serving Hull, Gatineau, and Aylmer, Quebec, Ms. Guérin left her homeland to study at the University of Ottawa, taking a B.Admin., 1971, B.Comm., 1972, and becoming a Chartered Accountant, 1975. She held posts with George Welch & Co., 1975-79, was Director, Financial Services, Champlain School Board in Gatineau, 1979-84, and Financial Analyst at Des Draveurs School Board in Gatineau, 1984-87, prior to her present post. Married to Serge Monette, 1980, Ms. Guérin is a member of the Chartered Accountant Institutes of both Quebec and Ontario. [Photo, courtesy Gladys Guérin]

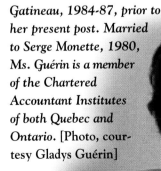

agencies, clothing outlets, book and music stores – created initially for the needs of the immigrant group – became both places of employment and the source of good things for other inhabitants of Montreal and the inner suburbs.

The economic development of the community was paralleled by the growth of Haitian institutional life. Great gathering places eased Haitian passage into society at large. Haitians formed a number of associations and organizations that first answered socio-economic and settlement problems and then helped newcomers obtain access to government and education services. Other associations, acting as agents of the modern concept of Haitian ethnicity, gave texture and definition to group identity. Haitian immigrants preserved Créole, their day-to-day language, through the establishment of drama and folklore groups.

Literature published by research and information centres, scholarly journals, popular magazines, and specialized works on Haiti and the diaspora contributed to the preservation of Créole. Community newspapers, radio programs, painting, sculpture, and music also exercised their right to define their own Haitian existence.

In addition, Haitians made a number of solid contributions both to Quebec and Canadian life in general. In politics, Jean Alfred, a Parti Québécois member of Haitian origin, represented Papineau riding in Quebec's National

After receiving B.Sc., École St. Louis de Gonzague, Haiti, 1962, and M.D., University Louis Pasteur, Strasbourg, France, 1970, Dr. Raymond Duperval, born, Jérémie, Haiti, 1944, and his wife, Mimose, moved to Sherbrooke, Quebec, on the recommendation of one of his former Louis Pasteur professors. There, Dr. Duperval interned and later attended University of Minnesota, Mayo Graduate School, where he specialized in Infectious Diseases, 1976, before returning to Sherbrooke as Assistant Professor of Medicine and Consultant, Centre Hospitalier Université de Sherbrooke. Named Associate Professor, 1981, and Head, Division of Infectious Diseases at the hospital, 1988, he became Full Professor, 1993, where in addition to his teaching he carried out research in Infectious Diseases and AIDS. Besides his medical work, Dr. Duperval is consultant of GAP-VIES, a community group aiding the more than 50,000 Haitians living in the Montreal Area. His other interest is Haitian music. With a few friends and two of his three sons, both graduate engineers, he participates in a band that has played numerous concerts, including the Faculty Club at his University, and has recorded two successful CDs. "It's our way to relax," Dr. Duperval explains. [Photo, courtesy Dr. Raymond Duperval]

Born, Haiti, 1950, Maryse Alcindor, M.A., LL.B., immigrated to Canada from Port-au-Prince, 1965. Settling, Montreal, Quebec, at first she became a teacher, 1967, then an attorney, graduating, Université de Montréal, LL.B., 1980. Today, she is Director, Education and Cooperation, Commission des droits de la personne et des droits de la jeunesse, an agency of the Government of Quebec since it was established, 1976. Her responsibilities include protecting the rights of individuals in an ever-increasing diverse Quebec society. Voted "Teacher of the Year" by her students at Henri Bourass Secondary School, Montreal, 1981, Maryse Alcindor consistently demonstrates exceptional dedication in everything she does. She was an integral member of two investigative teams that examined the disturbing conditions of patients at Rivière des Prairies Hospital in addition to the intolerable relations that existed between police and various ethnic and visible minority groups in Montreal. In order to overcome the intolerance that unfortunately had permeated some aspects of Quebec society, the two studies, both of which received wide media publicity, concluded that justice, peace, and equality were key missing links needed to build a more just society. An energetic volunteer, Maryse partakes in awareness workshops within her own community, striving to improve understanding and harmony among all groups living in a distinct Quebec society. Beyond Quebec, Maryse Alcindor is part of an international team setting up clinics in 19 different African countries to draw to the attention of women of African birth, their rights as world citizens. Proud of her origins, Maryse claims that her husband and three daughters are her inspiration. [Photo, courtesy Maryse Alcindor]

Assembly, 1976 and 1980, and was Quebec's first Black M.N.A. Many Haitians participate in the political life of Quebec at the grassroots by serving on a number of citizens' committees, anti-racism groups, and political action organizations.

Of note, Dany Laferrière, the well-known author of *How to Make Love to a Negro*, saw his popular work made into a successful feature film. As well, a number of Haitian journalists, anchors, and hosts have helped to give voice to French language print and broadcast media. In sports, Bruny Surin, athlete and world-class sprinter, has carried the hopes and dreams of all Canadians across the finish line at a multitude of track and field events. ⬙

Born, Port-au-Prince, Haiti, 1946, at 25 years, Keder Hyppolite immigrated to Canada, 1972, as did many Haitians that year, to escape the oppressive Duvalier regime which had ruled over Haiti since 1957. Settling, Montreal, where a majority of Haitian Canadians had taken up residence, over the past 28 years, Keder has devoted much of his time and energy as an activist for human rights, focusing on the integration of minorities and the resettlement of immigrants. After receiving a B.A., University of Quebec, Montreal, and acquiring a second degree in Social Administration and a Certificate in Human Rights, University of Prince Edward Island, Keder Hyppolite has passionately served his community. A Judge of the Human Rights Tribunal of Quebec and Member, Youth Centre of Montreal, Keder has run as an NDP federal candidate and twice has run for Montreal's City Council. President and Founding Member of both the National Council of Citizens of Haitian Origin and Alliance of Cultural Communities for Equality and Access to Health and Social Services, Keder is also a Member of the Board Quebec Movement to combat racism and is a Second Vice President, Harambee Centres Canada. For his efforts to serve and promote the Black presence in Canada, Keder was awarded the Commemorative Medal for the 125th Anniversary of the Confederation of Canada. He also received, February 2, 2000, The Round Table of Black History Month Award in recognition of significant contribution to compatriots, community, and to the city of Montreal. In this view, Keder shares a proud moment with Jean Doré, former Mayor of Montreal. [Photo, courtesy Keder Hyppolite]

Born, 1946, Port-au-Prince, Haiti, Fritzberg Daléus traces his family roots to such early Haitian surnames as Barthélemy, Innocent, Volcy, and St-Lot. A passionate artist with many talents, Fritzberg immigrated to Canada, 1972, settling, Montreal, after a brief sojourn in Toronto. In 1979, the romantic poet, singer, composer, painter, and passionate volunteer founded l'Association Culturelle et artistique des Haitiens à Montréal with the single purpose of promoting the untapped artistic talents of immigrant Haitians. In 1990, he founded le Centre de Union Multiculturelle et Artistique des Jeunes (CUMAJ) of which he is, today, the Director General. His driving force to share Haitian culture with Quebec society has made a positive impact. Fritzberg's enthusiasm in working with young people has been of great assistance to many Haitian immigrants, young people in particular, who have discovered their artistic talents and have been guided toward productive lives. On behalf of the City of Montreal, Mayor Pierre Bourque has cited Fritzberg for his energetic volunteer work ameliorating the quality of life in Montreal. Fritzberg has also been recognized by la Communauté Urbaine de Montréal for his generous contribution, 1997, à la premiere edition de la Semaine québécoise de la citoyennete. In this view, Quebec Premier Lucien Bouchard meets with Fritzberg Daléus, a Haitian immigrant determined to participate in Quebec's cultural and social heartbeat. [Photo, courtesy Fritzberg Daléus]

CANADA'S THAI community come from what today is a constitutional monarchy in Southeast Asia but formerly was the Kingdom of Siam. Census data for 1996 record the presence of only 5,015 Thais in Canada (single and multiple responses).

Although small in number, Canadians of Thai origin have settled in the provinces of Ontario (1,965), British Columbia (1,205), Quebec (855), and Alberta (680). Couples and small groups reside primarily in the major city centres of Toronto, Montreal, and Vancouver.

Thai Canadians are mostly well-educated professionals working as bankers, dentists, doctors, nurses, computer

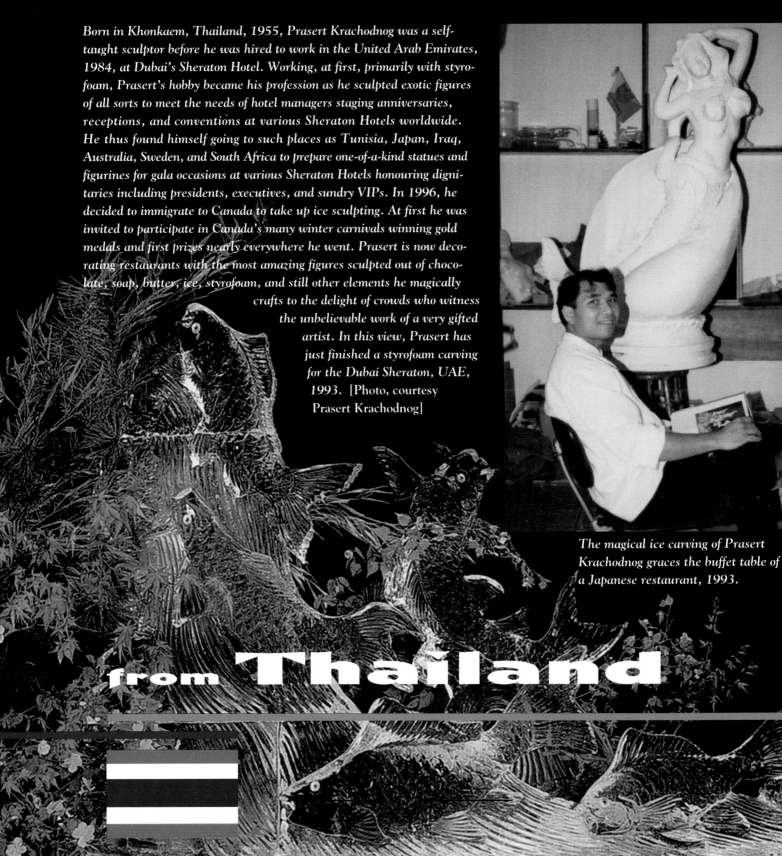

Born in Khonkaem, Thailand, 1955, Prasert Krachodnog was a self-taught sculptor before he was hired to work in the United Arab Emirates, 1984, at Dubai's Sheraton Hotel. Working, at first, primarily with styrofoam, Prasert's hobby became his profession as he sculpted exotic figures of all sorts to meet the needs of hotel managers staging anniversaries, receptions, and conventions at various Sheraton Hotels worldwide. He thus found himself going to such places as Tunisia, Japan, Iraq, Australia, Sweden, and South Africa to prepare one-of-a-kind statues and figurines for gala occasions at various Sheraton Hotels honouring dignitaries including presidents, executives, and sundry VIPs. In 1996, he decided to immigrate to Canada to take up ice sculpting. At first he was invited to participate in Canada's many winter carnivals winning gold medals and first prizes nearly everywhere he went. Prasert is now decorating restaurants with the most amazing figures sculpted out of chocolate, soap, butter, ice, styrofoam, and still other elements he magically crafts to the delight of crowds who witness the unbelievable work of a very gifted artist. In this view, Prasert has just finished a styrofoam carving for the Dubai Sheraton, UAE, 1993. [Photo, courtesy Prasert Krachodnog]

The magical ice carving of Prasert Krachodnog graces the buffet table of a Japanese restaurant, 1993.

from Thailand

technicians, engineers, and entrepreneurs. Thai women – exceptionally competent and hardworking – can also be found in the community's professional ranks. More recently, young Thai women have come to Canada to work as artists and entertainers, night club dancers, child care nannies, even as seamstresses in illegal enterprises.

Thai restaurateurs have carved out an important and popular niche in Canada's food service and hospitality industry. As more Canadians have become familiar with and knowledgeable about Thai cuisine through tourism and positive media accounts, Thai restaurants have increased greatly in number. It is believed that the first Thai restaurant in Canada opened in Toronto in 1978. There are now more than 30 Thai restaurants in the Greater Toronto Area (GTA). Thai restaurants, many family-owned and operated, have proven to be important stepping stones into the entrepreneurial ranks.

The Thai Community Association of British Columbia, the Friends of Thailand in Vancouver, the Thai Association of Ontario, the Thai Buddhist Community of Toronto, and the Thai Buddhist Association, Toronto, are all voluntary associations that meet regularly for social gatherings and religious celebrations. They teach Thai classical dance, raise money for relief and cultural efforts and Thai charities, and entertain visiting officials, including political leaders and monks. To those non-Thai Canadians who wish to understand and appreciate Thai culture, these Associations all have a welcome mat and an open door.

Group professional associations, in turn, are often North American in membership and governance. The Association of Thai Professionals Working in America and Canada, for example, is a Texas-based organization dedicated to linking Thai who are working in the scientific and technological fields.

Dr. Ekchai Vialpatar, born, Bangkok, Thailand, came to Canada via the United States, 1974, after graduating, Doctor of Chiropractic, from Northwestern College of Chiropractic, St. Paul, Minnesota. Establishing his practice in Toronto, Ontario, Dr. Vialpatar is a Member of the Canadian Chiropractic Association, Past President, Canadian Council of Chiropractic Sports Sciences, Fellow of the International Academy of Clinical Acupuncture, and a Member of the World Federation of Chiropractic. "Serving people, alleviating their pain and discomfort and bringing them health and wellness" is a motto which Dr. Vialpatar exercises while administering treatments. [Photo, courtesy Dr. Ekchai Vialpatar]

Pichet and Pien Tovich were born and raised in Thailand. Their respective parents were of Chinese origin, emigrating from South China to Thailand in the 1920s, due to economic hardship and frequent social unrest. Their parents were dedicated and hardworking people, whose constant sacrifices enabled their children to finish university. Both graduated, 1968, from the Faculty of Medicine, Chiangmai University, in Northern Thailand, opting to immigrate, 1970, to Canada where they began residency training, University of Toronto: Pichet in Neurology; and Pien in Pathology. Completing their training in 1975, during which time the instability in South East Asia caused much concern over their children's future in that region, they decided to remain in Canada. Pichet was able to establish a busy practice in Peterborough, Ontario, taking referrals from physicians in Peterborough and its surrounding area. Were it not for Pien's willingness to sacrifice her career to raise four sons, Pichet's practice would clearly have suffered. Instead it has since grown, with two other associate neurologists, and Pien acting as office manager. To date, the practice services an area populated [by] a quarter of a million residents. As with their parents, [their] success has been, in part, due to hard work, dedication, [and] sacrifice. But they are "very grateful for the opportunity, [fair]ness, and freedom Canada has provided them, to achieve [their] goals beyond anything they could ever have imagined." [In] this view, Pichet, left, Pien, centre, and the Hon. [C]huang Leekpai, Prime Minister of Thailand, attend [a] gala in Thailand, 1995. [Photo, courtesy Dr. [Pic]het Tovich]

Thai Couple from Oshawa Recognized by Spiritual Leader

Dr. Somchai Jiaravuthisan, in this view, left, was born in Chachoengsao, a small town in Thailand some 60 kilometers east of Bangkok. The son of parents who struggled to educate their three children, Somchai was successful in being near the top of his class all the way through school, including his pre-med training at Mahidol University, 1964-1966, and his medical school training at the same university, 1966-1970. Professor Athasit Vejjajiva, now the President, Mahidol University, was the mentor who guided Somchai to specialize in Neurology. Studying Neurology at Ramathibodi Hospital, Bangkok, Thailand's largest and oldest Psychiatric Hospital, Somchai was urged to go to McGill University in Canada to further his neurological studies. After stops at Dalhousie University, The Montreal Neurological Institute, and Saint John General Hospital, St. John, New Brunswick, Dr. Jiaravuthisan, today, is an active staff member in Neurology at the Oshawa General Hospital in Ontario. Somchai's wife, Yupin, next to her husband in this view, was also born in Chachoengsao, Thailand. To get to school each day, she had to travel one hour each way in a paddle boat. Accepted, 1963, to attend the Faculty of Dentistry, Mahidol University, Bangkok, Yupin obtained her D.D.S., 1971, the same year she married Somchai. When she came to Canada with Somchai, she passed, on her first attempt, the National Dental Examination, 1997, permitting her to work in Canada as a registered dentist. For the past 17 years, Yupin has worked at the Canadian Auto Workers Dental Clinic, Oshawa. In this view, Somchai and Yupin, together, receive a certificate from well-known Pra Rajadhammajetiyajan, Lord Abbot of Wat Dhammamongkol, Bangkok, taken at the Buddhist Temple, Richmond Hill, 1997. In the middle is Bill Dickinson, Honorary Consul General, Thailand. [Photo, courtesy Dr. Somchai and Dr. Yupin Jiaravuthisan]

Celebrating Wesak

In this Toronto view, 1996, Buddhists from the Yanviriya Temple, Richmond Hill, celebrate Wesak, an annual sacred festival commemorating the enlightenment of Siddhartha Gautama (Buddha) some 2,500 years ago. [Photo, courtesy Sompong Rogpradit]

วัดญาณวิริยา ๒
Yanviriya Temple II
166 Cedar Ave.

Theravada Buddhism also shapes Thai religious, ethnic, and cultural identity in Canada as it does in Thailand. Thai temples in Toronto and Vancouver also help to provide group solidarity. With the exception of the new pan-Buddhist celebrations such as Wesak, rituals in Canada often become occasions of community celebrations where weekend events promote social and cultural group awareness as much as religious identity. ♦

Wandee Young, right centre, was born at Puket, Southern Thailand, but grew up in Bangkok. Her father was in the restaurant business in Thailand so it was natural for Wandee, when she came to Canada, 1976, to follow in the footsteps of her father. Her first restaurant opened in Toronto, 1978. Called Young Thailand, Wandee claims it was the "First Thai Restaurant in Canada," a corporate slogan she has registered and trademarked. She sold the restaurant a few years later, but kept the name, and reopened another all-Thai restaurant, 1990. Today, Wandee has four Toronto eating establishments, all specializing in Thai foods, all called Young Thailand with the one on Church Street, downtown Toronto, the flagship of the exclusive chain. Because of her Buddhist background, her restaurants are discreetly decorated with artifacts, statuettes, figurines, and various images and carvings reflecting the religious background of her native land. In this view, Wandee stands between two distinguished Thai diplomats who paid a visit to one of Wandee's restaurants in 1999. On the right is Thailand's Ambassador to Canada, Mr. Sunai Bunyasiriphant and, left, is His Excellency M.R. Sukhumbhand Paribatra, M.P., Deputy Minister, Foreign Affairs, Thailand. [Photo, courtesy Wandee Young]

Channarong Ratanaseansuang, below right, born in Thailand, has been head badminton professional at the Glencoe Club, Calgary, Alberta, ever since he immigrated to Canada, 1967, the year Canada celebrated its 100th anniversary of Confederation. Since that time, Channarong has played a significant role in the development of badminton in Canada, guiding 21 athletes to Senior National Championships. He continues to bring out the best in teams under his leadership, including nearly 15 years as Canadian National Team Coach. As an athlete himself, Channarong competed at the very highest levels of badminton winning numerous individual championships throughout the world. These include being ranked #2 in the men's singles, 1963, and winning the World Masters for those 55 years or older in the Men's Doubles, Portland, Oregon, 1998. Channarong coached Canada's National Badminton Team at the Atlantic Olympics, 1996. In this view, Channarong competes in a match at Toronto's Granite Club, 1997. [Photo, courtesy Raphi Kanchanaraphi]

Born in Bangkok, Thailand, Raphi Kanchanaraphi, above, at the urging of his parents, concentrated on being a world-class badminton player at age 17. Before immigrating to Canada, 1969, age 32, he had been seeded the number one singles badminton player in the world. Settling first in Calgary, Raphi was offered the badminton coaching job for the new Granite Club, Toronto, 1973. Raphi has a long history of tutoring, instructing, and coaching champion badminton players. In Toronto, he was Jamie McKee's coach when Jamie became Pan American singles champion, 1978, and Canadian champion, 1977. The first President of the Thai Society of Ontario, 1975, Raphi, in this 1997 retirement party view, above, stands between Toronto brothers, Tom, left, and James Muir, right, both Canadian champions in the 1970s. The racquet they hold was used by Raphi in the 1958 Thomas Cup, a World Cup Tournament when Raphi was ranked the number one seed in the world. [Photo, courtesy Raphi Kanchanaraphi]

from **Brazil**

ONLY RECENTLY HAVE BRAZILIANS arrived in significant numbers in Canada. Between 1956 and 1991, approximately 15,000 Brazilians entered Canada. Many were not native-born Brazilians but Europeans who had migrated after the war and were now reuniting with kin. However by the 1990s, native-born Brazilian immigrants were 99 percent of the total. The lack of Brazilian emigration is partly due to the extraordinary size and economic variation within Brazil itself. Brazilians often chose to move within their own country. Moreover, migration is an expensive process and in Brazil those who could afford the journey preferred not to move partly because of the key role that close kinship relations play in Brazilian society.

Although Canada did not open an embassy in Brazil until 1942, economically there have been strong ties during this century. Brazilian Traction Light and Power Company (now Brascan) was founded in 1899 by Canadian engineers and investors such as Zebulon A. Lash, his son Miller, Sir William Mackenzie, Sir Alexander Mackenzie, E.R. Wood, and American Fred Stark Pearson – all of them interested in the railway and hydroelectric possibilities in Brazil. For a century Brazilian Traction has helped build Brazil's urban infrastructure and thus it has also been a conduit through which a small segment of Toronto's elite has established connections with Brazil, including marriage and children. Despite this link and others such as Alcan Aluminium and Massey-Ferguson, social and cultural ties were still limited between the two countries. It was not until the severe economic crises of the 1980s that the Brazilian middle class began to migrate to Canada in modest numbers. A number of working-class immigrants who sought economic opportunity and a strong social safety net in Canada also arrived from the state of Minas Gerais, a region between Brazil's industrial southeast and its agrarian north.

Most Brazilians have chosen southern Ontario's urban centres as their home, particularly Toronto. The city has offered work possibilities not only for the wealthier and educated classes but also for the working class who came in the late 1980s. Cleaning office buildings or working in construction and petty service industries provided employment for them. The significant Portuguese community in Toronto ensured important linguistic familiarity and job opportunities for some Brazilian immigrants whose official language is Portuguese. Yet the economic crisis of the early 1990s discouraged many Brazilians who entered after the economic crisis in Brazil in the early 1980s.

Before 1986 there were few Brazilian organizations in Canada. The most prominent was the women's organization, Samambaia Club, composed mostly of the wives of Canadian businessmen. The Grupo Brasil formed in

[Opposite] It all started in a church basement in 1966. Now, over 30 years later, the Brazilian Carnival Ball, held in Toronto each year, is the biggest annual Brazilian Ball held anywhere in the world outside Brazil. The 40 dancers who strut their stuff are "imported" to Canada to perform for the 1,600 guests who raise up to 1.5 million dollars in a one-night stand each year for such worthy causes as the Baycrest Centre for Geriatric Care, Alzheimer's Disease Research, the Sunnybrook Health Centre, Variety – the Children's Charity, and so much more. The costumes of the dancers, as viewed here, often cost more than $10,000 each. And when the Samba Brasil Samba Band explodes into its hot, throbbing beat, costumed dancers weave onto the floor to the tempestuous beat of drums and the infectious rhythm of the hottest dance music in the world. [Photo, courtesy Onnig Cavoukian]

Family Doctor for Montreal Brazilians

When Dr. Cinea de Souza immigrated to Canada from Belrizonte, Brazil, 1971, her plans were to attend a residency in Gastro-enterology at McGill University, Montreal. Her intentions, however, were short-lived as she met and soon married Lebanese-born Dr. Habib Daoud, a gastroenterologist himself. Halting her specialist career plans in medicine, Cinea, instead, established a family practice. Before retiring in 1998, Dr. de Souza Daoud was known as the "Family Doctor to all Brazilians" in Montreal. A mother of two, she now enjoys retirement while her husband still is a specialist, practicing gastroenterology in Montreal.
[Photo, courtesy Julia Souhami]

Choreographic Dancer

Newton Moraes had already studied dance with Anette Lubisco and Tony Seitz Petzhold in Brazil, his native home-land, before immigrating to Canada in 1991 to study at The School of Toronto Dance Theatre. Three years later he launched his career both as dancer and choreographer and has never looked back. In 1997 Newton Moraes Dance staged its very first show in Stuttgart, Germany, to a sold-out show at the Makal City Theatre. He now returns annually to Brazil to teach contemporary and Afro-Brazilian dance in the Province of Porto Alegre at the Federal University of Rio Grande do Sul as well as at the Casa de Cultura Mário Quintana. The company has been supported by the Canadian Embassy in Germany, by various Brazilian cultural sources, and in Canada by the Canada Council, the Ontario Arts Council, Toronto Arts Council, and the Laidlaw Foundation.
[Photo, courtesy Newton Moraes]

Founder of Brazilian Carnival Ball

Brazilians may not constitute a significantly large presence in Canada but their impact is significantly felt when the Brazilian Carnival Ball is held each winter at the Metro Toronto Convention Centre. Anna Maria Marcolini Guidi de Souza, the Brazilian-born Canadian who is the Founding President, has received for her many charitable causes the City of Toronto Medal of Merit for Community Service and Philanthropy, the Diamond Award from the Variety Club of Toronto, and, from the Governor General, the Queen's Medal of Honour. This view of Anna Maria de Souza, left, was taken at the Governor General's Residence in Ottawa on the occasion of the State Luncheon given in honour of His Excellency Fernando Henrique Cardoso, right, President of Brazil. [Photo, courtesy Anna Maria de Souza]

Combating Asthma

Noe Zamel was born in Rio Grande, Brazil. Before immigrating to Canada in 1972, he had served as an Instructor or Fellow or studied medicine at such places as Brompton Hospital, University of London, England; University Hospital, Groningen, Holland; University of Nebraska College of Medicine; and the University of California School of Medicine, San Francisco. Currently Professor of Medicine at the University of Toronto and Director of the Tri-Hospital Pulmonary Function Laboratories (Mount Sinai Hospital, Toronto General Hospital, and Women's College Hospital), Dr. Zamel has published over 200 original studies in the leading medical journals on respiratory diseases, including problems related to cigarette smoking and asthma. More recently he has been working on gene hunting for asthma, going to the ends of the world to obtain material from isolated inbred communities, including the loneliest island in the world, Tristan da Cunha, in the South Atlantic Ocean. Dr. Noe Zamel was elected Fellow of the Royal College of Physicians (Canada) in 1981. [Photo, courtesy Dr. Noe Zamel]

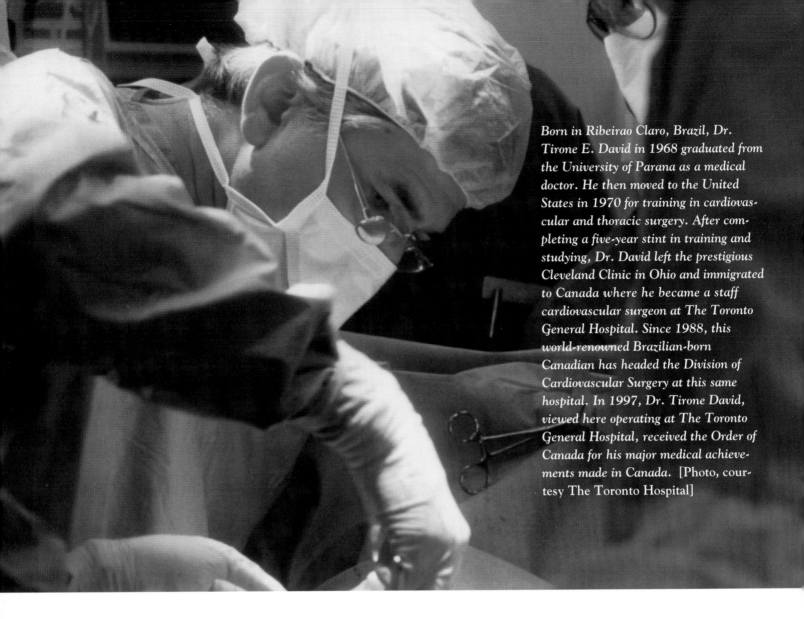

Born in Ribeirao Claro, Brazil, Dr. Tirone E. David in 1968 graduated from the University of Parana as a medical doctor. He then moved to the United States in 1970 for training in cardiovascular and thoracic surgery. After completing a five-year stint in training and studying, Dr. David left the prestigious Cleveland Clinic in Ohio and immigrated to Canada where he became a staff cardiovascular surgeon at The Toronto General Hospital. Since 1988, this world-renowned Brazilian-born Canadian has headed the Division of Cardiovascular Surgery at this same hospital. In 1997, Dr. Tirone David, viewed here operating at The Toronto General Hospital, received the Order of Canada for his major medical achievements made in Canada. [Photo, courtesy The Toronto Hospital]

the 1970s helped middle-class Brazilians ease their nostalgia for the homeland. In 1966, Anna Maria de Souza founded the Brazilian Carnival Ball that celebrates, in the midst of Toronto's winter, the popular African-influenced Catholic holiday. Especially known for its music and samba dance, the Brazilian Carnival Ball has become a major event on the social calendar of Toronto's elite, raising hundreds of thousands of dollars for charities and transcending its ethnic origins to become an English-speaking high society event.

Other associations have focused on such practical links between Brazil and Canada as BRASILNET's interest in creating commercial ties and the Brazilian-Canadian Association's interest in promoting culture. Among the many Brazilians in Canada, leisure time is spent watching futebol (soccer) or learning copeira (an athletic form of self-defence introduced to Brazil by African slaves). Several masters have set up academies to teach the sport in Halifax, Toronto, and Hamilton.

Brazilian music and dance have become quite popular in Canadian cities. Toronto has several professional bands such as Banda Dá, Banda Lua, San Sebastian Band, and Banda Sur. Women vocalists lead many of these. The band Unidos do Canada often performs in the Caribana festival. Two Portuguese-language newspapers, founded in the early 1990s, served the Brazilian community: the *Abacaxi Times* (founded in 1992) and *Hora H News* (1993). Now defunct, they have been replaced by *Brazil News* (1996). Although language, sport, and

A gala honouring
Brazilian President Fernando
Henrique Cardoso, above, was
hosted by Governor General Roméo
LeBlanc at Rideau Hall, 1997. Julia
Souhami, Chairman, Council of
Brazilians Living in Quebec, an orga-
nization preparing to celebrate 500
years of Brazilian history in the
year 2000, was one of the invited
guests who was presented to the
Brazilian President on his State
Visit. Julia came to Canada from
Brazil in 1974. She followed
husband-to-be, right, also from
Brazil, who began his medical career
as a radiotherapist in St. John's,
Newfoundland, that same year. Soon
these two adventurers were married,
spending their honeymoon near Cabot
Hill. Twenty-five years later, Dr.
Luis Souhami is Professor of
Oncology at McGill University, Montreal, where he and
Julia as Brazilian-Canadians have successfully raised a family in
Montreal. [Photo, courtesy Julia Souhami]

Carnival tie the small Brazilian settlement together, business and class interests are generally more important than any sense of cultural solidarity. Yet
Brazilian culture has had far-reaching influence on the Canadian imagination and that influence should only increase as national economies and
peoples become more integrated. ⛊

Maria José Apparecida de Almeida
was born at Conceição do Mato
Dentro, Minas Gerais, Brazil.
When she came to Canada, 1969,
as a graduate student, Maria José
Apparecida was a language specialist, having studied Philology in
Brazil, Spain, Portugal, Venezuela,
and Colombia. Upon coming to
Canada, she first studied
Linguistics, University of Ottawa,
completing her studies at University
of Montreal, graduating with a
Ph.D., Linguistics, 1980. A
respected teacher of both Portuguese
and Spanish, University of Montreal,
since 1972, Maria José Apparecida
is standing in this view with Mário
Soàres, when the former President
of Portugal attended a Montreal
gala, 1997. [Photo, courtesy Maria
José Apparecida de Almeida]

The largest and certainly one of the most colourful parades staged in Canada is the fabulous annual Caribana Festival. Conducted each year during the summer in downtown Toronto, nearly a million people enthusiastically gather to hear the calypso music and steel drums, to see the colour and to soak up the atmosphere of goodwill and cheer. Initiated to coincide with Canada's 1967 Centennial celebrations, Caribana is modelled on Trinidad's annual pre-Lenten celebration, "the greatest frolic on earth." A key musical instrument heard loud and clear during the Caribana week of festivities is the steel drum which made its first journey to Canada in 1954. "Pan" activity is now found across Canada, especially on university campuses where it is a magical instrument producing unique tone colours. Of course, the vibrant kaleidoscopic costumes, opposite, are a boon to the film processing industry as everyone brings a camera to the parade and takes pictures galore. [Photo, courtesy the Caribbean Cultural Committee]

from **Trinidad**

WITH ALMOST 150,000 people of Trinidadian origin in Canada, the impact of this small group on Canadian culture and social life has been profound. The most evident impact has been in the field of popular culture. The pre-Lenten festival, Caribana (celebrated in Canada during the summer), introduces many non-Trinidadians to the imaginative artistic and musical creations associated with this event. At the Mas (querade) camps expert artisans build wire-framed costumes while steel pan masters teach music to young students. Apart from these special Trinidadians are the thousands who have migrated to Canada in search of a better life. They have provided Canada with a wealth of teachers, nurses, civil servants, lawyers, doctors, engineers, skilled artisans, and an understanding of living in a multicultural society.

Trinidad and Tobago are two islands in the Caribbean off the coast of Venezuela. Most Trinidadians trace their origins to the island of Trinidad which has a population of 1.1 million people as compared to Tobago's 50,000. At various times outposts of the Spanish, French, and English empires, Trinidad and Tobago have a complex mix of peoples from those former empires. Although there are still some people of white and mixed race backgrounds in positions of power, most Trinidadians trace their ancestry to other groups. African slaves were brought in to work the sugar plantations. Indian Hindus and Muslims, Chinese, and Portuguese were offered free passage to Trinidad in the 1840s in return for a fixed wage for five years of work. Trinidad's social and cultural pluralism that has led to vibrant and extensive cultural activity has also created occasional tensions between the two largest groups – those of African and of South Asian heritage – who comprise almost evenly 80% of the population.

The earliest Trinidadians to come to Canada arrived in the 1920s to work in the Nova Scotian shipyards or as porters, labourers, or chefs on Canada's various railway lines. Before 1967 it was difficult for Trinidadians to enter Canada because of the country's rigid immigration laws. In the years between 1955 and 1965, for instance, just 100 Trinidadians entered Canada as domestics. A small group also came to Canada to study. Many enrolled at the University of Manitoba but often found Canada inhospitable. Until 1965 only 3,000 had immigrated to Canada. In the decades since the 1967 immigration rule changes, nearly 100,000 have immigrated to Canada from all racial backgrounds. Two-thirds have settled in Ontario, especially Toronto, Hamilton, and Windsor. Other communities flourish in Montreal, Vancouver, Calgary, and Edmonton. In the last thirty years, most have arrived highly educated but have found it difficult to find employment in their areas of expertise because of discrimination and their lack of Canadian experience.

Generating a Better Understanding of Canada's Justice System

Selwyn Reginald Romilly came to Canada in 1960 from San Fernando, the second largest city in Trinidad, choosing to settle in Vancouver because several friends who had earlier attended the University of British Columbia advised him that there was no snow in Vancouver. Receiving his undergraduate degree, 1963, Mr. Romilly furthered his studies at the University of British Columbia by graduating in Law, 1966. After practising at Smithers, British Columbia, 1967-74, Mr. Romilly was appointed to the Provincial Court Bench, Terrace, British Columbia, becoming a Provincial Court Judge there in 1974. In 1995, Judge Romilly was appointed to the Supreme Court of British Columbia. Mr. Justice Romilly is active in a number of key associations. He is an Honorary Member of the Harambee Foundation of Canada, an association involving aid to disadvantaged black youth. Active nationally in contributing to judicial and legal education, the Honourable Mr. Justice Romilly is known across Canada for making speeches and giving seminars aimed at generating a better understanding of Canada's justice system. [Photo, courtesy Mr. Justice Romilly]

A Family Doctor in the "House"

Born in San Fernando, Trinidad, 1941, Dr. Hedy Fry obtained her medical degree from the Royal College of Surgeons, Dublin, Ireland, 1968, before immigrating to Canada to establish a family medical practice in Vancouver. A medical practitioner in British Columbia for nearly 25 years, Dr. Fry was first elected as Member of Parliament, Vancouver Centre, 1993, and re-elected, 1997. Formerly Parliamentary Secretary to the Minister of Health, Dr. Fry was made Secretary of State (Multiculturalism) (Status of Women), 1996, and re-appointed, 1997, after the 1997 Federal Election. A Past President, British Columbia Medical Association, Dr. Fry was regularly featured on the CBC television series, Doctor, Doctor. A resident of Vancouver, Dr. Fry, in 1991, was recipient of the Caribbean Commonwealth Award. [Photo, courtesy Secretary of State]

Developing First Family Asthma Clinic in Manitoba

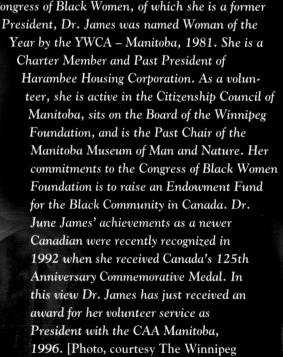

The story of Dr. June Marion James is impressive and inspirational. Born in Trinidad, she immigrated to Canada, graduating in Science from the University of Manitoba, 1963. She became the first Black Woman accepted at the University of Manitoba's School of Medicine, graduating M.D., in 1967. Her professional career in medicine has been extensive. First specializing in Paediatrics, she switched to Clinical Immunology and Allergy, joining the Winnipeg Clinic in 1976 as an Allergy Specialist. Today, she is a Partner at the Clinic and Assistant Professor of Medicine, University of Manitoba. Dr. James developed the first Family Asthma program in Manitoba. She has been active in many issues affecting women, including Family Law and Pension Reform. In addition to the Congress of Black Women, of which she is a former President, Dr. James was named Woman of the Year by the YWCA – Manitoba, 1981. She is a Charter Member and Past President of Harambee Housing Corporation. As a volunteer, she is active in the Citizenship Council of Manitoba, sits on the Board of the Winnipeg Foundation, and is the Past Chair of the Manitoba Museum of Man and Nature. Her commitments to the Congress of Black Women Foundation is to raise an Endowment Fund for the Black Community in Canada. Dr. June James' achievements as a newer Canadian were recently recognized in 1992 when she received Canada's 125th Anniversary Commemorative Medal. In this view Dr. James has just received an award for her volunteer service as President with the CAA Manitoba, 1996. [Photo, courtesy The Winnipeg Clinic]

Rita Cox proves that one does not have to be an astronaut or Olympic Gold Medalist to receive widely acclaimed recognition for one's accomplishments. As a young girl, at Port of Spain, Trinidad, she dreamed of moving to the United States. When the opportunity came, she made a beeline for New York City, graduating in Library Science from Columbia University, 1959, and taking a position with the New York Public Library. When she learned of Toronto's Public Library reputation, she got that itchy feeling and made her way to Canada, taking a position as an Assistant Librarian in Toronto. Bringing with her qualities which made her one of the best story tellers of her generation, she thrilled children of all backgrounds with stories about the Caribbean and began

assembling a library specializing in West Indian Literature. After 34 years with the Toronto Public Library, 22 years as Head of the Parkdale Branch Library, Rita Cox retired but not before she had created one of Canada's best community libraries and assembled one of the most comprehensive Black Heritage and West Indian collections in Canada. Affectionately called the Queen of Caribbean Heritage, Rita Cox has received many awards including honorary doctoral degrees from both York and Wilfrid Laurier Universities. This beloved storyteller, this much respected librarian, this builder of literacy among young people, was recognized for her lifetime achievements when Governor General Roméo LeBlanc, as viewed here, made her a Member of the Order of Canada, 1997. [Photo, courtesy Dr. Rita Cox]

Identifying Occupational Health Hazards

Dr. Roland Hosein, Vice-President, Environment, Health and Safety, General Electric Canada, is a native of Trinidad who took his B.Sc. and M.Sc. degrees at the University of London and completed his Ph.D. in Epidemiology at the University of Western Ontario, 1983. He did the epidemiology of lung disease's research at Yale University, and later led a team in Occupational Health, Government of Alberta. Dr. Hosein started the graduate program in Occupational and Environmental Health with the Faculty of Medicine, University of Toronto, 1978, and today maintains a part-time appointment as Associate Professor. A writer of two books as well as over 30 articles in various scientific journals, Dr. Hosein has been either editor or co-editor of several major studies identified with occupational health hazards. Dr. Hosein's corporate responsibility for health and environment covers Canada, Latin America, and India. He has assisted such governments as Egypt, Trinidad, and Grenada to develop Environmental Agencies, and today heads the Canadian Delegation on ISO 14000. He is involved in many community projects and currently is Chair of the Board of an ethnic theatre group, the Board of Prime Mentors Canada, Chair, Strategic Planning Committee, Alliance of Manufacturers and Exporters, Canada. His charitable works include Canadian, Caribbean, Indian, and Islamic organizations and he is funding the building of a technology wing of his primary school in his native Trinidad. Standing in this 1997 view with Sir Ellis Clark, President, Republic of Trinidad and Tobago, is Dr. Roland Hosein, right, on the occasion of the opening of the

Teacher with a Mission

The Bengali ancestors of Deo Kernahan, viewed right, came to Trinidad in the 19th century to work as indentured labourers on a sugar plantation near Felicity where the family adopted the surname of the plantation owner as their own. Three generations later, to take advantage of educational opportunities in Canada, Deo Kernahan migrated to Canada with his wife and daughter, 1968, to take an elementary school teaching post with the Etobicoke Board of Education, Toronto. Past President, Canadian Chapter the World Conference on Religion and Peace, the largest interfaith group i the world, and, currently, President, Canadian Council of Hindus as well as a broadcaster with Vision TV, Deo, in this view, is seen with Father R. O'Toole, middle, of the Scarborough Foreign Mission, and Father Nicola De Angelis, Auxillary Bishop, Multi-Religious Affairs to the Vatican, at ar Interfaith Conference at the Scarborough Foreign Mission, Toronto, 1999. [Photo, courtesy Deo Kernahan]

Martin Luther King Jr. Award Recipient

Born in Trinidad, Clarence Bayne came to Canada in 1954 to study Economics and Political Science at the University of British Columbia. After obtaining a Master's Degree, 1960, he worked as a transportation economist at CN in Montreal. Upon completing his Ph.D. in Economics at McGill University, he began teaching in the Faculty of Commerce and Administration, Concordia University, in the Decision Sciences/Management Information Systems Department. Currently, he is Director of the Graduate Diploma in Administration and Graduate Diploma, Sport Administration, and Director, Minority Entrepreneurship Institute at Concordia. For his distinguished contributions both as founder and leader of numerous cultural and community organizations, Dr. Bayne has received many awards including the Martin Luther King Jr. Award for general community service within the black community, in particular, and for cultural services, in general, and the Governor General's 125th Anniversary of Confederation Award. In addition to being President of the Black Studies Centre of Montreal and Vice President of the National Council of Black Educators of Canada, he is a Member of the Conseil des arts de la communauté de Montréal, on the Board of Directors of the Centre-West Community Health Corporation and the Quebec Board of Black Educators. Dr. Bayne is also the Founding Past-President of the Black Theatre Workshop, Montreal. [Photo courtesy Dr. Clarence Bayne]

Descendents of Michel de Verteuil in Canada

During the 14th century, one quarter of the French town of Bordeaux, France, was owned by la famille de Verteuil. A Royalist surname during the seige of Fortress Louisbourg as well as the French Revolution, a descendent, Michel de Verteuil (1773-1865), arrived in Trinidad in 1796 and became a plantation owner and Commandant of his Quarter. Five generations and over 170 years later, four de Verteuil brothers, descendents of Michel, all immigrated to Canada to continue their education and to make Canada their home. Viewed from left is Ian de Verteuil, Vancouver Island, B.C., and brothers, David, Oakville, Ontario, Maurice, Montreal, Quebec, and Michael, Oakville, Ontario. Their mother, Mary, along with her husband, Marcel de Verteuil OBE, followed her sons to Canada in the 1980s. [Photo, courtesy David de Verteuil]

One way to offset the problems faced in Canada has been to establish voluntary organizations, church groups, and service associations such as the Trinidad-Canada Association, Caribana Association and the Indo-Caribbean Association. Also, a common Caribbean experience links people to other pan-Caribbean or pan-Black organizations such as the National Black Coalition, the United Negro Improvement Association, the Black Heritage Association, and the Caribbean Canadian Business and Professionals Association. Equally, Trinidadians have an active religious life. In particular, churches of Roman Catholic, Anglican, Baptist, and Presbyterian denominations count many Trinidadians as participants, especially those of French and African heritage. Asian-Indian Trinidadians have created several Muslim mosques and Hindu mundirs to attend to their spiritual needs.

The cultural activities of Trinidadians flourish in the areas of literature, theatre, and dance with prominent individuals such as Ramabai Espinet, Jeff Henry, Frank Birbalsingh, Sam Selvon, and Neil Bissoondath. The Caribbean Theatre Workshop in Toronto brings theatre and dance groups from Trinidad and the Caribbean to Canada. Trinidadian music has had considerable impact on Canadian popular music culture in night clubs in Toronto, Montreal, and Vancouver with styles as diverse as calypso, steel band, soca, and has influenced the emerging Hip Hop Canadian sound. While there has not yet been a specific Trinidadian press, people from Trinidad have been involved with such British West Indian and Caribbean newspapers as *Contrast*, *Share*, *Indo-Caribbean World*, *Caribbean Camera*, and *Metro-World* as well as the magazine *Pride*.

As a result of their heritage in a diverse country, Trinidadians are well situated to play a critical role in Canada's emerging multicultural nation building in the new millennium. ⬥

Dr. Jameel Ali was born in Trinidad. A past student of St. Mary's College and Fatima College, he immigrated to Canada and enrolled in Medicine at the University of Manitoba, graduating, 1966. Following Fellowships at Boston University Medical Center and San Francisco General Hospital, Dr. Ali began his teaching career in Surgery at the University of Manitoba Medical School, 1973, leaving there, 1988, to become Full Professor of Surgery, University of Toronto Medical School. Internationally known and respected in the field of Trauma, Dr. Ali is also recognized as an excellent teacher of Surgery, for his research into and the understanding of Trauma Care, and as an examiner of post graduate studies in Surgery. In 1999, at the annual Gallie Day Dinner held in Toronto, Dr. Jameel Ali, as viewed here, left, received the Bruce Tovee Award from the Chairman of the University of Toronto's Department of Surgery, Dr. John Wedge, for his significant work as a teacher and, particularly, for his pioneering in the training of physicians in Canada and throughout the world in the principles of providing optimum care for injured victims. [Photo, courtesy Dr. Jameel Ali]

THE PORTUGUESE presence in Canada originates with the earliest European explorations of the Atlantic and the pursuit of abundant fish stocks off the east coast of Canada in the sixteenth century. Portugal's role as an imperial power over the last several centuries resulted in Portuguese immigration around the world to its colonies from Brazil and Goa to Mozambique and Macao. Under the leadership of Prince Henry the Navigator (1394-1460), trade routes and colonies were established. Canadian geographic place names testify to the importance of Portuguese navigators in mapping of eastern Canada. The name Labrador, one example among many, in all likelihood derives from a Portuguese explorer, one João Fernandes, a "lavrador" or farmer. A few individuals of Portuguese heritage settled in New France and early Canada: between the years of 1900 and 1949 only 500 Portuguese entered Canada.

For over a century, Portuguese have been migrating from their homeland in search of work. Three epochs of migration are discernable for Portuguese men and women. Over one million people left Portugal for Brazil between 1886 and 1950. It was not until the Canadian and Portuguese governments signed labour contract agreements to supply railway construction and agricultural workers after World War II that Canada became a popular option for Portuguese immigrants for the first three decades following the war. The third epoch saw large numbers choose migration targets closer to home in Western Europe. In the 1950s, almost 20,000 arrived in

Standing in front of the historical ceramic murals he created for a Toronto City Hall Exhibition, 1993, Américo Ribeiro, standing left, born, Lisbon, Portugal, is one of Canada's premier ceramista painters. At age 14, he began painting ceramic tiles, eventually immigrating to Canada from Nazaré, Portugal, settling, first, in Toronto's Portuguese community, working at odd jobs to raise the necessary monies needed to send for Estrela, his wife, and daughter, Maria Helena, eventually residing in Mississauga, Ontario. This view also depicts Portuguese-born Martinho Silva, centre, a former member of Toronto City Council, and António Sousa, an immigrant to Toronto from Portugal, 1953. The mural at left depicts Upper Canada's first Lt. Gov., John Graves Simcoe, landing at what is now Toronto Harbour, 1793; the mural, right, illustrates the first boatload of many hundreds of Portuguese immigrants, including António Sousa who landed at Halifax, Nova Scotia, 1953. [Photo, courtesy Américo Ribeiro]

from Portugal

Canada. The major Portuguese emigration was from the Azores and, in particular, the island of São Miguel. In the following two decades, in large part as a result of the family sponsorship program and chain migration, another 140,000 Portuguese chose Canada and by the 1996 census it was estimated that as many as 335,110 people of Portuguese heritage lived in Canada. Although they have settled in every province, Ontario is home to over two-thirds of that number and about 161,000 of those live in Toronto. Slightly under 50,000 live in Quebec, mostly in Montreal.

In many cities, Portuguese settled in traditional immigrant reception areas near jobs and transportation. Although often living near fellow Catholics such as Italian immigrants, they have been characterized by a high degree of residential segregation and active community institutional life. In 1991, 93 percent of Portuguese had less than nine years of school. Consequently, almost half of those Portuguese in the workforce labour in manufacturing and construction. Fairly often employment was found through kinship connections or the advice of other Portuguese Canadians. Portuguese women, although initially tending to the traditional needs of the home as they had been expected to in Portugal, were virtually forced by the economic pressures of Canada to find work so that the immigrant family could achieve its ultimate goal: home ownership. Many worked in the garment industry either toiling in factories or taking in piecework and still others experienced low wages and difficult work as cleaning staff in corporate office buildings. In 1974 Portuguese-Canadian women in downtown Toronto made their mark in the labour struggles of the decade by striking to avoid reusing dirty garbage bags. In turn, Portuguese construction workers moved gradually into union leadership positions.

As the community has become more settled, institutional life has emerged to fulfil the cultural and social expectations of Portuguese immigrants and their children. Some adopt the name Luso-Canadians for their local social and business clubs in reference to Lusitania, the ancient name associated with Portugal under the Roman empire. Organizations such as the Federation of Portuguese-Canadian Businessmen and the Association of

Mariano Rego was born in the Azores, 1921, on the island of São Miguel. With the help of his mother and father, he began playing the Portuguese Guitar at age five years. Soon he was playing in every theatre throughout the Azores. Winning first prize in Ponta Delgada in the prestigious Companheiros de Alegria Contest conducted at the famous Teatro Music Hall, 1952, he had no choice but to immigrate to the United States the next year where he excelled as a guitarist of renown. By 1957, he decided to re-immigrate, this time to Canada, bringing with him his family including his two daughters. At first he formed a band, calling it Os Toureiros de Portugal. After 12 years he was urged to go solo and played at such Toronto night spots as the Skyline Hotel, The El Mocombo, and Império and Vasco da Gama, two well-known Portuguese restaurants in Toronto. He has made some 40 recordings in a career spanning nearly half a century. Although he admits that it is a great pleasure to give solo performances for such personalities as Donald Trump, nevertheless, his greatest pleasure is knowing that all women love his music because, when they watch him play his famous Portuguese Guitar, he does so as if he were making love to it. In 1979, Mariano Rego donated to the Royal Ontario Museum his most famous guitar crafted by José da Silveira, an artist who lived on the Madeira Islands in the 19th century. [Photo, courtesy Mariano Rego]

"Distinguished Professor of the Year"

Professor Victor Da Rosa, B.A., M.A., M.Ed., Ph.D., was born in Portugal, 1947. A Professor at the University of Ottawa, where he has taught since 1971, Dr. Da Rosa has held various teaching and research appointments at such universities as Indiana, McGill (where he earned his doctoral), Concordia, Laurentian, Vaxjo (Sweden), Fernando Pessoa (Portugal), ULBRA (Brazil), and Witwatersrand (South Africa). A prolific writer of scholarly journals and books about ethnic relations, international development, and anthropology, in general, Dr. Da Rosa has received many honours and awards which include being made "Comendador" of the Order of Prince Henry the Navigator from the Portuguese government, 1989, being named the winner, 1988, of one OCUFA teaching award, recognizing Ontario professors making outstanding contributions in teaching and learning, and winning "Distinguished Professor of the Year, 1997," by the University of Ottawa. Dr. Da Rosa, in the year 2000, co-edited with Professor Carlos Teixeira The Portuguese in Canada. [Photo, courtesy Dr. Victor M. Pereira Da Rosa]

Active Union Leader

António Dionisio, above, right, first settled as a young boy in northern British Columbia when he and his parents immigrated to Canada from Portugal, 1962. After several years in the west-coast province, his family moved to Toronto where the majority of Canada's Portuguese community lived. Soon he was a licensed welder. He became a subway construction worker in Toronto, joining Local 183, 1969. He became an active member in the union almost immediately. After being trapped in a cave-in, 1976, he helped lead a city-wide strike, 1977. In 1982, by acclamation, he became President of Local 183, helping to organize many of the sectors of this well-known Union. Highly active in the Portuguese community, Tony was profiled in Maclean's Magazine for work in alleviating the Portuguese Refugee Crisis of 1988. Elected Business Manager, Local 183, 1996, Tony is a Board Member of Toronto Olympic Committee 2008. Tony, in this view, stands with Mike Colle, left, Provincial Liberal Member, representing Toronto's Eglinton/Lawrence Riding, who himself is an immigrant, having come to Canada from Italy (Puglia) at age five. [Photo, courtesy António Dionisio/Local 183]

First Portuguese Canadian Admitted to Quebec Bar

Arlindo Vieira was born at Serra de S. António, Portugal, 1951. Following education at the Catholic University of Portugal, Mr. Vieira immigrated to Canada. Settling in Montreal, Quebec, he was the first person of Portuguese descent to be admitted to the Quebec Bar, 1978. In 1986, he became a civil servant working for Quebec's Ministry of Culture and Immigration. In 1995, Arlindo Vieira was appointed by the Government of Quebec as President, Conseil des relations interculturelles, an autonomous organization created by the Quebec government, 1984, to assist immigrants settling in Quebec and to ease their integration into Quebec society. Mr. Vieira has always participated in the activities of the Portuguese community in Quebec, serving as Founding President, l'Alliance des professionnels et entrepreneurs portugais du Québec, 1990-1992, President, de la Caisse d'économie des Portugais, 1987-1989, and administrator, Centre portugais de référence et de promotion sociale, 1978-1980. Monsieur Arlindo Vieira was the official candidate for the Parti Québéçois in the provincial elections, 1985, for the riding of Saint-Louis. [Photo, courtesy Le Conseil des relations interculturelles]

Legacy of a Portuguese Painter

Alberto de Castro, born, 1952, of Portuguese parents, in Huambo, Angola, spent his formative years in Spain studying painting before immigrating to Montreal, 1969. Mounting several one-man exhibitions, Alberto won the commission to paint a mural for the Portuguese Pavilion at the 1976 Montreal Olympic Games. Alberto moved to Toronto, 1980,

Os PORTUGUESES NO CANADÁ
• UMA BIBLIOGRAFIA: 1953-1996 •

CARLOS TEIXEIRA • GILLES LAVIGNE

where his painting style followed the Näif school. Before he died, 1995, age 42, he felt that "Canada was to him what Tahiti was to Gauguin." Examples of his work are found in Europe, in the Ontario Provincial Legislature, Toronto's Our Lady of Lourdes Church, the Portuguese Consulate, Toronto, and in the corporate offices of Shell, IBM, Imperial Oil, and Sanyo. In 1985, his paintings were used on UNICEF Christmas cards and, in 1986, he exhibited at the third annual Salon international d'art näif, Paris. Many of his works are kept at the Casa do Alentejo, Toronto's Portuguese Community Centre, including this canvas called O Regresso do Emigrante, opposite, capturing the joy of a mother hugging her son upon returning to his birthplace in Portugal. [Photo, courtesy Casa do Alentejo]

Many Portuguese families migrated to Canada in the '50s and '60s from the Azores, a group of small islands in the Atlantic, some 800 miles off the west coast of Portugal. Collectively, these volcanic islands are administered as a political jurisdiction of Portugal. In order to seek a more secure future, many families from the Azores uprooted themselves and immigrated to Canada. José Martins and his family, as viewed here, are typical representatives of Canada's Portuguese community who made their way to Canada. After they arrived in Canada in 1964, they struggled with a new language, a new culture, and the absence of relatives and old friends. But they persevered. Today, they are making a substantial contribution to both Cambridge, Ontario, where they happily live, and to Canadian society, in general. In this 1995 photograph, José is standing, centre, back row, in front of his wife, Manuela, who is holding granddaughter Madelene, just baptized by Father Isabelle. The Martins family today consists of five children all of whom have gone on to complete post secondary school education. After living more than half of his life in Canada, José now runs his own insurance company, enjoys the Toronto Maple Leafs, has a pilot's licence, loves to fish, and oversees the traditional family dinner each Sunday. [Photo, courtesy José Martins]

Insuring His Family's Future

Portuguese Businesses in Winnipeg, and *Alliance des Professionels et Entrepreneurs Portugais du Québec* indicate the growth in small business throughout the community. Heritage language programs abound in community schools throughout Canada to ensure that immigrant parents and their Canadian-born children can communicate. By the early 1990s, over thirty such schools existed in Ontario. Education has been a critical issue for Portuguese-Canadian community activists and some parents have expressed concern over the lack of support offered to young Portuguese-Canadian students within the public and separate school systems and in homes where both parents work. The Toronto Portuguese Parents' Association, formed in 1981, has mounted a continued effort to encourage school boards, parents, and university students to help reduce dropouts, arbitrary academic streaming, and intergenerational misunderstandings.

The everyday life of Portuguese Canadians is enriched by the plethora of stores that cater to the culinary and consumption patterns of immigrants and their children. Fish stores with dried cod, restaurants with barbecued chicken, bakeries, and grape wholesalers add an energy and texture to such urban neighbourhoods as the one established around Dundas and College Streets in Toronto. To keep up with the neighbourhood bustle, community newspapers in Portuguese flourish such as the *Voz de Portugal* in Montreal or Toronto's *Correio Português*. Television and radio programs on CFMT, CIRV, or CHIN offer oral and visual testimony to the vitality of Portuguese community life in Canada's urban centres. In fact, some 50 Portuguese newspapers across Canada keep Canada's Portuguese community informed about ethnic and cultural life both at home and abroad.

Another significant aspect of neighbourhood life for many Portuguese Canadians is the active and vibrant pageantry of their Roman Catholicism. Almost 90 per cent of Portuguese are Catholic and, in the traditions of southern European Catholicism, their faith is often visually and publicly celebrated through the saints' feasts during which processions, prayers, offerings, sporting events, family reunions, and elaborate culinary preparations and their consumption are central features.

Since the first half of the 16th century, the Portuguese have been fishing the Grand Banks, a vast extension of the continental shelf off southeastern Newfoundland in the North Atlantic. It was natural, therefore, for young Valentim Arezes, born in Portugal, to follow in the footsteps of his ancestors. During the 1960s, he began working for a Portuguese trawler. After 12 years, because the political scene in his native land made working conditions unbearable, young Valentim decided to "jump ship." Thus, in 1972, he went to a travel agency, purchased a train ticket to Madrid, Spain, then purchased a plane ticket for Canada, arriving, St. John's Newfoundland, October 12, 1972. For the last 27 years, Valentim has been a fisherman. After stints with National Sea Products and Fishery Products International, he now is first mate on a vessel with a crew of 29 men plying the oceans for shrimp. Valentim calls Canada "the land of opportunity" and Newfoundland "a place to call home." In this view, First Mate Valentim Arezes stands in front of his shrimp vessel in the harbour of St. John's, Newfoundland, September 1999. [Photo, courtesy Valentim Arezes]

Portuguese-speaking priests preside over feast days for Our Lady of Fatima (*Nossa Senhora de Fátima*) sponsored by the Portuguese Catholic Mission in Vancouver or other such feasts in Winnipeg, Toronto, or Montreal. The Christ of Miracles feast staged outside St. Mary's Church was brought by Azorean immigrants to Toronto in 1966 and is one of the most elaborate religious events in the city.

While generally concentrated in the downtown core of Canada's major cities, recently significant numbers of Portuguese have moved to suburbs such as Mississauga and Oakville outside of Toronto and Laval outside of Montreal. This spatial and social move, aided by Portuguese-Canadian real estate agents who settle them into suburban communities with large concentrations of other Portuguese, indicates the gradual economic security and comfort with which Portuguese-Canadians address their everyday lives in Canada. With this move to the suburbs, there has also emerged an increase in Portuguese students pursuing university training for employment beyond the construction site or the factory floor to professions and small businesses. ⬥

Lillian Petroff/Carlos Teixeira

Born in Lisbon, Portugal, Dr. Manuel Tomás de Brito Ferreira was 35 years old by the time he immigrated to Canada to finalize his formal medical training at McMaster University, Hamilton, Ontario. A graduate in medicine with honours from the University of Lisbon, 1962, Dr. Ferreira trained in Pediatrics at the University of Glasgow, University of London, and Manchester Hospital, U.K, before immigrating to Canada. If anyone in Canada is dubbed "Mr. Portugal" it would have to be Dr. Ferreira. A family doctor in Toronto since 1972, Dr. Ferreira is a going concern within the Portuguese community, serving as President of the Portuguese Canadian National Congress, First Portuguese Cultural Centre as well as the Portuguese Credit Union. As a member of the Council of Communities, an elected body which advises the Portuguese Government on issues related to Portuguese abroad, Dr. Ferreira, since 1998, has served as President, as viewed here, addressing the Council in the Chamber of the Portuguese Senate, for the Regional Council for North America. A strong voice in the medical community, Dr. Ferreira has also served as Executive President of the Medical Staff for Doctor's Hospital, 1984-88. He has served as Clinical Elective Supervisor, Dept. of Community Medicine, University of Toronto, 1986 to present. He was instrumental in the creation of Toronto's Kensington Clinic to provide alcoholic and addiction treatment in the Portuguese language. He served as a member of the Medical Department of Amnesty International and was a founding member of the Canadian Centre for Victims of Torture. A man whose volunteerism has made him culturally very rich, Dr. Ferreira's weekly health program on CHIN Radio is now nearing 15 consecutive years. [Photo, courtesy Dr. Tomás Ferreira]

Born in São Miguel, the Azores, Eduardo Resendes, after becoming an ordained priest, 1958, was appointed Pastor of the Cathedral of Angra Do Heroísmo, Terceira, for four years before serving as Chaplain of the Portuguese Air Force, 1965-1978. Following his discharge, he came to Canada, settling in Mississauga where he built the first Portuguese Church of Santissimo Salvador Do Mundo, 1979. Shortly thereafter, he built a sister Church, Christ the King Roman Catholic Church. He currently serves both places of worship as Pastor. In recognition for his many services to the Mississauga community, Pope Paul II elevated Father Eduardo Resendes to the dignity of Prelate of Honour (Monsignor), February 27, 1996. [Photo, courtesy Monsignor Eduardo Resendes]

AMONG THE FIRST LITHUANIANS known to have settled in Canada were soldiers in the British army who fought in the War of 1812. Afterwards, these Lithuanian men took homesteads along the Canada-USA border and settled for good. However, it was only at the end of the nineteenth century that Lithuanians in growing numbers came to Canada. Some were men evading conscription into the Russian army (Lithuania was then part of the Czarist Empire), while others hoped to make money to buy land back in the homeland. Women came too, some with husbands, others lured by the promise of factory work. By the early twentieth century, there were Lithuanian communities in Sydney Mines, Nova Scotia, Montreal, and Toronto: the first Lithuanian mutual-benefit society appeared in Montreal in 1904 and the first parish, St. Casimir's (most Lithuanians were Roman Catholic), was founded in this city in 1907.

Lithuanian immigrants to Canada in the first half of the twentieth century were highly mobile. A number returned to Lithuania while many, in some years up to half, moved to the U.S.A. when jobs dried up in Canada. The most substantial early immigration to Canada directly from Lithuania occurred in the 1920s when the United States closed its doors to Lithuanians. By the 1930s about 8,000-9,000 Lithuanians lived in Canada, many widely scattered in mines and lumber camps while others grouped together in Montreal, Toronto, Sudbury, and Winnipeg, as well as in the farming community of Brooks, Alberta. Idealogical differences from left to right existed, and Lithuanian leftists even published a newspaper, but most Lithuanians were practising Catholics or Lutherans though they were tolerant of socialist ideas. Living through the Depression these men and women had little chance to rise economically. To maintain their ethnic identity, they organized choirs and theatrical productions while in Montreal they even had city-supported Lithuanian schools.

Dr.Biruté Galdikas, encouraged by the late Dr. Louis Leakey to study the great Asian ape with red hair, is a primatologist, world renowned for her nearly three decades of studying orangutans in the jungles of Borneo. Professor of Archaeology, Simon Fraser University, Biruté Galdikas, a trained social anthropologist with a Ph.D. from UCLA, was born in Germany, 1946, while her Lithuanian parents were en route to Canada as displaced persons. Growing up in Toronto, Ontario, she now lives in British Columbia, spending half of each year in Borneo studying the great ape that lives in the tropical rainforests of that Malayan island in S.E. Asia. She has been featured several times in National Geographic, profiled in Life and The New York Times, and in 1997 received the prestigious Tyler Prize for environmental achievement, along with Jane Goodall and George Schaller. Recently made an Officer, Order of Canada, Dr. Biruté Galdikas, a "Hero for the Earth," is currently President, Orangutan Foundation based in Los Angeles. [Photo, courtesy Filomena Galdikas]

from **Lithuania**

He was the former chess master of Lithuania. Born in Uzpaliai, 1911, Povilas Vaitonis graduated in Law, 1940, from Vilnius University, Kaunas, before immigrating to Canada, 1949, fleeing communist oppression in his homeland. Taking up residence in Hamilton, Ontario, within one year, Vaitonis became chess champion of that city. Between 1951-1961, he was chess champion of Ontario five times. He was Canadian national chess master in 1951 and again in 1957. He also wrote a much heralded chess column for The Hamilton Spectator, *1953-1956. Internationally, Vaitonis represented Canada in the semi-finals of the World Chess Championships in Saltjoebaden, Sweden, acquiring the international master's title. He also represented Canada in the Chess Olympics in Amsterdam, 1954, and in Munich, 1958. In this view, Vaitonis, in foreground, right, is at the Lithuanian Sports Club,* Vytis, *playing an Estonian Canadian player, mid-1950s.* [Photo, courtesy Lithuanian Museum, Mississauga]

After World War II, a new and much larger wave of immigrants came from Displaced Persons camps in Europe. Among these were many professionals and artists and, in the post-war economic boom, once they had completed labour contracts or took re-qualification examinations, many succeeded in re-establishing themselves professionally. These Lithuanians saw themselves as political refugees rather than immigrants in the true sense: they were quick to set up an intricate network of cultural, religious, and education organizations in Canada, centred in urban communities like Montreal, Toronto, Hamilton, Winnipeg, and Vancouver. An umbrella organization, the Lithuanian-Canadian Community, founded in 1952, united these far-flung "colonies" and represented them in relations with Canadian governmental agencies as well as with other communities in the world Lithuanian diaspora. Nearly 20,000 Lithuanian men, women, and children had moved to Canada between 1947 and 1953. The 1996 census reported a total Lithuanian population of 35,835 in Canada, with nearly two-thirds living in Ontario.

Lithuanians did not find it difficult to adapt to life in Canada. Northern Europeans, they adjust easily to the climate and greatly enjoy activities like camping, boating, and cottage life. Social structures within the communities are democratic, with parishes – such as three in the Toronto area, two in Montreal, and others in Edmonton, Winnipeg, Ottawa, and London, Ontario – often serving as the common organizational centre for many communities. Intermarriage with non-Lithuanians has grown steadily over the years but the family and its traditions have still remained the main propagator of Lithuanian identity. Young second, third, fourth-generation Lithuanian-Canadians are encouraged to explore their ethnic roots through summer camps, sports events, and Saturday schools, as well as membership in very popular choirs and folkloric dance ensembles.

Champion Table Tennis Player

At the age of 14 years, Violeta Nesukaitis became Canadian Women's Table Tennis Champion. When only 13 years old, she had already competed in the Toronto Table Tennis Club Championship, Women's Division, Open, and won! Violeta's father, born in Alvitas, Lithuania, leaving his homeland in 1944 to escape oppression, was her coach when she joined the table tennis elites of the world, in 1966, winning the U.S. National Women's Division Championship, the first non-American to do so. Winner of four North American Open Championships (1966, '68, '70, and '73), she travelled to Peking, China, 1971, with Team Canada, the first foreign table tennis team to be invited to play in China. Ranked nationally until she retired in 1976, Violeta Nesukaitis, in this 1971 view, below, in Peking, is seen with Chou En-Lai, China's Premier. Photograph, left, demonstrates Violeta's strength and power at the height of her career. [Photos, courtesy J. Nesukaitis]

From Playmaker to Playcaller

The son of Lithuanian immigrants, Leo Rautins, after attending high school in Ontario and participating as a member of the Toronto-based Lithuanian Athletic Club, Aušra, took a basketball scholarship to Syracuse University, New York, where the 6'8" forward for the Orangemen was an assist leader, an all-American in 1983 and, in the same year, picked 17th in the NBA first-round draft by the Philadelphia 76ers. Rautins is, today, a broadcaster for the Toronto Raptors of the National Basketball Association as well as National CBC broadcaster for the NBA Vancouver Grizzlies. [Photo, courtesy Lithuanian Museum-Archives, Mississauga]

Consultant to World Health Organization

Born in Kaunas, Lithuania, in 1920, Vytautas Pavilanis completed his medical degree at the University of Kaunas, 1942, receiving Diplomas in Microbiology, 1947, and Serology and Hematology, 1948, from the Pasteur Institute, Paris, before immigrating to Canada the same year to pursue a teaching and medical research career at the Institute Armand-Frappier in Montreal, Quebec. There he organized and was in charge of the production of vaccines for polio, flu, measles. A consultant to the World Health Organization, Dr. Pavilanis, now Professor Emeritus at the Institute Armand-Frappier since retirement, 1984, is viewed here, right, at the Pasteur Centenary with former Pasteur colleagues, Professor E. Wollmann, centre, internationally respected bacteriologist and Deputy Director of the Pasteur Institute, and, left, Professor D. Athanasiu, renowned Romanian virologist. [Photos, courtesy Dr. Vytautas Pavilanis]

Influential Graphic Artist

At the time he immigrated to Canada, via Germany, from Communist-oppressed Lithuania, 1949, Telesforas Valius was already an eminent illustrator and graphic artist. His early wrought wood engravings reflect such weighty themes as famine, fire, and funerals, subject matters which Telesforas Valius confronted in Lithuania as a young man bursting with artistic talent. Combining earlier skills he learned in Lithuania with the influential styles emerging in post-1945 America, the work of Telesforas Valius is today

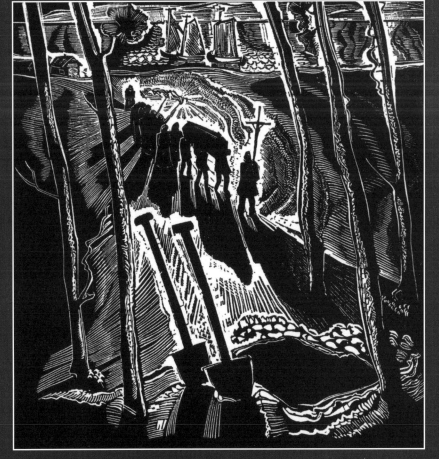

recognized as some of the finest graphic art of his generation. As a Toronto-based artist, Mr. Valius won many honours. He was elected Fellow of the International Institute of Arts and Letters in Switzerland; he was made Member of the Academy Tommaso Campanella in Rome; he also was elected Member of the American Color Print Society. In 1967, he was awarded Canada's Centennial Medal. Ed Bartram, one of Canada's outstanding printmakers, recently stated that Telesforas Valius, who died in 1977, "had immense knowledge about printmaking methods and a highly perfected facibility." Robert Duval, one of Canada's most respected art critics, claims that the art of Mr. Valius "represents a permanent resource for Canadians to enjoy in the future." Romas Viesulas, noted Professor at the Tyler School of Arts, Temple University, Philadelphia, has written that Telesforas Valius' 1942 wood engraving, Funeral Procession, as viewed here, from the cycle Tragedy of the Baltic Seashore III, "is a work of striking visual directness and of extraordinary psychological and graphic impact," claiming as well, that it is "one of the masterpieces of Lithuanian printmaking." [Photos, courtesy Lithuania Museum-Archives Mississauga]

Making Navigation Safer

When Joseph Vincent Danys fled Soviet oppression in Lithuania, 1944, little did he realize that Canada would make it possible for him to fulfil his dreams to become a hydrotechnical engineer. A graduate in civil engineering from the University of Vytautas, Kaunas, Lithuania, Joseph Danys settled with his family in Canada, 1949, first working for the C.N.R. and then Power Corporation. By 1955 he was Senior Foundation Engineer for the St. Lawrence River Power Project, one of the major engineering feats of the 20th century. From 1959-1979, he worked for the Ministry of Transport, Ottawa, designing and supervising the construction of a new generation of aids for navigation, the most striking of which, modern lighthouses, was chosen to figure on a series of Canadian postage stamps. Acting as a liason between the Lithuanian-Canadian community and the Canadian federal government, with representatives of the Latvian and Estonian communities, Mr. Danys, between 1973-1988, guided an all-party committee of Senators and M.P.s to organize an annual Baltic Evening in Parliament, a confirmation of Canada's refusal to recognize the Soviet incorporation of the Baltic nations. In this view, Joseph Danys, right, is standing, in 1986, with the Hon. Michael Wilson, Finance Minister, at one of these gala evenings which took place in the West Block on Parliament Hill, Ottawa. [Photo, courtesy Milda Danys]

Member of World's Elite Singers

Lithuanian-born Lilian Sukis had no reason to believe, after immigrating to Canada with her mother in 1949, that she would become an internationally known soprano voice. First settling in Val d'Or, Quebec, then Hamilton, Ontario, Lilia Sukis, upon earning certificates in piano and voice from the Royal Conservatory of Music, Toronto, entered the Faculty of Music, University of Toronto, studying voice under Irene Jessner, former prima donna with New York's Metropolitan Opera. Upon signing a contract as permanent American soloist with the Met, 1966, her North American career was launched by her singing leading roles in Rigoletto, Electra, Aida, Lucia di Lammermoor and Peter Grimes. The Director of the Munich Opera, Günter Rennert, then persuaded Lilian, some two years later, to make her European debut by opening the Munich opera season in the role of Fiordiligi. After her presentation of the role Sim Tjong in Isang Yun's opera by the same name, written for the Olympic Games in Munich, Lilian became a member of the world's elite singers. She then had leading roles in Mozart and Strauss, and began singing as a guest soloist performer in the world's leading opera houses including Berlin, Hamburg, Cologne, Düsseldorf, Frankfurt, Vienna, Prague, Lausanne, Geneva, Zürich, Paris, London, and Rome. Today, Lilian Sukis is Professor of Music at the Hochschule für Music, Graz, Germany. In this view, Lilian Sukis stands, right, with choir conductor, Stasys Gaitevicius, centre, and Dalia Viskontas, piano accompanist, at a Lithuanian commemorative service, Toronto, circa 1965. [Photo, courtesy Lithuanian Museum Archives, Mississauga]

Creating a Future for all the Tomorrows

Because of communist occupation of Lithuania, Petras Ažubalis was forced to flee his native land to Czechoslovakia where he was ordained as a Roman Catholic priest, 1942. At the invitation of Cardinal McGuigan of Toronto, he immigrated to Canada, becoming, in 1948, Pastor of St. John the Baptist, a Lithuanian parish in Toronto. Devoted to the many cultural and charitable activities of the Lithuanian community of greater Toronto, Rev. Ažubalis organized a Lithuanian Saturday School for children, established Caritas, a Lithuanian welfare organization, and founded a Lithuanian children's summer camp at Wasaga Beach, Ontario. A man of great energy, by 1959 he had embarked upon a project that would consume the rest of his life – the establishment of a cultural centre for Lithuanians of all religious faiths. Today, this centre in Mississauga, Ontario, is comprised of St. John's Lithuanian Cemetery (established, 1960); facilities for the Lithuanian weekly paper Tėviškės žiburiai; a large banquet/concert hall and an exhibition hall (built in 1972); the Lithuanian Martyrs' Roman Catholic Church (erected in 1978); and the Lithuanian Museum-Archives of Canada (completed after his death in 1989). This whole complex was given the name Anapilis, which means, in Lithuanian, "a city beyond." Rev. Petras Ažubalis, in this view, breaks ground for Mississauga's Lithuanian Martyrs' R.C. Church in the early 1970s. [Photo, courtesy Rev. Jonas Staškevičius]

The Dynamics of an Electrical Engineer

Left: Fleeing communist oppression, nine-year-old Gedas Sakus immigrated to Canada with his parents in 1948 from Chines, Lithuania. First settling in Winnipeg, the family moved to Toronto where Gedas, upon graduating in Electrical Engineering from the University of Toronto, began a 36-year career with Northern Electric in 1962, holding 21 different positions with the company, including President, Bell-Northern Research, 1986-1990; President, Northern Telecom Canada, 1990-1993; President, Public Carrier Networks, 1993-1996; and President, Technology, before retiring in 1998. This view, taken in 1993, shows Gedas Sakus, President, Northern Telecom Canada, making a presentation to Mr. Thu Rongji, the future Premier of China. [Photo, courtesy Gedas Sakus]

Politically, Lithuanian-Canadians today cannot be assigned to any particular Canadian party. So long as their homeland remained under Soviet rule, Lithuanians kept up steady pressure on Canadian politicians to continue the policy of non-recognition of the Soviet takeover. This lobbying involved very close cooperation with other Canadian ethnic groups, especially Estonians, Latvians, and East European groups. Since the re-establishment of Lithuanian state independence in 1990, Lithuanian Canadians have devoted a good deal of time, emotion, and funds to helping those in the homeland, though most have felt their ties to Canada are too complex to let them return to Lithuania.

The most recent wave of immigrants from Lithuania are mostly young professionals in search of better economic conditions. Their numbers are still too small for the creation of new ethnic organizations.

Milda Danys

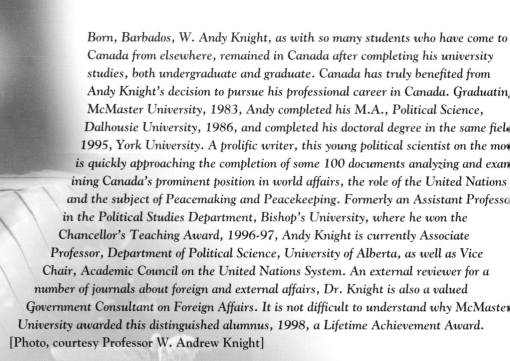

Born, Barbados, W. Andy Knight, as with so many students who have come to Canada from elsewhere, remained in Canada after completing his university studies, both undergraduate and graduate. Canada has truly benefited from Andy Knight's decision to pursue his professional career in Canada. Graduating McMaster University, 1983, Andy completed his M.A., Political Science, Dalhousie University, 1986, and completed his doctoral degree in the same field 1995, York University. A prolific writer, this young political scientist on the move is quickly approaching the completion of some 100 documents analyzing and examining Canada's prominent position in world affairs, the role of the United Nations and the subject of Peacemaking and Peacekeeping. Formerly an Assistant Professor in the Political Studies Department, Bishop's University, where he won the Chancellor's Teaching Award, 1996-97, Andy Knight is currently Associate Professor, Department of Political Science, University of Alberta, as well as Vice Chair, Academic Council on the United Nations System. An external reviewer for a number of journals about foreign and external affairs, Dr. Knight is also a valued Government Consultant on Foreign Affairs. It is not difficult to understand why McMaster University awarded this distinguished alumnus, 1998, a Lifetime Achievement Award.
[Photo, courtesy Professor W. Andrew Knight]

Born in Barbados, British West Indies, 1943, Anne Cools immigrated to Canada as a teenager, graduating from McGill University in the Social Sciences. Within 20 years, she became the first Black, male or female, to be appointed to the Canadian Senate. A respected Social Worker before entering politics, Anne Cools has been a passionate, innovative leader in creating services to assist battered wives, families in crisis, and families troubled by domestic violence. An unsuccessful Liberal candidate in the 1979 and 1980 Federal Elections, Senator Cools has served on numerous Senate Committees dealing with National Finance, Legal and Constitutional Affairs, and Official Languages. She was also a Member of the Senate Task Force on the Meech Lake Accord.
[Photo, courtesy Senator Anne Cools]

from **Barbados**

AFTER SLAVERY ended in the Caribbean, it became common for people to search elsewhere for better jobs or good, arable land. Migrants from the Caribbean region who left their homelands to work abroad, travelled to Britain and the United States. Migration became essential for the survival of family life, a practice that continues to this day. Only a handful of Caribbean migrants came to Canada before the 1900s, and these settled in such places as Nova Scotia, Ontario, and British Columbia.

Around the turn of the twentieth century, a small group of men were brought from Barbados to perform the hard and exacting work in the coal mines and in the blast furnaces of Sydney, Nova Scotia. With little money and no access to credit, these men congregated in a defined area of Whitney Pier separated from the rest of Sydney by the steel plant and the railway tracks.

An entirely new era of immigration from the Caribbean was the result of Canada's adoption of a nonracist immigration policy in the 1960s. Education and skills became the main conditions of admissibility, and "race" or ethnic origin was largely irrelevant. This opened the country to Barbadians and other people of Caribbean origin, especially from the English-speaking former British colonies.

In the 1996 Canadian census, 21,415 people identified themselves as either exclusively (10,240) or partially (11,170) of Barbadian ethnic origin. Of this total, 14,080 lived in Ontario; 4,185 in Quebec; 1,180 in British Columbia; and 980 in Alberta. The large majority of the ethnocommunity chose to live in the cities of Toronto and Montreal.

Barbadians often gather with their compatriots for social occasions. A variety of island-centred organizations such as the Barbados ex-Police Association sprang up to cope with the settlement problems of the Barbadians with many of their socio-cultural needs. (A number of former Barbadian law enforcement officers had chosen to come and settle in Canada.)

Barbadians today are very much a part of the rich mosaic of Canadian life. Committed to making life safer for children, Barbadian Seraphim ("Joe") Fortes at the turn of the century taught hundreds of Vancouver children to

It is not well known that the roots of Oliver Jones are traced to Barbados. Born, 1934, Montreal, Quebec, and growing up in Montreal's poor St. Henri district, like Oscar Peterson who lived in the same neighbourhood, Jones was a child prodigy who at three years could repeat songs on the piano he had just heard on the radio. When he was eight years, he was taking lessons from Oscar Peterson's sister Daisey. But instead of following in the footsteps of Peterson's soaring international fame, Oliver Jones, out of Puerto Rico, led a quartet backing Jamaican pop singer Kenny Hamilton, 1963-1980. Tired of the electric keyboard and playing top-40 material, Oliver returned to Montreal, 1980, to play jazz at Montreal's newest jazz room, a place called Biddle's. Three releases later, 1986, Oliver Jones started a nine-year trek travelling 350,000 miles a year, while working internationally, doing on average 130 concerts a year. By 1995, he decided that semi-retirement was in the best interest of personal health. Since his first public appearance some 60 years ago, Jones has stacked up 15 recordings, all with Justin Time Records Inc., an Order of Canada (1994), three Felix Awards, one Juno Award, the Oscar Peterson and Martin Luther King Jr. Awards, honorary doctorates, tours on five continents, appearances at most major festivals and the international respect of audiences, critics, and musicians. Not bad for someone who never had a jazz lesson in his life. [Photo, courtesy Justin Time Records Inc.]

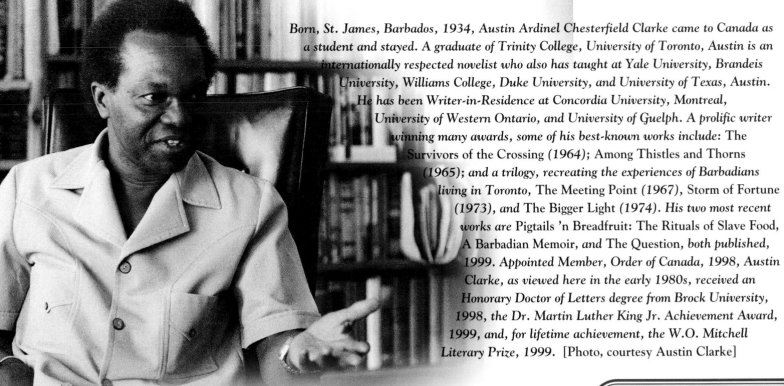

Born, St. James, Barbados, 1934, Austin Ardinel Chesterfield Clarke came to Canada as a student and stayed. A graduate of Trinity College, University of Toronto, Austin is an internationally respected novelist who also has taught at Yale University, Brandeis University, Williams College, Duke University, and University of Texas, Austin. He has been Writer-in-Residence at Concordia University, Montreal, University of Western Ontario, and University of Guelph. A prolific writer winning many awards, some of his best-known works include: The Survivors of the Crossing (1964); Among Thistles and Thorns (1965); and a trilogy, recreating the experiences of Barbadians living in Toronto, The Meeting Point (1967), Storm of Fortune (1973), and The Bigger Light (1974). His two most recent works are Pigtails 'n Breadfruit: The Rituals of Slave Food, A Barbadian Memoir, and The Question, both published, 1999. Appointed Member, Order of Canada, 1998, Austin Clarke, as viewed here in the early 1980s, received an Honorary Doctor of Letters degree from Brock University, 1998, the Dr. Martin Luther King Jr. Achievement Award, 1999, and, for lifetime achievement, the W.O. Mitchell Literary Prize, 1999. [Photo, courtesy Austin Clarke]

A pioneer in the historical sociology of sport, Professor Keith A. P. Sandiford, born, 1936, Bridgetown, Barbados, West Indies, began teaching History, University of Manitoba, 1966, the year he completed his Ph.D., University of Toronto. Born in Barbados and a graduate of both Combermere School (Barbados) and University College of the West Indies before immigrating to Toronto to pursue graduate studies, Dr. Sandiford is a keen cricket statistician who, in collaboration with Dr. Brian Stoddart of Australia, edited The Imperial Game: Cricket, Culture and Society, a seminal work published by Manchester University Press, 1998. Keith Sandiford's status as one of the world's leading cricket sociologists has led to numerous invitations to attend conferences and symposia in Australia, Canada, the USA, and the West Indies. A wide-angle historian, Keith has written on a variety of topics from Victorian politics and British diplomacy to examining Victorian culture, in general, and Barbadian education, in particular. An entertaining teacher, Keith earned two years in a row (1991, '92), the much coveted Merit Award from University of Manitoba. A community volunteer, Keith Sandiford has served as President, National Council of Black Education in Canada, the Canadian Ethnocultural Council, and the Canadian Labour Force Development Board. In this view, 1969, Dr. Sandiford was six short years away from becoming a Life Master with the American Contract Bridge League. [Photo, courtesy Dr. Keith Sandiford]

Before becoming a medical doctor specializing in cancer treatment, Anthony Lindsay Austin Fields, born, Barbados, 1943, had studied natural sciences at the University of Cambridge, U.K., 1962-65. Upon returning to Barbados, 1966, he was a teacher at both Queen's College and the University of the West Indies. Immigrating to Canada, 1968, Anthony Fields gained employment as a chemistry technologist at Hamilton-based Stelco. Recognizing the need to continue his education, he enrolled at the University of Alberta, first, to study Zoology, 1969-70, then, Medicine. Graduating in Medicine, 1974, Dr. Fields, after completing one year's internship at Edmonton's Royal Alexandra Hospital, moved to Toronto, 1975, to specialize in internal medicine, spending, first, three years at St. Michael's Hospital, then two more years specializing in Oncology at Princess Margaret Hospital, both hospitals being affiliated with the University of Toronto. When opportunity came, 1980, to return to Edmonton, Alberta, as member of the medical staff at the Cross Cancer Institute, with a full-time appointment to the Faculty of Medicine, University of Alberta, it was a dream come true. Since 1988, Dr. Anthony Fields, a Harrison College Old-Boy from beautiful Barbados, has been Director, Cross Cancer Institute, and, since 1998, a full professor, Department of Oncology and Department of Medicine, University of Alberta. A Board Member, National Cancer Institute of Canada, Dr. Fields has made major contributions to Canadian research in cancer and sits, today, on no less than 25 major committees at both the national and provincial levels, acting in advisory capacities for steering and liaison committees investigating the latest in cancer research. [Photo, courtesy Dr. Anthony Fields]

to swim. He saved scores of people from drowning and was given a public funeral at his death in 1922. His epitaph read: "Little Children Loved Him." The writer, Austin Clarke, born in Barbados in 1934, immigrated to Canada in 1955 and attended Trinity College at the University of Toronto. One of Canada's most prolific writers, Clarke expressed in his works the fears, struggles, hopes, and dreams of the African-Canadian community in Toronto. Through his writings, Clarke has become a powerful spokesperson for many immigrants, especially racial minorities. Barbadian Canadians, in sports, are well known for their cricket expertise but they are, as well, making an impact contribution to Canada's national pastime – hockey – in that Fred Brathwaite, Anson Carter, and Kevin Weekes all have Bajan roots. ♦

Born, Barbados, West Indies, 1941, Frank A. Maynard was educated at Combermere School (Barbados) and the Royal College of Music (London) before migrating to Canada. Following his graduation from Ryerson Polytechnic Institute and the University of Toronto, 1965, he entered the Ontario provincial service and rose rapidly to the rank of Supervisor, Administration, Department, Treasury and Economics. He moved to Winnipeg, Manitoba, 1969, as Director, Personnel Management, Department of Health and Social Development. Quickly establishing an enviable reputation as one of the most efficient administrators in the public service, Frank Maynard was appointed, 1981, Executive Director, Administrative Services, Manitoba Health. Later that same year he was made Assistant Deputy Minister of Health and from 1988 to his retirement, December 1994, he served as Deputy Minister in this department. Notwithstanding the frequent change of governments and shuffling of cabinets, Mr. Maynard was one of the chief Civil Servants in the provincial Ministry of Health for more than 13 years. He was the first Black administrator to rise to such heights in Manitoba. Now president of the Population Health Institute of Canada, Mr. Maynard serves often as a consultant whose advice is much sought after by corporate businesses. [Photo, courtesy Frank Maynard]

Robert A. Brathwaite worked in construction and in carpentry before he immigrated to Canada, 1961. Born, St. Philip, Foulis Bay, Barbados, Robert felt that Canada was a land of opportunity and quickly adapted to his new environs by taking a job at Canada Packers, Toronto. Now retired, Bob has been a very active volunteer with St. John Ambulance since 1966. Today a Sergeant Major in this 900-year organization, he plans all ceremonial activities for the Toronto Branch. Married to a Barbadian, Bob is also the proud father of four children, all of whom have grown up and are currently contributing to the growth of Canadian society. A Knight of the Order of St. John of Jerusalem, recognized in 1992 with the 125 Anniversary Medal celebrating Canada's 125th birthday, a recipient of the 1977 Queen's Silver Jubilee Medal, Robert Brathwaite received a very special award in 1999 for his many years of volunteer service. In part, the citation reads: "In recognition of your invaluable contribution to human welfare through your outstanding and dedicated volunteer service thereby enhancing the quality of life for fellow citizens." The certificate, an annual award sponsored by the Volunteer Centre, Toronto, was presented to Robert, as viewed here, by the Honourable Hilary M. Weston, Ontario's Lieutenant Governor, April 19, 1999. [Photo, courtesy Robert Brathwaite]

THE EARLY Iranians in Canada came as part of a massive flow of students to North American universities that began after 1965. Many would remain in Canada after completing their studies and having obtained immigrant status.

The freedom and political stability of Canada would also prove very attractive to the people of Iran, formerly known as Persia, in the aftermath of the revolution of 1978-1979 which toppled the government of Shah Mohammed Reza Pahlavi. The Islamic Revolution brought Iranians seeking refuge from the traditions of the Shiite Muslim religion as interpreted by the Ayatollah Khomeini. There would be an initial headlong flight to

Mehran Anvari's ancestral lineage goes back more than a millennium to the fall of the Persian Empire. Over hundreds of years, despite significant pressure and persecution, generations of Mehran's family remained Zoroastrian, that is, until the 1850s when they embraced the Baha'i faith. Born, Iran, 1959, both Mehran's father, Nooraldin, and mother, Noorangiz, were pharmacists in Tehran until the Islamic Revolution in Iran erupted, 1978. To avoid persecution and possible death, the family chose to migrate to Canada, settling in Grimbsy, Ontario. Mehran, who had earlier completed his formal education in England, returned there, the

same year his family immigrated to Canada, enrolling, University of Newcastle-on-Tyne, completing his medical degree there in five years. After completing one year's internship, Dr. Anvari returned to Canada, enlisted in postgraduate training at McMaster University where he completed a training program in surgery (1984-89). To further his studies in surgery, Dr. Anvari travelled to Adelaide, Australia, to work with Professor John Dent and Glyn Jamieson, pioneers in gastrointestinal mobility at the University of Adelaide. After three years additional training, Dr. Anvari graduated with a Ph.D. in "gastric motor function and the influence of gastric surgery." Anxious to rejoin his family in Canada, Dr. Anvari set up a clinical practice, 1992, at St. Joseph's Hospital, Hamilton, Ontario, and was appointed Associate Professor, with tenure, Department of Surgery, McMaster University. Recently made Director, Centre of Minimal Access Surgery (CMAS), McMaster University, 1999, Dr. Anvari is recognized internationally as an expert in the field of minimum access surgery. His revolutionary treatment for gastrointestinal disorders has brought lucrative offers to go elsewhere. He has remained in Canada, nevertheless, because Canada's multicultural policies are the closest to his own spiritual beliefs. In this view, Dr. Anvari, Director, CMAS, stands in the foyer of the recently opened centre, November 1999. [Photo, courtesy Dr. Mehran Anvari]

from Iran

Canada of members of the military, supporters and *apparatchiks* of the old regime. The Iran-Iraq War and both religious and political persecution subsequently provided the impetus for the middle class and the Baha'is, the largest religious minority in Iran, to follow in their footsteps. The imposition of the *hijab* (veiling) as a daily requirement of female attire, immediate dismissal from so-called "non-traditional" jobs, and limited occupational choices, forced women who did not share these values to chart a route elsewhere. Many chose Canada.

Born, Esfahan, Iran, 1949, Amir Etemadi, left, graduated, 1971, as an electrical engineer, Purdue University, and received his M.B.A., Loyola University, 1973, before immigrating to Canada, 1980, settling in Vancouver. Initially building or renovating a series of funeral homes, car dealerships, and custom homes in the Vancouver area, Amir discovered that his real niche was building ski resort accessories, such as lodges, villages, condominiums, townhouses, and restaurants for ski resort sites at both Whistler and Blackcomb Mountains north of Vancouver. When Amir's company, Amako, founded, 1983, built the 52,000 square foot Roundhouse Lodge Alpine, capacity, 1,750 patrons, atop Mount Whistler, it superceded another of Amir's creations, the 30,000 square foot Glacier Creek Restaurant, atop Mt. Blackcomb, as the world's largest mountain-top restaurant. Amako has recently expanded beyond British Columbia's acclaimed ski resorts, and currently is building a 327,000 square foot pedestrian village at Copper Mountain, Denver, Colorado. Amir's company is also completing a condominium-hotel at Utah's Solitude Mountain and is about to begin still another pedestrian village, this time at California's Squaw Valley. No question that Amir Etemadi's impact in the ski resort world offers ski buffs, worldwide, state-of-the art winter resort facilities unexcelled anywhere in the world. [Photo, courtesy Amir Etemadi]

Behrouz Tabarrok, right, was born in Tehran, Iran, 1939. His childhood years were spent playing by the Caspian Sea and wandering the great bazaars of the city of his birth. Sent to boarding school in England at age 13 years, Bez thrived in his new-found culture and married a British girl, Carolyn, 1963. After he earned his D.Philosophy from Oxford University, 1965, he and Carolyn immigrated to Canada where he was made Assistant Professor, Mechanical Engineering, University of Toronto. An exceptional teacher, scholar, and consultant, in 1977, Bez was made a full Professor. After another decade at University of Toronto, he was appointed Founding Chair, Department of Mechanical Engineering, University of Victoria, British Columbia. In addition to being an esteemed teacher, scholar of renown, and a distinguished researcher, Dr. Tabarrok chaired and organized many international symposia, congresses and conferences. He also served as President, Canadian Society for Mechanical Engineering. Before he died undergoing a heart by-pass operation, April 1999, Dr. Tabarrok was made Director, Institute for Integrated Energy Systems, University of Victoria. The Institute has been a pioneer in the creation of "fuel cells," the key component in what may be a technological and social revolution – the transformation of an oil-based economy to one based on hydrogen. During his life, Dr. Tabarrok wrote some 250 articles for a series of international journals and conferences. He received numerous awards including the Proctor & Gamble Award of Merit, the Robert W. Angus Medal and the CSME Best Paper Award. Posthumously, Dr. Tabarrok received from McMaster University the annual CANCAM Award, 1999. He leaves behind his wife, three children, and a grandson. In this view, Dr. Bez Tabarrok addresses an international symposium, Shanghai, 1987. [Photo, courtesy Carolyn Tabarrok]

Bombardier Stress Engineer

Seyed Hossein Miri's grandfather lived to see his 109th birthday. He used to say that "good luck is like a seed you find on your way home. Sooner or later, everyone finds one, but it is up to you to pick it up, eat it and survive another day or plant it, nourish it, and wait for it to bear you thousands of fruits." Seyed not only found seeds but nourished them and, today, his life must seem like a bowl of cherries. Born in Tehran, when Seyed graduated from high school, it was just in time to see all universities in Iran face closure. Facing a mandatory military draft, Seyed was at training camp when war broke out between Iraq and Iran. Such conditions made it impossible to plan a future or set a goal. But the desire for higher education burned brightly in his heart. One year after completing his two years of required military service, Seyed got married and, thanks to Canada's Immigration policy towards Iranians seeking opportunities in Canada, he and his wife and young daughter immigrated to

Canada, 1985. His first job was as a full-time "walking courier" in downtown Toronto. As a part-time painter, little seeds began appearing and Seyed, not forgetting his grandfather's advice, nourished every opportunity. Soon he was operating a CNC milling machine for P-Can Robotics. By 1989, the year he became a Canadian citizen, Seyed, now the father of two daughters, was working day and night to earn the right to attend Ryerson as an Aerospace Engineering student. From a class of 118 students who began the same program in 1993, only 13 graduated four years later, with Bombardier Aerospace snapping Seyed up as a potential employee. He has never looked back. Now a Stress Engineer preparing reports on creep, corrosion, crack propagation and fatigue life limits of various Bombardier aircraft components, Seyed's bowl is surely full of cherries. In this 1998 view, Seyed works in a Flight Safety Room. [Photo, courtesy Seyed Miri]

From Tehran to Toronto

It certainly is a remarkable story. A boy goes to work at age nine years to help his impoverished family in Tehran, Iran. Working for a man who ground magnifying glass from old window panes, Karim Hakim became versed in the optical field, from grinding glass to the maintenance of worn out equipment. By the time he was 19, he was in Germany grinding precious lenses for instruments. Before immigrating to Canada in the mid-1960s to pursue his career, he perfected his craft as a lensmaker in Switzerland. In 1967, he set up a laboratory in Toronto, purchasing old equipment, revitalizing it, and began selling his homemade lenses to opticians and optometrists. Before he knew it, hundreds of people wanted to buy lenses directly from him. Karim then began manufacturing frames, adding another dimension to his business, creating retail outlets and selling glasses directly to the public. Today, Hakim Optical has outlets across Ontario and into the Maritimes and is branching into the United States. On a good day, the company, with head-quarters in Toronto, sells as many as 1,000 pairs of prescription glasses at its more than 70 showrooms and 45 one-hour factory outlets. In fact, since he opened shop in the former Elmwood Hotel in 1967, Karim Hakim has sold over 14 million pairs of glasses! In this view, Karim, right, is viewed with Mayor Mel Lastman of Toronto, celebrating 32 years of entrepreneurship. [Photo, courtesy Karim Hakim]

Lotfollah Shafai, born, Maragbeh, Iran, 1941, became the first Iranian student ever to enroll in the Faculty of Applied Sciences and Engineering, University of Toronto. After completing his B.Sc. in engineering in his native homeland, he arrived in Canada, September 24, 1964, in the middle of the fall term and was given provisional acceptance to the Master's degree program, Electrical Engineering, completing his M.A.Sc., 1966, and was granted a Ph.D. in electrical engineering, 1969. After 10 years at the University of Manitoba, he was made full professor in the Department of Electrical and Computer Engineering. To enhance University of Manitoba's contact with Industry, Lot Shafai assisted in establishing The Institute for Technology Development and was its Director until 1987 when he was appointed Head of the University's Electrical Engineering Department. To enable national and international technical and scientific exchange, Professor Shafai established the Symposium on Antenna Technology and Applied Electromagnetics, 1986. Held every two years, it is the premier Canadian conference on Telecommunications, Antennas and Microwaves, attracting a number of international participants. At the University of Manitoba, Dr. Shafai has established a world-class Antenna and Microwave Laboratory. His early research contribution in 1976 resulted in satellite terminal miniaturization for Hermes Satellite. This work for the first time introduced CAD concept to reflector antenna design and subsequentially was adapted internationally. Professor Shafai's recent contributions were recognized, 1988, by the Institute of Electrical and Electronics Engineers of USA by electing him a Fellow. Author of some 700 books, technical papers and reports, an energetic Dr. Lot Shafai has received many awards. He knows that the stable and welcoming lifestyle of Canadian society has made it possible for him to have an uninterrupted career in teaching, researching, writing, and inventing (he has 12 patents). In this view, 1998, Dr. Jean-Pierre Wallot, right, President, The Royal Society of Canada, presents Dr. Lotfollah Shafai, left, with the prestigious certificate inducting him as a Fellow of Canada's most prestigious and respected scientific body. [Photo, courtesy Professor Lotfollah Shafai]

According to the 1996 census, there are 64,405 (single and multiple responses) Iranians in Canada. Members of this ethnocommunity live primarily in Canada's largest cities.

The earliest immigrants from Iran quickly joined the professional ranks as medical doctors, engineers, lawyers, nurses, and dentists. Those who came later chose entrepreneurship, focusing on the creation of construction companies, restaurants, bakeries, dry-cleaning shops, grocery stores, repair shops, and computer stores. Iranian women also offered a variety of community services, including catering, serving, and baking.

The Iranian business community has generously supported Iranian identity in Canada through financial means and promotion of Persian language journals, magazines, radio and television programs. Advertising revenues bolster the production and free distribution of many group publications and programs. The Iranian-Canadian business sector is also a leader in hosting a number of live cultural events including poetry readings and musical evenings. This intricate alliance and entwining of community enterprise and group culture remains a glittering hallmark of Canada's Iranian community. ✹

Marcus Aregawi graduated with a Bachelor of Applied Science, Civil Engineering, from Haile Selassie University, Addis Ababa, Ethiopia, where he was born. Before immigrating to Canada, 1972, Marcus first worked as a resident engineer in the Prime Minister's Office, Addis Ababa, moving to Germany, 1971, where he was engaged in the final designs for expressways (Autobahn), including many of its interchanges. By 1974 he had graduated in structural engineering, (M.A.Sc.), University of Toronto, at which time his career as a structural, design and consultant engineer took off. With Carruthers and Wallace, as project engineer, he was responsible for the design of many high profile buildings including Toronto's Eaton Centre; GM Plant, Oshawa; Dalhousie Sport Complex, Halifax; and Toronto's Roy Thomson Hall. With Quinn Dressel Associates, Marcus was responsible for the design of the Royal Bank Office Tower, Toronto; the Canada Centre, Alberta; Allstate Head Office, Markham; and part of the 68-storey Scotia Plaza complex, Toronto. In 1985, he joined Alex Tobias Associates and was responsible for the design of Palace Pier II, a 50-storey residential complex in Toronto. He also was responsible for the design of three 30-storey luxury towers in Toronto called the Palisades. Marcus Aregawi, many times an award-winning structural and design engineer, has been a building engineer with the City of Toronto since 1987. In this view, Marcus, wearing the traditional hard hat of a construction supervisor, surveys a Toronto building site in the 1980s. [Photo, courtesy Marcus Aregawi]

from Ethiopia

ETHIOPIANS come from the oldest independent country in Africa. Located in northeast Africa, Ethiopia was formerly known as Abyssinia. The Ethiopian presence in Canada is a recent phenomenon dating from the 1980s. Ethiopia's modern history has been marked by civil war, fighting against guerillas in the provinces of Eritrea (a separate country since 1992) and Tigray, and by repeated famines caused by drought. These factors have forced many to seek refuge abroad. Amharas, Tigrayans, Oromos, Jews, and others came to Canada from several countries of first asylum that included Egypt, Kenya, Italy, and Greece. The first group of newcomers to Canada was composed primarily of single English-speaking young men from middle- and upper-class backgrounds.

According to the Canadian census, there were, in 1996, 14,955 individuals of Ethiopian ethnicity in Canada (13,010 single response and 1,950 multiple response). There were no official statistics or separate categories for people who rejected identification as Ethiopians. (Canadian census data reported the presence of 6,225 individuals from the independent state of Eritrea.)

Ethiopians have tended to concentrate in Canada's urban centres, particularly within Toronto and its environs, because they have been more likely to find employment in a large urban setting. A small group of Ethiopian Jews (Falashas) made their way to Montreal where they struck up a good relationship with that city's Jewish community.

Daniel Gebretsadik was born in Tigray Province, Ethiopia, 1951. His inspirational story is one of survival and the grist for a Hollywood movie. Escaping oppression and poverty, Daniel fled Ethiopia, 1978, arriving in Dijbouti with a determined vision of immigrating to Canada. It took 18 months, but he made it to Canada, a smile on his face, settling, first, in Hamilton, Ontario, where he began attending Mohawk College during the day and drove a Toronto taxi at night. After three tough years, he was able to save enough money to return to Africa, via Sudan, and with the help of supportive rebels, was able to reconnect with his wife, Berhan, and both his son and daughter, and prepare them for their long journey to Canada. At the time, Ethiopia was facing very severe drought and famine. Rather than leave behind multitudes of expatriates seeking comfort and refuge in Sudan, Daniel spent nine months as a volunteer assisting fellow Ethiopians overcome the devastation of hunger and poverty. Re-established in a new world, Daniel, today, is a successful salesman for DaimlerChrysler Canada. His daughter attends the University of Windsor and his son is studying computer graphics at Sheridan College. Daniel and his wife are happy in their adopted homeland. [Photo, courtesy Charles J. Humber]

Establishing Toronto Medical Clinic

The ninth of ten children, Dr. Yemisrach Hailemeskel, CCFP, born, 1958, Harrar, Ethiopia, upon completing with honours her high school education at the Bible Academy, Narazeth, was offered a chance to go to Czechoslovakia on a scholarship, 1976, providing this Amharic-speaking Ethiopian learned to speak and read Slovakian. Upon completing this requirement, 1977, she enrolled at Safaric University, Faculty of Medicine, and continued her medical training at Comenius University, Bratislava, graduating, M.D., 1983. That same year she entered Canada as a visitor and applied for refugee status because the difficult political situation in Ethiopia prevented her from returning to her native land. While waiting for her landed immigrant status, Yemisrach worked for one year as a Research Fellow, Department of Pathology, Clinical Research Institute of Montreal. After successfully fulfilling all her requirements to practice medicine in Canada, by 1986, she was back in Toronto, where today she has an established medical clinic serving her community as a family physician. This scenic view was taken while visiting her sister in Switzerland as Dr. Yemisrach Hailemeskel was making her journey to Canada, 1983. [Photo, courtesy Dr. Yemisrach Hailemeskel]

Staff Surgeon from Addis Ababa

Ephrem Gebrechristos, M.D., F.R.C.S.(C), born in Makelle, capital of Ethiopia's Tigray Province, graduated in Medicine from Addis Ababa University at the time when a military regime was in power. Fleeing political repression in his native land, Dr. Gebrechristos found his way to Canada, 1986, and settled in Toronto where he continued his medical studies at the University of Toronto. Completing internship at St. Joseph's Health Centre, 1988-89, Dr. Gebrechristos received a series of surgical fellowships over the next six years, primarily at the Toronto East General Hospital where he was chosen Best Resident Teacher of the Year, 1993. Married and the father of one daughter, Dr. Gebrechristos, since 1995, has been Staff Surgeon at Humber River Regional Hospital. [Photo, courtesy Dr. Ephrem Gebrechristos]

Estifauos (Steve) Mengesha, left, and Jalye (Jay) Mengesha, right, are the sons of Princess Aida Desta Ras Mengesha Seyoam, granddaughter of Haile Selassie (1889-1975), former Emperor of Ethiopia, 1916-1974. Steve came to Canada, 1967, attending the University of Toronto. Jay followed his older brother to Canada, arriving in 1969, settling in British Columbia and graduating in Economics from Simon Fraser University. Today, Jay is Manager, Risk Management, Royal Bank of Canada, while Steve is an international business consultant. This photo was taken, 1988, following the release of the Royal Family who had been imprisoned for 14 years by the revolutionaries who overthrew Emperor Selassie, 1974. Steve, holding his son, is happy to learn that his mother, in picture held by Jay, has been released and is on her way to join her Ethiopian-born Canadian sons in Toronto. [Photo, courtesy *The Toronto Star*]

The occupational transition that has been difficult for many has resulted in a dramatic decline in their socio-economic status. This downward mobility can be attributed in part to the language barrier: it was all but impossible for Ethiopians in Canada to find other than low-skilled, manual, or service sector work until they became proficient in English. Another problem was that the training and experience acquired by individuals in Ethiopia tended to go unrecognized in Canada. Some Ethiopians responded to the obstacle of obtaining professional or skilled work by establishing businesses. A clustering of Ethiopian restaurants around Bloor and Christie Streets has helped create the ambience of an Ethiopian immigrant neighbourhood. Ethiopians also found that they could make a living in auto repair, furniture manufacturing, and commercial and instant printing services.

Although Ethiopian quest for decent housing and steady employment has been a preoccupation, various ethnocultural associations have helped to maintain local identities and to foster a larger sense of fellow feeling and cooperation. Eritreans, Amharas, Oromos, and Tigrayans have challenged themselves by working together to create a valuable and formidable complementary counterweight to the efforts of the Ethiopian government to deliver humanitarian aid to needy people at home. Ethiopians in Canada have also emerged as professionals in finance, engineering, and particularly in medicine.

The Ethiopian Orthodox Church in Toronto also played an important role. The Orthodox Church and even the Ethiopian Evangelical Church have helped Ethiopian Christians achieve a greater sense of nationality. Also, Ethiopian Muslims have found companionship and strength in many of Toronto's mosques. ⛊

The Hon. Sylvia Olga Fedoruk was born in Canora, Saskatchewan, the daughter of Ukrainian immigrants who came to Canada near the turn of the 20th century. A physicist and educator, Dr. Fedoruk is well known internationally in the world of medicine, science, and research: Fellow, Canadian College of Physicists in Medicine; former member, Atomic Energy Control Board, Canada; former Senior Physicist, Saskatoon Cancer Clinic; and a former consultant, Nuclear Medicine, International Atomic Energy Agency. She is also the author of nearly 40 major scientific papers. Dr. Fedoruk was named Lieutenant Governor, Province of Saskatchewan, 1988-1994. An avid follower of women's sports, she is Past President, Canadian Ladies Curling Association, and was inducted into the Saskatchewan Sports Hall of Fame as well as the Canadian Curling Hall of Fame. She was the YWCA Woman of the Year, 1986. A very busy Canadian proud of her Ukrainian roots, Dr. Fedoruk was a recipient of the Queen's Silver Jubilee Medal, 1977, was made an Officer of the Order of Canada, 1986, received the Toastmasters International Communications and Leadership Award, 1991, honoured with the Commemorative Medal, 125th Anniversary of Canada's Confederation, 1992, in addition to being recognized with the Taras Shevchenko Medal by the Ukrainian Canadian Congress, 1995. In this view, Lt. Governor of the Province of Saskatchewan, the Honourable Sylvia Olga Fedoruk, centre, stands with Ukrainian Canadians, members of a choir from St. Goretti School, Saskatoon, November 1, 1991, the date Roy Romanow was sworn in Premier of Saskatchewan. [Photo, courtesy Saskatchewan Tourism]

from **Ukraine**

ON SEPTEMBER 7, 1891, Vasyl Eleniak and Ivan Pylypiw stepped onto Canadian soil and became the first two officially recorded Ukrainian immigrants in Canada. Dressed in sheepskin coats they were pioneers of the Ukrainian Canadian community, the fifth largest ethnic group in Canada, now numbering over 1,000,000.

Canada had only seven provinces when the first Ukrainians arrived so they helped build Canada. They became pioneers of the Canadian West, breaking the virgin land and laying down a carpet of golden wheat. It was estimated by Senator Paul Yuzyk that Ukrainians pioneered 10 million acres of the prairies or 40 percent of Canada's wheat land.

An interesting twist of fate is that the "first immigrant" from Ukraine came in 1842. It was a Ukrainian strain of early ripening wheat, called Red Fife. Together with the variety Marquis derived from Ukrainian wheat, they formed the basis of Canada's early economic growth. It is fitting that Ukraine, known as the "Breadbasket of Europe" made Canada the "Granary of the World."

First Wave of Ukrainian Immigration 1891-1914

Ukrainian immigration to Canada grew after Professor Joseph Oleskiw visited Canada in 1895 and wrote a book *About Free Lands*. A flood of immigrants from Western Ukraine (Austria-Hungary) totalling 180,000 came to Canada from 1891 to 1914. Most settled in Manitoba and areas of the Northwest Territories which in 1905 became the provinces of Alberta and Saskatchewan. In 1999, there were two Ukrainian Canadian premiers, Roy Romanow in Saskatchewan and Gary Filmon in Manitoba.

In the early years Ukrainians were known by several names such as Ruthenians, Rusins, Carpatho-Rusins, Galicians, Lemkos, and Bukovinians. In 1897, the first Ukrainian Orthodox Church was built in Gardenton, Manitoba, and in 1898 the first Ukrainian Catholic church was erected in Star, Alberta. Many Ukrainians, however, have become affiliated with the Roman Catholic, Anglican, and Baptist churches. The Ukrainian churches, Orthodox and Catholic, celebrate Ukrainian Christmas on January 7th and Easter by the Julian Calendar. Ukrainian foods such as borshch beet soup, perogies (varenyky), cabbage rolls (holubtsi), kasha (buckwheat), kolach (chala), and bublyky (bagels) came to Canada with the pioneers. Edmonton's Cheemo Perogy Factory makes millions of perogies every week.

Unlike the Mennonites, Icelanders, and Russian Doukhobors, the early Ukrainian settlers received no financial assistance from the Canadian government. In fact, the government dumped trainloads of Ukrainians in the prairie wilderness and abandoned them to survive as best they could. The youngest suffered the most and deaths of babies were very high. In the NWT colony the death rate was 40 percent for infants under two years of age.

Life for the early Ukrainian settlers was extremely difficult. The agricultural season was short and many had to work in coal mines, in lumber camps, and laying railroad tracks. But survival was easier because of the bloc settlements of Ukrainians which stretched in a belt from southeastern Manitoba northwest into Saskatchewan and Alberta. It culminated in the 5,000 square mile Ukrainian bloc settlement around Vegreville northeast of Edmonton. Every new wave of Ukrainian immigrants found integration into Canadian life easier because the existing community was able to help until the New Canadians could survive on their own.

The first Ukrainian language newspaper was the *Canadian Farmer* (*Kanadiysky Farmer*) in 1903 and, in 1904, the first Ukrainian book, *Christian Catechism*, was printed in Winnipeg. In 1905 the first Ukrainian bookstore was opened.

First Canadian Woman of Ukrainian Descent to Receive the Order of Canada

Mrs. Catherine Crouse (nee Kolikowich) was born in Saskatchewan in 1906 to parents who had immigrated to Canada from Ukraine, settling in the Northwest Territories, 1896. As a young married woman in Winnipeg, this extraordinary Canadian of Ukrainian descent worked long and many hours to generate lasting interest in the heritage of her ancestral roots. She helped organize the Ukrainian Catholic Women's League, eventually becoming National President. For her active and dedicated work for the Ukrainian Catholic Church she was awarded, 1978, the Pro Ecclasia Et Pontifice medal by the Pope. For her 50 years of service to Canada's Ukrainian Community, in which she stressed the need for intelligent study of family life, Mrs. Crouse was made a member of the Order of Canada, 1979, with Governor General Edward Schreyer presiding over the ceremonies, as viewed in this photograph. This was the first time that a Canadian woman of Ukrainian descent had received this honour.
[Photo, courtesy Leona Crouse McDermid]

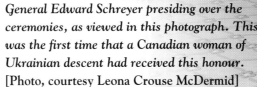
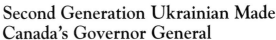

Second Generation Ukrainian Made Canada's Governor General

When the first two officially recorded Ukrainian immigrants settled in Canada, 1891, neither Ivan Pylypiw nor Vasyl Eleniak envisioned 100 years later that Canada's 24th Governor General would be a second generation Ukrainian Canadian. Installed as Governor General of Canada, January 29, 1990, the Rt. Hon. Ramon Hnatyshyn, in his installation speech, exclaimed that Canada "is a nation of immigrants" and that "Canada plays the fullest possible role internationally as a bilingual and multicultural nation." Speaking in English, French, and Ukrainian, the newly appointed Governor General, at the time, was unknowingly reinforcing a statement former Prime Minister Lester B. Pearson made to a gathering of Ukrainian Canadians at Elk Island National Park, July 17, 1966: "You have added something of value, of strength and colour to the Canadian character."
[Photo, courtesy Ukrainian Canadian Research & Documentation Centre]

Filmmaker with a Candid Eye

Of Ukrainian descent and born in Yorkton, Saskatchewan, Roman Kroitor joined Canada's National Film Board, 1949. Considered one of Canada's leading filmmakers, he was director-producer of Candid Eye, the world's first cinéma vérité television series, creating fascinating film portraits of public figures such as Stravinsky and Paul Anka. Labyrinth, the National Film Board's sensational 4.5 million dollar film at Montreal's Expo 67, was co-conceived by Kroitor, Kevin Low, and Hugh O'Connor. A resident of Quebec, Roman Kroitor joined Robert Kerr and Graham Ferguson in co-founding Multi-Screen Corporation to develop the IMAX process which produced Donald Brittain's Tiger Child at Expo 70, Osaka, Japan. Mr. Kroitor, left, is seen here, with Andrew Gregorovich, Senior Researcher, Ukrainian Canadian Research and Documentation Centre. [Photo, courtesy Ukrainian Canadian Research & Documentation Centre]

Following in the Footsteps of His Great-Great-Grandfather

In Canada in the late 19th and early 20th centuries, immigrants often felt compelled to anglicize their sur-names, the perception being, perhaps correctly, that if one had an Anglo surname, job opportunities were more accessible. Such is the case with Steven Peters. Recently elected to the Ontario Legislature for the Riding of Elgin-Middlesex-London, Steve's paternal grandparents immigrated to Canada, circa 1905, from the Horodenka area of Ukraine. Settling first in Saskatchewan, by the time the family migrated to Toronto, in the 1930s, the family surname, Pidwerbeski, had been changed to Peters. Steve's maternal family also immigrated to Canada from Ukraine. In fact, Steve's great-great-grandfather, on his mother's side, was Mayor of Werchrata for 10 years. As with his ancestor, Steve, from St. Thomas, Ontario, was elected Mayor of his hometown in 1991. The youngest Mayor in the city's history, he served three times before being elected a Liberal MPP, 1999. In this view, Steve Peters, Mayor of St. Thomas, is presented to Her Majesty The Queen on the occasion of the Royal visit to St. Thomas, June 27, 1997. [Photo, courtesy St. Thomas Times-Journal]

Passionate Investigative Journalist

Born, 1948, Lachine, Quebec, Victor Gregory Malarek has been a Canadian journalist since 1970. Of Ukrainian descent, Victor, co-host of CBC's Fifth Estate since 1990, and a senior reporter on social policy issues with The Globe & Mail since 1976, is a passionate journalist whose strong concerns about social issues have led him to two Michener Awards, 1985 and 1988, and a Gemini Award, 1997, as best Canadian broad-cast journalist. Author of several fascinating investigative books, Victor, who now lives in Toronto, in this view, speaks on the 1996 Tenth Anniversary of the Chernobyl nuclear disaster in his ancestral homeland, Ukraine. [Photo, courtesy Andrew Gregorovich]

After 100 Years – Still Remembering...

Todor and Vasylena Pawluk immigrated to Canada from Zadubrivka (Chernivtsi), Ukraine, 1899. The fourth generation descendants of these pioneering Ukrainian settlers gathered together, 1999, at the Shandro Church Cemetery, Alberta, to celebrate the centennial of their grandparents' long journey to Canada at a time when Alberta was a provisional district of the Northwest Territories. [Photo, courtesy Andrew Gregorovich]

Canada's Spiritual Landmarks

Ukrainian Churches are easy to identify when driving through various Canadian municipalities or passing through cities and towns of Canada's prairie provinces. Two examples of Ukrainian church architecture in Canada, are, above, the Ukrainian Orthodox Church, Vegreville, Alberta, now in the Ukrainian Heritage Cultural Village east of Edmonton, typical of hundreds of Ukrainian churches across Canada, and, right, St. Josaphat Ukrainian Catholic Cathedral, Edmonton, Alberta. [Photos, courtesy Andrew Gregorovich]

The first migration of Ukrainian immigrants to Canada was ended by the outbreak of World War I in 1914. Some 10,000 Ukrainians served in the Canadian armed forces in the War and one, Philip Konoval, won the Victoria Cross which was awarded by the King. Ukrainian Canadians have demonstrated a remarkable loyalty to Canada and many died on the battlefields of Europe.

However, the outbreak of World War I aroused suspicion of foreigners and Ukrainians, who had come from Austria-Hungary, were classified as "enemy aliens." Over 5,000 men, and some women and children, were interned for years in 25 concentration camps across Canada. They were incarcerated in places like Fort Henry and Banff National Park where they were forced to build roads, bridges, and other park development. These and other locations now have historical plaques marking the Ukrainian internment.

Second Wave of Immigration 1919-1939

The second period of immigration, 1919-1939, which brought approximately 70,000 Ukrainians to Canada, included many Ukrainian political refugees fleeing Communist oppression. With a Ukrainian Canadian community in place, they were warmly welcomed to established organizations, churches, and community halls. This interwar period was one of rapid growth. A whole string of local, provincial, and nation-wide organizations were established. For example, the Ukrainian National Federation of Canada was founded in Edmonton and soon had 100 branches and halls across Canada. The U.N.F. sponsored Ukrainian folk dance groups, like Edmonton's Shumka, and choirs. In 1939 it established the first Ukrainian credit union in Saskatoon.

Because Ukrainians had been excluded from politics in the old country, there was considerable interest in Canadian politics. In 1926 Michael Luchkovich of Vegreville was the first Ukrainian Canadian elected to Parliament; in 1955 Senator William Wall was appointed; in 1957 Hon. Michael Starr became the first Cabinet Minister of Ukrainian origin; in 1958 Hon. John Yaremko, Q.C. was appointed to the Ontario Cabinet; in 1970 Stephen Worobetz was appointed Lieutenant Governor of Saskatchewan; and in 1988 Mr. Justice John Sopinka was appointed to the Supreme Court of Canada.

Janice Kulyk Keefer was born in Toronto, Canada, 1952. Her mother Natalia Solowska emigrated from Halychyna, 1936; her father was born in Canada shortly after his parents emigrated from Halychyna, 1914. Educated at the University of Toronto, Kulyk Keefer won a Commonwealth Scholarship to obtain a D. Phil from Sussex University, England, 1983. Ever since, Kulyk Keefer has been published in Canada's leading magazines and anthologies, as well as in the United States, Germany, England, Mexico, France, the Netherlands, and Ukraine. She has published three novels, three collections of short stories, as well as a volume of poetry and two critical studies, one on Mavis Gallant and one on the fiction of Maritime Canada. Among the awards she has won are two first prizes in two consecutive years, in the CBC Radio Literary Competition. She has twice been nominated for Canada's most prestigious literary prize, the Governor General's Award. Professor of English Literature at the University of Guelph, Ontario, her most recent publications include Honey and Ashes *(Harper & Collins, 1998), a narrative of her maternal family's immigration to Canada, and* Marrying the Sea, *which was awarded the Canadian Author's Award for the best book of poetry published in Canada, 1998, the same year she co-edited* Two Lands: New Visions, *an anthology of contemporary fiction from Canada and Ukraine. In this view, Janice Kulyk Keefer is reading at the 1998 Eden Mills Writer's festival held annually near Guelph.* [Photo, courtesy Llewellyn Clarke]

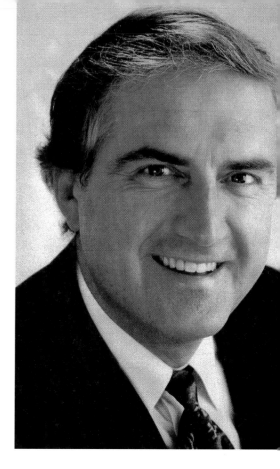

Born in Canada two generations after his ancestors immigrated to Canada from Ukraine, Roy Romanow was elected New Democratic Party Premier of Saskatchewan, 1991, and, subsequently, re-elected to that office in the succeeding general elections of 1995 and 1999. One of Canada's prominent politicians, Mr. Romanow, a graduate lawyer from the University of Saskatchewan, played a major role in the patriation of the Canadian Constitution, and in the formulation of the Canadian Charter of Rights and Freedoms. [Photo, courtesy Ukrainian Canadian Research & Documentation Centre, Toronto]

In 1999 the magnificent John Sopinka Court House opened in Hamilton, Ontario. In 1990, Rt. Hon. Ray Hnatyshyn became Governor General of Canada, our nation's highest honour.

The Ukrainian Canadian Congress was founded in Winnipeg in 1940 as the national voice of the Ukrainian community in Canada. It is also a member of the Ukrainian World Congress which promoted the independence of Ukraine from Soviet Russia and on August 24, 1991 Ukraine declared its independence.

Third Wave of Immigration 1945-1954

The inter-war immigration was disrupted by the outbreak of World War II in 1939. During this war some 40,000 Ukrainian Canadians served in the armed forces. From 1945 to 1954 the third and smallest wave of Ukrainian immigrants (about 35,000) arrived. Among them were displaced persons (DPs), refugees, survivors of Auschwitz, and Ostarbeiters from German slave labour camps. Hailing from all parts of Ukraine, this group included academics, engineers, teachers, and doctors. This small immigration settled mainly in the cities of eastern Canada.

Immigration Since 1954

Since 1954 there has not been a wave of immigration but a steady trickle of a few hundred Ukrainians every year. They have come to Canada from Australia, Great Britain, South America, the United States, and Europe. The 1991 independence of Ukraine has now opened up immigration. The population growth of Ukrainian Canadians is almost entirely based on natural increase and out of 1,025,000 in the 1996 Canadian Census, about 95 percent are Canadian-born. Ukrainian Canadians are no longer an immigrant community because they are now in their fifth Canadian generation.

Contributions and Achievements

Ukrainian Canadians are an active and vital force in this country. Builder William Teron in 1966 built the town of Kanata, which has become Canada's "silicon valley," and another builder, Toronto's Peter Jacyk, has become a prominent philanthropist. James Temertey is CEO of giant Northland Power.

Filmmaker Roman Kroitor was one of the founders of IMAX. Slawko Klymkiw is a senior executive at the CBC and Ivan Fecan is the CEO of the CTV Network. Comedian Luba Goy is noted for her role on the *Royal Canadian Air Farce*. Ted Woloshyn is a well-known personality on Toronto radio and Victor Malarek is a CBC TV personality. Some Ukrainian Canadians have found success in the USA such as Hollywood film director Edward Dmytryk and Alex Trebek, the host of TV's *Jeopardy*.

Intellectualizing Transculturalism

Ukrainian Prime Minister Yevhen Marchuk, left, meets two third-wave immigrants, Wasyl Janischewsky, right, President, Ukrainian Canadian Research & Documentation Centre, Toronto, and, centre, Professor Wsevolod Isajiw, Professor, Sociology, University of Toronto. Professor Janischewsky, who became a Canadian citizen, 1957, has taught engineering at the University of Toronto since 1954. Professor Isajiw has been teaching at the University of Toronto as Professor of Sociology, since 1957. [Photo, courtesy Andrew Gregorovich]

Patron of Ukrainian Culture

Born in Verkhnie Syniovydne, Ukraine, Petro Jacyk immigrated to Canada, 1949, becoming one of Toronto's most successful builders and land developers over the next 50 years. A noted philanthropist who never forgot his roots, he was instrumental in the establishment of the Harvard Ukrainian Research Institute. At the University of Toronto, he financed the Jacyk Collection of Ukrainian Serials, the Central and Eastern European Research Centre, and the Endowment for Ukrainian periodicals. At the University of Alberta, 1989, the Jacyk Centre for Ukrainian Historical Research was created with a one million dollar donation. He has endowed the Jacyk Ukrainian Studies Program at Columbia University, 1994, and the Jacyk Lectureship in Ukrainian Studies at the University of London, 1991. In 1996, President Leonid Kuchma of Ukraine honoured Petro Jacyk with the Presidential Prize of Ukraine for his patronage of Ukrainian culture, education, and scholarship. [Photo, courtesy Andrew Gregorovich]

In sports Wayne Gretzky traces his roots through his grandparents to Pidhaitse in Ternopil Province of Ukraine. World champion skier Steve Podborski and world champion curler Ed Werenich won honour for Canada. Edmonton's Michael Slipchuk was Canadian Champion Figure Skater in 1992. Canadian swimming champion Joanne Malar won three gold medals and set a record at the 1999 Pan Am Games. The Hockey Hall of Fame includes such Ukrainian Canadian notables as goalie Terry Sawchuk, John Bower, Bill Mosienko (who in 21 seconds scored the fastest three goals in professional hockey history), and John Bucyk.

Academics include Dr. Joseph V. Charyk, born into an Alberta Ukrainian pioneer family, who became an eminent space scientist. President Kennedy appointed him head of the Communications Satellite Corporation (Comsat). Charyk placed the first satellites in space which provided TV around the world and allowed us to see the first step of a man on the moon in 1969.

Writers such as Janice Kulyk-Keefer and Myrna Kostash, dramatist George Ryga, and poets Andrew Suknaski and Peter Kuzyk, are well known in Canadian literature and have written about their Ukrainian heritage.

Artist William Kurelek left a rich legacy of paintings and prize-winning books about the Ukrainian Canadian prairie experience. The prominent Canadian sculptor Leo Mol has left his mark on Canada with statues of Queen Elizabeth in Winnipeg, Prime Minister Diefenbaker in Ottawa, and Taras Shevchenko in Washington, D.C.

Although Ukrainian Canadians are patriotic citizens of Canada they have maintained a strong interest in their roots and pride in their ancestral heritage. This is evident in the work of the Shevchenko Foundation in Winnipeg which is dedicated to supporting Ukrainian heritage in Canada. There are Ukrainian museums and libraries in Toronto, Winnipeg, Saskatoon, Edmonton, and elsewhere. The large and fascinating Ukrainian Cultural Heritage Village in Alberta captures the history of the Ukrainian Canadian pioneers.

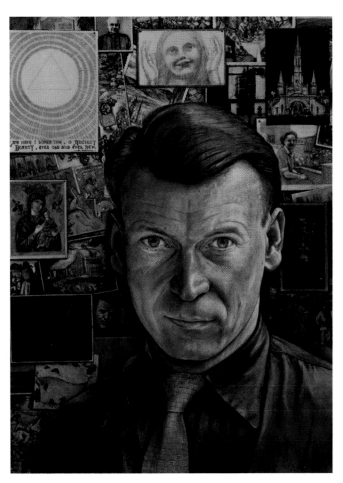

William Kurelek was the oldest of seven children born to a Ukrainian father who had immigrated to the prairie provinces from the village of Boriwtsi, Province of Bukovina, western Ukraine, 1924. Shortly after he arrived, he married a Canadian girl whose parents earlier had come to Canada from the same Ukrainian town. Born in a shack near Whitford, Alberta, 1927, William Kurelek not only experienced the hardships of growing up in a pioneering prairie settlement but the devastation of poverty brought on by the Great Depression of the 1930s. Wishing to be an artist, he studied art in Winnipeg, Toronto, and Mexico. By the 1960s, he was an established, well-known, and much respected artist living in Toronto. His earlier works, artistically narrative, depict sophisticated folkart scenes drawn from his prairie days and Ukrainian heritage. Because of his conversion to Roman Catholicism, his latter paintings enter a social-realism phase spotlighting mankind's original sin. This self-portrait of William Kurelek, completed a few years before his death, 1977, suggests characteristics of determination, concentration, and aggressive pensiveness, all of which are traits which have thrust him on the artistic stage as one of Canada's great triumphs in the world of canvas and brushstroke. [Photo, courtesy Jean Kurelek]

Ukrainian studies, including Ukrainian language, literature, and history have been offered at many Canadian universities since 1949. The Canadian Institute of Ukrainian Studies, at the University of Alberta since 1976, has provided a solid foundation for Ukrainian scholarship. Toronto's Infoukes (http://www.infoukes.com/) is the largest Ukrainian internet site in the world.

Many annual festivals, monuments, and historical plaques across Canada celebrate, mark, and preserve the history and heritage of Ukrainians in Canada. Canada's National Ukrainian Festival is held in Dauphin, Manitoba, every August. In 1961, a monument of Ukrainian poet, Taras Shevchenko, was unveiled by Prime Minister John Diefenbaker at the Manitoba Legislature. There is a monument of King Vladimir at the St. Vladimir Institute in Toronto. A large Ukrainian pioneer monument is on the grounds of the Alberta Legislature, and there is one at Hamilton City Hall. The largest Ukrainian monument is the giant Ukrainian Easter Egg (Pysanka) in Vegreville, Alberta, visited by Queen Elizabeth.

Ukrainian Canadians were the pioneers of the concept of multiculturalism which has been the official policy of the Canadian government since 1971. They have continued to preserve and develop their cultural identity in the Canadian mosaic. In the Greater Toronto alone, which has about 100,000 Ukrainian Canadians and is the most dynamic community in Canada, there exist some 150 organizations. Ukrainian Canadians are a very well organized community. ⬧

Andrew Gregorovich

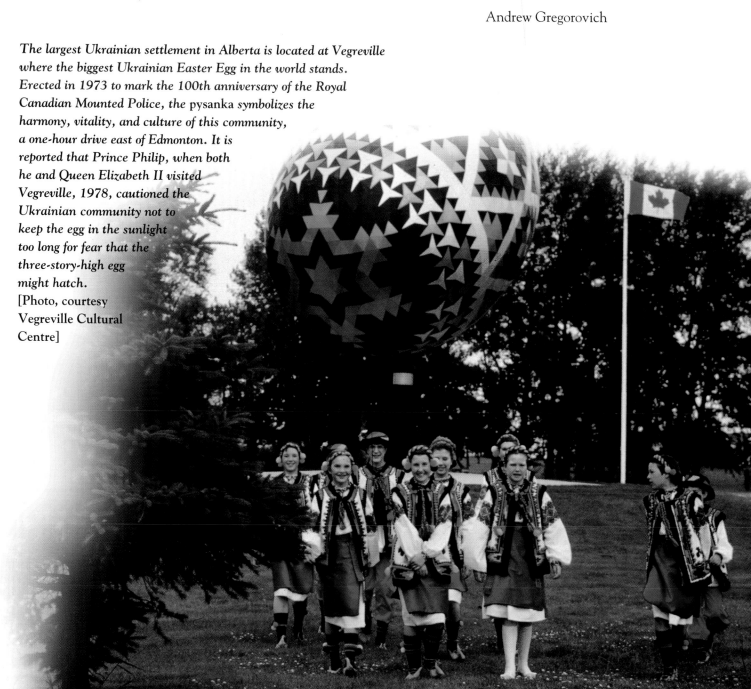

The largest Ukrainian settlement in Alberta is located at Vegreville where the biggest Ukrainian Easter Egg in the world stands. Erected in 1973 to mark the 100th anniversary of the Royal Canadian Mounted Police, the pysanka *symbolizes the harmony, vitality, and culture of this community, a one-hour drive east of Edmonton. It is reported that Prince Philip, when both he and Queen Elizabeth II visited Vegreville, 1978, cautioned the Ukrainian community not to keep the egg in the sunlight too long for fear that the three-story-high egg might hatch.*
[Photo, courtesy Vegreville Cultural Centre]

THE POPULATION of modern Canada includes immigrants with Indo-Portuguese history and culture. Goan settlement in Canada is relatively recent, the founding generation of Canadian pioneers coming in the 1960s from several parts of South Asia and East Africa.

All trace their origins to the small territory of Goa situated on the western Malabar coast of India, south of Bombay. Ruled by various Hindu dynasties and subsequently by the Muslim rulers of Mogul India, Goa was established as a Portuguese colony when it was seized by Alfonso de Albuquerque in 1510. Becoming an important commercial and trading hub between Europe and all other Portuguese colonies in Southeast Asia, Goa was returned to India in 1961. The demise of the Muslim ruling elite in the 1500s saw the local Hindu population convert to Roman Catholicism. Some four and a half centuries later, the colony became a separate Indian state with its own government in 1987.

Against this historical backdrop, Goan Christians, unlike their Hindu compatriots, began to seek opportunities for a better life in cities such as Bombay and Karachi during the mid- nineteenth century.

During the first ever International Goan Convention which took place over a two-week period in Toronto, 1988, a cultural extravaganza was staged at Roy Thomson Hall. This included traditional Portuguese dance ensembles as well as many modern colourful dance routines, as viewed below. [Photo, courtesy Albert J. Fernandes via the Multicultural History Society of Ontario]

from Goa

INDIA

GOA

As Christians proficient in English, which prevails in both the community at home and abroad, they were at ease with Western culture and armed with vocational training and clerical skills. Consequently, Goans were recruited by the British to work in the colonies of East Africa and a number of outports in the Persian Gulf. In the aftermath of Portugal's surrender of the colony, Canada, Australia, England, and the United States became targets of Goan migration.

The 1996 Canadian Census records the presence of 4,415 Goans in Canada (single and multiple responses); the sum total of individuals in Ontario is 3,565. However, it is estimated by community spokespersons that there are approximately 15,000 Goans in Ontario and approximately 5,000 in the rest of Canada.

Goans made a quantum leap into the professional world and the higher levels of commerce and industry. The Goan professional world includes lawyers, provincial court judges, senior corporate executives, educators, architects, physicians, and performing artists. Goans are also such semi-skilled workers as mechanics, machine-tool operators, and service industry employees.

Zulema de Souza, born in Goa, was the 14th and 17th and only female President of the Goan Overseas Association (G.O.A.) founded in Toronto, 1970. Ever since she immigrated to Canada, in 1971, she has energized the Goan community in her adopted country, organizing the first ever Goan International Convention, held in Toronto, 1988. This two-week Convention received international publicity and put Goans in Canada on top of the Goan world. Viewed here in the Office of Ontario Premier David Peterson, 1988, Zulema de Souza, viewed right of Mr. Peterson, centre, stands with a Delegation of Goan Canadians during the International Goan Convention of that year.
[Photo, courtesy Albert J. Fernandes via the Multicultural History Society of Ontario]

Canadian Gold Medalists in Scotland

Happy Goan members of the Canadian National Indoor Field Hockey Team celebrate winning the Indoor World Classic, Scotland, 1999, beating out Australia, Austria, Denmark, Scotland, South Africa, and the United States for the gold medal. In back row, left to right, stands Ken Pereira, whose Goan roots extend to Bombay, India, and who currently plays on Canada's National Team. Next to Ken is Scott Smith, not a Goan himself, but, as a member of Canada's National field Hockey Team, plays locally for the Toronto Goan Team. Holding the victory plaque is Louis Mendonca, Assistant Coach of Canada's National Field Hockey Team. His Goan roots are traced to Pakistan. Next to him is John de Souza, a Goan born in Uganda, and an ex-National Team player who is, today, President, Field Hockey Ontario. Far right, standing is Ed Fernandes, Vice President, Canada's National Team and, currently, captain, Goan Team of Toronto. Although Ed was born in Tanzania, his parents were born in Goa. Jeff Pacheco, bottom left, a player with Canada's National Junior Team, traces his Goan roots to Kenya. Bottom right is Wayne Fernandes, a member of Canada's National Field Hockey Team, whose Goan roots go back to Uganda, where his mother was born, and to Tanzania where his father, Ed, above, was born. [Photo, courtesy Ed Fernandes]

Contributing to the Cause of Multiculturalism

Dr. Colin Saldanha, of Goan descent, was born in Karachi, Pakistan, arriving in Canada, 1981, following completion of his medical degree, University of Karachi, 1979. Dr. Saldanha, today, practices Family and Occupational Medicine in Mississauga, Ontario. He also serves as a Corporate Physician to a number of business establishments and government agencies, including the RCMP, Transport Canada, Health Canada, and Immigration Canada. Involved extensively in community work, he participates in numerous forums on Race Relations and Equity, Policing and Social Justice Issues. A Past President, Peel Multicultural Council, Dr. Saldanha participated in the Spicer Commission on Canadian Unity. Appointed by Ontario's Solicitor General to Chair of the Peel Police Services Board, 1990, Dr. Saldanha later served as President of Canadian Association of Police Boards. Married with three children, Dr. Saldanha is a man with lots of service energy. He was awarded the Canada 125 Medal, 1992. In this view, Dr. Saldanha, with wife Sheila, receives a citation, 1991, for his "unselfish dedication and valued contribution to the cause of multiculturalism" from Ontario Premier Bob Rae on behalf of the Peel Multicultural Council. [Photo, courtesy Dr. Colin Saldanha]

Goan in Nova Scotia Meets Hockey Hall of Famer

Born to parents from Goa who had earlier immigrated to Uganda from Goa, Milu Fernandes was working for Coopers & Lybrand in Uganda at the time he and other Ugandan Asians fled Idi Amin's ethnic cleansing policies of 1972. Settling in Nova Scotia, Milu first worked for Bendix, then for Premdor, as comptroller, before this door manufacturing company merged with Sauder Industries. Now an administrator and manager of regional sales for Sauder, Milu is married to Plassey, a Ugandan-Goan herself. Their first wedding anniversary was celebrated in Amherst, Nova Scotia, where they have lived since 1972. Milu has served as an Amherst town councillor, serving as well as Deputy Mayor of this Nova Scotian community, the birthplace of Sir Charles Tupper, one of Canada's Fathers of Confederation. In this view, Milu chats with Darryl Sittler, Member, Hockey Hall of Fame, at an annual awards banquet in Amherst, 1988. [Photo, courtesy Milu Fernandes]

Canadians Celebrating their Goan Heritage

Since his parents were born in the Portuguese colony of Goa, John Nazareth is mindful that his roots, culturally, are Goan. Because the people of Goa are genetically Indian in origin, John recognizes that he is, in principle, Indian. Because he was Ugandan-born and lived in Uganda for the first 26 years of his life, there is no question in John's mind that he is also an African. Living in Canada since 1973, a Canadian citizen since 1981, the passport John carries assures the world at large that he is very much a Canadian. A graduate of Makerere University, Entebbe, Uganda, John Nazareth was one of thousands victimized by dictator Idi Amin's policy of expelling Asians from Uganda in the early 1970s. Taking up residence in Canada, 1974, John completed his M.Sc., University of Toronto, 1975, and earned his M.B.A., York University, 1985. John, his wife Cynthia, also a Goan from Uganda, and their two children live today in Mississauga. Currently working for Bombardier Aerospace as FRACAS Program Manager, John Nazareth has been a Reliability Engineer for the past 22 years. In this view, John, left, as President, Goan Overseas Association (Toronto), shares a G.O.A. Christmas Party with the then Secretary of State, the Honourable David Crombie, 1986. [Photo, courtesy John Nazareth]

Goan Doctor Honoured for Leadership in House-staff Education

Dr. Vincent Xavier DeSa's family roots are traced to the village of Moira, Goa, formerly a Portuguese colonial enclave located half way down the west coast of India. Born in Nairobi, Kenya, 1947, Dr. DeSa attended grade schools in Nairobi, received his medical education, University of East Africa, Uganda, and interned, Kenyatta National Hospital, Nairobi. Immigrating to Canada following Idi Amin's expulsion of Asians, 1972, Dr. DeSa and his family settled in Thunder Bay in northwestern Ontario, 1976, following post graduate training at both McMaster University, Hamilton, Ontario, and the Hospital for Sick Children, Toronto. Today, in addition to being the Medical Director, Perinatology, and the Chief of Paediatrics, Thunder Bay Regional Hospital, Dr. DeSa is also President, Medical Staff, St. Joseph's General Hospital, Thunder Bay, as well as Associate Professor, Department of Family Medicine, McMaster University. A keen volunteer in his Thunder Bay community, Dr. Vince DeSa is deeply committed to family medicine where, as a pediatrician, his interests focus on asthma, neonatal care, diabetes, and eating disorders. In this view, Dr. Vince DeSa, far right, is honoured with other of his colleagues practicing medicine in Ontario, by the Professional Association of Interns and Residents of Ontario (PAIRO) for his ongoing leadership in housestaff education. [Photo, courtesy Dr. Vince DeSa]

Goan Bringing Business Success to Brampton

Born to parents who had immigrated to Uganda from Goa, India, Eric De Souza, left, born 1936, became a civil servant in Uganda, first working for the Ministry of Education and then the Ministry of Finance as Head, Department of Tax and Industrial Promotion. Two of the five Tax Budgets he wrote there occurred when Idi Amin was in power. Fleeing Uganda, 1973, he first landed in the U.K., then Australia. Settling in Canada, 1976, Mr. De Souza was made President and CEO of Monarch Plastics Limited, the same year. Taking this Brampton, Ontario, business with 40 employees and sales of $1.5 million to a company in 1999 with some 250 employees, $40 million in sales and three plants – two in Canada and one in Kenosha, Wisconsin – Mr. De Souza's business acumen is much respected and appreciated as he accepts from two S.C. Johnson executives, Ed Furey, centre, and Ron Lenz, right, its fifth "Partners in Quality" Award, 1999. [Photo, courtesy Eric De Souza]

Fred D'Silva, left, was born in Karachi, Pakistan, to parents whose roots were Goan. Originally educated at missionary schools, Fred graduated in civil engineering, University of Karachi, 1955. Immigrating to Canada, 1958, to further studies in civil engineering, University of Toronto, Fred decided to remain in Canada upon completion of his studies and pursue his own career in construction even though the D'Silvas in Pakistan ran one of the largest construction and development companies in that country. After a short tenure with several construction companies, in 1967 Fred started, in partnership with Bramalea Development, a company called Bradsil, a name coined from the first three letters of Bramalea and the first four letters of D'Silva. Under the direction of Fred, Bradsil grew to be one of the largest general contractors in Canada, at one time employing over 500 people. Now retired and attending to other business interests, Fred, who is married to Melba, another Goan from Karachi, is pleased that his three children have launched their own independent businesses; Wendy, developing pre-school facilities and sons, Oscar and Darryl, in partnership, pursuing careers in construction. Most importantly, all three are keeping alive the D'Silva legacy of hard work, perseverance, and achievement. [Photo, courtesy Fred D'Silva]

Monsignor Peter Fernandes, right, was born in Goa, a small Portuguese colony on the west coast of India south of Bombay. He was ordained a priest, 1947, majoring in both Theology and Philosophy. After serving as a priest in Goa for 10 years, he moved, 1957, to Mozambique and for another 10-year period served as missionary in the former Portuguese colony. After a year's stay, Rome, Italy, where he studied Canonical Rights, Father Fernandes migrated to Canada, 1967, settling in Winnipeg where he founded the Portuguese Catholic Parish (Sacré Coeur) and then the Parish of the Immaculate Conception which holds, today, some 1,000 parishioners. For 14 years father Fernandes served as member, Canadian Immigration Board for Refugees. Appointed Monsignor by Bishop Adam Axner, 1993, Monsignor Fernandes, a Goan-Canadian, whose devotion to Winnipeg's Portuguese community inspired many thousands over a 30-year career in Canada, retired, 1997. [Photo, courtesy Paulo Jorge de Melo Pimental Cabral]

Established settlers and new immigrants created village associations through which senior Goans could reminisce and enjoy camaraderie and socialize with other Goans. They came together during the course of religious celebrations and feasts held in honour of the village unions' patron saints.

The community also sought to nurture ethnic persistence and encourage a Goan national identity by teaching its youth in Canada to speak Konkani, an Indo-Aryan language which became the official language of Goa in 1989. Today Konkani performances are enjoyed by Canada's senior Goans.

Founded in Toronto in 1970, the Goan Overseas Association (GOA) now stands at the head of the ethno-community's cultural and social life in the Greater Toronto Area. Each year, the Association organizes and orchestrates a full calendar of events including horseback riding, field hockey tournaments, track and field events, soccer matches, ballroom dances, symposia, and musical productions. Moreover, Goans in Montreal, Winnipeg, Calgary, and Vancouver can participate in the life of similar Goan organizations that together form a loose confederation.

Goans have found many opportunities to use their love of sports and field hockey expertise in service to their new homeland: they have represented Canada in many international matches. The sisters Michelle and Nicole Colaco played for Canada's Field Hockey Team at the 1994 World Cup.

Goans are noteworthy for their remarkably easy transition into mainstream Canadian society while retaining a deep affection for their Indo-Portuguese history and culture and their ties to the South Asian community at large. ☘

Elected a member of the Royal Canadian Academy of Arts, 1977, Ruth Tulviny, R.C.A., is an artist/painter/printmaker who was born in Estonia, came to Canada with her mother, Hilda Mikkelsaar, and worked as a domestic in order to attend the Ontario College of Art, where she won the Lt. Governor's Medal upon graduation in 1962. After completing other studies at l'Academie de la Grande Chaumière, Paris, and at the California College of Art, Oakland, Ruth embarked on a career of painting. Her solo exhibitions have travelled across Canada, U.S.A., France, England, Sweden, Estonia, and China. Ruth has also served as President, Ontario Society of Artists. Formerly a teacher of painting and printmaking, Ontario College of Art (1965-'73), Ruth received, in 1966, the National Academy of Design (U.S.A.) Award. In this view she is standing in front of "Butterfly of Davis #16," an acrylic painted in 1993 while she was artist in residence at the Neuroscience Centre, Davis Campus, University of California. [Photo, courtesy Ruth Tulviny]

from Estonia

ESTONIANS and their descendants in Canada hail from lands within the present-day independent republic of Estonia, which is located along the eastern coast of the Baltic Sea.

The first Estonians arrived at the end of the nineteenth century. Estonian fishermen established a small presence in Prince Rupert, British Columbia. Estonian farmers attracted by the promise of free land built homesteads in Alberta at Barons, Eckville, Foremost, Stettler, Walsh, and near Sylvan Lake. The interwar period saw Admiral John Pitka, a hero of the Estonian War of Independence, establish in 1924 a short-lived settlement near Fort St. Francis, British Columbia. Estonian immigration to Canada gained considerable momentum only after the Second World War. Large-scale immigration took place between 1948 and 1951: 11,370 Estonians arrived in this country. These postwar immigrants, many well educated, first had to complete a period of manual or other work in the rural and outlying regions before moving to the major city centres.

The Estonian ethnocultural group in Canada, according to the 1996 census statistics, consisted of 22,695 persons. By far the largest concentration of Estonian Canadians was in Ontario where 15,440 individuals resided. Smaller concentrations were found in British Columbia with 3,715 and Alberta with 1,735.

Many newcomer professionals were quickly able to resume their chosen careers. Estonian engineers, physicians, chemists, and professors, for example, helped to fill the void when many Canadian professionals left to pursue lucrative opportunities in the United States. Other Estonian Canadians, in turn, re-entered the professional ranks after upgrading their qualifications or after learning new skills or occupations. The continued growth of the Canadian economy during the 1950s, coupled with the creation of a supportive Estonian Credit Union, led to a growing Estonian presence in construction and manufacturing, most notably in plastics and textiles.

Born in Sweden shortly after his parents fled communist oppression, in 1944, in Estonia, Heino Lilles and his family immigrated to Canada when he was four years old, settling in Ontario where he graduated from Queen's University with a B.Sc. (1967) and M.Sc. (1971). Following completion of his Law Degree at Queen's, Heino attended University of London, England, obtaining his LL.M. before returning to Kingston, Ontario, becoming Associate Professor of Law, Queen's University, 1972-87. A specialist in Family and Children's Law, Heino Lilles was appointed a Territorial Judge of the Yukon in 1987. The Hon. Judge Heino Lilles is well known for involving the community in sentencing and for innovations in establishing aboriginal justice. Judge Lilles was a Visiting Scholar, University of New South Wales, Sydney, Australia, in 1994-95. This view depicts Judge Lilles swearing in Alice Frost from the Arctic community of Old Crow as a Senior Justice of the Peace. [Photo, courtesy the Hon. Judge Lilles]

Critically Acclaimed Artistic Director

A war baby born in Tallinn, Estonia, Urjo Kareda came to Canada from his native land via Sweden in 1949. Today, Artistic Director of Toronto's Tarragon Theatre, Urjo Kareda graduated from both the University of Toronto and King's College, Cambridge University, before becoming a well-known and much respected film and drama critic, university lecturer, and free-lance arts writer for such publications as the Globe and Mail, The New York Times, Maclean's Magazine, Saturday Night, among others. He has also success-fully co-directed several plays at the Stratford Festival, including Love's Labour Lost (1979) and The Seagulls (1980), in addition to being a successful CBC radio broadcaster. In 1995, Mr. Kareda was made a Member of the Order of Canada. [Photo, courtesy Tarragon Theatre]

Legendary Hydraulic Engineer

An international engineering legend, Hans Kivisild, P.Eng., Ph.D., was born in Tartu, Estonia, and grew up in the Estonian capital of Tallinn, fleeing his native land when it became reoccu-pied by the Red Army during World War II. With his wife, and upon completion of his education at the Royal University of Technology, Stockholm, he immigrated to Canada, 1950. In a short time he became known in Canada for his innovative engi-neering skills, designing the earthquake-proof George Massey Tunnel under the Fraser River in Vancouver. His engineering feats and impressive discoveries have been applied to a variety of projects, including the design of floating ice platforms for drilling oil in the Canadian Arctic, designing an arctic marine bulk cargo terminal on Hudson Strait and designing a year-round marine terminal on the St. Lawrence River. Overseas he has designed pillars to withstand ice flows for the Great Belt Link, a causeway connecting Copenhagen to the European mainland. Today, some 50 years after fleeing Estonia, his expertise as an hydraulics engineer is helping to turn the Estonian port of Paldiski into a year-round harbour for international tanker traffic. Dr. Kivisild, viewed here at Paldiski Harbour, 1997, is married to Livia Martna Kivisild, Ph.D., also born in Estonia. [Photo, courtesy Livia Kivisild]

6,500 Autopsies Later...

One of North America's most respected forensic pathologists, Dr. Hans Sepp, was born in Rakvere, Estonia. Before immigrating to Canada in the early 1950s, he attended medical schools in Tartu, his native land, and at the University of Hamburg, West Germany, before completing his medical examination at the University of Bonn, 1951. Dr. Sepp furthered his education at Toronto Western Hospital, the Banting Institute, Toronto General Hospital, the Hospital for Sick Children, among others, before he was certified as a Pathologist, 1957, by the Royal College of Physicians and Surgeons. A Professor at the Faculty of Medicine, University of Toronto, between 1958-1986, Dr. Sepp began his career as a forensic pathologist for the Ontario Solicitor General in 1964. It is estimated that Dr. Sepp, between 1964-1997, performed more than 6,500 autopsies, of which some 350 were homicide. One of his prized possessions is a diploma confirming that he is an Honorary Member of the Murder and Mayhem Society of North America. In this view, Dr. Sepp gives a guest lecture at his alma mater, University of Tartu in Estonia, 1988. [Photo, courtesy Dr. Hans Sepp]

Chess Player Becomes Oceanographer

Born in a fishing village on the shores of the Gulf of Finland, Helmuth Sandstrom fled Soviet occupation of Estonia, his native land, in 1944, resettling as a young lad with his family, first, in Finland, then Sweden, before migrating to Canada, as "swallows," landing at Halifax, Nova Scotia, 1950. As an undergraduate student in Physics at the University of Toronto, Helmuth became interested in glaciological studies which prompted him to join a scientific team venturing to Ellesmere Island in Canada's Arctic. Data collected there encouraged him to continue post graduate work at Scripps Institute of Oceanography at La Jolla, California. After gaining his Ph.D. there, he returned to Canada in 1966, taking a position as a research scientist at the Bedford Institute of Oceanography, Dartmouth, Nova Scotia. An internationally respected oceanographer, in this early view, Helmuth studies a chess board shortly after arriving at Pier 21, Halifax, 1950. [Photo, courtesy Helmuth Sandstrom]

Leading Folklore Scholar

The family of Martin Puhvel fled communism in their homeland, Estonia, in 1944, residing in Sweden for five years before migrating to Montreal, 1949. A Gold Medalist undergraduate at McGill University, Martin Puhvel completed his Ph.D. in English Literature at Harvard University, 1958. Before his 1996 retirement, Professor Puhvel had spent his entire teaching career at McGill, a span of nearly 40 years as one of the world's leading folklore scholars specializing in Old and Medieval English Literature. In this 1998 view, Professor Puhvel, left, receives his Emeritus Professorship certificate from Mr. Dick Pound, today, Chancellor of McGill University and, currently, Vice President of the International Olympic Committee. [Photo, courtesy Professor Martin Puhvel]

Toronto has become the centre of the Estonian ethnocommunity's organizational and institutional life. The postwar founders of both the Estonian Federation and the Estonian Central Council made that city the site of their national headquarters. The community has also created a large number of local clubs and specialized associations. The Estonian Boy Scout and Girl Guide movement; summer camps; and music, song, and folkdance ensembles have played an important role over the years in promoting heritage language retention and cultural identity. Tartu College in Toronto, a private and independent residence for students at the University of Toronto, quickly became a gathering place for Estonian-Canadian post secondary school students and academic organizations. Estonian sports enthusiasts and athletes soon appeared at many Canadian recreational centres and sports arenas; many became important at YMCAs and YWCAs as coaches and instructors, most especially of sports popular in Europe. Estonian-Canadian gymnasts played a pivotal role in making modern rhythmic gymnastics a nationally and internationally known sport. ⬇

Jakob Kembi, born in Parnu, Estonia, 1916, was forced to stop his education early and earn a living from the sea as a fisherman. He was very successful in his endeavours, but because Estonia was occupied and he was destined to be sent to Siberia, he voted with his feet and migrated to Sweden, where, once again, he became a successful fisherman. The waters around the east coast of Sweden were not safe for a recent émigré. He then took his family and moved to Canada in 1949. Fishing in Halifax was not productive so he took a train to Vancouver in 1951 to get in on the rich salmon harvest. Discovering that one had to be a Canadian citizen to obtain a fishing licence, to survive, he worked at Burrard Shipyards during the day and built toolboxes for Woodward Department Store at night. Eventually managing to obtain a piece of property on Vancouver's North Shore, Jakob built a house, sold it, then from the proceeds bought more property, built more houses, and became a home builder. These single family houses became multi-storied concrete apartments and then hotels. He built and now operates Days Hotel at Surrey Centre (formerly Surrey Inn) and, in 1999, at the age of 83, still goes to work every day and is actively involved in its management. In this view, Jakob Kembi supervises the building of one of his many concrete apartment buildings in the Greater Vancouver Area, circa 1965. [Photo, courtesy Alar Suurkask]

BULGARIANS have been arriving in Canada ever since the turn of the century. Most of the early newcomers were young men who had come, not as permanent immigrants, but as sojourners intending to return to their homeland. Overseas migration was a popular way for single and unaccompanied married men to make a living and fulfil their continuously rising expectations. The men had come to work – and work they did. As railroad navvies and road construction workers, they helped to create the infrastructure of Canada's ground transportation system. Working in mines, factories, paper and textile mills, they also helped to ensure the rapid development of Canada's industrial life and economy. This period of migration was interrupted by the Balkan Wars (1912-13) and the First World War. (Bulgaria supported the Central Power states of Austria, Germany, and Turkey.)

The interwar years (1918-1939) saw the attempt in Canada to establish communities. Having decided to settle in Canada, Bulgarian men dutifully made provision for brides, wives, and families to join them. Men who had been able to build up a stake often decided to go into business for themselves. The first entrepreneurial enterprises of the Bulgarians included restaurants, barber shops, shoe repair shops, tailoring and dressmaking establishments.

Kliment Dentchev, better known as "Klimbo" in the entertainment world, is a Bulgarian-born, Sofia-educated Canadian living in Montreal as an illustrator, story teller, actor, and multi-talented artist. Klimbo's Societé-Radio-Canada TV series between 1979-83 was sold worldwide to over 20 different countries and was the winner of over 10 international awards. Two of his best-known illustrated stories of this series are L'oeil Gauche du Roi *and* Le Lion et la Souris, *the latter winning the prestigious George Foster Peabody Award, ceremonies held in New York City, 1982, and administered by the University of Georgia School of Journalism and Mass Communication.* [Photo, courtesy Kliment Dentchev - Klimbo]

from **Bulgaria**

After the Second World War, Bulgarian immigration to Canada resumed on an even larger scale. The majority of the new immigrants, in addition to having the traditional economic motives, came as political refugees who wished to leave their homeland rather than live under the communist regime. The postwar economic boom attracted skilled workers, technicians, and professionals to Canada's rapidly growing metropolitan areas. And when democracy began to take hold of Eastern Europe in 1989, Canada once again became of primary interest to Bulgarian emigrants. Thousands began to arrive at airport points of entry at Gander, Newfoundland and Mirabel (Quebec), in the belief that several years of hard work could secure wealth and a comfortable life.

Today, according to the most recent government indices of population, there are at least 12,390 people of Bulgarian origin in Canada while sources in the ethnic group estimate over 30,000 members in Canada, arguing that the community has been imperfectly perceived in Canadian records. There are more people of Bulgarian origin in Ontario than in any other single province. Most live in Toronto and the industrial hinterland of southern and western Ontario. There are also several thousand Bulgarians in Quebec and in British Columbia, most notably in Montreal and Vancouver. Bulgarians can also lay claim to an historical presence in Canada's prairie provinces, early in the century, as a small but hearty group of Bulgarian farmers established homesteads in Manitoba, Saskatchewan, and Alberta.

Born in Sofia, Bulgaria, Daniel Damov was active in the Canadian insurance industry from 1951 until his retirement in 1994 as Chairman of the Board of both Zurich Indemnity and Zurich Life Insurance Company of Canada. A man of business prominence in the world of Canadian insurance, Mr. Damov, a graduate of the Faculty of Law, University of Paris, France, has served as Chairman of the Canadian Life and Health Insurance Association, Inc. and has served as director or member of many organizations including The Centre for Canadian-American Studies, University of Windsor; the Business Council on National Issues; Dean's Advisory Council, Faculty of Management, University of Toronto; Deans' Advisory Board, Insurance and Risk Management Programme, Faculty of Management, the University of Calgary; National Board, Arthritis Society; and the Sunnybrook Health Science Centre. Married and the father of two, Mr. Damov, today, is still active in Canada's business community as a director of four different insurance companies.

At the time of this 1983 photograph, Travelers Canada, of which Mr. Damov was President (1978-1988), and Wayne Gretzky had agreed to team up and assist Canadians to learn more about Travelers Canada umbrella of insurance protection. [Photo, courtesy Daniel Damov]

*Born during the first World War,
raised in various European countries, including Macedonia where
he was born, and Bulgaria
where he spent many of his
formative years, Kroum
Pindoff and Eva, his German-
born wife, both survivors of
the horrors of war, arrived in
Canada in 1955 as immi-
grants with one single purpose
in life: to make enough money
to aid innocent victims of war.
Forming a company called Pindoff
Record Sales in 1960, he began
selling records on consignment to
a variety of stores in Toronto.
By 1970, Eva became the
Founding President of Music*

*World, a company formed to market a variety of music products. Today Music World consists of 110 outlets Canada-
wide with over 1,000 employees. In the pink of life, these proud Canadians are capitalizing on the chance of a lifetime
to help the innocent victimized by the ravages of war. The couple, married 50 years in the year 2000, recently pledged
five million dollars to the Red Cross to help landmine victims become survivors. As philanthropists, both Kroum and
Eva paid to send more than 20,000 food parcels to senior citizens in Bulgaria following the implosion of the Soviet
Union in 1991. The Pindoffs recently built a home for 100 children in Orahavica, Gasinci, Croatia. They visit the
orphanage yearly and consider the children living there as part of their extended family. This recent view of the
Pindoffs reveals some of the ongoing Pindoff projects, including the development of homes for the aged in Bosnia.
[Photo, courtesy Eva and Kroum Pindoff]*

The Bulgarians are predominately Orthodox Christians, and their churches and parishes constitute major
centres of religious, social, cultural, and recreational activities. In 1910, Bulgarians joined hands with
Macedonians to found Sts. Cyril and Methody Church in Toronto's Cabbagetown neighbourhood. The first
priest of the church was the Archimandrite Theophilact, Demetrius Mallin, who had originally hailed from the
Bulgarian village of Vrachesh. Mallin resigned his position as parish priest in 1921 to pursue a long-standing
desire to perform medical missionary work in Toronto. After graduating from the University of Toronto's Faculty
of Medicine, Mallin emerged as a fine physician, a good man who had great compassion for the ill among the
working class of all nationalities. Other churches are located elsewhere in Toronto (St. George's and Holy
Trinity) and in Niagara Falls (St. Ivan Rilski). The churches offer a variety of services and activities including
Bulgarian heritage language classes for children, and social, athletic, and cultural clubs for teenagers and adults.
Folklore and dance groups attached to the churches also attract wide support from the ethnocommunity.

The Bulgarians, in spite of their comparatively small numbers, created a large number of associations and
clubs in this country. In 1921, Bulgarians partnered Macedonians in the United States and Canada in the
creation of the Macedonian Political (later Patriotic) Organization (MPO). In 1951, Bulgarians in Canada
established an important branch of the Bulgarian National Front. The BNF, founded in Munich, Germany, in
1947, promoted Bulgarian independence from Communist rule. The American-Bulgarian League for U.S.A. and

Widely Published Van Gogh Scholar

[Left] Born in Sofia, Bulgaria, Dr. Bogomila M. Welsh-Ovcharov is a full Professor at the University of Toronto, Mississauga Campus, where she teaches European and North American 19th and 20th Century Art History. She received her Ph.D. (cum laude) in 1976 at the University of Utrecht and today is recognized internationally as a much respected authority on Vincent Van Gogh. In this view, Professor Welsh-Ovcharov is seen with French Consul General Mr. Yves Doutrioux at a reception held in her honour when this widely published scholar was invested by the French Government in 1994 with the Order Chevalier dans l'Ordre Palmes Académique for her contribution to art history scholarship in French painting and, in particular, for her exhibition "Van Gogh à Paris" for the Musée d'Orsay in Paris. [Photo, courtesy Consulate General of the Republic of Bulgaria]

Community-spirited Businessman

[Right] Mr. Ignat Kaneff was born in the Region of Rousse in Bulgaria, and immigrated to Canada as a young man in 1951. When only 30 years old, he founded, in 1956, Kaneff Properties Limited, today a member of the Kaneff Group of Companies. Since 1967, Mr. Kaneff has been responsible for building over 3,500 family homes and over 8,000 hi-rise units, mainly in the City of Mississauga, but also in Oakville, Brampton, Toronto, and Barrie. A community-spirited businessman, Mr. Kaneff has received many honours. In 1992, he was named Mississauga's Citizen of the Year for his many years of voluntary service. In 1994, the University of Toronto awarded him an Honorary Degree of Doctor of Laws. In 1992, the Kaneff Centre for Management and Social Sciences was opened at the Erindale Campus, University of Toronto. A philanthropist since his arrival in Canada nearly 50 years ago, Mr. Kaneff has championed many causes including raising funds for hospitals in Canada. In his native land, Iggy's humanitarian aid is well-known as is his establishment of university scholarships. He is viewed here with his wife, Dimitrina Kostova, who is just as close to the various business enterprises of her husband as he is himself. [Photo, courtesy Dimitrina Kostova]

Born and educated in Zlatograd, Bulgaria, Dr. Konstantin Valtchev practiced as an obstetrician and gynecologist in Bulgaria, Ethiopia, and South Africa before immigrating to Canada, 1972. Today, Assistant Professor of Obstetrics and Gynecology, University of Toronto, Dr. Valtchev's private practice is affiliated with Toronto's Mount Sinai Hospital. A number of patents are registered in his name, including the Valtchev Uterine Mobilizer which is used worldwide in the fields of Gynecology and Endoscopy. This 1978 view portrays Dr. Valtchev, in Anaheim, California, as a newly elected Fellow of the American College of Obstetricians and Gynecologists. [Photo, courtesy Dr. Konstantin Valtchev]

Canada, founded in 1944 to lobby Allied governments in favour of Bulgaria at the end of World War II, had active chapters in Toronto and Montreal into the 1960s. The Bulgarian-Canadian Society, founded in Toronto in 1957, played a vital role in preserving group unity and ethno-cultural traditions. Its conferences, meetings, cultural festivities, parties, and picnics helped to build a newfound loyalty to Canada. In 1967, a "Bulgarian-Canadian Centennial Committee" was formed by community organizations across Canada to celebrate Canada's centenary. It published a com-memorative booklet, which won much praise for the way it expressed their attachment to Canada and their country of origin. In 1976, the community in Montreal founded the Association Socio-Culturelle Bulgare. In 1984, Bulgarians in Vancouver established the Bulgarian Home Society of British Columbia; in 1991 Bulgarian residents of Ottawa founded the Canadian-Bulgarian Society; and in 1992 the Canadian Bulgarian Association was created.

The contribution of Bulgarian Canadians to the business ranks of our country has been substantial. Among the leading members, past and present, of corporate Canada are Daniel Damov, Ignat Kaneff, Kamen Rustscheff, and Kroum Pindoff. Born in Sofia, Bulgaria, Daniel Damov, who studied law at the University of Paris, came to Canada in the early 1950s and became an insurance executive. Mr. Damov was President of Travelers Canada and Chairman of Zurich Canada before retiring and being elected to the U.S. Insurance Hall of Fame. Ignat Kaneff, a giant in the construction industry, has made a substantial impact on Mississauga, Ontario, by building thousands of homes and highrise units in Canada's sixth largest city. Other serious investments include retail commercial plazas, office administrative buildings, and golf courses including the internationally acclaimed Lionhead Golf & Country Club. A philanthropist, Kaneff endowed the University of Toronto in 1992 with a building on the University of Toronto, Mississauga Campus, at Erindale – the Kaneff Centre for Management and Social Sciences. The Ignat Kaneff Charitable Foundation, established in 1986, is today a key supporter of hospitals (Mississauga, Peel Memorial, and Oakville-Trafalgar hospitals), symphony orchestras, and community living centres of which Didi Kaneff is the President. As well, Kamen Rustscheff, now retired, was a general contractor in the Greater Toronto Area who was a top builder of schools, laboratories, and other institutional projects as required by all levels of government. Another influential Canadian of Bulgarian origin is Toronto music executive Kroum Pindoff, founder of Music World, a chain of 110 record store outlets that stretches across Canada. Typical of his imaginative philanthropy was his recent gift of $5 million to the Canadian Red Cross to aid victims of landmines.

A strong proponent for Canadian unity ever since he immigrated to Montreal, Quebec, in 1952, after studying law in Paris, Bulgarian-born Anton Tchipeff was elected Chairman of the Bulgarian National Committee created to coincide with Canada's centennial celebrations in 1967. From 1986-92, he was Assistant Deputy Minister for the Government of Quebec's Ministry of Immigration and Cultural Communications. In 1997, he received the award of the Agency of Bulgarians Abroad, in Sofia, and was decorated Knight of Madara, First Class, by the President of the Bulgarian Republic. This 1992 image of Anton Tchipeff, right, was taken in the Speaker's Office in Sofia, Bulgaria, with Stefan Savov, leader of the Democratic Party and Speaker of the Bulgarian Parliament, to the left. [Photo, courtesy Anton Tchipeff]

The contribution of Bulgarian Canadians to the social, cultural, and intellectual life of our country has been significant in every generation. Some, such as Torontonian Paul Christie, have served in elected political offices. Many have been active in the visual and performing arts. These include ethnomusicologist, Irene Markoff; sculptor, Maryon Kantaroff; a curator and art historian at the University of Toronto, Dr. Bogomila Welsh-Ovcharov; the fabulous Kotcheff brothers: television and film director, Ted Kotcheff, and his brother Tim, a television broadcast news executive. In addition, Bulgarian Canadians are also prominent in Canada's retail clothing (Golub Golubov is a premier producer of women's lingerie), while some are lawyers, medical doctors, and teachers at various levels in the academic community. In Montreal, Assen Nicolov Balikci was for many years professor of ethnology at the University of Montreal, famous for research work in Macedonia, Afghanistan, and Siberia (partly sponsored by the National Geographic Society), and in 1992 became Fellow of the Royal Society of Canada. Dr. Gloria Jeliu is Professor Emeritus of Pediatrics, Dr. Helen Gantchev a prominent child psychologist, and Dr. Jean Tchervenkov a leading researcher and specialist in organ transplants at McGill University. Yordan Nicolov established and still heads Cinelum, a leading Montreal studio for audio and video productions. Anton Tchipeff, along with a career in business management, is well known for his involvement in community organizations (e.g. president of the Montreal Citizenship Council), national unity causes, and with the Quebec Liberal Party. Between 1986 and 1992 he was Quebec Assistant Deputy Minister of Immigration and later member of the Immigration and Refugee Board of Canada. Bulgarian Canadians have contributed significantly to the growth and development of Canada and will continue to do so. ☙

Toronto's first International Caravan took place, 1969, the same year the Selyani Macedonian Folklore Group was founded. For the past 30 years, this well-known singing and dance group, in addition to performing at venues such as Toronto's Harbourfront, Mariposa Folk Festival, the Stratford Festival, the Ontario Science Centre, and the Royal Ontario Museum, has represented Canada on the world stage while participating at festivals in Wales, England, New York, Florida, and Macedonia. In this group view, the Selyani Macedonian Folklore Group is ready to perform at the Montreal Olympics, 1976. The backbone of the group is the husband and wife team of Jim and Dena Nicoloff whose ancestors immigrated to Canada from Macedonia in the early 20th century. In this view, Jim and Dena are seen with the Rt. Hon. Brian Mulroney when he, as Prime Minister of Canada, visited the Macedonian Home for Senior Citizens at Canadian Macedonian Place, Toronto, 1987. The Selyani Macedonian Folklore Group's aim has always been to preserve and share Macedonian folklore culture and to have an enjoyable time doing it. [Photo, courtesy Jim and Dena Nicoloff]

from **Macedonia**

ONE OF THE LARGEST GROUPS of non-British settlers to arrive in Canada at the turn of the century was comprised of villagers from the Balkan Mountains, then part of the Turkish Empire. These people and their descendants call themselves Macedonians, speak a Slavic language, and have their own churches, community organizations, and businesses – mainly in Metropolitan Toronto and the southern Ontario region.

The first Macedonians who came to Toronto were, in modern terms, "economic migrants for political reasons." The early ones, who hailed primarily from the provinces of Kostur (Castoria) and Lerin (Florina), once important *vilayets* of the Turkish Ottoman Empire but today portions of northern Greece, were driven by a search for a better quality political and socio-economic life and by the varying degrees of expulsion, or sense of expulsion, political and socio-economic.

They formed pockets of linguistic and cultural otherness in the city, living an almost completely isolated existence in a distinct set of neighbourhoods centred around their church, stores, and boardinghouses. They moved with little awareness of the city around them since the needs of their families in the old country and political events in the homeland were more important to them than developments in Toronto and Canada. A greater interest in Canada took root only after Macedonians began to think less like sojourners and more like settlers. This transition was often accompanied by a move from industrial labour to individual entrepreneurial activities.

Official statistics and population indices are not helpful in determining the size of the community in Canada because Macedonians fell under the general headings of the Ottoman Empire, Greece, Serbia (or Yugoslavia), and Bulgaria. Few Macedonians entered this country before the turn of the century. Sources from within the community tallied the presence of 1,090 Macedonians in Toronto by the year 1910. Thirty years later, readers of various Macedonian almanacs were informed that there were upwards of 1,200 families in the city. The mass departure of Macedonians from Aegean Macedonia continued in the aftermath of the Second World War and the Greek Civil War (1946-49). The 1950s witnessed the arrival of about 2,000 Macedonian refugee children to Canada. Significant exodus from Vardar Macedonia (now the Republic of Macedonia), or from towns and cities, began in the post-Depression years and gained momentum in the postwar period.

John Bitove Sr. was born in Toronto's east end, 1928, to parents Nicholas and Vana who had immigrated to Canada, 1919, from Gabresh, a village located in Aegean Macedonia. By 1949, young John had opened "The Java Shoppe," the first of many restaurants which he would operate over the next 34 years, including ownership of the Big Boy Family Restaurant chain as well as the first "true" Toronto nightclub with atmosphere called "The Gaslight Tavern," in Yorkville. By 1983, York County Foods was created to serve the Lester B. Pearson International Airport. Then, in 1986, John Bitove created CitiDome to serve the Toronto SkyDome. Both companies were amalgamated, 1987, and the name, Bitove Corporation, was created to handle all the operations of a very busy Canadian entrepreneur. Noted for his philanthropy, including his generous support of displaced persons from the Balkans and for giving to the Hurricane Relief Fund in the 1950s, John also assisted in the reorganization in Skopje, Macedonia, after the disastrous 1963 earthquake in his parent's homeland. He was the Founder and prominent Chairman of the Board, Canadian Macedonian Place, a senior citizen's complex in Toronto. In this view, John Bitove Sr. is presented with the Order of Canada by Governor General Jeanne Sauvé, 1989. [Photo, courtesy Vonna Bitove]

The most recent Canadian census (1996), which provides for self-declaration of ethnic origin, records 30,915 Macedonians in Canada, the sum total of individuals making single- or multiple-group responses; 24,340 of these people lived in the Toronto census metropolitan area.

Small clusters of Macedonians could also be found elsewhere in Ontario in Cambridge, Guelph, Hamilton, Kitchener-Waterloo, Markham, Mississauga, Newmarket, Niagara Falls, St. Catharines, Thornhill, Thorold, and Windsor. Community spokespersons believe there are actually 100,000-150,000 Macedonians in the Greater Toronto Area (GTA) and the outlying regions, creating the largest Macedonian settlement outside the Balkans.

At the turn of the century, Macedonians arriving in Toronto went to Cabbagetown in the city's east end because of the many industrial work opportunities to be found there. Settlements in West Toronto Junction and the area of Niagara and Wellington Streets were established later as the west end became the site of Toronto's meat-packing industry and new job opportunities opened up.

Initially, Macedonians lived in substandard roughcast or frame boardinghouses. Rooms in many of these dwellings were insufficiently lighted and badly ventilated. Overcrowding was also a problem. Four- and five-room houses were known to have accommodated as many as 20 residents at a time. And yet, a complex order emerged in most establishments with house rules and codes about residents' responsibilities. In many boarding-houses, tenants often cooked and did other household chores on a rotating basis.

By 1940, however, Macedonians had begun the trek away from the old neighbourhoods. Confidence, experience, and ambition put small entrepreneurs and restaurateurs in the forefront of movement from the original settle-ment areas. The growth and development of housing projects such as Regent Park, coupled with an explosion of commercial and industrial developments, also served to push out most of those who had remained in the area. The community's first and second generations in turn were being drawn by opportunity and acculturation to the suburbs and to neighbouring cities as much as they were leaving because of Toronto's industrial expansion and declining neighbourhoods.

With their skills, brawn, and biceps, the Macedonian immigrant work force would help to ensure the industrial takeoff of the city of Toronto. Macedonians, unlike Chinese, Italians, and Jews, were mainly factory hands and labourers in the city's abattoirs and meat-processing plants, sheet-metal industries, iron and steel foundries, and leather and fur-processing companies.

Casual work on the intercity and street railways opened up for them as well. Armed with pick and shovel, they could be found working on the various street-railway projects in the city. Railway work also drew Macedonians out into the Canadian bush to perform a variety of tasks. They laboured in such regions as Hearst and Copper Cliff in northern Ontario clearing tracts of land for the railway or for mine spurs.

Industrial employment opportunities in sugar-processing plants and knitting mills brought Macedonians into southern and western Ontario as well. Able-bodied men also performed dangerous and demanding work constructing a new Welland Canal.

Macedonians' ascent into the merchant class gained momentum after 1920. Many men soon realized that it would be not only more profitable to operate their own business than to toil as labourers but also physically safer. At first, the world of enterprise was the preserve of the community's steamship agents and bankers. Below the bankers were those who filled the community's entrepreneurial ranks: restaurateurs, shoeshine parlour operators, butchers, and grocers. From the humble diner to the elegant dining room, Macedonians would come to distin-guish themselves as restaurateurs and would dominate the trade in Toronto during the 1950s and 1960s.

Macedonian women were also ready to work when they came to Toronto. Many became boardinghouse keepers. Young brides cooked meals, washed clothes, scrubbed floors, and tended to a host of other family and tenant needs. By collecting board and rent money and minimizing household expenses, these women helped to build their family's income. Wives of storekeepers assisted their husbands at work. At first, Macedonian women found it difficult to deal with strangers or to assist in the business without fully comprehending the English language or business practice, but, over time, many seemed to take the place of their husbands as the chief proprietors of small businesses, freeing the men for other enterprises.

Macedonian entrepreneurs and their descendants eventually used their strength in the food service industry as a springboard into a variety of larger and more sophisticated ventures. In general, most Macedonians were content to expand and solidify their position within the middle class as accountants, contractors, computer consultants, florists, machine shop operators and industrial manufacturers, printers, importers, travel agents, and jewellers. The community remained under-represented in the professions until the third generation. Postwar immigrants from northern Greece and the Republic of Macedonia added to the group's professional ranks. Today, Macedonians also

Born in Drenoveni, Kosour, Macedonia, Phillip Meanchoff (1912-1993), right, immigrated on his own to Canada when only 16 years old. By 1930, he had opened his first restaurant in Toronto's east end. At the height of his career, he had five restaurants in partnership with a brother who followed him to Canada. As viewed, right, Waller's Snack Bar at Gerrard and Sackville Streets in east end Toronto made Phil Meanchoff's soda bar the top place to be for lunch in postwar Toronto. [Photo, courtesy Ron Meanchoff]

When the Bulgarian Holy Synod in Sofia sent Dr. Mallin to Toronto, 1910, to be the spiritual leader of the Macedonian community there, Toronto Macedonians, at that time, saw little difficulty in defining their religious life as Bulgarian and their culture and nationality as Macedonian. Born in Vrachesh, Bulgaria, 1882, and first priest of Sts. Cyril and Methody Macedono-Bulgarian Orthodox Church, Toronto, this important leader, left, of Toronto's Macedonian community during the first half of the 20th century, was elevated from Theophilact to Archimandrite, 1913. Anxious to keep Macedonian immigrants within the Macedonian cultural and religious sphere, the Archimandrite understood that New World demands would slowly but surely erode Old World ways. When the Archimandrite graduated in medicine from the University of Toronto, 1921, he reluctantly resigned his position as parish priest and spiritual leader. Dr. Mallin, nevertheless, continued his service to the expanding Macedonian community as "a medical missionary doctor" for the rest of his life. Throughout his long career, as both a religious leader and a practising doctor, Dr. Mallin, until he died in 1949, was devoted to Canada's Macedonian community. [Photo, courtesy Sts. Cyril and Methody Macedono-Bulgarian Orthodox Church]

Building Canada's First Lasers

Boris Peter Stoicheff was only five years old when his father, a Macedonian immigrant who had worked variously on the railways and in restaurants for five years in Canada, sent for his wife and two children to join him in Toronto, 1929. Soon there were six children for Peter and Vasilka Stoicheff to feed, clothe, and put through school. In the end, each of the six Stoicheff siblings graduated from the University of Toronto, with Boris obtaining his Ph.D. in Molecular Physics, 1950. Today, Boris Stoicheff, born in Bitola, Macedonia, 1924, is an Emeritus University Professor of Physics at the University of Toronto where he has taught since 1964. Before joining the faculty at the University of Toronto, Professor Stoicheff had been a Research Officer in the Physics Division of the National Research Council, Ottawa. While there, in late 1960, he built Canada's first lasers. His career research interests in light, the interaction of light and matter, spectroscopy, lasers and their application in science still continue in the world of physics where he is internationally respected and esteemed as a physicist. A Past President of the Optical Society of America (the first Canadian to be President of this international society), Professor Stoicheff, an Officer of the Order of Canada, has received many honours and awards including the William F. Meggers Award and the Frederic Ives Medal of the Optical Society of America, the Gold Medal for Achievement in Physics of the Canadian Association of Physicists, and the Henry Marshall Tory Medal of the Royal Society of Canada. In this view, Professor Arthur Schawlow of Stanford University, a 1983 Nobel Laureate who co-invented the Laser, 1959, visits his friend Boris Stoicheff, in shirt, at his laboratory, University of Toronto where Dr. Schawlow had earlier been a student. [Photo, courtesy Dr. Boris Stoicheff]

Nurturing Care for the Aged

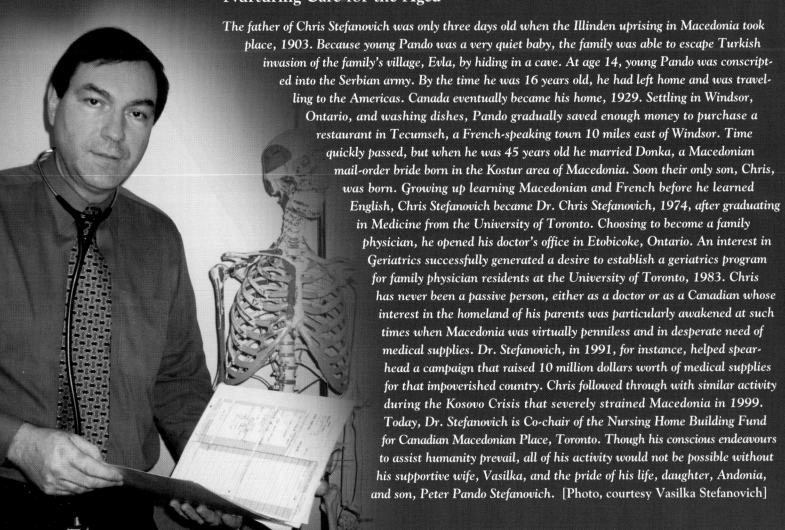

The father of Chris Stefanovich was only three days old when the Illinden uprising in Macedonia took place, 1903. Because young Pando was a very quiet baby, the family was able to escape Turkish invasion of the family's village, Evla, by hiding in a cave. At age 14, young Pando was conscript- ed into the Serbian army. By the time he was 16 years old, he had left home and was travel- ling to the Americas. Canada eventually became his home, 1929. Settling in Windsor, Ontario, and washing dishes, Pando gradually saved enough money to purchase a restaurant in Tecumseh, a French-speaking town 10 miles east of Windsor. Time quickly passed, but when he was 45 years old he married Donka, a Macedonian mail-order bride born in the Kostur area of Macedonia. Soon their only son, Chris, was born. Growing up learning Macedonian and French before he learned English, Chris Stefanovich became Dr. Chris Stefanovich, 1974, after graduating in Medicine from the University of Toronto. Choosing to become a family physician, he opened his doctor's office in Etobicoke, Ontario. An interest in Geriatrics successfully generated a desire to establish a geriatrics program for family physician residents at the University of Toronto, 1983. Chris has never been a passive person, either as a doctor or as a Canadian whose interest in the homeland of his parents was particularly awakened at such times when Macedonia was virtually penniless and in desperate need of medical supplies. Dr. Stefanovich, in 1991, for instance, helped spear- head a campaign that raised 10 million dollars worth of medical supplies for that impoverished country. Chris followed through with similar activity during the Kosovo Crisis that severely strained Macedonia in 1999. Today, Dr. Stefanovich is Co-chair of the Nursing Home Building Fund for Canadian Macedonian Place, Toronto. Though his conscious endeavours to assist humanity prevail, all of his activity would not be possible without his supportive wife, Vasilka, and the pride of his life, daughter, Andonia, and son, Peter Pando Stefanovich. [Photo, courtesy Vasilka Stefanovich]

Shopping for Home Runs

Stan Thomas traces his roots to that part of Macedonia which had been annexed by Greece at the end of the First Balkan War, 1912-13. His father's Macedonian surname, Bozinov, was hellenized to Bozinis and when he immigrated to Canada, 1930, settling in Windsor, Ontario, his name was anglicized to Thomas. It was 17 years before Boris (Stan's father) was able to send for his wife and family to join him because of the intervening Depression and World War II, but once the war was over, his wife and two children joined him in Windsor. The very next year, Boris and Dana Thomas became the proud parents of Stan, today, Senior Executive Vice President, Marketing, Shoppers Drug Mart. A graduate MBA, York University, Stan is an individual who has not neglected his Macedonian roots. When the Kosovo crisis erupted, 1999, Stan Thomas spearheaded a drive to send four million dollars worth of pharmaceutical supplies to Macedonia which had been flooded by thousands of Kosovo refugees. Director, Canadian Macedonian Senior Citizen's Centre, Toronto, since 1979, and President, 1990-93, Stan Thomas assists in guiding many of the charitable activities of Shoppers Drug Mart which, in consort with the Blue Jays Charitable Foundation, has teamed up to help kids in distress across Canada. Thanks to this partnership, Kids Help Phone received $500 from Shoppers Drug Mart and the Blue Jays Charitable Foundation for every Blue Jay homerun hit out of the park, 1999. In this view, Stan, left, shares a moment with Toronto Blue Jay All-Star, Shawn Green, unveiling Shoppers Drug Mart/Toronto Blue Jays 1999 calendar. [Photo, courtesy Shoppers Drug Mart]

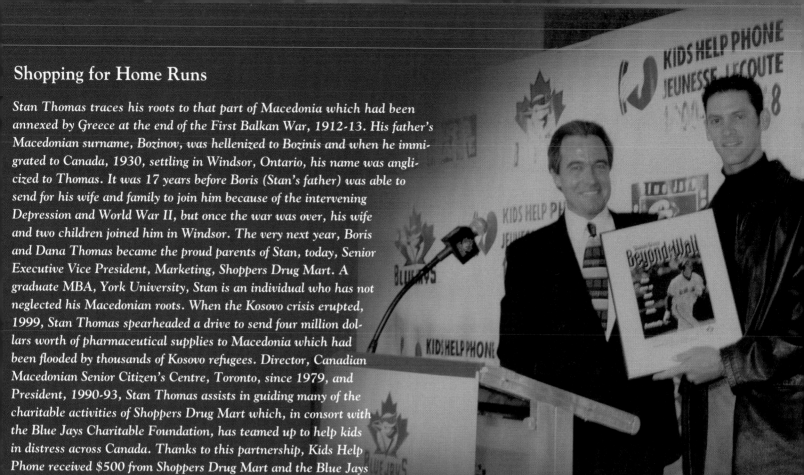

Fighting for Human Rights Worldwide

A senior partner in the Toronto office of the international law firm of Gowling, Strathy & Henderson, Toronto, Chris Paliare received his LL.B., Osgoode Hall, 1970, his LL.M., University of Texas, 1971, and was called to the Ontario Bar, 1973. He was articled to and then a partner of Ian G. Scott, Q.C., one of Canada's finest advocates, who went on to become Ontario's Attorney General. Chris specializes in commercial litigation, Constitutional and Charter Rights litigation, public law, and employment law, at all levels of Court, including the Supreme Court of Canada. Committed to Macedonian issues in Canada and abroad, Chris has been on the Board of Directors of Canadian Macedonian Place, a senior citizen's residence for Macedonian Canadians since its creation, 1979, and has served as its president for five years. On the international stage, he has fought for human rights conferences in Moscow, Helsinki, and Warsaw. He was also active in assisting the Republic of Macedonia achieve international recognition as a sovereign state following the break-up of Yugoslavia in 1991. This 1979 view of Chris and his wife, Eva Marszewski, also a lawyer, illustrates Tsena Paliare (Balkou), the paternal grandmother of Chris who was born, 1889, in Tyrsca, a village in the portion of Macedonia now part of Greece. She immigrated to Canada, 1935, to join her husband, George, and Chris' father, Norman, who earlier had immigrated to Toronto, 1927. She passed away in 1994 at age 95. Chris' commitment to Macedonian issues stems from the close relationship he had with his grandparents. [Photo, courtesy Chris Paliare]

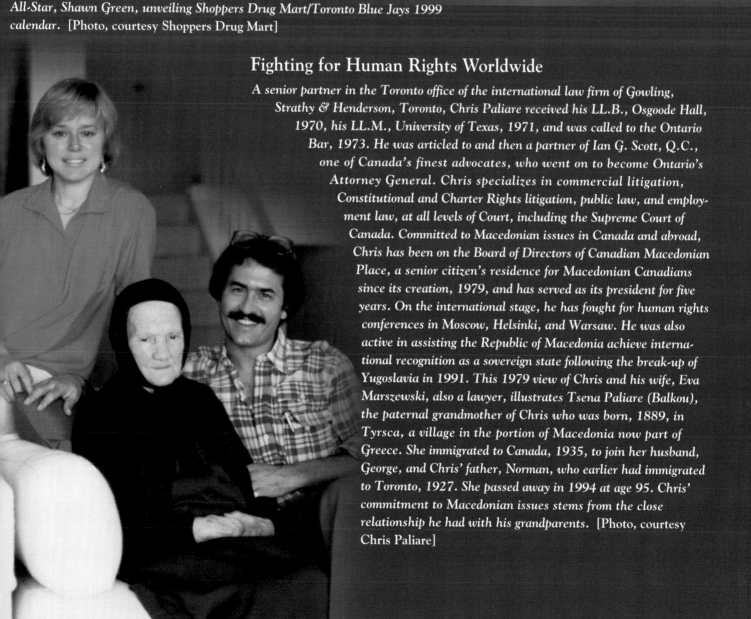

Macedonian Boarding House

Typical Macedonian boarding-house, Toronto, 1917. The planting of seeds in a new land often meant sharing accommodations, living in stark conditions, and dreaming of a secure future. This painting by S. Tomev is part of the permanent collection of the Multicultural History Society of Ontario.
[Photo, courtesy MHSO]

Recognized Internationally as Eastern European Scholar

Historian Andrew Rossos was born, 1941, in the Aegean or the Greek part of Macedonia. At the age of seven, during the Civil War in Greece (1947-1949), he and his two older brothers and sister were among the many Greek and Macedonian children who were evacuated for their safety (kidnapped, as the Greek government said at the time) to the Communist countries of Eastern Europe. He and his siblings were taken to Czechoslovakia. A year later, their mother ended up in Poland. Their father, who immigrated to Canada at the end of the Civil War in Greece, did not succeed in reuniting the family again until the very late 1950s in Toronto. With the aid of graduate fellowships, Andrew completed his education at Stanford University, California, where he obtained his Ph.D. in Russian and East European history, 1970. Today, Andrew Rossos, born in Vambel (Maskohori in Greek) a small, picturesque, but no longer existing Macedonian village, is a Professor of History, University of Toronto, where he has taught since 1967. Over the years Professor Rossos has been the recipient of research grants and fellowships from the American Council of Learned Societies/the Social Science Research Council, the Canada Council, and the Social Sciences and Humanities Research Council of Canada. His research interests have ranged from Russian-Balkan relations to Czech historiography, Balkan nationalism, and the history of Macedonia and the Macedonians. His scholarly work has been published by well-known academic publishers and in leading scholarly journals. Professor Rossos is recognized internationally as an authority on Eastern Europe and as a leading specialist on Macedonia and the Macedonians. [Photo, courtesy Dr. Andrew Rossos]

figure prominently in the professional fields of law, medicine, science and technology, education, sports and recreation, and the arts and entertainment industry.

Participation in Toronto's civic life and the Canadian community at large failed to interest the group at first. Macedonians were content to remain on the periphery of the Canadian way of life. They created such flexible institutions as boardinghouses, coffeehouses, and mutual benefit and burial societies to tend to their needs. The boardinghouse and the coffeehouse quickly emerged as informal centres of community life. They became all-important repositories of job information and workplace strategies.

As Christians and adherents of the Eastern Orthodox faith, Macedonians also founded a number of churches – often divided along Bulgarian and Macedonian Orthodox spiritual jurisdictions – in Toronto and neighbouring cities. They looked to the church to tend to their spiritual needs and recreated its traditional role as a bulwark of national identity serving to focus their political and communal actions and their loyalties.

Administered by elected executive committees, all churches organized or supported – as they still do today – various educational, athletic, and cultural programs. They became centres of heritage language instruction. They hosted teas, dances, and entertainment evenings and mounted elaborate celebrations of the major religious holidays, including Easter and those held in honour of patron saints.

The need for newcomers to provide for themselves what we would now call social insurance and worker compensation was met by establishing mutual aid and benevolent societies on the basis of village or place of origin. Such organizations operating in Toronto obliged their working members to assist needy comrades in finding a job. In times of illness, the societies encouraged members to seek professional medical help and to submit to hospital care if necessary. The societies themselves were prepared to assume the cost of transporting a sick member back to the homeland if that was his wish. The member was obliged, once he was sufficiently recovered and suitably employed, to reimburse his particular benevolent organization fully for the expenses incurred on his behalf.

When members' working conditions and incomes became the responsibility of the government, insurance companies and labour unions, mutual benefit societies and brotherhoods evolved into social clubs, playing a role as centres of immigrant culture. The increased emphasis on encouraging "Macedonian-ness" in the Balkans and in North America formed part of the tactic of organizational survival. Updating the purposes of societies and extending membership to women also helped the ethnocommunity stay together.

A number of business and professional organizations, student and youth groups have been established. The community has also created and continues to support a number of newspapers, radio and television programs, folkdance groups, sporting organizations, and historical and literary societies.

Leadership in these and other Macedonian institutions comes from among entrepreneurs, the working class, youth, and women. The community continues to respond as individuals, as families, or collectively to the opportunities and challenges that shape group life in Canada. ⌖

Both sets of Lillian Petroff's grandparents were born in Macedonia before they immigrated to Canada, the males immigrating prior to the outbreak of World War I and the females arriving shortly after Armistice in a state of combined fear and happiness as hand-picked brides. Graduating from the University of Toronto with a Ph.D. in History, Lillian works today as Co-ordinator of Educational Programs for the Multicultural History Society of Ontario, a non-profit organization located on the campus of St. Michael's College, University of Toronto. In this view, Lillian is seen with Robert Fulford, well-known Canadian journalist and columnist, after winning an Award of Merit, 1996, for her publication: Sojourners and Settlers: the Macedonian Community in Toronto to 1940. *[Photo, courtesy Lillian Petroff]*

Mike Wiegele, inset, born in Feistritz, Austria, 1938, grew up in Lading Kärnten, Austria. Today he is considered the godfather of the helicopter ski industry in British Columbia. Since his immigration to Canada, 1959, Mike has become the dynamic leader of Mike Wiegele Helicopter Skiing. His warmth, kindness, and generosity extend far beyond his love for the mountains, to include the care and protection of his family, the community, and the many employees who work for him. Much of Mike's dream to give others the chance to experience the majestic mountains of British Columbia was formalized when, as a young man, he became Director of Lake Louise Ski School, 1965. In 1970, Mike scheduled the first helicopter skiing trip to the Cariboo mountains. Mike's helicopter service now lifts skiers to slopes in the heart of the Cariboos and Monashees. Glistening with fresh, deep powder snow, these conditions host skiers who seek the ideal. Today, Mike's ski village at Blue River, British Columbia, is known the world over as home to the best powder skiing. That people of fame and prominence travel halfway around the world to experience a heli-lift to a mountain top of pristine snow is testimony to Mike Wiegele's ability to predict that powder snow is a desirable marketing commodity. However, Mike's dream was not yet complete. In 1992, Mike decided to start summer operations at the Resort. Guests now come to Blue River during the summer to be whisked off to remote lakes and beautiful mountain vistas for heli-hiking, fishing, and summer skiing. In 1993, "The Grizzly Hut" was built. The Grizzly Hut is enjoyed by hikers in the summer and is used as an education centre for research and a safety post for guides and visitors in the winter. In this view, skiers, after having been helicoptered to the top of the mountain in the background, are caught in a moment of euphoria as they ski down the majestic slope covered by virgin powder snow. [Photo, courtesy Mike Wiegele Helicopter Skiing]

from Austria

He came to Canada, age 22, from the town of Weiz in the foothills of the Austrian Alps. He had grown up in a working-class neighbourhood ravaged by war and depression, leaving school at 14 years to apprentice as a tool and die maker. Driven by a desire to travel the world, he arrived in Montreal, 1954, travelled by bus to Kitchener, Ontario, where he landed a job as a dishwasher in a local hospital. After saving enough money, he moved to Toronto, 1957, purchased some second-hand lathes and milling machines and set up shop. Within one year, he had ten employees. Several decades later, Frank Stronach, the young man who immigrated to Canada, had parlayed his business into Magna International Inc., the world's most diversified automobile parts supplier with some 54,000 employees and annual sales over 14 billion dollars. Creating a revolutionary new economic culture known as Fair Enterprise, the cornerstone of which is a Corporate Constitution guaranteeing the rights of employees, management, and investors to share in profits, Frank Stronach is more than a household name in Canada. A distinguished Canadian who has helped bring to Canada international recognition with his racing stables, Frank Stronach, Member, Order of Canada, is very much a visionary world figure charting Magna's growth as a prominent global leader in the automotive industry. [Photo, courtesy Magna International]

AUSTRIA'S association with Canada is a long-standing one: it dates as far back as the seventeenth century. The first Austrians linked with Canada were the soldiers who participated in the defence of New France. The mass emigration from the Austro-Hungarian Empire to Canada began at the end of the nineteenth century. No single explanation can account for the rapid demographic change, the over-division of arable land, a dearth of industry, military conscription, growing ethnolinguistic persecution, and political instability were all factors motivating the peasants from the eastern provinces to come to Canada. During this first wave from 1880 to 1914, German-speaking people from the regions of Galicia, Bukovina, and the Banat made their way to the Canadian West. They were lured by the Dominion government's promise of free land, by steamship companies, and by the various agents involved in the emigration process. Some prairie settlers did not come directly from the homeland but, instead, immigrated from the United States where they had originally settled. With land restrictions in the American West and few new opportunities for expansion, the Canadian prairies offered new opportunities for making a living. Settling near Langenburg, Meberg, Qu'Appelle, and Kendal in Saskatchewan, and near Edmonton, Josephsburg, Spruce Grove, Golden Spike, and Stony Plain in Alberta, these people welcomed the collapse of an oppressive eastern empire and began to assert their cultural identities as, for example, Czechs, Serbs, Croatians, Ukrainians, Hungarians, Jews, and Romanians.

Living conditions became particularly challenging in Austria after the First World War when the country was reduced to a portion of its former size. As a result, the flow of immigrants to Canada from three states of the Federal Republic of Austria – Carinthia, Styria, and Burgenland – was relatively large between 1926 and 1938. With Germany's occupation of Austria in 1938, thousands of political refugees, mainly from the educated,

Born, Vienna, 1924, Eli Kassner, in his early years as a teenager, sang in a synagogue choir and received a Jewish education from his father before he escaped persecution of Jews in Austria, 1939, by joining a Jewish women's organization, Hadassah, as part of a group of 60 youths who had been given permission to emigrate to Israel. In the process, Eli left behind his mother, father, and sister, all of whom would later perish in a Nazi concentration camp. Between 1939-1951, while living in various kibbutzes, Eli's interest in guitar music escalated. By 1951, he made a decision to join his brother, who had also survived Nazi persecution, and found passage to Canada. Soon Eli was teaching guitar lessons in Toronto. In 1958, Andrés Segovia, the famous classical guitarist, invited Eli to Spain to study with him. The next year, 1959, Eli returned to Canada and joined the Royal Conservatory of Music, Toronto, and began teaching at the University of Toronto, Faculty of Music. He also opened his own guitar academy, teaching such students as Norbert Kraft and Liona Boyd. Today, Eli Kassner is renowned throughout the guitar world, not only as a musician and teacher but as the person who organized the Guitar Society of Toronto and who formed the University of Toronto Guitar Ensemble. An international juror and lecturer, Eli Kassner has been the catalyst behind the classical guitar renaissance that has taken place around the world. [Photo, courtesy Eli Kassner]

Immunologist Passionate about First Nations Peoples' Art and Culture

Dr. Berhard Cinader was born in Vienna, Austria, 1919. An internationally respected immunologist with two doctorates, Dr. Cinader immigrated to Canada, 1959, after completing his formal education, at University of London's Lister Institute of Preventative Medicine. From 1958-69, Dr. Cinader was Head, Subdivision of Immunochemistry, Ontario Cancer Institute, Toronto. While President, International Union of Immunological Societies, 1969-74, Dr. Cinader was also full Professor, University of Toronto, Medical Cell Biology, Medical Genetics, and Clinical Biochemistry between 1969-71. An Advisory Panel Member on Immunology for the World Health Organization since 1965, Dr. Cinader, President, 6th International Congress of Immunology, 1986, has received, over many years of intense research, numerous awards and medals for his scientific medical research and important discoveries and findings. These include the prestigious Pasteur Medal, 1960; Ignac Semmelweis Medal, Budapest, 1978; Thomas W. Eddie Medal (Royal Society of Canada), 1982; Officer, Order of Canada, 1985; and Landsteiner Medal, Sixth International Congress of Immunology, 1986. Author of over 300 scientific articles on immunology, oncology, and gerontology, over a 55-year professional career, Dr. Cinader also served as President, Royal Canadian Institute, 1989-90, and has given distinguished lectures in such places as Bombay, India; Beijing, China; Bankok, Thailand; Zagreb, Yugoslavia; Tashkent, U.S.S.R.; and Prague, Czechoslovakia. Retired as Professor Emeritus, University of Toronto, 1992, Dr. Cinader's keen interest in Canada's first nation peoples has led him to investigate, with passion, native art and culture, making his new-found discoveries a second career. In this mid-1980s view, Dr. Cinader addresses an Ontario conference celebrating and honouring native culture. [Photo, courtesy, Dr. Berhard Cinader]

International Guest Conductor

She started her professional musical career as a concert pianist touring for five years the U.S., Canada, Europe, the Middle East, and Japan, until an injury to her right hand, 1973, forced her to retire as a solo pianist. Born, Vienna, Austria, Agnes Grossmann first studied piano with internationally renowned Choral Conductor, Ferdinand Grossmann, her father. Graduating, Hochschule für Musik, Vienna, Ms. Grossmann, after her accident, studied orchestral and choral conducting in Vienna, 1974-78, before becoming Assistant Conductor, Vienna Jeunesses Choir. Ms. Grossmann's first tenure in Canada came, 1981, when she was Visiting Professor, Choral and Orchestral Activities, Ottawa University. Returning briefly to Austria, 1983, she was made Artistic Director, Vienna Singakademie, 1983, before being appointed Artistic Director, Chamber Players of Toronto, 1984-90, and simultaneously, Artistic Director and Conductor, Orchestre Metropolitain de Montréal, 1985-1995. A conductor with great energy, Agnes Grossmann was chosen "Woman of the Year" in the Arts in Montreal, 1987, the same year she made her debut with both Ottawa's National Arts Centre Orchestra and Salzburg's Mozarteum Orchester, 1988. Appointed Artistic Director, Vienna Boys' Choir, 1996-98, she guided the very successful 500th Anniversary Tour of this internationally famous vocal group throughout the great music halls of North America. Recipient, Honorary Doctor of Laws Degree, Mount St. Vincent University, Halifax, 1991, Conductor Grossmann received, 1992, the Silver Honorary Cross for Outstanding Artistic Achievement from the Austrian Government, 1992, as well as the Golden Honorary Cross of the City of Vienna, 1995. Resuming, 1999, her international guest-conducting career, Dr. Grossmann made her debut with the Montreal Symphony Orchestra, 1999, and was reappointed Artistic Director of the Orford Arts Centre, Montreal, the same year. [Photo, courtesy Agnes Grossmann]

"The Best Pianist Currently Playing" in Canada

Although he was born in Vienna, Austria, and although his formative years were spent in the United States, 62-year-old Anton Kuerti has lived half his life in Canada and now calls Canada home. At age 11, he performed the Grieg Concerto with Boston's famous conductor, Arthur Fiedler. He was still a student when he won the famous Leventritt Award, the prestigious Philadelphia Orchestra Youth Prize, 1957, the same year he debuted with the New York Philharmonic Orchestra, Carnegie Hall. Anton Kuerti has toured 31 countries, including Japan, USSR, and most European countries. In Canada, Kuerti, "the best pianist currently playing," according to Fanfare Magazine, has appeared in 115 communities and has played with every professional Canadian orchestra including 35 concerts with the Toronto Symphony. He has won many prizes and honorary doctorates, and is an Officer of the Order of Canada (1998). Founder, Festival of Sound, Parry Sound, Ontario, Anton Kuerti's vast repertoire includes some 50 concertos, including all the Beethoven Concertos and Sonatas and a six-CD set of the Schubert Sonatas. [Photos, courtesy Anton Kuerti via Paul J. Hoeffler]

Holocaust Survivor Finds Career in Emergency Services

Immigrating to Canada as a 14-year-old holocaust survivor, Paul Tuz, born, Vienna, Austria, 1929, was taken under the wing of Captain F.W. Beattie and his wife, both ardent members of St. John Ambulance, Toronto Branch. This association, for Paul, was a timely open window for him to assimilate into Canadian society, affording Paul an opportunity to serve St. John Ambulance, an association which has lasted in excess of 55 years. He helped establish the first postwar First Aid tent at the Canadian National Exhibition. He also organized first aid posts along the Humber River during Hurricane Hazel, 1954. At the height of the "Cold War," in the late 1950s and early '60s, Paul was appointed North Zone Controller of Metro Toronto's Emergency Measures Organization (E.M.O.) to prepare and coordinate all emergency services in North York, Leaside, Weston, and Etobicoke in the event of a foreign nuclear or missile attack. During this time, Paul trained over 5,000 people in Emergency First Aid. A major result of Paul Tuz's service was the systematic creation of an efficient ambulance service located strategically in various communities throughout Metro Toronto to serve an evergrowing population in need of efficient emergency service. For his farsightedness in creating a community ambulance system, now a national concept followed by every government in Canada, Paul was made a Member of the Order of Canada, 1979. After serving Chrysler Canada for 10 years and making his mark in industrial accident prevention, Paul assumed the presidency of the Better Business Bureau which during his 20-year tenure became North America's largest BBB. Living in semi-retirement, Paul Tuz is now Honorary Consul General of Mali and still serves on the Advisory Committee of the St. John Ambulance. In this view, as President of the Better Business Bureau, Paul Tuz, right, interviews the Rt. Hon. J.G. Diefenbaker, circa 1975, former Prime Minister of Canada (1957-1963). [Photo, courtesy Paul Tuz]

business, and professional classes, arrived in Canada. A much larger flow of immigrants began after the Second World War when Austria again went through challenging times with her economy at a low ebb and the occupation troops of Britain, France, the United States, and the Soviet Union on her soil.

Data on ethnic origin from Canada's 1996 census indicate that 140,520 people were wholly (28,085) or partially (112,435) of Austrian origin. Austrian Canadians settled principally in Ontario (48,710), British Columbia (33,980), and Alberta (24,925). Smaller concentrations were also found in Saskatchewan (13,700), Manitoba (9,155), and Quebec (7,230). Austrians became urban dwellers during the postwar period. Toronto accounts for 10,510; Vancouver, for 8,800; Montreal, 5,695 (virtually the entire sum of Austrians in the province of Quebec). Also, in 1996 Canadians having at least some Austrian ancestry still resided on the prairies, albeit no longer living on farms in the old settlement blocs. Edmonton has an Austrian community of 4,875. Although not so large as Edmonton's settlement, Calgary also has a group settlement of 4,305. The same census reported 1,470 people of Austrian background in Victoria and 1,410 in Saskatoon.

Most of the early immigrants from Austria were farmers and artisans who played an active role in the early development of Canada, particularly in the opening of some of the most arid and isolated parts of the West. Members of the interwar and postwar periods arrived with a variety of skills and professional training. Among

Born, 1941, outside Vienna in Lower Austria, Karl J. Kaiser spent his youth in the shadow of Stalin's Russia, thanks in large part to the carving up of Austria by the Allies following World War II. Still being in public school, Karl enrolled in a private school run by Cistercian monks. Intending to become a monk, Karl, however, thrived in chemistry, even finding himself helping his teachers in the preparation of laboratory work. After graduation from high school, he worked for several years for the government. Soon he became a teacher in a vocational trade school in one of Austria's wine regions. Becoming more and more interested in the winemaking process, especially after befriending a local gentleman vintner, then marrying his visiting granddaughter whose family had earlier moved to Canada, Karl and his wife, Sylvia, were destined to immigrate to Canada. After the birth of their first daughter, Magdalena, 1969, the Kaiser family thence migrated to St. Catharines, Ontario, moving in with Sylvia's parents. Karl, anxious to upgrade his educational

qualifications, graduated with an honours B.Sc. in chemistry and biochemistry, the necessary background qualifications leading to partnering with Donald Ziraldo to co-found Inniskillin Wines Inc. When this partnership, 1974, was granted a licence to make wines, it was the first time that an Ontario Government had granted such a licence since 1929! Thanks in large part to Karl Kaiser, left, master winemaker, Inniskillin Wines is a recognized international winery, specializing, today, not only in award-winning icewines but in premium quality red and white wines. In this view, Karl Kaiser, left, stands in the Inniskillin wine cellar with Bernard Repolt, a wine consultant from Beaune, France, who works closely with Karl Kaiser and Inniskillin Wines in producing a joint venture wine named Alliance. [Photo, courtesy Dawn Grundy, Inniskillin Wines]

Immunologist Dr. Josef Martin Penninger and his research team at the Ontario Cancer Institute, 1999, ended a 30-year worldwide search for the gene that determines and causes a particular cell to eat away bone. Not only has Dr. Penninger and his team uncovered the reasons for the osteoporosis condition, but his laboratory in the future promises to discover a way to end this debilitating disease affecting millions worldwide. Born, Gurten, Austria, 1964, Dr. Penninger graduated from the Medical School, University of Innsbruck, Austria, 1990, and came to Canada as a postdoctoral fellow, the Ontario Cancer Institute, Princess Margaret Hospital, Toronto, where, 1995, he was made Assistant Professor, Department of Immunology and Medical Biophysics, University of Toronto, and, 1999, Associate Professor. A specialist in a very demanding and rewarding field, Dr. Penninger has received many prestigious awards in both his native land and his adopted homeland. For his outstanding contributions to cancer research, Dr. Penninger was given, 1999, the William E. Rawls Prize from the National Cancer Institute of Canada. At 35 years, the young medical researcher from Austria was a key member of a research team that led to identifying, among other matters, 1) the osteoporosis gene; 2) the molecular motor that allows cells to change their shapes; 3) the cells in our body that kill tumor cells; 4) the molecular principle of joint destruction in arthritis and complete prevention of arthritic crippling using a natural hormone called OPG (protector of the bone) that is to bones what insulin is to diabetes. OPG completely prevents bone loss in osteoporosis, arthritis, and essentially all other diseases associated with bone loss; and 5) how cells sense stress. This "newer" Canadian is sure to become, in the 21st century, a figure of research prominence on the world stage. In this view, Dr. Penninger is in his research lab at the Ontario Cancer Institute, 1999. [Photo, courtesy Dr. Josef M. Penninger]

the immigrants were skilled tradesmen, technicians, and professionals (including medical doctors and engineers). At the same time, many Austrians were also establishing themselves on a relatively large scale in business and industry. A number of factors led to their success. Chief among these were a highly developed work ethic with emphasis on self-employment, risk taking, and resourcefulness. Of note, one of the most successful entrepreneurs to emerge from the community is Frank Stronach, founder of Magna International, the auto parts manufacturing giant. Stronach is Canada's pre-eminent breeder of thoroughbreds: this successful sportsman has stood in the winner's circle numerous times, having won the Belmont Stakes, the Kentucky Derby, and two Queen's Plates.

In many of Canada's largest urban centres, there is at least one Austrian club or organization. Most of these organizations, of a social or cultural nature, were formed initially to meet the social and economic needs of the refugee communities. Today, they also serve as a point of contact for other Canadians interested in the cultural life and heritage of Austria.

Many Canadians of Austrian origin have enriched our cultural life in the fields of music, theatre, and the decorative and visual arts. Among them are the classical guitarist Norbert Kraft, harpsichordist Greta Kraus, pianist and composer Anton Emil Kuerti, and choreographer Anna Wyman.

Angelica Escobar, born state of Morelas, village of Tlaquiltenango, Mexico, some two hours south of Mexico City, immigrated to Canada, 1989, eventually settling in Brampton, Ontario. Before she came to Canada with three of her four children, Angelica had been a local folklore dancer in community and cultural centres in her home town. Her passion for music led her to co-found Alianza, a Mexican folklore group specializing in popular music and dance. In the seven years since the group was founded, 1994, Alianza has performed at many local venues including numerous Festivals and Fiestas staged with Caravan, Carabram, Carassauga, at the University of Toronto, Sheridan and Seneca Colleges, Ontario Place, and various galas at numerous hotels. In this view, Angelica's daugher, Thania, struts and clicks her stuff at a hot venue where Mexican music and colour captivate an enthusiastic audience. [Photo, courtesy Angelica Escobar

José Zamorano was born in Mexico. After completing an undergraduate degree in finance, in Mexico City, José travelled to France, completing his doctoral degree in Economie Agroalimentaire, 1990. Convinced an economic relationship between Canada and Mexico was going to get stronger, and desiring to participate in the future developing process, he, his wife, Concepcion, and two children immigrated, 1997, to Montreal where he felt important opportunities in that city existed for him and his family. He was right. Today, he works as an executive for Provigo, a huge Quebec grocery store conglomerate. As a manager with Provigo's Produce Division, Boucherville, P.Q., José assists in importing fruits and vegetables from Mexico and Latin America. He also lectures at Écoles d'Hautes Etudes Commerciales, University of Montreal. Formerly an agricultural economist with the Mexican government, José enjoys working for Provigo in the private sector. His wife has her own business, importing and selling Mexican furniture in the heart of downtown Montreal. [Photo, courtesy José Zamorano, Ph.D.]

from Mexico

Born in Zamora, State of Michoacan, Mexico, Eleazar Noriega graduated as a Medical Doctor, 1967, from Universidad Nacional Autonoma de Mexico, Mexico City. Serving the Central Military Hospital, 1967-68, and completing postgraduate work at the School of Medicine, University of Miami, Miami, Florida, 1970, Dr. Noriega and his wife immigrated to Canada, 1971, serving at several Toronto area hospitals before establishing his own private practice, 1977, in Pediatrics, downtown Toronto. Dr. Noriega has been teaching Pediatrics, University of Toronto, School of Medicine, since 1977. An active staff pediatrician, Division of Adolescent Medicine, Eating Disorders Program, The Hospital for Sick Children, since 1988, Dr. Noriega's contributions have been immense, especially for teenagers and young adolescents with problems associated with anorexia nervosa and eating disorders in general.
[Photo, courtesy Dr. Eleazar Noriega]

He was 31 years old when he arrived in Canada as a landed immigrant. Born in Monterrey, Nuevo Leon, Mexico, Roberto Cruz Cid, his wife and two children chose Montreal as their destination, 1989, because the whole family could speak French as well as Spanish. Because he had worked in the tourist and trade sectors in Mexico before coming to Canada, Roberto had acquired the necessary geographic and cultural knowledge of Mexico to make him an asset in Canada, especially for companies seeking to establish meaningful trade links with Mexico. To upgrade his qualifications, Roberto took international trade courses in Montreal, becoming a much sought out qualified candidate to guide and direct international trucking transportation between Canada and Mexico. Today, Roberto works for SGT 2000 Inc., an international transport company where he helps manage the import and export of goods between Mexico and Canada. He also assists Canadian companies on the lookout for trade opportunities, thereby facilitating business relationships between Canadian and Mexican companies. In this view, Roberto stands next to a SGT transportation vehicle, one of many he guides and tracks under the NAFTA trade agreement.
[Photo, courtesy Roberto Cruz Cid]

MEXICANS are among the newest residents in Canada. They began to arrive in this country in the 1950s in very small numbers. Over the years, the number of immigrants has steadily increased, particularly from the 1970s on, and they now represent an interesting cross section of the Mexican population: urban and rural dwellers of various social and economic backgrounds. Significant Mexican immigration began with the coming of a cadre of professionals, managers, technicians, and students studying at Canadian universities, largely city folk from Mexico City, Puebla, Guadalajara, San Luis Potosi, and Acapulco. Like the many highly qualified immigrants from other countries, they left their homeland, often with families in tow, to obtain better income, job satisfaction, and career mobility.

The migration or immigration of Mexican Mennonites occurred in a different and remarkable way. Between 1920 and 1940, a number of Canadian Mennonites left their self-contained world of agriculture here and moved to northern Mexico. During this period, a certain amount of return migration also took place. Drought and economic hardship were some of the prime reasons for many Mexican-born descendants of the original migrants to move back to Canada between the mid-1980s and the early 1990s.

According to the 1996 census, there were at that time 23,295 people of Mexican descent in Canada. The highest proportions can be found in Ontario (8,210) and British Columbia (5,560), followed by Quebec (5,195), and Alberta (2,455). The main destinations were this country's major urban centres and metropolitan areas.

Maria Guadalupe Barrios de Abalos was born in the state of Hidalgo, Mexico, on the beautiful plateau of the Sierra Madre where, together with Veracruz, San Luis Potosi and Tamaulipas, it has survived centuries of cultural invasion. Since her immigration to Canada, 1972, Maria Abalos has found her niche in the Hospitality Industry, gaining confidence over a 20-year period working for others by establishing Xilonen Catering and Consulting Services to meet the needs of fiesta lovers craving authentic Mexican foods. Founded with passion, Xilonen Catering affords Maria Abalos the opportunity to supply Canada's fast growing Hospitality Industry seeking the best of zest in Mexican foods. Founder and first President of the Mexican Canadian Association, Maria is proud of her Mexican roots and, as a happy Canadian, knows that she is educating Canadian taste buds by introducing such new food products as pasilla, serrano, arbol, guajillo and smoked jalapeña. In this view, Maria Abalos stands in her food booth promoting Mexican sauces at Hostex 99, Mississauga's International Trade Centre, as well as giving support to an important Mexican Import Company. [Photo, courtesy Charles J. Humber]

Educating Canadian Taste Buds

Operating Private Dental Clinic

A dental surgeon, Dr. Nelly Jinich's thesis when she graduated, cum laude, from the Faculty of Dentistry, Universisidad Technológica de México, Mexico City, 1976, was called "Haematological Management of Hemophiliac Patients." When she first came to Canada, 1978, she did dental radiographic research work at Toronto's Hospital for Sick Children. Nevertheless the route to certification as a Canadian dentist was a struggling uphill climb. Upon completing her Doctor of Dental Surgery, University of Toronto, 1991, Nelly received a prize for being an outstanding student in Clinical Paedodontics. Today, married to Simha Mendelsohn, a computer/business systems engineer, also from Mexico, Nelly, the proud mother of three boys, manages her own dental practice in Toronto while operating a private clinic. [Photo, courtesy Simha Mendelsohn]

Specialist in Theory of Architecture

He received his B.A. in Architecture, National Polytechnic Institute, Mexico City, 1971, his M.A. in Architecture, University of Essex, Colchester, England, 1975, and his Ph.D. in the History and Theory of Architecture, University of Essex, 1979. A distinguished architect, Alberto Pérez-Gómez, born, Mexico City, Mexico, 1949, is, today, the Saidye Rosner Bronfman Professor of History and Theory of Architecture at McGill University where he has supervised the graduate program in the History and Theory of Architecture since 1987. He has taught in Great Britain at the Architectural Association in London and at universities in Mexico, France, Switzerland, Austria, Finland, Denmark, Norway, Spain, and Sweden, in addition to many universities in the USA. Formerly Director, School of Architecture, 1983-86, Carleton University, Dr. Alberto Pérez-Gómez was also Director, Institute de recherche en histoire de l'architecture, Montreal, 1990-94. His first book, Architecture and the Crisis of Modern Science (MIT Press, 1983), won the Alice Davis Hitchcock Award for architectural history, 1984. His most recent book, co-authored with Louise Pelletier and entitled Architectural Representation and the Perspective Hinge, was published by the MIT Press, 1997. Dr. Pérez-Gómez, as viewed in this recent photograph, is co-editor of CHORA: Intervals in the Philosophy of Architecture. [Photo, courtesy Dr. Alberto Pérez-Gómez]

Born in Mexico City, Dr. Leopoldo Chagoya, left, graduated, M.D., University of Mexico, and specialized in Psychiatry at Montreal's McGill University. Working for five years there, he became Head, Family Therapy, Jewish General Hospital, returning, 1972, to Mexico City where he co-founded the Institute of the Family with Mexican colleagues. In 1982, Dr. Chagoya re-immigrated to Ontario. He became the first Head of Family Studies, McMaster University, and is now Associate Professor, University of Toronto. At present he combines private practice in Psychotherapy, Psychoanalysis and Couple Therapy with teaching and supervising psychiatric residents in Individual and Couple Psychotherapy, Mount Sinai Hospital, Toronto. He has published extensively many scientific articles, book chapters, and one book called Techniques of Family Therapy. Translating texts is another of his specialities. Over the last two years he has re-awakened his early love for writing fiction, film dialogue, and film scripts. [Photo, courtesy Dr. Leopoldo Chagoya]

Laura Ochoa, far right, is an International Trade Consultant living in Laval, Quebec. Born in Mexico City, she immigrated to Canada, 1984. Today she assists companies by introducing their products to the North American market. In this context, Mrs. Ochoa met, 1998, with Montreal Mayor Pierre Bourque, left, at a gala in honour of the Mexican Consul, M. Celso Delgado, who was based in Montreal when this photograph was taken. [Photo, courtesy Laura Ochoa]

In contrast, Mexican Mennonites chose to establish homesteads in southwestern Ontario, settling in Aylmer, Leamington, Chatham, St. Catharines, and in the vicinity of Kitchener.

Mexicans in Canada have integrated well into Canadian economic life. They can be found throughout the labour force as professionals, entrepreneurs, manufacturers, clerical and construction workers, salespeople, and agricultural workers. Home and family life are a sustaining force for Mexicans in Canada. The family provides the individual with security and economic stability. Although their family in Canada is primarily a nuclear unit, the spirit of an extended family is important to many Mexicans.

Once they became established in communities in Canada, the Mexicans developed their own institutions to meet the social and cultural needs of their members. Organizations founded by the group include the Mexican-Canadian Association, the Mexican-Canadian Alliance, and the Association of Mexican Professionals. Mexican immigrants are enriching the multicultural character of Canadian society. Mexican cooking and foodstuffs have helped to change our home eating habits. Vitally interested in maintaining their social and cultural heritage, Mexican Canadians seek to pass it on to the younger generation and to other Canadians. ❂

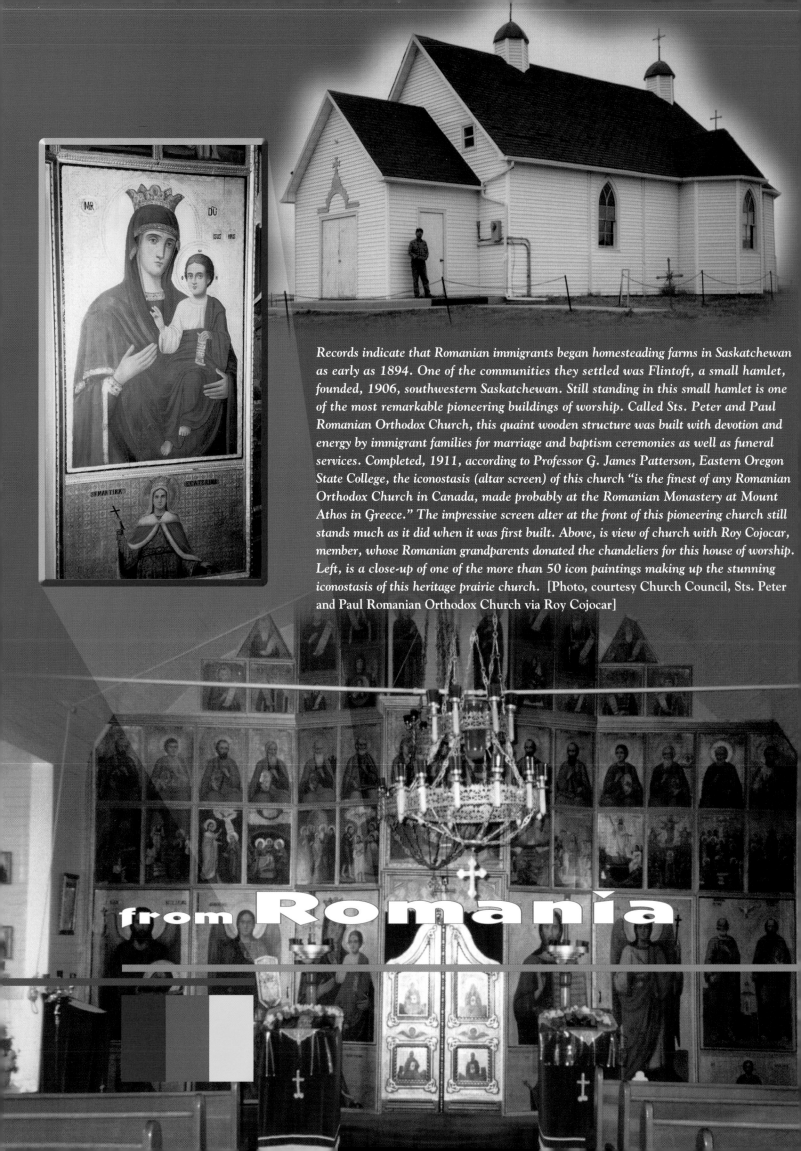

Records indicate that Romanian immigrants began homesteading farms in Saskatchewan as early as 1894. One of the communities they settled was Flintoft, a small hamlet, founded, 1906, southwestern Saskatchewan. Still standing in this small hamlet is one of the most remarkable pioneering buildings of worship. Called Sts. Peter and Paul Romanian Orthodox Church, this quaint wooden structure was built with devotion and energy by immigrant families for marriage and baptism ceremonies as well as funeral services. Completed, 1911, according to Professor G. James Patterson, Eastern Oregon State College, the iconostasis (altar screen) of this church "is the finest of any Romanian Orthodox Church in Canada, made probably at the Romanian Monastery at Mount Athos in Greece." The impressive screen alter at the front of this pioneering church still stands much as it did when it was first built. Above, is view of church with Roy Cojocar, member, whose Romanian grandparents donated the chandeliers for this house of worship. Left, is a close-up of one of the more than 50 icon paintings making up the stunning iconostasis of this heritage prairie church. [Photo, courtesy Church Council, Sts. Peter and Paul Romanian Orthodox Church via Roy Cojocar]

from Romanía

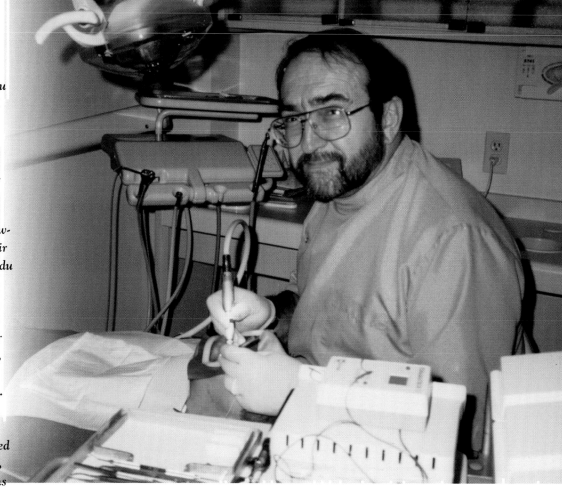

While travelling as Romanian tourists in Turkey, 1969, Sandu and Elena Dumitrescu applied for and were granted political asylum, leaving behind their 18-month-old, Romanian-born son in the care of grandparents. Some three months later, the Dumitrescus were sent to a refugee centre in Italy, not knowing the true whereabouts of their son. Almost one year later, Sandu and Elena entered Canada as landed immigrants, settling in British Columbia. It was also inevitable that Sandu, in order to practice dentistry in Canada, would be required to upgrade his earlier dental qualifications. Enrolling as a second-year student, 1972, University of British Columbia, Sandu excelled as a dental student, graduating, 1974, approximately five months after both he and Elena were reunited with their son. Setting up his own practice in Burnaby, British Columbia, Sandu now employs a staff of eight, including Elena, who despite being a Chemist with a Master's Degree, has found life easier managing her husband's business than working for free in order to gain employment experience or working a long 40-hour week at half pay in order to give her resume appealing credentials, at the expense, of course, her family. In this contemporary view, Dr. Dumitrescu prepares to treat a patient in his office. [Photo, courtesy Dr. Sandu Dumitrescu]

ROMANIANS have been coming to Canada from their magnificent ancestral homeland in central, south-eastern Europe north of the Danube River, west of the Black Sea and the Prut River, and making their home here since the last half of the nineteenth century.

At the centre of Romania and stretching to its northwest is the Transylvanian Plateau surrounded, in the form of an arc, by the Carpathian Mountains which comprise about 30 percent of the entire country. Romania consists of a number of distinct regions, each of which has its own unique history – Walachia, Moldavia, Transylvania, Banat, Oltenia, Dobruja, Bukovina, Crisana, and Maramures.

Romanians whose ancestors lived there in ancient times are believed to be descendants of two closely related peoples – the Dacians and the Getae. Through association with Romans early in the first century A.D., when part of ancient Dacia was subdued and became a province in the Roman Empire, their language took on certain Latin characteristics which it shares with French, Italian, Portuguese, and Spanish.

Gradually, despite the ongoing violence of marauding forces for nearly a thousand years, three distinctive Romanian states began to develop during the Middle Ages: Walachia, Moldavia, and Transylvania. At the end of the sixteenth century A.D., Michael the Brave, a Walachian leader, brought these three Romanian states together under his control. Unfortunately, Michael was soon overthrown and killed. His union of Romanian states collapsed. At long last, in mid-July 1878, the union of Walachia and Moldavia, as the sovereign state of

Romania, was recognized internationally through the signing of the Treaty of Berlin by representatives of the Great Powers of Europe and of Turkey.

Precisely why and when Romanians first began to immigrate to Canada cannot be established, definitively, from the public records.

While the records lack clarity on some matters concerning early Romanian immigration to Canada, other matters are quite clear. When the Treaty of Berlin was signed, it provided, specifically, that the Government of Romania would protect the Jews. But the Jews were not guaranteed Romanian citizenship. By the early 1870s in Canada, however, Jews had the legal right to full Canadian citizenship even though they were often not given equal treatment with Gentiles in particular circumstances. Nonetheless, they did have the right to vote and to be elected to and to hold public offices. In Romania, Jews did not have these rights.

This difference in the legal status of Jews in Canada as compared with their legal status in Romania may have motivated some Romanians to immigrate to Canada. We know from personal and family accounts that Jews

Cristina-Delia Suciu, born in Cluj-Napoca, Romania, is the daughter of an agricultural engineer and of a mother who is a medical doctor. Graduating from the University of Cluj-Napoca Medical School, Cristina immigrated, on her own, to Canada, 1984, settling first, in Winnipeg, interning for one year at the University of Manitoba, then practicing for one year in that city before transferring to Hamilton, Ontario, where she attended McMaster University, becoming certified as an anaesthesiologist, 1993. Cristina worked as an anaesthesiologist in various southwestern Ontario cities, including hospitals in Hamilton, Windsor, Burlington, and Oakville before taking on a permanent position at Brantford General Hospital. In this view, Cristina is seen at the 80th anniversary celebrations of the Romanian Orthodox Church, Boian, Alberta, 1985, the year after she immigrated to Canada. Cristina, left, is standing next to the Rt. Hon. Don Mazankowski, M.P. for Vegreville, His Eminence Archbishop Victorin, Cristina's uncle and Archbishop of the Romanian Orthodox Archdiocese in America and Canada, and Father Mircea Panciuk, Parish Priest of St. Mary's Romanian Orthodox Church, Boian, Alberta. [Photo, courtesy Dr. Cristina Suciu]

immigrated to Canada from Romania before the substantial general immigration began in the late 1890s. It is estimated that, in the last half of the nineteenth century, some 15,000 Jews arrived from Europe as immigrants in Canada. Some settled in southern Saskatchewan and established their own distinctive communities there in the 1890s.

In 1898, Iachim Yurko and Elie Ravliuk, two Romanians from Boian in Bukovina in northern Moldavia, chose land in a new rural settlement northeast of Edmonton. This new settlement had been begun the previous year by Ukrainians who had come from villages near Boian. By January 1901, nearly a hundred Romanian families had settled in this "Boian" district near what is now the community of Willingdon, Alberta. Many more Romanian families came. Some settled in the Boian area, others in rural districts in Alberta and elsewhere in various places on Canada's western prairies.

Born in Hairy Hill, Alberta, 1926, William (Vasile) Yurko was the first Canadian of Romanian descent to be elected to either a provincial legislature or to Ottawa's House of Commons. His grandparents, Nazarie and Acsenia Yurko had arrived in what is, today, Boian, Alberta, from Bukovyna, 1899, at that time part of the Austrian Empire but, today, a Romanian-speaking section of both Romania and Ukraine. Serving two years in the Canadian Air Force as a World War II gunner before graduating as a Chemical Engineer from the University of Alberta, 1950, Bill spent 17 years in the private sector, including a stint of six years with Atomic Energy of Canada, before being elected in a by-election to the Alberta Legislature, 1969. Re-elected, 1971, he was appointed Environment Minister, the first politician anywhere in Canada to hold this portfolio. In 1979, Bill left provincial politics and was elected federally as a Member of Parliament for Edmonton-East. After his re-election, 1980, he moved in Parliament to "patriate" the Constitution, a motion receiving unanimous consent three times in the House of Commons and resulting in patriation of the Canadian Constitution from Great Britain, 1982. After leaving politics, 1984, Bill was made a Member of the Senate and Board of Governors, University of Alberta, 1985-91. In this 1987 view, the Hon. William Yurko, whose ancestral home has been restored at the Ukrainian Cultural Heritage Village, Vegreville, Alberta, is seated next to Jean Chrétien at which time Canada's future Prime Minister was granted an Honorary Degree in Law from the University of Alberta. [Photo, courtesy Bill Yurko]

A vigorous campaign by the Government of Canada was responsible for this substantial influx of settlers. The centrepiece of this campaign was the Dominion of Canada Lands Policy. Under that policy, every adult immigrant arriving in Canada's northwest was entitled to 160 acres of public land – a homestead – on payment of the required fee of ten dollars. The homesteader was required to live on the land chosen, build a dwelling, and cultivate a certain amount of land within a three-year period. If these requirements were met, full title to the homestead was granted to the homesteader.

This arrangement, whereby an immigrant could acquire land by living on it and working it was attractive to Romanian peasants. They could never have acquired land that way in Romania, but they could in Canada. Thus thousands of Romanians immigrated to Canada in the hope of acquiring land. By 1914 there were more than 8,000 people of Romanian origins living in Canada.

The Romanians who came to Canada before the First World War were primarily farmers. Those who came after the war, usually had either practical skills as tradesmen or technicians or special professional qualifications. Many who came in the 1920s settled in major cities including Montreal, Toronto, Hamilton, Windsor, and Kitchener-Waterloo. Between the two World Wars, the percentage of Romanians living in western Canada reached its high point. As agriculture was increasingly mechanized, many who had been working on farms moved into the developing cities on the prairies and sought employment there.

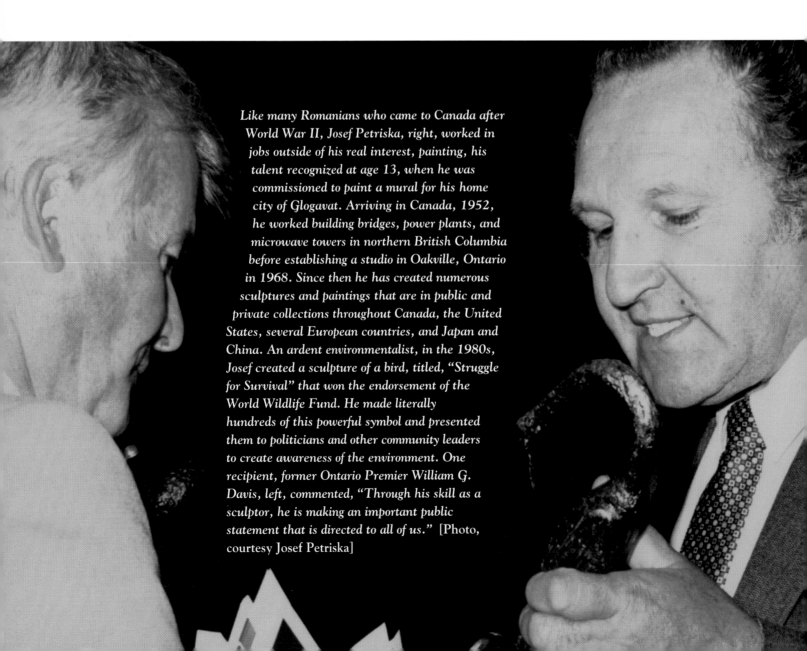

Like many Romanians who came to Canada after World War II, Josef Petriska, right, worked in jobs outside of his real interest, painting, his talent recognized at age 13, when he was commissioned to paint a mural for his home city of Glogavat. Arriving in Canada, 1952, he worked building bridges, power plants, and microwave towers in northern British Columbia before establishing a studio in Oakville, Ontario in 1968. Since then he has created numerous sculptures and paintings that are in public and private collections throughout Canada, the United States, several European countries, and Japan and China. An ardent environmentalist, in the 1980s, Josef created a sculpture of a bird, titled, "Struggle for Survival" that won the endorsement of the World Wildlife Fund. He made literally hundreds of this powerful symbol and presented them to politicians and other community leaders to create awareness of the environment. One recipient, former Ontario Premier William G. Davis, left, commented, "Through his skill as a sculptor, he is making an important public statement that is directed to all of us." [Photo, courtesy Josef Petriska]

Hydrological Engineer

Monica Crisan was born in Bucharest, Romania, 1954. A graduate hydrological engineer, University of Bucharest, 1983, Monica is typical of those immigrants who came to Canada in the 1980s from eastern European countries, bringing with them professional skills which Canada urgently required to meet the growing needs of a world demanding more and more scientific and technological skills. Arriving in Hamilton, Ontario, 1985, with husband Myron, Monica, now residing in Brampton, Ontario, is a much respected civil engineer who has shared her skills with several engineering firms in need of expanding expertise and valued experience. [Photo, courtesy Charles J. Humber]

Internationally Ranked

Born, Bravov, Romania, 1952, Gabriel Neacsu, left, was a member of the Romanian National Tennis Team for five years before defecting to Belgium during a Tennis Tournament, 1972. As a professional tennis player, Gabriel was ranked one of the top 200 tennis players in the world. With his racquet, Gabriel targeted the tennis courts of the world until he met and married a Canadian from British Columbia. Settling in Vancouver, 1980, since that time Gabriel has worked for a number of Tennis Clubs, including the prestigious Hollyburn Country Club, West Vancouver. Over the past 19 years, Gabriel has helped develop some world-class players, including Helen Kellesi and Grant Connell, whose doubles team was ranked #1 in the world, 1993. He also coached and travelled for nearly two years with W.T.A. player Sandra Wasserman, Belgium's top tennis player. Currently working as Head Pro, the New National Youth Tennis Centre at People's Courts, Coquitlam, British Columbia, Gabriel now runs a very successful junior academy where he trains more than 100 children, ages 5-18, including coaching full time the top British Columbia player, Sanjan Sadovich. [Photo, courtesy Gabriel Neacsu]

because of the havoc which had rocked Romania immediately after the war. Like those who came between the wars, immigrants arriving immediately after the Second World War settled, for the most part, in major Canadian cities. Most of them had completed their secondary education and some had completed advanced studies. Despite the difficulties of having, in most cases, to learn a new language and to gain technical and professional acceptance, they were generally successful in securing employment in Canada's postwar economy. But there were major impediments to be overcome by Romanian-trained medical doctors who came after the Second War and wished to continue to serve in their chosen profession in Canada. These problems still continue.

The violence that accompanied the takeover of Romania by the Communists late in 1947 was another key factor in stimulating the immigration of many thoughtful people. A considerable percentage of the Romanians who came during this phase had spent time in refugee camps in Europe. Romanians who came in the second phase of immigration after the Second World War often faced major perils for themselves and their families since it was often difficult to obtain legal permission to immigrate from Romania. Many Romanians, particularly professionals, were often refused permission to go abroad. For them, Romania had become a prison. Many were determined to escape despite the dangers. Some finally arrived and gained employment in Canada. Others were caught and severely punished. Some lost their lives.

A third phase in the post-Second War Romanian immigration to Canada began when the despotic Ceausesco regime was ended in late December 1989. By that time there were, according to the Canadian census, over 70,000 persons of Romanian origin living in Canada. Of these, less than half are reported to have been born in

Romania. Since the early 1900s, additional thousands of Romanians have come to Canada as immigrants.

When the first Romanian immigrants arrived in the late nineteenth century, Canada was still, primarily, an agrarian society. Through their work as farmers in Western Canada, Romanians and their fellow immigrants from eastern Europe and elsewhere helped to develop Canada's vast agricultural potential. Gradually, through combined efforts,

Born in Botosáni, Romania, 1924, Valerie Miclea was only five years old when her father, Georghe, who had earlier come to Canada in search of opportunities, sent for his family to join him in Windsor, Ontario, where he had found a job. Valerie's destination was to become an executive secretary to mining presidents at a time when Canada was a world leader in producing minerals. She was Richard V. Porritt's executive assistant, 1965-1974, when he was President of Noranda Mines. Following an executive secretarial position at Hawker Siddeley, Valerie was made executive assistant to President Alfred Fairley when he guided Hollinger Mines Limited during the 1970s. Valerie married Charles W. Clark, 1976, and retired, in 1979, as "executive assistant to presidents." [Photo, courtesy Valerie Clark]

Canada became an agricultural superpower and was transformed into an urban, increasingly mechanized society.

As life in Canada has been and is being transformed through the development and application of increasingly sophisticated technologies and sciences, Romanian specialists have played key roles in many areas. They have contributed to advances in the manufacturing and service sectors of the economy through their skill and knowledge in the automation and now the cybernation of many activities.

Romanians have also played important roles in the development of Canada as a transcultural society. In fact, most Romanians settling in Canada have endeavoured to understand the generally accepted customs and conventions of their neighbours in both English and French language sections of Canada and to adapt thoughtfully to them. Many Romanians can speak both of Canada's official languages in addition to their mother tongue.

Through the dedication of many individuals working in Romanian churches and synagogues and the various other Romanian cultural agencies, efforts are ongoing to sustain and foster appreciation of historic cultural and moral values in the several Romanian traditions. These activities, which have been carried forward now for over a century by succeeding generations of Romanians who have chosen Canada as their new homeland, have enhanced the quality and the richness of the life Canadians are privileged to share. ♻

D. McCormack Smyth

When Romanian-born Dan S. Hanganu arrived in Canada, 1970, he brought with him his newly wedded bride, Anca, a degree in architecture from the University of Bucharest, and a vision that he would establish his architectural career in Quebec. A Fellow of the Royal Architectural Institute of Canada and a Member of the Royal Canadian Academy of Arts, Dan Hanganu is a diversified architect with a professional practice ranging in scale from single family houses to entire city blocks. A sample of his projects include McGill University's New Law Library; a state-of-the-art head office for Cirque du Soleil; Ecole des Hautes Études Commerciales, Université de Montréal; Pointe-à-Callière Museum of Archaeology, built to celebrate the 350th anniversary of the founding of Montréal; Abbey Church at St-Bênoit-du-Lac; and Galleria Dorchester, Montreal, a mixed-use complex of retail stores, offices, and 700 units of housing located in downtown Montreal. Teaching architecture at both McGill University and Université de Montréal, Professor Hanganu has been a visiting lecturer in France, U.S.A., Argentina, China, Mexico, Italy, and Colombia, among other places. He has won over 40 architectural awards in such places as Switzerland, Morocco, Romania, and more recently in Canada. A prolific architect, his works have been celebrated internationally in various exhibitions, including a recent show held, 1998, Buenos Aires, Argentina. [Photo, courtesy Dan Hanganu]

A chance meeting with Mr. Ian Clark, Canada's cultural attaché attending the first solo art exhibition of Croatian-born Anton Cetin, Paris, 1968, resulted in the now internationally recognized painter immigrating to Canada that year. He and his wife Milka arrived in Paris, 1966, after Anton had studied mural techniques at the School of Applied Arts, Zagreb, 1954-59, and graphic arts and painting, Academy of Fine Arts, 1959-64.

In Paris he was a freelance artist and illustrator until French authorities told him to get a permanent job or leave the country within months. He mentioned this to Canada's Ian Clark, who said if they wish, they could immigrate to Canada. Within months they were in Toronto. There Anton worked as a freelance illustrator while creating his archetypal Eve, "who universally represents the feminine, the spirit of peace and harmony, the giver of life and nurturing force." In the 1980s he added a bird to "represent both the fragility of nature and the power of nature in its ability to fly." This dual theme in hundreds of his paintings have been shown at more than 80 solo and 150 group shows worldwide. His works hang in numerous galleries and corporate boardrooms in Canada and in more than a dozen countries, including the Vatican and his native Croatia, where he was awarded the Order of Croatian Danica and the Order of the Croatian Wattle by the President of Croatia, 1995.

Rendered in his Toronto studio, 1997, Hi!, an acrylic on canvas (22"x26") depicts the two strong motifs, Eve and bird, which characterize the later paintings of Anton Cetin. [Photo, courtesy Anton Cetin via Mel James]

from Croatia

CROATIANS accompanied many of the earliest European voyagers to Canada, both as explorers and crew. Legend persists that Croatians were aboard the third expedition of Cartier and Roberval in 1541-42. There is an early account of a Slavonian miner, Jacques, who accompanied Champlain, 1605-06, on his voyages to Acadia.

Less flamboyant or notable were the Croatian soldiers, miners, and fishermen who arrived in those early years. Croatian soldiers who served the French in Austrian military units helped defend New France in 1758-59. Croatian sojourners came with the fur trade to the Western interior and to the Pacific Coast and joined the Cariboo gold rush of the 1850s and the Yukon rush of 1898. A group of miners made their way from the United States to Ladysmith on Vancouver Island. Others followed shortly thereafter, settling in Nanaimo, Cumberland, and Wellington. At the same time, Croatians established Canada's first authentic group settlement around the Fraser River salmon grounds where they quickly adapted themselves to the ways of the Canadian fishing industry.

Frank Mahovlich's father immigrated to Canada from Gornji Ostrc, a farming community in Croatia, during the interwar years, eventually settling in the mining community of Timmins, northern Ontario. Born, Schumacher, Ontario, 1938, young Frank played his Junior Hockey at St. Michael's College, Toronto, joining the Toronto Maple Leafs, 1957-58, winning the Calder Trophy as Rookie of the Year. Known throughout his career as "The Big M," Frank's explosive slap shot guided the Maple Leafs during the early 1960s to four Stanley Cups. In 17 seasons in the National Hockey League, including stints with Maple Leafs, Detroit Red Wings, and Montreal Canadiens, this Hockey Hall of Famer amassed 533 total goals and 570 assists. Made Officer, Order of Canada, 1994, Frank also captained the Toronto Toros of the World Hockey League, 1974-75, before retiring from the Birmingham Bulls, 1978. In this 1998 view, The Honourable Frank Mahovlich, son of a Croatian immigrant, addresses the Toronto media after being appointed to the Canadian Senate. [Photo, courtesy The Toronto Star/inset, photo, courtesy, C.J. Humber]

Eight-Month Journey to Pier 21

Born, Bratovajnci, near Karlovac, Croatia, 1937, Branko Culig was a machinist at the time he married Dragica (Carol) Sut, a seamstress, born, Novaki, Croatia, 1943. In 1965, Branko and Carol fled Yugoslavian oppression by entering Italy on a day pass. They then were guided into Switzerland before slipping into Germany where they were placed in a Displaced Persons camp. There they waited to learn what country would accept them as refugees. After six months, Branko and Carol were given the good news that Canada would take them in. They crossed the Atlantic by boat, arriving, Pier 21, Halifax, Nova Scotia, 1966. From that place of entry, a boat took them to Welland, Ontario, where relatives lived in nearby Fonthill. After settling, Toronto, Branko, a tool and die maker with Canada Packers, and Carol, a caregiver, raised two sons. One, a graduate of Humber College, works as a manager for United Parcel Services, British Columbia, while the other son, a York University graduate, currently works as a financial planner. In this view, Branko and Carol prepare to leave their native land, 1965, on an eight-month journey that would lead them to a new world, a new homeland where opportunity embraced them. [Photo, courtesy David and Danny Culig]

"He was the toughest man I ever fought"
Muhammad Ali

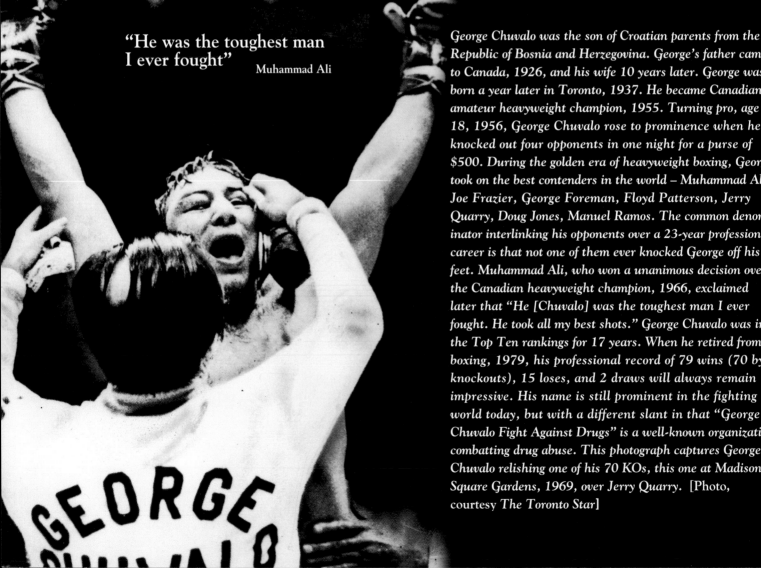

George Chuvalo was the son of Croatian parents from the Republic of Bosnia and Herzegovina. George's father came to Canada, 1926, and his wife 10 years later. George was born a year later in Toronto, 1937. He became Canadian amateur heavyweight champion, 1955. Turning pro, age 18, 1956, George Chuvalo rose to prominence when he knocked out four opponents in one night for a purse of $500. During the golden era of heavyweight boxing, George took on the best contenders in the world – Muhammad Ali, Joe Frazier, George Foreman, Floyd Patterson, Jerry Quarry, Doug Jones, Manuel Ramos. The common denominator interlinking his opponents over a 23-year professional career is that not one of them ever knocked George off his feet. Muhammad Ali, who won a unanimous decision over the Canadian heavyweight champion, 1966, exclaimed later that "He [Chuvalo] was the toughest man I ever fought. He took all my best shots." George Chuvalo was in the Top Ten rankings for 17 years. When he retired from boxing, 1979, his professional record of 79 wins (70 by knockouts), 15 loses, and 2 draws will always remain impressive. His name is still prominent in the fighting world today, but with a different slant in that "George Chuvalo Fight Against Drugs" is a well-known organization combatting drug abuse. This photograph captures George Chuvalo relishing one of his 70 KOs, this one at Madison Square Gardens, 1969, over Jerry Quarry. [Photo, courtesy The Toronto Star]

Croatians who came as part of the massive prewar flow to Canada lived by manual labour in mines, forests, and factories. They showed a remarkable degree of dispersion, settling in almost every region including British Columbia, Alberta, Saskatchewan, and Ontario. In Saskatchewan, Croatian farm families lived near the towns of Bladworth, Hanley, and Kenaston while others established homesteads in Lesack and Duck Lake near Prince Albert. In Alberta, Croatians located in Taber, Lethbridge, and Iron Springs. By 1910, Edmonton was also home to Croatians. During this same period, Croatians who migrated to Winnipeg from the United States formed the basis for later community growth and development. In Ontario, Toronto, as well as smaller centres such as Hamilton, Thorold, Welland, Sault Ste. Marie, Port Arthur, Fort William, and Windsor attracted Croatians to work in industry. Croatian miners sought opportunities in the new mines in both northern Ontario and Quebec. In the Atlantic provinces, by the mid-1920s, Croatians had settled in New Waterford, Reserve Mines, Stellarton, and Sydney in Nova Scotia. The better-educated immigrants began coming to Canada during the interwar period and generally sought employment in the industrial cities and towns of central Canada. Most of the post-1945 displaced persons from refugee camps in Austria and Italy – Croatian educators and other professionals, skilled tradesmen, businessmen, and industrialists – were assigned to remote resource towns to work as bushworkers, miners, and railroad navvies. They tended to move south to Canada's major cities after completing their contracts.

The 1996 Canadian census listed 84,495 Croatians in Canada (single and multiple responses combined). The ethnocommunity group has established itself in Toronto, Calgary, Edmonton, Hamilton, Kitchener-Waterloo, Montreal, Vancouver, and Windsor. Croatian communities in the hinterland and resource frontier towns and cities include those in Nanaimo, Rouyn-Noranda, Sault Ste. Marie, Sudbury, Thunder Bay, and Timmins. Croatians usually settled in distinct neighbourhoods in these cities and towns.

Fraternal, literary, and cultural societies, language schools, musical ensembles, sporting clubs, and political organizations were formed that involved large numbers of the immigrant community and provided a framework in which the children of the immigrants could be educated to the dreams and ways of their parents and grandparents. Croatian halls and churches were required. The first Croatian Catholic parish was established in Windsor, Ontario, in 1950. Other parishes and missions were located in Toronto, Mississauga, Hamilton, Sault Ste. Marie, Winnipeg, Calgary, and Vancouver.

Croatians have played an important role in many aspects of this country's development. Early Croatian migrant work gangs helped build the transcontinental railroad and development Canada's mining, forestry, agriculture, and fishing industries. During the interwar period, many became hardworking factory hands in Canada's growing industrial sector. The third generation have enjoyed considerable upward mobility, building careers in the service, industrial, private, and professional sectors of Canadian society. They have been active in the visual and performing arts – Nenad Lhotka headed the Royal Winnipeg Ballet during the 1950s and Joso Spralja excelled as a painter, sculptor, photographer, and folk musician during the 1960s.

Croatians have enhanced many professional sports in Canada and the United States. Frank Mahovlich (appointed to the Canadian Senate in 1998), his brother, Peter, Joe Sakic, and Marty and Matt Pavelich have left indelible marks in the National Hockey League. In the boxing ring, George Chuvalo, Canadian and Commonwealth Heavyweight Champion, was inducted into the Canadian Sports Hall of Fame in 1992. Football player John Mandarich of Thunder Bay, Ontario, played on the defensive line of both the Edmonton Eskimos and Ottawa Rough Riders in the Canadian Football League during the 1980s. His younger brother, Tony, became

At Forefront of Permafrost Engineering

Since coming to Canada as Assistant Professor, Civil Engineering, Laval University, 1962, Prof. Branko Ladanyi has carried out research on frozen soils and ice that has improved the design of engineering structures in the permafrost regions of Canada, United States, Scandinavia, Russia and China. Born, Zagreb, Croatia, 1922, the son of a Hungarian father, he was a civil engineering graduate, University of Zagreb, 1947, and taught there 11 years before earning a Ph.D., Geotechnical Engineering, University, Louvain, Belgium, 1959. As a research engineer, Belgian Geotech Institute, Ghent, 1959-62, Professor Ladanyi received an invitation from Laval University which brought him to Canada, 1962. In 1967, he was made Professor, Mining Engineering, École Polytechnique, Montreal, and, 1977, Professor of Civil Engineering until his retirement, and appointment as Professor Emeritus, 1994. As the Co-founder of the Northern Engineering Centre, École Polytechnique, 1972, he continues to conduct research in his particular field of permafrost engineering, rock mechanics and tunnelling, his work resulting in the co-authorship of An Introduction to Frozen Ground Engineering, 1994, and major contributions to three other volumes and to more than 160 other scientific papers dealing with geotechnical engineering in cold regions, permafrost engineering and rock engineering. Pictured here on the west coast of Newfoundland where he and students were testing the strength of sea ice, 1990, Dr. Ladanyi, Fellow, Royal Society of Canada, has received awards, among others, from the Province of Quebec, the Canadian Geotechnical Society, the E.E. De Beer Award, Belgian Geotechnical Society, the American Society for Testing and Materials, and the Canadian Northern Science Award, Department of Indian Affairs and Northern Development.[Photo, courtesy Professor Branko Ladanyi]

Researching Nerve Cells and Brain Synapses

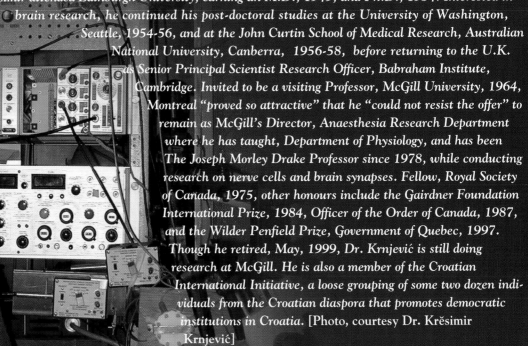

Dr. Krěsimir Krnjević had a "complicated early life history" because his father had been active as a Croatian politician in the 1920s and '30s. Born Zagreb, 1927, he was the son of Juraj Krnjević, General Secretary of the Croatian Peasant Party and youngest elected member of the Yugoslav Parliament who, 1930, left Croatia to appeal for Croatian democracy at the League of Nations, Geneva, Switzerland, after King Alexander took power. With substantial autonomy granted in 1939, the family returned to Zagreb but when Germany invaded Yugoslavia, 1941, Juraj, as a senior government official, left Zagreb, first for the Middle East, then England, while Krěsimir and his sister attended high school, Capetown, South Africa. Reunited with his father, 1944, Krěsimir attended Edinburgh University, earning an M.D., 1949, and Ph.D., 1954. Interested in brain research, he continued his post-doctoral studies at the University of Washington, Seattle, 1954-56, and at the John Curtin School of Medical Research, Australian National University, Canberra, 1956-58, before returning to the U.K. as Senior Principal Scientist Research Officer, Babraham Institute, Cambridge. Invited to be a visiting Professor, McGill University, 1964, Montreal "proved so attractive" that he "could not resist the offer" to remain as McGill's Director, Anaesthesia Research Department where he has taught, Department of Physiology, and has been The Joseph Morley Drake Professor since 1978, while conducting research on nerve cells and brain synapses. Fellow, Royal Society of Canada, 1975, other honours include the Gairdner Foundation International Prize, 1984, Officer of the Order of Canada, 1987, and the Wilder Penfield Prize, Government of Quebec, 1997. Though he retired, May, 1999, Dr. Krnjević is still doing research at McGill. He is also a member of the Croatian International Initiative, a loose grouping of some two dozen individuals from the Croatian diaspora that promotes democratic institutions in Croatia. [Photo, courtesy Dr. Krěsimir Krnjević]

an All-American offensive lineman during his senior year at Michigan State. Born in Oakville, Ontario, he was drafted by the Green Bay Packers of the National Football League in 1989. In figure skating, the brother and sister pairs team, Val and Sandra Bezic of Toronto, captured the 1980 World Professional Championship. Sandra subsequently became a highly successful and innovative choreographer for legions of top-ranked figure skaters.

Croatians have also succeeded in the political arena. At the municipal level, Joseph Mavrinac served as Mayor of Kirkland Lake and Frank Krznaric served multiple terms on the Timmins city council. In provincial politics, Peter Sekulic of Alberta, David Stupich of British Columbia, and John Sola of Ontario proved victorious. The 1993 federal election produced four Croatian-Canadian office-holders: Janko Peric (Liberal-Cambridge), Jan Brown (Reform-Calgary Southwest), Roseanne Skoke (Liberal-Central Nova Scotia), and Allan Kerpan (Reform-Moose Jaw-Lake Centre, Saskatchewan). ♧

The Mavrinac family story is typical of how a father left his wife and children behind, in this case, Croatia, to find a job in Canada. Ivan Mavrinac was hired to work in a gold mine in the Kirkland Lake area of northern Ontario where he saved enough money in three years to send for them, 1929. One of his sons, Joseph, five when he arrived, has since become one of Northern Ontario's most noted citizens as owner of motels and hotels between 1948 and 1980, and then as a well-known politician, serving six consecutive terms as Mayor of Kirkland Lake. In March, 2000, Joseph completed a two-year term as Chair of the Ontario Reality Corporation. He has served as President of three hotel/ motel associations, President of the Ontario Association of Municipalities of Ontario, and Director, Federation of Canadian Municipalities. In World War II he served on corvettes HMCS Trail and Battleford, on convoy duty in the North Atlantic, and is a life member and recipient of the Royal Canadian Legion 50-year and Meritorious Service Medals. Joe, as he likes to be known, is also a Paul Harris Fellow, Rotary International, and proud of his roots in that he is a Fifty-Year member of the Croatian Fraternal Union. Here, His Worship Joe Mavrinac wears Kirkland Lake's Chain of Office. [Photo, courtesy Major Joe Mavrinac]

Born, 1930, Bruges, Belgium, Paul M. Soubry was educated in his native land before immigrating to Winnipeg, Manitoba. He continued his education by enrolling at Angus Business College in Winnipeg, and later in Advanced Marketing and Sales Management at the University of Waterloo, 1951. Mr Soubry started his 45-year career in the Farm Equipment industry, as an Export Trainee for Cockshutt Plow Co. As a result of mergers and acquisitions he worked in senior executive positions for White Farm Equipment Co., Versatile Farm Equipment Co., and Ford New Holland Canada Ltd., retiring, 1995, as Vice President and General Manager, New Holland Canada Ltd. Today, Mr. Soubry is Chairman of the Board of Governors, University of Manitoba; Chairman, Victoria Hospital; Winnipeg Member Industrial Technology Centre, Province of Manitoba; Former Chairman, Canadian Exporters Association and Canadian Farm Industrial Equipment Association. In this 1994 view, Paul Soubry, right, VP-General Manager, and Paul Zanetel, left, Chief Engineer, accept on behalf of Versatile Farm Equipment Operations, the Canada Export Award for the second time, from the Minister of Agriculture, Mr. Ralph Goodale. [Photo, courtesy Paul Soubry]

P EOPLE OF BELGIAN ORIGIN have been involved in virtually every aspect of Canadian life but they have probably made their most important and obvious contribution in agriculture. Many of the Belgians who pioneered in the West or established farms in Ontario and Quebec were experienced farmers in their home country. Their expert knowledge of dairy farming, tobacco and sugar beet growing, fruit and market gardening, has been of considerable importance to Canada. Belgian farmers made a number of improvements in rural land use that included the reclamation of swamp lands, a better system of drainage, wider application of fertilizer, and more intensive cultivation.

from **Belgium**

At the turn of the century, Belgian capitalists and investors were attracted by the possibilities open to them in pulp and paper production, in railway construction, and in public works. For example, the Shawinigan-based Belgo-Canadian Paper Company, founded in 1902, enjoyed a long and successful run until its union with Consolidated-Bathurst in 1975.

Belgo-Canadian land and development companies played a leading role in promoting settlement in the prairies and in developing the urban centres of Winnipeg, Edmonton, and Calgary. They were also closely associated with the development of the Okanagan Valley into a prime fruit-producing area.

When Belgians moved into urban centres, they branched out into a variety of occupations and enterprises. Some distinguished themselves in the diamond-cutting business; others became insurance agents, salespeople, retailers, or owners of hardware stores, lumber yards, plumbing, building, and electrical supply outlets. Of particular note is Michael DeGroote's trucking company in Elliot Lake, Ontario, which evolved into the Laidlaw group of enterprises.

Belgian Canadians have held many important positions in the field of education. In Quebec, Belgians excelled as school organizers and administrators. Auguste-Joseph de Bray of Louvain founded the École des Hautes Études Commerciales in Montreal in 1908. Alfred Fyen, a former officer in the Belgian army, headed a new institution for the training of surveyors in Quebec City in 1907 and became a director of the prestigious

Roger Vermeulen's grandparents were born in the village of Marie-Aalter, Belgium. Following World War I, Roger's grandparents, Peter and Emerence Vermeulen, with their three-year old son, Andrew, immigrated to Canada, settling near Bothwell in southwestern Ontario where they began working in the sugar beet fields. A few years later, the family moved into the region south of Delhi, in southwestern Ontario, where Andrew Vermeulen, Roger's father, became a successful tobacco farmer. Educated in Simcoe, Ontario, Roger Vermeulen was first elected to public office, 1969. Since that time, and while working full time for the Federal Department of Employment and Immigration, Simcoe, Roger has served the township of Delhi as Councillor, Deputy-Mayor, and, since 1995, Mayor. In 1992, Mayor Vermeulen, father of two daughters, Past President, St. Williams Lions Club, and Member, Royal Canadian Legion, was presented with the Governor General's Commemorative Medal for the 125th Anniversary of Canada. In this photograph, Mayor Roger Vermeulen, sitting with Chain of Office, hosts HRH Prince Phillippe, standing, Crown Prince of Belgium, at a gala dinner at the Delhi Belgium Hall, December 8, 1998. Far right is Belgium's Ambassador to Canada, the Hon. Claude Laverdure. [Photo, courtesy Mayor Roger Vermeulen]

Bilingual Head-Hunter

Toronto's Anne Whitten Bilingual Human Resources Inc. is a well-known specialty agency recruiting and placing bilingual staff in various positions at various levels, including management. Established by a Belgian-born, highly motivated and energetic entrepreneur, Anne Whitten found success indirectly. While visiting her sister in Toronto, 1960, Anne learned English so rapidly that she stayed for a year, discovering that there was a real need in Canada for translators. Born in Louvain, 15 miles east of Brussels, Anne graduated from the prestigious Université Catholique de Louvain with a degree in Philosophy and Letters. In Canada she founded the Belgian Canadian Business Association and has taught French at such private schools as Loretto Abbey and Havergal College, both in Toronto. In this view, Anne Whitten visits with his Excellency, Mr. Luc Carbonez, Ambassador to Canada from Belgium, at the National Club, Toronto, 1999. [Photo, courtesy Anne Whitten]

Marketing Aerospace Technology

Born, 1949, Angleur, Belgium, Jean Colpin has spent nearly an equal amount of time on three continents. Raised in the Belgian Congo where his father was pursuing an expatriate career, Jean Colpin returned to Belgium to attend university, completing his M.A. in Mechanical Engineering, Université de Liège, 1973, graduating with a doctoral degree in Fluid Dynamics from the Von Karman Institute, 1977, and teaching there until 1981 when he joined F.N., a Belgian Aerospace firm. When he had an opportunity to join a market leader in engine propulsion, Pratt & Whitney Canada, and participate in the design and development of their products, he and his entire family journeyed as immigrants to Canada, 1985. Today, Jean Colpin is Vice President, Engineering, for Pratt & Whitney which today is the world leader in small gas turbine engines. Mr. Colpin has never regretted making Canada his home. Like their father, his daughter and son are both engineers. As Jean says, "Canada has been for us a land of opportunity where we have been, my family and I, able to develop, have fun, and contribute." In this contemporary view, Jean Colpin conducts a seminar on site at Longueuil, Quebec.
[Photo, courtesy Pratt & Whitney]

George Wybouw was born in Brussels, Belgium, August 27, 1944, exactly six days before the British liberated the city. A good portion of his youth, in addition to schooling, was spent visiting western European countries. When completing his B.Com. and B.Ed. degrees at University of Antwerp, George became involved in the International Association of Students in Economics and Commerce, spending internships in Spain and Czechoslovakia which provided him with still greater interest in other cultures, other countries. This was probably why he initially travelled to Montreal and McGill University to study Business, completing his M.B.A. there, 1970. Invited to join the Faculty of Business Administration, Université de Moncton, New Brunswick, at age 25, was an offer he could not refuse. Such an offer in his own country would have taken 20 or 30 years! So, he jumped at the chance and has been, consequently, a teacher/administrator at this Moncton, New Brunswick, institution for nearly 30 years. During the 1980s, Dr. Wybouw took a sabbatical, graduating, Ph.D., Erasmus University, Rotterdam (the Netherlands). While teaching Management Information Systems, George became Director of the M.B.A. program, 1991, Université de Moncton, and launched the first French-speaking M.B.A. distance program via videoconferencing and the internet. Appointed Dean, School of Business Administration, Université de Moncton, 1996, George Wybouw is involved, today, with the Greater Moncton Multicultural Association. In this view, 1999, George, right, visits Aziz Bouslikhan, CEO of Isiam, in Morocco, where the Moncton M.B.A. program is offered. [Photo, courtesy George Wybouw, Ph.D]

École Polytechnique in Montreal in 1908. This human dynamo went on to found the École des Arts Decoratifs et Industriels in 1912 and subsequently the École d'architecture. And Charles De Konick, as Professor and Dean of the faculty of Philosophy from 1934 to 1965, played a long and important role as a liberal thinker and educational reformer in the life of Laval University.

Throughout the rest of Canada, Belgians contributed to the quality of existing separate school systems. The Sisters of Notre-Dame-de-Namur came from Cincinnati to open schools in eastern and northern Ontario in the 1880s. In 1914, another Belgian order, the Ursuline Sisters from Tildonk, took charge of the village school in Bruxelles in southern Manitoba. Members of the community were active in the public school system, vigorously championing the right of French language instruction and the creation of bilingual schools. Louis Hacault played a prominent role in the Manitoba Schools Question of the 1890s as the representative of francophone Catholics.

As well, Belgian Canadians made important contributions in the world of arts and letters. Music in Canada owes a great deal to the priest, Father P.J. Verbist, who helped to found the Academie des Beaux-Arts in Montreal in 1873. Composer Guillaume-Joseph Mechtler, the organist of Notre-Dame church in Montreal

Marc F.G. Vanden Bussche's grandfather immigrated to Canada from Geluwe, West Flanders, Belgium, where he had supplemented his work on the family farm by cycling professionally. Seeing greater opportunities for himself in Canada, he set sail from Antwerp, 1926, aboard the Melita, an immigrant ship carrying 1,500 passengers to Quebec City. Young Gerard made his way to Chatham, Ontario, where other people of Flemish background had settled as farmers. Nearly 30 years later, Gerard Vanden Bussche and his family migrated to Delhi, Ontario, where Gerard and son, Roger, a recent graduate, Ontario Agricultural College, Guelph, established a business specializing in irrigation systems, supplying irrigation equipment as well as design and installation services for local farmers. Nearly 21 years after his father had co-founded the Belgian Club of Delhi, 1948, Roger Vanden Bussche died prematurely, 1979, age 49. His wife initially carried on the business operations. At age 18, however, Marc, Roger's son, left school, 1980, to begin working for the family business, eventually taking control of the operations, 1991. As General Manager of the business co-founded by his grandfather and father, Marc, former President, Canadian Irrigation Association, has mandated a millennium goal: to make Vanden Bussche Irrigation & Equipment Limited a North American leader in supplying and installing irrigation systems. In this view, Marc Vanden Bussche, left, and the Vice President of Shanxi Province toast each other, Feb 7, 1999, while the Vanden Bussche team from Delhi toured China on a trade mission trip. [Photo, courtesy Marc Vanden Bussche]

between 1792 and 1832, is believed to be the first Canadian to be paid for his compositions. Joseph-Jean Goulet helped to found the Montreal Symphony Orchestra in 1894.

The visual arts are an aspect of Canadian cultural life to which Belgians have contributed much. Henri Leopold Masson is a painter, well known in international art circles, who opened the eyes of Canadians to the splendour of the Gatineau region near Ottawa. Among sculptors are Marcel Braitstein, Yosef Gertrudis Drenters, Auguste Hammerechts, and Pierre Hayvert whose work was featured at the Quebec Pavilion at *Expo 67*.

Belgians played a useful part in helping develop the Canadian Roman Catholic Church. Belgian bishops helped to solidify a Catholic presence in Canada's Far North and on the Pacific coast. Religious orders from Belgium were important in many rural and isolated communities. For example, Trappist monks established a monastery in Oka, Lower Canada (Quebec), in 1862. Here, building a grist mill, saw mill, and cheese factory, they devoted their lives to the community.

According to the 1996 census, 123,595 people of Belgian origin live in Canada with 31,375 persons declaring a single ethnic origin and 92,225 indicating multiple ethnic origins. Belgian immigration consisted mainly of two groups: the Flemings who hailed from the northern half of the country including Antwerp and Limburg and spoke Flemish, a Dutch dialect; and the Walloons, who came primarily from the southern provinces including Hainaut, Namur, Liege, and Luxembourg and spoke French.

The first major movement of Belgian peoples took place between 1906 and 1914. The liberalization of Canadian immigration criteria brought Belgians to the prairie provinces. A small colony of Belgians and Dutch settlers was established at Davidson, Saskatchewan. Belgian settlements were also founded in Manitoba surrounding Winnipeg and St. Boniface and to the southwest including the towns of Bruxelles, St. Alphonse, and Swan Lake. Another wave of immigrants followed in the decade after World War I when thousands came at the behest of railway company recruiters, sugar beet manufacturers in Ontario and Alberta, and tobacco companies. Many of the immigrants made their way to the tobacco fields of southwestern Ontario including Kent, Essex, and Lambton counties, settling in the communities of Tillsonburg, Delhi, Simcoe, and Aylmer. After World War II, Belgians followed the general trend to urbanization, settling in the "golden horseshoe" of Ontario's commercial and industrial development. Ontario is now home to 39,640 Belgians: 30,075 reside in Quebec, primarily in the urban setting of Montreal (18,405); 16,445 live in the province of Manitoba.

As the Belgians had a tendency to integrate rather easily into the English or French-Canadian way of life, they did not form many organizations of their own to maintain their identity in Canada, choosing rather to form local social clubs for mutual help and recreation as well as for the promotion of cultural relations between Belgium and Canada. ✪

Archie Verspeeten's family immigrated to Canada from Belgium, 1925. Settling in the Chatham region of southwestern Ontario, Isidoor and Aimee Verspeeten, some five years later, became the proud parents of Archie who would grow up in Norfolk County learning tobacco farming. After Archie married Irene Clarysse, 1951, he foresaw opportunities in the trucking business. He left his farm operations, and established Verspeeten Cartage Limited, 1957, the year he moved to Dehli. At first trucking agricultural crops, Archie saw further opportunities, 1967, and purchased a competitor in the trucking business. Now the proud father of five sons, Archie got into the general commodity freight hauling business. By 1989, all operations were shifted from Delhi to Tillsonburg where grounds for a new terminal on a five-acre site was purchased. Business continued to grow rapidly, especially when General Motors awarded VCL a contract large enough that Archie was obliged to establish, 1992, a trucking terminal in Oshawa to accommodate the shipping needs of the General Motors plant there. Additional terminals have since been opened in Whitby (1994), Flint, Michigan (1994), and Dayton, Ohio (1996). As well, a state-of-the-art terminal along Highway 401 at Tillsonburg was opened in 1999 to serve the ever-growing needs of a trucking fleet in excess of 1,500 pieces of equipment. Verspeeten trucks travelled some 142 million kilometres in 1998, serving both Canada and the U.S.A. Archie's five sons are all established in the business and Archie, today, nearly 50 years after purchasing his first truck, 1952, is still running the growing operations as president. In this view, Archie, sitting, centre, is flanked, first row, by sons, Alan, left, and Mark, right. In back row, left to right, stand Brian, Ron (Vice President), and Dennis. [Photo, courtesy Archie Verspeeten]

EGYPTIAN IMMIGRATION to Canada did not begin until the 1950s. A unique combination of many people and cultures, it reflected the human variety that was Egypt for much of the nineteenth and twentieth centuries. The vast majority of the early immigrants were members of Egypt's minority communities: Jews, Armenians, Lebanese, Syrians, Greeks, and Italians. Many of these groups first became interested in Canada when the government of Gamal Abdel Nasser passed a new series of nationalization laws that cut into their dominance of Egypt's industry and commerce, banking, the service sector, even the administration and operation of the Suez Canal. (This led to a war with Great Britain, France, and Israel in late 1956.) Large-scale emigration of native Egyptians took place after 1970 as university and college graduates began to yearn for a better way of life. This continued throughout the eighties as both Muslims (mainly Sunnis) and Christian Copts, who shared a

Zaher Abd Elmeged Masood, one of five children born and raised in Alexandria, Egypt, was three years old when his father died. Growing up in a close family environment with a mother determined to raise five children who would make a contribution to the world at large, Zaher vigorously pursued education, graduating in Production Engineering, University of Alexandria, 1971. After three years as a part-time tool designer and part-time lecturer, University of Alexandria, Zaher and his Egyptian-born wife decided that Canada was the place to raise a family. Enrolling as a graduate student in Mechanical Engineering, McMaster University, Hamilton, Ontario, Zaher completed his M.Eng., 1974, taking a job, for ten years, as a Senior Piping Engineer, with Stone & Webster, Toronto, before gaining employment, 1990, with Atomic Energy of Canada Limited – CANDU Operation. By 1996 he had become a Team Leader, Piping Task Force, in Naari, North Korea, and in 1997 was made a Section Head, Process Design and Piping Engineer, Taejon, Korea. Proud father of four sons, in this recent view, Zaher and members of his family, stand together on the grounds of Royal Military College, Kingston, Ontario, where one of his sons, Omar, in uniform, middle, is pursuing an undergraduate degree in engineering. [Photo, courtesy Zaher Masood]

from Egypt

World-Class Architect

Born, Cairo, Egypt, 1943, Medhat Abdou graduated in architecture from the University of Cairo, 1964, immigrating to Canada, 1966. Summer training in West Germany during university years was the main reason for leaving Egypt to work abroad after graduation. Travelling through Europe was an awesome experience for Medhat in that the future architect with Webb Zerafa Menkes Housden was seeing the same buildings all over Europe that he had studied as a student. Facing uphill challenges, Canada became his land of destiny. Medhat had one suitcase and $150 when he left Egypt. By the time he arrived in Montreal, 1966, $25 was all that was left. Gaining a job was easy in 1966 as Montreal was booming. Once the Expo 67 boom had come and gone, Medhat left Montreal for Toronto joining a multidisciplinary firm as Assistant Architect working on projects in Abu Dhabi, U.A.E. until the start of the 1967 War. In August, 1969, Mehat joined the WZMH Partnership, an internationally respected architectural firm. A partner himself since 1985, Medhat Abdou, over a 30-year career, has been involved in the design of no fewer than 25 major projects worldwide which have honed his skills and taught him how to put complex projects together. After the 1992 Gulf War, Medhat took on his first major architectural commission to design

four buildings in Abu Dhabi for Etisalat, the telecommunications giant of the United Arab Emirates. Other projects in the Middle East which Medhat Abdou has designed include Kuwait's 85-million-dollar Headquarters for the Public Institution for Social Security; Beirut's 100-million-dollar Trade Centre in Lebanon; Alexandria, Egypt's 200-million-dollar San Stefano mixed-use complex on the Mediterranean Sea, including a 125-room Four Seasons Boutique Hotel; and the 300-million-dollar Nile Plaza Four Seasons Hotel overlooking the Nile River in Cairo. With Hisham T. Mostafa, owner, looking on, in this view, Medhat Abdou, left, on behalf of WZMH, signs the contract commissioning him and his Toronto-based firm to design the spectacular Nile Plaza. [Photo, courtesy Medhat Abdou]

Coptics in Canada

Pursuing a lifelong career of spiritual service, Father Angelos Mikhial Saad, born in Alexandria, Egypt, first graduated as a medical doctor from the University of Alexandria, 1973, then began an intensive five-year period studying theology, becoming ordained in 1978 as a Coptic Orthodox Priest. After completing 10 years of spiritual service in Alexandria, he took a pastoral post in Seattle, Washington, 1988. When His Highness Pope Shenouda III, Pope of Alexandria and Patriarch of the See of St. Mark in Alexandria, Egypt, suggested that Father Angelos go to Canada and direct the building of a Canadian Coptic Centre, Father Angelos went to Mississauga, Ontario, 1989, and immediately initiated a fundraising campaign to build a major spiritual and cultural centre to complement the church of the Virgin Mary and St. Athanasius which earlier had been established in Mississauga, 1974. Today, under the guidance of Father Angelos, this dynamic Coptic Centre is actively preparing to meet the spiritual and cultur-

al needs of working parents, the aged, and the sick by establishing schools, daycare centres, and a sports centre for the community in the heartland of one of Canada's fastest growing municipalities. Father Angelos also established three new churches in Ontario, the Church of Archangel Michael and St. Takla, Brampton; Church of St. Mina, Hamilton; and the Church of St. George and St. Marcorious, St. Catharines. In this view, Father Angelos, centre, stands with His Highness Pope Shenouda III, left, and Mississauga's Mayor Hazel McCallion, right, at the time when the Canadian Coptic Centre was celebrating its official opening, 1998. [Photo, courtesy the Canadian Coptic Centre, Mississauga, Ontario]

Specialist in Neurodegenerative Diseases

Born in Egypt, Dr. Mohamed M. Khalifa, Chairman, Division of Medical Genetics, Department of Paediatrics, Queen's University; Director, Medical Genetics Unit, Kingston General Hospital; and Associate Professor, Paediatrics as well as Department of Pathology, Queen's University, received his M.D., Cairo University, 1974, M.Sc, Human, Medical Genetics, Ain-Shams University, Cairo, 1980; and M.Sc., Paediatrics/Genetics, University of Saskatchewan, 1985. Director, Post-graduate Fellowship Program in Medical Genetics for Canadian College of Medical Geneticists Certification in Clinical Genetics/Cytogenetics and Molecular Genetics, since 1992, Dr. Khalifa, one of Canada's leading molecular genetic researchers, a prolific contributor to many publications, is in demand as an invited lecturer to many conferences, seminars, symposia, and conventions, sharing his knowledge on such diverse topics as genetic disorders, neurodegenerative diseases, metobolic disorders, genetics and ovarian cancer, genetic counselling in breast cancer, bioethics, genetic disorders in Arab populations, the Noonen Syndrome, Pallister-Killian Syndrome, Fragile X Syndrome, Harlequin Syndrome, and the Aicardi Syndrome. Migrating to Canada, 1983, Dr. Khalifa, who has been associated with Queen's University since 1985, is the proud father of son, Hady, as illustrated in this recent view, Kingston, Ontario. [Photo, courtesy Dr. Mohamed Khalifa]

In Vogue

Immigrating to Canada in 1980 shortly after graduating in public relations and business from the University of Cairo, Egyptian-born Afrah Gouda became one of Canada's leading fashion models. While upgrading her education at York University, Ryerson Polytechnic Institute, and Seneca College, specializing in marketing and computers, Afrah has found time to volunteer with a number of nation-wide organizations, in particular the Children's Wish Foundation of Canada and the Canadian Hemophilia Society. [Photo, courtesy Afrah Gouda]

Rifaat Fares was born in Elbaliana, an Egyptian town in the Province of Souhag, less than 100 miles north of Luxor, the ancient city of Thebes on the Nile River where the boy-king Tutankhamun (1352-1343 B.C.) lived and Ramses II (died 1223 B.C.) ruled. One of 10 children, all of whom attended and graduated from university, Rifaat completed his degree in Pharmacy, University of Alexandria, 1976. After working as a pharmacist for over 10 years in his native land, marrying Magda, and becoming the father of two children, Ramez and Kareem, he chose to immigrate to Canada, 1987. Rifaat, now living in Mississauga, Ontario, worked for over two years at the Mississauga Hospital, a challenge, he says, that gave him a higher level of clinical experience. He established his own pharmacy in Oakville, 1995, calling it St. Mark after one of the Apostles who preached Christianity in Egypt and North Africa. A second pharmacy, United Drug Mart, was opened in Toronto, 1998, to serve nursing homes and the Centre for Addiction and Mental Health. [Photo, courtesy Rifaat Fares]

Ezzat Fares Abd-Elmessih was born in Elbaliana, Egypt, and is an older brother of Rifaat Fares. After attending the University of Alexandria, Egypt, where he graduated in Medicine (M.B.Ch.B.), 1961, he continued in Medicine, receiving a Diploma in General Surgery. Immigrating to Canada, 1968, he worked in the Surgical Department, Santa Caprini Hospital, Montreal, Quebec, before moving to Regina in 1969 to intern at the Regina Grey Nuns' Hospital. He was appointed Senior Resident, Surgery, Regina General Hospital, 1970. Since 1971, Dr. Abd-Elmessih has practiced in Saskatchewan as a Family Physician. Active in professional associations, Dr. Abd-Elmessih has served on the executive of the Regina & District Medical Society, elected president, 1992. He served as executive member, Vice President, 1996-97, and President, 1997-1999, Regina Health District Medical Staff Association. Dr. Abd-Elmessih served as Medical Health Officer for the R.C.M.P. Training Academy, 1990-1992, and remains an honorary member of the South Saskatchewan Officers Mess. Dr. Abd-Elmessih is active in his community having served on the Albert Park Community Association as Soccer Coordinator and coach. He is also a Life-member of the Regina Maple Leaf Lions Club, a volunteer with Scouts Canada, and High School Athletics as team doctor for Luther Lions Football team. Married for 25 years to his wife, Pat, Dr. Abd-Elmessih has two children, Samir and Esther, both at university. He is a founding member of St. Mark and St. George Coptic Orthodox Church, Regina, 1996. [Photo, courtesy Dr. Ezzat Fares Abd-Elmessih]

Following in the Footsteps of St. Mark

Community-Minded Physician

common language and history, complained of conditions at home including the growing secularization and pro-Soviet thrust of the government. The introduction of the immigrant investor program attracted a particularly high component of wealthy native Egyptians after 1985.

In 1996, Statistics Canada recorded the presence of 35,570 persons of Egyptian origin (single and multiple responses combined). The largest concentration of Egyptian Canadians was found in Ontario with 16,120, followed by Quebec with 14,740. The next largest Egyptian populations were found in Alberta (1,865) and British Columbia (1,735). The largest single centre of Egyptian population was Montreal (13,980), followed by Toronto (5,450). Egyptians have also been attracted to Ottawa-Hull with 925.

The large urban and economic centres were the most popular areas for settlement; within these metropolitan areas, however, Egyptians are widely dispersed. The majority have a university education or a high degree of technical training. This fact, as well as knowledge of English and/or French that has enabled them to garner

Born in Banha, Egypt, Faisal Zekry immigrated to Canada in 1970, bringing with him skills as a chemical engineer, having graduated from the Faculty of Engineering, University of Cairo. After a five-year stint with American Standard, Cambridge, Ontario, Faisal, in 1976, took a position with Ashland Canada Inc. where today he is Mississauga Plant Manager as well as an Officer of the company. Living on a farm north of Toronto, Faisal and his wife, Nellie, have been volunteers, since 1978, at a weekend school for teaching children Arabic language and Islamic religion. In this view, Faisal, left, presents an award to Mississauga Mayor Hazel McCallion in recognition of the City's involvement in Excellence in an Emergency Response Exercise. Next to Mr. Zekry, is Carl Spratt, Inspector of Police, Peel Region, followed by James Bertram, Deputy Chief of Police, Region of Peel, Cyril Hare, Mississauga Fire Chief, and Joseph Moore, Emergency Program Manager, Region of Peel. [Photo, courtesy Ashland Chemical Inc.]

Marie Tadros, after completing her high school education in Alexandria, Egypt, chose to immigrate to Canada in 1967 to reconnect with a brother who had earlier immigrated to Canada. Fluent in many languages, including Arabic, Italian, Greek, French, and English, Marie entered the teaching profession at the elementary school level. After completing degrees at both York and Brock Universities, Marie spent many devoted years to teaching French Immersion and Core French with the Etobicoke Board of Education in Ontario, before retiring from the teaching profession in 1998. [Photo, courtesy Marie Tadros]

many types of employment in the white collar sector as professionals, administrators, teachers, clerical workers, and salespeople, has helped to ensure a comfortable lifestyle and considerable geographical mobility.

Egyptian Canadians exhibit a distinctive variety of religions, sects, and rites. Within the community are Muslims (Sunni and Shiite), Coptic Christians (Orthodox and Catholic), Maronites, Melchites, Antiochian Orthodox, Protestants, Syrian Catholics, Armenians, Roman Catholics, and others. And each of these groups has its own houses of worship in Canada along with the requisite social and religious organizations. Members of the Coptic Orthodox Rite, for example, founded their first church in Montreal in 1967 (St. Mark's Church). Today, Montreal is home to three such churches. In Ontario, Coptic Orthodox churches can be found in Toronto, Ottawa, Kitchener, and Mississauga. Alberta, Saskatchewan, and British Columbia also have one each.

As well, during the late sixties and early seventies, the Canadian Coptic Association and its sister organization, the Egyptian-Canadian Association, supplemented the work of the church by publishing a host of magazines and other reading materials for this group and providing a number of services and social activities. Egyptian Muslims, in turn, participate in a number of established Islamic centres and mosques that serve many nationalities in Canada. Additionally, a large number of non-religious, non-political organizations have been established by the ethnocommunity with varying degrees of success. They aspire to promote Egyptian culture and socio-economic development in the homelands, to strengthen ties between Canada and Egypt, to conduct Arabic heritage language classes, and to increase social cohesion between various segments of the ethnocommunity such as Egyptian-Canadian businesspeople. While many Egyptian Canadians have been able to reach a high level of success in Canadian cultural and professional circles, it can also be said that the growing number of professionals, skilled technicians, business leaders, and administrators is another indication of their ready desire to contribute to Canadian society and business.

Ezzat Fattah, born Assiout, Egypt, 1929, graduated, from Faculty of Law, University of Cairo, 1948, and worked in capacities such as District Attorney, Public Prosecutor, and Chief Prosecutor for various Egyptian cities, including Alexandria, 1949-54, and Cairo, 1958-61, before enrolling at University of Vienna Institute of Criminology, 1961, pursuing graduate studies and undertaking research under the guidance of Professor Roland Grassberger who introduced Ezzat to the new discipline of Victimology. Ezzat Fattah became a Research Assistant in Criminology at the Université de Montréal, 1965- 68, as well as an Assistant and Associate Professor of Criminology at the same institution while he was pursuing graduate work there, receiving his M.A., 1965 and Ph.D., 1968, in Criminology, the first student in Canada to be awarded a doctorate in this discipline. Currently, Professor Emeritus of Criminology, Simon Fraser University, since 1974, Professor Fattah was the University's Founding Chairman of the Criminology Department, 1974-78. Author or co-author of several important books and some 100 scholarly papers in learned journals, Dr. Fattah received the Konrad Adenauer Research Award in the Social Sciences and the Humanities, 1992; the Commemorative 125th Anniversary of Canada Medal; and is a Fellow, Royal Society of Canada. Staunch defender of human rights and keenly aware of the need to protect citizens against the abuses of power, Dr. Ezzat Fattah was one of many leading the successful fight in Canada against the death penalty. His well-known association with Amnesty International has caused him to be invited to a number of international conferences to crusade for the abolition of the death penalty and the commutation of sentences for those on death row. Recognizing that "crime is normal, even natural behaviour," Dr. Ezzat Fattah, a pioneer in victimology, argues strongly for a new body of criminal law for the 21st century, reflecting the social realities of post-industrial society. [Photo, courtesy Professor Ezzat Fattah]

Born in Lindesberg, Sweden, Eva Svensson took her early violin training with the legendary John Fernström and later with Gert Crafoord, formerly Concert Master with the Stockholm Philharmonic. Before immigrating to Canada, Eva Svensson had studied violin in Salzburg, Austria. Offered a full scholarship to Boston University, 1963, upon graduating both undergraduate and graduate in Violin Performance, and working with such notable musicians as cellist Aldo Parisot, Eva took her first professional job with the Montreal Symphony, 1969, and has been, ever since, a member of that internationally respected musical body. Since arriving in Canada, Eva has been active in the Montreal music community, performing as soloist for both radio and television, serving as a member of various orchestras, including L'orchestre Symphonique de Radio-Canada, the McGill Chamber Orchestra as well as the Montreal Symphony. Sitting on numerous juries, teaching at the Faculty of Music, McGill University, recording over 85 solos for London Decca, Vox, and EMI labels, Eva Svensson's musical career is reinforced by her husband who, as a violinist, is Professor of Violin, McGill University, and her two children, Erik, a cellist and Karl, a percussionist. [Photo, courtesy Eva Svensson]

from Sweden

THE FIRST SWEDISH immigrants to Canada arrived in the early 1870s as part of the mass migration to North America. Most of these early settlers entered Canada by way of the United States, via Minnesota and North Dakota, as land settlement policies became more restrictive in the American West. Facing mounting debts and few opportunities for expansion, thousands of Swedish immigrant farmers moved from the United States initially to Winnipeg, then fanned out across the prairies. The vigorous advertising campaign mounted by land agents of the Canadian Pacific Railway and the Dominion Government had struck a deep chord with Swedes, now wise in the ways of prairie farming and looking for a second chance. Swedish rural settlement in Manitoba first began in 1885 at a colony named Scandinavia, near the present-day town of Erickson. During the first decade of the twentieth century, other Swedish settlements, such as Smoland, would be established in the area between the towns of Teulon and Inwood in Manitoba's Interlake district. Saskatchewan would also have a long history of Swedish settlement. One of the first Swedish settlers in Saskatchewan was Emmanual Ohlann, who founded the community of Stockholm north of the Qu'Appelle River in 1905. Here, Swedish immigrants engaged in mixed farming, some lumbering, and fishing. Other Saskatchewan communities that drew Swedish settlers include Broadview, Buchanan, Canwood, Elfros, Hendon, Kipling, Percival, Prince Albert, Melfort, and Wadena. In Alberta, Swedes were highly concentrated in local farming communities such as Wetaskiwin, New Sweden, Calmar, Falun, Malmo, Thorsby, and Westerose, communities situated between the cities of Calgary and Edmonton. In turn, Swedish Canadians involved in railway building and logging would make their way to

Farmer, politician, premier of Alberta, Harry Edwin Strom was born in Burdett, Alberta, the son of parents who immigrated to Canada from Sweden early in the 20th century. First elected to the Alberta Legislature in 1955, he was re-elected in 1959, 1963, 1967, and 1971 as a Member of the Social Credit Party. In December 1968, after the retirement of Premier E.C. Manning, he became Premier himself, holding that office until 1971 at which time the Social Credit Party was defeated by Peter Lougheed's Progressive Conservative Party. Following the provincial election of 1975, the only Premier of Swedish descent of any Canadian province, retired from provincial politics. In this view, Premier Strom confers with students, 1970, at Fort Vermilion, Alberta, 150 miles northeast of Edmonton.
[Photo, courtesy Provincial Archives of Alberta/PA 6461]

Innovative Choreographer

Born, Stockholm, Sweden, Bengt Jörgen, after graduating from the Royal Swedish Ballet School, decided to further his studies in Canada at the National Ballet where, for several years (1982-85), he was a member. Leaving the National Ballet to pursue his own choreographics career, Bengt Jörgen established, 1987, Ballet Jörgen to expand and improve opportunities for ballet choreographers. Under his directorship, Ballet Jörgen has emerged as Canada's leading presenter of original ballets. In 1989, Bengt Jörgen was appointed resident choreographer of Toronto's George Brown College where today he is the Artistic Director, Dance Programs. Ballet Jörgen, under Bengt's direction, has consistently won rave reviews. A young dancer who risked everything to build an innovative choreographic company, Bengt's troupe presents original works at Toronto, its home base, and on tour at such places as New York where the New York Times, 1995, exclaimed that "freshness, authority, and intelligence are hallmarks" of this innovative dance troupe. In 1998, Ballet Jörgen's new production, Romeo and Juliet, premiered in Banff, Alberta, and toured Canada and the United States. To date, Bengt Jörgen has created over 30 ballets. Some 50,000 people annually see the Ballet Jörgen in action. In this view, Bengt Jörgen and Tara Butler play Romeo and Juliet, 1998. [Photo, courtesy Andrew Oxenham, photographer, via Bengt Jörgen]

Composer Exchanging Culture

Bengt Hambraeus, born Stockholm, Sweden, 1928, graduated M.A., 1950, and Ph.D., 1956, from Uppsala University where his concentration centred on Musicology, History and Psychology of Religion, and the History and Theory of Fine Arts. He studied the organ with Alf Linder; he also studied Composition with Günter Raphael; in Germany, he studied with Wolfgang Fortner, Olivier Messiaen and Ernst Krenek, 1951-54. Since 1948, Dr. Hambraeus has been active both as writer and composer and, as a young musician, became internationally recognized in both disciplines. Working for National Swedish Broadcasting Corporation, 1957-72, Dr. Hambraeus introduced foreign cultures and experimental Western Music for the first time to a Swedish audience. However, it was not until 1971 that Bengt Hambraeus discovered Canada. Selected by the Swedish Music Information Centre to give an eight-week North American lecture tour offering Swedish contemporary music, Dr. Hambraeus was made an offer, following the tour de force lecture circuit, by McGill University, 1972, to teach at the Faculty of Music as a Professor. Upon retirement, 1995, Dr. Hambraeus was made Emeritus Professor. His commitment to Swedish and Canadian cultures, including ethnical, aboriginal, and transcultural internationalism, are well known. He was awarded, 1986, Sweden's highest honour, the Royal Medal "Litteris et Artibus" presented by the Swedish Ambassador on behalf of the King of Sweden. In 1996 he received the rare award, The Swedish Tribute, from the Swedish Embassy in Ottawa, for his contribution to cultural exchange between Sweden and Canada. Many of his latter compositions such as Nocturnals (1990), Piano Concerto (1992), and the Horn Concerto (1997) were created with strong inspiration from both the Glengarry County landscape, eastern Ontario, and the heritage and integrity of native peoples in different worlds. [Photo by Michael B. Hambraeus (the late), courtesy Dr. Bengt Hambraeus]

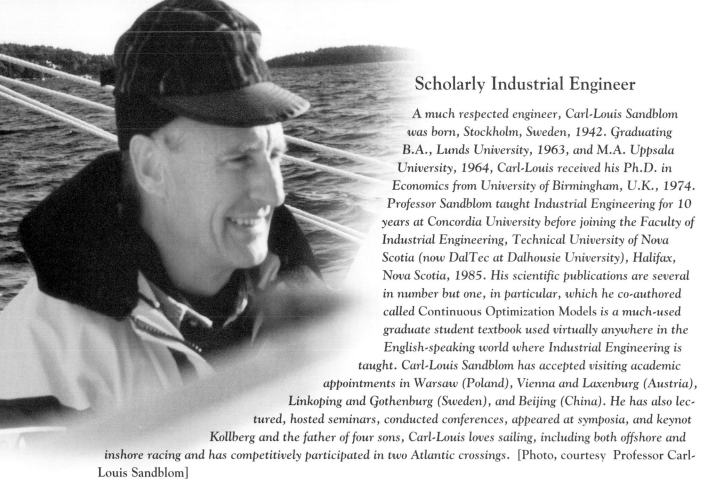

Scholarly Industrial Engineer

A much respected engineer, Carl-Louis Sandblom was born, Stockholm, Sweden, 1942. Graduating B.A., Lunds University, 1963, and M.A. Uppsala University, 1964, Carl-Louis received his Ph.D. in Economics from University of Birmingham, U.K., 1974. Professor Sandblom taught Industrial Engineering for 10 years at Concordia University before joining the Faculty of Industrial Engineering, Technical University of Nova Scotia (now DalTec at Dalhousie University), Halifax, Nova Scotia, 1985. His scientific publications are several in number but one, in particular, which he co-authored called Continuous Optimization Models is a much-used graduate student textbook used virtually anywhere in the English-speaking world where Industrial Engineering is taught. Carl-Louis Sandblom has accepted visiting academic appointments in Warsaw (Poland), Vienna and Laxenburg (Austria), Linkoping and Gothenburg (Sweden), and Beijing (China). He has also lectured, hosted seminars, conducted conferences, appeared at symposia, and keynot Kollberg and the father of four sons, Carl-Louis loves sailing, including both offshore and inshore racing and has competitively participated in two Atlantic crossings. [Photo, courtesy Professor Carl-Louis Sandblom]

Reigning Ballerina Retires

Today, Annette av Paul is artistic consultant, teacher, and coach of classical ballet. Born, Stockholm, Sweden, 1944, she studied at Royal Swedish Opera's Ballet School, before joining Royal Swedish Ballet, 1962. She was a sensational hit almost immediately when Bolshoi choreographer, Yuri Grigorovich, visiting Stockholm, 1962, plucked her out of school to play the lead role of Katerina in The Stone Flower which was touring Sweden at the time. Two years later, Canadian Brian Macdonald, at the time choreographer of the Royal Winnipeg Ballet, entered her life. After they were married, they shared together their artistic talents, she as a ballerina, he as choreographer, and together, as well as independently, they have made a major contribution to international ballet. During her career as a professional dancer, the last 14 years as reigning ballerina with Les Grands Ballets Canadiens, Annette performed with Nureyev, Fonteyn, Bruhn, and Orlando Salgado from Cuba. She danced in the CBC's first colour spectacular, Rose La Tulippe, and for Swedish TV and the BBC. She has done Sugar Plum, Swan Lake, Sleeping Beauty, Giselle, and Romeo and Juliet. She has starred in ballets by George Balanchine, Jerome Robbins, Anthony Tudor, Kenneth MacMillan, Anton Dolin, Glen Tetley and José Limon, among others. Retiring, 1984, she became the founding artistic director, 1986, Ballet British Columbia. Today Annette is the associate director of the Dance Program, Banff Centre for the Arts. Former principal ballerina with the Royal Swedish Ballet, the Harkness Ballet of New York, the Royal Winnipeg Ballet, and Les Grands Ballets Canadiens, Annette av Paul Macdonald, 32 years a ballerina, today lives in Stratford, Ontario. In this view, Principal Dancer Annette av Paul is performing in The Hangman's Reel, choreographed by Brian Macdonald for Les Grands Ballets Canadiens, Montreal, 1984. [Photo, courtesy of Ron Diamond]

British Columbia, establishing a group presence in Revelstoke, Campbell River, Cranbrook, Greenwood, Kimberley, Malakwa, Matsqui, Nelson, Port Alberni, Prince George, Prince Rupert, Rossland, Silverhill, Smithers, and Trail. The main concentration of Swedes in Ontario at this time was in the northwestern districts of Kenora, Rainy River, Sudbury, and the Lakehead. Only a handful of these early arrivals could be found in eastern Canada, around and about the city of Montreal and in the Maritimes.

By the eve of the First World War, Winnipeg had emerged as the leading centre for Swedish culture and activities in Canada. The initial community network was developed in Winnipeg to meet the needs of Canadians of Swedish origin. The first Swedish-language newspaper and community church were founded in Winnipeg in 1886 and 1889 respectively. As well, various Swedish national and community organizations got their start in the city. The interwar period, however, marked the beginning of a gradual shift of population from the farms to this nation's urban centres and industrial areas. Swedish workmen and industrial labourers, as well as a later phalanx of postwar arrivals including engineers, businessmen, and representatives of Swedish export industries, all gravitated to Canada's major cities and the economic opportunities to be found there. The 1996 Canadian census reports 31,200 individuals of wholly Swedish origin and another 247,775 who describe Swedish as one of their ethnic origins, for a total of 278,975. A total of 90,490 had settled in British Columbia, 71,910 in Alberta, 54,525 in Ontario, 30,775 in Saskatchewan, and 19,885 in Manitoba, representing the major Swedish provincial centres in Canada. Swedish communities range in size from Vancouver's 18,690 through such centres as Edmonton, Calgary, Toronto, and Winnipeg, with 6,000 to 11,000, to cities like Montreal, Victoria, Saskatoon, Regina, and Thunder Bay with 2,500 to 4,800 members.

Her maternal grandmother was born in a railway camp in Lapland while her maternal grandfather left home at eleven years and worked in mining camps. Her paternal grandparents were farmers in middle Sweden and a great uncle of Ingrid Arvidsdotter Bryan worked the Klondike, made a fortune and donated most of it to a Baptist Church in Los Angeles. Born, Jukkasjarvi, Sweden, Ingrid's undergraduate studies were far and wide in that she attended Austin College, Texas, University of Lund, Sweden, Trinity College, Dublin, and completed her undergraduate degree in Economics, University of Sheffield, England, 1967. During that time, she married Rorke Bryan and when he got a job as Assistant Professor, University of Alberta, Edmonton, they immigrated to Canada. While he was teaching, she continued with her studies in Economics completing both her M.A. (1968) and Ph.D. (1972) before she and the family moved to Toronto where Ingrid taught, first, University of Toronto, Scarborough Campus, and, secondly, Ryerson Polytechnic University (formerly Ryerson Polytechnical Institute). Ingrid, a popular teacher at Ryerson since 1976, has developed two programs at Ryerson, one implementing a combined major program between Business and Economics and the other creating a new degree program in International Economics. She has served as Chair of the Economics Department (twice) as well as Dean of Arts, 1987-92. Mother of two children, author of two influential books, Ingrid, as with most first generation immigrants, has stayed close to her Swedish roots in that the family returns every summer to their cottage south of Kalmar (Djursvik). In this view, Ingrid Arvidsdotter Bryan hands out a prize at a Ryerson Awards Gala in the mid 1980s. [Photo, courtesy Professor Ingrid Arvidsdotter Bryan]

Several groups form the institutional structure of the Swedish-Canadian community. Canadian lodge members of the Vasa Order of America, such as those belonging to the Strindberg Lodge of Winnipeg, founded in 1913, dealt with the sick, the maimed, the dead, and forgotten during the early and vulnerable settler period. Only with the growth of unionism, occupational diversity, and improved safety conditions on the job did the Order grow into a social and cultural club. Members of the ethnocommunity were also strong supporters of the temperance movement in Canada. Swedish chapters of the International Order of Good Templars (IOGT), in conjunction with their temperance program efforts, soon expanded the scope of their work by sponsoring reading circles and other literary activities and putting on plays, bazaars, and picnics. More recently, modern organizations such as the Swedish Women's Educational Association, the Svenska Klubbeni Montreal and the Svenska Herrklubban (Vancouver), continue to advance Swedish traditions and celebrate the culture of the homeland.

As well, Swedes quickly and successfully gained acceptance in Canadian society. The group contributed much to cooperatives, credit unions, and wheat pools in the West. It also played an important role in the struggle to establish a union in the lumber industry in British Columbia during the 1930s. It follows that Canadians of Swedish origin would eventually be drawn into Canadian politics, beginning as citizen electors and as brokers between their community and Canadian parties. The Swedish Liberal Club of Winnipeg, which was founded in 1908, encouraged many to become naturalized or to take full advantage of their rights as citizens, and to know and understand the workings of the Canadian political process. British Columbia provides an illustration of the political maturity reached by the Swedes during the interwar period. Liberal candidate Olof Hanson, for example, was elected to the House of Commons in 1930. Rolf Wallgren Bruhn, first elected to the provincial legislature in 1924, became minister of public works in 1931. Swedish Canadians also made political strides in Saskatchewan as supporters of the Cooperative Commonwealth Federation (CCF) and in Alberta as supporters of Social Credit. Of note is Alberta-born Harry Strom who grasped a political brass ring when he became premier in 1968. ☘

Graduating in architecture from a private school in Stockholm, Swedish-born Kjell Orrling began working for a lighting fixture company in his native city when he was spotted by a European company who offered him a job in Canada, 1973, as a lighting fixture designer. When his contract was up two years later, rather than return to Sweden, he applied to stay as a landed immigrant and set up his own business designing and manufacturing lighting fixtures. Some 13 years later, Kjell successfully sold his business so he could

paint full time. Kjell has never looked back, forging ahead with his career as a full-time artist. He certainly had no doubt that he would be a success when his first solo show, in Sweden, sold out in a couple of hours. Orrling's truth-to-nature water colours, such as Nefertiti, left, are very much in the tradition of trompe l'oeil, as most viewers assume his masterpieces are collages or fragmented images, not accurate renderings of balanced colouring, contextual contrast, and spatial images contained in illusionary three dimension. In 1995, Kjell Orrling was elected Member, Royal Canadian Academy of Art. [Photo, courtesy Kjell Orrling]

This interior view of St. Nicholas Serbian Orthodox Cathedral, Hamilton, Ontario, records members of the Queen Mary Circle of Serbian Sisters gathered together with the Very Reverend Djuro Vukelic, centre, flanked by the Very Reverend Stevo Stojsavljevic, left, and the Very Reverend Lazar Vukojev, right, on the occasion of the Circle's 50th anniversary, 1984. Founded, 1917, the congregation of the church is the second oldest in Canada, preceded only by Svete Trojice, Regina, built in 1916. The stunning iconostasis (altar screen) was donated by the Chelar family, in the 1960s, and its beautiful frescoes were rendered in the 1990s. [Photo, courtesy Mrs. Milica Chelar]

DURING the late nineteenth and early twentieth centuries, Serbs living mainly in the territories under the dictates of Austro-Hungary left their villages and towns, driven by government oppression and the lack of economic opportunity, to seek a better life in the new world. Many chose Canada as their destination. Serbs from Serbia-proper emigrated much less often than Serbs from other jurisdictions.

Able-bodied, single, young Serbian men first arrived in British Columbia, via California, during the 1850s. Serbs moved freely across western Canada or crossed over from Montana, Idaho and Washington to form ethnic enclaves in Lethbridge, Edmonton, and Calgary. Serbian farmers were also among the first settlers of the Canadian prairies.

from Serbia

After completing his Ph.D., Materials Science, University of Toronto, 1990, within seven years, age 35, Doug Perovic was appointed Chair of his alma mater's Metallurgy Department. Dr. Perovic, born, Toronto, 1962, is the son of Serbian parents, Rajko and Senka, both born in Montenegro in Yugoslavia. Following completion of his doctorate, Dr. Perovic took a Postdoctoral Fellow at the world-renowned Cavendish Laboratory, Cambridge University, U.K. Today, Dr. Perovic has received worldwide acclaim for developing new electron microscopy techniques to study the structure of chemistry of advanced semiconductor materials. Professor Perovic, using the electron microscopy facilities at the University of Toronto, discerned that secondary electron contrast is caused by electron band bending due to the surface state of dopant atoms, a discovery that is "at the leading edge of a highly competitive field of research." As a result, Professor Perovic's contribution to the materials science of semiconductor and metals systems has made him an international figure of prominence, causing him to be in demand at scientific conferences worldwide. In 1997, he was, in fact, the only Canadian invited as an International Advisory Committee member and invited lecturer for the "International Centennial Symposium on the Discovery of the Electron" at Cambridge University, U.K. [Photo, courtesy Dr. Doug Perovic]

At the turn of the century, Serbs shifted their settlement to central Canada, mainly Ontario. In 1903, a small group of Serbs settled in Toronto. By 1914 this community consisted of approximately two hundred settlers. Other Serbian settlements in Ontario prior to the outbreak of the First World War included Hamilton, Welland and Niagara Falls, where immigrants laboured in steel mills and helped build Ontario Hydro generating stations and the Welland Canal.

Serbian immigration to Canada virtually ended with the start of the Great War. In 1916 Bozidar Markovich, an early and prominent Serbian leader in Canada, was delegated to recruit Serbs for the war effort. Indeed, some recruits returned to defend their homeland against the advancing Austro-Hungarian and German armies. Little Serbia's heroic defence against the Central Powers' juggernaut won much sympathy from Canada and the world alike.

Both the Canadian establishment and the growing Serbian communities worked diligently to raise money for Canadian and Serbian war efforts. For instance, the Serbian National Shield Society of Canada, the first Canadian Serbian organization, established in 1916, collected humanitarian aid for Serbia. The Serbian Red Cross sent Helen Losanitch to North America to enlist help for her war-torn native Serbia. The first official reception at the Ontario Lieutenant Governor's new residence, Toronto, was an appeal for Serbia.

During the interwar years, large waves of Serbs immigrated to Canada. They were primarily single men or married men who left their families in the Krajina region and other impoverished areas of Yugoslavia, with plans to bring them to Canada when their financial positions had improved. Serbs from this group settled in the industrial centres of Ontario and in the mining and mill towns of both northern Ontario and Quebec. By 1928 it was estimated that the Serbian community in Central Canada had reached one thousand in number.

A remarkable variety of Serbian immigrant enterprise began to emerge between the two world wars. Serbs applied their entrepreneurial skills by opening grocery stores, barbershops, shoe repair and tailor shops, restaurants, coffeehouses, small bars and taverns. At this time, Serbs also gained an initial foothold in Canada's emerging hospitality and tourist industry, dominating the hotel and motel tourist business in Niagara Falls.

By 1934, the first Serbian newspaper in Canada, *Glas Kanade*, later named *Voice of Canadian Serbs*, was established and still continues under the auspices of the Serbian National Shield Society. Bozidar Markovich was its first editor. Today, the commercially-based *Novine* has a very wide readership among recent immigrants.

You name it and he's done it as a photographer! A graduate of Belgrade's Cinematographic Institute, Boris Spremo was born of ethnic Serb origin in former Yugoslavia, immigrating to Canada, 1957. After several years freelancing, he gained employment with The Globe and Mail, 1962, before joining The Toronto Star, 1966. For the past 34 years, Boris Spremo has won over 280 major national and international awards as a photojournalist. He was the first Canadian to capture a First Prize Gold Medal (1966) in the World Press Photo Competitions held at The Hague. A four-time National Newspaper Award winner, Boris Spremo has won the Canadian Press Picture-of-the-Month Award 18 times. The Toronto Fire Fighters have honoured Boris with Best Picture of the Year Awards three times, and the Toronto Police have awarded Boris the Best Picture of the Year Award on four separate occasions. His works have been published in some of the world's best-known maga-zines: Life, Sports Illustrated, Reader's Digest, The National Enquirer, and Maclean's. In the course of his many world-wide assignments, Mr. Spremo was picked to accompany Prime Minister Trudeau on offi-cial state visits through South East Asia, the Soviet Union, and to Latin America. He has photographed some of the 20th century's most prominent personalities including The Royal Family, Pope Paul II, Charles de Gaulle, Premier Kosygin, Haile Selassie, Fidel Castro, The Beatles, Gorbachev, Boris Yeltsin, among others. He has covered 30 Royal Tours, the '86 World Cup Soccer, the funeral of Robert F. Kennedy, the War in Vietnam, Canada's Peacekeeping troops abroad, hostilities in Northern Ireland, Israel, the Kurds in Turkey and Iran, the funeral of Princess Diana and famine in Ethiopia. One of the keen eyes of the 20th century, Boris Spremo was made a Member of the Order of Canada, 1998, for his work as a photojournalist. In this view, The Toronto Star photographer takes time out while on location in El Salvador. [Photo, courtesy Boris Spremo]

Post-World War II immigrants of the 1947-53 period came with a variety of occupations. Most were refugees victimized by an entrenched Communist regime and aggressive Croatian policies. Professionals, upon arriving in Canada, studied long hours for recertification in order to continue their professional careers. By the mid-60s, the reunification of divided families had become an important objective and many Serbs sponsored their families and new mates. This new wave of immigrants quickly achieved economic affluence and success. The sudden break up of Yugoslavia, 1991, and the subsequent civil wars, caused Canada's Serbian community to grow dramatically. More than 25,000 Serbs arrived in Canada with most educated professionally and fluent in English.

The 1996 Canadian census recorded 40,200 Serbs in Canada. Community spokespersons, in turn, argue that the community remains underrepresented in official records and believe that there are at least 250,000 Serbs in Canada, since many Serbs arriving in the '70s, '80s, and '90s identified themselves by their former citizenship, Yugoslav, and not by their ethnic heritage and/or roots.

Almost all Serbs belong to the Serbian Orthodox Church and as such have built a number of architecturally splendid churches in Canada since the first was built in Regina in 1916. Hamilton's St. Nicholas Cathedral, the first in Ontario, was built in 1917. Other parishes were also established in Toronto, Windsor, London, Kitchener,

Niagara Falls, Montreal, Vancouver, and other centres. Churches in Hamilton and Windsor and the Holy Transfiguration Monastery in Milton are enriched with magnificent frescoes on their interior walls.

In order to maintain and propagate their language and culture and to pursue recreational, political, athletic, and other interests, many community organizations were established, such as the Serb National Federation and Chetnik War Veterans.

Among them, music and folklore organizations in Canada perform Serbian national dances to appreciative audiences everywhere and host folklore festivals. The first was Toronto's Strazilovo. Toronto's Hajduk Veljko delighted visitors to the Montreal Olympics, 1976, and at *Expo 86* in Vancouver. The Hamilton group, Kolo, garnered cheers for performances at the 1978 Commonwealth Games, Edmonton, and at New York's Lincoln Centre. The Serbian Cultural Association 'Oplenac' dancers performed at *Expo 86* in Vancouver and at Ottawa's Canada Day 1997 festivities. Michael Pepa, who entered Canada at Pier 21, Halifax, 1953, as founding artistic director of the Toronto-based Les Amis Concerts since 1982, has promoted Canadian twentieth century repertoire performances. The first Serbian orchestra was formed by the Yoksimovich brothers in Hamilton. The major annual community event for Canadian Serbs remains Serbian Day in Canada which has been continuously celebrated in Niagara Falls since 1946 under the auspices of the Serbian National Shield Society of Canada.

In sports, Canadian Serbs have represented this country in international chess, swimming, fencing, and rowing competitions and they have professionally played Canadian football, soccer, basketball, golf, and hockey.

Since 1981, the Serbian Heritage Academy has organized many academic lectures and conferences, but its most ambitious undertaking has been the formation of the Ontario Centre for Newcomers in Ontario, a service which assists new immigrants to integrate into Canadian life. As tensions and civil wars erupted in former

Lilana Novakovich, President, Celebrity Events Network, one of Canada's largest and most successful booking agencies, was born, Toronto, to Nikola and Zivana, Serbian immigrants who arrived in Canada, 1952. She represents many celebrities including most of The Young and the Restless *cast, television personalities from Life Network, Home and Garden Television, and children's events (Dudley the Dragon and Noddy). A syndicated columnist for 16 of the 20 years she has been in business, her weekly columns appear in many Canadian dailies. She is a regular on Global Television. Formerly, Lilana was Advertising and Publicity Director, Prentice-Hall Publishing, responsible for many high-profile book launches. Lilana considers her involvement with the St. Sava Serbian Church community, Toronto, while in her teens and early twenties, as the foundation for much of her success today. In this view, left to right, Lilana participates in a Hospital for Sick Children Telethon (Toronto) with Dini Petty, Jeanne Cooper (Kay on Y&R) and Jess Walton (Jill on Y&R), an event Lilana participates in each year. [Photo, courtesy Lilana Novakovich]*

Triumphing Over Odds

Dragi Zekavica was born in a displaced persons' camp, West Germany, 1948. His parents, whose ethnic roots were Serbian from Yugoslavia, were victimized throughout most of the 1940s by two different forces: the Third Reich of Germany and the Communists who took control of Yugoslavia after World War II. Thus it was that Predrag and Branka Zekavica, with their new-born son, Dragi, forfeited any hopes of ever returning to their native homeland. Instead, as displaced persons, they landed at Pier 21, Halifax, October 8, 1949. When Dragi was only 16 years, he was tragically struck by a truck in his hometown of Niagara Falls, losing all sight in both eyes. Recuperating at the Toronto General Hospital, Dragi was able to complete his secondary education, thanks in large measure to Toronto teachers whose generous tutoring helped him graduate from high school and gain admission to university. When he graduated from Carleton University, he became the first visually-impaired student to graduate from there with an Honours Degree in Constitutional History and Political Science. After much resistance and objection, Dragi was admitted to the Faculty of Law, Queen's University. Upon graduation, he became the first blind student to complete all requirements for an LL.B. from that school. It is not well known that Dragi challenged authorities requiring visually impaired students to pass examinations that they couldn't write because of blindness. Thanks in large part to Dragi Zekavica, blind students in Ontario are no longer required to write L.S.A.T. entrance examinations. Since his admittance to the Ontario Bar, 1978, Dragi has been practising criminal law. He was the first Barrister without sight to appear before the Supreme Court of Canada. He is a Director, Canadian National Institute for the Blind. As a criminal lawyer, Dragi Zekavica has incorporated Street Link, an organization acting as liaison between prison inmates and families. He is affiliated with Toronto's Serbian Centre for Newcomers in Ontario (since 1993), to assist Serbs who, like his mother and father, fled war zones in Yugoslavia. For his contributions to the Serbian community, the Minister of Citizenship and Culture recently presented an Ontario Volunteer Service pin to Mr. Zekavica for his 20-year service to the Serbian radio program "Sumadija" on CHIN radio. In this view, Dragi Zekavica stands in front of his alma mater with his law degree diploma. [Photo, courtesy Dragi Zekavica]

Designing Automotive Components

Born, Krusevac, Serbia, 1941, Jim Bekcic graduated, University of Belgrade, Faculty of Mechanical Engineering, 1966. His dedication to Mechanical Engineering began with a stint in the Military where he published several books in Statics, Kinematics, and Material Tensile Properties. Professionally, his career started with industrial cable car design for various lead/zinc ore refineries. Immigrating to Canada, 1973, with his family, Jim worked on specialty equipment including a unique Sugar Cane Separation System for Barbados. In 1978 he founded Beckar Engineering Ltd., a consulting firm in Windsor for the automotive sector. Beckar Engineering designs machines for deburring, transferring and defining automotive components, as well as assembly lines for truck frames. Beckar Engineering made it possible for Jim to participate in the 1986 Canadian Trade Mission to Africa and network there with officials from Kenya, Zimbabwe, and Botswana. In 1988, Jim founded Arbec Tool & Machine Ltd., to manufacture all of the machines and systems that Beckar Engineering designs. Jim has successfully presented products of Arbec-Beckar Group to the Canadian, American, and Mexican markets, allowing Arbec-Beckar Group to participate in very challenging and successful projects throughout North America. Arbec-Beckar Group has received several awards for excellence from Ford Motor Company, in particular for pioneering work in core definning and head deflashing systems. [Photo, courtesy Jim Bekcic]

Entertaining with Elegance and Ease

Nikola Manojlovich's mother, born, Silbas, Serbia, came to Canada with her parents via the Orient Express and a Cunard Liner, landing, Pier 21, Halifax, before journeying onwards as a landed immigrant to Windsor, Ontario, 1938. Nik's father, also an ethnic Serb, was waiting in a displaced persons camp, West Germany, before being given papers, 1949, to immigrate to Canada. Because of the large Serbian community in Windsor, Nik's father settled in this southwestern Ontario city where he would meet his future wife, and together producing a son, Nikola, 1963. Nik was keenly involved in the Serbian community during his formative years. An active member of Windsor's Serbian choir and folkloric dance troupe, he also participated each Sunday as an altar boy at the Serbian Eastern Orthodox Church Gracania. After graduating, University of Western Ontario, Nik ventured into the hospitality industry, 1983, working as Catering Manager and Director of Banqueting and Convention Operations, Sheraton Hotels, Toronto. By 1995, Nik with a partner opened a company specializing in social and corporate event planning and continues to establish a niche in this service industry. Nik is also the host, writer, and co-creator of HGTV's "Savoire Faire", a successful series of programs, now three seasons long, leading viewers through the ageless art of entertaining with elegance and ease. "Savoire Faire" is a runaway TV hit show which is now shown in homes of 32 million American viewers. A fourth season promises to garnish a greater audience in that the show is syndicated and shown in Hong Kong and Singapore. In his spare time, moreover, Nik still finds time to conduct the St. Sava Serbian Orthodox Choir in Toronto. [Photo, courtesy Nik Manojlovich]

Niagara Falls Visionary

George Yerich, born, 1930, Niagara Falls, Ontario, is the son of Serbian parents who immigrated to Canada from their native land early in the 20th century. After graduating, University of Toronto, 1953, George continued with the development of his father's motel business which had begun in Niagara Falls during the Depression. Playing an early role in developing the Niagara tourist industry, George served as a charter member and president, Niagara Resort and Tourist Association. In 1968, George and Violet, his wife, acquired The Skylon Tower, a well-known Niagara Falls tourist attraction. Today, George has visionary plans to help make Niagara Falls a world-class destination. He plans on doing this by expanding the facilities of The Skylon Tower and the 22 acres surrounding it into an integrated complex showcasing two full-service hotels with 700 rooms in total; building over 400,000 square feet of cinema seating, including a state-of-the-art IMAX theatre; introducing international dining with theme restaurants and a variety of entertainment venues; and building parking facilities for 5,000 vehicles. George Yerich also owns Holiday Inn by the Falls, independent from the well-known American hotel chain of the same name in that the Yerich family business, founded in the 1930s, preceded the name of the American-owned business. The auditorium at Niagara College, Niagara-on-the-Lake, is named Yerich, reflecting the respect the family has generated in the community. The family, too, has generously donated to the Greater Niagara General Hospital and has contributed significantly to the two Serbian Orthodox Churches in the Niagara region. In this view, George Yerich stands next to two bells of the St. George Serbian Orthodox Church, Niagara Falls, which were donated by the Yerich family to commemorate his parents, Pane and Katherine Yerich, pioneer Serbs of Niagara Falls. [Photo, courtesy George Yerich]

Award-Winning Architect

Born, Belgrade, Yugoslavia, 1922, Michael Kopsa graduated, University of Belgrade, Faculty of Architecture, 1948. Immigrating to Canada, 1951, Mr. Kopsa settled in Toronto. Taking an active role in the Ontario Association of Architects, Mr. Kopsa designed the Yugoslav Pavilion at Montreal's Expo 67. During his early years, he took part in a number of architectural competitions. In 1957 he was one of six finalists in a design competition for the new Winnipeg City Hall. He won second prize for the Mendel Art Centre, Saskatoon, and an honourable mention for Charlottetown's Fathers of Confederation Centre. He was one of four finalists in the competition for the Royal Canadian Air Force Memorial, Trenton, Ontario. For the design of the new Brantford City Hall, 1964, he won first prize. One of his largest projects was designing the entire university campus in Jehda, Saudi Arabia. His latest work, now under construction, is the Serbian Orthodox Church, Mississauga, designed in the Byzantine tradition.
[Photo, courtesy, Michael Kopsa]

Stellar Sixteen Years in NHL

Peter Zezel is proud of his Serbian heritage. His father, who came to Canada, 1948, lost his own father at age 11, survived the ravages of World War II, and crossed the Atlantic, landing on the soil of a brand new country at 18 years. Peter's father, at first worked on a farm, then various lumber camps. After learning a trade, he then started his own business. Marrying a Canadian girl, Peter Sr. settled down and helped raise a family. Young Peter started playing hockey at 5 years. He also inherited his love for soccer from his father. In the under-21 category, Peter Jr. represented Canada on the Junior Canadian National Soccer Team. Peter's hockey career began, 1983, when he was drafted by the Philadelphia Flyers. During his 16 years as a centre in the National Hockey League, Peter also played for St. Louis Blues, Washington Capitals, Dallas Stars, New Jersey Devils, Vancouver Canucks, and Toronto Maple Leafs, scoring overall 608 points, including 219 goals. An immigrant's son who was taught early the value of the work ethic, Peter lived out a dream that most Canadian boys only dream about. [Photo, courtesy Peter Zezel]

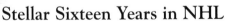

Yugoslavia in 1991 a wide cross-section of groups organized street demonstrations which helped the community remain strong in the face of negative stereotyping. The newest of these organizations is the Centre for Peace in the Balkans. The Serbian Brothers' Help, formed in the 1950s, has been especially active, along with several other humanitarian groups, in sending aid overseas. The Association of Serbian Women has been represented at UN women's conferences via membership in a Canadian NGO. "Radio Sumadija and Radio Ravna Gora", broadcast on CHIN-Radio, have both been instrumental in keeping the Serbian community informed over the past 30 years.

Many Serbs continue to contribute to Canada in a variety of ways. The late Nikola Budimir, a Windsor businessman, was honoured when a branch of the Windsor Public Library was named after him. Nikola Pasic, grandson of Serbian Prime Minister Nikola Pasic and a founder of the Serbian Heritage Academy, has delivered papers at numerous conferences conducted by Canadian learned societies. Today, Rad Simovic is the first Serbian manager of one of the largest thermoelectric generating stations in Canada. Author Dan Mrkich, who joined the Department of External Affairs, 1982, is Trade Commissioner for Poland, Hungary, Czech Republic, and Slovak Republic. Mila Mulroney, nee Pivnicki, wife of former Prime Minister Brian Mulroney, is the daughter of Dr. Dimitrije Pivnicki, a Montreal psychiatrist. Olga B. Markovich, daughter of Bozidar Markovich, is the first

Stanislava Markovich, born, Krusevac, Serbia, 1919, has the distinction of founding, 1987, the Serbian Heritage Museum in Windsor which promotes the history and the culture of Serbs both in their ancestral land and in Canada, the first Serbian museum of its kind in North America. Stanislava had a most successful career as a municipal librarian, working 22 years for the Windsor Public Library. Before she retired, she was the Library's Assistant Director, 1967-79. Recipient of the Ontario Senior of the Year Award, 1993, Stanislava, before immigrating to Canada, had been a teacher in Kraljevo, Serbia, 1939-50. Married, 1939, her husband, Vukasin, an officer in the Royal Yugoslav Air Force, was taken prisoner by the Germans during World War II. After the hostilities, he immigrated to Canada, leaving Stanislava and their son behind the iron curtain. Eventually settling in Windsor, Stanislava rejoined him by escaping from Yugoslavia, 1950, bringing with her their 10-year old son, Bozidar. Soon another son, Slobodan, was born. Both sons are now grown, one an urban geographer, while the other is an economist. In this view, Stanislava sits at her desk in the Windsor Public Library, circa, 1975. [Photo, courtesy, Stanislava Markovich]

Canadian Serbian journalist and a long-time magazine editor with Southam News. Jasna Stefanovic is the first Canadian Serb nominated for a Gemini (1998). Bora Dragasevich was the first Serb appointed by Prime Minister Pierre Trudeau to the Canadian Consultative Council on Multiculturalism and was one of the co-founders of the Canadian Ethnocultural Council. Paul Pavlovich became the first Toronto school administrator with Serbian roots. Vida Radovanovic, author and publisher, is the founder of *Coffee Culture Magazine*. Lolita Davidovich from London is a successful film actress in the U.S. The list of doctors, lawyers, engineers, and other professionals goes on.

The evolving presence and positive contribution of Canadians of Serbian origin have greatly enriched the physical and cultural development of Canada, and they will continue to do so into the new millennium. ⬇

Draga Dragasevich

AMONG THE THOUSANDS of U.E. Loyalists who arrived in British North America at the conclusion of the American Revolution were a large number of Dutch colonists who chose not to side with the revolutionary forces of George Washington. It was not until the late nineteenth century, however, that the Dutch once again migrated to Canada, this time as agricultural homesteaders flooding the prairie provinces where they assisted in opening up the "last best west." Still another wave of Dutch farmers came to Canada during the interwar period, mostly settling in rural Ontario where they helped secure the agricultural base of the province as trailblazers for market gardening and sugar beet and tobacco farming that would grow extensively in the following decades. During this time Dutch farmers significantly contributed to the development of the Holland Marsh, north of Toronto, into one of the largest and most productive vegetable-growing centres in Canada.

The postwar fifties and sixties witnessed a great surge in the growth of Dutch immigration to Canada. The Second World War saw Canada forge an important bond with The Netherlands when it became a safe haven for Crown Princess Juliana of The Netherlands and her family and when Canadian soldiers played a pivotal role in the liberation of The Netherlands from Nazi occupation. After the war, Canada looked with great favour upon The Netherlands, ready to welcome the immigration of thousands of Dutch nationals – war brides of Canadian servicemen and a badly needed agricultural work force. By the mid-1950s, the Canadian government saw fit to issue a clarion call for Dutch skilled industrial workers, technicians, business people, and professionals.

According to the 1996 census, 916,215 Canadians of Dutch origin lived in Canada. Ontario was home to nearly half of the Dutch Canadians. Only 18,665 were residents of Quebec. British Columbia topped the list in the West with 176,235, followed by Alberta with 136,835, Manitoba with 51,595, and Saskatchewan with 35,305. In the Maritimes, 41,475 lived in Nova Scotia and 14,650 in New Brunswick. Among cities, Toronto was the leading settlement area with 44,040, followed by Vancouver with 33,095. Other main centres of Dutch

from the
Netherlands

Gratitude of a Thunder Bay Dutchman

Born in the Netherlands, 1921, Derk Maat was an active player in the underground movement throughout World War II in western Europe for which he received a special commendation from U.S. President Dwight D. Eisenhower expressing "the gratitude and appreciation of the American people for [his] gallant service in assisting the escape of Allied soldiers from the enemy." After immigrating to Canada, 1949, he settled at Fort William (Thunder Bay), Ontario, and began working on a farm for 35 dollars a month, purchasing, 1951, a small nursery and greenhouse, the basis for a landscaping business he established, 1952. Grossing $3,500 in his first year of operations, by 1998, this same company grossed 15 million dollars. Four of his six children now run the family business, Wilco Landscape Contractors, with operations spreading westward from Thunder Bay to Vancouver. Active in public life for over 50 years, Derk Maat is a Rotarian, a Life Member of the John Howard Society, and a major figure in the Dutch Canadian Association. A faithful Progressive Conservative Party supporter for over 45 years, in this view, right, he is seen with former Prime Minister the Rt. Hon. Joe Clark, P.C. In gratitude to Canada and his adopted country's hospitality to Queen Juliana and other members of the Dutch Royal family who were given refuge in Canada during World War II, Derk Maat, with great support from the local Dutch Association, planned, designed, and constructed a windmill in Thunder Bay dedicated to "Prinses Margriet," who was born in Canada at the time the Netherlands was occupied. After it was built it was presented to the City of Thunder Bay, 1986. The windmill carries a plaque stating "May the relationship between the Netherlands and Canada be a symbol of friendship and peace to all." The windmill is recognized today by the City as the most outstanding monument at the International Friendship Gardens in that municipality. [Photo, courtesy Derk Maat]

A Man Called "Anne"

Anne De Boer, who had learned the retail trade from his father during the Second World War, was determined to forge for himself a business career in Canada after making a trip to The Canadian International Trade Fair, 1950. Although he didn't speak English, he knew that his future plans were in Canada. A man of resolve, born in Hoogeveen, The Netherlands, Anne immigrated, by boat, to Canada, 1951, with wife Tine, and five of their six children, settling in Toronto where business opportunities in post-war Toronto were the greatest. He first ventured into the wholesale business, but a retailer at heart, Anne changed course, opening several stores experimenting with retail products, including appliances, baby carriages, children's clothing, brooms and brushes, before discovering furniture was his real niche. Today, De Boer's furniture stores consist of a series of six retail stores specializing in upscale home furnishings catering to people who want to decorate their homes with furnishings reflecting classical yet upbeat styles. In this view, Chairman of the Board, Anne De Boer, "advertises" his former homeland and his furniture business in the Muskoka vacation region of Ontario. [Photo, courtesy John De Boer]

Tempting Taste Buds with Cookies

The Voortman cookie factory, located on the north side of the busy Queen Elizabeth Way curving along the western end of Lake Ontario between Toronto and the Niagara Peninsula, has been a highway landmark in Burlington, Ontario, since 1975. Two Dutch-born brothers, Harry and Bill Voortman, originally got their feet wet as bakers in a dreary room located at the back of a Hamilton house. A two-story building in Hamilton was their next stop. Then it was a 4,600 square foot building, on to an 18,000 square foot site and finally to their present site which has dramatically expanded over the years to 210,000 square feet. Born, Hellendoorn, in Overijssel, the two brothers immigrated to Canada, 1948, with their widowed father, John, and two other siblings, settling, first, at Picton, Ontario, but moving to Ontario's Golden Horseshoe, 1951, to establish their baking business. Brother Bill has since retired from the business and Harry and the Voortman clan have forged ahead with the family business, making 120 different cookie styles. Produced by nearly 500 employees and distributed throughout North America, Voortman cookies are a well-known household name with a distinct Dutch taste. In this recent view, Harry Voortman says his cookies are "so tempting." [Photo, courtesy Voortman Cookies, Ltd.]

First Dutchman to be Elected to Canada's House of Commons

The eldest of 13 children, John Oostrom was born in Utrecht, in the central Netherlands, and came to Canada with his entire family, 1952, settling on a farm near Kemptville in eastern Ontario. Moving to Toronto, 1955, John took late afternoon and early evening courses at the University of Toronto, proudly graduating from there, 1959, in political science. After working for nearly 20 years, primarily with Philip's Electronics, "the political bug hit him," 1979, and he won the nomination for Toronto's York South-Weston riding to run as a Progressive Conservative candidate in the upcoming federal election, 1980. Not only did he lose the election of 1979 but a subsequent election in 1980. Nevertheless, a true perseverer, he was victorious at the polls in the 1984 general election when Brian Mulroney's Progressive Conservative Party swept into Parliament. In this view, Parliament Hill, John Oostrom, right, the first Dutch Canadian elected to Canada's Parliament, and Charles J. Humber, Publisher, Heirloom Publishing Inc., meet with Prime Minister Brian Mulroney, 1986, to present him with an illustrious book celebrating Canada's rich history and heritage. [Photo, courtesy John Oostrom)

World Champion Figure Skater

Born in Amsterdam, the largest and capital city of the Netherlands, 1946, Petra Burka came to Canada with her parents, 1951. Ten years later, she was the Junior Canadian Skating Champion and the Senior Canadian Champion, 1964-66. World Champion Figure Skater, 1965, the first Canadian to win this event since Barbara Ann Scott's achievement, 1947, Petra represented Canada at the 1964 Olympics and won the Bronze Medal. She was also two times World's Bronze Medalist. For her accomplishments as one of the world's pre-eminent figure skaters, Petra was voted Canada's Outstanding Athlete of the Year, 1965, and Canada's Outstanding Female Athlete of the Year, 1964 and 1965. A frequent colour commentator on skating events for CBC and CBS for Olympic, World, European, and Canadian championships, Petra Burka brought great glory to Canada in the 1960s and, after her retirement, took on coaching responsibilities at the Toronto Cricket Skating and Curling Club, giving back to a country that helped to spotlight her on the world stage. [Photo, courtesy Petra Burka]

205

Woman on the Move

Annette Verschuren's parents arrived in Canada, 1951, migrating from their home in Oploo, in Noord Brabant, the Netherlands, for a dairy farm in Cape Breton, Nova Scotia. Shortly after her parents arrived, Annette was born, the middle of five children. At an early age this farmer's daughter knew she would eventually have to leave the beautiful rural surroundings of Cape Breton for opportunities awaiting her in a wide-open business world. Upon graduating Business Administration from St. Francis Xavier, Antigonish, Nova Scotia, Ms. Verschuren's destiny with business success came quickly. Gaining employment with senior level responsibilities at business establishments such as Canada Development Investment Corporation and Imasco, Annette grasped early that innovative retailing concepts in Canada were lagging. After acquiring the Canadian rights for Michaels, a series of arts and craft chain stores in the USA, she became founding President, 1993, and quickly became known as an executive with business smarts whose star was rising fast. Romanced by The Home Depot offering her a once- in-a-lifetime opportunity, she left Michaels of Canada, 1996, after much consideration, tc head up, as President, the fast expanding Canadian division of the largest American hardware retail chain. She has been honoured with the Women on the Move Award, 1994, the Canada 125 Medal, and an honorary Doctorate from Mount Saint Vincent University. [Photo, courtesy The Home Depot]

One of North America's Most Respected Freelance Photographers

Born, Veghel, North-Brabant, the Netherlands, John de Visser came to Canada as a keen-eyed, 22-year old immigrant and since his arrival, 1952, has become one of North America's most respected freelance photographers. His credits are seen in some of the world's best-known magazines: Life, Time, National Geographic, Sports Illustrated, Maclean's, Fortune, Esquire, Der Stern, Paris Match, and virtually every Canadian magazine of importance in print since the 1960s. Over the past 40 years, John has contributed to more than 100 books, including such internationally acclaimed Canadian publications as Canada, Year of the Land (NFB,1967) and Between Friends/Entre Amis NFB (1976). One of the founding photographers of the Image Bank of Canada (now Masterfile), John's awards are many including NFB Gold Medal for Still Photography, Kodak Medal for 1964 New York World's Fair, and Time-Life Achievement Award. He has published over 50 books in collaboration with many prominent Canadian personalities, including Morley Callaghan, Farley Mowat and Hugh MacLennan. [Photo, Ted Amsden, courtesy John de Visser]

settlement in Ontario include Ottawa-Hull, Hamilton, St. Catharines-Niagara, Kitchener, and Oshawa. Sizable numbers can also be found in Edmonton, Calgary, Winnipeg, Montreal, and Halifax. There are also settlers from the northern province of Friesland in the Netherlands. Frisians numbering approximately 10,000 in Canada today choose to identify themselves as a subset of the important Dutch-Canadian community.

Dutch women have played an indispensable role in the economic life of the *ethnie*. Single women who migrated to Canada for economic betterment filled the insatiable demand for domestic servants. These women profited from sharing the ethnicity of the dominant groups in the population. The Dutch were secure in the support of their ethnic community and in their high reputation among employers. The women could move in and out of domestic service in accordance with its advantages and disadvantages. Marriage and a family thrust new responsibilities on the women: shopping, cooking, laundering, knitting, sewing clothing, caring for the children, and, commonly, managing the family purse. Women also contributed to the family economy initially through work on the farm and in the fields. By the 1950s, Dutch women could be found on factory assembly lines. Education of their daughters in the 1960s and 1970s eased entry into the technical and professional worlds.

Postwar immigrants showed remarkable initiative in the creation of group clubs and community associations established to provide cultural, educational, social, and sports activities for the Dutch community. The community also dutifully supported dance and chorale groups, Dutch-language print and broadcast media. Additionally, the community spearheaded the establishment of co-operative savings and group lending institutions, providing

Netherlands-born Christina Mahler is Principal Cellist of a group of 18 permanent performers with Toronto-based Tafelmusik specializing in historical performance practice. The musical instrument she plays for baroque repertoire was made by a craftsman nearly 250 years ago. She studied cello with Anner Bylsma at the Royal Conservatory in the Hague, and performed extensively at fine musical centres in Europe before immigrating to Canada, 1981, to join Tafelmusik, Canada's leading orchestra on period instruments founded, 1979. Ms. Mahler also teaches cello at University of Toronto and at the Royal Conservatory of Music, Toronto. Together with Anner Bylsma, Christina is featured in a Tafelmusik recording of Vivaldi's Concertos for Strings (Sony Classical Vivarte, 1992). Spending an average 12 weeks a year on the road with annual tours in Europe at such concert halls as the Concertgebouw, Amsterdam; the Musicverein, Vienna; Symphony Hall, Birmingham; and Barbican Centre, London, Christina has travelled extensively as principal cellist with Tafelmusik in Belgium, Czech Republic, Denmark, France, Germany, Latvia, Lithuania, the Netherlands, Poland, Portugal, Slovenia, Spain, Switzerland, and the United Kingdom. Urjo Kareda, renowned Music Critic, The Globe and Mail, exclaimed, 1995, that Christina Mahler, as soloist performer, plays "with passion and persuasion...the concert's truest singing." [Photo, courtesy Christina Mahler]

From Pier 21 to Ontario Cabinet Minister

The Hon. Elizabeth Witmer, Minister of Health and Long-Term Care, Government of Ontario, was born, one of 13 children, to Josef and Sientje Gosar, Kethel, Holland, the Netherlands, 1946. Immigrating to Canada with her family, March 1951, and landing at Halifax, Nova Scotia, aboard The Volendam, the Gosar family migrated to Picture Butte, Alberta, before settling in Exeter, southwestern Ontario, January 1952. Upon graduating from University of Western Ontario, 1968, Elizabeth, now married, began teaching high school. In 1990, Elizabeth Witmer was elected Member of Parliament for Waterloo North, 1990. Past Chair, Waterloo Board of Education, 1985-89; former Minister of Labour in the first Mike Harris Government, 1995-97; recognized, 1987, Kitchener-Waterloo Woman of the Year; and a recipient of the Canada 125th Medal, Ms. Witmer was sworn in as Minister of Health, 1997, and reappointed Minister of Health and Long-Term Care, 1999. Married to Cameron and the proud mother of Scott and Sarah, Elizabeth Witmer is an influential member of the provincial legislature of Ontario in that she has been a Member of the Policy and Priorities Committee, since 1995, and was formerly Deputy Chair of the Progressive Conservative Caucus. In this view, the Hon. Elizabeth Witmer visits with pre-schoolers, Ottawa, 1998. [Photo, courtesy Ministry of Health, Government of Ontario]

Canada's First Premier of Dutch Ancestry

The Hon. William Vander Zalm, born in Noordwykerhout, Holland, immigrated to Canada, with his parents, 1947, attending high school in Abbotsford, British Columbia, before becoming president of his own nursery business, 1956. Entering politics a decade later as an alderman for the Surrey Municipal Council, Mr. Vander Zalm, before being elected to the B.C. Provincial Legislature, 1975, served as Mayor of Surrey, B.C., 1969-1975. In 1986, he was sworn in as the Social Credit Premier for British Columbia, and served in this capacity until 1991. In this view, Premier Vander Zalm is seen with Queen Beatrix of the Netherlands when she visited Victoria in 1988.

badly needed economic aid and capital in the face of unsympathetic Canadian bankers. Of note, the DUCA Community Credit Union of Toronto (founded 1954) began as an immigrant mutual benefit society only to become a multi-faceted computerized financial services organization offering its members retirement plans, foreign currency transactions, personal and mortgage loans.

Immigrants from the Netherlands have enriched the political, intellectual, athletic, and cultural life of Canada, often applying their religious values to their adopted country's cultural life. Dutch Canadians serve on municipal and provincial boards and in various capacities in both the provincial and federal governments. Educator Egerton Ryerson (Ryersoon), of Loyalist descent, solidly laid the foundations for Ontario's educational system while serving as Chief Superintendent of Education for the province from 1844 to 1876. The arts in Canada have been enhanced by painter Cornelius Krieghoff (1815-72) and a number of sculptors, designers, weavers, pottery makers, and craftspeople working in stained glass, mosaics, and jewellery. Canadians of Dutch origin have also brought honour to Canada as figure skaters – Petra Burka won the Canadian, North American, and Women's World Figure Skating Championships in 1965; as car racers – Eppie Wietzes earned considerable recognition for his awesome driving skills and unquenchable thirst for speed; and as filmmakers – Patricia Rozema's recent adaption of Jane Austen's *Mansfield Park* (1999) received international acclaim. ♥

To win the Stanley Cup is the dream of every budding hockey player. Not only did Joe Nieuwendyk fulfill that dream by playing for a team that won the Stanley Cup but the Dallas Stars' exciting forward also won the Conn Smythe Trophy as the Most Valuable Player of the 1999 Stanley Cup finals. Born, the Netherlands, the parents of Joe Nieuwendyk immigrated to Canada, 1959. Settling, Oshawa, Joe was born just before the family re-located to Whitby where he grew up playing two sports: lacrosse and hockey. He was just as proficient in both games, but Cornell University offered him a chance to play hockey at an Ivy League school and Joe leaped at the opportunity to lace up for the Red Machine. Chosen 27th overall in the 1985 NHL Draft, Joe left Cornell University to play professional hockey for the NHL's Calgary Flames. Voted Rookie of the Year, 1986, Joe has gone on to prove that an immigrant's son from the Netherlands is just as good as any player who ever laced up and skated on a frozen pond. [Photo, courtesy, Gordon Nieuwendyk]

THE FIRST-KNOWN KOREAN contact with Canada came in 1898 as the result of the Canadian mission movement and its pastoral, medical, and educational work in the historic Hamgyong Province and neighbouring China (Manchuria). There was little Korean immigration to Canada before the Second World War although a small group of students and Christian converts, deeply influenced by Canadian missionaries, had come during the prewar period. More substantial immigration began at the close of the Korean War. The increasing numbers of Koreans included northerners who, having fled headlong from political persecution and became refugees in the south, decided to seek a fresh start.

When Canada adopted a more liberal immigration policy in 1967 whereby applicants would be officially judged on the basis of individual skills and the needs of the Canadian economy, and formal diplomatic relations were established, Koreans began to arrive in even greater numbers. In the 1996 census of Canada, a total of 66,655 persons claimed Korean ancestry. A geographical breakdown of Korean settlement in Canada showed that the vast majority – 36,515 – reside in Ontario. Other provinces with a substantial Korean settlement

With a bedsheet spread over straw on the household floor in front of a warm stove in Siberia, the future Moderator, United Church of Canada, was born, 1924. His parents had earlier fled Japanese repression in their native Korea. Their forced journey took them, first, to Siberia, then to China, each time migrating to avoid repression, oppression, and political revolution. When communism clashed with young Sang Chul Lee's new-found Christian faith, he escaped alone into Korea, his ancestral home, and never saw or heard from his parents again…. Wishing to pursue studies in Theology, Sang Chul Lee enrolled in Hankak Theological Seminary, graduating, Bachelor of Divinity, 1951. Marrying, 1953, Shin-Jah, daughter of the principal, Hankak Seminary, Lee completed his Master of Theology, Hankak Seminary, 1956, then attended Ecumenical Graduate School, Switzerland, 1963, before graduating with a Master's Degree in Systematic Theology, 1964, Union College, Vancouver, British Columbia. Moving with his wife and three young daughters to Richmond, B.C., 1965, Rev. Lee took a post as Pastor, Steveston United Church, where he preached each Sunday in English, Korean, and Japanese. In 1969, Rev. Sang Chul Lee moved with his family to Toronto where for the next 20 years he served as Pastor of Toronto Korean United Church. When he was elected Moderator, United Church of Canada, 1988, he became the first visible minority to hold that post. At the time he became Chancellor, Victoria University, University of Toronto, 1992-98, the Very Rev. Dr. Sang Chul Lee had spent his life as an outspoken advocate for human rights, both in his adopted homeland of Canada and his ancestral homeland of Korea. One of the great honours bestowed upon the Very Rev. Dr. Lee was the Korean Overseas Compatriots Prize, 1999, in recognition of his inspiring leadership and significant contributions to Korean-Canadian society. In this view, Rev. Lee and his wife, Shin-Jah, enjoy a Cape Breton vacation during the mid-1990s. [Photo, courtesy the Very Rev. Dr. Sang Chul Lee]

Young Sup Chung, born, Inchon, Korea, 1937, went to Purdue University, Indiana, to pursue undergraduate work in the biological sciences. Upon graduating, B.Sc., 1960, he travelled to Giessan University, Giessan, Germany, graduating, Ph.D., 1964. While a Research Associate, Frankfurt University, Young Sup married In Hi, 1965, then travelled to California where he was a Post-Doctoral Fellow, Palo Alto Medical Research Foundation, 1966-69. Since 1970, Dr. Chung has been Professor, Department, Biological Sciences, University of Montreal. He has received numerous awards, including Order of Korea for Science, 1999, and Prix d'Excellence (Government of Quebec), 1993. Author/co-author of over 140 scientific articles, Dr. Chung was made Chevalier, Ordre National de Québec, 1993, and Chevalier, St-Sépulcre de Jérusalem, 1996. He also received the National Merit Services award from the President of Korea, 1992. The father of piano virtuoso, Lucille, and Rex, a financier, Young Sup Chung, on four separate occasions, has been visiting professor at the world-renowned Pasteur Institute, France, 1980, '87, '91, '94. [Photo, courtesy Dr. Young Sup Chung]

Sandra Oh's father, Joon Soo, and mother, Young Nam, were married in Seoul, Korea, before moving to the United States to attend university. Upon completing their education in Michigan, the Oh family then moved to Toronto, 1967, where, as graduate students, University of Toronto, Joon Soo studied Economics and Young Nam specialized in Biochemistry. Upon completing their education, the Oh family then moved to the Ottawa suburb of Nepean. From there, Joon Soo worked as an Economist with the Federal Government while Young Nam worked at the University of Ottawa. Sandra, born, Nepean, 1971, upon graduating from high school, enrolled at the National Theatre School of Canada, Montreal, and following her training there as an actress, became recognized almost immediately as a film star, winning, 1994, FIPA d'Or, Cannes, France, for her lead role in Runaway: The Diary of Evelyn Lau. The next year, she won a Genie – Canada's version of the Oscar – as best actress for her lead role in the film, Double Happiness. For her performance in Last Night, played at the Cannes Film Festival, 1998, she won the coveted Prix de la Jeuness. In the middle of shooting her third season in the HBO Television comedy series, Arli$$, Sandra won the best actress award for her portrayal of Rita Woo, a quirky, oddly sexy, obsessive-compulsive with somewhat exaggerated human problems. According to Larry Tazuma, Associate Editor, KOREAM, Sandra stands out as one of the few Asian actors, "good enough to stand up to the likes of Hollywood's leading talents." In 1999, Sandra won the Theatre World Award for Outstanding New York Debut for her role in Stop Kiss. [Photo, courtesy John Oh]

Dr. Hak-Yoon (Hal) Ju, Professor, Plant Science, Nova Scotia Agricultural College, Truro, Nova Scotia, was born, 1938, Kyunggi Do, Korea, immigrating to Canada, 1969, after graduating, first, in Agronomy, Seoul National University, and specializing in agricultural science, Malling Agricultural College, Denmark. Completing both his M.Sc. 1976, and Ph.D., 1980, MacDonald College, McGill University, Dr. Ju gained employment, 1981, with Department of Plant Science, Nova Scotia Agricultural College, where, since 1989, he has been Full Professor. Although he teaches traditional agricultural courses such as Small Fruit Crops, Tree Fruit Crops, and Plant Physiology, his specialty research areas, especially in ginseng and mushroom cultivation, frost survival of lowbush blueberry, the study of cold apple hardiness, the investigation of weed control , and the research into stevia (natural sweetner) production have made his work an international success story. In this recent view, Dr. Hal Ju addresses a gathering of agriculturalists exploring and learning new opportunities for specialty crops. [Photo, courtesy Dr. Hak-Yoon Ju]

Esteemed
Microbiologist

Genie Award Winner

Exploring New
Opportunities
for Specialty Crops

Psychiatric Epidemiologist Investigating Stress

Although occupation of Korea came to an end, 1945, the 40-year repressive Japanese regime was soon replaced by Russian occupation and communism, the spoils of World War II. This is the troubling scenario into which Samuel Noh was born, 1946. Fleeing North Korean oppression, the young Noh family migrated to South Korea, settling, Seoul, 1947. Soon the Korean War (1950-53) engulfed their lives. Young Sam lost his father, an uncle, and grandfather in this nasty conflict. He, his mother and sister, for 10 years, lived in a refugee camp-like postwar housing project. When it was time for young Sam and his sister to pursue serious education, the fatherless family returned to Seoul where Sam enrolled at Yonsei University. Deciding that a better life awaited him across the ocean, Sam Noh and his beautiful bride, Kyoung, immigrated to Canada, 1971, settling in Toronto. With $600 to his name, a pregnant wife, and no knowledge of English – only high hopes – the only job he could find was working as a labourer at a disposable diaper factory. He also learned that immigrants carried with them loads of stress and had difficulty coping, in general, with a new environment. Recognizing the need to get more education, between 1973-84 Sam attended University of Western Ontario, receiving his B.A. and M.A. degrees in Sociology and his Ph.D. in Epidemiology and Biostatistics. A Senior Research Scientist, Clarke Institute of Psychiatry, Toronto, and Associate

Professor, Institute of Medical Science, University of Toronto, Dr. Noh, today, is widely recognized and cited for his significant contribution to stress processes through which experienced stress is manifested as either physical or mental pathology. This formula has made Dr. Noh one of a select few who are professionally called psychiatric epidemiologists in that they investigate, among other matters, the prevalent societal stresses which are at the root of many psychological ailments associated with immigrant populations. Recipient, New Pioneers Award, Science and Technology, 1997, and currently President, Korean Canadian University Professors' Forum, Dr. Samuel Noh, left, is recognized worldwide for his scholarly investigations into the mental health of immigrants and is in demand as a keynote speaker at international conferences, forums, symposia, and seminars. [Photo, courtesy Dr. Samuel Noh]

Exploring Causes of Social Change

Yunshik Chang, right, born, Inchon, Korea, 1936, came to Canada shortly after graduating from Seoul National University, 1958, to study Sociology at the University of British Columbia. His interest in the cause of social change, particularly in a democratic society, peasant life, folk religion, and Korea, in general, prompted Mr. Chang to pursue post-graduate studies at Princeton. Upon completion of his Ph.D. at that Ivy League school, Dr. Chang returned to University of British Columbia where he was made Full Professor, 1980, and Director, Centre for Korean Research, Institute of Asian Research, since 1993. His numerous publications examine the currents of social idealism, rising commercialism, the role of women, religion, and print media in Korea, all suggesting that Professor Chang has created bridges of communication, making it possible to understand better an emerging Korea and its role as an important state on the Pacific rim. [Photo, courtesy Professor Yunshik Chang]

include British Columbia (19,610), Alberta (4,845), and Quebec (3,925). The largest single Korean concentration was found in Toronto where 15,525 reside; other large centres for Korean settlement included Vancouver (9,055) and Montreal (3,510). Of note, Canada's first permanent settler was Tae-yon Hwang, a mission-sponsored medical intern who came to Alberta in 1948. He chose to remain after his training, settling in Blind River, Ontario. Hwang was soon to be joined by other students and by independent immigrants.

Most of Canada's Koreans are highly skilled workers or professionals including physicians, nurses, dentists, accountants, college and university teachers. A number of Koreans have also climbed into the entrepreneurial class, opening small businesses – specialty food shops, restaurants, travel agencies, and real estate offices. The community has also dominated the managerial ranks of convenience chain stores. In Toronto, a Korean small business neighbourhood emerged on Bloor Street West between Bathurst Street and Dovercourt Road. Restaurants, bakeries, gift shops, grocery stores, and travel agencies dot the street. Toronto also became home to three Korean banks – Korea Exchange, Chohung, and Hanil – credit unions, and industrial branch plants of several major Korean industrial corporations including Hyundae and Samsung.

Koreans who have come to Canada have shown remarkable initiative in creating community associations. These associations in Toronto, Winnipeg, Edmonton, and Vancouver organize and administer a wide range of social and cultural activities. They also do the community proud by participating in numerous multicultural and municipal events including Caravan in Toronto,

Hyung-sun Paik began playing the violin, age six. Born, Seoul, Korea, after graduating from Ewha Girls' High School, she furthered her studies in violin under the guidance and tutelage of Professor Eudice Shapiro, University of Southern California, 1971. Before graduating magna cum laude, *U.S.C., Bachelor of Music in Violin Performance, 1975, Hyung-sun performed solo with U.S.C. Symphony Orchestra. Upon graduation, she returned to Korea to play Tchaikovsky Violin Concerto with Seoul National Symphony Orchestra. The next year, 1976, she studied violin with the world-renowned musician/teacher, Josef Gingold, Professor of Violin, Indiana University. Upon graduating with a Master's Degree in Music, with Distinction, Indiana University, 1979, she performed Sibelius Violin Concerto, Seoul Philharmonic Orchestra, Seoul. During the 1979-80 season, she played first violin with the Los Angeles Chamber Orchestra, then moved permanently to Toronto, Ontario, with Thomas Min, her Korean-born husband, who, upon receiving his Ph.D., Nuclear Engineering, UCLA, gained employment with Atomic Energy of Canada. Hyung-sun, since 1980, has played first violin with the Toronto Symphony Orchestra and has played many musical recitals, both solo and chamber, in many cities in the United States, Korea, and Canada. After the untimely death of her husband, 1996, Hyung-sun Paik was left to raise two children, Paul and Elise.*
[Photo, courtesy Hyung-sun Paik]

Rising Musical Star

Born, Montreal, 1973, to Korean parents who immigrated to Canada, 1969, Lucille Chung, age 10, made her piano debut, 1983, with the Montreal Symphony. When 15 years, she was invited to tour Asia as featured soloist with the Montreal Symphony Orchestra, 1989. That same year, she won first prize at the Stravinsky International Piano Competition. Before she was 25 years old, she had performed with the Philadelphia Orchestra, the Moscow Virtuosi, the Seoul Philharmonic, the Budapest and Weimar orchestras in addition to performing throughout Canada. Her recital credits include the Kennedy Center, Washington; New York's Carnegie Hall; Amsterdam's Concertgebouw; Great Hall of Franz Liszt Academy, Budapest; Salzburg's Mozarteum; Montreal's Place des Arts; and Toronto's Ford Centre for the Performing Arts. A graduate of the Curtis Institute of Music, B.M., Philadelphia, and the Juilliard School, M.M., New York, she has studied, among others, under Seymour Lipkin, Karl-Heinz Kämmerling, and Lazar Berman. Lucille Chung has brought as much fame to Canada for her accomplishments as a pianist as to herself. Canada has recognized her achievements as a musician with the 1999 Canada Council for the Arts Virginia Parker Prize. Currently, Fellow, Accademia Pianistica (Incontri col Maestro) di Imola with Giovanni Valentini, Lucille Chung has been called by The Washington Post an "exciting" and "gutsy" pianist. Perhaps the Budapest Sun said it best when she performed in Hungary: she's "a rising musical star." [Photo, courtesy Lucille Chung]

Medical Team Committed to Healthcare

Drs. Sang Whay Kooh and Rak Hay Kim were born and raised in Korea. They met as medical students, Yon-Se University, Seoul, marrying shortly after obtaining their M.D. degrees. After post-graduate training in the United States, 1956, they, with three small children, came to Toronto, 1962, and completed their medical specialties, pediatrics for Dr. Kooh, and internal medicine for Dr. Kim. After obtaining his Ph.D., Physiology, University of Toronto, Dr. Kooh has continued to work as a Research Scientist and Pediatrician, Hospital for Sick Children, since 1962. He is an internationally recognized expert in children's bone disease, specializing in rickets and Vitamin D

deficiency. In the Korean-Canadian community he is better known for his leadership role in many community organizations. At one time or another, he has served as President or Chairman of Korean-Canadian Cultural Association of Metropolitan Toronto; Toronto-Korean Educational Society; Korean YMCA; Korean Scholarship Foundation; Korean Heritage Award Society; Korean United Way Committee; and Korean Mental Health Centre. He was a member of the Race-Relations Committee and Heritage Language Advisory Committee, Toronto Board of Education and has been a Director of Korea Exchange Bank of Canada since its inception. He also edited Koreans in Ontario, 1986. For outstanding Service to Canada's Korean Community, Dr. Kooh received a commendation from the President of the Republic of Korea, 1991. Dr. Kooh also received, 1973, a citation for Community Service from the Minister of Foreign Affairs, ROK. Dr. Kim has been in private practice in internal medicine in Toronto since the late 1960s. She will be remembered by many Koreans as the first Korean-speaking doctor looking after patients who could not speak English. Her practice over the past 10 years has been exclusively endocrinology, treating diseases such as diabetes and thyroid conditions. This 1998 photograph of Dr. Kooh, right, and Dr. Kim, left, includes three of their six grandchildren. [Photo, courtesy Dr. Sang Whay Kooh]

The parents of Juliette Kang immigrated to Canada from Seoul, Korea, 1968, sojourning in Montreal, Winnipeg, Calgary, and Vancouver before settling, Edmonton, 1974, one year before Juliette was born. Beginning violin studies at age four, by the time she was nine years old, she was studying with Dr. Jascha Brodsky of the Curtis Institute of Music, from where she graduated, B.Mus., 1991, one of the youngest ever to earn a bachelor's degree from that famous Institute. At the Juilliard School, from where she gained her Master's Degree in Music, 1993, Juliette studied under Dorothy Delay, Hyo Kang, and Robert Mann. She came to international attention as Gold Medal Winner in both the Yehudi Menuhin and Indianapolis International Competitions, 1994. An especially accomplished recitalist, Ms. Kang's invitations include New York's Carnegie Hall, the Kennedy Center, Tokyo's Suntory Hall, Boston's Gardner Museum, and New York's 92nd Street Y. At age 7, she made her concerto debut in Montreal, and when only 13 years, she became the youngest ever to win the Young Concert Artist International Auditions (1989). She was featured, 1994, in New York Times Magazine as one of the people under age 30 "the most likely to change the culture." Her mastery of the violin assures her a prominent place on the international stage as one of the world's great talents whose performances, night after night, blend opulent tones, heroic flair, and romantic sensibility with sheer virtuosity and astonishing technical aplomb. [Photo, courtesy Matthew Sprizzo, New York]

Folklorama in Winnipeg, Heritage Festival in Edmonton, and Asian Music Festival in Vancouver. Korean Canadians also organize around common or shared interests and kinship ties. School and college graduates come together in support of one another through membership in alumni associations.

The first Korean newspaper published in Canada was *Hanka Jubo* (*Korean Canada Times*) which, started in Toronto, was published from 1971 to 1972. Present-day newspapers include the *Korea Times Daily*, *New Korea Times*, and the *Korea News*. Korean-language broadcasting can also be found in the larger settlement areas.

Korean community life revolves heavily around its religious institutions. The most important are largely Protestant (United and Presbyterian) although there are also a substantial number of Roman Catholics and Buddhists – devoted adherents of Korea's dominant religion. The Protestant Church, having been very influential in Korea, no doubt influenced the choice of religion for the many who came to Canada. The first Korean Protestant church in Canada was established in Montreal in 1965 in the basement of that city's First Presbyterian Church. It should come as no surprise, therefore, that the community soon produced a Protestant religious leader, the Reverend Sang Chul Lee, minister of the Toronto Korean United Church, who was named Moderator of the United Church of Canada in 1988.

Koreans are a people rich in folk traditions. Their contributions to Canada range from dance, music, and Tae Kwon Do (the art of self-defence) to the many glories of Korean cuisine. Canadian broadcasting has been enriched by the presence of second-generation Korean-Canadian journalists based in Toronto including Ben Chin of City TV, Monica Kim of the Global Television Network, and Son-Kyung Yi of the Canadian Broadcasting Corporation. ♉

TURKISH IMMIGRATION TO CANADA began as early as 1880, but the first substantial group arrived between the years 1956 and 1975. Initially, Turkish migration was the result of uncertainty about political and economic conditions in Turkey and the unease about the world economy in general. The new migration included a large number of professionals. Turkish engineers and doctors, immigrant arrivals of the late 1950s and early 1960s, remain an important and influential segment of the Turkish-Canadian community.

After 1960, skilled workers arrived in large numbers. From 1980 on, however, unskilled villagers immigrated because of dire economic need and because Canada had liberal immigration policies and a reputation as one of

Burhan Türkşen, born, 1937, Turgutlu, Manisa, located some 40 kilometers from Izmir, Turkey, on the Aegean Sea, received his primary and junior high school education at Cumhuriyet Ilkokulu and Turgutlu Ortaokulu. He continued his education in 'Izmir Atatürk Lisesi' for his senior high school, then attended the University of Pittsburgh, USA, 1957-64, receiving his B.Sc. and M.S. degrees in Industrial Engineering, as an honour student, before returning to Turkey for his military service, 1964. After being "honourably discharged" from military service, 1966, as First Lieutenant, Burhan returned to University of Pittsburgh to complete his Ph.D. in Operation Research and Systems Management Engineering. In 1969, he was made Assistant Professor, University of Toronto, 1970, and full Professor, University of Toronto, 1983. A specialist in Computational Intelligence, Knowledge Acquisitions, and Information Technology, Dr. Türkşen's understanding of computing technologies and artificial intelligence have taken him around the world to conferences, symposia, and seminars where he is in demand as an expert on Fuzzy Sets, Systems, and Logic. Author or co-author of some 120 papers since 1993, Dr. Türkşen still finds time to volunteer in several Turkish Canadian Associations, including Türkish Culture and Folklore Society of Canada and the Council of the Federation of Turkish Canadian Associations. In this view, Dr. Türkşen, far right, poses with friends at a memorial meeting for Turkey's founding president Kemal Atatürk, whose picture is in the middle. Other honourable members of Turkish Culture and Folklore Society at the ceremony are, from right continued, Mrs. Esin Akalin, Mr. Nüzhet Önen, Mr. Osman Baran, and Mrs. Sevim Önen. [Photo, courtesy Professor Burhan Türkşen]

from **Turkey**

Businessman Motivated by Volunteerism

Born, Sakarya, Turkey, Turan Kalfa, following high school graduation, 1978, took to the high seas and worked as a navigator on
merchant ships before docking permanently in Canada, 1984,
retiring as a sea merchant. Over the next several years, Turan
experimented in the restaurant business, worked in a bagel
factory, was in the security guard business, and even tried
direct marketing before settling, Montreal, 1985. While studying
computer programming, Concordia University, Turan started a
truck pick-up and delivery service business. By 1994, age 33,
he had created one of the largest independent moving van lines
in Canada. At the same time, he successfully went into the
business of self-storage. By 1996, Turan had sold his moving
company to concentrate on developing his thriving self-storage
business. Today, Turan has six major locations in Quebec,
with 15 partners. The company is now the largest of its kind
in Quebec, proving the old adage that one has to make and lose
money three times before making it big time.... Volunteerism is
a big part of Turan's life. Proud father of two young daughters,
Turan is a Past President, Friendly Anatolians of Montreal
Association, 1993-94. He was President, Kentspor Soccer
Team, 1995. He was also Vice-President, Turquebec Culture
and Friendship Association, 1996-97. As Member, Political
Action Committee, Turan, since 1996, has been part of a team
successfully lobbying for the creation of a Peace Garden, year
2000, for the Botanical Gardens of Montreal. The Founder,
Turkish Info Line, which has translated all Canadian immi-
gration laws into Turkish, Turan Kalfa financially backed the
posting of this translation on the Internet, making such material
available to help newcomers from Turkey adjust to Canadian
society. Winner, Best Business Award for Self-Storage in
Montreal, 1996-1999, and prominent candidate for Canadian
Turkish Businessman Award, 2000, Turan is destined to
become the first Turkish Canadian to run successfully for politics.
In this view, Turan, left, greets Jean Charest, centre, Leader,
Liberal Party of Quebec, at a Liberal Fundraising Gala,
Montreal, 1998. Also present is Yusuf Kutlu, President,
Turquebec, and Fadima Houda-Pepin, Liberal M.P. [Photo,
courtesy Yusuf Kutlu]

Newer Canadians Toasting Canada

When Bora and Selmin Hinçer and their two young sons left
Turkey for Canada, 1979, the temperature was plus 20
degrees Celsius. When they arrived in Toronto, the same day,
the temperature was minus 20 degrees Celsius! They looked
at each other and exclaimed "Will we survive here?" Selmin
Hinçer brought with her, to Canada, a B.Sc., Pharmacy. To
work in Canada as a pharmacist, however, she had to complete
further courses and pass exams. Upon completing these
requirements, 1983, she began practicing her profession in
Kingston, Ontario, where today she is the head pharmacist
at one of the largest drug store chains in Kingston. Bora came
to Canada with a B.A., Sociology, from the University of
Istanbul, where he was a marketing manager for a large
company. Upon entering Canada, he quickly established his
own business, Ephesus Trading, specializing in import, wholesale, and retail marketing. Active in Turkish-Canadian relations, Bora is Past President, Federation of Canadian Turkish
Associations. As a freelance writer, his articles and editorials
have been published in many urban centres. A member, as
well, of The Kingston Whig-Standard Community Editorial
Board, one article that Bora wrote celebrating Canada Day
(1997), states that "the country I was born in is like my
mother, and I love her. Canada, on the other hand, is like my
wife. I love her too. I had no control over being the son of my
mother, but I have chosen my wife and will spend all of my life
with her. Canada, my darling, Happy Birthday." Bora and
Selmin's sons are both successful Turkish Canadians. Ilkim
studied Law, and currently works as a corporate lawyer for a
large downtown Toronto law firm. Ilke, who won most public
speaking contests he ever entered, currently is working for a
national newspaper in Toronto and is an aspiring actor. In
this view, left to right, Ilke, Bora, Selmin, and Ilkim Hinçer of
Kingston, Ontario, toast their good fortune and family health.
[Photo, courtesy Bora Hinçer]

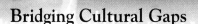

Making Daily Deposits into Emotional Bank Accounts

Born, Izmir, Turkey, Faruk Bahadirli came to Canada from his native land in the late 1960s as a computer programmer. Having graduated in Electrical Engineering, Middle East Technical University, Ankara, Turkey, Faruk has worked over a 30-year period in Canada as a Programmer Analyst/Systems Analyst in Information Systems for a number of Canadian companies, including Snap-on-Tools, Jacuzzi, Dr. Scholl's-Maybelline, Canadian Standards Association, and Business Depot where he currently is employed as a Programmer Analyst. Active in a wide cross-section of community service, Faruk has been Board Member, Rexdale (Etobicoke) Home Day Care, for seven consecutive years. He is a volunteer producer and announcer for the Turkish Radio called Radyo Merhaba, AM 1540/FM 101.3, Toronto. He is also a Founding Board Member of the Turkish Canadian Community Centre. To keep relationships healthy and to maintain high levels of trust, Faruk Bahadirli makes "daily deposits" into the "emotional bank accounts" of others. In this view, Faruk is addressing the largest-ever gathering of Turkish Canadians (1,500) who assembled at Seneca College, 1998, to celebrate the 75th anniversary of the Founding of the Republic of Turkey, 1923. A picture of the Republic's first President, Kemal Atatürk, is propped up against the flag of Turkey. [Photo, courtesy Faruk Bahadirli]

Bridging Cultural Gaps

Born, Bozdoğan (Aydin), Turkey, 1936, Özer Aksoy studied, Işiklar Military College, Bursa, and Air Force Academy, Izmir, graduating as Lieutenant in the Turkish Air Force before coming to Canada, 1957, to be trained by the RCAF as a NATO jet pilot. After a two-year training period, stationed at such places as Crumlin and Centralia, southwestern Ontario, Moose Jaw, Saskatchewan, and Gimli, Manitoba, Lt. Aksoy returned to Turkey where, because of an accident, he was grounded as a pilot. In 1960-61, Özer began working for the U.S. Army Corps of Engineers, Çiğli guided missile base, Izmir, Turkey, as interpreter/translator for the U.S. Army Commanding and Administration Officers. In 1962 he immigrated to Canada, settling, London, Ontario, where he gained employment over the next 35 years with 3M Canada, retiring, 1996, as Senior Engineering Purchasing Agent for 3M plants across Canada. Özer established, 1962, the first Turkish Canadian Association at London, Ontario. He was instrumental in assisting Turkish communities throughout Ontario to organize social and cultural groups. In so doing, he became a leader within Canada's Turkish community, helping to found the Federation of the Turkish Canadian Association of which Mr. Aksoy was President, 1992-93. Not content with assisting Turkish immigrants adjusting to their new life in Canada, Özer Aksoy was a key founder of the World Turkish Congress in New York, 1992. Located at United Nations Plaza, Özer, today, serves as Vice President of the Congress. Married to Ann McKeon of London, Ontario, Özer is the proud father of Tulin, a public relations manager, and Davut Erol, a physician. In this view, Turkish Canadian Özer Aksoy, Vice President, World Turkish Congress, leads a parade section down Madison Avenue, New York, 1998. [Photo, courtesy Özer Aksoy]

Specializing in Women's Issues

Aysan Sev'er came to Canada, 1971, from Istanbul, Turkey, her birthplace. Settling in Windsor, Ontario, she attended University of Windsor, completing her undergraduate degree, Psychology, 1978, and an M.A., Sociology, 1980, before attending York University where she graduated with a Ph.D., Sociology, 1983. Since 1984, Professor Sev'er has taught at the University of Toronto as a much respected member of the Sociology Department where she specializes in Issues Pertaining to Women. The author of three books and many scholarly articles in various professional journals, Professor Sev'er was recognized, 1998, with the Annual Persons' Day Award honouring the Supreme Court's Decision, 1929, legally making all Canadian women, persons. [Photo, courtesy Professor Aysan Sev'er]

Creating a Family Business

Züleyha Erkoc, born, Tokat, Turkey, a village near Ankara, was educated in nursing at Hacettepe Hemşire Kolej. In 1973, as a practicing nurse in Istanbul, Züleyha met her future husband, Mehmet Tukoff, who had fled communism in his native Bulgaria. After their betrothal, he immigrated to Canada, settling in Toronto, where he worked for two years before sending for his wife-to-be. One month to the day after Züleyha's arrival, June 6, 1975, Züleyha and Mehmet were married, choosing to settle in fast growing Mississauga, Ontario, where they have established a thriving business cleaning offices of commercial establishments. Together, they have raised two daughters and a son: Özlem, centre, a graduate of Humber College, İnci, left, an undergraduate at Queen's University, and Tolga, right, still in high school but anticipating a career in law. Together, the family sponsors a Guatemalan boy, through World Vision. [Photo, courtesy Züleyha Tukoff]

Establishing a Private Family Practice

After Dr. Erdoğan Sartekin, a Turkish-born orthopaedic surgeon, immigrated to Canada, 1967, his wife, Saadet, left their native homeland to join her husband, bringing with her their son, Kemal, born, Eskişehir, Turkey, 1960. Living, first, at Hull, Quebec, then Montreal, young Kemal attended Marianopolis College before enrolling, University of Ottawa, graduating B.Sc., Biology, 1982. Returning to Turkey the same year, Kemal entered Istanbul University's Faculty of Medicine. After graduating M.D. and returning to Canada, Kemal successfully passed Canada's Medical Evaluation Exam and was accepted, 1990, to a rotating internship and family practice residency, St. Paul's Hospital, Vancouver, British Columbia. With dual citizenship, Dr. Kemal Sartekin enrolled in the Medical Officer Training Program, Canadian Armed Forces. Upon completing his residency training, 1993, he served, at Captain's rank, three years at Valcartier Military Hospital as Chief Surgical Resident. Upon completing his contract with the Military, Dr. Sartekin returned to British Columbia, 1995, where he worked out of various medical clinics until 1997, at which time he opened his own Private Family Practice, Port Coquitlam, British Columbia. In this view, Dr. Sartekin stands in his Port Coquitlam Clinic, 1999. [Photo, courtesy Dr. Kemal Sartekin]

Halit Anginer, born, Manisa, Turkey, 1944, earned both his B.A. and M.S. (1969) degrees from Middle East Technical University, Ankara, then took on a number of professional positions in his homeland including a position with the Turkish government, before immigrating to Canada, 1992. Settling in Toronto, Halit and his family established a business selling apparel and unisex clothing in downtown Toronto's fashion strip near Bloor and Yonge Streets. Married to the girl he met at university, Halit, together with Gönül, has raised three children, each of whom helps in building the family business which now includes three retail outlets. In this view, Halit and Gönül stand in front of their Greater Toronto Area home and are pleased that they chose Canada as their new homeland.
[Photo, courtesy Halit Anginer]

the world's major immigrant and refugee-receiving nations. More recently, Turks have been both political and economic refugees fleeing unrest and oppression in neighbouring states, in particular, from terrorist activities carried out by some Kurdish groups that have claimed up to 30,000 lives in eastern Turkey since the early 1980s, and from ethnic cleansing policies carried out by Greek-Cypriots, until 1974, against Turkish Cypriots, all of which has contributed to global Turkish immigration.

It is difficult to assess the size of the Turkish-Canadian community today because the available data rely on self-identification by Turks who came to Canada from a variety of regions including neighbouring countries once part of the Ottoman Empire that still have a Turkish-speaking minority. The 1996 Canadian census data indicate that there are 18,130 Turks (single and multiple responses) in Canada. There are 9,770 Turks in Ontario, and 4,805 in Quebec. Most have settled in Montreal and Toronto with lesser concentrations in Calgary, Edmonton, London, Ottawa, and Vancouver. Small clusters of Turks from Cyprus and Bulgaria can also be found in Ontario in Hamilton, Kitchener, and Mississauga.

There are Turkish Canadians in all sectors of the Canadian economy. Engineers, doctors, computer scientists, teachers, and administrators – both male and female – make up the group's professional ranks. Skilled and semi-skilled industrial workers and taxi drivers constitute the largest segment of the group's employed workers. Also, in an effort to provide for the needs of their families, a number of Turkish women and homemakers have entered the job market as cleaners, factory workers, and seamstresses.

Most Turks have retained a high degree of emotional and intellectual attachment to their homeland and are proud of its recent educational and economic achievements. For Turkish immigrants, even the highly educated, most of whom have adapted successfully to Canadian life, dual citizenship is the norm.

The Turkish community has its own radio program, *Radyo Merhaba*, broadcasting in Turkish every Saturday from *CHIN AM 1540/FM 101.3* since 1995. *Radyo Merhaba*, operated by volunteers with Turkish background, serves as a cultural umbrella for the Turkish community in Canada and it is presently the largest Turkish organization in Canada with over 1,000 members. *Radyo Merhaba* also has a quarterly newsletter being mailed to over 10,000 private addresses, as well as a monthly newsletter for its members. It prepares the community's *Business Directory* each year and maintains a webpage (*www.radyomerhaba.com*) to help the newcomers and to enhance intra-community relations.

The chief form of entertainment for the members of the ethnocommunity is getting together with friends and sharing a meal. Relations within the social and economic subgroups common in Turkey continue to prevail within the immigrant community and often dictate the style and activities of the communal organizations. Probably

Dr. Aydin and Mrs. Tülin Yurtçu were both born in the Republic of Turkey. When they immigrated to Canada, they settled in Montreal where they have lived since 1961. Tülin, a seamstress and a graduate of Ankara Institute of Art, has worked, in Canada, in various fashion stores, as a couturière. Dr. Yurtçu, today, is a retired psychiatrist who graduated from the Medical Faculty, Ankara University. He received his psychiatric residency training as a staff psychiatrist and clinical director in both rural and urban hospitals, until his recent retirement. Both Dr. and Mrs. Yurtçu have been directly involved in various community activities with fellow Turkish Canadians. Both have served as President, Turkish Cultural Association of Canada, which was founded in Montreal, 1963. They are also co-founders of the Turquebec Cultural and Friendship Association since its inception, 1993. They continue to promote a better knowledge and understanding of their native country through cultural exhibitions, conferences, media coverage, TV appearances, and debates. Ambassadors of goodwill, the Yurtçu family focuses on the significance of multi-ethnic diversity, mutual tolerance, harmony, and reconciliation among peoples who make up Canada. Very important to the Yurtçu family is living in a society where peaceful co-existence, tolerance, and mutual respect are national hallmarks. [Photo, courtesy Dr. Aydin Yurtçu]

the earliest Turkish community organization in Canada was the Canadian Turkish Friendship Association that a group of Turkish immigrants from Germany founded in Toronto in 1964. Active until the early 1980s, its headquarters on Bathurst Street in Toronto served as a welcome centre for newly arrived immigrants and as a community centre for the Turkish community of Ontario. As the community grew and diversified, other organizations appeared. In 1976, the Turkish Culture and Folklore Society of Canada, created in Toronto, eventually eclipsed the Canadian Turkish Friendship Association. Since its inception, the aims of the Turkish Culture and Folklore Society have been to promote, through its culture, a knowledge and understanding of Turkey. The organization has been involved at various times with folk dancing, exhibitions, and theatre.

Since the late 1970s, various community organizations have emerged to represent various subgroups and regional Turkish settlement areas. These include the Association of Canadian Turkish Cypriots (Mississauga), the Canadian Association for Solidarity of Turks from Bulgaria (Mississauga), the Turkish Canadian Association of London, and the Canadian Turkish Cultural Association of Hamilton. The Montreal community is currently represented by the Association Culturelle Turque du Québec.

The various associations across Canada are now represented by an umbrella organization, the Federation of Canadian Turkish Associations founded in Toronto in the mid-1980s with its executive director and offices located in Toronto. The Federation serves as a referral and communications centre for Turkish news, local events, business and governmental inquiries, and intergroup relations.

Prior to 1980 Turkish-Canadian immigrants came primarily from urban and secular backgrounds. While religious practice was not altogether neglected by the early settlers, for they hailed from a country where well over 90 percent of the inhabitants are Muslim, it remained a matter of individual conscience. Later arrivals have brought with them their commitment to regular and significant participation in religious life, especially through the mosque. This may include Friday prayers, but it generally means communal participation in the various festivals of the Muslim calendar. Presently there are four Turkish mosques in Toronto.

The Turkish community's political participation in Canada has been limited. The small size of the community, its limited financial resources, its political fragmentation, the urban and rural experiences within and outside Turkey, and the lack of experience in the organizational and cultural life of Canada have all been contributing factors. Lately, especially through Turkish Radio's efforts, these are all in change. ⚜

Görsev Pristine

THE INITIAL contacts between Spain and Canada go back several centuries to the voyages of the Basque fishermen and whalers to Canada's Atlantic coastal waters and to Spanish exploration of the Pacific coast. Basques, along with Portuguese, Bretons, and others reached the plentiful fishing grounds on the Grand Banks in the sixteenth century. Port aux Basques on the south shore of Newfoundland and Ile aux Basques in the St. Lawrence River help to mark this distant chapter in Canadian history. On the west coast of Canada and the United States during the eighteenth century, the Spaniards were the first to discover and chart many of the straits, islands, and gulfs for a distance of four thousand miles. That explains why Spanish names such as Galiano Island, the Strait of Juan de Fuca, Navarez Bay, and Mount Bodega abound in the British Columbia coastal area. After this early age of exploration ended, there was little contact between Spain and Canada until very recent times.

After immigrating to Canada, 1982, Esmeralda Enrique formed Esmeralda Enrique Dance Company which, today, has emerged as one of Canada's acclaimed dance ensembles. Based in Toronto, the saluted dance company fuses contemporary music and modern dance forms with the essentials of true flamenco, earning critical and popular recognition at yearly festivals. The Globe and Mail's Deirdre Kelly exclaimed in a recent interview that the Spanish Dance Company's "virtuostic display is wild and dizzying ... like a spontaneous show of unbridled energy in the back rooms of a late-night cafe." [Photo, courtesy Esmeralda Enrique]

from Spain

Specialist in Spanish Medieval Literature

As Visiting Professor, University of British Columbia, 1968-69, Arsenio Pacheco, born Barcelona, Spain, 1932, and his wife, Mercedes, decided they wanted to stay in Canada, "a truly new and open world where it would be possible for our two sons to learn and develop the personal and social values that we wished them to have." The opportunity came a year later when UBC engaged Professor Pacheco to teach Spanish Language and Literature, with emphasis on his particular field of research, Catalan Medieval Literature and the Spanish l7th Century Novel. He became a Full Professor of Spanish, UBC, 1980, a post held until his retirement, 1997. A University of Barcelona M.A. graduate, l954, Ph.D., 1958, Professor Pacheco took a position as Assistant Lecturer, University of Glasgow, for two years before becoming Lecturer, University of St. Andrews, Scotland, 1959, a position he held until moving to British Columbia, 1968. Professor Pacheco became involved in the Canadian Association of Hispanists, serving as President, 1978-81. He was a member, Executive Committee, Canadian Federation for the Humanities, 1984-85, was elected Member, Royal Society of Canada, 1981, and received the UBC Issac Walton Killam Memorial Senior Fellowship for research on the evolution of Catalan and Spanish narrative literature. "It is a long and ambitious project that still keeps me busy today," he concedes. [Photo, courtesy Professor Arsenio Pacheco]

Highly Respected Law Professor

Law Professor Ernest Caparros has written some 50 chapters in collective works as well as six books dealing with Canadian Law since immigrating to Canada from his native Spain, 1967. Born, Malaga, 1938, he earned an LL.L, University of Zaragoza, 1961, and spent two years, University of Navarra, obtaining his doctorate degree, J.C.D., before immigrating to Canada where he became Editor, Les Cahiers de Droit, 1965-70, and Assistant Professor, Law, Laval University, 1966. He was Adjunct Professor, 1967; Associate Professor, 1970, Professor 1975, and twice served as Vice-Dean, 1971-74 and 1976-77. At Laval he also earned an LL.D., 1973. In 1981, he moved to University of Ottawa as Professor of Law, and Professor, School of Graduate Studies and Research. Besides teaching, Ottawa University, Professor Caparros has been a visiting Professor at such universities as Toronto, Dalhousie, Calgary, McGill, and Sherbrooke, in Canada, and has served in similar roles in Mexico, Columbia, Spain, Italy, Chile, Argentina, and France. He was a consultant on Canada's Law Reform Commission, 1971-75, Civil Code Revision Office, 1975-76, and Legal Council, Assembly of Bishops, Quebec, 1982-90. Since 1986, he has also been a Judge, Ecclesiastical Appeal Tribunal of Canada, and served as Canadian President, Canon Law Societies of America, 1991-93. Honours and distinctions include Fellowship, Royal Society of Canada, 1985; Knight of Magistral Grace, Order of Malta, 1992, and Associate Member, International Academy of Comparative Law, 1994. [Photo, courtesy Professor Ernest Caparros]

Combining Religion, Law, and Language into a Distinguished Career

Born, Madrid, 1922, and brought up in Cuba after the death of his father, Leslie Dewart, right (whose surname Duarte, was anglicized), began to study medicine at the University of Havana but gave it up, 1942, the year he came to Canada to join the RCAF. As a pilot, he served in bomber-reconnaissance operations over the North Atlantic remaining in the RCAF until 1947 when he enrolled at University of Toronto, and discovered he loved Philosophy and wanted to teach. On earning an M.A, 1952, and Ph.D., 1954, he taught, University of Detroit, 1954-56, returning to the University of Toronto where he taught in the Department of Philosophy, St. Michael's College, until 1968. That year the University of Toronto established a Department of Religious Studies and Dr. Dewart spent the next 20 years there before his retirement. He also gained an LL.B., 1979, and was called to the Bar of Ontario, 1981. Author of five books between 1963 and 1989, and more than 30 papers on religion, language and law, Professor Dewart became a Senior Research Associate, Faculty of Divinity, Trinity College, 1995, and is at present writing his sixth book on the philosophy of the mind. Here he enjoys a reunion with his oldest Canadian friend, Dr. Ralph Yorsh, of Vancouver, British Columbia, a pioneer in the use of hypnosis in dentistry. [Photo, courtesy Professor Leslie Dewart]

The first mass emigration of Spaniards began in the mid-1950s. The reasons were rural overpopulation, the collapse of certain occupations, industrial expansion, the quest for adventure, and the simple desire to better one's lot in life. There was even a political edge to Spanish emigration as people sought to escape the rigours of the Franco regime. Under an arrangement between the Spanish and Canadian governments, a group of 150 farm families immigrated to Canada in 1957. Another project worked out by the two governments involved bringing a group of young, single Spanish women from different walks of life to work for a year as domestic servants.

José Evangelista, born, Valencia, Spain, 1943, was enrolled, University of Valencia, while simultaneously attending Valencia Conservatory of Music, studying harmony and composition with Vincent Asencio. He received a Diploma in Composition, 1967, the same year he graduated L.Sc. (Physics), University of Valencia. Later work in computers led him to immigrate to Canada, 1969, working as a systems analyst, Ministry of Transport, Ottawa. Settling in Montreal, 1970, he abandoned his scientific career and initiated composition studies with André Prévost and Bruce Mather. Graduating, McGill University, M.Music, 1973, and D.Music, 1984, José Evangelista, since 1979, has been Professor of Music, Université de Montréal. Dr. Evangelista pursues an artistic path exploring ways to make music based exclusively on melody. He has developed heterophonic writing, both for instruments and orchestra, in which the

melodic line generates echoes of itself and creates an illusion of polyphony. At the Université de Montréal, 1979, Professor Evangelista created the Balinese Gamelan Workshop, 1987. Composer-in-residence, Montreal Symphony Orchestra, 1993-95, José Evangelista has received numerous commissions, among others, from Groupe vocal de France, Itineraire (Paris), the Kronas Quartet (San Francisco), the SMCQ and the CBC. His music has been performed in Canada, the U.S., Europe, Asia, and Australia by groups such as EnsembleModern (Frankfurt), Nieuw Ensemble (Amsterdam), Music Projects (London), and the Nouvel Ensemble Moderne (Montreal). [Photo, courtesy Professor José Evangelista]

Dr. David Munoz, right, born, Jerez, Spain, 1953, in addition to graduating M.D., 1976, Universidad de Navarra, Spain, earned a M.Sc., Pathology, 1984, Queen's University, Kingston, Ontario. As medical student, physician, and professor, Dr. Munoz has served in various capacities, either as resident, fellow, or teacher, at Universidad de Navarra, Queen's University, University of Vermont, University of Saskatoon, and University of Western Ontario where, currently, he is Professor, Pathology and Clinical Neurological Sciences, since 1998. Author of some 100 peer-reviewed articles in scientific journals, Dr. Munoz is a recognized authority in the study of Alzheimer's disease, specializing in the role of aluminum, education, and infarcts. Additonal areas of interest as a medical researcher include the characterization of alternative causes of dementia and the role cerebral Chromogranin A has in health and disease. Currently on leave of absence and researching in Spain, Dr. David Munoz's research in the new millennium is destined to have positive impact in the world of science. [Photo, courtesy Dr. David Munoz]

The group included nurses, teachers, a cartoonist, a bookbinder, several stenographers, dressmakers, saleswomen, and even a mechanic who made truck parts for a Spanish firm. Many of the Spanish immigrants who came in the mid-1960s were skilled workers who gravitated to Canada's urban centres. They were, for example, technicians, welders, electricians, and mechanics. A small but growing number of white-collar workers and professionals also came during this period.

Official figures on the number of Spaniards in Canada vary. According to the 1996 Canadian census, 204,360 reported that they were entirely (72,470) or partly (131,895) Spanish by ethnic origin. But only 11,240 people indicated that their country of birth was Spain. Clearly, many people from Spanish-speaking countries other than Spain declared themselves to be Spanish by ethnic origin.

Spaniards are heavily concentrated in six major cities: Toronto, Montreal, Winnipeg, Vancouver, Calgary, and Edmonton. In these large urban centres they tend to cluster in identifiable areas with people from other Latin countries such as Portuguese, Italians, and Latin Americans. In Montreal, Spaniards reside in a number of suburbs including Greenfield Park, Laval, Brossard, and Dollard-des-Ormeaux. As well, a cluster of Spanish ethnocommunity organizations and storefronts on the Rue Saint-Laurent have served to increase the group's visibility in that city. In Toronto, a group of Spanish stores and a medical centre run by Spanish-Canadian physicians have helped to form a relatively small and compact business district on College Street.

Educational, cultural, leisure, and welfare organizations such as the Association Cervantes-Camoens of Quebec City (1945) and the Club Hispano of Toronto (1964) have also been founded in the larger Spanish communities. These clubs serve many of the immigrants' needs of body and soul. Activities include soccer and bowling, theatre, music, art classes and recitals, lectures, and the celebration of important Spanish holidays. The bold and innovative decision by the Hispano-Canadian Association of Kitchener-Waterloo (Ontario) to build two housing developments to assist lower-income Spaniards and non-Spaniards helps to remind us that tending to the needs of one's own does not hinder or impede the desire and ability to contribute to the larger community. 🍁

After receiving two M.A. degrees, one in Spanish, the other in French, University of Chicago, 1964, Professor Teresa Kirschner spent one year lecturing at Indiana University before beginning her teaching career at Simon Fraser University, 1967. On obtaining a Ph.D., Spanish Literature, University of Chicago, 1973, she was made Assistant Professor, Simon Fraser, 1974, Associate, 1981-90, and Full Professor, 1990, until her retirement, 1998, when she became Professor Emeritus. Besides winning the Excellence in Teaching Award, 1988, Dr. Kirschner, born Barcelona, Spain, 1936, has thrice won the Canadian Association of Hispanists Award, once for the book El protagonista colectivo en Fuenteovejuna de Lope de Vega, *1979. She has also written or edited numerous books and articles on both 17th and 20th century Spanish and Latin American literature, and has been active in numerous organizations, including serving terms as President, Canadian Association of Hispanists; Chair, Department of Spanish and Latin American Studies, Simon Fraser University; Member, Social Sciences and Humanities Research Council of Canada; and Member, Executive Committee, Canadian Commission for UNESCO. Another of her interests is the Vancouver Spanish Pacific Historical Society, founded to promote through lectures, symposia, and exhibits, interest in Spanish activities along the northwest coast during the 18th century. At her retirement party, 1998, Dr. Kirschner received a contemporary totem pole, a reminder of the towering contribution she has made to Canadian Hispanic Studies.* [Photo, courtesy Professor Teresa Kirschner]

Born, Kagawa, Japan, 1944, Warabé Aska is one of those gifted artists who also writes and has found way to combine his enormous talents through the publishing of children's books. A graduate of Takamatsu Technological School, Kagawa, Japan, where he developed and enhanced his artistic skills Warabé immigrated to Canada, 1979, becoming a landed immigrant, 1982. Since 1972, Warabé has supervised solo exhibitions of his art in Japan, England, the U.S., and Canada. His art has also achieved global acclaim in exhibitions staged in the Czech Republic, Germany, Spain, Italy, France, Yugoslavia, and Iran. His works have appeared on UNICEF greetings cards, are part of the permanen collections of Japan's Imperial Family, Hino Motors Co., Japan, Corporation of the City of Toronto, as well as in many prominent private collections. In 1993, he created the Official Event Poster for Earth Day. In 1993, as well, Warabé won first prize for his art at the Tehran International Biennale of Illustrations, Iran. Winner many awards and cited in n less than eight Who's Whos Warabé's latest book, Lulie the Iceberg, published in Japan, the U.S., the U.K., Canada, Italy, Taiwan, and Korea, in collaboration with UNICEF and Her Imperial Highness Princess Takamad who wrote the text, was offi cially launched at New Yor Carnegie Hall, October 25, 1998, generating much pub lic awareness about the nee to preserve our fragile Ocea Planet. The paintings of Warabé Aska are often dra matic, symbolic, and morali tic such as the striking oil, 1991, on this page, entitled Mother Goose vs. Cloud's Eagle which reveals a Cana goose defending her goslings (Canada's ten provinces) fr a menacing eagle. In the photograph above, Warabé Aska, left, stands with Her Imperial Highness, Princes Takamado of Japan, at the Carnegie Hall launch of Lu the Iceberg. [Photo, courte Warabé Aska]

from Japan

ETWEEN 1877 and 1928, Japanese men moved elsewhere to help overcome the dire consequences of life in poor, overcrowded fishing and farming villages. During this period, Canada was essential for the survival of Japanese family life.

Manzo Nagano, the first-recorded Japanese immigrant at the turn of the century, was soon followed by many young, single, or unaccompanied married men with a desire either to survive or to improve family and village life at home in Japan and eventually return there.

British Columbia was the first choice for the pioneer migrants or *Issei*. There, they worked in the mines, logging camps, or sawmills, on the railway, or as fishermen in coastal villages.

As Japanese men progressed from sojourning to settling, they began sending for brides, wives, and families. They then entered the entrepreneurial ranks as merchants and shopkeepers in Vancouver and Victoria. Others used their farming experience in the fertile Fraser and Okanagan valleys; then, as they gained skill and knowledge, they moved into the front ranks of the fruit and market garden industries.

The early immigrants, including veterans of the Canadian Army from the First World War and their Canadian-born children (the *Nisei*), were victims of racism. Subject to massive discriminatory legislation, they were denied the right to vote. All Japanese Canadians were also excluded from employment in certain industrial sectors, trades, and most professions including the civil service and teaching.

Thomas K. Shoyama was born, 1916, Kamloops, British Columbia, to parents who, as refugees, immigrated to Victoria, British Columbia, near the turn of the last century, from Kyushu, Japan. A distinguished Canadian who has lived an exemplary life of public service, Mr. Shoyama graduated in Economics (B.A.) and Commerce (B.Com.), University of British Columbia, 1938. Between 1939-1945, Mr. Shoyama worked as the editor and publisher of a civil rights weekly newspaper in Vancouver and Kaslo, B.C. Briefly serving in the Intelligence Corps of the Canadian Army following the end of World War II, Mr. Thomas Shoyama gained employment between 1946-64 with the Saskatchewan government, first as a government research economist and later as an economic advisor to the Premier of the Province. By 1964, he had moved to Ottawa to join the Economic Council of Canada as a senior economist. Upon transferring to the Department of Finance, 1968, he served as Assistant Deputy Minister, 1968-74, in successive branches of the Department. By 1975, Mr. Shoyama had become Deputy Minister of Finance, retiring, 1979, to act as Special Advisor on the Constitution in the Privy Council Office. He was also elected Chairman, Atomic Energy of Canada Limited, the same year. Before retiring from the Government of Canada, 1980, Mr. Shoyama was recognized with the Outstanding Achievement Award of the Public Service of Canada. He then started a new career, age 64, by accepting a professorship at the University of Victoria, School of Public Administration and Centre for Pacific and Oriental Studies, positions he held until he was 76 years old. The year he retired from teaching, 1992, he was appointed by the Government of Japan to the Order of the Sacred Treasure, Gold and Silver Star. Elected Officer of the Order of Canada, 1978, Mr. Shoyama is the honoured recipient of the Vanier Medal, 1982, and holds honorary degrees from both the University of British Columbia and the University of Windsor. In this view, Thomas Shoyama, Deputy Minister, Finance, 1975-79, sits at his desk in Ottawa. [Photo, courtesy Thomas K. Shoyama]

A few months after Japan bombed Pearl Harbor on December 7, 1941, the Canadian government used the War Measures Act to strip all those of Japanese origin, including those who were Canadian nationals, of their civil rights and property and to order their removal from the West Coast. In 1942, over 20,000 Japanese Canadians were rounded up and shipped to internment camps in the interior of British Columbia or to sugar beet farms in Alberta

Because Raymond Moriyama, inset, was born to parents of Japanese origin, he and his family, along with thousands of other Japanese families, were removed for national security reasons from their home during World War II, processed through a temporary camp in Vancouver, and then held in isolation for the remainder of World War II. Some 20,000 Japanese Canadians were processed similarly and it was not until 1949 that they were re-enfranchised and could begin rebuilding their lives. Raymond Moriyama was no exception. Graduating in Architecture from both the University of Toronto and McGill University, Montreal, Raymond Moriyama has made giant steps in the world of architecture, generating an internationally respected reputation since he opened for business, 1958. Over the next 40 years his firm has created many award-winning projects such as the Japanese Canadian Cultural Centre, Toronto; Scarborough Civic Centre; Science North, Sudbury; Toronto Reference Library; Canadian Embassy, Tokyo; and, most recently, the Saudi Arabian National Museum, Riyadh. Recipient of eight honorary degrees and made an Officer, Order of Canada, 1985, Dr. Raymond Moriyama believes that "Architecture is a backdrop for worthwhile human activity." The Saudi Arabian National Museum, below left, the result of an International Design Competition won by Moriyama & Teshima Architects, was officially opened, January 22, 1999, by King Fahad to celebrate the 100th anniversary of the unification of Saudi Arabia. [Photos, courtesy Moriyama & Teshima Architects]

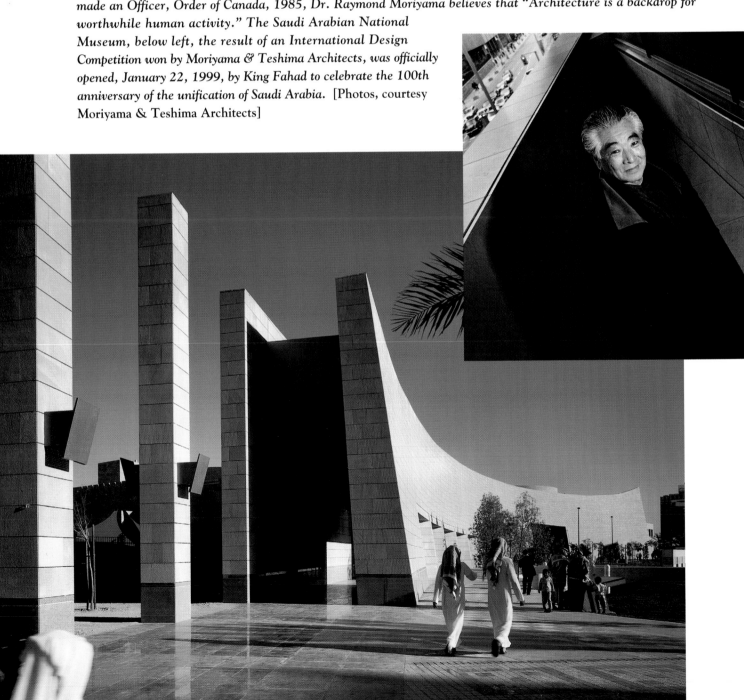

and Manitoba. After 1945, the Canadian government's repatriation efforts resulted in 4,000 "voluntarily" returning to Japan and the remainder choosing to relocate east of the Rocky Mountains. These Japanese moved to Ontario, Quebec, and the Prairie provinces. All wartime restrictions were lifted from Japanese Canadians only in 1949 when full civil rights, including freedom to live on the Pacific coast, were restored and the community was granted full voting rights.

As a result of the postwar dispersal, a large proportion of Japanese Canadians now live in Ontario. The 1996 census recorded a total of 77,130 Japanese Canadians (single and multiple responses). Some 33,245 live in British Columbia and 27,825 live in Ontario. Among the cities, Vancouver was the leading choice of settlement with 13,360, followed by Toronto with 10,030.

The immigrant generation from Japan has made an indelible mark upon Canada's resource-based and service industry sectors. Perhaps their greatest influence has been in the West coast fisheries and agriculture. Many of the techniques and much of the gear used in the fishing industry were introduced and developed by the *Issei*. Drawing upon a wealth of experience in fruit and market gardening, they helped to introduce better systems of farming in the agricultural districts around Mission, Haney, Kelowna, and Vernon, British Columbia.

Joy Nozomi Kogawa, born, 1935, Vancouver, British Columbia, faced discrimination during World War II when she and her parents and thousands of other Japanese Canadians were removed from their coastal area homes and forced into supervised isolation in the interior of British Columbia and elsewhere in Canada. Prior to the publication of her novel, Obasan, 1981, which covers her experience as a Japanese Canadian who lost her civil rights as the result of harsh government policy, Joy Kogawa was better known as a poet. Instrumental in influencing the Canadian government to make settlement, in 1988, with Japanese Canadians for their loss of liberty and property during World War II, Joy Kogawa has been the recipient of many awards, including the Canadian Authors' Association Book of the Year Award, 1982. A Member of the Order of Canada, this distinguished poet, novelist, and writer has received several Honorary Doctoral degrees including one, in 1999, from Knox College, University of Toronto, as shown in this photograph. [Photo, courtesy Joy Kogawa]

The second generation of Japanese Canadians (*Nisei*) and the third generation (*Sansei*) include many more professionally trained and educated people who have been able to enter a variety of administrative and managerial jobs and merge successfully with the Canadian community at large.

The most recent group of immigrants to Canada consists primarily of highly skilled and educated engineers and managers. They began to arrive after 1967 to work in the branch plants of many Japanese corporations and industries. Most settled in Toronto and Canada's other major urban centres.

Before the Second World War, in order to maintain the social cohesion of the group, Japanese Canadians formed a number of organizations, both religious and secular. These included language schools, credit unions, trade associations, friendship groups, prefectural or village district societies.

Canada's Mr. Judo

During World War II, because the Canadian government considered Japanese Canadians a security threat, Jim Kojima's fisherman father and other families of Japanese origin were removed from their homes at Steveston, British Columbia, and transferred to sugar beet farms in Alberta. It was at this time that Jim was born. Not until the 1950s did the Kojima family return to Steveston where a judo school (dojo) had been reopened and where Jim enrolled in judo classes. Although he received his black belt in judo, age 19, he never became a recognized international contender so he threw himself into administration and by 1957 was sitting with the Senior Judoka of British Columbia as the secretary treasurer of Judo, B.C. Over the last 40 years, Jim Kojima has served as President, Judo Canada, 1988-94, Chairman, 1993 World Judo Championships, Hamilton, Ontario, has received the Order of Canada, 1983, was the Fundraising Chairman for Judo/Kendo, the only Japanese-style judo hall anywhere in the world outside Japan, became the first Canadian-born citizen to receive an international licence to referee with the International Judo Union, and was awarded an honorary third degree black belt in Karate by the Mayor of Wakayama, Japan. Whether it is in Hawaii, at the Pan American Games, the Fukuoka Cup, Japan, at the Olympics (since 1976), Rio de Janeiro, Paris, Helsinki, Barcelona, Belgrade, Panama City, Seoul, London or elsewhere, Jim Kojima is an internationally celebrated Canadian who energetically has put Canada on the Judo map! [Photo, courtesy Judo Canada]

Pioneering Neuroscientist, Compassionate Physician, Esteemed Mentor

Dr. Juhn A. Wada has devoted his entire professional life to epilepsy as a clinician, scientist, and advocate. Born, Tokyo, Japan, 1924, Dr. Wada's father was a distinguished Professor of International Law, Hokkaido Imperial University, and his brother, Juro, Founding Chancellor, World Society of Cardio-Thoracic Surgeons, performed Japan's first heart transplant, 1968. A graduate, M.D., Hokkaido Imperial University, 1946, and a graduate, Doctor of Medical Science, 1951, Dr. Wada had spent time at the University of Minnesota and the Montreal Neurological Institute, McGill University, before being appointed to the Faculty of Neurological Research, University of British Columbia, 1956. From then until 1998, Dr. Wada spent his academic career, other than leaves of absence, at UBC. An Associate, Medical Research Council of Canada, 1966-94, Dr. Wada's main interest as a neurologist has been researching Human Brain Asymmetry and Neurobiology of Epilepsy. One of the recognized world leaders in these areas of research, his major contributions have been the development of the Wada Test, a carotid amytal test for cerebral speech lateralization and short memory assessment. He is also renowned for the discovery of human brain asymmetry re language as genetically dictated as a prenatal rather than a postnatal (speech) development, and for the identification of anterior callosal section as a rational, safe surgical treatment modality for difficult generalized epilepsy. Recipient of many internationally renowned awards, Dr. Wada, author of 11 books and over 300 papers in referred journals, was awarded the Wilder Penfield Gold Medal, 1988, the Order of Canada (Officer), 1992, the Order of Japan (Sacred Treasure, Gold and Silver Star), 1995, and, in 1998, the William G. Lennox Award from the American Epilepsy Society, for his many years as a pioneering neuroscientist who, as a compassionate physician, was an esteemed mentor for generations of students and fellows. [Photo, courtesy Dr. Juhn Wada]

Born, Kobe, an important city-port in pre-war Japan, Dr. Fumiko Ikawa-Smith remembers growing up in a cosmopolitan community, attending kindergarten and elementary school with Indian and Chinese children whose parents were merchants and diplomats. Her father was an historian. Her mother's mission was making sure her children got the very best of the very best in education. After graduating, Tsuda College, B.A., 1953, Fumiko chose to study Anthropology at the graduate school level. She attended Radcliffe College, Cambridge, Massachusetts, graduating, M.A., 1958. Marrying, 1959, Canadian-born Philip Smith, they moved to Canada, eventually settling, Montreal, where Fumiko's teaching career at McGill University began, 1967. Upon completing her Ph.D., Harvard University, Dr. Ikawa-Smith was made Associate Professor, McGill University, 1974, and Full Professor, 1979. Recently serving as Associate Vice Principal, Academic Affairs, McGill University, 1991-96, Professor Ikawa-Smith has served, over the years, as Director, Centre for Asian Studies, Chair, Department of East Asian Languages and Literature, and Chair, Department of Anthropology. As a scholar whose works are internationally respected and well known, Dr. Ikawa-Smith, President, Japanese Studies Association of Canada, 1999-2000, is a leading authority in the origins of the Japanese, the prehistory of Pacific Northeast Asia, and studies on the archeology of Japan's past, having contributed to many acclaimed encyclopedias, dictionaries, and prominent journals specializing in archeology and anthropology. In this view, she is addressing the National Research Institute of Cultural Properties of Korea, Seoul, 1992. [Photo, courtesy Professor Fumiko Ikawa-Smith]

Leading Authority on Prehistory of Pacific Northeast Asia

Building Cultural Bridges

Shortly after graduating, Waseda University, where he majored in languages, Tokyo-born Toyoshi Yoshihara joined Sumitomo Corporation, a huge and very successful Japanese conglomerate. Sent to Canada, 1970, Yoshi's purpose was to introduce Japanese heavy equipment to an untapped Canadian market. At the time, Japan was famous for transistor radios, toys, and textiles but Japanese heavy equipment was, as yet, undiscovered in Canada. Originally, Yoshi's stay was meant to be temporary, probably two or three years. But, he fell in love with Canada and insisted on staying, becoming, 1972, Founder of Komatsu Canada Ltd. Within 10 years, Yoshi created a nationwide marketing network turning Komatsu Canada into the second largest Canadian supplier of bulldozers, excavators, loaders, graders, and mining trucks. Now retired as Chairman, Komatsu, Yoshi spends much of his new-found time translating Canadian plays into Japanese productions. Over the years, as a passionate hobby, he has, to date, translated some 30 Canadian plays into Japanese, one play, in particular, drawing about 200,000 theatre-goers in Japan to a production run exceeding five years. Toyoshi Yoshihara believes he is building cultural bridges between his native land and his adopted homeland. In this view, Yoshi stands on a heavy duty piece of equipment, the type he successfully marketed across Canada over a 30-year period. [Photo, courtesy Toyoshi Yoshihara]

The Honourable David Hiroshi Tsubouchi's parents immigrated to Canada from their native Japan long before the outbreak of World War II. Because of their Japanese heritage, during the war they were quarantined in a northwestern Ontario camp with other Japanese Canadians. David was born, Toronto, several years after his parents were reintroduced into Canadian society following end of hostilities, 1945. A man who has worn many hats in active public life, David was first elected Councillor, Town of Markham, 1988, then acclaimed, 1991, becoming Chair, Markham Planning and Development, 1991-94. Throwing his hat into provincial politics, he was first elected to the Ontario Legislature for Markham, 1995. A graduate B.A., York University, 1972, and LL.B., Osgoode Hall Law School, 1975, David Tsubouchi was sworn in as Minister of Community and Social Services, 1995, and appointed Solicitor General, Province of Ontario, June 25, 1999. While Minister of Community and Social Services, Mr. Tsubouchi did much to promote Ontario's wine and grape industry including the introduction of the Vintner's Quality Alliance Act (VQA) and the direct delivery of VQA wines. In recognition of these efforts, he received the wine industry's "Business Citizen of the Year" award, sponsored by the Royal Bank. Former Chair, Society of Markham Poets, Markham Historical Museum, and Canadian Artists Federation, David's hobby is collecting books signed by authors. Proud of his heritage, David is former Director, Japanese Canadian Cultural Centre. In this view, the Hon. David Tsubouchi holds a frame containing barbed wire which was used to contain his father in an internment camp at Anglin, Ontario, during World War II. Presented to the Minister, 1999, by the Board of the Thunder Bay Military Museum, it serves as a reminder of those injustices which Canadian society in another era inflicted on minorities during times of national stress, strife, and strain. [Photo, courtesy the Hon. David Tsubouchi]

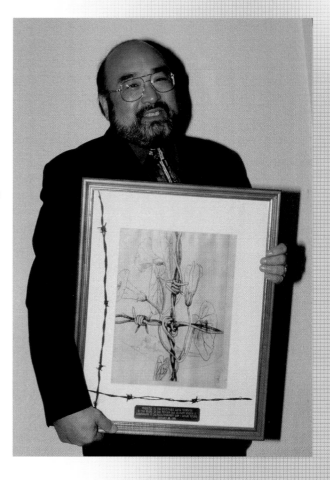

Three Christian religious affiliations are prominent. The Methodist Church and its successor, the United Church of Canada, have the most numbers but Anglicans and Roman Catholics are highly prominent as well. Congregations of Buddhists and other affiliations also exist.

The early Japanese published a number of Japanese-language newspapers which appeared daily; these included *Canada Shimpo* (Vancouver, 1924-41), the *Tairiku* (Vancouver, 1907-41), and the *Minshu* (Vancouver, 1924-41). The Japanese-Canadian community is now served by several Japanese- and English-language publications including the *Nikka Times* and the *New Canadian*. Japanese-speaking residents of Vancouver, Toronto, and Ottawa are also served by a weekly television program.

Japanese Canadians founded community centres in Montreal and Toronto. The Japanese Canadian Cultural Centre of Toronto, which opened in 1963, seeks to promote a sense of community among the generations of Japanese Canadians as well as to forge strong social and cultural links with the other peoples of Canada.

During the 1980s, the Japanese-Canadian community focused much of its energy on the struggle for the redress of wartime wrongs. Spearheaded by the National Association of Japanese Canadians (NAJC), the community succeeded

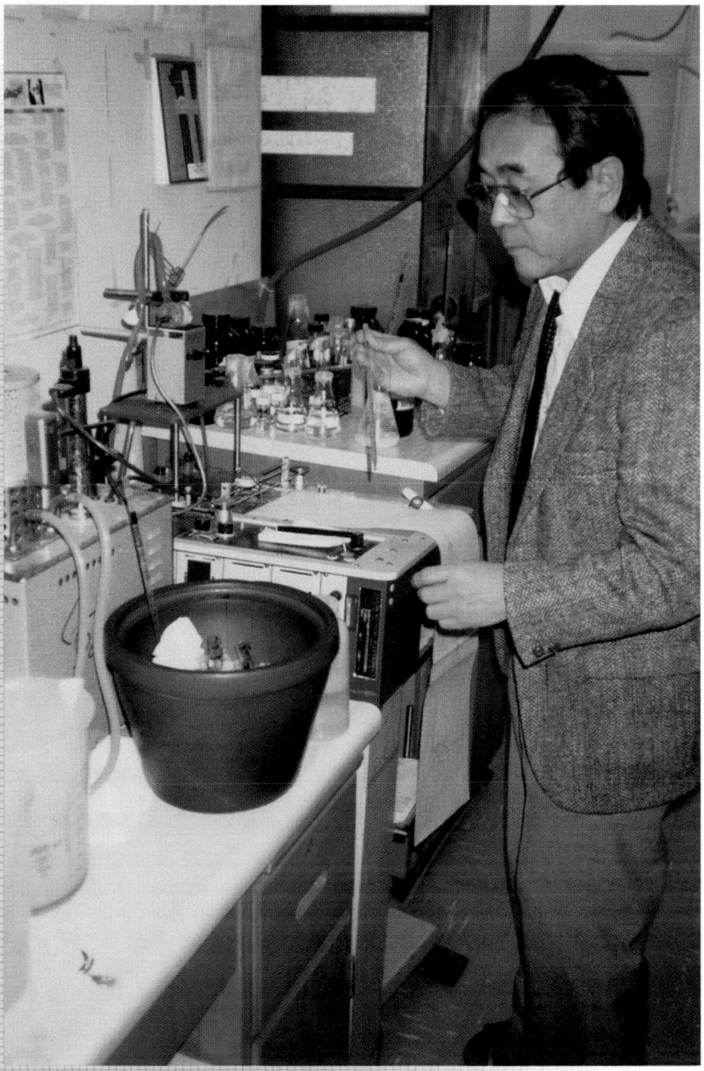

After completing his Ph.D. in Physiology and Bacteriology, Iowa State College, 1958, then completing post-doctoral work, Western Reserve University, Dr. Isamu Suzuki returned to Japan where he was born, 1930, teaching, University of Tokyo, 1960-62, before accepting a National Research Council of Canada Postdoctoral Fellowship at University of Manitoba, 1962-64. By 1972, Dr. Suzuki was Chair, Department of Microbiology, University of Manitoba, where he quickly established himself internationally as a noted authority on sulfur metabolism, sulphur oxidation, ammonia oxidation, and bacterial leaching. Over a 40-year career as teacher, researcher, and author, Dr. Isamu Suzuki's laboratory studies have concluded that the bacteria he investigates, Thiobacilli, are not only responsible for sulfur oxidation but also oxidize iron and are responsible for metal leaching from sulfide ores which can be used to extract metals such as copper, zinc, uranium in "bacterial leaching." Until recent times, this leaching was only known to cause acid mine drainage problems in the environment. A noted speaker at international conferences on sulfur metabolism and bacterial leaching, in this view, 1989, Dr. Suzuki is in his laboratory studying the bacterial activity in "Oxygraph" with an oxygen (O_2) sensitive electrode. [Photo, courtesy Dr. Isamu Suzuki]

in persuading the federal government to acknowledge wartime wrongs, to pay compensation to those who had been deprived of their rights and freedoms in Canada, and to promote human rights and multiracial harmony.

In terms of Japanese-Canadian representation in Canada's political life, a number have been elected to municipal office and school boards in British Columbia. In Ontario, the Honourable David H. Tsubouchi, a Sansei, was elected to the provincial legislature in 1995 and serves as minister of community and social services.

People of Japanese ancestry play a part in just about every aspect of Canadian cultural life. Writers and poets include Roy Miki, Joy Kogawa, and Rick Shiomi. Terry Watada of Toronto shines as a songwriter and performer. Artists, painters, and photographers who have won wide recognition include Kazuo Nakamura, Takao Tanabe, Shizuye Takashima, and Tamio Wakayama. Raymond Moriyama is one of Canada's outstanding architects. His designs include the Japanese Canadian Cultural Centre (1969), the Ontario Science Centre (1969), the Canadian Embassy in Tokyo, and the Saudi Arabian National Museum, Riyadh. Finally, geneticist, educator, and environmentalist, Dr. David Suzuki, has won much international attention as a broadcaster.

WHEN JUAN DA FUCA or Yannis Phokas, a Greek mariner from Cephalonia, surveyed the British Columbia coast in 1592 in the service of the Spanish monarch, this was the first recorded instance of a Greek presence in North America. It was not until the nineteenth century, however, that Greeks began to migrate here in greater numbers to develop Canada's railway lines. By 1931, almost 10,000 Greeks had settled in Canada, mostly in Montreal and Toronto. Between 1945 and 1971, of the 107,000 Greeks who entered Canada, nearly 80 percent were sponsored by relatives or co-villagers. The vast majority were unskilled workers who came to work in factories, restaurants, and maintenance. Almost 15 percent were young women who came as domestic workers. Greek immigration peaked in 1967 but dropped off dramatically to be only slightly raised by the refugee movement of Greek Cypriots in 1974 which saw tradesmen and professionals flee the Turkish invasion. By 1996 the census reported 203,000 Greeks in Canada. Over half were in Ontario.

Greeks have tended to settle in large cities. The large settlements in Montreal (54,415) and Toronto (39,600) have resulted in concentrations of small businesses such as restaurants, coffeehouses, pastry shops, greengrocers, travel agencies, social clubs, and professional offices. Toronto's Danforth Avenue and Montreal's Jean Talon Street and Park Avenue are the loci for Greek Canadians and the general public in search of Greek culture and institutions.

Born, Argos, Greece, Eleni Bakopanos immigrated, as a preschooler, from Greece to Canada with her parents who chose to settle in Montreal in the 1960s. Eleni Bakopanos is the first Greek-born Canadian woman to be elected to Canada's Parliament. First elected to the House of Commons, 1993, representing the riding of Saint-Denis, Montreal, Mrs. Bakopanos was returned to Parliament, 1997, representing the Montreal riding of Ahuntsic. Currently, Member, Standing Committee on Procedure and House Affairs and Associate Member, Standing Committee on Foreign Affairs and International Trade, Mrs. Bakopanos is also a member of the Sub-Committee on Human Rights and International Development. A McGill University graduate with an Honours Degree in Political Science and History (where she also studied law), Mrs. Bakopanos worked on the 1980 Quebec Referendum and assumed the position of Provincial Co-ordinator, Ethnic Groups Commission, for the Quebec Liberal Party. Subsequently, she was policy advisor to various Quebec ministers responsible for Cultural Communities and Immigration. Decorated, 1997, Grand Officer, Infante D. Henrique, the highest honour given to a civilian by the Portuguese government, Mrs. Bakopanos also received the Golden Cross of the Order of the Phoenix, February 2000, awarded by the President of the Hellenic Republic. Mother of two daughters, Mrs. Bakopanos, in this view, participates, 1997, in the annual Greek Independence Day Parade, Montreal, with Mayor of Athens, Dimitrios Avramopoulos, at her side. [Photo, courtesy Eleni Bakopanos]

from Greece

Nephrologist Develops New Technique for Treating Kidney Disease

The family of Dr. Dimitrios G. Oreopoulos fled as refugees from political turbulence in Asia Minor, 1922, settling in Alexandroupolis, just inside Greek territory next to the Turkish border. After his birth there, 1936, his family migrated to Athens where Dimitrios completed much of his formal education, graduating from the Medical School, University of Athens, 1960. Receiving a scholarship to attend Queen's University, Belfast, Dr. Oreopoulos graduated from that Northern Ireland university, 1969, earning a Ph.D. researching and becoming a specialist in kidney stones. He crossed the Atlantic, 1969, settling in Toronto, where he accepted a permanent position, Division of Nephrology, Toronto Western Hospital, in addition to being appointed Assistant Professor, University of Toronto. Over the next 30 years, Dr. Oreopoulos has gained international prominence as an authority in continuous ambulatory peritoneal dialysis. As a noted nephrologist, he has had much satisfaction in knowing that his technique for treating kidney disease is now adopted worldwide by nephrologists whose patients numbering close to 100,000 have benefited from his research. Recipient of many awards including, 1981, the prestigious Charles Mickel Fellowship; the National Torchbearer Award, 1994, from the American Kidney Fund; Distinguished Physician of the Year Award by the Hellenic Medical

Society of New York, 1993; and, most recently, the Scribner Award, 1998, from the American Society of Nephrology, Dr. Oreopoulos' volunteer work as President, the Hellenic Home for the Aged, assisted in raising three million dollars for the construction of a 75-bed apartment and an 82-bed nursing home. Contributing to the knowledge of Nephrology has been a passion for Dr. Oreopoulos, exemplified by his contribution of more than 300 articles published in medical journals and various periodicals. He has written three books about Geriatric Nephrology and for 11 years pub-lished the Journal of Humane Medicine. *In addition to all these achievements, Dr. Oreopoulos's greatest pride has been, with his wife, raising four children, all Canadian achievers. For his service to medicine and the community, Dr. Oreopoulos, left, as viewed here, at the Polymenakeion Centre, Toronto, 1998, was invested with the Order of Honour, Republic of Greece, by the Hon. John Thomoglou, Ambassador to Canada from Greece. [Photo, courtesy Dr. Dimitrios Oreopoulos]*

His Eminence Metropolitan Archbishop Sotirios Athanassoulas was born to George and Anastasia in Lepiana Arta, Greece, 1936. He graduated, University of Athens School of Theology, 1961, and obtained a Master's Degree in Theology, University of Montreal, 1971. Speaking Greek, English, and French, he has served as a clergyman in Canada since 1962. Elected Bishop of the Greek Orthodox Church in Canada, December 18, 1973 and ordained, 1974, he was elevated to the rank of Metropolitan Archbishop of Toronto, 1996. The Archbishop has served as Member of the Governing Board of the University of Toronto, 1975-78. He visited China, 1981, with The Canadian Council of Churches, and Australia with the World Council of Churches, 1982. When he assumed duties as Bishop in Canada, there were 22 Parishes. Now there are 75. During his Archieratical service, the Diocese, and now Metropolis, established the annual Youth Assemblies, 1980; the monthly newspaper, Orthodox Way, 1982; the Social Services of the Diocese, 1984; Metahomes, 1984, providing transitional housing for the homeless; The Greek Orthodox Order of Canada, 1987; the weekly television program Orthodox Voice, 1990, which is broadcast across all of Canada; the School of Byzantine Music, 1991; the Convents of St. Kosmas of Aitolos, Ontario, and the Virgin Mary of Consolation, Quebec, 1993; the Greek Orthodox Education of Ontario (Day Schools), 1996; and the Toronto Orthodox Theological Academy (1998). He has composed and published Catechism of the Greek Orthodox Faith in English, and in both Greek verse and prose. He was honoured with the Centennial Medal of Canada, 1967, and the Queen's Jubilee Medal, and the "125 Canada" Medal, 1992. [Photo, courtesy Greek Orthodox Metropolis of Toronto]

Iconostasis is Hidden Canadian Treasure

Approximately 95 percent of Greek Canadians belong to the Greek Orthodox Church, headquartered, Toronto, Ontario. The earliest Greek Church in Toronto is St. George Greek Orthodox Church whose cathedral-like sanctuary is majestically enhanced by a series of breathtaking religious iconographic paintings making the interior of this church one of the hidden treasures of Canada. [Photo, courtesy St. George Greek Orthodox Church]

Vintner Cultivating Taste Buds

Born, 1955, in the northern Greek village of Panteleimon, a town in the region of Florina near Thessalonika, Tom Noitsis barely remembers the time when his father, in 1958, said goodbye to Aphroditi, his wife, and his son and daughter, before leaving Greece for Canada. Settling in the southwestern Ontario town of Galt, for three years he worked hard in the restaurant business, the time it took him to save enough money to send for his family. Arriving, 1961, Tom quickly learned English and aspired to be an investment banker from a young age, so much so that he left Ryerson Polytechnical Institute before graduating to take a job with Dominion Securities. After five years, Tom's thirst for new opportunities took him from a series of jobs where his natural communication skills developed at such places as Famous Players, CN Real Estate, Beckers, and Tridel before he found his niche in the wine business. Establishing a company, 1993, called Eurovintage International Inc., Tom has taken giant steps over the last seven years to introduce the latest and newest wines and spirits to the Ontario market. He has also demonstrated leadership in being at the top of his business as a celebrated wine agent in one of the most competitive markets in North America. In this view, Tom Noitsis, centre, along with Zen Kucharski, Hamilton representative, stands and pours a glass of wine in his Eurovintage booth at Hamilton's Royal Botanical Gardens, 1999, during an evening of charitable fundraising.
[Photo, courtesy Tom Noitsis]

Aerospace Executive Promotes Canada

Basile Papaevangelou, right, born Eleftheroupolis, Kavala, Greece, came to Canada with his parents at age two, landing at Pier 21, Halifax, Nova Scotia, 1953. Because of the large Greek community living in Montreal, the Papaevangelou family settled in Quebec's largest city where young Basile received all of his schooling, graduating, B.Eng., McGill University, 1973, and earning his M.B.A. from that same institution, 1982. Former President, AlliedSignal Aerospace Canada, Basile, in this mid-1990s photograph, taken at the Paris Air Show, chats with James A. Lovell Jr. who commanded the unsuccessful Apollo 13 Moon Mission (1970) and returned the spacecraft to Earth following a potentially disastrous explosion on board. Since his retirement, Basile has been deeply involved in a special all-Canadian millennium project called The Canada Tree, a magnificent tree sculpture composed of woods from each province and territory telling fascinating stories of ordinary and extraordinary Canadians. A towering symbol, The Canada Tree celebrates the extended roots of the fascinating Canadian experience.
[Photo, courtesy Basile Papaevangelou]

His father immigrated to Canada from Spili Vrisi, Greece, in 1920, to enter the restaurant business and earn enough money to send for his wife and only son as soon as the necessary funds became available. When his family came to Canada in 1925, their destination was Guelph, Ontario. There young Gus Mitges proceeded with his education, graduating from the Ontario Veterinary College as Doctor of Medicine (D.V.M.), 1942. With a successful veterinary practice in Owen Sound, Ontario, Gus Mitges was urged to throw his hat into the political arena. Elected to the House of Commons in 1972 as a Progressive Conservative, it was the first of six successive elections he would win. For harmonizing relationships between his native land, Greece, and his adopted country, Canada, Gus, in 1995, was made Commander of the Order of the Phoenix, the highest civilian award given out by the Government of Greece. In this 1985 view, in his 14th year as a Member of Parliament, Gus confers with the Leader of the Progressive Conservative Party of Canada, the Rt. Hon. Brian Mulroney, Prime Minister of Canada. [Photo, courtesy Dr. Gus Mitges]

Winning Six Successive Elections to the House of Commons

Excavating Hellenistic Civilization

Born, Athens, Greece, 1963, Michael Cosmopoulos completed his undergraduate degree, University of Athens, graduating summa cum laude, 1985, and received his M.A. and Ph.D., Washington University, St. Louis, 1986 and 1989, respectively. He also studied at University of Sorbonne, Paris, and received from the Council of Europe a Diploma in Underwater Archaeology before immigrating to Canada, 1989, to take a teaching position, Department of Classics, University of Manitoba, where today he is Professor of Archaeology in the Departments of Classics and Anthropology. His research interests are the social, political, and cultural history of Greece from the Bronze Age to the Hellenistic period. He has excavated at several ancient sites in Greece and Ukraine, including Mycenae, Pylos, Epidaurus, Ancient Corinth, Ithaca, Oropos, and Olbia. Director of the new excavations at the sanctuary of Demeter at Eleusis, Dr. Cosmopoulos is currently directing a new interdisciplinary archaeological project near Pylos, aiming at the origins of the federal system of government. In recognition of his teaching, the University of Manitoba awarded him a Merit of Excellence in Teaching, 1999. Director, Centre for Hellenic Civilization, University of Manitoba, Dr. Cosmopoulos is Vice President of the Archaeological Institute of Canada. He has also authored eight important books germane to his research interests and some sixty articles and papers in international journals in addition to addressing various national and international conferences on ancient Greek social, political, and cultural history. [Photo, courtesy Dr. Michael Cosmopoulos]

Internationally Respected Neonatologist

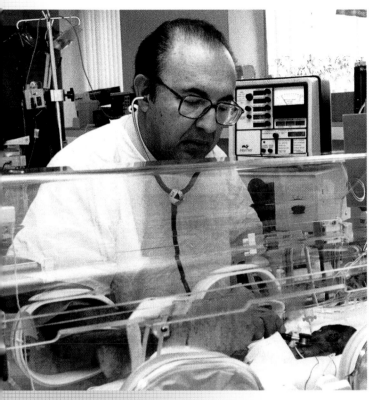

Dr. Apostolos Nicolas Papageorgiou immigrated to Canada shortly after graduating from the Medical School at the University of Sorbonne, Paris, France, 1966. Born, Volos, Greece, 1937, Dr. Papageorgiou migrated to Canada to take post graduate work in Pediatrics at both University of Montreal and McGill University, 1966-73. Since 1974, Dr. Papageorgiou has been Director, Neonatology, Jewish General Hospital, Montreal. He is Full Professor, Pediatrics, Obstetrics and Gynecology, McGill University, since 1988; Pediatrician-in-Chief, St. Mary's Hospital; Pediatrician-in-Chief, Jewish General Hospital. President, Society of Neonatologists, Province of Quebec, and Past President of the section of Neonatal/Perinatal Medicine of the Canadian Pediatric Society, Dr. Papageorgiou is the recipient, Osler Award for Outstanding Teacher, Faculty of Medicine, McGill University, as well as the Kaplan Award, Best Clinical Teacher, Department of Pediatrics, McGill University. Voted outstanding member of the Montreal Greek community by Hellenic Ladies Benevolent Society, and recipient, the Hellenic Scholarships Foundation Award for Academic Excellence, Dr. Papageorgiou was co-ordinator of the International Committee of Experts on the Revision of the Health Care System in Greece, 1993. A Fellow of the Royal College of Physicians and Surgeons of Canada, Dr. Papageorgiou has addressed conferences, symposia, and conventions in 22 countries, clearly demonstrating the international respect he has as a Neonatologist since immigrating to Canada. [Photo, courtesy Dr. A.N. Papageorgiou]

From NHL Arenas to Sports Analyst

George Nicholas Kypreos was born, Xirokamapion, a village outside Sparta, Greece. Growing up on a farm with olive trees, goats and vegetables, he lived through World War II, Greek civil war, and difficult economic times, finally leaving his homeland, 1951, immigrating to London, Ontario, saving money, and bringing his family, one by one, to Canada. It was inevitable that George would meet Theodora, the daughter of Greek immigrants. She was born in Amikle, still another village outside Sparta. She, too, immigrated to Canada and settled, like her future husband, in London, Ontario. After their marriage, they moved to Toronto where son Nick was born. Raised by a family who worked hard to overcome culture and language barriers, Nick benefited from parents who desired he should pursue dreams with passion and determination. Playing professionally in the minor leagues for four years, by 1989, Nick Kypreos was skating for the Washington Capitals of the National Hockey League. Finishing his career with the Toronto Maple Leafs, 1997, by the time he left the NHL as an efficient, hard-nosed winger, he had amassed 1,210 penalty minutes. Today, Nick is a polished CTV Sports Analyst, still demonstrating the passion instilled in him by immigrant parents who wanted only the very best of the very best for their son. [Photo, courtesy Nick Kypreos]

While obtaining his Ph.D., State University of New York, Buffalo, N.Y., Christos Hatzis, born, Volos, Greece, 1953, visited Toronto and decided to make Canada home upon completing his Ph.D., 1982, because of "the country's mosaic concept of culture." He has since added to that mosaic by composing over 40 major works which include a number of compositions based on Inuit music and culture that has received international attention through concerts and broadcasts worldwide. Following a Halifax concert celebrating his Inuit works that included performances by Baffin Island throat singers, a local critic wrote, "if that is not sublime, what is?" Dr. Hatzis, Associate Professor, Faculty of Music, University of Toronto, since 1995, has composed music for some of Canada's and the world's best-known artists, and orchestras. The Tafelmusik Baroque Orchestra of Toronto, commissioning the work of a living composer for the first time, performed his Farewell to Bach, under his direction, 1998. The same year, his 70-minute choral work, Kyrie, was performed in Toronto. In 1998, as well, his Confessional for cello and orchestra was given its world premiere by Cellist Shauna Rolston and the CBC Vancouver Orchestra. The English Chamber Choir of London, sang his Heirmos to "sold out" audiences the same year. Later the score was recorded by Sony. Other labels that have recorded his music are Naxos, Marquis, CBC and Centrediscs. Dr. Hatzis won the Prix Italia, 1996, for Footprints in New Snow, the Prix Bohemia, 1998, for the same work, the Jules Leger Prize, 1996, for Erotikos Logos, and the Jean A. Chalmers National Music Award, 1998, for his composition Nunavut. [Photo, courtesy Dr. Christos Hatzis]

The Greek Orthodox Church has been central to the maintenance of culture and Greek-language programs among second and third generation Greek Canadians. Social service and community activities have often been organized around the clergy but have links to early mutual benefit societies such as Anagenisis in Montreal and the Saskatoon Greek Society. By 1980 nearly 40 parishes existed in Canada. Some civic leaders in Greek

After receiving an M.Sc., Plant Pathology, from the Agricultural University of Athens (where her grandfather, Stavros Papandreou, had been President, 1919-1959), Dr. Leda Raptis, born, Athens, Greece, 1950, attended McGill University, 1973, to continue her Plant Virology studies. A Ph.D. from Sherbrooke University was followed by postdoctoral studies at Princeton and Harvard universities before joining the National Research Council, Ottawa, 1984. In 1986, she joined Queen's University's Microbiology Department as Assistant Professor, becoming Associate, 1992 and Full Professor, 1997. With her Canadian-born husband, Kevin Firth, a systems design engineer, they developed an apparatus for the electroporation of adherent cells. She has co-authored more than 50 papers on cancer viruses and edited and written two chapters of a book on Simian Virus 40, scheduled for publication in year 2000. An older and younger brother followed Dr. Raptis to Canada for their university education. The younger one, Stavros, is now a pathologist at Montreal's Santa Gabrini Hospital. In this view, Dr. Ledas Raptis is in her Queen's University laboratory with the electroporation apparatus both she and her husband developed. [Photo, courtesy Dr. Leda Raptis]

*Jim Karygiannis, M.P., born, Athens, Greece,
immigrated to Canada as a teenager with his family, 1966, settling in
Toronto, Ontario. Graduating in Industrial Engineering from the University of Toronto, he
worked in the family business until 1988 at which time he ran for political office, winning a seat in the House of
Commons as a Liberal Member of Parliament. Representing one of the most ethnically diverse federal ridings in
Canada – Scarborough-Agincourt – Mr. Karygiannis has been an effective voice for small business, immigration,
and multicultural matters in the House of Commons. Married and the father of five daughters, Mr. Karygiannis
was awarded, in 1999, the decoration of the "Officer of the Order of Phoenix" by the President of the Hellenic
Republic. The three-time elected Member of Parliament, middle, is seen in this recent Riding gathering, with a
representation of loyal constituents.* [Photo, courtesy Jim Karygiannis]

communities have sought, since the late 1960s, to limit the power of the clergy especially in such non-religious matters as social services and schooling. In part this secular activity was influenced by the presence of Prime Minister Andreas Papandreou, a lecturer at York University in Toronto after he had been dismissed by King Constantine and his right-wing allies in 1965. The Greek Orthodox clergy in Canada tended to support the dictatorship because of its strong support of Christianity. In turn, this alienated a significant portion of secular Greek Canadians. Secular organizations such as the Greek-Canadian Community of London, Ontario, set up women's athletic and youth programs in the 1980s. Greek-language schools are now integrated into Ontario's international languages programs and receive financial assistance from the province as well as from the Greek Ministry of Education. The largest nonsectarian Greek organization in Canada is the American Hellenic Educational Progressive Association (AHEPA) which started a Canadian chapter as early as 1928, in Toronto, and today has a about 22 chapters across the country. Other important social agencies are the Greek Canadian Labour Association, in Montreal, that helps Greek immigrants to understand their rights as workers, and the Centre for Social Services for Greek Canadians in Toronto that offers family services. In 1981 the Hellenic Canadian Congress was founded as an umbrella organization for all Greek-Canadian communities.

Newspapers such as Montreal's *Elleniko Vema* and Toronto's *Ellenikos Tachidromos* cover the news and politics of both Canada and Greece. In Quebec, Greek heritage candidates from the NDP, Liberals, and Conservatives have attempted to win seats in the Quebec legislature. At the federal level Eleni Bakopanos, a Liberal Member, Quebec, has served in the last two Chrétien governments. Though the campaign of Montreal shopkeeper and broadcaster John Kambites was unsuccessful, several Greek Canadians from Ontario, such as Liberal MP Jim Karrygiannis and Conservative MP Gus Mitges, have successfully served in Ottawa. ✿

Donovan Bailey, born, Manchester, Jamaica,1967, moved to Canada at age 13. After attending Queen Elizabeth Park High School, Oakville, Ontario, Donovan attended Sheridan College, graduating in Economics. Although between 1990-1994 he participated in track events at the international level, he did not take track seriously until he began working with trainer Dan Pfaff, 1995, the same year he became World Champion in the 100m. On July 27, 1996, he became an international sensation when, at the Summer Olympics, Atlanta, Georgia, he won the 100 metres in the world-record time of 9.84. He was also a member of the men's 4x100m Olympic relay team, capturing a second Gold Medal. The same year, Donovan set a world indoor record of 5.56 over 50 metres at Reno, Nevada. A complete rupture of his Achilles tendon, in the fall of 1998, put a temporary halt to his career. It certainly will surprise no one, however, to see Donovan overcome adversity in the year 2000 and once again represent Canada, this time at the Sydney, Australia, Olympics. In this historic photograph taken by Peter Thompson of Mississauga, Ontario, Donovan Bailey crosses the finish line first in the 100-metre finals at the 1996 Olympics. His win in world-record time gave credence to his claim that he was, in 1996, the world's fastest human being. [Photo, courtesy Peter J. Thompson]

from Jamaica

JAMAICAN immigration to Canada has been a major phenomenon only for the past four decades, but Jamaica's long-standing association with Canada dates back to the late eighteenth century. Jamaican Maroons, descendants of escaped slaves who had zealously guarded their freedom in the mountains of Jamaica, are known to have arrived in Halifax on July 22, 1776. There they helped to reinforce Nova Scotia's defences by building the Halifax Citadel, 1795-1800.

During the nineteenth century, the immigrants' enterprise showed itself in the variety of work they did. Jamaican John Robert Giscome came to Canada when gold was discovered along the Fraser River in 1858. When the boom days of the California Gold Rush ended, Giscome trekked north to make his fortune in the Cariboo gold fields of British Columbia. Imbued with an adventurous spirit, he also explored and charted much of the Fraser and Peace River water system. In Victoria, James Barnswell used his great skill as a carpenter to build some of that city's most fashionable residences. Another remarkable member of the early Jamaican-Canadian community was Robert Sutherland of Ontario. A graduate of Queen's University (1852) and Osgoode Hall (1855), Sutherland became Canada's first black lawyer. Upon his death in 1878, this bachelor legalist bequeathed his entire estate, in the amount of $12,000, to Queen's University, Ontario.

Mavis Elaine Burke came to Canada in 1970 to work with a firm of Ottawa-based educational consultants. This was a change of career from her position as lecturer in education with the University of the West Indies from which she graduated with distinctions in theory and practice of education (Dip. Ed., 1962). Her M.A. (Education) was earned at the University of London, U.K., 1965. After completing her Ph.D., University of Ottawa, 1975, Dr. Burke became an Immigrant Education Consultant with the Toronto Board of Education. She became well known and respected for her contribution to multicultural issues. From 1977-81, she was an Education Officer with the Ministry of Education, Government of Ontario. She also became a valuable resource to the diverse groups in the society. She served as Chair and President, Ontario Advisory Council on Multiculturalism and Citizenship (1981-85) and was Advisor to the Ontario Women's Directorate (1987-88) and to the Ontario Ministry of Education (1988-1992) on issues relating to human rights and equity. Mavis Burke has also contributed to other sectors of society. She chaired the Social Assistance Review Board (1985-87). She was a member, Government of Canada Immigration and Refugee Board (1992-93). Her volunteer contribution was highlighted by the registered charitable organization she founded in 1987 to promote early childhood care and education in Jamaica and in Canada – Women for P.A.C.E. (Canada). Dr. Burke has received many awards including, as viewed in this photograph, being awarded the Order of Ontario from Ontario's Lieutenant Governor, the Honourable Hilary Weston, October 1999. [Photo, courtesy Mavis Burke, Ph.D.]

As the twentieth century began, Jamaican Canadians helped to fill the demand for railway porters, domestics, blacksmiths, and foundry workers that an expanding Canadian economy necessitated. At the same time, Jamaican-Canadian activists began to search for alternative strategies to help liberalize postwar Canadian society and its immigration laws. A Canadian government scheme to recruit female domestics of African descent was established in 1955. To be eligible, an applicant had to be a single female in good health aged between eighteen and thirty-five. After working as a domestic for at least a year, a woman would be granted landed immigrant status. By 1965, over 1,000 women had arrived from Jamaica under this scheme. Jamaican nurses soon followed, gaining admission as "cases of exceptional merit" in response to medical labour force needs.

Since 1967, two aspects of Canada's immigration policy encouraged the growth of the Jamaican-Canadian community. Canada started admitting immigrants on the basis of a "point system" that allowed it to select people who were educated and skilled. An "independent" applicant received points for his or her level of education, ability to speak English or French, work experience, and other factors. As a result, many Jamaican immigrants who were trained in management, a profession, or a trade were able to come in through the "independent" class. Canada also continued its policy of reuniting families, and so immigrants who became landed residents could apply to bring over members of their immediate family. Many women who came during this time gravitated to work in service and clerical occupations. The combined admissions of independent and family-class immigrants resulted in the steady growth of Canada's Jamaican population.

According to the 1996 census, there were 188,770 persons of Jamaican origin in Canada. Of this total, the largest concentration of Jamaican Canadians (159,465) resided in Ontario. They could also be found in Quebec (10,075), Alberta (7,815), British Columbia (6,030), and Manitoba (2,925). Jamaican immigrants usually settled in the large urban centres of Canada with Toronto (73,865) and Montreal (9,605) being the most popular cities. In these and other metropolitan areas, they were widely dispersed through the suburbs and downtown areas albeit in small concentrations downtown.

Graduating, Bachelor of Architecture, University of Manitoba, 1964, Jamaican-born Richard Henriquez continued with post-graduate studies, Massachusetts Institute of Technology, Boston, receiving an M.A., Architecture and Urban Design, 1967. In 1969, he opened a firm in Vancouver, and has since designed many notable projects such as The Justice Institute, New Westminster, Capilano College Library and Birch Building, North Vancouver, the Environmental Sciences Building, Trent University, Peterborough, and was jury co-winner, United Nations Peacekeeping Monument, Ottawa, 1990. Other projects have included the heritage restoration of the Sinclair Centre, the Eugenia and Sylvia Hotel Towers, and three luxury condominiums, all in downtown Vancouver. His awards and prizes include two Governor General's Awards for Architecture, 1990 and 1994, two Lieutenant Governor of British Columbia Awards, 1990 and 1992, and two City of Vancouver Heritage Awards, 1986 and 1988. His "Memory Theatre" was exhibited at the Venice Biennale, 1996, and in 1998, he represented Canada, at the Biennial of Architecture, Buenos Aires. Mr. Henriquez, who says that "It is a privilege to live in this country [Canada]," is a Fellow, Royal Architectural Institute of Canada. [Photo, courtesy Chick

Jamaicans of West African ancestry traditionally have been the largest group to immigrate from Jamaica to Canada. Reflecting the ethnic heterogeneity of Jamaica, a percentage of immigrants of European origin include Sephardic Jews from Spain and Portugal, English and German Jews, as well as Jamaicans of Chinese, East Indian, or Lebanese origin. Representatives from these minority groups include Michael Lee-Chin of the Berkshire Group; Montrealer Ray Chen, photographer; Dr. Ronald Wong, family doctor, Surrey, B.C.; Ophthalmologist, Dr. Garth Taylor of Cornwall, Ontario; and Vancouver architect, Richard Henriquez.

Today in Canada there are Jamaican Canadians in all walks of economic life. Retail and fast-food outlets, restaurants, hairdressers, and barbershops created for the needs of the Jamaican-Canadian community have become natural commercial centres for other members of the Caribbean community. Jamaican Canadians can be found in the public sector, medicine and health-care delivery, law, banking, and the financial services industry. Mary Anne Chambers, a vice president at the Bank of Nova Scotia, is typical of the many women who have made significant achievements in their chosen field.

Jamaican Canadians have also seen fit to nurture their own culture within the Canadian mosaic. The church has been a major instrument providing this outlet. Jamaicans have also showed remarkable initiative, forming organizations among themselves for social, cultural, and educational purposes including the Jamaican Canadian Association (JCA), Council of Jamaicans, and National Council of Jamaicans and Supportive Organizations in Canada (NCJSOC). Jamaica's firebrand political activist and thinker, Marcus Garvey, founder of the Universal Negro Improvement Association, struck an important chord in the immigrant community during the interwar period with his encouraging message of Black pride and achievement.

As a tribute to his outstanding volunteer service, John Brooks Community Foundation and Scholarship Fund was established, 1981, to address, among other matters, the high drop-out rate of Black students in the Metropolitan Toronto School System. Upon immigrating to Canada, 1963, Clovis John Brooks co-owned and operated the Latin Quarter, a Caribbean-oriented night club, making its facilities available as a community drop-in for West Indian immigrants, especially domestics who had no place to go on their day off. As a member of St. Charles Anglican Church, Toronto, John organized sports activities for the St. Clair Youth Council in conjunction with the Police to promote better understanding between the two groups. In cooperation with the Toronto District School Board, John also helped to establish the Regal Road Public School Day Care Project. The John Brooks Scholarship Fund, named in honour of this Jamaican-Canadian, has presented annual awards to students who achieve excellence in academic studies or artistic and athletic activities. Although the majority of students recognized each year are drawn from Greater Toronto's Black Community, the awards are open to all ethnic groups. Since 1981, nearly 500 students have been recognized for their scholastic achievement and have received scholarships. Many recipients return each year to participate in the annual presentations. In 1984, the Ontario Government awarded Mr. Brooks the Ontario Medal for Good Citizenship. He received the Canadian Birthday Achievement Award, 1985, and was given a lifetime membership in the Jamaican Canadian Association. In 1991, he received the MacDonald-Cartier Award from Prime Minister Brian Mulroney. He was made, Member, Order of Canada, 1993, and received an Honorary Degree from Queen's University, 1992. Determined to improve the lives of those around him, the chief concern of John Brooks continues to be the success and future of the Scholarship Fund. [Photo, courtesy John Brooks]

Lobbying for a Better Society

He immigrated to Canada, 1955. After graduating,
B.Sc., McGill University, and earning an Ontario
High School Teacher's Certificate, Brandeis Denham
Jolly, born, Green Island, Jamaica, worked on nutri-
tion research for the Government of Jamaica and air
pollution research for Metropolitan Toronto before
becoming a teacher of Chemistry and Physics, Forest
Hill Collegiate, Toronto. He then went into business,
owning and operating two medical diagnostic companies,
1978-83, and a Days Inn, West Toronto, 1987-97. At
present, he is President, Denham Corporation Ltd. and
Tyndall Nursing Home Limited which owns a Nursing Home
by that name as well as Tyndall Estates Retirement Home,
Mississauga, Ontario. B.D. Jolly Holdings is another company
with real estate properties in both Mississauga and Toronto.
Between 1982-85, he was the publisher of Contrast, a weekly Black
Community newspaper, and was the founder and first President of the
Black Business and Professional Association of Toronto, one of the many
community activities Mr. Jolly has been involved in as an Ontario businessman. These include: Member, Board of
Governors, Central "Y", 1993-95; Committee for Due Process; Jamaican Canadian Association; Harriet Tubman Games;
Caribana; the Daphne Dacosta Cancer Association; Black Inmates Organization; Black Action-Defence Committee; Jane-
Finch Concerned Citizens; and a founding member of the Cornwall College Old Boys Association, Toronto. A strong lobbyist
for an all-Black radio station in Toronto, Mr. Jolly's involvement has been recognized by a number of organizations including
the Black History Society's Daniel G. Hill Community Service Award, 1998, and the Governor General's Commemorative
Medal on the 125th Anniversary of the Confederation of Canada. In this view, Denham Jolly meets with Mel Lastman,
Mayor of Toronto, at the opening of the Jamaican Canadian Community Centre, Downsview, Ontario, 1999. [Photo,
courtesy B. Denham Jolly]

Neurosurgeon Toiling for Others

Dr. Renn Holness was born in Kingston, Jamaica, towards the end of World War II. As a high school student,
he showed potential stardom in track events by winning the 100-, 200-, and 440-yard sprints in the Jamaican
College Track and Field Championships, both 1960 and 1961. Rather than pursue sports, however, he chose
a career in Medicine. Trained on a Centenary Scholarship, University of West Indies, 1961-68, Dr. Holness
spent 1964 at Guy's Hospital Medical School, UK, studying Anatomy, and returning to Jamaica with a
B.Sc. in that subject, the first UWI student to achieve this honour. Upon graduating MB, BS (Honours),
he walked away with medals in Pathology, Microbiology, Paediatrics, Obstetrics, and Gynaecology and
was the overall Gold Medalist of the Class of 1968 at UWI. Before moving to Halifax, Nova Scotia,
where today he is Professor and Head, Division of Neurosurgery, Department of Surgery,
Dalhousie University Medical School and QE II Health Sciences Centre, Dr. Holness had
been involved in a Fellowship in Paediatric Neurosurgery and Peripheral Nerve Surgery,
Toronto General Hospital. President, Canadian Neurological Society (1992-95), Dr.
Holness has become increasingly involved in third world medical education, particularly
in the Caribbean where he helps to train students as well as to bring them (and
patients) to Halifax. In 1998, Dr. Holness received the Distinguished Graduate Award
during the 50th anniversary celebrations of the University of the West Indies. Married
to Deidre, a former nurse, and the father of five children, Dr. Holness's very busy day-to-
day activities also include serving on a Task Force to promote admission of indigenous
Black and First Nation students to medical school. In year 2000, Dr. Holness took a
six-month sabbatical to become a Director of a Clinical Program, UWI Medical School,
Nassau, Bahamas. [Photo, courtesy Dr. Renn Holness]

First Afro-Canadian Appointed Citizenship Judge

Born, St. Mary, Jamaica, Pamela Appelt was raised in her home village by her maternal grandmother after her parents left for England to complete their education. Spending school holidays and her university years in England where her father worked for the BBC and her mother ran a printing business, Pamela, 1965, travelled to Montreal on holiday, and liked Canada so much that she applied for landed immigrant status. Working first as a biochemist, Queen Elizabeth Hospital, Montreal, she then worked as a researcher in medical biochemistry, McGill University. After marrying lawyer David Appelt, they moved to Oakville, Ontario, 1979, raising two children, Melanie and Michael. In 1987, Pamela was appointed to the Court of Canadian Citizenship, the first female Judge of Afro-Canadian descent to be so named. A cultural bridge builder, especially since her recent retirement as a Citizenship Judge, Pamela serves on many volunteer committees. She is the recent Chairperson of the allocation committee on violence against women with the United Way of Greater Toronto. She is also a member of the Custody Review Board whose role is one of negotiation and dispute resolution. An energetic and enthusiastic volunteer, Pamela was a Canadian Delegate to the United Nations' Decade for Women Conference, Nairobi, Kenya, 1985. A community activist, she has served on numerous boards, including the Community Foundation of Oakville, the Canadian Multiculturalism Council, the B'nai Brith League of Human Rights, Annual Harry Jerome Awards, and the Black Business and Professional Association. In this view, she is shown being congratulated by Prime Minister Brian Mulroney, 1987, on the occasion of her being appointed a Canadian Citizenship Judge. [Photo, courtesy Pamela Appelt]

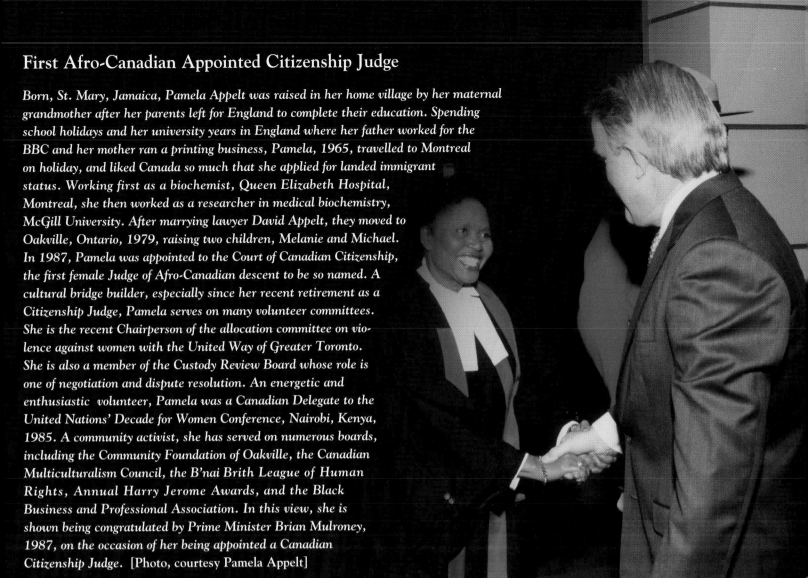

Building Social Safety Nets

After graduating from the College of Science and Technology, Kingston, Jamaica, Alvin Curling, born, 1939, was actively involved in youth work and had a career in housing management and land settlement before immigrating to Canada, 1965. In Ontario, both these skills were recognized when, as the first Liberal M.P.P. elected in the riding of Scarborough-Rouge River, he was named Minister of Housing 1985-1987, Minister of Skills Development, and member of the Premier's Council on Science and Technology, 1987-89, and Parliamentary Assistant to the Minister of Intergovernmental Affairs, 1990. On arriving in Canada, Mr. Curling worked for several companies: White Motors, Go Transit, Confederation Assurance, and Prudential Insurance, besides being a volunteer immigration counsellor. Alvin also attended Seneca College of Applied Arts and Technology and York University. In 1972 he joined Seneca as Director of Student Services and remained there until his election, 1985, a seat he has held since. Dedicated to improving literacy at all levels, Mr. Curling was President, World Literacy of Canada, 1981-84, and continues to take an active role in that organization as well as the Jamaican Canadian Association. In 1997-98, he was Chair, Advisory Board to the Caribana Cultural Committee. [Photo, courtesy Alvin Curling, M.P.P]

Two older brothers joined the Canadian Army during World War II, one of the reasons Bromley Armstrong, centre, immigrated to Canada in 1947 at age 21 after working for five years in his native city of Kingston, Jamaica. In Canada he joined the Massey Harris Company and got involved in a war of his own when he observed that few Blacks were hired and only in the most menial jobs with no chance for advancement. He joined the trade union and by 1954, was one of the participants in the "March on Ottawa" demanding changes in racist immigration laws. He became financial secretary and represented Local 439, United Auto Workers of America, in the Toronto and District Labour Council where he personally identified acts of discrimination against Blacks and Jews, and provided such evidence to pressure provincial and municipal governments to enact new laws. It led to the enactment of the Fair Employment Practices Act, a forerunner of the Ontario Human Rights Code. Mr. Armstrong also found time to take business courses, and in 1969, opened his own insurance agency. In 1973, he founded the Islander newspaper. Other community activities include being a founding member, Jamaican Canadian Association and its President, 1970-1972. He served as an Ontario Human Rights Commissioner, 1975-80, was a founding member, Urban Alliance for Race Relations, a member of the Ontario Labour Relations Board, 1980-1996, and founder and President, National Council of Jamaicans and Supportive Organizations in Canada, 1978. In 1998, Bromley Armstrong received the annual Baha'i National Race Unity Award for his pioneering fight against racism. In this view, Mr. Armstrong is flanked, left, by Reg Newport, former Executive Director, Baha'i Faith Canada, and the Hon. Roy McMurtry, Chief Justice, Ontario Court of Justice. [Photo, courtesy Ron Fanfair via Jamaican Trade Commission]

Jamaicans have also joined hands with other Caribbean people to found the Organization for Caribbean Cultural Initiatives (OCCI), the Black Business and Professional Association (BBPA), the West Indian Social and Cultural Society (WISC), and the John Brooks Community Foundation. Members of the Jamaican Canadian diaspora have also generously provided assistance to the homeland, supporting the island's schools, colleges and universities, various hospitals, and patient clinics.

Jamaican Canadians played a substantive and important role while serving in Canada's armed forces during both World Wars. They were also on the front lines in the war against racism and discrimination, working hard for various government measures to ensure an environment in which all immigrants and racial minorities can live and work together as equals. An early community leader, Harry Gairey, who came to Canada from Jamaica, via Cuba, in 1914, helped to organize the Brotherhood of Sleeping Car Porters to aid against unfair treatment and lack of opportunity in the workplace. The same can be said for Bromley Armstrong, Labour Relations

Though they had known each other in their native Jamaica, Byron and Violet Carter of Pickering, Ontario, immigrated to Canada separately, he via the United States to study mechanical engineering, and Violet to work as a nurse and further her education while working at the Toronto Western Hospital. Violet was already a graduate of the Public Health School in Kingston, Jamaica, with a Royal Society of Health Certificate from the U.K., when she came to Toronto, 1961, and later served with the Victorian Order of Nurses, Toronto, 1963-65, before moving to the Scarborough General Hospital, 1965-1992, where she spent her time in the gynaecology and later the nursery wards. Byron, who graduated from the Milwaukee School of Engineering, moved to Toronto and married Violet, 1961. For the next 19 years he worked at Canadian General Electric, Toronto, then briefly managed Don Park Sheetmetal Company before opening his own home renovation business, B.C. Renovations in Pickering, Ontario. He retired in 1992. Active in the Jamaican community, Violet was a founding member of the Jamaican Canadian Association, 1962, and has served on a number of committees, while Byron has served as Treasurer and Vice President of the group that has some 2,000 members. He was also president of the now defunct Credit Union of the Jamaican Canadian Association. They are the proud parents of four children, two boys, one an architect and the other an engineer, and two girls, a lawyer and a rehabilitation counsellor. [Photo, courtesy Byron Carter]

Officer, and Herman Stewart, Trade Unionist. It should therefore come as no surprise that a number of Canadians of Jamaican origin including Bev Salmon, Rosemary Brown, and Alvin Curling participated in municipal politics, sat in provincial legislatures and the federal parliament and in cabinets at both levels. In 1968, Lincoln Alexander, whose mother immigrated to Ontario from Jamaica during World War I, became the first Black elected to the House of Commons where he served as the Progressive Conservative member for Hamilton West until 1979. It was during his final year in Parliament that he became the federal Minister of Labour, marking the first time a Black had been a Cabinet Minister at the federal level. In 1985 he became the first Canadian Lieutenant Governor of colour, serving the people of Ontario in that capacity until 1991.

In the sporting arena, Jamaican-born track and field stars such as Milt Ottey and Mark Boswell in the high jump, and Molly Killingbeck and Charmaine Crooks in the relays and long sprint events have carried the athletic hopes and dreams of all Canadians at international track and field events. So did Ben Johnson. But, when sprinter Donovan Bailey became "the fastest man in the world" after winning the 100-metre event at the Atlanta Olympics, 1996, all Canadians were euphoric. ♥

The largest annual festival in North America, and the second largest in the world, is celebrated each October in the twin cities of Kitchener-Waterloo, southwestern Ontario. Called Oktoberfest, the nine-day festival, named the "Number One Tourist Event in Canada," 1998, by the American Bus Association, is widely known for its spirit of Gemuetlichkeil. Founded, 1968, Oktoberfest features all the fun and flavour of the original Munich Oktoberfest in Germany. Enthusiastic revellers, in excess of 700,000, watch day-long parades; eat schnitzel, roasted pigtails, bratwurst and sauerkraut; drink suds from colourful beer steins in the many Festhallen; dance in banner bedecked halls to the brassy strains of oompah bands; and visit the numerous cultural centres celebrating Canada's diversity, in general, Germany's heritage, in particular. In this view, the mascot of Oktoberfest, Onkel Hans, greets the enthusiastic crowds, lining the streets of Kitchener-Waterloo's Oktoberfest, 1998. [Photo, courtesy Kitchener-Waterloo Oktoberfest Inc.]

from Germany

The town of Lunenburg, Nova Scotia, designated a UNESCO World Heritage Site, is one of the few municipalities in all of North America that has kept its 18th century Georgian charm intact. A large immigration of German Lutherans to this community in mid-18th century Georgian Canada brought with them the legacy of German architecture associated with four kings of Great Britain, all named George and all of German descent. This Georgian building at 69 Fox Street, Lunenburg, today named the Lennox Tavern, was built by German-born Andreas Jung, circa 1790. Jung was one of the early German immigrants who helped found the Town of Lunenburg, Nova Scotia, 1753. [Photo, courtesy Pierre St. Jacques/E. Patricia MacDonald, Town of Lunenburg]

WHEN IT WAS RECORDED IN 1664 that Hans Bernard had purchased land near Quebec City, this was the first recognition of the German presence in Canada. Between the sixteenth and eighteenth centuries, German-speaking immigrants who established homesteads in New France, included demobilized soldiers who had served in the French military forces at Port Royal, Louisbourg, and Quebec.

Between 1750 and 1753, some 2,400 German newcomers landed at Halifax. These "foreign Protestants" spearheaded a movement that resulted in the creation of the largest German-speaking community in British North America before the American Revolution. The settlers who were part of this initial immigration came from the region known as the Palatinate and they could recite a litany of disasters in the form of war and famine. In Halifax, they were supplied with provisions and accommodation and put to work on the city's fortifications. In 1753, some 1,400 of them demanded and were given land on the coast southwest of Halifax. There, in Lunenburg, they became expert fishermen and boat builders renowned for the *Bluenose* schooner. Their legacy, today, was honoured in 1995 when UNESCO declared Lunenburg a World Heritage Site.

Between 1760 and 1770, Germans from Europe and from Pennsylvania (a principal hub of German settlement in the Thirteen Colonies) came to Annapolis County (Nova Scotia) and to several other areas including Albert County, Coverdale Parish, Elgin Parish, and Hillsborough Township, which later became part of New Brunswick.

The American Revolution motivated many United Empire Loyalists of German origin to move to British North America. German-speaking people from New York and Georgia, Mennonites from Pennslyvania, militia men and members of German regiments, Hessians, who had fought for the British Crown – these made their way to Upper Canada (Ontario) where they founded settlements along the St. Lawrence River, in the Ottawa valley, and in small packages along the north shore of Lake Erie, setting the stage for those who would soon come after them in still larger numbers.

Gold Medalist Architect

Eberhard Heinrich Zeidler was born in Germany and educated, among others, at Weimer during the Bauhaus revival, post-1945. Mr. Zeidler immigrated to Canada, 1951, where he continued his architectural interests as Associate-in-Charge of Design and, later, a Partner, Blackwell & Craig, which has evolved into the present firm, Zeidler Roberts Partnership/Architects. His landmark buildings in Toronto include Toronto's Eaton Centre, Ontario Place, The Atrium at the Hospital for Sick Children, Ontario Cancer Institute/Princess Margaret Hospital and the Ford Centre for the Performing Arts. Other projects include Canada Place (Vancouver), McMaster University Health Sciences Centre (Hamilton), Living Arts Centre (Mississauga), Media Park (Cologne), Columbus Centre of Marine Research and Exploration (Baltimore), Liberty Place – Phase II

(Philadelphia), and the Yerba Buena Gardens (San Francisco). His works are also part of the London, Moscow, Beijing, Shanghai, Kuala Lumpur, Jakarta, and Barcelona cityscape. Mr. Zeidler won the prestigious Gold Medal from the Royal Architectural Institute of Canada (1986), was made an Officer of the Order of Canada (1984), and was elected an Honorary Fellow of the American Institute of Architects (1981). In this 1991 view, at the Art Gallery of Ontario, Mr. Zeidler, right, is conversing with Prince Charles, left, whose own interest in architecture is as well known internationally as is Mr. Zeidler's architectural designs which span three continents. [Photo, courtesy Art Gallery of Ontario]

In the Shadow of Dinosaurs

Like many others who have immigrated to Canada, Hans-Dieter Sues came as an exchange student to take post-graduate work after completing undergraduate studies, in this case, Johannes Gutenberg University, 1975. Born in Rheydt, Germany, the 19-year-old graduate added an M.Sc., University of Alberta, 1977, then moved to Harvard, completing a second Master's program, 1978, and Ph.D., 1984. He worked and carried out post-doctoral studies in Canada and the United States for the next eight years before being appointed, 1992, Associate Curator, Vertebrate Palaeontology, Royal Ontario Museum, and Assistant Professor of Zoology, University of Toronto. Made Associate Professor two years later, he was appointed Curator, Vertebrate Palaeontology, ROM, 1996. Author of more than 50 articles and book chapters, and co-editor of two books, Terrestrial Ecosystems Through Time, 1992, and In the Shadow of the Dinosaurs, 1994, Dr. Sues also serves as associate editor of the Canadian Journal of Earth Sciences. [Photo, courtesy Dr. Hans-Dieter Sues]

Born, Hamburg, Germany, 1904, Gerhard Herzberg was an exceptional student graduating, Darmstadt Technical University, in addition to the University of Gottingen, where he graduated with honours and studied under such notables as Max Born, one of the fathers of the quantum theory, and James Frank, who was instrumental in developing that theory. By the time he was in his early 30s, Dr. Herzberg was known as one of the pioneers in molecular spectroscopy and structure. However, because he had married a Jewish woman, Dr. Herzberg was declared unfit by authorities to teach Germany's youth at the time. Prospects for a teaching job, therefore, were dim, especially since the Depression offered little opportunity for work of any kind. A former colleague, however, was suc-

cessful in helping to secure a job for him at the University of Saskatchewan, 1935. The Herzbergs consequently immigrated to Canada, remaining for 10 years in Saskatoon where his reputation spread internationally as a scientist. Following cessation of hostilities, 1945, and a brief academic hiatus, University of Chicago, 1945-48, Dr. Herzberg was invited to head up Physics at Canada's National Research Council, Ottawa. Over the next 50 years, he became internationally known as the father of modern molecular spectroscopy. Made Companion of the Order of Canada, 1968, his research paid off, 1971, when he was awarded the Nobel Prize in Chemistry for his contributions to the knowledge of electronic structure and the geometry of molecules, particularly free radicals. The NRC's Herzberg Institute of Astrophysics, Victoria, British Columbia, is named after this prominent German Canadian, one of the leading scientists of the 20th century. In this view, Dr. Herzberg celebrates his 80th birthday, 1984, with former Governor General Jeanne Sauvé. [Photo, courtesy National Research Council of Canada]

Between 1792 and 1837, German settlers (a high percentage of them Mennonites) arrived from New Jersey and Pennsylvania. Popularly known as "Pennsylvania Dutch," the group sought not only free land but also religious freedom and exemption from military service. They founded communities in the Niagara district in Welland, Lincoln, and Haldimand counties. They also contributed to the growth and industrial development of the Grand River settlement and substantially helped to make the twin cities of Berlin (Kitchener) and Waterloo into the centre of Ontario's German community. Extolling the community's German heritage is Oktoberfest, an annual celebration which today has become a national tourist attraction.

German-born William Berczy (1744-1813), artist, teacher, and land speculator and his "German Company" brought out settlers to Markham Township, north of York (Toronto), 1794. There, these immigrants cleared land, cultivated fields, and erected a church and school. They also cut a road (Toronto's Yonge Street) through a virgin forest from Lake Ontario to Lake Simcoe, thereby creating a model settlement. The visionary Berczy is acknowledged to be not only one of the leading portrait painters of his day but also the co-founder of Toronto and the architect of some of its earliest public buildings.

Reaching for the Sky

Born in Germany, 1942, Wolf Haessler came to Canada, 1952, with parents, one sister, and four brothers. They settled, first, Montreal, then Richmond Hill, Ontario. Wolf graduated in engineering from the University of Guelph, 1966. He also graduated, University of Western Ontario, with a graduate degree in Mechanical Engineering. Co-founding a machinery building business, 1969, Wolf and his company, Haessler & De Way, initially specialized in manufacturing equipment for food processors and handling materials. Realizing a need for scissor-type work platforms, the company envisioned becoming a work platform manufacturer and Skyjack Inc. was born, 1981. By 1985, Wolf had purchased all of the shares of Haessler & De Way not owned by him. Today, Wolf is continually on the road in Europe and Asia expanding the sales of Skyjack scissor platforms, one model of which he stands upon in this recent view. [Photo, courtesy Skyjack Inc.]

Esteemed Mechanical Engineer

Educated, Martin Luther University and University of Karlsruhe, Germany, Friedrich Paul Johannes Rimrott, born, Halle, Germany, 1927, arrived as a mechanical engineer aboard the M.V. Italia, Pier 21, Halifax, 1952. With $50 in his pocket, Fred soon learned that if he was going to continue with engineering in Canada it would be wise to pursue a post graduate education. By 1955, Fred graduated, University of Toronto, M.A.Sc., and thence travelled to Pennsylvania to pursue his Ph.D. at Penn State University in Engineering Mechanics. By the time he had finished a Postdoctoral Fellow at École Polytechnique, Montreal, 1960, the University of Toronto invited Dr. Rimrott to be Assistant Professor, Mechanical Engineering. It was a lifelong association in which Dr. Rimrott became well-known, both nationally and internationally, in Theoretical and Applied Mechanics. When he retired, 1993, as Professor Emeritus of Mechanical Engineering, University of Toronto, Dr. Rimrott had served the Toronto school since 1967 as full Professor. In 1980, Dr. Rimrott became President, 15th International Congress of Theoretical and Applied Mechanics. In earlier years, Dr. Rimrott gathered together a group of like-minded engineers in Canada to form the Canadian Congress of Applied Mechanics. Better known as CANCAM, their meetings have been held biannually ever since he became Founding Chairman, 1967. Dr. Rimrott also organized and chaired the first Canadian Society for Mechanical Engineering, 1990. Recipient of Honorary Degrees from University of Victoria, British Columbia, University of St. Petersburg, Russia, and University of Magdeburg, Germany, F.P.J. Rimrott's immigration to Canada, 1952, has helped to spotlight Canada as a world leader in Mechanical Engineering. Winner of the prestigious Alexander von Humbolt Research Prize, and either author or co-author of several major publications in Dynamics, Dr. Rimrott, left, in this view, visits with Nguyen Van Khang, distinguished professor at University of Hanoi, while in Halong Bay, Vietnam, 1995. [Photo, courtesy Professor F.P.J. Rimrott]

Performance
of the Year

Victor-Johannes Kraatz was born in Berlin, 1971, and came to Canada with his grandparents, mother, and sister as landed immigrants, 1986. Victor shares much of his fame on the world stage with Canadian-born Shae Lynn Bourne, with whom he has paired at Canadian and international competitions since 1991, the year they burst on the figure skating scene as a very up-beat ice-dancing duo. Four times they have been World Bronze medalists (1996,'97.'98, and '99), and from 1993 through 1999 were celebrated paired Canadian Champions. Although he trains full time at Stamford, Connecticut, Vancouver, British Columbia, remains his hometown. In this view, Victor Kraatz with partner Shae Lynn Bourne perform their sensational Riverdance routine which brought them honoured international recognition. This same routine was voted Performance of the Year, 1998, by the People's Choice Awards. [Photo, courtesy IMG]

Courage in Motion

Four months after competing in her very first race, Silken Laumann tried out for the National Rowing Team, 1982, and won a spot. The second child of Hans and Sigitta Laumann, who immigrated to Canada from Germany, 1960, Silken epitomizes the meaning of hero and competitor, courage and dedication, inspiration and passion. Born, Mississauga, Ontario, 1964, Silken, Bronze Medalist with sister Danielle, Double Sculls, Los Angeles Summer Olympics, 1984 Bronze medalist, Single Sculls, Barcelona Summer Games, 1992 (10 weeks after a serious leg injury in a regatta accident) and a Silver medalist, Single Sculls, Atlanta Summer Olympics, 1996, was voted Canada's Athlete of the Year, 1991, after winning the World Cup Title. Recipient of many awards, including the Harry Jerome Comeback Award and the Wilma Rudolph Courage Award, 1997, Silken Laumann, who retired from competition, 1999, was inducted into the Canadian Sports Hall of Fame, 1998. [Photo, courtesy The Toronto Star]

During the nineteenth century, Canada experienced a large influx of German Catholics and Amish people. Most who emigrated at this time were drawn to Ontario, particularly to Perth, Huron, Bruce, and Grey counties. Others, including a substantial number from Prussia, chose to settle along the Ottawa River in Renfrew County and in Quebec's Pontiac County. The prosperity of the newly established German Empire served to bring about a substantial drop in German immigration in the middle of the 1870s. Thus, it was the large number of German-speaking Mennonites from the Ukraine who helped Canada's Minister of the Interior, Clifford Sifton, to realize his dream of aggressively peopling the prairie provinces. They were among the first settlers to arrive in Manitoba after it became a province in 1870. During the last two decades of the nineteenth century and the first decade of the twentieth, thousands of settlers of German origin from eastern Europe including Austria-Hungary, the Russian Empire, and the Balkans settled in Manitoba, Saskatchewan, and Alberta.

A small number of German settlers made their way to British Columbia under the auspices of the Hudson's Bay Company at the time of the Fraser River gold rush in 1858 and, later, of the Cariboo gold rush, to achieve success only later as grocers, farmers, craftsmen, shopkeepers, and brewers.

The outbreak of the First World War prompted the Canadian government to restrict direct immigration from Germany. During this period, a small group of German-speaking Hutterites did, on religious grounds, immigrate to Canada from the Dakotas. They settled in Manitoba and Alberta where locals and neighbouring residents regarded their distinctive communal way of life as a threat to society.

During the interwar period, 97,000 German-speaking immigrants came to Canada from Poland, Austria, Czechoslovakia, and Germany. Farmers and agricultural workers settled in the vicinity of older German settlements on the Prairies. A smaller number of artisans, labourers, and shopkeepers who had had only limited success in the urban centres of eastern Canada and the prairie provinces moved on to British Columbia.

During the late 1930s, a small group of Sudeten Germans were permitted to come to Canada from

Following studies at the University of Göttingen, 1962-65, and the Free University of Berlin, 1966, Margrit Eichler, born, Berlin, Germany, 1942, won several grants and fellowships, including a Fulbright Travel Grant and a Woodrow Wilson Fellowship, that enabled her to complete both her M.A. (1968) and Ph.D. (1972) programs at Duke University, before moving to Canada to lecture in Sociology at the University of Waterloo. In 1977, she was appointed Associate Professor, Sociology, Ontario Institute for Studies in Education, University of Toronto, and full Professor three years later. Author of a number of books on women's concerns and family life, these include The Double Standard *(1980),* Canadian Families Today *(1983),* Misconceptions *(1994), and* Family Shifts, *(1997). Professor Eichler has also written numerous articles, book chapters, and reports and has served on numerous advisory boards, including the Ontario Law Reform Commission (1989-95), and the Addiction Research Foundation. She has also been President, Canadian Research Institute for the Advancement of Women, was founder and coordinator of the Canadian Coalition for a Royal Commission on New Reproductive Technologies, 1987-89, held the Nancy Rowell Jackman Chair in Women's Studies at Mount St. Vincent University 1992-93, and has won numerous honours, including the YWCA Woman of Distinction Award, 1990, and an Hon. LL.D., from Brock University, 1991. [Photo, courtesy Professor Margrit Eichler]*

Czechoslovakia in order to escape Nazi persecution for their Social Democratic political affiliation.

Significant German immigration did not occur again until the movement of displaced persons after the Second World War. Between 1947 and 1950, immigration to Canada included many German-speaking refugees from Romania, Yugoslavia, and the former Austria-Hungary. When the ban on immigration of German nationals was lifted in 1950, the number of Germans entering the country increased dramatically. Between 1950 and 1961, 250,000 arrived; they tended to settle in the urban areas of Canada, particularly in Ontario, Quebec, and western Canada.

The 1996 Canadian census recorded the presence of 2,757,140 persons of German descent living in Canada of whom 726,145 identified themselves as being exclusively of German origin while 2,030,990 claimed German as one of their origins. As we have seen, few Canadians of German origin came from the German nation-state. Most came to Canada from central or eastern Europe and from the United States.

The largest number of German Canadians live in Ontario, followed by Alberta, British Columbia, Saskatchewan, and Manitoba. In 1996, there were 95,545 Germans living in Vancouver; 78,760 in Edmonton; and 57,520 in Winnipeg. In Ontario, there were 116,955 living in Toronto; 47,675 in Kitchener; and 26,540 in St. Catharines-Niagara. A total of 60,765 of the 102,930 German Canadians in the province of

With $25 in his pocket, he immigrated to Canada, 1951, from Baden Baden in the Black Forest region of West Germany as a 22-year-old engineering school dropout. An immigrant with a vision, by 1953 Robert Schad and several partners had formed a company called Husky Manufacturing and Tool Works, a business operating out of a small garage in Willowdale, north of Toronto. It was not long before a Husky snowmobile was buzzing up and down Toronto's Yonge Street, and turning lots of heads. This was six years before Bombardier patented its famous Ski-Doo. Although the ambitious venture failed, Schad took control of the company and has never looked back. Turning to custom designing and precision manu-

facturing, Schad received his first major order for a mold for manufacturing plastic parts, 1959. Envisioning rapid growth in the plastics industry, Schad and his company turned to specializing in molds. Soon Schad was developing and building high-speed injection molding machinery to produce vending cups. Because his processing apparatus was so fast, Schad was on the verge of cornering a great portion of the market share and took the company to accelerated growth. Relocating operations to Bolton, Ontario, 1969, the company made several major breakthroughs in automated machinery for counting, sorting, stacking, and preparing plastic products for packaging with minimum labour. The company's growth ever since has been phenomenal. A hands-on founder, Schad's skills at handling people are just as legendary as is his business acumen. Robert Schad's company, now called Husky Injection Molding Systems Limited, generated 1999 sales in excess of 700 million U.S. dollars. With customers in over 70 countries, Husky's state of the art equipment produces a wide range of plastic products. Some 2,800 employees worldwide work together as the result of a German immigrant's leadership skills, corporate culture values, and proactive concern for the environment. [Photo, courtesy Husky Injection Molding Systems Limited]

Designer, visual artist, and calligrapher Friedrich Peter of Vancouver, B.C., was born in Dresden, Germany, 1933. His hopes to study at the College of Graphics and Book Arts, Leipzig, East Germany, were dashed because he failed the political interview of the entry examination. He moved to West Berlin, a free enclave behind the Iron Curtain, where he was accepted by the Academy of Visual Arts. Graduating six years later, 1957, with his wife Christine, a refugee from East Germany, he explored leaving Germany. The U.S.A. required sponsors and possibly military service; New Zealand meant working on a sheep farm for one year, and his wife serving as a domestic for nine months. A Canadian Rockies poster enticed them to seek out the Canadian consulate. There an immigration official listed them as sign painters "to make them more employable" and recommended they move to Vancouver. Immigrating to Canada, 1957, from Montreal they took a train to Vancouver. Friedrich became an instructor at the Vancouver School of Art in 1958 and continued to teach at its successors, the Emily Carr College and the Emily Carr Institute of Art and Design, until 1998. Besides teaching, Friedrich worked creatively in different areas of visual design and art. He continues to be actively involved in design, painting and exhibiting, calligraphy, typeface design, drawing and book illustration. He designed postage stamps, coins, and medals including the issues commemorating Canada's National Anthem, 1980; patriation of Canada's

Constitution, 1982; and the Terry Fox Marathon of Hope, 1982. His winning designs include the 1998 four 50-cent proof coin Sports Series of the Royal Canadian Mint, $100 gold coins for the Constitution, the XV Olympic Winter Games in Calgary, 1988, and its official Sports Medal. His typeface design work has been awarded in several international Typeface Design Competitions. The widely used "Vivaldi" and "Magnificat" fonts, publications, and travelling exhibitions of his calligraphy as well as his book illustrations, made his work known abroad. He was elected member, Royal Canadian Academy, 1974. Commissions include large banner murals for the Sixth Assembly of the World Council of Churches, the MacPherson Centre, Burnaby, B.C., murals for Trinity Western University and Regent College, the University of B.C., and street banners for the City of Vancouver. Friedrich and Christine who have raised three children, all born in Canada, believe that "God's guidance, not our dreams of freedom ... brought us to Canada." In this view, Friedrich Peter stands in front of a Scripture mural-painting for the Trinity Western University, Langley, B.C., unveiled, year 2000. Inset is the Marathon of Hope stamp commemorating Terry Fox's historic run across Canada, 1982. [Photos, courtesy Friedrich Peter/Canada Post Corporation]

Quebec lived in Montreal. And in the Maritimes, there were 101,050 in Nova Scotia and 30,450 in New Brunswick.

Since the beginning of their settlement in Canada, Germans have contributed much to the growth and development of our country. Initially, as missionaries, soldiers, fishermen, boat builders, and farmers and, later, as artisans, engineers, manufacturers, entrepreneurs, professionals, and artists, German Canadians have made a dramatic impact on the economic sector. German immigrant work gangs were a necessary precondition to the growth and development of packing houses, machine shops, mills, railway yards, and construction sites in such western cities as Edmonton, Calgary, and Medicine Hat. Farmers began grape growing in the Niagara Peninsula, and craftsmen established themselves in wood processing and furniture production, tanning, brewing, and in the production of rubber goods and textiles.

An important pioneering industrialist was Alfred Freiherr von Hammerstein of Alberta, founder of the *Alberta Herald*, the Athabasca Oil and Asphalt Company, and early developer of the Alberta Tar Sands. In British Columbia, the daring investor and speculator, Gustav Constantin Alvo von Alvensleben, was believed to have pumped $7 million into the provincial economy in the pre-World War I period. As well, Montreal exporter Wilhelm Christian Munderloh is remembered for helping to initiate the first steamship connection between Canada and Europe in the 1860s.

In 1906, Adam Beck, E.W.B. Snider, and D.B. Detweiler of Ontario combined their business savvy and community effort to create a public utility, the Hydro-Electric Power Commission of Ontario, later changed to Ontario Hydro. In the nineteenth century, music proprietors, Abraham and Samuel Nordheimer, followed by Theodore August Heintzman, became Canada's leading piano manufacturers.

No less important is the role that Canadians of German origin have played in the food industry (notably, J.M. Schneider Inc., of Kitchener, Ontario), in science, in music, and the political arena. Henry Sittler and Walter Hachborn, moreover, descendents of nineteenth century German immigrants, helped co-found one of Canada's great success stories when they created Home Hardware Stores Limited, 1964, which today has over 1,000 stores across Canada.

Among the scientists of distinction on the international scene is Gerhard Herzberg. This physicist, who was awarded the Nobel Prize in 1971, helped to establish the reputation of the National Research Council of Canada as a scientific "centre of excellence."

Many other Germans who came to Canada as musicians with the early British regimental bands stayed on as music teachers. These men and others such as Joseph Hecker, who founded the Winnipeg Philharmonic Society in 1880, and Dr. Augustus Vogt, founder of the Mendelssohn Choir in Toronto, did much to develop Canadians' appreciation of good music. The late Elmer Iseler, a native of Kitchener, made a great contribution to choral music in Canada as conductor of the Mendelssohn Choir and as the founder and director of the Festival Singers of Toronto. Postwar arrival Herman Geiger-Torel helped make opera a lively part of the Canadian arts scene as general director of the Canadian Opera Company.

We would do well to remember that Germans have been active in the public life of Canada from the earliest days of their settlement. At least two of the Fathers of Confederation – Charles Fisher of Fredericton and William Henry Steeves of Saint John – were of German origin. Over the years, many have also been elected as members of the federal and provincial governments. The Right Honourable John G. Diefenbaker, of mixed German and Scottish descent, was Prime Minister of Canada from 1957 to 1963. As well, the Right Honourable Edward Schreyer was to serve as Canada's Governor General from 1979 to 1984. ⬇

from **India**

Born, 1930, Agra, India, home of the Taj Mahal, Dr. Saran A. Narang made his way to Canada after graduating, Ph.D., Calcutta University, 1961, completing post-doctoral work, The Johns Hopkins University, 1962, and after spending three years as Research Associate under Professor Harbobind Khorana at the Enzyme Institute, University of Wisconsin, 1963-66. Made Assistant Research Officer, Division of Chemistry, National Research Council of Canada, 1966, Dr. Narang has spent his professional career at the NRC where, since 1981, he has been the Principal Research Officer, Institute for Biological Sciences. Renowned as one of the world's most notable molecular biologists, Dr. Narang and his team at the NRC played a significant pioneering role during the 1970s in the development of efficient and rapid methods of chemical synthesis of DNA. This work originally began in the laboratories at the University of Wisconsin where future Nobel Laureate Dr. Khorana supervised Dr. Narang's experiments in nucleotide synthesis which became a major contribution to the elucidation of the genetic code. The current work of Dr. Narang, who was made an Officer of the Order of Canada, 1985, involves the development of molecular evolution technology which is of great value in the treatment of cancer. His pioneering work of synthetic DNA has had a great impact on the development of PCR, site directed mutagenesis, and DNA sequencing for which several Nobel Prizes have been awarded. In this contemporary view, Dr. Saran Narang examines laboratory results with a research assistant. [Photo, courtesy Dr. Saran Narang]

As THE WORLD embraces the millennium, some 750,000 people living in Canada can trace their cultural roots to South Asia, including present-day India, Pakistan, Bangladesh, and Sri Lanka. It is safe to say that a great percentage of this number have immigrated to Canada from Asia's sub-continent. And although Hinduism is the dominant tradition in India, that great region of south central Asia, nevertheless, is home to many religious cultures which are, today, also prominently found in Canada.

The first South Asians, mostly Sikhs from Punjab, settled in British Columbia at the turn of the century. By 1908, chain migration had encouraged over 5,000 Punjabi pioneers to find work in British Columbia; evidence of their presence there can be seen in the establishment of two community organizations in Vancouver: the Khalsa Diwan Society and the Hindustan Association. In 1907, nativist opposition to an Indian presence and fear of "the Asian peril" encouraged a range of discriminatory legislation: it restricted migration by requiring

[Opposite] Bharata Natyam, along with other classical art forms of India, has its origins in the manuscript called the Natya Shastra which was written by Sage Bharata around 4000 BC. It was primarily conceived out of the urge to express one's emotions and exuberance. Originally this form of dance was strictly prevalent in temples but it later came under the patronage of Kings of southern India. It was only in this century that Bharata Natyam revolutionized and gained attention and regard as a Hindu classical art form. The centre of all arts in India is Bhakti or devotion and, therefore, Bharata Natyam, as a dance form, and the Carnatic music set to it, are deeply grounded in Bhakti. Bharata Natyam, it is said, is the embodiment of music in visual form, a ceremony, and an act of devotion. This art form is very popular in Canada and all over the world. In this recent view, Anila Sitaram expresses the classical art form of the Bharata Natyam. [Photo, courtesy Mohan Mahidhara, photographer, via Sadhana Nagnur]

If he had the opportunity all over again, Anil Rastogi would not hesitate to choose Canada as his new homeland. Born in Delhi, India, 1950, the son of a middle-class Hindu businessman, Anil, age 17, left his birthplace, travelling to Oslo, Norway, 1967, to work as an off-set printer. Quickly learning Norwegian, Anil began working for IBM as a programmer/analyst. A visionary, Anil realized that a university education was a necessary requisition for advancement in business management. Taking a year's leave of absence from IBM, Anil acquired a Diploma in an International Management Programme in Oslo. With eyes wide open, but confident to overcome the worst, he applied for and was admitted into the MBA program at the University of Western Ontario, 1975, even though he did not have a formal undergraduate degree. When he graduated, 1978, he won the Gold Medal among a class of 240. He has never looked back. The young man who immigrated to Canada from India via Norway is now Vice President and Chief Information Officer, McCain Foods Inc., responsible, with a staff of 370 in 10 countries, for IT function throughout the company. Formerly V.P., Systems and Technology, AT&T; Chief Information Officer, William M. Mercer Limited; Senior Vice

President, Wellington Insurance; Vice President, Morgan Financial Corporation, among others, Anil and his wife Indu, also from Delhi, are proud parents of two sons, Shetil and Shelly, both of whom are following in the footsteps of their father in business management.
[Photo, courtesy Anil Rastogi]

additional personal wealth, limited political rights, and stipulated that one must arrive by "continuous journey" from India and not from other ports such as Hong Kong. The hostility to South Asian immigration crystallized in 1914 when a ship called the *Komagata Maru* entered Vancouver harbour carrying 376 potential immigrants of East Indian origin, the majority being Sikh veterans of the British Army. For two months the passengers were denied the right to disembark until finally they departed, unable to enter a Canadian port.

Although wives and children were allowed in 1919, the Indian community in Canada did not grow for almost a half century until, in 1951, Canada developed a quota system to allow some Indian emigrants to help with postwar economic expansion. Over the next decade, more Indians, mostly Sikhs from Punjab, joined families living in Canada since before the restrictions. Gradually, professionals and higher-educated immigrants came. By 1961 there were still only about 7,000 South Asians of Indian origin in Canada, but a decade later – after racial discrimination was formally removed from Canadian immigration legislation and the point system introduced – that number jumped to 70,000 and the diversity increased dramatically.

Dr. Vangi S. Ramachandran, Distinguished Researcher/Researcher Emeritus, National Research Council of Canada (NRC), is an acknowledged world leader in the fields of cement science and technology, having made many scientific and technological breakthroughs in Concrete Science over a 45-year career. Born, 1929, Bangalore, India, upon completing his Ph.D., University of Calcutta, Dr. Ramachandran gained status as a Senior Research Officer at the Indian Central Building Research Institute before taking a post-doctoral fellowship, 1962-65, at NRC. Returning to work in India, Dr. Ramachandran was invited, 1967, to return to the NRC where an appropriate world-class Construction Materials Research Laboratory would be available for him to undertake research of international importance. After accepting this invitation, in 1968, he and his wife, Vasundhara, and their two children, immigrated to Ottawa where he continued his career as a renowned world scientist. Dr. Ramachandran has more than 200 publications, including 10 books, some of which have been translated into Russian and Chinese. He also writes short stories and articles on music and poetry. He has won many international prizes and has travelled worldwide delivering key presentations to many scientific organizations. He appears in many international biographical works. His biography appears in the 2000 Outstanding Scientists of the 20th Century, published by the International Biographical Centre, Cambridge,

U.K. In this view, NRC President Dr. Larkin Kerwin, left, 1989, presents Dr. V.S. Ramachandran with the President's Medal, citing that this Canadian from India "has contributed significantly to NRC's reputation as a world centre of excellence in Cement Science." [Photo, courtesy R.S. Ramachandran]

Emigrants from India today enjoy success in all fields within the economy. While there is some concentration in British Columbia in agriculture and forestry, for the most part people from India living in Canada have settled in major cities and, since the 1960s, many highly skilled workers and professionals have energized Canada's universities, the civil service, hospitals, and high-tech industries. Still others have felt the sting of discrimination within the workplace or faced, as have other immigrants, the barrier to job placement, phrased vaguely as the lack of Canadian experience, that many industries impose. Despite some setbacks, Indian Canadians as a group have an average income approximately equal to the Canadian average.

The most vibrant evidence of the Indian emigrant impact on the urban landscapes of Canada can be seen in the establishment of extensive and bustling commercial districts that cater to the desires of ethnic Canadian communities for distinctive foods, clothing, and music. In Toronto the self-proclaimed India Bazaar on Gerrard Street offers a cacophonous array of colours, sounds, and smells for those in search of a saree, bhangara of

Hindu Temple Reinforces Ottawa's Diversity

The concept to build the Hindu Temple of Ottawa-Carleton was developed at a meeting of the community held on February 29, 1984. Regular religious activities commenced, September 1986, after the first phase of construction. The nine inner Temples to house the Deities were built during the second phase and completed in October 1989. Three Shikharas (domes) adorn the top of this Hindu Temple. There are two resident priests to serve the needs of the community. During the Festival of Light (Deepavali), the Temple may hold a thousand people. All funds for the Temple have been raised through generous donations by the people of the district and the surrounding areas.
[Photo, courtesy Mohan Mahidhara, photographer, via Sadhana Nagnur]

Director, Kidney Transplant Program

Shiv Lal Jindal was born in the village of Dhanaula, in that part of northwest India called Punjab. Prior to university, Shiv was educated in Nabha, then completed his undergraduate work at Government College, Ludhiana, 1952-54, and received his Medical Degree, Punjab University, Chandigarh, 1959. Interning, Rajendra Hospital, Patiala, Punjab, 1960-61, Dr. Jindal's initial residency was at Royal Victoria Hospital, Belfast, N. Ireland, 1961-64. Dr. Jindal was also resident, Springfield Hospital, Springfield, Massachusetts, before becoming Permanent Resident, and Fellow, Ottawa Civic Hospital, 1967. Since 1969, Dr. Shiv Jindal has become a much respected Nephrologist, Ottawa Civic Hospital, and has served on the teaching staff, University of Ottawa, where since 1973 he has been Director, Kidney Transplant Program. As Acting Head, Division of Nephrology, Ottawa Civic Hospital, since 1995, Dr. Jindal's interests in Renal and Heart Transplant have brought much positive recognition to the Ottawa Civic Hospital, to Ottawa University where he teaches, and to himself. A member, past and present, of many influential committees associated with organ transplanting, Dr. Jindal, married to Sarita, his wife of nearly 40 years, the father of three children, all embarked on professional careers, still has found time to be active in Canada's influential Indo-Canadian Community. Founder, Indo-Canadian Community Centre, 1971, and the Hindu Temple of Ottawa-Carleton Inc., Dr. Jindal has been the President of the Hindu Temple of Ottawa-Carleton since 1984. A Fellow, Royal College of Physicians, Canada, and the American College of Physicians, Dr. Jindal's decision to make Canada his new homeland, 1967, is a clear indication that transculturalism will be the heartbeat of Canada's 21st century. [Photo, courtesy Dr. Shiv Jindal]

Reeling in International Acclaim

The New Yorker Magazine *reviewed her most recent film, claiming that* Earth (1999) *"… has an urgency and narrative economy like Casablanca" and that it was reinforced by "hypnotic score" and "passionate cinematography." Deepa Mehta's Hindu parents hailed from Lahore, now a major city in Pakistan, but before the 1947 Partition, a major city in northwest India. Born, Amritsar, India, 1950, Deepa Mehta received a degree in Philosophy from the University of New Delhi before beginning her cinematic career writing scripts for children's films. At 23 years, Deepa immigrated to Canada. Her first feature film,* Sam & Me, *won Honourable Mention in the Prestigious Camera D'Or Category, 1991, Cannes Film Festival. She directed, 1992, a one-hour episode of the* Young Indiana Jones Chronicles *for ABC Television. Produced by George Lucas, the "Benares" episode was filmed on location in India.* Camilla, *her second feature film, 1993, starred the late Jessica Tandy, in addition to Bridget Fonda, Graham Greene, and Hume Cronyn.* Fire, *1997, first of a trilogy, was launched at the Toronto International Film Festival, 1997, where it tied for the Air Canada People's Choice Award. It was one of 29 films selected from over 1,400 films for the New York Film Festival that same year.* Fire *has been sold to more than 30 countries worldwide. The impressive second film in the trilogy,* Earth, *received a standing ovation when it was launched at the Toronto Film Festival, 1998. It won the Prix Première du Publique at the Festival du film Asiatique de Deauville, France, March 1999. The New York Times calls* Earth *a film "bathed in a deep golden light that recalls the orange sky … in* Gone With the Wind *during the burning of Atlanta." Deepa Mehta, who divides her time between Toronto, her home base, and Delhi, is currently completing the final episode of her trilogy, a production called* Water *which explores the human condition in the India of the 1930s, an area, today, inhabited by more than one billion people.* [Photo, courtesy Dilip Mehta, Contact Press Images]

Generating Employment in Southwestern Ontario

Born, India, K.C. Vasudeva graduated in instrument technology from the Indo-Swiss College of his native land before he and his bride, Susan, immigrated to Canada, 1971. Settling in Waterloo, Ontario, "Kacee" worked for three separate companies before he invested $2,000 to open a screw machine shop in 1977. Kacee's company, Maxtech, by year 2000, will generate over 100 million dollars in annual sales with more than 500 employees at seven different Maxtech divisions, the conglomerate he successfully guides in southwestern Ontario. In this view, left, K.C. Vasudeva, with Prime Minister Jean Chrétien, participates as a member of the 1996 Canadian Trade Mission Team to Korea, the Philippines, and Thailand. [Photo, courtesy June Hintz/Maxtech Manufacturing Inc.]

International Futurist and World Visionary

Born, 1944, Delhi, India, young Naseem Javed and his family, along with many thousands of other families, left partitioned India for the newly created Islamic Republic of Pakistan, 1947. Graduating, University of Karachi, B.A., 1964, Naseem gained valuable experience in the family-run printing and publishing business, learning marketing street smarts and the necessary sales skills required to embark on a marketing career in Canada. Immigrating to Montreal, 1967, Naseem's graphic skills, international vision, and general marketing pizazz caught the eye of Montreal Mayor Jean Drapeau, quick to discern that Naseem's communication abilities would be a valuable asset to the Montreal Summer Olympics, 1976. He became an integral part of the new team, promoting and staging the

hugely successful international sporting event during the hot summer of 1976. At the conclusion of the Montreal Olympics, Naseem was recognized as an international futurist and a world visionary. He then migrated to Toronto, Ontario, to establish ABC Namebank, a product and corporate consultant firm specializing in the creation of new corporate identity names. Over the last 20 years, Naseem and his company have productively guided clients to such recognized names as Telus, Gentra, Genexxa, Maximum, Celistica, and Minnova. In this view, Naseem Javed, centre, advises Mayor Jean Drapeau, left, and architect Roger Taillbert, right, on the marketing of various programs for the 1976 Montreal Summer Olympics. [Photo, courtesy Naseem Javed]

Committed to Universal Human Rights

Below, right: Canada's Human Rights Commissioner, since 1995, Robinson Koilpillai was born, Madras, India, 1923. A retired international teacher and high school principal, Mr. Koilpillai had been an educator in Ceylon (Sri Lanka), India, Ethiopia, and the U.S.A. before coming to Canada, 1960. Edmonton, Alberta, in particular, and Canada, in general, have been the beneficiaries of his inexhaustible energy. A high school Social Studies Curricular builder for the Edmonton School Board, as well as Alberta Department of Education, Mr. Koilpillai was administrator with the Edmonton School Board, 1970-88. For his services to education, he received, 1987, the National Award for Outstanding Education from the Canadian Council for Multicultural and Intercultural Education. In 1981, he was acknowledged with the Alberta Achievement Award and received, 1992, the Canada 125 Medal. A Member of the Order of Canada and President of the Canadian Multicultural Education Federation since 1987, Mr. Koilpillai is affiliated with numerous international federations and institutions including the Canadian Council for International Cooperation. In this view, Canadian Human Rights Commissioner, Mr. Robinson Koilpillai, right, poses with delegates to the International Human Rights Conference, Edmonton, Alberta, November 28, 1998. Archbishop Desmond Tutu, Nobel Laureate, 1984, left, was present to support the Edmonton Resolution, which, in part, was to reaffirm the Conference's commitment to the universal and inalienable rights enshrined in the Universal Declaration of Human Rights, sometimes referred to as the "Magna Carta of Mankind." [Photo, courtesy Robinson Koilpillai]

Specialist in Steam Systems

Above, left: Born, Baroda (now Vadodra), India, 1945, Farokh K. Pavri, a Zoroastrian who attended a Jesuit school before graduating in engineering from Pune University, 1971, began a life-long career as an engineer specializing in steam systems. After three years of employment with Spirax/Sarco, in Pune, his company transferred him to Iran. There he met and married Shirin, another Zoroastrian. They lived in Tehran for nearly six years before immigrating to Canada, 1980. Settling in the Toronto area, over the last 20 years, Farokh, past president, Toastmasters' Club, Streetsville Chapter, has worked for the largest steam ancillary equipment manufacturer in the world. Regional Sales Manager for Spirax/Sarco, Farokh has been involved in the sales, marketing, and installation of virtually all major steam systems in southern Ontario since immigrating to Canada. Both Farokh and Shirin are proud parents of two sons, both of whom are following the boating interests of their parents. Both sons are recognized Gold Sailors with the Canadian Yachting Association and both teach sailing and sail racing. In this view Farokh and Shirin stand next to their 36-foot yacht (aptly named Sails Call to honour his passion for sailing and selling), moored at Etobicoke Yacht Club. [Photo, courtesy Farokh Pavri]

Annual National Entrepreneur Award Nominee Meets Canada's Finance Minister

Born, 1942, the Punjab, India, Gian Singh Sandhu joined the Indian Air Force as a young Sikh of 18 years. Envisioning greater opportunities for him and his young family in Canada, Sandhu set out in 1969 to start a new life in a new land half way round the world. Within a week he gained employment at Williams Lake, central British Columbia. A man of vision, Sandhu embarked on an ambitious program of self-development, taking specialized courses at such institutions as University of Western Ontario. Earning an M.B.A. energized his leadership, organizational, and planning skills. Moving quickly up the management ladder, by 1981, he had his own sawmill business and by 1987 Jackpine Forest Products Ltd. was established with the help of two venture capitalist friends. Diversifying from door and window manufacturing to high-lined engineered wood products, Jackpine has made Sandhu a proud employer of 250 Canadians. He forecasts that the millennium year will generate $140 million in sales for Jackpine. Committed to the Sikh community,

Sandhu has served as President of both the International and National World Sikh Organizations. He has also served as President of both the Western Singh Sabha Association and the Guru Nanak Sikh Temple in Williams Lake. Nominated for the Annual National Entrepreneur Award, Sandhu has vowed never to forget his roots and will always be thankful for the opportunities God and Canada have given to him, his wife and four children. In this view, the Hon. Paul Martin, Minister of Finance, meets with Gian Singh Sandhu at Parliament Hill, Ottawa, Fall, 1999. [Photo, courtesy Gian Singh Sandhu]

Wilderness Gurdwara

The Western Singh Sabha Gurdwara, Williams Lake, British Columbia, was built, 1984, to meet the needs of a growing Sikh community. It recalls pioneer days when some 150 Sikhs mined the Cariboo fields during the gold rush days a century ago. [Photo, courtesy Western Singh Sabha Gurdwara Temple]

First Turbaned Member of Parliament in Western World

Gurbax Singh Malhi, left, is the first turbaned Member of Parliament in the western world. Initially elected to the Canadian House of Commons, 1993, Mr. Malhi was re-elected in the 1997 general election, serving constituents in the Ontario riding of Bramalea-Gore-Malton-Springdale. Born in India, Gurbax Malhi received his Bachelor of Arts degree from Punjab University where he specialized in Political Science, English, and History. Upon immigrating to Canada, Mr. Malhi became a real estate broker and established himself as an active member of the Toronto Real Estate Board in addition to the Canadian Real Estate Association. Prior to the 1993 election, Mr. Malhi served as the Founding

Director, Canadian Sikh Cultural and Sports Centre, and was an energetic volunteer member of the Peel Police Ethnic Race Relations Committee as well as a hardworking President of the Bramalea-Gore-Malton Federal Liberal Association. In Ottawa, today, Gurbax Malhi is Chairman, House of Commons Standing Committee for the Library of Parliament and is also a member of several parliamentary associations. In the past, Mr. Malhi served on the powerful Justice, Legal Affairs and Human Rights Committee. Married to Devinder and proud father of son, Gurinder, and daughter, Harinder, Mr. Malhi, in this House of Commons setting, greets Canada's Minister of Fisheries and Oceans, the Hon. Herb Dhaliwal, who, like his caucus colleague, was born in the Punjab. [Photo, courtesy Gurbax Singh Malhi]

Bollywood musicals (musicals made in Bombay), and vegetarian or meat thalis. Numerous jewellery shops that carry the distinctive, orangey, 22-carat gold line the streets as South Asian Canadians from Toronto's suburbs and southern Ontario – but also from all over the United Sates and Canada – converge to shop, eat, meet friends, and see Hindi- and Tamil-language movies.

Throughout the suburban communities that ring Canada's major cities, community organizations representing the needs of parts of Asia's sub-continent community have been solidly established. Political candidates of Indian heritage have successfully run at the local, provincial, and federal levels. At the federal level are British Columbia politicians the Hon. Herb Dhaliwal, M.P., Minister of Fisheries and Oceans, and Reform Party member, the Hon. Gurmant Grewal. Indo-Canadians Deepak Obhrai and Rahim Jaffer represent ridings in Alberta as Reform M.Ps. In Ontario, Gurbax Malhi has served the federal riding of Malton over the last two general elections as a Liberal Party Member. Provincially, British Columbia has four Indo-Canadian M.L.A.s, including Sindi Hawkins, Moe Sihota, Harry Lali, and Ujjal Dosanjh who, as leader of British Columbia's NDP, became Premier of British Columbia, February 20, 2000, the first Indo-Canadian to hold that office in Canada.

Religious centres, temples, mosques, and gurdwaras established by the faithful of the many religions that converge in India have been important social and community institutions in Canada as well as places of worship. Hinduism, Sikhism, Islam, Buddhism, Christianity, Jainism, Judaism, and Zoroastrianism all have adherents within Canada's Indian population. In Ontario, some 50 temples serve the needs of Hindus; Sikhs have used gurdwaras notably in British Columbia and Ontario as focal points for community development. Malton, Ontario, has the largest such gurdwara. Prominent also among the expanding Muslim community in Canada are the Ismailis who have created an extensive network of social institutions and who are linked internationally to the Aga Khan and his institutions.

The presence of Indo-Canadian voices in understanding multi-ethnicity within the public search for Canadian culture and national meaning has been outstanding in recent years. Writers in Urdu have nourished a flourishing of traditional poetry. Filmmakers such as Deepa Mehta have crafted powerful, if not controversial, films about the human condition within the Indo-Canadian context and have enjoyed a mainstream, international audience. Moreover, major news reporters and production personnel of Indian descent, including Monika Deol, formerly of CITY TV, now occupy prominent places in many of Canada's television and radio markets. ✪

Rights of Sikhs Affirmed

From 1986 to 1996 the World Sikh Organization participated in the alteration of the Royal Canadian Mounted Police Dress Code Policy to include the rights of minorities to wear their religious head-gear. These efforts culminated in an official policy, announced in 1990, by then Solicitor General Pierre Cadieux, allowing Sikhs to wear turbans in the RCMP. On May 13, the first turbaned Sikh officer, Baltej Dhillon, viewed here, graduates from the RCMP College. [Photo, courtesy World Sikh Organization]

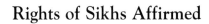

Traditional Sikh Wedding Ceremony, Oakville, Ontario

Prabh (Bob) Singh, left, a chartered accountant, and Rana Dhaliwal, studying to be a teacher, were married in a beautiful, traditional Sikh ceremony at the Oakville, Ontario, Gurdwara, August 2, 1998. The proud parents of the wedded couple immigrated to Canada in the early 1970s, producing families who have grown up as Canadians, yet cherish their ancestral roots which extend halfway around the world to Asia. [Photo, courtesy Bob and Rana Singh]

THE NUMBER OF PEOPLE of Italian heritage living in Canada topped the one million mark in the last decennial census. The presence of Italian men and women in politics, the arts, education, and business has been increasingly evident in recent years. Today, Italian communities exist throughout the country. More than three-quarters of Italians have chosen to live in Canada's cities and have been central in the physical and cultural transformation of these urban areas. As labourers, many Italians did the backbreaking work of construction and manufacturing to fuel Canada's booming postwar economy. Later, as purveyors of Italian cultural foods, fashion and styles, especially in cities such as Montreal, Toronto, Calgary, and Vancouver, significant multigenerational Italian communities have recast these cities.

Before the Great Depression, almost 150,000 Italians entered Canada to earn enough money to buy some land back in Italy. Following World War II, almost 500,000 Italians entered Canada to work and to make a life for themselves and their children. By 1981, almost 87 percent had settled in Quebec and Ontario with the majority of those in Montreal and Toronto. Almost 70 percent came from Italy's south, 12 percent from central Italy, and 18 percent from the north. Many arrived from areas such as the provinces of Cosenza and Catanzaro in Calabria, L'Aquila in Abruzzo, Campobasso in Molise, and smaller numbers from Sicily, Lazio, Puglia, Veneto, and Friuli. Of all officially counted Italian immigrants to arrive in the United States over the last century, half immigrated before 1910; for Canada, the median year was 1955!

Every four years, Toronto's nearly 500,000-strong Italian population follows with great interest the results of the World Cup. When Italy's National Soccer Team won the 1994 semi-finals, Toronto's "Little Italy" exploded with enthusiasm, gathering along St. Clair Avenue near Dufferin Street shouting "Viva Italia" and waving tri-colour flags, as viewed in this Ron Bull photograph for The Toronto Star. *Even though the Italian team lost the World Cup final, Torontonians from all walks of life were unified in celebrating the world achievements of an adopted "home team."* [Photo, courtesy The Toronto Star]

from Italy

In the 1920s and '30s, one of the largest Italian communities in Canada was at Sault Ste. Marie, Ontario. In Italy, at the same time, Benito Mussolini was implementing social programs in the homeland aimed at, among other matters, supporting old age groups, assisting impoverished mothers, and making education compulsory. Some Italian expatriates in Canada tended to support, from afar, Mussolini's early social programs by raising funds to assist the Italian government of the day to fulfil its welfare policies, believing monies sent back home would be used to assist needy relatives left behind. This mid-1930s Giuseppi Verdi Lodge picnic held in Sault Ste. Marie typifies the gathering of a local "black shirt" group concerned about financially strapped parents and other relatives left behind in a country on the verge of economic collapse and impending war. The parish priest of the Holy Rosary Church, today called Our Lady of Mount Carmel, Sault Ste. Marie, sits in the middle of this historic view which preserves for posterity an intriguing epic from Canada's visible past. [Photo, courtesy Angela Dea Cappelli]

Although the vast majority of Italians can trace their origins in Canada to the postwar period, there have been more than four centuries of different forms of interaction between Italians and Canada. First, before the birth of either the Canadian or Italian states in the 1860s, individuals working for English, French, or Spanish monarchs journeyed to Canada. Later, in the nineteenth century, northern Italians with specialized skills such as music and language teachers, hoteliers, or masons provided services for the general society. After the 1880s, Italians (many of them peasants from southern Italy) began to migrate to Canada in massive numbers as part of the great trans-Atlantic migrations of Europeans that continued up to the Great Depression. Many came to work seasonally but still

Serving and Protecting Canada's Largest Municipality

Police Chief of Toronto, Julian Fantino, was born, 1942, in Vendoglio, a village in northern Italy. He came to Canada, 1953, the year after his father had preceded other family members to work as a labourer. His first home was one shared with another family, and one of his first jobs was as a security officer for a department store chain before joining the Metropolitan Toronto Police Force as a Constable, 1969. Over the next 23 years, he served in Uniform Patrol, Undercover Drug Enforcement, Detective Branch, Criminal Intelligence, Homicide, and was a Division Commander when he moved to London, Ontario, as Chief in 1991. In 1998, he returned to the Toronto area as Chief, York Regional Police, in the suburban area north of the City of Toronto with a population of 665,000. His appointment as Chief of Toronto Police Service was confirmed, December 1999. In his 31-year career, Chief Fantino has lectured and written extensively on police-related matters and has served as President, Ontario Association of Chiefs of Police, 1998. Past Chair, Criminal Intelligence Services of Ontario, Chief Fantino is an active member, International Association of Chiefs of Police, the Canadian Association of Chiefs of Police Law Amendments Committee and Crime Prevention/Community Policing Committee. He has also attended meetings of the Interpol Standing Working Party on Offenses Against Minors. As well as being named Volunteer of the Year, 1993, London Urban Alliance on Race Relations, he is the recipient of several awards of recognition from a variety of community groups including the Order of Merit, 1994, National Congress of Italian Canadians, and the Award of Excellence, 1997, Criminal Intelligence Service Canada. Interviewed by The Toronto Star, at the time of his appointment to York Region, Chief Fantino observed, "I think the thing that drives me is not the fame or the position. What drives me is living up to the good fortune that I have been able to attain." [Photo, courtesy York Region Police]

From Salsomaggiore to Westmount

Following World War II, like hundreds of thousands of Italians, Adriano Bussandri of Salsomaggiore left his homeland with his wife and two-year-old son, Claudio, to seek a better life in Canada. They arrived in Montreal, 1949, where Adriano got a job with a textile company and his wife Emma became a seamstress. Claudio, whose father died when he was 14, placed second in the province in his high school graduating year, receiving a scholarship to McGill University, where he obtained an Hons. B. Eng., 1969. He worked for Gillette of Canada, then Nabisco Brands Ltd., where he rose to be a Vice-President, 1976, the same year he earned an M.B.A. through evening studies at McGill. In 1980, he was named President and General Manager, Nabisco's Club Coffee companies, Vice-President and General Manager, Food Service Division, 1984, and President and CEO of Lantic Sugar, 1987-95, at which time he was recruited to become President and CEO of Medis Health & Pharmaceutical Services, Inc., with annual sales in excess of $3.5 billion. A member of the Business Council on National Issues, Mr. Bussandri is also Chairman of the Board of the Canadian Wholesale Drug Association, Vice Chairman of the Board, Montreal Children's Hospital Foundation, and on the Board of Governors, Conseil du Patronat du Québec. A brother, Canadian-born Fulvio, is President of Microcell Solutions, a subsidiary of Teleglobe Canada. [Photo, courtesy Adriano Bussandri]

Government Deputy Leader, House of Commons

For the last 16 years, Italian-born Alfonso Gagliano has been a federally elected Liberal Member of the House of Commons, Ottawa, the last six of which have been as a member of the Cabinet, first as Secretary of State for Parliamentary Affairs, 1994-96, Minister of Labour, 1996-97, and Minister of Public Works and Government Services since 1997. Born, Siculiana, Italy, 1942, he came to Canada, 1958, and took courses at Sir George Williams College (now Concordia University) to become a Certified General Accountant. His first political victory was election as School Commissioner, St. Jerome/LeRoyer, 1977, becoming its President, 1983. In 1984, he was elected M.P. for St. Leonard-Anjou, and as a member of the Opposition, was named Opposition Spokesman for Small Business, Revenue Canada, and Canada Post. In 1988, he was reelected to the new riding of Saint Leonard and appointed Chair, Quebec Liberal Caucus, then Chief Opposition Whip, 1991. Re-elected, 1993, Prime Minister Chrétien named him Chief Government Whip, followed by his appointment to the Cabinet, 1994, as Secretary of State and Deputy Leader of the Government in the House of Commons. Re-elected, June 1997, to the riding now named Saint-Leonard/Saint-Michel, The Hon. Mr. Gagliano, in addition to his role as Minister of Public Works and Government Services, has continued his role as Deputy Leader of the Government. He is also responsible for the Canada Information Office, Canada Post Corporation, Canada Mortgage and Housing Corporation, the Royal Canadian Mint, and Canada Lands Company Limited.
[Photo, courtesy Office of the Minister of Public Works and Government Services]

Veritable Viticulturist

Born in Pisticci, a small town in the Province of Matera, Italy, Grace Cisterna, as a child, immigrated to Canada with her family, 1952, following the trail of an uncle who had earlier immigrated to Canada. After completing her formal schooling, she married Angelo Locilento, and began working as a hairdresser. By the time she owned her own salon, she chose to stop working in order to raise three sons. By 1985, she returned to work but this time joining her husband's company, Vin Bon Juice Co., a distributer of fresh juice for the home wine-making business that was booming. The business acumen she learned from managing her husband's flagship store prompted her and her husband to establish their own Ontario winery. Calling it Cilento Wines Ltd., Grace took over as managing director and has never looked back. By 1995, Cilento Wines had its first vintage. Today, Grace is proud that the wine company she and her husband established in the City of Vaughan, Ontario, is already producing winning wines worldwide. She now has completed a series of certificate and diploma courses, furthering her hands-on education in viticulture, wine tasting, and the overall study of wine. If Grace has anything to do with generating international respect for Canada's wine industry, Cilento Wines will command the same prestige and respect as wines produced from the Italian vineyards where she was born. In this view, Mayor Lorna Jackson, right, City of Vaughan, Ontario, has just presented Grace and Angelo Locilento with a certificate following the official opening of the 36,000 square foot Cilento facility in Woodbridge, 1995.
[Photo, courtesy Cilento Wines]

others settled and created the foundation for postwar communities. Following World War II, mass immigration to Canada from Italy recommenced at historically unprecedented levels that continued up until the early 1970s.

As early as 1497, with the arrival in Newfoundland of Giovanni Caboto (John Cabot) in the service of the English King Henry VII, individuals from the Italian peninsula began to come to Canada. Other notable figures included Francesco Bressani, the Jesuit priest whose *Relazione Breve* written in Italian about his experiences among the Huron in French Canada was published in 1653. As military men in the service of France in the New World, several men of Italian heritage played prominent roles. Enrico di Tonti was La Salle's lieutenant in the 1680s during the expansion of the fur trade. General Carlo Burlamacchi helped defend New France against the British in 1759-60. Captain Filipo de Grassi served the British in the West Indies and was later given a land grant in Upper Canada where he settled in to teach Italian. Throughout the centuries of migration to Canada, Italians arrived as people with ability in search of opportunity whether as language or music teachers, vendors, hoteliers, itinerant artisans, stonecutters, tailors, or labourers.

While the history of Italian migration to Canada finds its antecedents in these individuals, the story of Italian settlement here really begins with the arrival of Italians to work in Canada's resource-based economy, mining

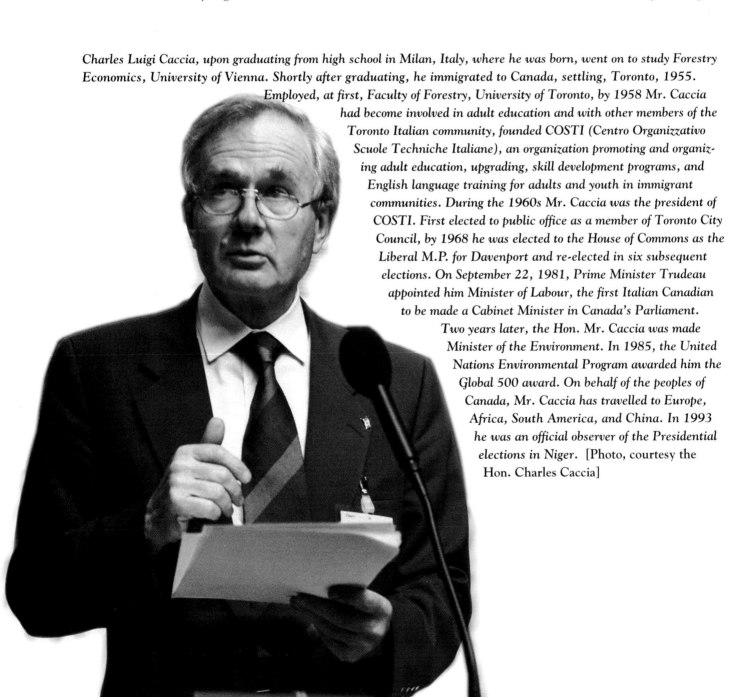

Charles Luigi Caccia, upon graduating from high school in Milan, Italy, where he was born, went on to study Forestry Economics, University of Vienna. Shortly after graduating, he immigrated to Canada, settling, Toronto, 1955. Employed, at first, Faculty of Forestry, University of Toronto, by 1958 Mr. Caccia had become involved in adult education and with other members of the Toronto Italian community, founded COSTI (Centro Organizzativo Scuole Techniche Italiane), an organization promoting and organizing adult education, upgrading, skill development programs, and English language training for adults and youth in immigrant communities. During the 1960s Mr. Caccia was the president of COSTI. First elected to public office as a member of Toronto City Council, by 1968 he was elected to the House of Commons as the Liberal M.P. for Davenport and re-elected in six subsequent elections. On September 22, 1981, Prime Minister Trudeau appointed him Minister of Labour, the first Italian Canadian to be made a Cabinet Minister in Canada's Parliament. Two years later, the Hon. Mr. Caccia was made Minister of the Environment. In 1985, the United Nations Environmental Program awarded him the Global 500 award. On behalf of the peoples of Canada, Mr. Caccia has travelled to Europe, Africa, South America, and China. In 1993 he was an official observer of the Presidential elections in Niger. [Photo, courtesy the Hon. Charles Caccia]

Gio-batta Garlatti was born in the village of Forgaria, province of Udine, Italy, 1935. As a qualified cabinetmaker, at age 22 he set out to make a name for himself. After travelling ten days by boat from Genoa, Joe landed in New York, June 19, 1957. He then made his way directly to Canada, settling, first, in Toronto, quickly gaining a reputation as a first-class cabinetmaker. Within five months he had saved enough money to send for his wife, Angela. Soon they relocated to Markham, Ontario. Known as "that Italian immigrant who could make or fix any piece of furniture," Joe became a charter member of the Canadian Antique Dealers' Association (C.A.D.A.). In 1976 he was commissioned by the National Film Board of Canada to craft a wooden box for Between Friends/Entre Amis, *a special publication used as the official gift from Canada to the United States to celebrate the American Bicentennial. Joe was also commissioned to craft still another presentation box, this time for* LOYAL SHE REMAINS, *the acclaimed publication produced by the United Empire Loyalists' Association of Canada and officially presented to Her Majesty The Queen, 1984, to commemorate Ontario's Bicentennial Celebrations of that same year. Joe Garlatti, whose antique tool collection is the envy of cabinetmakers, in this 1976 view, discusses with then Prime Minister Pierre Trudeau the commemorative box he has just crafted for him.* [Photo, courtesy Joe Garlatti]

and railway construction – from the 1880s until laws in Canada and Italy restricted migration in the 1920s. Between the years 1901 and 1911, almost two million Italians arrived in the United States as compared to only 60,000 who came to Canada. Labour recruitment programs developed by Canadian Pacific Railway, Canadian National Railway, and Dominion Coal Company, with the help of paid labour agents, or *padroni*, brought workers in to work on railway construction along the Grand Trunk, in the steel mills in Sydney, Nova Scotia, in mining at Crow's Nest Pass or the Kootenay district in British Columbia and in Sault Ste. Marie, Ontario. Some cleared bush in Canada's hinterland, engaged in agricultural development in Manitoba, or were truck farmers in Lethbridge or Montreal. Many others, as sojourners, participated in any form of manual labour that earned them enough money to send home to their families in Italy or establish a foothold in Canada's urban centres. Since much of this work was seasonal, gradually small urban settlements were established to service workers returning from Canada's frontier. At first, settlements of Italians in Canadian cities tended to consist predominantly of male seasonal workers who returned to the cities after clearing brush, setting rails, or mining.

Gradually, as Toronto and other cities addressed the need for the urban infrastructure of sewers and trolley lines, Toronto's Italian population grew and settled more permanently. By 1910 many seasonal workers became settlers finding work as stonemasons, greengrocers, tailors, or cobblers. Canadian cities developed neighbourhoods known as "Little Italies" during this early period and these formed the basis of the huge settlements of

Honouring Patron Saint of Workers

Gaetano Gagliano, born, Cattolica Eraclea, Agrigento, Sicily, 1917, is the son of a God-fearing family believing in one very important credo: family is the foundation upon which a future is built. In 1928, and at the urging of his mother, 11-year-old Gaetano travelled to Alba, in the Piedmont, to learn the printing trade. His promising career, however, had to take a back seat, as sickness, impending war, and family needs forced him to return to the family farm where, 1945, he married Guiseppina, not quite 16 years of age. Together they farmed and started a family. Because postwar Sicilians faced growing communism, Gaetano and his wife decided, in the best interests of their young family, to immigrate to Canada. Four days after landing, Toronto, 1954, their fifth child was born. Capitalizing on his earlier years of training to be a printer, Gaetano began working for a small printing company. By 1956, however, he was on his own, buying a printing press, and running his own business from the basement of his house. Thirty-five years later, Gaetano's small printing company has grown into a 23,000 square metre printing house located north of Toronto in the City of Vaughan. Today, St. Joseph Corporation, named for the patron saint of workers, is a multipurpose, highly integrated printing house with state-of-the-art facilities second to none in Canada. A number of the ten Gagliano children are a part of the family business as are some in-laws and a few grandchildren. One of Canada's most successful business stories, St. Joseph Corporation, with over 1,400 employees, is much more than the story of a God-fearing, visionary immigrant whose hard work has made the company he founded, 1956, one of the most productive all-Canadian printing companies. It is also the story of an immigrant man who never forgot the principle that family is the foundation upon which one builds success. In 1998, Gaetano Gagliano received the Order of Canada, the highest honour bestowed upon Canadian citizens by their government. In this family portrait, Gaetano and Guiseppina proudly sit surrounded by their 10 children, four of whom were born in Sicily, six of whom were born in Canada. Tony Gagliano, standing back row, middle, is Executive Chairman and CEO. [Photo, courtesy St. Joseph Corporation]

"Greatest Living Interpreter" of *Madame Butterfly*

[Opposite] After receiving a Governor General scholarship, Maria Pellegrini, born 1945, Pescara, Italy, entered the Conservatory of Music, University of Toronto, and made her debut with the Canadian Opera Company as Gilda in Rigoletto. A year later she was chosen to audition for the Royal Opera House, Covent Garden, and remained their "Principal Soprano" for eight years. Her debut role, 1967, Covent Garden, was Lui in Turandot, opposite the famed Birgit Nilsson and James McCracken. World renowned for her Cio-Cio-San in Madame Butterfly, England's leading critic, Lord Harwood, publicly declared "Maria Pellegrini is the greatest living interpreter of the role of her generation." Her performances of Cio-Cio-San have earned the Puccini Medallion commemorating both her and the composer Giacomo Puccini. The Canadian Broadcasting Corporation featured her in two films: Madame Butterfly and a biographical artist profile that has been aired on major networks worldwide. Miss Pellegrini's fame includes royal performances for The Queen, the Pope, and the incarnations Violetta in La Traviata; Puccini's Manon Lescaut; Desdemona in Othello; Nedda in Pagliacci; Lucia in Lucia di Lammermoor; and Mimi in La Bohème in which a recording exists with tenor Luciano Pavarotti. She has worked with such distinguished conductors as Solti, Colin Davis, Mackerras, Downes, Sinopoli, Guadagno, and Barbini. Recordings include Covent Garden Anniversary, Passione Arias, and Madame Butterfly, 1996. Engagements in 2000 include many returns to her native Italy where she has already received the prestigious Caravella d'Oro, Puccini Medallion, and citations from the City of Rome. She also was honored with the 1995 Woman of The Year Award from the Canadian Ethnic Press Council. In this recent photograph, Maria Pellegrini plays the title role of Manon Lescant by Giacomo Puccini. [Photo, courtesy Remigio Pereira, Ottawa]

The success of Inniskillin Wines is directly related to two co-founders: an Austrian Canadian vintner and a very successful entrepreneur. The latter, Donald J.P. Ziraldo, was born, St. Catharines, Ontario, 1948, receiving his B.Sc. in Agriculture, University of Guelph, 1971. Recognizing that wine makers in Canada faced extinction following the signing of the American Free Trade Agreement, late 1980s, Donald Ziraldo innovatively spearheaded a drive to create Vintners' Quality Alliance (VQA) assuring potential customers and consumers alike that Canadian wine came with the guarantee of a quality assurance program based on the French appellation of origin system. A dapper wine-making pioneer, Donald helped organize a tourist wine route that linked together and showcased vintners particularly in the Niagara region. He helped launch Cool Climate Oenology and Viticulture Institute, Brock University, named Inniskillin Hall. By the late 1990s, Canadian wines, thanks largely to a relentless promoter, had shed the general perception that they were not worthy of comparison to European labels. The son of immigrant parents who came to Canada from Friuli, northern Italy, Donald Ziraldo, a man on a mission, tirelessly promotes, 24 hours a day, Inniskillin wines, in particular, and Canadian wines, in general. Capturing the coveted Grand Prix d'Honneur award at the 1991 VinExpo, Bordeaux, France, the president and co-founder, Inniskillin Wines, has made icewine a North American household name. Voted as one of the 25 Canadian CEOs of the Century by National Post Business Magazine, 1999, Donald Ziraldo was made, 1998, Member, Order of Canada, and is rightly proud to have been a major part of a growth industry which has helped spotlight Canada on the world stage. In this view, Donald Ziraldo basks in the snow with bottles of award-winning Inniskillin icewine. [Photo, courtesy Dawn Grundy, Inniskillin Wines]

The Icewine Cometh

Italians in Toronto's west end and of Montreal's St. Léonard's district. Although the term "Little Italy" can be used disparagingly, it also indicates that Italians were establishing a permanent presence in the life of Canada's cities. Immigrants from Sicily used their peasant agricultural skills, knowledge of fruits and vegetables, and their access to the railways to establish a niche in the wholesale and retail fresh food trades. As these sojourners became more settled, they sent for wives in Italy, and, by 1921, the female population in Toronto was only slightly less than the male population.

Italian-Canadian community life during the period between the two wars was centred around commerce, Italian national Catholic parishes such as Our Lady of Carmel in Toronto, Our Lady of Sorrows in Vancouver, or St. Rita's in North Bay. Other activities developed out of social clubs and mutual benefit societies that were established during these years to encourage Italians to unite for their political and social self-interest. Prominent among these were the Sons of Italy lodges throughout central Canada; the *Tirolese Italiana* in Lethbridge, Alberta; the *Umberto Primo* Society in Montreal; or the *Comitato Intersociale* that was the umbrella group of Italian organizations in Toronto. During the interwar years, many of these clubs received aid from Mussolini's Italy. This coloured the view of Canadian government officials when World War II was declared. Several hundred Italians were interned during the Second World War at Camp Petawawa, and others faced prejudice during the war as a result of their heritage. In 1947, when finally the Enemy Alien Act was lifted, Italians were again permitted to enter Canada.

Born in Palermo, Italy, Lino Saputo's father immigrated to Canada, took odd jobs, saved money and sent for his wife and eight children to join him in Montreal, 1952. Lino was 17 years old at the time. Some two years later, 1954, Lino started making cheese in the corner of a downtown Montreal factory. This was the year the Saputo Group was founded. His father and mother made the cheese and Lino made deliveries by bicycle. After buying out several Quebec dairies and cheesemakers in Ontario, Manitoba, and New Brunswick, Lino was in the position to corner the Montreal market by the 1970s. Now he has 40 percent of the total Canadian cheese market and nearly 10 percent of the U.S. market. With annual sales approaching two billion dollars, it is no wonder that Mr. Saputo is called "Canada's King of Mozzarella." [Photo, courtesy Saputo Group Inc.]

In the postwar period, the small Italian settlements were rapidly transformed by the incredible numbers of new immigrants arriving to work in manufacturing, construction, and development of Canada's industrial base. It is estimated that as many as 80 percent of Italian immigrants who arrived in this period came through the family sponsorship program. Family life was altered as women became more active in the formal labour market. While kin connections were central in helping Italians migrate here, they also aided many Italian men and women to find work in factories or construction sites with cousins and people from their original hometowns. In southern Italian society, women had worked at home or in groups farming in the fields. The economic needs of Canadian life forced women to double their workday both in their traditional caregiver roles in the home and now out in Canada's booming industrial and manufacturing economy. The large numbers of Italians enabled the kinship systems to find places in which Italian women could work together. This assuaged cultural and gender fears about the New World.

To cope with this influx, communities established new associations with the help of some prewar elites. In Vancouver there was the *Comitato Attività Italiane*; in Montreal and Toronto, the Italian Immigrant Aid Society helped new immigrants adjust to Canadian life through counselling, provisioning of goods, and interpreting. Later, in the 1960s, *Centro Organizzativo Scuole Tecniche Italiane*, or COSTI, aided Italian immigrants and many other immigrants to adjust to the Canadian labour market through recertification of skills, language classes, family counselling, and aid to injured workers. The Canadian Italian Business and Professional Association (CIBPA) and the Federation of Italian Canadian Clubs and Associations (FACI), later known as the National Congress of Italian Canadians, were two organizations instrumental in helping to organize community events, lobby governments, and assist with raising funds for victims of earthquakes or disasters back in Italy.

In 1971 FACI and CIBPA in Toronto created the Italian Canadian Benevolent Corporation later known as Villa Charities to build Villa Colombo, a home for the aged. Over a quarter of a century later, a new cultural centre, Columbus Centre, and several seniors' apartments were built to establish a locus for Italian community activity in the city. In Vancouver, the Italian Folk Society representing over 50 clubs constructed the Italian Cultural and Recreational Centre, in the late 1970s. Other Italian communities across the country built similar community centres such as the Casa d'Italia in Montreal, the Calgary Italian Club, the Italian Community Hall in Dominion, Cape Breton Island, and the Da Vinci Centre in Thunder Bay.

The vitality of postwar Italian communities is not limited to their extensive institutional structure. While the number of social services offered to Italian speakers and their children through community activities is impressive, Italian Canadians have made their presence felt in other social arenas. In politics three members of its current government immigrated to Canada within a year of each other (1957/58). The Hon. Charles Caccia has served in the House of Commons consecutively since 1968; The Hon. Alfonso Gagliano has been elected to the House of Commons since 1984; The Hon. Maria Minna, Minister, International Cooperation, has served in the House of Commons since 1993. In the 50 years since the end of World War Two, over 60 Italian-language newspapers have been published in Toronto alone. Writers such as Nino Ricci, the poets Mary Melfi and Antonino Mazza have explored the immigrant experience and life as Italian Canadians. New cultural magazines such as the *Eyetalian* magazine in Toronto or *Vice Versa* in Montreal offer cultural venues for hundreds of thousands of Italian Canadians. Italian immigrant economic mobility in the postwar period has set the stage for the second and third generation to explore ways to create "Italian-ness" within a Canadian setting. ⬇

SRI LANKA, formerly known as Ceylon, is an island off the southeast tip of India. It is inhabited by about 17.5 million people made up of four groups: Sinhalese (75 per cent), Tamils (19 per cent), Moors and Malays (6.5 per cent), Burghers of mixed European (Portuguese and Dutch), Sinhalese, and Tamil blood, and others (less than 1 per cent). They speak three languages: Sinhala, Tamil, and English and follow four religions: Buddhism, Hinduism, Christianity, and Islam. The Sinhalese are mostly Buddhist and the Tamils mostly Hindu, but there are Christians in both communities. Moors are exclusively Muslim, and the Burghers almost exclusively Christian but with a few well-known Buddhists among them. While in general the linguistic and ethnic boundaries overlap, a sizeable number, primarily urban, speak English. The Burghers use English as their mother tongue and the Moors speak the language of their local community but more commonly Tamil than Sinhala. The four ethnocommunities, the three languages and the four religions are all represented in the Sri Lankan Canadian community, though in disproportionate numbers.

Sri Lankan immigration to Canada began after the Second World War. It is known that 27 Sri Lankan Burghers had immigrated to Canada by 1955. The numbers would increase dramatically after Canada revised its immigration policy in 1967 from an ethnic European basis to a point basis (education, language, ability, professional training) benefiting people of Asian descent.

It is difficult to calculate the size of the Sinhalese and Burgher communities in Canada. In the 1996 Canadian census, 31,435 persons indicated that they were of Sri Lankan ethnic origin. It is likely that this figure is made up primarily of Sinhalese and Burghers. As well, 30,065 individuals declared themselves to be of Tamil origin in census reports as a special category.

The coming of the Burghers to Canada followed changes in the Sri Lankan government and the dethroning of English, and the groups' perception of restricted cultural marginalization in the homeland. The Sinhalese, mostly English educated, too, came in search of employment and social opportunities, bringing with them many skills.

from Sri Lanka

The Pandam-paaliya is one of many masks of the Sinhalese Tovil (dance group) repertoire of Sri Lanka. Distinct from religious ceremonies, Tovil is performed, to much psychotherapeutic effect, in a home setting when a family or community member falls seriously ill, or when a woman is approaching childbirth. [Photo, courtesy C.J. Humber/ Private Collection, Professor Suwanda Sugunisiri]

Contributing to Canada's Literary Heritage

Michael Ondaatje came to Canada from Ceylon (Sri lanka, 1972). Immigrating to Canada via England, 1962, Mr. Ondaatje, born, Colombo, 1943, graduated, first, University of Toronto, B.A., 1965, then Queen's University, M.A., 1967. For over 30 years, Michael Ondaatje has indelibly contributed to Canada's rich literary heritage as a respected poet, novelist, film maker, editor, anthologist, publisher, and teacher. An early book of poetry, The Collected Works of Billy the Kid: Left Handed Poems, won the Governor General's Award, 1970, and was adapted for the stage and produced at Stratford, Toronto, and New York. He won another Governor General's Award, 1979, for his collected poetry, 1963-78, There's a Trick with a Knife I'm Learning to Do. As a novelist, he won a Trillium Award, 1987, for In the Skin of a Lion. The English Patient, 1992, which brought Michael Ondaatje considerable international fame, won a third Governor General's Award, plus the prestigious Booker Prize, and still another Trillium Award. After it was turned into a film, The English Patient captured nine Academy Awards, 1997. His critical examination of Leonard Cohen's poetry, 1968, was one of the early literary studies of this well-known Canadian poet. Michael Ondaatje's teaching career began at York University where he still lectures at Glendon College. [Photo, courtesy The Toronto Star]

Straddling Two Cultures

Hemamali Gunasinghe, before immigrating to Canada, 1970, with her husband, Siri (poet, well-known filmmaker, and scholar), and their family, was an instructor in English as a Second Language, University of Ceylon, Peradeniya, Sri Lanka, her native homeland. Settling, Victoria, B.C., Hemamali earned an M.A., Linguistics, and a Ph.D., Applied and Psycholinguistics, University of Victoria, and while raising daughter, Manjula, and son, Ravi, was a Sessional Lecturer in Applied and Psycholinguistics, Department of Linguistics, University of Victoria. Since 1992, Dr. Gunasinghe has taught full time in the Department of English, Camosun College, Victoria, B.C. Active in theatre, both in Sri Lanka and Canada, Hemamali has performed as an actor both on stage and in film. She has translated poetry and drama from English into Sinhala, and has directed stage drama, including Deirdre by W.B. Yeats, Blood Wedding by Frederico Garcia Lorca, and Twilight Crane by Gengi Kenoshita. She has translated several key publications from Sinhala into English and from English into Sinhala. These include An Anthology of Modern Sinhala Literature for the University of Michigan Press and Anthology of Modern Sinhala Prose for UNESCO. In 1999, Hemamali received from the Ministry of Cultural Affairs, Sri Lanka, the Literary Academy Award for translating The Cart, an anthology of short stories by Somaratne Balasooriya. (Her husband, a year earlier, received from the Government of Sri Lanka the Sinhala Film Award as one of Sri Lanka's Ten Best Movie Directors of all time.) Dr. Hemamali Gunasinghe also founded Rasanjalee, an ethnocultural youth group showcasing Sri Lankan culture at such venues as the Commonwealth Games, Victoria Folk Fest, and Saanich All One Family Festival. At Camosun College, 1998, she staged, as viewed here, "Come Dance With Serendipity," an evening of Sri Lankan dance, food, and music commemorating Sri Lanka's 50 years of independence. Although Hemi, like most immigrants, straddles two heritages, she exudes that Victoria is a "warm" home to the entire Gunasinghe family. [Photo, courtesy Dr. Hemamali Gunasinghe]

Three Special Reasons to be Proud Canadians

Kandiah Chandrakumaran was born in the ancient capital of Anuradhapura, Sri Lanka. Minority Tamils living among the Sinhala, because of escalating political tension, the family moved to Jaffna, a district in northern Sri Lanka where Tamil presence was strong. Graduating, Mechanical Engineering, 1974, University of Ceylon, Chandra soon gained employment with the Government's Ministry of Irrigation, Power and Highways. After completing his efficiency bar examination, Chandra was made Regional Director, Mechanical Engineering, but when ethnic conflict disrupted the country in the mid-1970s, Chandra eventually chose employment elsewhere, settling in Nigeria, 1979. Briefly returning to Sri Lanka, 1981, to get married, Chandra and his wife, Usha, a civil engineer, immigrated to Nigeria. Seeking opportunity and ongoing stability, they immigrated to Canada, 1989. Chandra's first job was as an engineer with a firm building Terminal 3 at Lester B. Pearson International Airport, Mississauga. Employed, since 1994, with Crossey Engineering, Toronto, Chandra and his wife have become Canadian citizens. They are also the parents of triplets, two boys and a girl, and are proud to raise them in a country where freedom, tolerance, and opportunity are national characteristics. [Photo, courtesy Kandiah Chandrakumaran]

Lyrical Palaeontologist

Poet and palaeontologist best describe the interests of Asoka Weerasinghe, a native of Colombo, Sri Lanka, who after 12 years in England and Wales, moved to St. John's Newfoundland, 1968, graduating Memorial University, M.Sc. in Palaeontology, 1970. He then became Head Thematic Researcher, National Museums of Canada, Ottawa, and remained in various government posts as an exhibits specialist, until 1989, at which time he joined the Office of the High Commissioner of Sri Lanka, Ottawa, as Director of Communications. Since 1994, he has been a consultant and visual arts curator and dealer. Poetry, however, has sustained his interest since his student days at the University of Wales, B.Sc., 1967, with 11 volumes of

prize-winning works published in Canada and the U.K., and appearances in anthologies in several countries. He has won numerous awards from a number of universities and various Poetic Societies, including the Welsh University Eisteddfod Award, 1966, and the Newfoundland and Labrador Arts and Letters Gold Medal for Poetry, 1969. Professor D. Freeman, Newfoundland Arts and Letters Society, claims that Asoka Weerasinghe "has an excellent ear for language, a sensitivity to musical patterns of vowels and consonants, and a highly original lyrical sense." Mr. Weerasinghe is also founder/organizer, Gloucester Spoken Art, Poetry and Storytelling Series, since 1995. [Photo, courtesy Asoka Weerasinghe]

Librarian Articulating Immigrant Experience

A retired librarian, Rienzi Crusz, a native of Galle, Sri Lanka, published, 1999, his ninth book of poetry – a second major interest since he first arrived in Canada, 1965. Before immigrating, he had graduated, University of Ceylon, 1948, the Morley School of Librarianship and Archives, University of London, U.K., and was Chief Research Librarian, Central Bank of Ceylon, 1951-63. After coming to Canada, he worked in the Catalogue Department, University of Toronto, while taking a Bachelor of Library Science, University of Toronto, 1967. Joining the University of Waterloo as Senior Reference and Collections Development Librarian, 1966, he pursued his interest in poetry. His first book, Flesh and

Thorn, was published, 1974. Both his poetry and prose have appeared in numerous anthologies and journals in the United States and Europe, one critic describing him as having "invented a precise, ironic, yet sensuous language to articulate the multiple dimensions of the immigrant experience." Retiring, 1993, Rienzi Crusz won the City of Kitchener-Waterloo Cultural Award, 1994. [Photo, courtesy Rienzi Crusz]

Born Tangalla, Sri Lanka, 1936, Dr. Suwanda Hennedi Jayasumana Sugunasiri, married to Swarna and father of son, Shalin, and daughter, Tamara, attended Buddhist schools in Colombo, Sri Lanka, before completing his B.A., University of London, M.A., University of Pennsylvania, and Ph.D., University of Toronto, 1978. A civil servant, 1954-64, Dr. Sugunasiri has taught at Vidyodaya University, Sri Lanka; Humber College, Toronto; Ontario Institute for Studies in Education (OISE), Faculty of Education, and Trinity College, University of Toronto. A U.S. Fulbright Scholar, 1964-66, arriving in Canada, 1967, he is a Founding Co-Editor, Toronto South-Asian Review, author of non-fiction, poetry and plays, producer/actor and dancer. Currently

Founding President, Toronto College of Buddhist Studies and, formerly, President, Buddhist Council of Canada, Dr. Suwanda Sugunasiri has served on a variety of committees including the Ontario Advisory Council on Multiculturalism and Citizenship and an ad hoc Interfaith Committee on the Canadian Constitution, 1992. Dr. Sugunasiri, in this view, right, stands with wife Swarna, recently retired Head of English as a Second Language, York Board of Education, daughter, Preeti Tamara, a lawyer who was called to the Bar, February 2000, and son, Shalin Manuja, Assistant Professor of Law, Dalhousie Faculty of Law, and formerly (acting) Senior Policy Advisor to the Minister of Justice of Canada. Together, this family has earned 15 degrees and has amassed 35 years of university education. [Photo, courtesy Dr. S.H.J. Sugunasiri]

During the 1980s, the number of Tamils grew rapidly as a result of the bloody civil strife and anti-Tamil riots. Prompted as well by the Canadian government's special Tamil refugee resettlement program created in 1989, they arrived in Canada as both genuine refugees and economic refugees. Over 1,800 Tamils were admitted during the first year of the program. Thousands more would follow to build new lives for themselves and their families in Canada.

Nearly all Sinhalese, Burgher, and Tamil immigrants in Canada have settled in urban areas. Most of the new arrivals went to Ontario. Small numbers also contributed to the growth of urban communities in Quebec, Alberta, and British Columbia.

Most of the early immigrants who had British educational or professional qualifications and experience have continued in professional, technical, or managerial positions in Canada. Many of the post-1983 arrivals established small businesses. Tamils, for example, climbed into the entrepreneurial class by becoming grocers and restaurateurs who specialize in South Asian cuisine and foodstuffs, marriage and insurance brokers, real estate and travel agents.

The early Sinhalese, Tamil and Burgher communities used to come together to celebrate the New Year and various other social events organized by the Canada-Sir Lanka Association in particular. Unfortunately, as civil unrest continues in Sri Lanka, the ability to maintain public ties among the groups has become increasingly difficult, although personal contacts continue. All, however, have consistently made efforts to integrate with and contribute to Canadian society at large. Among Sri Lankan Canadians, the poet and writer Michael Ondaatje is probably the most well known. He has helped put Canadian literature on the world map and garner international acclaim. ☙

Born, Velky Ruskov, Slovakia, at 16 years, Stephen Roman, below, decided to immigrate to Canada. When he first came to Canada, young Stephen worked as a farm labourer before enlisting in the Canadian Armed Forces, 1942. After developing a medical condition, he was discharged, 1943, disappointed that he was unable to help free his conquered homeland. Going from farm labourer to foundry worker to munitions employee, eventually to speculating investor and financier, Stephen Roman went on to become the founder, Denison Mines. During his day, it would become the largest independent uranium mining company in the world. He was a Canadian delegate to the Atlantic Community Conference, 1962. There, Mr. Roman introduced a resolution calling for all governments of the Free World to confront growing Communism by working together to assist less fortunate countries to attain economic and political stability. Recipient of honorary degrees from St. Francis Xavier University and University of Toronto, Mr. Roman was made Knight Commander of the Order of St. Gregory the Great by Pope John XXIII and was made a Member of the Order of Canada, 1988. A former Director, John G. Diefenbaker Memorial Foundation, formerly Director, Royal Agricultural Winter Fair, Toronto, Honorary Member, Royal Canadian Military Institute, and Canadian Mining Hall of Fame Inductee, 1977, Stephen Roman was the spearhead behind the vision and building of the Slovak Cathedral of the Transfiguration of our Lord, Unionville, Ontario. Consecrated by His Holiness, Pope John Paul II, 1984, before it was completed, the Cathedral, today, is a prominent landmark north of Toronto. In this view, Mr. Roman, July 1986, surveys the second largest bell peal in the world. One of three bells is waiting to be hoisted into the 210 foot central tower, a triumphant monument signifying renewal and hope, and a reminder that Stephen Roman, who died in 1988, never forgot his Slovak spiritual heritage. [Photos, courtesy Helen Roman-Barber/The Toronto Star]

from

Czech/Slovak

Republics

They were the children of a prominent Czech family from Prague whose father was a prosperous cork manufacturer. Otto, born 1940, and Maria, born, 1943, were too young to remember Nazi occupation of their native land during World War II, but when Communists, after the war, nationalized their father's business, they certainly recall travelling with trepidation and forged passports through Europe until they landed as immigrants in Canada, 1951. Although they had earlier begun pairs skating in their homeland, it was not until they settled in Oakville, Ontario, that Otto and Maria Jelinek seriously took up pairs figure skating. Success first came, 1955, when Otto, age 15, and Maria, age 12, won the Canadian Junior Pairs Championship. By 1958, they had placed third at the World Championships, Paris, and second, 1960, at the World Championships, Vancouver. The climax of their career as skating partners came,1962, when the brother/sister team won the World Championship in Prague, their native city. Retiring from amateur compe-tition, 1962, the couple skated professionally for six years with the Ice Capades. Otto Jelinek went on and ran success-fully for political office, first, 1972, as a Progressive Conservative representing his home riding of Halton, then over the next decade, serving in several cabinet posts during the Mulroney years. Maria, in turn, works for a travel agency in Oakville. In this view, the Jelineks skate to the World Championship, 1962. [Photo, courtesy Maria Jelinek]

SUBSTANTIAL Czech immigration to North America did not begin until after 1860. In its initial phases, it was not motivated to any great extent by political discontent over the fate of the Czech nation within the Austro-Hungarian Empire, but moreso to escape poverty and embrace opportunity. Czechs leaving the provinces of Bohemia, Moravia, and Silesia mainly went to the United States and established communities in Nebraska, Texas, Oklahoma, Minnesota, and Illinois. Czech immigration to Canada began on a small scale only towards the end of the nineteenth century. Most of the early immigrants settled on the prairies, establishing small farming communities in southeastern Saskatchewan, including Kolin in 1884, and, later on, Derdard, Glenside, and Dovedale. In 1900, a few Czech families who came via the United States founded Prague (Viching) in Alberta. The first urban settlements to receive prewar Czech immigrants were Edmonton, Kingston, and Windsor. Toronto attracted only a small transient group of Czechs at this time, Winnipeg emerged as the early centre of Czech activities in Canada. The Czechs worked as artisans, entre-preneurs, construction workers, and railroad navvies.

The name Bata Shoes is known world-wide. Thomas Bata at age 24 left his Nazi-occupied homeland, Czechoslovakia, to immigrate to Canada, 1939, where he purchased an old factory and 1,500 acres of land north of Trenton, Ontario, christened it Batawa, and with 100 relocated employees from the company his father founded at the turn of the century, began manufacturing shoes in Canada. The Batas, who had been cobblers for generations, had, through Thomas' father, developed shoe manufacturing into a major industry at Zlin, Czechoslovakia, by 1932, the year Tom's father died in an airplane crash. Young Thomas, who attended an English prep school and a French boarding school in Switzerland and had already apprenticed as a shoemaker, held increasingly responsible positions within the company, but, having no wish to live under the Nazi regime, came to Canada. Through his entrepreneurial skills and business acumen, the company grew rapidly, and despite World War II and its aftermath which inflicted heavy losses on the Bata company, particularly its Eastern European assets that were either destroyed or seized by Communist regimes, Mr. Bata succeeded in rebuilding the organization which at its peak employed 70,000 people and manufactured 300 million shoes annually. Retiring at age 75 in favour of his eldest son, Tom Jr., Mr. Bata continued being active in international organizations including the International Chamber of Commerce, the Business and Industry Advisory Committee (formed to advise OECD), and the panel of "expert advisors" to the U.N.'s Commission on Transnational Corporations. Named a Companion of the Order of Canada, 1971, Mr. Bata holds honorary degrees from University of Economics, Prague, the Technical University, Brno, and York University, Toronto. He is a Paul Harris Fellow of Rotary International and a Honorary Colonel of the Hastings and Prince Edward Regiment with which he served as Lieutenant and later Captain during World War II. His Swiss-born wife, Sonja, also a recipient of the Order of Canada, 1994, has been deeply involved in the Girl Guides, the National Design Council, and the World Wildlife Fund. She has honorary degrees from four Canadian universities, serves as an honorary captain, Royal Canadian Navy, and has founded and endorsed the Bata Shoe Museum which is a major tourist attraction in downtown Toronto. In this view, Tom and Sonja Bata are greeted by U.S. Vice President George Bush at a World Wildlife Fund meeting in Washington, D.C., in the 1980s. [Photo, courtesy Sonja Bata]

The first significant emigration from Slovakia (then situated within the framework of the Kingdom of Hungary) occurred in the early 1870s and was the direct result of the numerous work opportunities to be found in the coal mines, steel mills, and oil refineries of the United States. Almost a decade later, many of these same immigrants moved from the United States into western Canada. Some were attracted by the heady prospect of obtaining free homesteads while others hoped to earn a better living in the coal fields of Alberta in the Crow's Nest Pass area near Blairmore and at Lethbridge. In 1885, immigration agent Paul Esterhazy brought a group of Slovaks and Hungarians from Pennsylvania to settle the Minnedosa district in Manitoba and, in 1886, the area north of the Qu'Appelle River in Saskatchewan. In time, many began the trek eastward to Fort William and other small urban communities in northern Ontario.

The end of the First World War and the founding of the Czechoslovak state brought many changes to the Czech and Slovak peoples, but the immigration of both groups continued. While a small percentage of the Czechs who began coming to Canada around 1921 were farmers who specialized in sugar beet production and

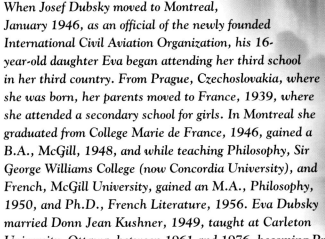

Former University President

When Josef Dubsky moved to Montreal, January 1946, as an official of the newly founded International Civil Aviation Organization, his 16-year-old daughter Eva began attending her third school in her third country. From Prague, Czechoslovakia, where she was born, her parents moved to France, 1939, where she attended a secondary school for girls. In Montreal she graduated from College Marie de France, 1946, gained a B.A., McGill, 1948, and while teaching Philosophy, Sir George Williams College (now Concordia University), and French, McGill University, gained an M.A., Philosophy, 1950, and Ph.D., French Literature, 1956. Eva Dubsky married Donn Jean Kushner, 1949, taught at Carleton University, Ottawa, between 1961 and 1976, becoming Professor of French and Comparative Literature there, 1969. Dr. Eva Kushner returned to McGill as Chair, French Department, 1976-80, and Professor of French and Comparative Literature until 1987 when she became President, Victoria University, Toronto, 1987-94. In addition to teaching, Dr. Kushner has headed several learned societies and other organizations: President, Académie des lettres et sciences humaines; Vice-President, Royal Society of Canada, 1980-82; President, Humanities Research Council of Canada, 1970-72; and President, International Federation for Modern Languages and Literatures, 1996-99. She was a Member of the Canada Council, 1975-1981, and Member and Vice-President, Social Sciences and Humanities Research Council of Canada, 1983-1986, and is a life-time Member, Canadian Research Institute for the Advancement of Women. She has written, edited and co-edited books and articles in Renaissance studies, Comparative Literature, as well as in French and French-Canadian Literature of the 20th century. Dr. Kushner, acclaimed academic, administrator, and intellect, has also co-edited the proceedings of several international congresses. In this recent view, Dr. Eva Kushner, while attending a conference in South America, visits Iguazy Falls, the Niagara Falls of Brazil. [Photo, courtesy Dr. Eva Kushner]

Award Winning Geodetic Research Scientist

Internationally renowed scientist and professor, Petr Vaníček, Department of Geodesy amd Geomatics Engineering, University of New Brunswick, as conference convenor, addresses, in this view, the Geodetic Aspects of the Law of the Sea Conference, Bali, Indonesia, 1996. He came to Canada, 1969, as a post-doctoral fellow of the National Research Council, Ottawa. A native of Susice, Czechoslovakia, Dr. Vaníček, was a Senior Scientific Officer, Tidal Institute in Liverpool, U.K., 1967-69, during which time he received his Ph.D., Mathematical Physics, Czechoslovak Academy of Science. In 1969, he applied for a post-doctoral fellowship in Canada. In 1971, he became Associate Professor, University of New Brunswick, and Professor, 1976. In the early 1980s, he was Full Professor, and later Adjunct Professor in four departments: Survey Science, Geology, Physics, and Civil Engineering, University of Toronto. Numerous invitations as a visiting scientist and professor have included universities in Brazil, Germany, Sweden, the U.S.A., and South Africa. Author of over 300 articles, conference papers, and editor of the proceedings of numerous symposia, Dr. Vaníček, was author of Geodesy: the Concepts, now in its tenth printing, as a standard textbook used in Geodesy courses, worldwide. He has won numerous awards: Fellow, American Geophysical Union, the first Canadian scientist to receive the Humboldt Foundation "Distinguished Senior Scientist Award" (1990), and one of the few to receive the U.S. Academy of Science/ National Research Council "Visiting Senior Scientist Award." He is also winner, the J. Tuzo Wilson Medal for outstanding contributions to Canadian geophysics, 1996, and was named O'Connor Fellow, Curtin University of Technology, Perth, Australia, 1998. A former President of the Canadian Geophysical Union and member of several other geophysical societies, Professor Vaníček, was awarded a Dr. Sc. (Mathematical and Physical Sciences) by the Czech Academy of Science, 1993, and has raised more than $2 million in support of his research. He was appointed Honorary Research Professor at U.N.B., 1999. [Photo, courtesy Professor Petr Vaníček]

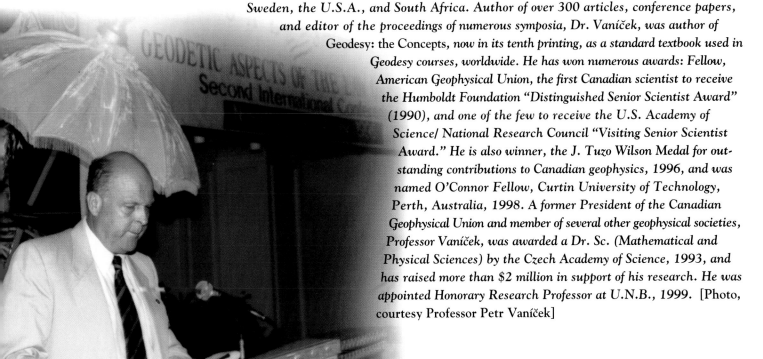

A specialist in the history of immigration and ethnic groups in North America, Professor Mark Stolárik, right, born St. Martin, Slovakia, 1943, immigrated to Canada, 1951, with his parents, settling first, Hull, Quebec, then Ottawa. He earned his B.A., 1965, and M.A., 1967, University of Ottawa, where he is currently Full Professor and Chair, Slovak History and Culture, after spending a number of scholarly research years in the United States. He earned a Ph.D., 1974, University of Minnesota, then taught history at Cleveland State University, 1972-76, before returning to Ottawa for a year as Head of the Slavic and Eastern European Programme, National Museum of Man, Ottawa, 1977-78. Returning to the United States as President and CEO, Balch Institute for Ethnic Studies, Philadelphia, 1978-91, he published several books there before re-entering Canada when the University of Ottawa established a Chair, Slovak History of Culture, 1992. Professor Stolárik has published several volumes on Slovak history, immigration and ethnicity, and has written more than 50 articles in learned journals about the Slovak experience. He was a consultant and contributor to the Harvard Encyclopedia of American Ethnic Groups, *1980, and the* Encyclopedia of Canada's Peoples, *1999. Currently preparing the definitive study of the history of Slovaks in North America, he is seen here with Dr. Ivan Gasparovic, left, Speaker of the Slovak Parliament who visited Ottawa and met Dr. Stolárik in his office, 1993. [Photo, courtesy Professor Mark Stolárik]*

would establish large agricultural concerns near Lethbridge, Alberta, and Chatham, Ontario, the vast majority of postwar arrivals came to the cities, particularly to Montreal, which quickly replaced Winnipeg as the largest Czech settlement area in Canada until the Second World War. Still others were attracted by the possibilities of work open to them in the mining and smelting areas of Quebec and Ontario, especially in Timmins, Sudbury, Noranda, and Arvida.

After the Nazi occupation of the Czechoslovak state in 1938, many refugees fled the country and settled in Canada. In 1939, businessman Thomas J. Bata relocated staff from the Bata shoe factories in Moravia to Canada,

"One of the Most Creative Geologists of his Time"

In 1992, when Ján Veizer of the Earth Sciences Department, University of Ottawa, won the Gottfried Willhelm Leibniz Prize, the German Research Foundation's highest honour, worth some $2.1 million (Canadian) to be spent on research, judges called the Geoscience Professor, born, Pobedim, Slovakia, 1941, "one of the most creative geologists of his time." They were referring to his research into the 4.5 billion years of earth evolution and his claim, through the study of rocks and layers of sediment, that the planet evolved in cycles similar to the birth and death of living things. Besides this study, Professor Veizer is deeply involved in studying the geochemistry of waters, waste disposal sites plus the ecology of rivers and lakes. A Ph.D. graduate, 1968, Slovak Academy of Sciences, Bratislava, he taught there until proceeding to Australia to take a second Ph.D., 1971, at the Australian National University, Canberra. Before joining the University of Ottawa, 1973, he taught and did research at UCLA, California and Göttingen, Germany. Made Full Professor, 1979, appointments have taken him back to Australia, Germany, the United States and Israel, and guest lectures have taken him around the world. Besides the Leibniz Prize of 1992, Professor Veizer is a Fellow, Royal Society of Canada, and has won the Canada Council Killam Award and the Logan Medal, most prestigious award of the Geological Association of Canada. [Photos, courtesy Professor Ján Veizer]

Only Canadian Journalist Given the Olympic Order

George Gross, who has been a full-time sports writer in Toronto for 40 years, arrived in Canada, 1950, unable to speak a word of English and with $4.50 in his pocket. Born, 1923, Bratislava, Slovakia, George made a daring escape to Austria across the Danube and, in Canada, worked one year on a farm for $30 a month with room and board. He then worked in the Dispatch Department of Eaton's before embarking on a freelance career as a sports writer and broadcaster with The Toronto Telegram and CKFH, Toronto, doing three radio shows, one in Slovak, one in Hungarian, and another about sports. After covering the Soccer World Cup in Sweden, 1958, he was hired full time by the Telegram. On its demise, 1971, he joined the Toronto Sun as Sports Editor. Now Corporate Sports Editor, George won a National Newspaper Award, 1974, and the Sun's Dunlop Award twice, has written three books, Torontolympiad For The Handicapped (1976), Donald Jackson, King of Blades (1977), and Hockey Night in Canada (1982-83). George was inducted into the Hockey Hall of Fame, 1985, and is the only Canadian journalist given the Olympic Order. A member of Variety Village, he Chaired the Conn Smythe Sports Celebrities Dinner for Handicapped Children, for seven years, and has received such honours as the Ontario Achievement Award, 1973; Ontario Medal for Good Citizenship; Gold Medal of the International Ice Hockey Federation, 1980; City of Toronto Medal; and was the first recipient of the Promises of Hope Award, on behalf of the Canadian Save the Children Fund. In 1999, he was named Member, International Olympic Committee's Press Commission, and is a Director of Toronto's Olympic Bid for the 2008 Games. He is also President, Sports Media Canada, and Vice-President, Association Internationale de la Presse Sportive. [Photo, courtesy George Gross]

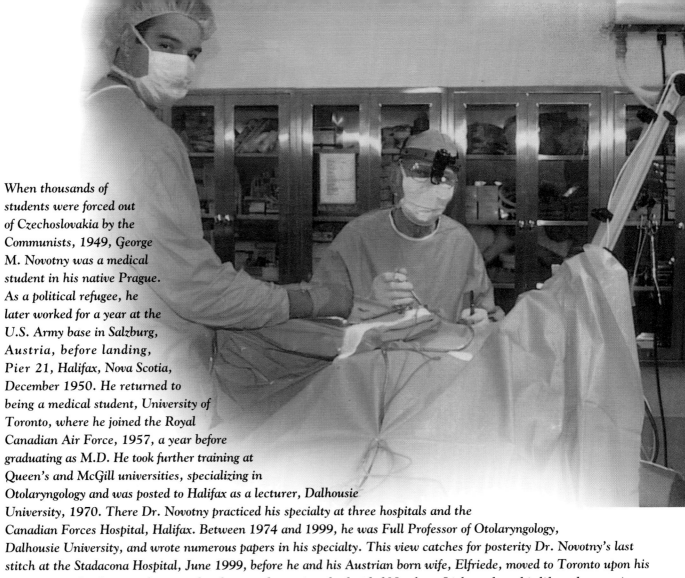

thereby establishing a safe haven and the town of Batawa near Frankford, Ontario. With "liberation" in 1945 and a Moscow-dominated regime, free exit from Czechoslovakia ended but not until thousands of Czech and Slovak exiles and refugees had settled in Canada between 1947 and 1958. This well-educated group of immigrant professionals chose to settle in cities, especially those in Ontario and Quebec. An exodus of Czechs and Slovaks to Canada began again after the Soviet invasion of Czechoslovakia in 1968, an invasion that came to be known as "Prague Spring." This group of young professionals settled in central Canada as well as in Edmonton, Calgary, and Vancouver. Their economic and social integration has been successful.

The 1996 census figures, based on self-declared ethnic origin rather than place of birth, recorded a total of 71,915 Czechs (single and multiple response), 45,230 Slovaks and even 39,185 persons who were content to be labelled Czechoslovakian.

Czechs and Slovaks have formed a multitude of ethnocommunity organizations in Canada. Some are fraternal and mutual benefit societies, others are cultural, political or social groups. Organizational homes or halls, the meeting place of choice for both communities, soon dotted the Canadian rural and urban landscapes. Events celebrated include religious, historical, and patriotic anniversaries and special days.

Czechs and Slovaks have contributed in many different fields in Canada. Many Czechs have been attracted to business and industry. A relatively large group have established factories of their own, thus introducing new products and methods and providing many employment opportunities. The Bata family's shoemaking empire, for instance, made and sold one million pairs of shoes per day during the 1960s. Czechs have also contributed much to the world of the performing arts through the talent and efforts of conductor Walter Susskind, composer Oskar Morawetz, pianist Antonin Kubalek, and singer/actor Jan Rubes and his actor wife, Susan Rubes. And émigré writer Josef Skvorecky played a pivotal role in helping to save, preserve, and enhance Czech language and literature.

Slovak immigrants have also played a significant role in the life of Canada as businessmen, political figures, professionals of all walks, and sporting and cultural figures. Stephen B. Roman achieved meteoric success as the owner of the richest uranium mine in the world (Denison Mines). An outstanding Catholic layman, Roman was

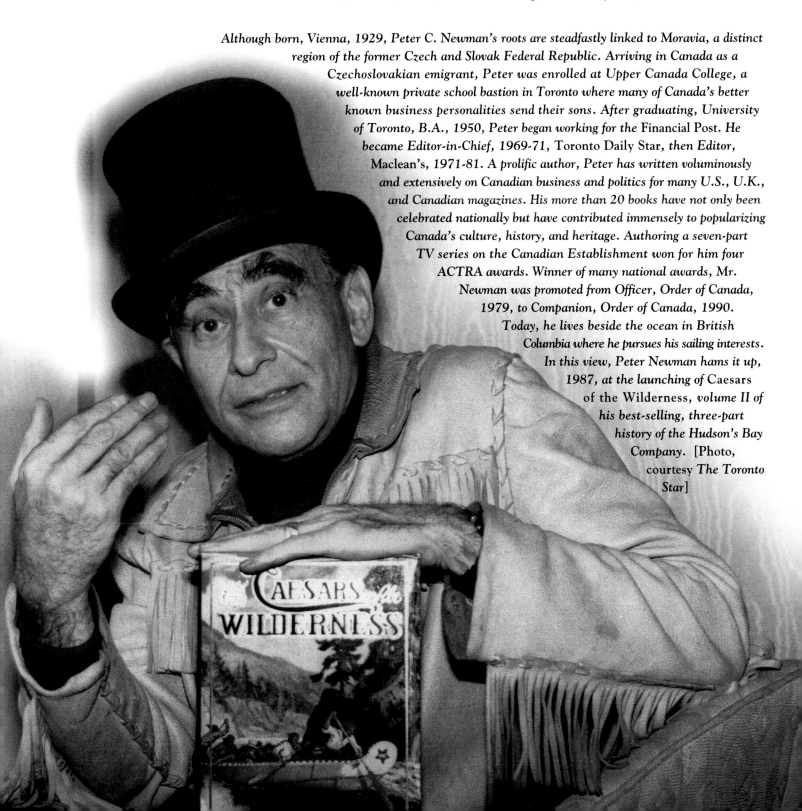

Although born, Vienna, 1929, Peter C. Newman's roots are steadfastly linked to Moravia, a distinct region of the former Czech and Slovak Federal Republic. Arriving in Canada as a Czechoslovakian emigrant, Peter was enrolled at Upper Canada College, a well-known private school bastion in Toronto where many of Canada's better known business personalities send their sons. After graduating, University of Toronto, B.A., 1950, Peter began working for the Financial Post. He became Editor-in-Chief, 1969-71, Toronto Daily Star, then Editor, Maclean's, 1971-81. A prolific author, Peter has written voluminously and extensively on Canadian business and politics for many U.S., U.K., and Canadian magazines. His more than 20 books have not only been celebrated nationally but have contributed immensely to popularizing Canada's culture, history, and heritage. Authoring a seven-part TV series on the Canadian Establishment won for him four ACTRA awards. Winner of many national awards, Mr. Newman was promoted from Officer, Order of Canada, 1979, to Companion, Order of Canada, 1990. Today, he lives beside the ocean in British Columbia where he pursues his sailing interests. In this view, Peter Newman hams it up, 1987, at the launching of Caesars of the Wilderness, volume II of his best-selling, three-part history of the Hudson's Bay Company. [Photo, courtesy The Toronto Star]

Internationally Respected Quantum Chemist

Born 1935, Northern Bohemia, Czechoslovakia (today the Czech Republic), Josef Paldus, in this view, centre, took his undergraduate and Master's degrees in Mathematics and Physics, Charles University, Prague, and a Ph.D., Czechoslovak Academy of Sciences, 1961, that led to post-doctoral studies in Chemistry at the Division of Pure Physics (since renamed Herzberg Institute for Astrophysics), National Research Council, Ottawa, 1962-64. As a quantum chemist, he returned to the Institute of Physical Chemistry, Czechoslovak Academy of Sciences, Prague, where, 1966, he won further awards in Chemistry while continuing collaboration with the NRC. When Russia

invaded Czechoslovakia, 1968, Dr. Paldus decided to remain permanently in Canada, and accepted an offer from the Department of Applied Mathematics, University of Waterloo, as Visiting Associate Professor. He has remained there ever since, becoming Professor, 1975. As a Visiting Professor he has taught in Canada, France, the Netherlands, Israel, Germany, Spain and, since 1984, has also served as Adjunct Professor, University of Florida, Chemistry Department. Dr. Paldus has written more than 250 papers, primarily for the Journal of Chemical Physics, and chapters in a number of monographs. His honours, which began in his student days, more recently include, Fellow, Royal Society of Canada, 1983; Member, International Academy of Quantum Molecular Science, 1984; a Killam Research Fellowship, 1987-89; the J. Heyrovsky Gold Medal, Czechoslovak Academy of Sciences, 1994; Honorary Membership in The Learned Society of Czech Republic, 1995; and the prestigious Alexander von Humboldt Senior Scientist Award, 1996. [Photo, courtesy Dr. Josef Paldus]

One of Canada's Leading Agricultural Scientists

Dr. Jan S. Gavora worked for 26 years (1971-97), Research Branch, Agriculture and Agri-Food Canada (AAFC), Ottawa, where he was Principal Research Scientist. Born, Brezova pod Bradlom, Czechoslovakia, 1933, Dr. Gavora obtained his M.Sc., University of Agricultural Sciences, Nitra, Slovakia, 1957. After 11 years in industry and research, he left Czechoslovakia following the Russian invasion of his homeland, 1968, immigrating to Canada "because I had always admired it and knew it was a great agricultural country." Dr. Gavora spent two years as a Post-doctoral Fellow, University Manitoba, 1969-71, before joining the Animal Research Institute of AAFC, Ottawa, 1971, and being made Auxiliary Professor, Animal Science, McGill University's Macdonald College. A lead author of Animal Breeding: Recent Advances and Future Prospects, 1989, Dr. Gavora has also written over 170 scientific articles, book chapters, and technical publications, edited two books, and has spoken at numerous scientific and industrial meetings throughout the world. He obtained a D.Sc., University of Agricultural Science, Nitra, Slovakia, 1991. One of Canada's leading agricultural scientists and internationally recognized expert in inheritance of resistance to diseases in poultry and farm animals, he received the Public Service of Canada Merit Award, 1984, Tom Newman International Award, U.K., 1985, the Japan Society for the Promotion of Science Travel Award, 1988, and the Canadian Society of Animal Science Merit Award, 1989, the AAFC Aggcellence Award for Leadership, 1997, and on his retirement that same year, was named Scientist Emeritus at AAFC. [Photo, courtesy Dr. Jan Gavora]

greatly responsible for the building of the Cathedral of the Transfiguration near his estate in Unionville, Ontario. Notables in journalism include George Gross, former sports editor, *Toronto Sun*, and Robert Reguly, former writer for *The Toronto Star*. Both Stan Mikita and Elmer Vasko of St. Catharines played hockey for the Chicago Blackhawks during the Golden Era when the National Hockey League consisted of only six teams. Slovaks have also taken their place on the Canadian political stage. Politicians of note include William A. Kovach, who sat as a Social Credit member in the Alberta legislature from 1948 to 1966. In Ontario, Toronto alderman George Ben was elected as a Liberal member in the Ontario Legislature in 1965. He was followed by Peter Kormos, who was first elected to the legislature in 1987 as a member of the New Democratic Party. Finally, in the federal arena, Anthony Roman was elected to the House of Commons as an independent in 1986 and Paul Szabo was elected as a Liberal to the House of Commons in Ottawa in 1993. ❦

As a book designer and publishing consultant, Frank Newfeld, RCA, has won 140 Canadian and 39 International awards. As well as having designed over 650 books, he has written and illustrated three children's books (published by Oxford University Press and Groundwood Books). Born, Brno, Czechoslovakia, Frank moved to England with his mother, 1938, and, at 19, visited Canada, 1947. He graduated from the Central School of Arts and Crafts, London, 1954. He returned to Toronto the same year where he opened a studio and taught part-time at Central Tech, Ryerson, and later at the Ontario College of Art. In 1963 he joined McClelland & Stewart as Art Director, becoming a Director of the company, 1964, and Vice President, Publishing, 1969. He left, 1970, to be President, Macpherson Newfeld Limited; and, 1980, joined the faculty of Sheridan College, later becoming head, Illustration Program. His clients have included CIL, the Art Gallery of Ontario, the National Gallery of Canada, the Royal Ontario Museum as well as numerous publishing houses in Canada, the U.S., and the U.K. His work has been exhibited in Canada, the U.S., a number of European countries as well as Israel and Japan. A co-founder of the Society of Graphic Designers of Canada, his honours include three medals for design from Germany as well as the Centennial Medal for Canada and the Queen Elizabeth II Jubilee Medal. In this view, Joan and Frank Newfeld are presented to the Rt. Hon. Pierre Trudeau, Prime Minister of Canada, by Dr. Jean Sutherland Boggs, Director, National Gallery of Canada, on the occasion of the opening of the Jordaens Exhibition, Ottawa, 1968. [Photo, courtesy Frank Newfeld]

DURING THE NINETEENTH CENTURY, the first immigrants to leave China for the west coast of the North American continent came mainly from the Pearl River Delta in southern China.

Disasters in the form of typhoons, earthquakes, famine, and floods periodically destroyed the delicate balance between nature and the Chinese people. But even without such natural disasters, migration, if not immigration, was necessary. First came local seasonal migration, then overseas migration, and finally permanent settlement away from home. In these ways villages and towns traditionally tried to avoid the total dislocation born of over-population, the collapse of certain occupations, a weakened economy, civil war, and foreign invasions.

Some of the first Chinese migrants to Canada came from the California Gold Rush. When gold was discovered in 1858 along the Fraser River, the interior of British Columbia was flooded with immigrants, many Chinese included. During the 1860s and 1870s, others came directly from China as independent miners and workers or were recruited as contract or indentured labourers.

The second wave of Chinese immigration came between 1880 and 1885 with the construction of the western section of the Canadian Pacific Railway (CPR). Thousands were recruited directly from China to build the last segment of Canada's transcontinental railroad from Eagle Pass to Port Moody.

After the completion of the CPR, most Chinese railroad navvies faced unemployment, hardship, and discrimination. Nearly a thousand men went back to China. Others went into industries such as forestry, sawmills, fish canning, coal mining, and into domestic service. Many, in search of job opportunities, moved eastward to other provinces.

The Mississauga Chinese Centre was designated an Official Ontario Tourist Attraction, 1998, making it the only mall in Ontario, and perhaps in all of Canada, to receive such status. The 43-foot high Main Entrance Gateway is built from 17,000 cubic metres of timber and uses only wooden studs in its prominent architecture. [Photo, courtesy Mississauga Chinese Centre]

The strong anti-Chinese sentiment of the day gave rise to immigration policies that restricted further Chinese immigration to Canada. After 1885, the Act to Restrict and Regulate Chinese Immigration required that all Chinese entering Canada pay a series of head taxes: $50, $100, and finally $500. In 1923, the Chinese Immigration Act (the Exclusion Act) prohibited Chinese immigrants, with few exceptions, from entering Canada. Until its repeal in 1947, many wives and children in China were unable to join their husbands and fathers in Canada. It was not until Canada's 1967 Centennial that the point system was introduced and Chinese people could enter the country under democratic immigration policies. Chinese immigration to Canada started to increase in the postwar decades with people trickling in from many different locations including Hong Kong. A sizeable number of Chinese also came to Canada in the 1980s as refugees from Vietnam, Laos, and Kampuchea (Cambodia). Today, the majority of recent Chinese immigrants in Canada are from Hong Kong, coming as students, entrepreneurs participating in the immigrant investor program, or as members of the family reunification program. New groups of immigrants have also migrated from South America, South Africa, the Caribbean, Singapore, Malaysia, and the Philippines.

Between 1858 and 1967, Canadians of Chinese origin settled in every province, though by far the most lived in British Columbia. After 1967, settlement shifted towards central Canada, with Ontario a favoured destination. The 1996 census records the presence of 921,585 persons of Chinese origin (single and multiple responses) in Canada. Major settlements were established in Ontario (422,770), and British Columbia (312,330). Today, people of Chinese descent make their home in all of Canada's big cities.

In the early period, many Chinese settled in the mining communities of British Columbia where they established areas characterized by Chinese shops and residential buildings. As more immigrants arrived in Victoria, New Westminster, and later Vancouver, so-called Chinatowns developed. Major settlements were also

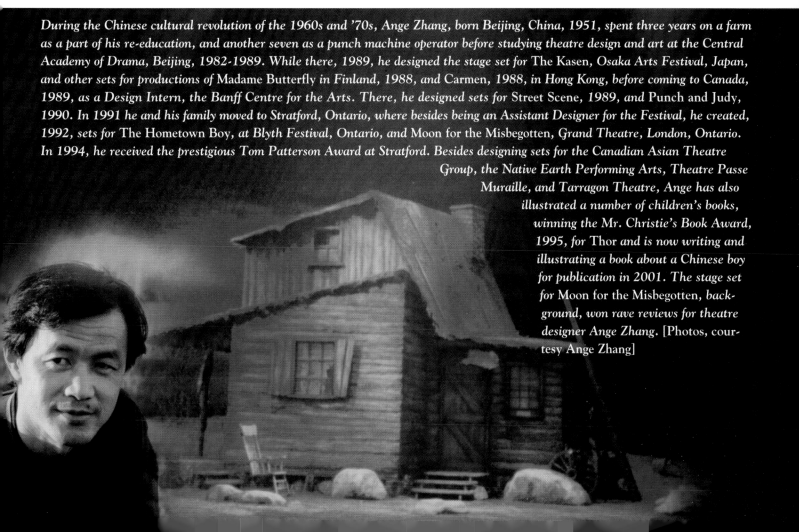

During the Chinese cultural revolution of the 1960s and '70s, Ange Zhang, born Beijing, China, 1951, spent three years on a farm as a part of his re-education, and another seven as a punch machine operator before studying theatre design and art at the Central Academy of Drama, Beijing, 1982-1989. While there, 1989, he designed the stage set for The Kasen, Osaka Arts Festival, Japan, and other sets for productions of Madame Butterfly in Finland, 1988, and Carmen, 1988, in Hong Kong, before coming to Canada, 1989, as a Design Intern, the Banff Centre for the Arts. There, he designed sets for Street Scene, 1989, and Punch and Judy, 1990. In 1991 he and his family moved to Stratford, Ontario, where besides being an Assistant Designer for the Festival, he created, 1992, sets for The Hometown Boy, at Blyth Festival, Ontario, and Moon for the Misbegotten, Grand Theatre, London, Ontario. In 1994, he received the prestigious Tom Patterson Award at Stratford. Besides designing sets for the Canadian Asian Theatre Group, the Native Earth Performing Arts, Theatre Passe Muraille, and Tarragon Theatre, Ange has also illustrated a number of children's books, winning the Mr. Christie's Book Award, 1995, for Thor and is now writing and illustrating a book about a Chinese boy for publication in 2001. The stage set for Moon for the Misbegotten, background, won rave reviews for theatre designer Ange Zhang. [Photos, courtesy Ange Zhang]

established in Ontario, Alberta, and Quebec. Their Chinatowns served as commercial areas and community centres. Businesses drew their customers from the residents of the district and from a transient population of Chinese miners and labourers from more remote areas. Chinatowns were not all restaurants and laundries. These were flanked by a rich assortment of establishments serving many more aspects of the immigrants' needs of body and soul. Traditions and ties to China were maintained, and politics, entertainment, family life, sports, and battles against racism were organized there. Today, the growth of Canada's Chinese community can be seen in the renewal of old Chinatowns and in the emergence of thriving commercial centres and shopping plazas in the suburbs of major urban areas. Toronto now has the largest Chinese community in Canada and the third largest in North America. Vancouver has the second-largest Chinatown in Canada, and Montreal's Chinatown was revitalized in the 1980s with community development projects to build senior citizens' homes, community centres, and housing and business complexes.

After having settled in all areas of British Columbia, early Chinese arrivals worked in key industries such as gold mining, salmon canning, and coal mining. They also laboured on frontier projects such as railway building and land clearing. In central Canada's towns and cities, restaurants and laundries provided both a haven for many Chinese and an ideal economic opportunity since such businesses did not require much start-up capital,

The youngest player ever to win the Grey Cup was Calgary Stampeder Normie Kwong, an 18-year-old fullback whose parents had immigrated from Canton, China, in the early 1900s. Born in Calgary, 1929, Normie was the first Chinese Canadian to play in the Canadian Football League. By the time he retired, 1960, Normie held over 30 CFL records, had won the Schenley Award, 1955 and 1956, as the CFL's most outstanding Canadian player, and was voted Canada's Athlete of the Year, 1955, beating out luminary runners-up such as Cliff Lumsden, Jackie Parker, Rocket Richard, and Stan Leonard. In 13 seasons, the 5'10", 170-pound fullback played in seven Grey Cup Finals, winning four. Nicknamed the "China Clipper," both on and off the playing field, at the age of 69 years, Norman Kwong was awarded the Order of Canada, 1998. When he joined the CFL, 1948, it was one year after Chinese Canadians finally won the right to vote and one year after Ottawa had lifted a 24-year effective ban on Chinese immigration to Canada.

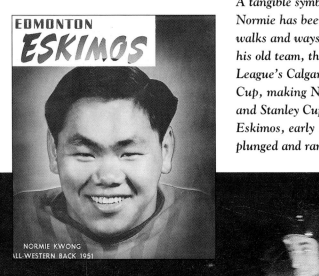

NORMIE KWONG
ALL-WESTERN BACK 1951

A tangible symbol of hope and dreams for the Chinese Canadian youth of his day, Normie has been an important role model throughout his life for immigrants of all walks and ways. From 1988-91, Normie was President and General Manager of his old team, the Calgary Stampeders. He was also co-owner of the National Hockey League's Calgary Flames, 1989-94, during which time the Flames won the Stanley Cup, making Norman Kwong, C.M., the only Canadian to win both the Grey and Stanley Cups. In this view, Normie Kwong lunges forward for the Edmonton Eskimos, early 1950s. In his 13-year career as a fullback, Normie Kwong, inset, plunged and ran for 9,022 yards. [Photo, courtesy Normie Kwong]

new language skills, or special training. The restaurant trade was to remain an important source of employment and self-employment for members of the community after the Second World War even when opportunities in professional and technical occupations opened up.

By the 1960s, new opportunities in the professional and technical fields emerged with the decline of the relative importance of the service sector as a source of employment. After 1967, the arrival of Chinese immigrants with professional qualifications contributed to the growth of a distinct Chinese middle class. Chinese immigration increased after policy changes were made favourable to business immigrants in 1985. The growth of the Chinese population in Toronto by the mid-1980s, for example, increased the demand from Chinese proprietors for ethnic cuisine and for cultural products. In particular, the growing middle class created an ongoing need for professional services and quality products from Chinese professionals and entrepreneurs. As well, the injection of capital by Chinese business immigrants and off-shore capital corporations stimulated the growth of large-scale, capital-intensive ethnic enterprises in Canada.

Chinese Canadians have shown remarkable initiative in forming strong clan and district associations based on place of origin in China, surname, and common heritage. These associations have provided support, information, and assistance in dealing with immigration, taxes, and employment opportunities. They have organized legal aid, arranged loans, set up credit unions, and housing for bachelor immigrants. They have also served as meeting places and cultural centres and have assumed a leading role in organizing social events such as picnics, dances, New Year's celebrations, and performances of Chinese operas. During the challenging days of World War II, the associations raised millions of dollars for the Canadian war effort through parades and social events. As the Chinese community grew, service agencies were formed to help non-English speakers find work.

Kuo Nan Kao, has, in the words of the Royal Society of Canada "led the world in solving central problems in artificial hybridization of plants using tissue culture," work carried out since joining the National Research Council, Saskatoon, 1970. Born in Jen Yee, Kiangsu, China, 1934, his parents moved the family from that war-torn country to Taiwan where Kuo Nan admits he was an indifferent student upon graduating from Chung-Hsing University, B.Sc., 1956. When he became research assistant at Chung-Hsing University, he had no thought of studying overseas until urged to do so by his girlfriend and now wife, Wen-Jou, 1962. Admitted to the Ontario Agricultural College, now the University of Guelph, he received an M.S.A., 1964, and a Ph.D., University of Saskatchewan, 1968. A year of post-doctoral studies at Guelph and a year of research at the National Research Council's Prairie Regional Laboratories followed before joining the NRC as Assistant Research Officer, 1970-74, Associate, 1974-80, and Senior Research Officer, Plant Biotechnology since 1980. The recipient of the Distinguished Graduate Award in Agriculture, 1986, and recently recognized with a commendation for his scientific achievements by the Royal Society, Dr. Kao attributes his success to his professors at the two Canadian universities where he studied and the freedom to do research in good facilities. He is pictured here with NRC President, Dr. Arthur Carty, right, and the citation given him, 1998, by the Royal Society for 25 years of pioneering scientific research in the production of cell cultures from protoplasts. [Photo, courtesy Dr. Kuo Nan Kao]

Canadian Senator

The first person of Chinese descent to sit in the Canadian Senate, the Hon. Vivienne Poy, born, Hong Kong, 1941, came to Canada as a university student, 1959, graduating in History from both McGill University and University of Toronto, before entering the business world as a fashion designer. Member of the Canadian Senate, since 1998, Vivienne Poy, author of two books, is active in the Chinese community as Honorary Patron, Chinese Cultural Centre of Greater Toronto, is advisor to the Canadian Multicultural Council on contemporary issues concerning Asian countries, and is an Advisory Board member, Canada-Hong Kong Resource Centre for Asia Pacific Studies, University of Toronto – York University. Formerly Trustee, Art Gallery of Ontario and the National Gallery of Canada, and former Director, Canadian Stage Company, the Hon. Vivienne Poy has served as a fundraiser for the Kidney Foundation and, Member, Famous People Players (U.S. Board). In 1997, the sister-in-law of current Governor General of Canada, Adrienne Clarkson, Vivienne Poy received the Arbour Award for outstanding volunteer service to the University of Toronto. [Photo, courtesy the Hon. Vivienne Poy]

Contemporary Chinese Canadians have contributed much to Canada. Among Canada's most prominent architects is Bing Thom, who designed the Canadian pavilion for the 1992 World's Fair in Seville, Spain. And in the field of construction, engineering, and property development, Michael Huang is a vigorous force. As partner of Huang and Danczkay, his firm built Terminal 3 at Pearson Airport and skyscrapers at Harbourfront.

Canadian fiction, nonfiction, and poetry have been enriched by writers of Chinese background including Wayson Choi, Denise Chong, Winston Kam, Evelyn Lau, Sky Lee, Fred Wah, and Paul Yee.

Remarkable figures in Canada's film industry include such writers, artists, and filmmakers as Brenda Lem, Keith Lock, and Mina Shum.

Canada's Governor General

In early 1942, fleeing the Japanese invasion of Hong Kong, William and Ethel Poy and their two immigrant children, settled into a cramped apartment in downtown Ottawa. On October 7, 1999, one of those two children was sworn in as Canada's 26th Governor General. A popular investigative journalist and media commentator, Governor General Adrienne Clarkson is the first member of a growing visible minority to be appointed Canada's representative Head of State. Between 1982-87, she served as Ontario's Agent-General in Paris. After a brief stint as President, McClelland and Stewart Publishing House, she returned to CBC fame, hosting Adrienne Clarkson Presents, 1989-99. A graduate B.A. and M.A., English Literature, University of Toronto, Governor General Adrienne Clarkson is sure to transform Canada's highest office into an intellectual and cultural Camelot. Two weeks before her installment as Governor General, Adrienne Clarkson, who was made Officer, Order of Canada, 1992, shares a happy moment with her proud father, William Poy. [Photo, courtesy Boris Spremo, C.M./The Toronto Star]

Quintessential Ballerina

Chan Hon Goh, Principal Ballerina, received her dance training,
Vancouver, British Columbia, at the Goh Ballet Academy and
began performing with the Goh Ballet Company while
still in her teens, quickly establishing a reputation for
being a dancer with breathtaking technique.
The Vancouver Province reported, when she
was in her teens, that "The company jewel is
Chan Hon Goh, unmistakably world-class material in the making." Born, Beijing, China, 1969, by
the time she was 17 years, Ms. Goh was a prize winner
at the Prix de Lausanne International Competitions of
Dance, Switzerland. She was the first Canadian ever awarded
the Silver Medal at the prestigious Adelaide Genee Competition,
London, U.K., 1988. Joining the National Ballet of Canada, 1988, she
was promoted to Second Soloist, 1990, First Soloist, 1992, and Principal
Dancer, 1994. Possessing the grace and beauty of the quintessential ballerina, her
many stunning performances include the title roles in Giselle; Swan Lake; Don Quixote; Ben
Stevenson's Cinderella; Sugar Plum and Snow Queen in Kudelka's The Nutcracker; Juliet, her favourite role,
in John Cranko's Romeo and Juliet, 1998; Princess Aurora in Rudolf Nureyev's The Sleeping Beauty, 1994,
and Tatiana in Onegin, 1996, reported by Deirdre Kelly, The Globe and Mail, as one of the dance highlights of
the year. Living in Toronto and married to Chun Che, a former principal dancer in China and now a master ballet
teacher, Chan Hon Goh, a breathtakingly gifted dance actress, also acts as Culture Advisor to the Chinese Cultural
Centre in Greater Toronto. [Photo, courtesy National Ballet of Canada]

First Chinese Canadian to Receive Order of Canada

Like the mighty dragon in Chinese mythology, Jean Lumb's spirit and determination have made her a symbol to be admired.
Her father came to Canada from China, 1899, to work as a farm labourer. After saving enough money to send for his wife
and their six-year-old son, the family grew 11 more in number. Jean was born, 1919, Nanaimo, British Columbia, at a time
when Chinese families in Canada faced discrimination, had no right to
vote, attended segregated schools, and were not permitted to become
professionals. By the time Jean was 16 years, she, with sister Dorothy,
was travelling by train from Vancouver to Toronto to help an older sister
and husband in their grocery store. When she married Doyle Lumb,
1939, they were the first Chinese in Toronto married in a church.
Establishing their own business, together they worked for 20 years in
their grocery store, at the same time raising three sons and three
daughters. In 1959, they opened a restaurant, Kwong Chow, in
Chinatown which became famous for its Cantonese cuisine. But Jean
Lumb had another mission: to end all restrictions on Chinese wanting
to immigrate to Canada, especially that part of the legislation that kept
Chinese families in Canada separated from family across the seas.
A member, 1957, of a Chinese Delegation lobbying Prime Minister
John Diefenbaker to pass laws permitting the rejoining of families long
separated one from the other, Jean Lumb was happy to see the repeal
of such discriminating legislation. Jean also led the fight to save
Toronto's Chinatown and then fought successfully to save Chinatowns
in both Vancouver and Calgary. Over the years, Jean became an important link between non-Chinese Canadians and Chinese people, helping
to share Chinese thoughts and feelings with government officials. She
did the same when volunteering in hospitals, old-age centres, and
women's organizations. Serving as a Citizenship Judge, Jean Lumb's
greatest moment came, 1976, when she received the Order of Canada,
the first Chinese-Canadian to be so honoured. [Photo, courtesy
Cavouk Portraits via Jean Lumb]

Award-Winning Immunologist

The first Canadian to win the prestigious Alfred P. Sloan Prize was a biochemist from Toronto's Ontario Cancer Institute. Born, China, 1946, Dr. Tak Mak came to Canada after completing undergraduate and graduate studies, University of Wisconsin, 1969. Graduating Ph.D., Biochemistry, 1972, University of Alberta, Dr. Mak, since 1974, has been a senior staff scientist, Ontario Cancer Institute, and a staff member, since 1984, Department of Immunology, University of Toronto. In 1997, he was made a University Professor. Co-author of over 400 scientific papers, Dr. Mak is best recognized for the co-discovery, 1984, of the T-cell receptor, which acts as a plasma police force, identifying intruders and calling out troops of antibodies against them. "T-cells are basically detectives. They go and check the IDs of everything that they come into, like going down a subway and checking everybody," says Dr. Mak. "And 24 hours a day there are at least a trillion T-cells in the body, constantly surveying every tissue of the body, looking for something that is foreign." Dr. Mak has also made significant contributions in the area of virology, immunology, genetics, molecular signaling, and cancer biology. The Sloan Prize, worth $100,000, was awarded to Dr. Mak for the implications his discovery has made in the battle against malignant diseases. Dr. Tak Mak's honours include, among others, the E.W.R. Steacie Award, 1985; Emil von Behring Prize, 1988-90, from Phillips-Universitat Marburg, Germany; Gairdner International Award, 1989; Canadian Foundation for AIDS Research Award, 1991; King Faisel International Prize for Medicine, 1995; McLaughlin Medal, University of Texas, 1997; and the Novartis Immunology Prize, 1998. [Photo, courtesy Princess Margaret Hospital]

Genetic Engineer

Cancer research and genetic engineering are the major interests of Dr. Wei Xiao, now Professor, Microbiology and Immunology, University of Saskatchewan, who recalls that when he finished high school in his native city of Xuzhou, Jiangsu, China, 1975, he was sent, as part of the Chinese Cultural Revolution, to be "re-educated" on a farm. Three years later, he went to Nanjing Agricultural University, obtained a B.Sc., 1982, then came to Canada on a scholarship, graduating, M.Sc., University of Toronto, 1984. With further scholarships, he obtained a Ph.D, University of Saskatchewan, and pursued post-doctoral studies, Harvard University, 1990-92, before returning to the University of Saskatchewan as Assistant Professor, 1992. In 1998, he returned to China as Visiting Professor at both Zhejiang University and Nanjing University, and, in 2000, was named Full Professor, Microbiology and Immunology, University of Saskatchewan. A winner of the National Cancer Institute Research Scientist Award, Dr. Xiao is also active in multicultural and community activities in Saskatoon. [Photo, courtesy Dr. Wei Xiao]

Dr. Lap-Chee Tsui, O.C., was born in Shanghai, China, 1950. He was raised and educated in Hong Kong. He then moved to the United States to continue his studies at the University of Pittsburgh. After receiving there his Ph.D., Molecular Biology, 1979, he trained briefly in the Biology Division at Oak Ridge National Laboratory before joining Department of Genetics, Hospital for Sick Children, 1981, as a Post-doctoral Fellow researching cystic fibrosis, a fatal, inherited disorder that affects about 1 in 2,500 Caucasian children around the world. In 1989, Dr. Tsui attracted international attention when he announced that he and colleagues had identified the defective gene responsible for cystic fibrosis. He was appointed the Hospital's Geneticist-in-Chief, 1996. In recognition of his work, Dr. Tsui has received numerous honours including the Cresson Medal, Franklin Institute (Philadelphia), 1992, Dr. Jonas Salk Award, 1997, the Gairdner International Award, the Medical Research Council of Canada Distinguished Scientist Award, the Canadian Confederation Medal, and has twice been named a Howard Hughes Medical Institute International Research Scholar. He is an Officer of the Order of Canada, 1991, a Fellow of the Royal Society of Canada, and a Fellow of the Royal Society of London. Recipient of four honorary doctorates, Dr. Tsui is the inaugural holder of the H.E. Sellers Chair in Cystic Fibrosis at The Hospital for Sick Children. He is also Professor, Department of Molecular and Medical Genetics, University of Toronto. In 1994, he was appointed a Full Professor, University of Toronto. [Photo, courtesy The Hospital for Sick Children]

In the performing arts, composer Alexina Louie, and rocker and video jockey Sook-Yin Lee continue to gain recognition in their respective musical fields. In the world of classical dance, Chan Hon Goh became the first Chinese-Canadian principal dancer with the National Ballet of Canada.

Chinese Canadians have gained and continue to gain considerable recognition in Canadian broadcast and print journalism. Of special note are journalist, novelist, and publisher Adrienne Clarkson, who, in 1999, was invested as Canada's 26th Governor General; television business correspondent Der Hoi-Yin, newscaster Wei Chen, and journalist and writer Jan Wong.

Designer Alfred Sung built a fashion business empire under the Club Monaco label, creating a variety of product lines that includes luggage, perfume, furs, and household linens.

In the world of computer technology, entrepreneur Kwok Yuen Ho of ATI Technologies Inc. has become an industry powerhouse in the design and production of sophisticated computer graphics.

Of great importance to the medical research community are the scientific achievements of Dr. Tak Mak, leading Canadian investigator of the immune system, and Dr. Lap-Chee Tsui of the University of Toronto, who identified the gene responsible for cystic fibrosis.

When he was only 12 years, Arthur Lee, born, Canton, China, 1953, moved with his family to Canada, settling, Sudbury, Ontario, where his father became a successful restaurateur. Mr. Lee, today, holds a B.A., Business Administration, Ryerson Polytechnic University. With his wife, Esther, Mr. Lee co-founded Solidwear Group of Companies, a clothing manufacturer based in Toronto. The Group has grown from 20 employees, at inception, 1995, to over 400 employees working out of 6 locations in Southern Ontario. The Group's activities are carried out in over 190,000 square feet of production, warehouse, and office space. In 1997, Mr. Lee acquired at auction and donated to the McCrae House Museum, Guelph, Ontario, the war medals of the late Lt. Col. John McCrae, the author of the world-famous poem, In Flanders Fields, thereby ensuring that the valuable medals would remain in Canada. In recognition of his service to Canada, Arthur Lee was awarded the Meritorious Service Medal by the Governor General of Canada. Mr. Lee is also the recipient of the Arbour Award from the University of Toronto, an Honorary Doctorate of Laws from Ryerson University, and an Alumni Award of Distinction from Ryerson. Mr. Lee co-chairs the Yee Hong Centre for Geriatric Care, is a Member, Board of Directors, Upper Canada College, is a Member, Board of Directors, Ontario Heritage Foundation, and is Member, Fashion Advisory Board of Ryerson. Mr. Lee has been active in sponsoring the Foster Parents Plan, St. John Ambulance, and the Hospital for Sick Children. Mr. Lee and Esther have been married for over 20 years and have three children: Jennifer, Andrea, and Adrian. In this view, Arthur Lee holds up a portrait of Col. John McCrae, a thank-you gift from Guelph's Mayor Joe Young who is recognizing Mr. Lee for donating the highly prized war medals he purchased at a much publicized auction, 1997, and then donated to the McCrae House Museum. This photograph was taken at the McCrae House Museum on the occasion of the 125th anniversary of the birth of Col. John McCrae, M.D., 1998. [Photo, courtesy the McCrae House Museum]

In sports, Normie Kwong, "The China Clipper," played on four Grey Cup championship football teams during the 1940s and 1950s. As a fullback, this gridiron great set thirty Canadian Football League individual records and was the first player to rush for over 9,000 yards. Vancouver athlete Lori Fung brought home the gold in rhythmic gymnastics from the 1984 Olympics.

The postwar period witnessed an increased participation of Canadians of Chinese origin in Canadian politics. In 1957 Douglas Jung became the first Chinese Canadian to be elected to the House of Commons serving the riding of Vancouver Centre from 1957 to 1962. Vancouver lawyer and native Albertan, Art Lee, followed in his footsteps in 1974. Raymond Chan, an immigrant from Hong Kong, was elected to the House in 1993 and was subsequently named Secretary of State for Asia and the Pacific.

Chinese Canadians have also entered provincial politics. Bob Wong of Fort Erie, Ontario, was elected to the provincial legislature in 1987. He was the first Chinese named to a cabinet post in Canada when he served as Ontario's Minister of Energy and Minister of Culture and Citizenship in the government of Premier David Peterson.

Chinese Canadians have figured prominently in municipal government. Mayors include Peter Wing of Kamloops, British Columbia (1966-1971); Wayne Mah of Eston, Saskatchewan (1984-1985); and Peter Wong, who was elected mayor of Sudbury, Ontario, in 1983.

The Chinese community has also helped address such issues as racial equality and minority rights. Lawyer Susan Eng served as Chair of the Metropolitan Toronto Police Services Board from 1991 to 1995. Dr. Joseph Wong served as Chairman of the United Way of Greater Toronto in 1990 and was named to the Order of Canada in 1993. Born and bred in Nanaimo, British Columbia, Jean Lumb of Toronto was a member of the committee that successfully lobbied the Diefenbaker government in 1957 to change the immigration law to improve family reunification. For her long and sterling career in community service, she was awarded the Order of Canada in 1976, the first Chinese Canadian woman to receive this recognition.

Other activists of note include restaurateur Bill Wen, founding president of the Toronto Chinese Restaurant Association and a leader of a gritty save Chinatown campaign; Valerie Mah, the first Chinese-Canadian elementary school principal in Toronto; Cheuk C. Kwan, human rights activist and project director of the National Movement for Harmony in Canada; Dock Yip, community sage and neophyte actor at age 80, and the first Chinese Canadian called to the bar; and Dora Nipp, lawyer, historian, documentary filmmaker, and policy analyst with the Ontario Human Rights Commission.

Philanthropist David Lam was appointed Lieutenant Governor of British Columbia in 1988 and served until 1995. Toronto residents Evelyn Huang and Vivienne Poy, the latter of whom is the first person of Chinese descent to sit in the Canadian Senate (1998), in turn, have proved indefatigable fundraisers and supporters of numerous cultural causes.

As Canadians embrace the new millennium, Chinese influence will continue to shape and influence the development of Canada as a global player in the twenty-first century. ⬇

Master Moy Lin-shin, a Taoist master, studied Taoism and the internal arts with highly respected teachers in China and Hong Kong for nearly 30 years. Born, Toishan, China, 1931, he dedicated his life to compassion and service to others, inspired by the example of the Bodhisattva Kuan Yin. He integrated his knowledge into a widely accessible set of movements he called Taoist Tai Chi in order to acknowledge the source of his teachings. Shortly after arriving in Toronto, 1970, he founded the Taoist Tai Chi Society to promote health in the community, and then the Fung Loy Kok Institute of Taoism, 1981, to promote Taoist spiritual traditions, and the Gei Pang Lok Hup Academy, 1988, to encourage the study of other Taoist internal arts. These are all non-profit volunteer organizations, totalling over 500 branches in 28 countries worldwide. Master Moy lived a simple life with few worldly possessions. As a teacher, he instilled in his students the fundamental Taoist principle of cultivating both body and spirit; as a healer, he personally assisted countless individuals to recover their health. His efforts to help people of all health conditions culminated in the establishment of the first Taoist Tai Chi Health Recovery Centre at Orangeville, Ontario, 1997, a focal point for research and training in the therapeutic value of the Taoist arts. Master Moy, as viewed in this 1979 photograph taken at the Bathurst Street Club, Toronto, passed away in 1998, but the organizations he founded continue to flourish through the efforts of thousands of volunteers inspired by his life of selfless service. [Photo, courtesy Chris Farano/Taoist Tai Chi Society via David Lucas/Kane Design]

Janusz Zurakowski was born, 1914, Ryzawka, in once Polish territory that had come under control of Russia. When his family moved to independent Poland, Janusz after completing high school, joined the Polish Air Force, 1934. At the outbreak of World War II, Jan was a flying instructor and when Poland fell to enemy forces, Jan escaped to England, joined the Royal Air Force and during the Battle of Britain was credited with destroying three enemy aircraft. Later, he joined Polish Squadrons, serving as Flight Commander and Squadron Leader. For his wartime services he was awarded the Polish Virtuti Militari Cross and the Polish Cross of Valour with three Bars. At the end of the war, Jan graduated from the Empire Test Pilot's School and began testing airplanes in England, including one of the world's first jet fighters, the Vampire. He also worked in the development of the Meteor and the Javelin fighter aircraft. By 1950, he established a new air speed record between London-Copenhagen-London. In 1952, he immigrated to Canada to join Avro Aircraft in Malton, Ontario, as chief development pilot. That same year he became the first to break the sound barrier, in Canada, flying a CF-100 fighter aircraft. When the Avro Arrow, Canada's pride in aeronautical engineering and design achievement, was ready for testing, Jan Zurakowski, March 25, 1958, completed the much heralded first flight of this supersonic aircraft. In recognition for his many experimental achievements in the air, Jan was awarded the prestigious McKee Trophy and became a member of Canada's Aviation Hall of Fame. In 1960, he retired to the heart of the 19th century Polish community in Renfrew County, near Barry's Bay, where he and his wife Anna established a tourist business. In this double view, Jan, background, boards the Avro Arrow, 1958, and, inset, is viewed receiving the J.C. Floyd Award from Jim Floyd, whose acclaimed design of the Avro Arrow afforded Jan Zurakowski, as a test pilot, an opportunity to showcase Canada's world leadership in both aircraft design and aeronautical engineering. [Photos, courtesy J.C. Floyd]

from Poland

POLES have long played a role in Canadian history. Dominik Barcz, who arrived in Lower Canada around 1750, served on the Legislative Council and later published two newspapers. The partition of Poland among Russia, Prussia, and Austria in 1795 would contribute to the continual growth of this New World settlement. The wish to flee political or religious oppressions and a poor economy also sparked the emigration of Poles to Canada.

The sons of Polish immigrant arrivals would fight with distinction on the battlefield in the War of 1812 and the Rebellions of 1837. By the middle of the nineteenth century, Alexandre Eduard Kierzkowski would serve on the Legislative Council from 1858, in the Legislative Assembly from 1861, and in the House of Commons from 1867. Mr. and Mrs. E. Brokovski ameliorated life in Winnipeg by helping to establish the Dramatic and Literary Association in 1876 and by sponsoring the Philharmonic Society.

Sir Casimir Gzowski, an exile of the 1830s who reached Ontario in the early 1840s, was knighted for services to his Queen both as a military and a civil engineer. Gzowski was responsible for seven bridges (including one

Possibly the smallest group of early settlers to establish a distinct cultural tradition in Canada were Polish immigrants who came to Ontario in the late 1850s and by the 1890s had established an ethnic community of some 325 families in Renfrew County, northeastern Ontario. They came from a region in Poland known as Kazuby lying west of the Vistula River and touching the Baltic Sea. They brought with them Old World ways and built log houses and filled their rustic homes with country furniture unexcelled in decorative charm and charming beauty elsewhere in Canada. Two examples, viewed here, of Polish-Canadian furniture, include the skrynia or storage chest, and kreddens or kitchen cupboard, very useful household furnishings in any century and pursued by a growing gamut of passionate Canadiana collectors.
[Photos, courtesy Howard Pain]

connecting Fort Erie, Ontario, with Buffalo, New York), ports, canals, railways, Yonge Street between Toronto and Simcoe, the Niagara Parkway, and numerous other engineering projects. He also served as President of the Dominion Rifle Association, Colonel in the Militia, Administrator and Deputy Lieutenant-Governor of Ontario and an Honorary aide-de-camp to Queen Victoria. His great-grandson – broadcaster, editor, and writer Peter Gzowski – became one of Canada's best-loved media personalities.

Within two decades of Gzowski's arrival, a group of Poles – Kashub peasants from Prussian-occupied Poland attracted by land and railway developers' advertisements – arrived in Renfrew County on Ontario's lumbering and farming frontier. They were émigrés with a fierce desire to maintain their regional Polish culture that, in the decades before they migrated, had been undermined by German administration. At Wilno, Ontario, in 1876, the

Since 1981, Tony Ruprecht, M.P.P., has represented Toronto's west-end riding of Parkdale as a Liberal Member of the Ontario Legislature. Born, Konstantinow, Poland, 1942, Tony came to Canada, 1949, after attending school in Germany. Graduating, Laurentian University, B.A. (Hons), 1969, and Wichita State University, 1971, Tony entered the political arena in the 1970s, serving first on the Toronto City Council before his election to the Ontario Legislature, 1981. In 1985, Tony was appointed Ontario's first Minister Responsible for Disabled Persons. He has also served as Minister Without Portfolio for Citizenship and Culture, and was Parliamentary Assistant to the Minister of Community and Social Services. Tony has also taught International Politics, Brandon University, and Public Administration, York University. In 1990, Tony made a unique contribution to Ontario's historic heritage and cultural life by publishing Toronto's Many Faces, a 400-page guidebook to more than 65 diverse cultural communities in Toronto. The same book was updated and republished, 1998. Tony is the recipient of numerous international honours, including Knight of Malta, Sovereign Military Order Saint John of Jerusalem; Estonian Gold Medal of Honour; Medal of Valour & Merit, Government of Portugal; Polish Gold Cross of Merit; and Medal of Honour, Government of the Philippines. In this view, centre, Tony Ruprecht, M.P.P., meets Pope John Paul II at the Vatican to present His Holiness with a large Copernicus painting on behalf of the Canadian-Polish Congress. [Photo, courtesy Tony Ruprecht, M.P.P.]

Kashubs founded what has become the oldest continuous Polish parish in Canada. They persisted in their faith, their dialect, and group life over a number of generations.

By the turn of the century, there were Poles in Toronto, Hamilton, Sudbury, and many smaller cities of the Niagara Peninsula and the Ontario North. There were over 1,000 Poles in Winnipeg before 1895, and smaller groups in Montreal, Vancouver, and Sydney, Nova Scotia.

Prompted by the vigorous policies of Clifford Sifton, Minister of the Interior in Wilfrid Laurier's government, some 115,00 Polish settlers came to Canada between 1896 and l918 to settle the newly opened prairies. The First World War temporarily disrupted the flow of Poles to Canada, but, in 1919, after the Polish republic had been established, a growing number of newcomers chose to make their way to Ontario, with Toronto gradually replacing Winnipeg as the centre of Polish life in Canada.

While the Depression slowed the movement of Poles into Canada, the outbreak of the Second World War further inhibited Polish immigration. Between 1939 and 1944 almost 1,000 Polish engineers, technicians, and other skilled refugees came to Canada and contributed to the war effort. In 1946 and 1947, ex-soldiers, who had served with the Allies, entered Canada on the strength of one-year contracts to work on beet farms, in factories and hospitals, and as domestics and railway builders.

Born, 1924, Ustrobna, Poland, Stan Jasinski, during the early war years, worked in the same stone quarry as Jozef Wojtyla, still another Polish-born citizen who would, in 1978, become His Holiness, Pope John Paul II, the first Polish Pope of the Roman Catholic Church to be elected in 450 years. Stan escaped Communism in Eastern Europe, 1966, after acquiring an engineering degree in Germany and a Master of Science Degree in Poland. Immigrating to Canada, 1967, Stan's twofold dream was to begin anew in a world where people respected and treated each other equally and to establish his own company where such ideals could be introduced. After a month in Canada, Stan sent for his wife, Ruth, and after brief stops in Welland and Toronto, founded in Woodstock, Ontario, Hyd-Mech Engineering Ltd., 1978. Sales were a meagre $80,000 in 1980. But over the next three years, Stan's company was on the move breaking $3 million in sales. By 1995, with facilities in Woodstock, Ontario, Houston, Texas, and Pueblo, Colorado, Hyd-Mech was clearly a company with a future and at the forefront of metal sawing technology and in the top tier of bandsaw manufacturers in the world. Stan, in this view, one year after his arrival in Canada, exclaims today that Canada has been very good to him. It gave him the required freedom to develop his own business. When he semi-retired, 1997, Stan left a considerable number of shares to his Hyd-Mech employees and turned the company's operations over to a new management team. [Photo, courtesy Hyd-Mech Engineering Ltd.]

Born in the Baltic Sea port of Gdynia, Poland, Marek Michalak obtained his elementary and secondary school education in Warsaw. Graduating, M.Sc., Cell Biology, University of Warsaw, 1973, Marek then earned his Ph.D. in Muscle Biochemistry at Warsaw's Nencki Institute for Experimental Biology, studying under world-renowned Dr. Sarzala-Drabikowski, a research scientist highly connected with "the outside world." Marek was only 27 years old when he left Poland, 1978, to study as a post-doctoral fellow under the guidance of Dr. David MacLennan, internationally respected as a scientist in muscle structure and function at the University of Toronto. Upon completing his research there, he and his wife travelled to Zurich, Switzerland, where Marek studied and researched the role of calcium in cell physiology with world-leading pathologist and cell physiologist, Dr. E. Carafoli. After completing his training there, he began his scientific career at Toronto's Hospital for Sick Children, 1984, moving to Edmonton, 1987, where there was a dynamic research environment developed by the Alberta Heritage Foundation for Medical Research. Currently, Dr. Michalak is a Professor of Biochemistry, University of Alberta, and a Director, Medical Research Council of Canada, Molecular Biology Division. Dr. Marek Michalak feels fortunate to be residing in Canada where he has been given exceptional opportunities to develop his medical research career. In 1986, he was awarded the Young Investigator Award from the Canadian Cardiovascular Society and, in 1999, the Astra/Zeneca Award in Molecular Biology for investigative studies into the role of membrane proteins in cardiac pathology. [Photo, courtesy Dr. Marek Michalak]

Most of the postwar migrants were political refugees from a Communist regime. Many were well-educated and qualified physicians, lawyers, teachers, engineers, and other professionals who chose urban life in Ontario and Montreal. Between 1957 and 1980, over 40,000 Poles came to Canada as part of an effort to re-unify divided families. Many others who came as visitors, performers, or athletes claimed refugee status. Finally, from 1981 until 1989, Canada opened its doors once again to allow a great wave of *Solidnosc* (Solidarity) political émigrés and economic migrants seeking better social and economic opportunities.

The 1996 census counted 786,735 people of Polish origin in Canada with Ontario having 370,455, the bulk of the community. These well-educated and better-trained individuals rejuvenated community organizational life and introduced new measures of voluntary action.

Thomas Anthony Brzustowski, born, Warsaw, Poland, 1937, is President, Natural Sciences and Engineering Research Council of Canada, (NSERC), Ottawa. He was 11 when his father, an Aeronautical Engineer, came to Canada to join A.V. Roe Company, Toronto, 1948. He graduated with a B.A.Sc. (Engineering Physics), University of Toronto, 1958, earning at Princeton University an A.M., 1960, and Ph.D. (Aeronautical Engineering), 1963. In 1962, Dr. Brzustowski began his career, Department of Mechanical Engineering, University of Waterloo, teaching and carrying out research in thermodynamics and combustion. Between 1967-1970, he served as Chairman, Mechanical Engineering Department, and was Vice-President, Academic, University of Waterloo, 1975-87. Appointed Deputy Minister, Colleges and Universities, Province of Ontario, 1987-91, he then became Deputy Minister, the Premier's Council, for another four years before being appointed President, NSERC, which makes strategic investments in Canada's capabilities in science and technology by providing grants in aid of basic university research, assistance to university-industry partnerships, and support for the advanced training of researchers in both areas. Awarded the Angus Medal of the Engineering Institute three times, Dr. Brzustowski holds honourary degrees from University of Guelph, Ryerson Polytechnic University, and the University of Waterloo. Dr. Brzustowski is also the recipient, Engineering Alumni Medal of the University of Toronto. In this view, Dr. Brzustowski, right, receives a certificate of appreciation from Dr. Ron Duhamel, Canada's Secretary of State for Science, Research and Development, May 1999. [Photo, courtesy Dr. Tom Brzustowski]

Newly arrived physicians, dentists, and other medical practitioners were required by Canadian licensing bodies to undertake examinations, internships and other forms of probationary work. Skilled tradespeople also endured trial periods and examinations. Mathematicians, scientists, and engineers benefited from the universal language of their disciplines, but lawyers, civil servants, and other white-collar workers had less chance to continue in their occupations. Some drove taxis, became short-order cooks or hospital aides, or worked at anything available.

Before 1920, the Polish entrepreneurial class in Canada had established corner groceries, bakeries, barbershops, and the shops of shoemakers and blacksmiths. By 1935, these small entrepreneurs were joined by a

Canada's First Minister of State for Muilticulturalism

The Hon. Stanley Haidasz, P.C., M.D., centre, is the son of a Polish immigrant who was born in Stanislovow, eastern Poland, and who came to Canada, 1910, and worked his entire life in the new world for CP Freight. Appointed Canada's first Minister of State for Multiculturalism, 1972, the Hon. Stanley Haidasz was first elected as a Liberal to the House of Commons for Trinity (Toronto) in the 1957 general election, and continuously served that riding through eight successful general elections. Graduating in Medicine, University of Toronto, 1951, Dr. Haidasz has served Canada with distinction in many capacities throughout a very busy professional career. He headed the Canadian Delegation to the World Food Program, Geneva, 1964, the same year he was Delegate to the United Nations General Assembly. He was also a member of the Canadian Delegation to the World Health Organization, Geneva, 1970 and 1972. Knight Commander Grand Cross of the Sovereign Order of St. John of Jerusalem (Knights of Malta) and Chancellor of its Priory in Canada, Dr. Haidasz was appointed to the Canadian Senate, 1978, serving in many Senate Standing Committees over a distinguished 20-year span, including Banking, Energy, Environment, Foreign Relations, and Science and Technology. Former National Chairman, Canadian Polish Millennium Fund, 1962-72, Dr. Haidasz was a Member, 1966, to Poland's Millennium in Warsaw. Founding President, Canada-Poland Chamber of Commerce, Dr. Haidasz is an excellent example of how the children of immigrants to Canada have served as cultural links and bridges where their parents were born and where they themselves were born. This view, taken two hours before the assassination of J.F. Kennedy, November 22, 1963, shows Dr. Haidasz in the Ottawa office of Prime Minister Lester B. Pearson with Witolda Malcuzynskiego, right, virtuoso pianist, the last and one of the most famous students of Ignacy Paderewski (1860-1941), former President of Poland's provisional parliament, 1940. [Photo, courtesy Dr. Stanley Haidasz]

handful of physicians, dentists, and lawyers as well as the millionaire owner of the Sisco Mine in Amos, Quebec, and a highly successful building contractor in Hamilton, Ontario. Together with the more successful farmers, these constituted the economic elite of the ethnocommunity. Skilled workers, tradespeople, civil servants, professionals, administrators, and other white-collar occupations were under-represented until the postwar period.

Polish patriotism informed the lives of the immigrants. By the turn of the century, Polish communities began to demand a priest of their own, to organize mutual aid societies for the well-being of their co-nationals and to create patriotic societies to support the cause of their suppressed nation. Because banks were reluctant to advance funds to immigrants with meagre jobs and because loan companies charged exorbitant interest rates, parishes and secular bodies across Canada created credit unions. The first, St. Stanislaus Credit Union, was organized in Toronto in 1945. By 1993, it was the largest parish-affiliated credit union in Canada, with ten branches, over 30,000 members, and assets of $200 million.

At 16, Peter Paul Koprowski, born, Lodz, Poland, 1947, had written his orchestral In Memoriam Karol Szymanowski, *and in 1967, the young composer completed his first renowned* String Quartet. *With an M.A. from the Krakow Academy of Music, 1969, he took up studies with Nadia Boulanger, Paris, 1970-71, and later that year arrived in Canada where he became Assistant Professor, Faculty of Music, McGill University, 1973-74, then Professor of Composition, Faculty of Music, University of Western Ontario, 1974. Besides teaching and obtaining a doctorate, University of Toronto, 1977, Dr. Koprowski has received commissions to compose over 40 works for orchestras, ensembles and artists, including the Berlin Philharmonic Wind Quintet, Sinfonia Varsovia, and the National Arts Centre, Ottawa. Dr. Koprowski's* Flute Concerto *was premiered by the Oslo Philharmonic and Per Oien, 1983, and his works have been presented by such artists as Pinchas Zukerman, Jukka-Pekka Saraste, Trevor Pinnock, Okko Kamu and Rivka Golani. Dr. Koprowski has also given concerts, conducted and recorded in Canada, United States, South America, Europe and Asia. Twice he received the Jules Leger Prize, 1989 and 1994. He also received the Victor Martyn Lynch-Stanton Award, 1990, and the Jean A. Chalmers National Music Award for four orchestral works, 1997. He has been called Canada's "composer laureate" and one of the country's "foremost artists" whose wide-ranging compositional voice does not preclude music that comes, in his words, "straight from the soul."*
[Photo, courtesy Dr. Peter Paul Koprowski]

Making Cultural Impact

The expulsion of some intellectuals and artists by the Polish government, 1968, brought Tadeusz Jaworski, a prize-winning film/TV producer/director, in his homeland, and his wife, Tamara, a world-renowned tapestry-gobelin artist, to Canada. Arriving in Canada, 1969, Tad, MFA graduate, 1951, State Academy of Film and Theatre Arts, Lodz, Poland, has taught at both Humber College and York University, Toronto, and has worked as a celebrated independent producer/director of docudramas and various documentaries over the last 30 years. His written and directed six-hour CBC TV production, The Jesus Trial, starring Christopher Plummer, Douglas Campbell, and Robin Gammell, was described by "the Pope" of French critics, Jean Jacques Gauthier, of La Figaro, as a work of "great research, of great interest and of great intelligence." His docudrama Selling Out, 1972, based on social and family changes in Prince Edward Island, was nominated for an Academy Award, 1973, and won a Golden Etrog (Genie), Canadian Film Festival, 1972. Tad Jaworski's accomplishments both as a film and TV producer/writer has led to more than 35 major and/or international awards he has won in Europe, the U.S., Australia, and Canada. Producer of over 200 feature TV dramas, docudramas, and cinema verité documentaries, Tad was elected to the Royal Canadian Academy of Arts, 1978. Tamara, Tad's internationally acclaimed wife, has, over the past 40 years, been featured as a tapestry artist in numerous solo and group exhibitions worldwide. Her skill and artistry in tapestry/gobelin weaving, an art form dating back more than 500 years, is considered part of the great renewal of this art in Poland and throughout Europe. She is the only North American artist represented at the Centre National de la Tapisserie d'Aubusson in Paris. The Louvre's Francois Mathieu, curator, Decorative Art, describes her work "at the peak of modern art weaving." Exhibitions of her tapestry/gobelin have been widely acclaimed in more than a dozen European countries and her tapestries hang in such galleries as the Pushkin National Museum, Moscow, Warsaw's National Museum, National Museum of Textile Arts, Lodz, and the Scottish Art Institute. Numerous private collectors and corporations in Canada have commissioned her to weave major works, two of the largest on display being the four tapestries, each 9'x15', titled "Quartet Modern" at the First Canadian Place, Bank of Montreal Tower, Toronto, and a much celebrated 22'x33' tapestry, "Unity," in the lobby of Place Bell Canada, Ottawa. Three international competitions have awarded her gold medals, including one in Milan and another in New York. Los Angeles Times critic Leon Whiteson has described her as "one of Canada's proudest cultural treasures," a fact also recognized by the Governor General, 1994, when Tamara was made Member, Order of Canada, the citation reading in part, "an artist and weaver at the forefront of the renaissance of the 16th century of French gobelin tradition, Tamara Jaworski is renowned for her ability to marry this medieval craft with contemporary design." In this view, left, Tamara works at her loom in her Toronto studio executing the 8'x8' tapestry-diptych, "Spheres," now hanging in the John Molson Executive Reception Hall, Toronto. Tad Jaworski, above, prepares to direct a scene from The Jesus Trial, a six-hour documentary, completed, 1978. [Photos, courtesy Tad Jaworski]

As curator of the Egyptian Department of the Royal Ontario Museum, Krzysztof Adam Grzymski was the person primarily responsible for the successful exhibition of Egyptian antiquities at the ROM in the year 2000, the only Canadian showing of this tour de force exhibition. Born, Kalisz, Poland, 1951, Dr. Grzymski won a scholarship to the University of Calgary after obtaining an M.A., Archaeology, University of Warsaw, 1976. He taught and did research at the University of Calgary while earning his Ph.D., 1981, and was a Research Fellow and Assistant Director of the Dongola Reach Survey, 1982-84, and Director of the project in the Sudan, 1984-86. He was appointed Senior Curator, Egyptian Section, ROM, and Associate Professor, University of Toronto, 1984. As an esteemed archaeologist, he co-directed the Pelusium West excavations, Egypt, 1994-95, and has been Director of the ROM Expedition to Nubia since 1986. Dr. Grzymski is the author of Archaeological Reconnaissance in Upper Nubia, 1987. *He also co-authored* Ancient Egypt and Nubia, *Royal Ontario Museum, 1994, and* Egyptian Art in the Age of the Pyramids, *New York, 1999. Since 1998, he has been Vice-President, Canadian Institute in Egypt.* [Photo, courtesy Dr. K.A. Grzymski]

Before the establishment of the Polish Republic after World War One, Poles drew leaders from their own ranks, but especially from among the Roman Catholic clergy: Oblates, Redemptorists, Resurrectionists, and the Felician nuns.

The willingness to support a parish or language school, drama group, community print and broadcast media reflected the immigrants' commitment to the maintenance of Polish folkways, language, and values. Polish pride swelled after the election of Pope John Paul II, the choice of Czeslaw Milosz in 1980 for the Nobel Prize for literature, and the selection of Lech Walesa in 1983 for the Nobel Peace Prize.

The few Poles who helped govern Upper and Lower Canada or the Dominion of Canada after 1867 had no successors until Dr. Stanley Haidasz of Toronto was elected as a Member of Parliament in 1957. Haidasz later became Minister of State (Multiculturalism) in the Trudeau government of 1972 and the first Polish member of the Senate in 1978. Other Liberal M.P.s, past and present, include Jesse Flis of Toronto and Stan (Kazimcerczak) Keys of Hamilton. Progressive Conservative Pat Sobeski represented Cambridge, Ontario; Don Mazankowski, M.P. for Vegreville, Alberta, served in the cabinets of both the Rt. Hon. Joe Clark and the Rt. Hon. Brian Mulroney and held positions as Minister of Finance and Deputy Prime Minister.

A number of Poles have served in municipal and provincial governments. Toronto and a number of other cities and towns have had Polish-Canadian aldermen. Ontario and the western provinces have had Polish MLAs and ministers, most notably Gary Filmon, former Premier of Manitoba. ♖

RUSSIAN settlement in Canada began as early as the nineteenth century when Doukhobors, members of a Russian Christian sect similar to the Society of Friends, assisted by British and American Quakers and novelist Leo Tolstoy, migrated to Canada in the late 1890s after persecution for refusing miliary service. The group settled in the Prince Albert and Yorkton areas of Saskatchewan. By 1908, a group of Doukhobors had moved west to British Columbia and established residence there in the Kootenay and Grand Forks areas.

Ambassador, author, diplomatic advisor, and University Chancellor, George Ignatieff, born St. Petersburg, Russia, 1913, became, after immigrating to Canada and attending schools in both Montreal and Toronto, a distinguished statesman who joined Canada's Department of External Affairs, 1940, shortly after attending Oxford University as a Rhodes Scholar. Son of Count Paul Ignatieff, last Minister of Education under Tsar Nicholas II, as a young man, George developed an expertise in East-West relations, particularly at the United Nations where his service included terms as Canadian Ambassador and President of the Security Council. He was also Ambassador to Yugoslavia, 1956-58, and Permanent Representative of Canada to NATO, North Atlantic Council, Paris, 1962-66. A distinguished statesman, George Ignatieff received honorary degrees from Brock University, University of Toronto, University of Guelph, University of Saskatchewan, York University, Bishop's, and Victoria University. Provost, Trinity College, University of Toronto, 1972-79, Dr. Ignatieff was appointed Chancellor, University of Toronto, 1980-86. Named Companion, Order of Canada, 1973, before he died, 1988, Dr. Ignatieff wrote his memoirs, The Making of Peacemongers, 1985.
[Photo, courtesy The Toronto Star]

from Russia

The political, social, and economic conditions prevailing in the Russian lands during the early twentieth century encouraged the emigration of good peasant folk – Russians proper – as well as Russian Jews and other subjects from the western territories of the Empire including Belarus, Lithuania, Ukraine, and Moldova. The majority of these early immigrants were attracted to such Canadian cities as Montreal, Toronto, Windsor, Timmins, Winnipeg, Vancouver, and Victoria. Many found employment in industry, for it was factory jobs that guaranteed the community's income.

Emigration to Canada was halted by the Russian Revolution of 1917 in which the Tsarist regime was overthrown and replaced by Bolshevik rule and then by the outbreak of the Russian Civil War of 1918-21. This conflict, which led to the defeat of the counter-revolutionary White Russians by members of the Bolshevik Red Army, resulted in thousands of refugees having to seek safety and new lives in France, Britain, Switzerland, China, and other countries for a number of years before eventually coming to Canada. Russians also came to Canada after the Second World War as part of the great mass migration of people which followed the Allied victory.

Russian immigrants of the inter- and postwar periods represented a broader movement of professionals, people of education and culture with experience and training in many different fields. Because of their privileged position, these newcomers were able to integrate with relative ease into Canadian society. Among them were such individuals as Leonid I. Strakhovsky, who helped create a Slavic Studies Department at the University of Toronto; physician Boris P. Babkin, a gastroenterologist at Dalhousie and McGill universities; and the talented clan of Count Paul Ignatieff, the last minister of education under Tsar Nicholas II. The 1970s had special

During the 1920s some immigrants, offered important posts in Canada because of their skills were trapped into more menial, sub-professional jobs because of changing circumstances and/or the devastating depression afflicting employment in the 1930s. An example is the Diakonoff family who moved to Vancouver, B.C., in 1921, when the Hudson Bay Company, in search of new fur sources, arrived at Petropavlovsk on the Kamchatka Peninsula of Siberia and hired Gurey Diakonoff. As manager of the Churin Company's trading compound at Petropavlovsk, since 1915, Gurey was an expert fur trader with Siberian natives, but he jumped at the chance of leaving a war-torn Russia as a result of the Bolshevik Revolution. Gurey, with his wife Olga, children Nina, eight, Olga, six, Igor, four, and their grandmother, Anna Kostinsky, arrived aboard the Casco in Vancouver, November 1921, where, for several years, Diakonoff played a key role in organizing an annual Hudson Bay Company expedition, each Spring, and sailing with it to the Kamchatka Peninsula to buy furs. But in the mid 1920s, Russia closed its borders to trade and that, coupled with the Great Depression, changed what had been a comfortable life in Vancouver, to one of hard times. Siberian-born Diakonoff, unable to speak English fluently, was demoted to a menial post in the Hudson Bay fur storage department; his wife who had never worked and was used to household help, ironed clothes for a dry-cleaner; the children found jobs after leaving high school to augment the family income. The older members of the family continued to speak Russian and enjoy the Russian Orthodox Church which they later helped establish in Vancouver, but their children, as students of Vancouver's public school system and sent to St. Mark's Anglican Sunday School for religious and social activities before the Orthodox Church was established, were quickly assimilated into Vancouver social life. The sisters, Nina Donnelly, and Olga Morris, now in their 80s (shown in this view with their mother before leaving Petropvlovsk), now live in Toronto and Guelph, Ontario, where they retain fond memories of their Siberian-born parents and life in the Churin Company compound along the Kamchatka coast. They are also proud of their Canadian-born children, five grandchildren and five great-grandchildren.
[Photo, courtesy Mel James]

Renowned Russian Orthodox Choir

*Christ the Saviour Orthodox Cathedral Choir was formed in
Toronto, 1940. The Russian Orthodox Church, where this choir
performs, was established, 1915, three years before the
Bolsheviks in Russia executed Tsar Nicholas II and the Romanov
family. Serge Boldireff, centre, was the choirmaster of this prominent group for 17 years, leading them in both Russian religious
music and folk songs. Today he is conductor of the Russian
Orthodox Church of St. Nicholas, Washington, D.C. Serge's
father, the Rev. Oleg Boldireff, immigrated to Canada early in the
20th century, settling in Montreal and was a priest there for man
of the 64 years he served as a Russian Orthodox clergyman. The
Choir itself has performed in Montreal, Ottawa, Buffalo, New Yo
City, Connecticut, and Pennsylvania, in addition to Toronto
Caravan. Recently, it made its European debut by performing in
Poland. [Photo, courtesy the Very Reverend Nicolas Boldireff]*

Russian Mennonite Watercolourist

*Artist Peter Goetz was 11 years old when he came to Kitchener,
Ontario with his Mennonite family who immigrated from Slavgorod, Russia, 1929. His father, whose Russian roots are
traced to the reign of Catherine the Great (1729-96), first worked as a labourer helping to construct Westmount Golf
and Country Club. He later became a greenskeeper there while Peter attended the local high school, then Waterloo
College, now the University of Waterloo, and became, 1947, a student of the famed Group of Seven artist, F.H. Varley.
Since 1957, Mr. Goetz has mounted an annual show of his work which has been included in exhibitions by the Royal
Canadian Academy, Ontario Society of Artists, Canadian Society of Painters in Watercolour, Montreal Museum of Fine
Arts, the National Gallery, Ottawa, and the Western Art League. Since 1957, Peter Goetz has established solo shows
annually. He is a Fellow, International Institute, Arts and Letters; International Platform Association; Centro Studie
Scambi International, Rome; and a member of the Canadian and Ontario Society of Artists, as well as the Canadian
Society, Painters in Watercolour. [Photo, courtesy Peter Goetz]*

Celebrated Iconographer

As an Iconographer, Igor Suhacev, has worked in Ethiopia, the United States and Canada. Born in Zagreb, Yugoslavia, 1925, the son of Russian parents who fled their homeland after the Russian Revolution, Igor recalls that the family elected to leave Belgrade before the Soviet Army occupied Yugoslavia during World War II. While living in a displaced persons camp near Hamburg, Germany, 1945, Igor, who like his father Petr, was an iconographer, studied secular art at the Hamburg Academy of Art and completed further studies in iconography at a Russian icon school, also in Hamburg. In 1949, the family left Europe and immigrated to Ethiopia where Igor and his father designed and painted a number of churches, stained glass windows, and the throne for Emperor Haile Selassie. At the urging of Petr's sister, Elizabeth, who immigrated to Toronto, 1949, and worked in Toronto's garment district, the family decided to move to Toronto, 1957, where Igor, after a brief stint with an architect, returned to his first interest as an iconographer, painting five churches in Toronto, five in Hamilton, and others in St. Catharines, Ontario; Montreal, Quebec; Roblin, Manitoba; and Yorkton, Saskatchewan. Other major commissions – some taking years to complete – took Igor to Chicago, Illinois, and South Bend, Indiana. Igor's wife, Sylvia, born in Smolensk, also immigrated from Russia following World War II, worked as a domestic for a year before meeting Igor in Toronto. They now live in Mississauga where Igor, having retired from the tough physical demands of painting walls and ceilings, now paints landscapes on canvas. In this view, Igor Suhacev, well-known Canadian iconographer, completes a frescoe in one of many churches he has embellished with religious themes and holy figures. [Photo, courtesy Igor Suhacev]

Dedicated Volunteer

Following World War II, thousands of people, uprooted from their homes, reached Canada where they were commonly referred to as DPs, short for "Displaced Persons." Maria Blagoveshchensky was one of them, a 20-year-old native of Pskov, a city 200 miles west of St. Petersburg, Russia, where her mother and grandmother were killed, 1944, when Russian planes dropped bombs during the recapture of their territory lost to Germany in 1941. A high school graduate in her native city, on her Canadian arrival, January 1948, she spent a year working as a nurse's aid, Brockville Ontario Hospital, before electing to move to Toronto to study bookkeeping and accounting. Over the next 40 years, Maria was employed as a bookkeeper by two companies, Yolles Furniture and Nubar Graphics. Active in Toronto's Russian community for years, she has been Chair, Russian Canadian Cultural Aid Society, since 1982, Treasurer, Russian Orthodox Holy Trinity Church and Vice-Principal of its Church School for the past 25 years, and a member of the Russian Orthodox Immigration Services of Canada. Her dedication to helping people, young and old, was recognized, 1995, when a surprise party, attended by more than 500 people, saluted and honoured Maria, above right, for her many years of dedication to Ontario's Russian community. [Photo, courtesy Maria Blagoveshchensky]

importance with the defections of Russian seamen and performing artists. As well, the emigration of Soviet citizens of the Jewish faith added to the community's ranks. Migration to Canada was renewed only in 1991 following the breakup of the Union of Soviet Socialists Republics.

With regard to the question of ethnic origin, according to the 1996 Canadian Census, a total of 272,325 persons responded they were wholly (46,885) or partially (225,450) of Russian background. The larger urban centres of Canada such as Montreal, Toronto, and Vancouver continue to be the most popular areas for settlement. In addition, Russians have settled in Calgary, Edmonton, Winnipeg, Saskatoon, Regina, and Hamilton.

Rich in symbolism, the Russian Orthodox Church acted as a bastion of national identity, the centre around which many Russian Canadians rallied, most especially the post-1917 White Russian emigrants. The ethnocommunity group founded at least 20 Russian Orthodox churches in Alberta, Saskatchewan, and Manitoba during the first decade of the twentieth century. As expected, Toronto and Montreal also have a highly developed Orthodox religious life. In Montreal, the Church of Sts. Peter and Paul was founded in 1907; the Church of St. Nicholas was established in 1927. In Toronto, Christ the Saviour Russian Orthodox Cathedral, founded, 1915, became the hub of Russian Orthodox church life in Toronto – with choirs, dance groups, children's orchestras, youth concerts, cultural groups, and sisterhoods. Every Sunday after liturgy, the faithful gathered downstairs in the church hall around the Russian classical library over *chai* (tea) with glorious food like *piroshki*, pelmeni and borscht lovingly prepared by the sisterhood. And more often than not, it was a time of joyous fellowship, lectures, and talks with discussions on what was going on in Russia. In addition, there were a number of Russians belonging to other religious groupings including the Doukhobor, Roman Catholic, Protestant, Mennonite, and Hutterite sects.

Galina Komarow, daughter of Captain Constantine Martemianoff and Zinaida Klugloff, was born, St. Petersburg, Russia, 1918, the same year that Tsar Nicholas Romanov and his entire family were brutally executed by Bolshevik revolutionaries. The next year, Galina and her parents escaped Bolshevik-led persecution, fleeing to Europe. For the next 20 years, they were European sojourners, travelling through Poland, Germany, France, and Austria, as displaced persons, surviving the ravages of depression and war. Eventually migrating across the Atlantic aboard the TSS

Nea Hellas, the family arrived, Pier 21, Halifax, July 1949. First settling, Ajax, Ontario, then Toronto, Galina quickly established a Hair Dressing Salon on Gerrard Street in Toronto's east end. Because Galina's parents had loyally served the Romanovs before the fall of Tsarist Russia, a sister of Tsar Nicholas II, Olga, chose to finish out her last days with loyal friends in the flat above Galina's Gerrard Street Salon. Galina carried on her hair dressing business for many years after the death of "the last Duchess," retiring shortly after her own mother passed away, 1989. In this view, circa 1955, Galina Komarow, right, visits with Her Imperial Highness, the Last Grand Duchess of Russia, who, in exile, resided, Cooksville, Ontario, throughout the 1950s. [Photo, courtesy Galina Komarow]

Russia's Last Grand Duchess

Alexander III (1845-1894), Tsar of Russia, 1881-1894, and his wife, Empress Marie, had four children, two sons, Nicholas and Michael, and two daughters, Xenia and Olga. Nicholas Romanov, who became Russian Tsar, 1894, the year his father died, lived in unbelievable opulence. At the height of his power, the Imperial Palace outside St. Petersburg, where he was raised and ascended to power, had 900 rooms and 5,000 indentured servants. It was here that Olga, 14 years younger than her brother Nicholas, grew up exposed to the intrigues of the infamous Mad Monk Rasputin who became the "spiritual advisor" to her sister-in-law. After Olga married Peter of Oldenburg, this unhappy marriage was dissolved by her brother, one of the last acts he performed as Tsar before he abdicated, 1917. Soon after, Olga, a woman of passion, married Lt. Col. Nicolai Kulikovsky, a commoner who completely swept her off her feet. After Nicholas II and his entire family were brutally assassinated, 1918, Olga and her family were given asylum in Denmark. Fearing Communist aggression and expansion in the Baltic at the end of World War II, after years of happiness she left Denmark, 1948, and immigrated to Canada with her husband and two sons. Briefly farming near Campbellville, Ontario, the family settled, 1950, Cooksville (Mississauga), Ontario. Olga became a member of Christ the Saviour Russian Orthodox Cathedral, Toronto, where her portrait, as Last Grand Duchess of Russia, hangs in the Cathedral, today, and where her works as an artist embellish the beautiful interior iconostasis. In 1960, after 10 years living in Cooksville, Olga was taken in by close Russian friends and died six months later, age 82, in an apartment above a hair dressing salon on Gerrard Street in Toronto's east end. In the view above, Her Imperial Highness Grand Duchess of Russia, Olga Romanov-Kulikovsky, stands next to an icon of Mary which she painted for Christ the 7mid-1950s. Left, she stands in her Cooksville, Ontario, home beside a portrait of her father, Tsar Alexander III. [Photos, top and left, courtesy Galina Kamarow]

Centre photograph depicts final resting place of Olga Romanov-Kulikovsky, the Last Grand Duchess of Russia (1882-1960), York Cemetery, Toronto, Ontario. [Photo courtesy, C.J. Humber]

Dimitry Vladimirovich Pospielovsky was born, 1935, Rovno, Russia, a city in that part of eastern Europe that has changed its nationality four times during the 20th century. He was 14 years old when he, his mother, and two sisters immigrated to Canada from Europe to escape Russian Communism, first settling, Kirkland Lake, northern Ontario, then, Montreal, where Dimitry completed his high school education. An activist during his student days, Dimitry joined a Russian anti-communist organization, the Labour Alliance of Russian Solidarists, and upon graduating from Sir George Williams College, Montreal, 1957, he moved to West Germany where that organization's headquarters was located. There he worked for a "Free Russia" short-wave Radio station and distributed anti-communist literature. After two years, Dimitry enrolled, University of London, U.K., graduating, M.A., 1961. Upon graduating, London School of Economics and obtaining a M.Phil., 1967, Dimitry, over the next five years, worked as a Programmer/Broadcaster for the BBC and as a Research Associate Writer, Hoover Institution, Stanford University, before he accepted a teaching position, University of Western Ontario, 1972. He retired from University of Western Ontario, 1997, after teaching there for 25 years as Professor, Russian and Modern European History. Professor Pospielovsky has taught variously at Harvard University's Russian Research Centre; London School of Economics; School of Slavic Studies, University of London; Oaklahoma, Carleton, and Wilfred Laurier universities; and Moscow and St. Petersburg Theological Seminaries. A recognized world authority specializing in the history of Soviet atheism, the Russian Orthodox Church of the 20th century, and the Russian Church under the Soviets, Dimitry Pospielovsky currently spends much of his time in Russia researching and investigating the new emerging states of Eurasia. In this view, Professor Pospielovsky takes time out during his 1997 retirement party at the University of Western Ontario. [Photo, courtesy Mirjana Pospielovsky]

Russians have made numerous contributions to Canadian life. The early Russian immigrants helped to ensure the physical development of this country. Later waves of immigration brought the most educated, politically conscious, and culturally active. From their ranks have come scholars, musicians, and artists including muralist Bill Perehudoff, the son of a Doukhobor farmer in Saskatchewan; portrait and still-life artist Parashkeva Clark; and Nicholas de Grandmaison, a portraitist specializing in First Nations subjects. During the 1930s, Boris Volkoff trained dancers and aroused interest in ballet. In 1955, Ludmilla Chiriaeff, born in Latvia of Russian parents, founded Les grands ballets Canadiens in Montreal. It is therefore only fitting that ballet star Mikhail Baryshnikov chose to defect while on tour in Canada in 1974. Finally, the five sons of Count Paul Ignatieff have made an extraordinary number of contributions in the academic arena and diplomatic corps. The Count's youngest son, George, served as Canadian Ambassador to Yugoslavia, Deputy High Commissioner in London, and as the permanent representative of Canada to the North Atlantic Council of NATO in Paris and the United Nations. A theatre at the University of Toronto was named after Ignatieff, who also served as Chancellor of the University of Toronto. It follows that his son, Michael, has gone on to distinguish himself as a writer, historian, and broadcaster both in Canada and abroad. ♦

Music, Mathematics, Psychology, and Peace are among the academic expertise of Professor Emeritus Anatol Rapoport, University of Toronto, who, at 88, still teaches a course in the Psychology Department on his long-standing interest in "game theory." Born, Lozovaya, Russia, 1911, Professor Rapoport earned diplomas in piano, composition and conducting at Vienna Hochschule für aMusik, 1934, before moving to the U.S.A. to obtain his S.M., 1940, and Ph.D., Mathematics, 1941, University of Chicago. Captain, U.S. Air Force during World War II, between 1947 and 1954, Professor Rapoport taught Mathamatics, University of Chicago, was Fellow, Stanford University Center Advanced Study Behavioral Sciences, 1954-55, before becoming Professor of Mathematics and Senior in Research Mathematics, Mental Health Research Institute, University of Michigan, 1955-70. Professor of Mathematics and Psychology, University of Toronto, 1970-80, and, since 1984, Professor of Peace Studies, same institution, his long interest in Peace studies led to his election as President, Canadian Peace Research & Education Association, 1972-1975, and President, Science for Peace, 1984-86. Dr. Rapoport has been a visiting or guest professor throughout his professional career at such institutions as University of Warsaw; Vienna Institute for Advanced Studies; Technical University of Denmark; Wissenschaftszentrum Berlin; University of Hiroshima, and Ludwig Maximilian University, Munich. He is the author of more than 300 articles. In 1976 he received the Lenz International Peace Research Prize and holds honorary degrees from the Universities of Western Michigan, Toronto, Royal Military College, and the University of Bern, Switzerland. [Photo, courtesy Dr. Anatol Rapoport]

The surname Khan has been identified internationally with squash over the last half of the 20th century. And although Hashim Khan has been labelled by the New Yorker as "... the greatest athlete for his age the world has ever seen," his son Sharif, winner of the North American Squash Championship record setting 15 times, was often considered, during his prime, the Jerry West or Jack Nicklaus or Joe Namath or the Bobby Orr of squash. Born in Peshawar, Pakistan, 1945, Sharif attended Millf Academy, England, moved to Detroit, 1967, upon graduation, to be with his father, the professional at the Uptown Athletic Club. Sharif moved to Toronto the next year, gaining employment as professional at the Skyline Racquet Club. He continued playing from Toronto, his home base, retiring from competition, 1982. Today he is Master Pro, The Racquet & Fitn Academy, Etobicoke, Ontario. He is also Director, the Sharif Khan Children's Squash Foundation affiliated with both the Big Brothers and Sisters of Peel. Eight members of the Khan family have combined to win 29 British Open titles. Sharif hopes that his daughter Sheena Mahria, age 17, will continue to add to the Khan Dynasty in World Squash. [Photo, courtesy Sharif and Karen Khan]

THE TERM PAKISTANI is commonly used to describe all citizens of Pakistan, regardless of their ethnic background. Today, the idea of being Pakistani is as much a matter of perception, volition, and generation as it was half a century ago.

The Islamic Republic of Pakistan is characterized by great ethnic and linguistic diversity. Flanked by Iran and Afghanistan in the west and China in the north, Pakistan also shares a border with India to the east. Within its 796,000 square kilometres live 138 million people including Punjabi, Pathan, Baluchi, and Sindhi groups. In contrast to its ethnic and linguistic variety, Pakistan is homogeneous in terms of religion: fully 98 percent of the population is Muslim; the remaining 2 percent includes Hindus, Christians, and Zoroastrians.

Settlement in Canada from that part of India today known as Pakistan began at the turn of the century with the migration of perhaps 200 pioneers from what would become

from **Pakistan**

Building Cultural Bridges

Since arriving in Canada from his native Pakistan, 1968, Asaf Shujah has been one of the most active members of the Pakistani community of Toronto. Now President of the Pakistan Canada Cultural Association, Mr. Shujah immigrated to Canada after obtaining a London, U.K., diploma as a computer programmer. He worked at the Bank of Montreal and Ryerson Polytechnic University, Toronto, 1970-1984, before becoming involved in motel and residential property management as President, Gold Bloom Management & Investment Co. Ltd. Since 1990, he has also been proprietor of East Pole Trading Co., importers of equestrian riding equipment. His extra-curricular activities, on behalf of the Pakistani community, include being a founder of the Pakistan Canada Cultural Association, 1972, and founder of the Urdu-English monthly newspaper, AZAD, 1990. He has served on committees of the Toronto Board of Education; helped Ontario's Ministry of the Attorney General design the terms of reference for the Commission on Race Relations in Criminal Justice, 1992; was appointed Chairman, National Federation of Pakistani-Canadians, 1993; and in 1997, organized the "50th Anniversary Independence Day Celebrations," the same year he served as Chair, Pakistan-Muslim League of Canada. Mr. Shujah's volunteer work has been recognized by several organizations, including the Ontario Government who recently awarded him a certificate marking 15 years of voluntarism. [Photo, courtesy Asaf Shujah]

North America's Largest Muslim Cultural Centre

Muslims are great mosque builders. The largest Muslim mosque in Canada, below, built at a cost of over seven million dollars, is the 53,000 square-foot mosque built by the Islamic Foundation of Toronto. In addition to being a place of worship and prayer, the Islamic Foundation of Toronto is North America's largest Muslim Cultural Centre attracting Muslims who have come to Canada from some 50 different countries, including Pakistan. [Photo, courtesy Charles J. Humber]

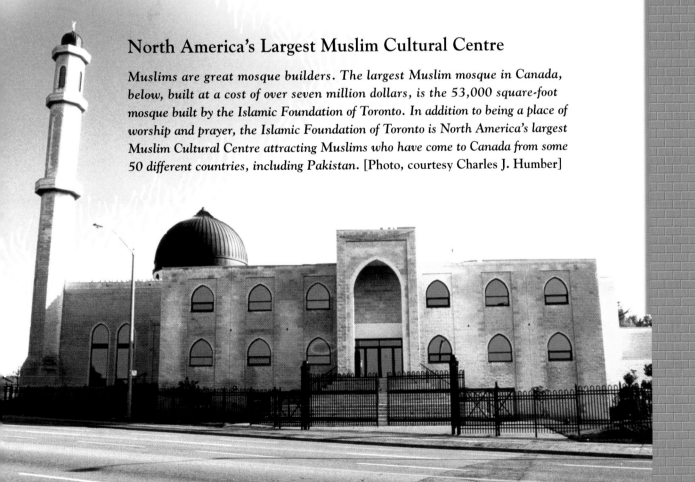

Sociologist Focusing on the Family

Professor Parvez Wakil, who came to the University of Saskatchewan, Sociology Department, 1964, planned to return to Pakistan with his wife, Farkhanda, after a year, but his research kept him there for three years and they decided "the city and country seemed the best place in the world to live in and raise our family." Born in Gujart, Punjab,

1935, Professor Wakil attended Government College and University of Punjab, Lahore, before attending Washington State University, 1959-63, under the Inter-University Teachers Exchange Program. Named Most Outstanding Pakistani Student in the United States by the American Friends of the Middle East, 1962, he returned to Pakistan as Senior Lecturer, Sociology, 1963-64, before arriving in Saskatoon. Since then, he has taught and been involved in research in Canada, the United States, and elsewhere. His particular interest has resulted in such books as Marriage, Family and Society: Canadian Perspectives, 1975; Marriage and Family in Canada, 1976, and numerous articles on the family in a number of professional journals. He has also edited and/or authored four books on the society and culture of South East Asia. An advisor to the Canadian government, 1966-67, he also wrote a Report for Health and Welfare Canada, 1992. Professor Wakil was a founder and later President, Islamic Association of Saskatchewan and the Pakistan Canada Cultural Association. Between 1983-86, he served as a member, Canadian Commission for UNESCO. He is also a Member, Canadian Bar Association, on the Board, Canadian Asian Studies Association, and a member, Canadian Sociology and Anthropology Association, Vanier Institute of the Family, and the National Council of Family Relations. His community work has earned him a life membership in the National Council of Pakistani Canadians and his participation and research in sociology in over 200 national and international conferences has led to his induction as a Haultain Fellow. He is also a Gilmore Fellow of Research. [Photo, courtesy Professor Parvez Wakil]

Celebrated Montreal Pakistani

"I immigrated to Canada in 1968, with the intention of discovering the world and furthering my education," recalls Zaheer A. Abbasi, now Manager of Production/Development, Axcan Pharma Inc., Mont St. Hilaire, Quebec. Graduating B.Sc., Pharmacy, University of Karachi, Pakistan, 1967, Mr. Abbasi took additional technical and business courses over a number of years while serving as Production Manager, Howett & Moore, Ltd., 1968-76. Following a reorganization of the company, he served in three executive positions in the Manufacturing, Product Development, and Production Departments, Beecham Laboratories Inc., 1976-1991, before joining Axcan Inc., 1991. As a young man in Montreal, he helped form and played for the Pakistan Cricket Club, Montreal, serving the club in various capacities, 1979-1991. Past President, Pakistan Association of Quebec, Inc., 1993-95, he was on its Board of Governors, 1995-1999. A former Chairman, Constitution of Bylaws Committee, National Federation of Pakistani Canadians, Ottawa, 1996-98, Mr. Abbasi also serves as Canadian Director, Institute of Overseas Pakistanis, Lahore, Pakistan. In 1995 and 1997, he was the Canadian delegate at international conventions of overseas Pakistanis held in Islamabad. A former Secretary, Pakistani Community of Quebec, Mr. Abbasi's numerous activities on behalf of his countrymen have been recognized by the Pakistan Cricket Club of Montreal, 1993; by the Board, National Federation of Pakistani Canadians, 1994; and from members and Board of Directors of the Pakistan Association of Quebec, the Meritorious Services Award, 1995. [Photo, courtesy Zaheer Abbasi]

the Pakistani part of Punjab. Within a few years the majority of these sojourners returned to the Asian sub-continent or made their way into the United States. What followed may be described as the exclusion era because, as a result of the 1907 immigration ban, no South Asians, including people of Muslim and Sikh origin, from what is now Pakistan, were allowed to immigrate to Canada until after the Second World War. In 1951, the Canadian government introduced a quota system for South Asian immigrants that allowed for the immigration of 100 Pakistanis a year. As quota places were taken up by students and a cadre of extremely well-educated professionals, the postwar arrivals set the stage for a marked increase in emigration from Pakistan. From 1967 to 1975, immigration statistics recorded the presence of 13,811 immigrants of Pakistani origin in Canada. These could only be described as the cream of the crop – educators, doctors, engineers, accountants, and scientists who

On obtaining his fifth degree, Mohammad A. Qadeer settled in Canada as Associate Professor, School of Urban and Regional Planning, Queen's University, Kingston, and Full Professor, 1978. Born, Lahore, 1935, before the Partition of India, in 1947, Mohammed received a B.Sc., 1953, and M.A., 1959, University of Punjab, earned an M.S., School of Ekistics, Athens, Greece, 1963, and while teaching in the United States, obtained an M.A., Community Planning, University of Rhode Island, 1966, and a Ph.D., his fifth degree, Columbia University, 1971.

Besides teaching at Queen's University, his specialization in such areas as Social Development Programs, Urban Land Economy and Real Estate Development and Urban Planning for Multicultural Cities, has led to consulting and research assignments for the United Nations Development Programme, Canada Housing and Mortgage Corporation, Ontario Ministry of Housing, Ontario Hydro, and other consultant roles in his native Pakistan. Co-author of Towns and Villages in Canada, *and author, of* Urban Development in the Third World, 1983, *Professor Qadeer has also written eight book chapters dealing with such diverse subjects as "Urban Planning and Multiculturalism in Ontario," and "Why Family Planning is Failing." More than 100 articles have also appeared in academic and professional journals and daily newspapers and magazines in Canada and Pakistan. Appointed Professor Emeritus, Urban and Regional Planning, Queen's University, 2000, Dr. Qadeer received the Peter Nash Award for Achievement in the Practice of International Planning, University of Rhode Island, 1989. [Photo, courtesy Dr. Mohammed Qadeer]*

Friendship with a Canadian post-graduate student also attending the University of London, England, brought Professor Om Parkash Malik to Canada where, since 1974, he has been Professor of Electrical Engineering, University of Calgary. Born, Sargodha, Pakistan, 1932, before going to London, he obtained, 1962, a Master of Engineering, Roorkee University, in the province of Uttar Pradesh in northern India, and between 1953 and 1961, worked as Assistant to the Chief Engineer, Punjab State Electricity Board. After graduating, Ph.D., University of London, 1965, Om immigrated to Canada as Assistant Professor, Electrical Engineering, University of Windsor. After two years he

was appointed Associate Professor, Department of Electrical Engineering, University of Calgary, Alberta. Author/co-author of over 350 research papers in international professional journals and conferences, Professor Malik recalls that the decision to move to Canada "was rather easy," as he always had "a soft spot to see this country." Dr. Malik has earned many awards as a professional engineer, including the Engineering Institute of Canada's Canadian Pacific Railway Engineering Medal 1996-97. He also serves as Director, Calgary Indo-Canadian Centre Association. In this view, Dr. Malik, in China on a teaching excursion, raises his arm to explain technical matters at a large electric power station. [Photo, courtesy, Dr. Om Malik]

settled throughout Canada, with the majority settling in Ontario, followed by Quebec, British Columbia, Alberta, Manitoba, and Saskatchewan. By the mid-1970s, Pakistani immigration came to be characterized by a significant number of skilled or semi-skilled workers. By the late 1970s, the occupational range of Pakistani immigrants was very wide indeed.

According to the 1996 Canadian census, 38,655 individuals said that they were wholly or partially of Pakistani origin. The major distribution of Pakistanis (single and multiple responses), according to the census data, was as follows: Ontario, 24,895; Quebec, 5,150; British Columbia, 4,180; and Alberta, 3,470. Pakistanis in Canada lived mainly in the large cities of Toronto, Montreal, and Vancouver, where they were dispersed across the residential areas of these urban centres.

With an M.A. in Fine Arts, Lahore University, Tehzib Morad immigrated to Canada from her native Pakistan, 1979. Settling, Montreal, she and her husband, Omer, raised three children before Tehzib intensified her desire to work as a freelance artist and illustrator. Since her teenage years, Tehzib has carried out research in Asian art traditions. Incorporating age-old techniques to meet the needs of her own style, which uses vibrant colours associated with her Pakistan culture and the detailed simplicity of 16th century Persian and Mogul miniatures, she has genuinely applied this formula to her renderings of Canadian landscape, especially the cold winter scenes of Quebec. Tehzib's snow is often pink or red, turquoise or yellow, generating feelings of warmth, cordiality, and affection evident in the colours associated with her heritage. Today, Tehzib's niche is producing multicultural greeting cards for enthusiastic clients, mainly newer Canadians who seek out and discover her work for occasions such as Eid-al-Fitr, Diwali, or Christmas. Her silk-screen greeting cards, printed by hand, are in great demand. By winning prizes at local exhibitions and participating in a variety of community functions, her miniatures are gaining wider recognition, especially beyond Quebec where they have reaped praise at places such as Royal Ontario Museum, Toronto Convention Centre and the Sheraton Centre where her works have been exhibited. Revealing Tehzib's Asian heritage is this unnamed miniature, typical of her Canadian winter landscapes. The quaint Quebec village in the background reflects her passion for the deep, rich colours of the Asian sub-continent. The mauve snow is reminiscent of silk colours worn by the Muslim women of Pakistan. The skaters garbed in exuberant colours recall the intense colours worn by women shopping at Pakistani bazaars half way round the world. [Photo, courtesy Tehzib Morad]

Opening of Ismaili Jamatkhana, Burnaby, British Columbia

His Highness the Prince Karim Aga Khan, whose accession in 1957 made him the 49th hereditary Ismaili Imam, is the spiritual leader of the Shia Imami Ismaili Muslims, generally known as Ismailis, who live today in 25 countries worldwide, including Pakistan, Canada, and the U.S. Throughout the course of history, Ismailis have made significant contributions to Islamic Civilization in those parts of the world either where they have emerged or where they have settled. They have built such world cities as Cairo where University of Al-Azhar, built by Ismailis, is reputed to be one of the oldest institutions of higher learning in the world. In the 1970s, political changes in the early '70s in Asian and African countries led to the arrival of large numbers of Ismailis in Canada. It is estimated that nearly 75,000 Ismailis live in Canada as we enter the new millennium. The Ismaili community in Canada today is governed by volunteers under the aegis of His Highness Prince Aga Khan Shia Imami Ismaili Council of Canada. In 1985, the local Ismaili Council in British Columbia unveiled and dedicated the new Ismaili Jamatkhana and Centre, Burnaby, B.C. In this view, Mawlana Hazar Imam, second from left, and former Prime Minister, Brian Mulroney, centre, participate in the opening ceremonies of this British Columbia Jamatkhana. The Premier of British Columbia, Bill Bennett, is second from right. [Photo, courtesy Government of Canada]

Jousting Journalist Activating Cultural Awareness

Born in Pakistan, Raheel Raza received her primary and secondary education in convent schools before graduating from University of Karachi, majoring in English and Psychology. Growing up in a culture where women were supposed to be seen and not heard, Raheel, nevertheless, combatted such attitudes and participated in drama, debating, and writing contests throughout her formative years. In 1979, Raheel and her husband, Sohail, and their family, moved to the United Arab Emirates where Raheel was invited to work with the Ruler of Sharjah to develop tourism. As the only Asian woman working for the Ruler's Office, Raheel gained valuable experience writing for the Khaleej Times, a leading English newspaper in the Arabian Gulf. As the first Asian female journalist in the area, Raheel focused on interviewing multinational women living in the Arabian Gulf, highlighting their special talents. When both Raheel and Sohail and their two sons, Zain and Saif, moved to Canada, 1989, Raheel brought with her valuable experience in journalism. Now a media consultant and free-lance writer, in addition to working for the Ontario Heritage Foundation, Raheel (she has contributed to almost every section of The Toronto Star) addresses the many issues facing the South Asian community and Muslim women in Canada. An experienced and exceptional public speaker, Raheel participates in forums, seminars, conferences, and symposia as a well-known personality who bridges the gulf between East and West. Ready to participate in dialogues dealing with media stereotypes, gender equality, racism, discrimination, and multiculturalism, Raheel is an active Muslim woman committed to erasing the misconception that Islam is a rigid faith based on inequality and fundamentalism. She is proud to wear shilwar khameez, her national dress, and argues that mutual interfaith and understanding can only lead to better understanding and greater harmony. In this view, Raheel and her husband visit their native homeland, Pakistan. [Photo, courtesy Raheel Raza]

British Columbia Entrepreneur

Before coming to Canada, 1980, Rashid A. Aziz, a native of Peshawar, Pakistan, became a Chartered Accountant, England, working there and in Iran until unrest in the Islamic Republic forced him and his wife to return to England. At the time, England was suffering high inflation and labour unrest, so they immigrated to Canada, settling, Vancouver, British Columbia, where Rashid worked as a Manager for Deloitte & Touche, 1980-87, before moving on to Quadra Logic Technologies as Vice President, 1988-93, and Inflazyme Pharmaceuticals Inc. as Executive Vice President and Director, 1993-94. That year he elected to open his own consulting and investment firm, now known as RAA Consulting Services. A resident of Vancouver, Rashid has been a Director, St. John Ambulance, Burnaby Branch, Camp Coordinator, French Camps in B.C., and a member of the Finance Committee of the Children's Telethon. He is part owner of an environmental company and a director of four early-stage public companies in businesses ranging from pharmaceuticals to health and beauty care. In this view, Rashid Aziz is holidaying in Aix-en-Provence, France, June 1998. [Photo, courtesy Rashid Aziz]

Zia Chishti and his wife, Zeb, now live in Canada after a life that started in India, then Pakistan, following the Partition of India, 1947. After six years in London, England, Zia and his family immigrated to Canada, settling, Charlottetown, Prince Edward Island, 1982. That's because two of their six sons lived in P.E.I., one of them teaching at the University of P.E.I. and another, a practicing accountant. Zia, whose ancestors settled more than 400 years ago in the historic town of Fatehpur-Sikri (India's capital between 1569-1609), was born in 1926 and married Zeb at 19. In 1953, Zia left Zeb and two sons with family members to study law and work at the office of the High Commissioner of Pakistan, London, England. Returning, 1956, he practiced and taught law at both Karachi and Lahore Universities, 1961-1973, before returning to London with his wife and two youngest sons to be with the four older boys attending university. In London, he resumed the practice of law, arguing on occasion, cases in France for the United Nations. When two of the Chishti sons got jobs in Canada, the other family members decided to join them in P.E.I. where Zia discovered he had to spend 18 months attending law school at Mount Allison University, New Brunswick, take his exams at Dalhousie University and spend still another year articling with a law firm in P.E.I., before being able to open his own office in Charlottetown. He did so, opening his own firm at age 66, and has since established himself as a respected member of the legal profession as well as a devoted Muslim in the community of some 20 Muslim families in the Charlottetown area.
[Photo, courtesy Badar Chishti]

With the growth of the communities, an entrepreneurial infrastructure began to develop where traders and a plethora of import-export firms came to predominate. The community has also established a noteworthy presence in the food franchise industry and in accounting and finance.

Pakistanis created a host of cultural vehicles to provide support and to ensure a sense of continuity and survival. A number of journals, periodicals, and newspapers are published by and for Pakistani immigrants in Canada. Urdu, the national language of Pakistan, has become popular, and is highly celebrated. Pakistanis have proven to be ardent supporters of South Asian classical music, films whether on video or in specialty movie houses, as well as an adoring audience for visiting South Asian celebrity performers. In terms of the Muslim faith, Pakistanis, as members of the Muslim community-at-large have helped to establish parochial centres and numerous mosques and congregations in almost every city where they have settled in substantial numbers. In addition to life centred on mosques or Islamic centres, the community, in an attempt to establish a firm cultural base in the Canadian diaspora, has also supported such secular organizations as the Pakistan-Canadian Association and, on various university campuses, the Pakistani Student Association. ♣

Special Message

The Honourable John Manley, Minister of Industry

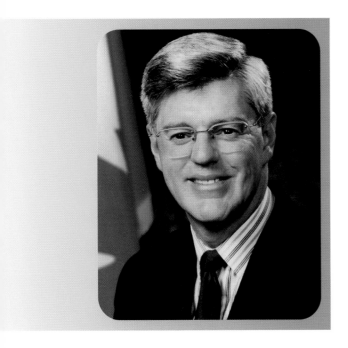

First elected in 1988 and re-elected in 1993 and 1997 as Member of Parliament for Ottawa South, John Manley was appointed Minister of Industry in November 1993. He was given additional responsibilities as Minister responsible for the Atlantic Canada Opportunities Agency, the Canada Economic Development for Quebec Regions Agency, and Western Economic Diversification in January 1996. Mr. Manley is assisted in these duties by three Secretaries of State.

The Minister is also responsible for a number of Government agencies including the Standards Council, the Canadian Space Agency, the National Research Council, Statistics Canada, the Business Development Bank of Canada, the Canadian Tourism Commission, the Natural Sciences and Engineering Research Council and the Social Sciences and Humanities Research Council.

Supported by these organizations, Mr. Manley and his colleagues, among other matters, have been given an important part in making technology work for Canada.

As Minister responsible for telecommunications policy, Mr. Manley has led the development of a strategy for Canada's Information Highway.

On March 9, 2000, the Hon. John Manley received the Intenet '99 Person of the Year Award from Skynet Internet Collective.

I AM DELIGHTED that corporations from a cross-section of Canadian industry are partnering with Heirloom Publishing to present volume VII, CANADA *at the Millennium: A TransCultural Society*, honouring Canada's multicultural heritage. This volume of the nationally acclaimed CANADA *Heirloom Series* celebrates the many contributions over 50 ethno-cultural groups have made to Canada. They have immeasurably contributed to Canada's industrial and commercial growth, its cultural and social evolution and its academic and professional development. Corporate support is especially appropriate in this era of globalization, when Canadian businesses are benefitting from a diverse work force as they expand their markets.

I know that the volumes of the CANADA *Heirloom Series* make excellent gifts for Canadian trade missions to present to their hosts abroad. The volumes highlight our country's achievements and demonstrate why the United Nations has recognized Canada as the best nation in the world in which to live, five times over the last six years. This timely volume celebrates the contribution of diversity to our strength as a nation.

I am pleased to acknowledge Heirloom Publishing's generosity in allowing Industry Canada's Digital Collections program to hire young people across Canada to produce a digital version of the CANADA *Heirloom Series* for display on SchoolNet. I know that Heirloom Publishing's corporate partners will be pleased to learn that the articles featuring their firms in the *Heirloom Series* will be accessible at the Canada's Digital Collections web site **(http://collections.ic.gc.ca)** which Yahoo Canada has called the best educational site in the country.

I extend my congratulations to Heirloom Publishing and to its co-venturer, the Multicultural History Society of Ontario, in this celebration of the millennium, as well as to those corporations whose assistance helped make CANADA *at the Millennium* a showcase of Canada's rich multicultural heritage.

Corporate Sponsors

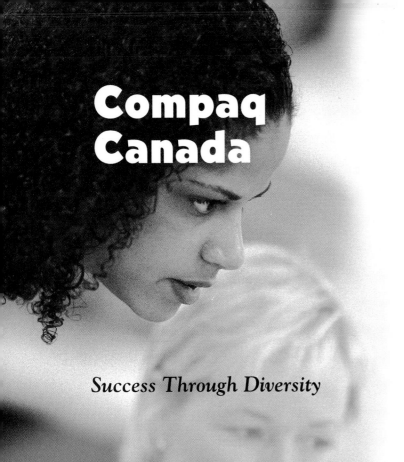

Compaq Canada

Success Through Diversity

THE RAPIDLY CHANGING WORLD of the new millennium is driven by technologically-based innovations and increasing needs for better understanding amongst all peoples.

Thanks to the World Wide Web, connectivity is occurring on personal, commercial, ideological and political levels. A trillion-dollar Internet-driven economy is being created. World commerce, driven by new markets, new products, and new trade agreements is flourishing.

Indeed, the Web has also dramatically reduced hierarchical, geographical and time zone boundaries enabling the sharing of energies and ideas across previously impenetrable strata. Diverse peoples are able to create synergistic bonds that transcend yesterday's barriers.

This connection amongst people has played a key role in the success of Compaq Canada Inc., the fourth largest subsidiary of Compaq's international family. By helping all employees leverage ideas and knowledge, Compaq has become the largest overall manufacturer of computers in the world.

Compaq, founded in 1982, helped spark the emergence of the personal computer marketplace. By the 1990s Compaq had become the world's largest supplier of PC and server products. Compaq manufactures, markets, and services NonStop(r) eBusiness hardware, software, solutions and services. These include industry-leading enterprise computing solutions; fault-tolerant, business-critical solutions; enterprise and network storage solutions; commercial desktop and portable products; and consumer personal computers.

Compaq's unique market approach is built on long-standing strengths including: a full range of quality products based on a long-term commitment to industry standards; strong partnerships with industry leaders to deliver comprehensive, cost-effective solutions; a deep understanding of integration and management with intelligent, differentiating tools and services; and people who are striving toward achieving the highest level of customer satisfaction.

To further its success, Compaq Canada has developed a proactive policy of cultural diversity and is creating supporting programs that embrace four major initiatives to recognize and support the talents of its people.

Compaq defined cultural diversity: how Compaq employees think and act based on their history, training, experience and beliefs. Initiatives were created to acknowledge and deal with heritage, race/nationality, gender and company.

Heritage – the strength of roots

Through acquisitions, Compaq Canada has grown from 280 employees in the mid-1990s to more than 3,000 people in 38 sites across six Canadian time zones. The merging of four high technology companies – Neo-Dyne Consulting, Tandem Computer, Digital Equipment and Compaq – meant developing a strong team spirit amongst employees was crucial to forming a united company with a singular business vision. This was realized through an umbrella curriculum called: "Quest for One Compaq."

A comprehensive business strategy was developed and disseminated through its employee engagement initiatives. These delivered information and teambuilding tools to every Compaq employee ultimately flowing through to 100 percent of Compaq employees.

"Compaq's 13 Values" were communicated to all employees. Commitment to cultural diversity and across-the-board knowledge of the company's goals channelled efforts so that they were consistent with its business direction.

In addition, to foster solidarity and the unencumbered exchange of ideas amongst employees, "bottom-up" social committees were set up to acknowledge and celebrate the strengths of corporate diversity.

Race/nationality – forging strong bonds

The second diversity issue centered on helping the more than 50 nationalities working at Compaq understand each others views, work habits, and experiences. Since Compaq's 3,000 people reflect a microcosm of the world's workforce, Compaq set up an environment to embrace visible minorities and other nationalities.

The goal was simple: to value individual differences and maximize the opportunities for people and to make a contribution regardless of differences.

Compaq implemented recruitment and remuneration practices that identified the best candidate for employment, advancement or reward regardless of race/nationality, culture or heritage. Senior executives, managers and employees at Compaq currently reflect the success of this initiative since they cross heritage, race/nationality, and gender lines.

In addition, multiculturalism was embraced through celebration of a wide variety of cultural festivities. Cultural events were organized and promoted. In December alone these include: Judiasm, Islam, Baha'i, Russian, Christian, Afro Canadian/American, Scottish, Zoroastrianism, and native Canadian celebrations.

Gender - equal opportunities and respect

Creating a cohesive environment for both sexes to work together in harmony and trust means a happier work force and better business results. Compaq has addressed this through comprehensive programs such as maternity and parental leave for new parents, a guaranteed job after maternity or parental leave, equal pay for jobs of equal value, and an harassment-free environment that stresses respect and trust.

In addition, Compaq has educational and developmental initiatives for employees, and actively supports external programs such as "Women of Influence." It also encourages informal mentoring to enable employees to gain first-hand business knowledge of the corporate world from experienced people.

Company – valuing its greatest resource

Finally, Compaq worked to create a company that values its people as its greatest resource and visibly demonstrates this through programs and action.

Employee programs leading to a more desirable work environment include initiatives such as the Virtual Office, Flexible Working Hours, Flexible Dress, and Results-based Measurements. These help employees maintain productivity by allowing them to plan their own work and to achieve the optimum balance for career, home life, and experience. Compaq provides tangible support such as equipment and extra phone lines for a Virtual Office and a supportive and effective management team dedicated to all programs.

Surveys show that Compaq's support for a culturally diverse workforce is helping employees achieve high job satisfaction and, in turn, deliver product and service excellence to customers. The company can only look forward to greater success.

Royal Bank

Asset Diversification

Bill Clementi, Teresa Zoccoli, and Roberto Ciasca: Team Italian is heard and seen all over Toronto's Italian community.

ON FRIDAY afternoons shortly before two o'clock, Roberto Ciasca, an investment advisor for RBC Dominion Securities, takes his seat behind the microphone in the studio at CHIN radio – located in a landmark building on Toronto's diverse and ethnic College Street. While financial advice is commonplace on radio shows across Canada, Ciasca's talk show is different from others. It's spoken in Italian and aimed exclusively at the city's enormous Italian population.

Italian talk shows offering financial advice and bilingual financial newsletters illustrate only two of the ways Royal Bank Financial Group is serving and interacting with its multicultural client base.

Royal Bank employees in Toronto have taken their jobs outside of the branch and assumed a more visible role within the city's large Italian community. This team of bankers and financial advisors, Royal Bank's so-called Team Italian, are heard and seen all over Toronto, participating in cultural and community events. "We have fun together," says Teresa Zoccoli, manager, personal banking. "We help out. And the community appreciates our efforts – they've told us so."

Team Italian bridges the gaps between language, generation, and culture, forging relationships with older Italians who may not be comfortable speaking English. "While the younger generation is more informed when it comes to investments, many retired

Italians have special financial needs and often look to their sons and daughters for help," Zoccoli explains.

Canada has been called "a community of communities." Nowhere is this more obvious than in its cities, which are home to people from around the world. New Canadians come from an extraordinary variety of ethnic backgrounds and are busy establishing new communities of their own.

Canada's multicultural identity benefits where dealings with other countries are concerned. If trade and investment links can be established on a broader scale, the potential is there for Canada someday to boast an economic diversity to match the diversity of its population.

Reflecting the Canadian Community

Royal Bank Financial Group's goal is to be an organization which recognizes the benefits of differences within the workplace. This diverse workforce can anticipate the need for a variety of ethno-cultural markets nationally as well as globally.

Acknowledging diversity allows RBFG to establish a mutually beneficial business relationship with its workforce as well as with its clients. For the group, implementing and integrating diversity means going beyond mere acknowledgement to honing its understanding of the group's fit in the global jigsaw puzzle.

Look to Calgary for a further example of this team

Josephine Ching and Cindy Tong: "Teambuilding strategy in action."

"... become flexible enough to value differences ..." and "encourage and listen to a range of ideas, perspectives and solutions"

building strategy in action. Josephine Ching and Cindy Tong run a branch in a huge Chinese supermarket. "We're the new wave of banking," declares Ching. "You can find us opposite the frozen fish." While the majority of their time is spent advising customers about financial products, they may also be found translating English into Cantonese for a newcomer. "It's our way of helping," explains Ching. "Our customers have become our friends."

Diversity: An off-balance sheet asset

Establishing strong community relations throughout the country continues to be a high priority for everyone at RBFG and a key to the corporation's future success. The challenge lies in embracing differences in order to set them apart as a socially responsible corporate leader – not only to its employees, but also to its customers and communities.

Exemplifying their corporate identity, RBFG employees consistently involve themselves with their communites on several levels, nationwide.

These relationships lead to market opportunities for financial services and skilled employees for the Canadian workforce.

Diversity: Canada's national resource

As Canada's leading lender to small business, Royal Bank Financial Group works with aboringial entrepreneurs not only to offer financial products and services, but also to provide the information and tools to help grow these businesses, in turn, encouraging Canada's growth.

Royal Bank Financial Group is striving toward establishing strong relationships at the grassroots level with Aboriginal youth as they prepare to lead their communities. Since 1993, the bank's Native Student Awards Program has provided recipients with $4,000 for each year of their post-secondary education. This past summer, 191 students participated in a national Stay-in-School program.

These efforts are milestones along the path to achieving the equal representation of Canada's multicultural society in our workplaces as well as in the economy.

Royal Bank Financial Group's customers demand that it expand its offerings beyond the one-size-fits-all methodology to become flexible enough to value differences. To do so, it must encourage and listen to a range of ideas, perspectives, and solutions. In turn, by incorporating differences from all the cultures found in Canada, Royal Bank Financial Group not only will be better able to meet its customers' needs today, but will be better poised to attract and retain the best employees to compete in the future.

IN 1954, a young Austrian tool and die maker immigrated to Canada with nothing more than a suitcase, a few hundred dollars, and a penchant for hard work. Within several years, he parlayed his tool-making know-how into a small company that would become one of the world's largest automotive parts suppliers.

His name: Frank Stronach. His company: Magna International Inc., the world's most diversified supplier of automotive components and systems. His vision: the creation of a new corporate culture known as Fair Enterprise, which guarantees the rights of employees, management and investors to share in the profits they help produce and which gives employees and managers ownership in the company.

The Magna story begins in 1954 with the arrival to Canada of Frank Stronach. In 1957, three years after immigrating to Canada, Frank was able to fulfil a life-long dream by opening his own business. It was a small, one-man tool and die shop in a rented gatehouse in downtown Toronto. Frank worked long hours and slept on a cot next to his lathe and milling machinery. By the end of the first year of operation, Frank had ten employees. Just three years later, his

company, Multimatic, landed its first automotive contract – an order to produce metal-stamped sun visor brackets for General Motors. The company never looked back.

Frank began to expand his growing firm by offering profit and equity sharing partnerships to key managers. In doing so, he was able to harness their entrepreneurial energy and enthusiasm and place the company on a path of phenomenal growth. Initially, only managers participated in the profit and equity sharing arrangement. But Frank wanted to give every employee a share of the company's profits and ownership as well, making each of them a part-owner with a tangible stake in the company's success.

In the late 1960s, Frank finally got the opportunity to do so. His company merged with Magna Electronics, a publicly-traded aerospace and defense firm, in 1969. As Chairman of the public company, Frank was able to expand his profit and equity participation plan to include every employee, and his unique operating philosophy known as "Fair Enterprise" was born.

By the early 1970s, Magna's automotive operations had expanded to include a greater number of stamped

and electrical components and the company name was changed to Magna International Inc. Magna implemented a major product diversification strategy and divisions were organized into product groups. By the end of the decade, Magna surpassed the $200 million sales mark and had developed a growing reputation for its can-do attitude and innnovative solutions to customer problems.

During the 1980s, Magna formally adopted a governing Corporate Constitution, guaranteeing the rights of employees, investors and management to share in the profits they help produce. Profits are allocated to the employees in the form of cash payments and shares held in trust. Shareholders and senior management also receive a predetermined percentage of annual pre-tax profits, and a minimum of seven percent is allocated to research and development to ensure the company's long-term growth. A maximum of two percent of before-tax profit is donated to various charitable, cultural and educational groups and causes. Magna is believed to be the only company in the world with such a Constitution. The Employee's Charter,

formalized in 1988, strives to create a quality work environment by guaranteeing employees a safe and healthful workplace, job security, competitive wages and benefits, and fair treatment.

In recognition of his unique business philosophy and visionary style, Frank Stronach was inducted into the Canadian Business Hall of Fame in 1995. The honour was a tribute to his Fair Enterprise philosophy of sharing profits and ownership with Magna's key stakeholders. In 1999, he was awarded the Order of Canada for his dedication to community, country and compatriots.

Today, Magna is a key player in the fiercely competitive global automotive industry. The company sells to every major automaker in the world and employs more than 59,000 people at manufacturing divisions and product development centres throughout North America, Europe, South America and Asia. As the industry continues to change, Magna is committed to remaining at the forefront of that evolution, and Frank Stronach continues to play a key role in charting Magna's course as a Fair Enterprise corporation.

Connecting Canadians

ON NOVEMBER 7, 1885 the last spike was driven in the Canadian transcontinental railway at Craigellachie, B.C. Canadians have come a long way since this fundamental step to overcome distance and diversity. This nation's history is marked by the melding of cultures and the rise of strong communities across the land. In more recent times, barriers of distance and often inclement weather have been overcome by the development of modern transportation systems and one of the world's best telecommunications systems. This stellar progress will certainly continue in the 21st century.

We have moved into yet another phase of our history, often called the *Information Society* or the *Knowledge-based Economy and Society*. In today's global economy, knowledge is as important as physical capital, financial capital, and natural resources as a source of economic growth. Information and communications technologies are the new engines of this growth, transforming the way we do business, expanding our learning environments and providing new opportunities for Canadians to participate in the social, cultural, and economic life of their country.

Helping make Canada more competitive in the knowledge-based economy is Industry Canada's mission. Innovation, investment, productivity and exports are our main concerns but so too are the quality of skills, creativity, and learning capabilities of Canadians. Making progress in any of these areas requires effective partnerships with organizations from all sectors and communities, working together in their areas of expertise.

March 30, 1999 – a milestone in Canadian history

Like the Canadian railway more than 100 years before, the last virtual spike for Canadian school and library connectivity was driven on March 30, 1999, when a tiny three-student Nova-Scotian school on Pictou Island, in the Northumberland Strait was connected to the Information Highway. The children living on this isolated island gained access to an entire nation and an entire world on that day. They now have the opportunity to experience first-hand the rich diversity of Canadian culture and language by working collaboratively with other children through the Internet. In the words of nine-year-old Laura Banks: "It will take us wherever we want."

This final link in the SchoolNet partnership made Canada the first country in the world to connect its schools and libraries to the Internet and a world leader in developing and using an advanced information infrastructure to achieve social and economic aims. This achievement may help change the way Canadians learn, communicate, and do business in the future every bit as much as the railway and highway systems have in past decades.

Canada's SchoolNet is a crucial part of the

Industry Canada

Driving the last spike of the C.P.R., connecting Canadians east to west, Craigellachie, B.C., 1885.
[Photo, courtesy NAC/C-011371]

Government of Canada's *Connecting Canadians* strategy to make Canada the most connected nation in the world by the year 2000. *Connecting Canadians* is designed to meet the challenges posed by the new economy and is a commitment to a dynamic economy, a life-long learning culture and the promotion of social cohesion, cultural expression, and new linkages between citizens and government.

The private sector has the main responsibility for building the Information Highway, but Industry Canada is helping to create the right environment to encourage this growth and ensure that all Canadians have opportunities to share in the benefits.

Through our support to *CANARIE*, we are helping the private sector build the next generation Internet in Canada for faster and better service. Policy and regulatory reform also encourages private sector development of both infrastructure and network applications.

A big part of *Connecting Canadians* means getting *Canada On-line*. Through the *Community Access Program*, 5,000 rural and remote communities and 5,000 urban areas will be connected to the Internet by March 2001. Building on Canada's success in connecting its schools and libraries to the Information Highway, *Canada's SchoolNet* will work with its provincial and private sector partners to extend connectivity from schools to the classroom by March 31, 2001, bringing the benefits of the Information Highway to Canadian learners. To ensure schools and public libraries have the equipment and software they need, the *Computers for Schools* program promotes the donation of surplus but still valuable computers from governments, businesses and individuals.

VolNet, a joint private and public sector initiative, will link 10,000 voluntary and charitable organizations to the Internet and to each other by March 2001.

Young Canadians are gaining entrepreneurial and technology-based job experience through programs such as *Digital Collections* and *Aboriginal Digital Collections* which have created a web site with more than 250 multimedia collections of significant Canadian contemporary and historical content. Young college and university graduates find work through on-line job matching with employers in the *National Graduate Register* and *Campus Worklink*.

Smart Communities will encourage communities to become leading-edge users of information technologies so that all sectors and community members work towards developing their communities. The goal is a *Smart Community* in each province, in the North, and in an Aboriginal community by March 2001.

Electronic Commerce will create a legal and regulatory framework to make Canada a location of choice for developing electronic commerce products and services, enabling us to capitalize on the phenomenal growth of on-line business.

Through *Strategis*, Industry Canada provides Canadians with direct access to valuable business and consumer information resources, time saving interactive tools, and a growing number of on-line and electronic commerce services.

You can learn more about *Connecting Canadians* by visiting *http://www.connect.gc.ca*.

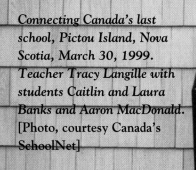

Connecting Canada's last school, Pictou Island, Nova Scotia, March 30, 1999. Teacher Tracy Langille with students Caitlin and Laura Banks and Aaron MacDonald. [Photo, courtesy Canada's SchoolNet]

City of Toronto

Toronto speaks your language

www.city.toronto.on.ca/busine

THINKING of expanding your business in North America? Think Toronto. Whether you do business in e-commerce, biomedical engineering, digital media, or robotics, Toronto speaks your language.

The fifth largest city in North America, Toronto is Canada's financial and industrial centre. Canada's top five banks and 90 percent of the country's top foreign banks are headquartered in Toronto. Toronto leads the country in manufacturing, marketing, employment, new building activity, retail sales, tourism, and small business growth. Last year, Toronto generated 25 percent of all job growth in Canada and broke its record for building-permit issuance.

Toronto is consistently ranked one of the world's best cities in which to live and do business. At a fraction of what it would cost to expand in the U.S., we can enjoy Toronto's unbeatable business climate and very attractive foreign exchange rates. Not to mention that Toronto is within a "trucker's day" of more than half the American population.

Toronto is competitive and works hard to provide business with all the essentials. These include an excellent transportation network and a superb telecommunications infrastructure. In fact, Toronto has the highest concentration of fibre optic cable of any North American city. A highly skilled workforce, the majority of whom specialize in science, engineering, or business administration, is behind Toronto's dynamic spirit. A dynamism that is reflected in all sectors. With a scientific record that includes the discovery of insulin and the Alzheimer's and cystic fibrosis genes, it is no surprise that the University of Toronto's medical faculty is the largest on the continent.

Toronto speaks your language in other ways. Toronto has the highest proportion of immigrants of any city in the world. On any given day, Toronto's 2.4 million residents speak 100 languages, giving the city a clear competitive advantage in the international marketplace, and a good reason to celebrate. Annual festivals such as the Chinese Dragon Boat Races on Toronto's spectacular waterfront, Taste of the Danforth, and Caribana Festival are part of the reason Toronto's quality of life is unsurpassed.

Toronto's streets are clean and safe, its neighbourhoods strong. The downtown core is a thriving business centre by day and a vibrant entertainment and residential centre by night. Toronto's publicly funded health-care system is among the best in the world.

This portrait of Toronto tells a story that can be read in any language. It's a picture of prosperity. Put yourself in the picture. Then watch your investment and your family grow.

Top Languages by Mother Tongue (in addition to English and French)

Chinese	286,460	Spanish	72,795
Italian	202,440	Punjabi	64,625
Portuguese	107,795	Tagalog	58,255

Toronto: One Great, Big City

Toronto is no longer simply Canada's business capital. Now a major force on the international scene, the new Toronto is where the business world meets to do business.

New York, London, Paris, Rio de Janeiro: great cities by their very nature that conjure up images with the mere mention of their names. Toronto is rapidly proving itself as the city for business development, innovation, and success.

Those familiar with Toronto are not the least bit surprised to see Toronto is consistently being recognized as an international city with a high quality of life by expert sources like the Geneva-based Corporate Resources Group and acclaimed business publications like *Fortune* magazine.

And, when asked, most Canadians readily think of Toronto as Canada's corporate and creative centre. Toronto's imagination and creativity is gaining world renown. Its designers, animators, performers and other artists, film makers, and scholars are second to none.

Forecasts of economic growth for the Toronto Area are among the highest of any city region in the developed world. The GDP is approximately $77 billion and retail sales were $33 billion in 1999. Of 42 locations studied by a recent KPMG study, Toronto ranked in the top two most competitive major urban areas in North America and ahead of all the European cities.

Toronto attracts new businesses and residents from all corners of the world in droves. In fact, by 2001, more than 50 percent of Torontonians will have been born outside Canada. With so many languages spoken and a very diverse economy, it is simple to get around and do business no matter what part of the globe was once called home or what kind of business you are in. It is easy to see why in Toronto we say, "Toronto speaks your language."

Torontonians are known for their hospitality and the city is known for its restaurants, theatres, and clubs. The world's tallest free-standing structure provides a bird's-eye view of our beautiful city with its office towers, tree-lined streets, shopping districts, beautiful lake, parks, and diverse neighbourhoods. The 21-million visitors who walk the city's streets each year will attest that Toronto really is One GREAT Big City.

Toronto's downtown core has the third highest retail sales in North America. The Eaton Centre, with its indoor walkway system, is only one reason why.

St. Lawrence Market, Toronto, Ontario.

Maxtech Manufacturing Inc.

K.C. Vasudeva, Chairman and CEO

WHEN K. C. VASUDEVA invested $2,000 in 1977 to open a screw machine shop, he was founding a company that today consists of eight divisions with more than 500 employees and annual sales of more than $100 million. That tells the story of Maxtech Manufacturing Inc., which today is a respected producer of a diverse array of automotive components as well as hand tools and power tool accessories. Born in India, Kacee graduated in instrument technology before he and his bride immigrated to Canada in 1971 and settling in Waterloo, Ontario.

A strong desire to establish his own business was realized in 1977 when he discovered a need for a particular kind of screw machine part in the automotive industries. He bought one screw machine and, while continuing to work part time, he and wife Susan spent every available hour turning out screw machine parts before landing contracts with two companies. This enabled Kacee to buy a second machine, devote all his time to the business, and hire his first employee. New emission control laws for automobiles passed in the United States during the mid-1980s were the real catalyst for launching Maxtech into today's multi-faceted, multi-million dollar business. Ever alert to technological change and skilled at improving on it, Kacee developed improved emission gas reutilization (EGR) fittings which are used in all automobiles made in North America. From 1989 to 1994, Kacee purchased three bankrupt manufacturing companies. They include a CNC shop specializing in machining automotive parts, a thermoset molding company, and an injection molding company. Today, these companies are Maxtech Precision Products, Maxtech Plastics, and Thermoset Molding. In 1995, Maxtech Inc., in Roseville, Michigan, was added to make cold formed stainless steel components.

Another division, Precitech Inc. at Ste. Foy, Quebec was added in 1998 to produce powdered metal components.

Maxtech Enterprises Inc. formed a joint venture in 1999 with an international automotive parts manufacturer based in Germany to create Woco-Maxtech Inc., a manu-facturer of noise vibration harshness components in Michigan. Kacee attributes the success of Maxtech Manufacturing Inc. to one important maxim: "Look after the customer at any cost." If there is a problem, the Maxtech employees don't ask who is at fault. They first solve the problem and then discuss what went wrong. As a result, *Financial Post*/Arthur Anderson has named Maxtech one of Canada's 50 Best Managed Private Companies for 1994 through 1999. In 1998, Kacee was named Wilfrid Laurier University's Outstanding Business Leader. The year before, the Indo Canada Chamber of Commerce named him Businessman of the Year. Kacee, as CEO and Chairman, was selected as a finalist in the Manufacturing Industrial Products category for Ontario's 1999 Entrepreneur of the Year program. Kacee has 16 patents to his credit.

Despite these many corporate and individual awards, Kacee maintains that the company's achievements cannot be attributed to him alone. "Yes, we are successful because of a strong and motivated management team, but the real heart of the company is our diverse and dedicated employees."

Jackpine Forest Products Ltd.

Engineering New Wood Products

DIVERSITY and versatility are two vital qualities that help Jackpine Forest Products establish dominance in the remanufacturing and value added industry in Canada. Diversity of products enables the company to identify and fill niche markets, while cultural diversity at both management and operational levels strengthens the total community, a teamwork approach that recognizes the value of different approaches. Versatility encourages the ability to assess trends, adapt to their effects on the forest industry, and respond to a changing world.

From a well-established, value-added plant to a bright new engineered wood products operation, Jackpine has shown steady growth coupled with faith in the forest industry and in the community of Williams Lake, central British Columbia.

The original plant utilizes lumber down to seven inches in length to produce value-added components for the North American and overseas market. The new plant is also marketed on an international level. Between the two plants, Jackpine provides enough materials to supply the needs of about 5.5 percent of Canada's total housing starts per year.

The main plant has four operational areas under a 35,000 square foot heated building – a planer and moulder combination, a second moulder line, a small block finger jointing line with an automatic chop line and a notcher and resaw line. State-of-the-art dry kilns bring products to 8 or 10 percent moisture content.

The new engineered wood products plant produces

Gian Singh Sandhu, President & CEO, centre, with partners, Prem Singh Vinning, left, and Avtar Singh Sandhu, right.

a variety of new product lines such as long-length, finger jointed rafters, floor joists, flanges, and edge glued panels. Nearly double the size of the original plant, it is designed for future expansion. The equipment in the plant is the latest technology geared to produce unique products. The plant will finger joint high grade 2x3-2x12 lumber to 60 feet in length. This is the first plant of this size in Canada.

Gian Singh Sandhu, Jackpine's energetic President and CEO, came to Canada 30 years ago from India with his wife and young family, looking for more opportunities. While his background was in the Air Force, he saw an opportunity in the forest industry, first in working for a major sawmill operations and then striking out on his own. As one of a few practising Sikhs in a small town, Sandhu stood out. As with any newcomer to a new land, he felt he would have to work twice as hard to get ahead.

Jackpine was established in 1987 by the Sandhu family with financial help from venture capital friends (Prem Singh Vinning and Avtar Singh Sandhu), and has grown steadily. The future looks bright to Sandhu, with unlimited potential for more growth, more markets, and more opportunities. Now, with his own business booming in a time when the forest industry has had to face many challenges, he and his company still stand out as leaders in the remanufacturing process.

The company is targeting its millennium sales to exceed $140 million. The combined workforce for the three operations will be greater than 250.

illiams Lake, B.C.,
ckpine employees

Mississauga is fortunate to have a cosmopolitan mosaic of cultures and neighbourhoods.

Festivals and special events encourage Mississauga residents to have fun while learning more about each other's culture.

IN MISSISSAUGA, we are proud of our cultural diversity. In every shopping centre, in every school, you will see a microcosm of the world's peoples. At the Mississauga Civic Centre there are 32 languages spoken in addition to English, not really a surprising fact, since 43 percent of Mississauga's population are immigrant families. Interestingly, the various cultural groups are scattered throughout Mississauga's many residential districts, learning and working together – becoming proud citizens of our city and country.

The first years can be difficult for new Canadians, especially if English is not their mother tongue. But, the various ethnic organizations, churches, and the City's community development staff work together to help ease the transition. Mayor McCallion considers multicultural harmony so important that she hosts an annual breakfast, bringing together leaders from all the cultural organizations to exchange ideas.

Our festivals strengthen the sense of community. Every June, Philippine Independence day is celebrated with a parade, entertainment, and games. In July, the Can-Sikh Sports and cultural festival features competitions in kabodde (a hard tackling, rugby-type sport), weightlifting, tug-of-war, and volleyball. Italian, Chinese, Portuguese, Polish – most groups hold annual festivals with City staff participation and assistance.

Of the many festivals held each year, one stands out as a celebration of friendship and understanding –

Carassauga. The 16 pavilions reflect the pride of each community as they share their food and culture with the broader public. For example, this year (1999) at the Caribbean Pavilion, children of all cultures participated in storytelling and were treated to a magic show. At the Chinese pavilion, visitors created their own original illustrations under the guidance of Chinese brushpainting artists. This well-attended festival started 14 years ago, has been self- supporting since 1995, with corporate sponsorships increasing every year.

In a multicultural environment, effective law enforcement requires sensitivity and teamwork. Peel Region Police are working to develop relationships with each of the many groups. Our police service is proud to have officers from Caribbean, Polish, Serbian, Ukrainian, and other ethnic backgrounds, all actively involved in promoting better cultural relations.

We, in Mississauga, have long realized that the vitality and creativity of our cultural mix play a big part in the growth and prosperity we have experienced. Businesses have benefited, especially those companies operating call centres or selling globally. Then there are the countless successful small businesses operated by new Canadians, creating employment and building our City. The majority are savvy, enthusiastic, hard-working, and talented – all the right ingredients to contribute to the general prosperity and well-being of this city and our country. Welcome and we thank you for enriching our society!

All The Right Connections

Mississauga

Metzler & Company

Recruiting Outstanding Executives

J. MICHAEL METZLER, president and CEO of Metzler & Company, whose corporate client list includes at least 50 of Canada's top 100 corporations as well as an impressive number of fledgling start-ups, states, "Our approach to recruiting outstanding executives can best be described as a process that is a subtle blend of both art and science."

The scientific approach is clearly established at Metzler & Company by maintaining an up-to-date customized computer system that now contains the names of some 48,000 potential candidates, while the more subtle, artistic aspect is based on finding a candidate who not only has the necessary skills but also suits the client's specific company culture.

To meet these requirements, Metzler & Company's professional recruiters and research staff begin a search only after a detailed consultation with a client that leads to a comprehensive position description outlining the background, skills, and personal characteristics that collectively define the ideal candidate. "We then take a holistic approach in the assessment of potential candidates to ensure that the all-important right fit will be achieved," says Michael, adding, "Every client has different needs just as every person is different."

Michael's career began in the 1980s when he joined Deloitte & Touche and became the firm's top producer in Canada and winner of the "Principal of the Year" award in 1986. Later he was the youngest partner in the world of Ward-Howell International at Toronto before opening his own firm in 1991.

Metzler & Company's clients include companies in finance and investment, real estate, telecommunications, internet, marketing and sales, and retail management, to name only a few. "We don't try to serve every type of business," Michael admits. "It's our rule never to take on anything we don't understand or can't bring value to."

Observing that it's a leap of faith for a business establishment to hire an executive search organization to find them a key executive, Michael claims in return, "It's our responsibility to identify people who are not only highly accomplished, but also individuals whose attitudes and personal values are compatible with those of the client's corporate culture. When we succeed in doing this for a client, we too have succeeded."

With more than 98 percent of candidates proving successful for at least one year, Metzler & Company seldom has to fulfill its firm commitment to replace any within that time frame free of charge.

Being the owner of a successful corporate executive search firm has convinced Michael that, in the final analysis, what really determines whether a company will succeed or fail is the people – the women and men who transform the organization into a living, breathing enterprise. "Human talent is the rarest and least appreciated commodity in the world," he says and predicts that successful organizations of the future will be those that possess people talent and make a point of asking with sincerity, "How may I help you?" This philosophy, which Michael describes as "customer intimacy," is certainly an essential element in the success of Metzler & Company.

Husky

A Canadian Success Story in Injection Molding

FOUNDED IN 1953 by Robert Schad, Husky started out as a small machine shop in a Toronto garage. The first product, a single-track snowmobile, called the "Huskymobile," failed, however the name remained. The company continued on as a machine shop making thinwall molds for the plastics industry. When the existing injection molding machines in the 1960s could not run the Husky molds at their full potential, the company developed its first injection molding machine for thinwall applications, which was the fastest in the world. To recover its significant investment in this development, Husky looked for markets beyond Canada, and was quickly the leading global supplier of high speed injection molding systems.

After struggling through the 1970s oil shock, Husky applied its expertise in high speed injection molding in the fast-emerging market for plastic (PET bottles). In the latter part of the decade, the company had developed the leading edge injection molding system to manufacture PET preforms. From the late 1970s until today, Husky has continually led the advancement of injection molding systems for the production of PET preforms. As the large scale conversion of glass to plastic progressed, Husky once again positioned itself as the leading global supplier of high speed/high volume equipment for the packaging industry.

Today, Husky is the largest brand name supplier of injection molding equipment in the world. The company has significantly broadened its scope beyond the packaging market serving customers in the automotive, technical market, and general purpose market. Its core products include injection molding machines, molds and integrated systems for polyethylene terephthalate (PET) bottle preforms, part handling robots, and hot runner systems. The company's focus is providing manufacturing solutions aimed at maximizing customer productivity – not simply selling hardware. In 1999, total sales were $708 million (US) with 2,800 employees worldwide. Husky has built the most extensive service and sales network in the industry, with 33 regional sales offices in over 25 countries and technical centers in North America, Latin America, Europe, and Asia.

Since 1953, Husky's growth and global success has been achieved without acquisitions, thereby preserving the core of its entrepreneurial spirit and cultural identity. The company's purpose is to be a role model of lasting business success based on its core values:

Through a heritage of continual product development, Husky has become the world leader in high output PET preform systems as shown here at one of its customers' operations.

- Make a contribution
- Proactive environmental responsibility
- Passion for excellence
- Uncompromising honesty

Husky is actively engaged in developing solutions that reduce plastic consumption and facilitate the use of recycled plastics. In 1999, Husky completed building an 8,000-ton injection molding machine – the largest of its kind – to mold plastic car bodies in a joint project with DaimlerChrysler. This project, which is a significant investment for Husky, holds the potential to lead the automotive industry towards an era of more environmentally sustainable practices. Its manufacturing operations have aggressively continued to reduce ozone depleting substances (HCFCs), chlorinated solvents, and volatile organic compounds (VOCs) by converting its metal part cleaners and painting process to water-based applications. Husky's waste diversion rate from its operations is 93% compared to the government's standard of 50%, and all of its landscaping is pesticide and herbicide free. Husky also donates 5 percent of its pre-tax profit to charitable causes involving community, environment, and education.

Manufacturing facilities are state of the art with the latest engineering and manufacturing tools to enhance employee effectiveness. New facilities maximize natural lighting while the cafeterias offer healthy foods. Its manufacturing facilities are concentrated on campuses,

located in Bolton, Ontario; Milton, Vermont; and Dudelange, Luxembourg. The campuses facilitate team work across businesses, open communication, and an economy of scale to provide leading employee services such as wellness and fitness programs, and a child development centre on its Bolton, Ontario, campus. In addition to global career opportunities, the campus environment allows employees to develop their careers locally without uprooting families. People are challenged early on in their careers with rewarding projects. The organization's emphasis on product innovation and stretch goals means an exciting environment for talented people to grow and make a contribution. These initiatives, along with a strong corporate culture, help Husky to attract and retain individuals who are dynamic, fast paced, entrepreneurial, and have a purpose beyond making money. Husky is proud of the team it has built and knows that its largest source of competitive advantage is its people.

AWARDS

1993	*Canada Award for Business Excellence*
1993	*Canada Export Award for Outstanding Export Performance*
1994	*Canada Export Award for Outstanding Export Performance*
1996	*50 Best-managed Private Companies in Canada*
1997	*Margaret Fletcher Award for Early Childhood Education (child development centre, Bolton, Ontario)*
1998	*Financial Post Gold Environmental Leadership Award*
1998	*National Occupational Health and Safety Award for Excellence*

Husky's campus in Bolton provides employee services such as wellness, fitness, and a childcare centre.

Glendan
Mould Inc.

Steve Spick, Founder and President, Glendan Mould Inc., with blueprint for multi-cavity stack unit.

Stainless steel, six-cavity mould made at Glendan Mould for production of plastic flowerpots.

PLASTIC CONTAINERS for ice cream, margarine, yogurt or prescription pill bottles may not look like works of art, but the engineering required to produce such containers demands precision-made molds carefully carved out of raw steel. A successful company carrying out such high speed injection mold building is Glendan Mould Inc.

In its six-year history, Glendan has produced molds for the plastic industry in the food, pharmaceutical, and horticultural sectors both in Canada and the United States and, in 1999, explored expanding its customer base by attending a trade show in Bejing, China.

After graduating from the mold building course at Seneca College, Glendan's founding president, Steve Spick, joined a major mold-making company in Toronto, learning all aspects of the mold industry by working in several departments and operating the numerous machines required to produce a variety of molds. He then started Glendan in 1994.

Steve opted to specialize in high speed, thin wall, multi-cavity molds. Ever since, his company not only has been successful in Canada, but also has entered into a working alliance with a major American mold making company, Dollins Tool Inc. This has made the two companies a substantial international operation capable of bidding more successfully for international customers.

Glendan, like Dollins, offers a complete line of services to customers with its engineering department taking careful note of the special needs of plastic manufacturers then creating state-of-the-art molds to meet those special needs. Although the final product may be a small two-cavity mold or a complex multi-cavity stack unit capable of producing up to 64 units at a time, the labour-intensive engineering graphics and the first working models often take three to four months to complete.

"A successful mold is precision-made so that each cavity is identical, requiring a minimum amount of plastic but is strong enough to be totally reliable," says Steve, claiming some molds may be required to produce as many as 10 million units before being serviced. "With those kinds of quantities, a saving of five percent in the thickness of the plastic required can be significant," Steve adds.

So far, Glendan has produced molds for numerous foodstuffs, such as tubs for whipped cream, ice cream, and grated cheeses, and has been involved in developing several promotional drink cup molds for internationally recognized fast food outlets. Glendan also manufactures molds for the bio-medical industry, and a line of particularly light, thin plastic flower pots for the horticultural industry.

Now providing some 25 to 30 plastic molders with a variety of molds, Glendan in conjunction with its American working affiliate, Dollins Tool Inc., is poised to expand its sales and marketing efforts globally.

Brampton

A Great Place to Call Home, for Business, for Pleasure

THE CELEBRATED City of Brampton combines the textures of a small, history-rich Ontario town with the dynamics of a growing city numbering more than 300,000.

Some 150 years ago, Brampton was no more than a tavern named Buffy's Corners. After two Englishmen arrived in the area, they took up land, opened an ashery, a store, a copper shop, and a distillery, establishing a community which they named after their birthplace in England.

By 1969, Canada's first satellite community was built on 8,000 acres east of the Town of Brampton. Five years later, The Town of Brampton, The Township of Chinguacousy, The Toronto Gore, and parts of Mississauga amalgamated to form the City of Brampton.

When Brampton topped the 300,000 mark in 1998, the city became Canada's thirteenth largest municipality. Brampton's strategic location in the GTA, sitting atop one shoulder of Toronto and adjacent to Canada's largest airport and a maze of highways, has generated steady industrial and commercial growth.

Brampton's role as a car manufacturing centre dates back to 1960, when the first Rambler rolled off the line of the American Motors Assembly Plant. Today, Daimler Chrysler's Assembly Plant builds 1,500 Chrysler Concorde, LHS, 300M, and Dodge/Chrysler Intrepid models each day, shipping them around the globe.

Jaguar has its Canadian corporate headquarters in Brampton, housing both the executive offices and the training facilities for Jaguar dealerships across North America.

Auto-affiliated Magna International has strong presence with its new 400,000 square foot plant that combines two Magna enterprises: Massiv Automated Systems – a robotics assembly firm – and a technical training centre.

Other outstanding businesses in Brampton include a division of SKD Co. which manufactures metal stampings and welded assemblies for automotive manufacturers, including Daimler Chrysler; ABB, one of the world's largest engineering and technology firms which consolidated three Toronto-area facilities at its new $25-million Brampton operation; MacDonald Dettwiler Space and Advanced Robotics Ltd., formerly Spar Aerospace where the Canadarm for the NASA space shuttle was developed, currently making a special manipulator system for use in constructing and servicing the International Space Station; Siemens Electric Ltd., a global leader in the field of electrical and electronic engineering with its Canadian headquarters located in Brampton.

Brampton has more parks per capita that any other municipality in Canada. Three of the most notable are Chinguacousy Park, with its 100 acres, Professor's Lake, a 100-acre lake with sandy beach and docks, and Gage Park, a 5-acre park with a temperature-controlled, artificial ice surface winding in and about century-old trees and a landmark gazebo.

The City of Brampton currently operates 35 recreation facilities, one of which is a Wellness Centre, one of only two of its kind in Canada, emphasizing physical and mental well-being.

Brampton boasts one of the highest adult sports participation rates per capita in North America. Three successful sports franchises play out of the Brampton Centre for Sports and Entertainment.

To get the latest information about Brampton, visit www.city.brampton.on.ca/economic-development.

Ford of Canada

FOR MANY CANADIANS, the new millennium brings the opportunity to reflect on our country's rich history and the possibilities that lie ahead. At Ford of Canada, the history is long and full, and the future promises to be even brighter.

Ford of Canada's past originates from August 17, 1904, when Henry Ford, who had launched Ford Motor Company a year earlier, presided over the company's first expansion outside of the United States, with the incorporation of Ford Motor Company of Canada, Limited. The fledgling company produced 114 cars and its 17 employees generated a total payroll of $12,000 in its first year.

From those humble beginnings, Ford of Canada grew to play a leading role in the country's economic development throughout the twentieth century, touching the lives of hundreds of thousands of Canadians from all walks of life. In contrast to the company's first-year results, Ford of Canada's annual production of cars and trucks now exceeds 685,000 and employment of over 17,400 employees in its corporate and Canadian Auto Workers family generates a payroll of over $1.5-billion. Since 1990, Ford has invested over $7-billion in Canada, and in 1999 parts purchases from Canadian suppliers topped $5-billion. Windsor is the engine capital of the Ford world and in 1999 produced 1.5-billion engines.

The past century has been an exciting one for Ford and indeed for all Canadians. Now as we enter a new era, reflecting on our heritage and contemplating the future, Ford of Canada is prepared to embrace the unparalleled opportunity shared by all Canadians. Ford is focused on providing Canadians with innovative, thoughtful products and services that make their lives easier and respect their time, developing talented employees who contribute to the company and society as a whole, and adding value to the communities in which we all live and work.

Employment

Ford of Canada is striving to maintain a dynamic work environment, attracting, developing, and retaining many talented employees. The company's recently implemented Ford 2000 program is revolutionizing the way Ford does business on a number of fronts, including people management. As such, the company values and promotes three core ideals – empowerment, diversity and teamwork.

At Ford of Canada, each employee is empowered to have a direct impact on the quality and desirability of the company's products and its productivity. By empowering every employee, the overall strength of the company is multiplied. Ford also values a workforce that reflects the diversity of its markets and the Canadian landscape as a whole. By maintaining a diverse workplace environment, Ford is able to have a better understanding of the wants and needs of its customers, which leads to greater success that is shared by each and every employee. And by working together, sharing ideas and communicating openly, Ford is well equipped to move towards the company's common goal – to become the world's leading consumer company for automotive products and services.

Retail Locations

For many Canadians, the face of Ford is their local Ford retail team, identified by the familiar blue Ford oval. It's the most recognized automotive brand symbol in the world, and today it appears over all of the 567 Ford dealer locations across Canada. The retail team includes 22,000 people nationwide, from all walks of life.

The Ford blue oval – the most-recognized automotive brand sign in the world – which appears over all Ford of Canada retail locations.

Marketing

Ford also reaches out to a diverse group of Canadian consumers in the marketing and sales of all its car and truck models. Ford print, radio and television ads are produced in a number of different languages and geared towards many different segments of the consumer marketplace.

Ford of Canada has even created a management position and marketing department dedicated specifically to special markets. The company believes it is important to recognize and understand the mindset of all Canadian automotive customers, regardless of background. By ensuring that marketing communications address the specific needs of each customer, Ford is reaching out to a wide cross-section of Canadians.

Vehicles

Ford of Canada offers a range of vehicles which appeal to every taste. From the exciting new Ford Focus to Canada's best-selling F-Series pickup trucks, from the sporty Ford Mustang to the complete line-up of Sport Utility Vehicles (SUVs), there is a Ford car or truck for everyone.

Ford takes great care in the design of its vehicles to accommodate the distinct needs of its customers. For example, Ford developed the "Third-Age Suit," which restricts the physical agility and reduces the strength of designers who wear the suit by 25 per cent. The Third-Age Suit is changing the way Ford designs cars by helping design engineers understand the physical limitations and ergonomic requirements of a wide range of drivers and incorporating these needs into new and improved vehicle designs.

Ford of Canada President and CEO Bobbie Gaunt with the new 2000 Ford Escape SUV.

Environment

In the new millennium, Ford will strengthen its focus on being a leader in practical environmental innovations for its products and facilities. Ford employees worldwide stand behind a commitment to use innovation and technology to help preserve the environment for future generations, which is embodied in the company's environmental pledge and policy.

Ford Environmental Pledge

"Ford Motor Company is dedicated to providing ingenious environmental solutions that will position us as a leader in the automotive industry of the 21st century. Our actions will demonstrate that we care about preserving the environment for future generations."

Ford's Environmental Policy

"To protect the environment by striving to continually improve processes that minimize waste and pollution, and by setting environmental objectives and targets which meet or exceed all legal requirements."

The company backs up its strong environmental stance with action. Ford offers the widest selection of Low Emissions Vehicle (LEV) and Alternative Fuel Vehicle (AFV) cars and trucks in Canada and these technologies are having a significant real-world impact on the environment today in the form of reduced smog-forming vehicle emissions. With this industry-leading selection of LEVs and AFVs, as well as its support of the Auto Maker's Choice fuel endorsement program, Ford of Canada is assured of maintaining its position at the environmental forefront.

Ford Focus, 2000 North American Car of the Year.

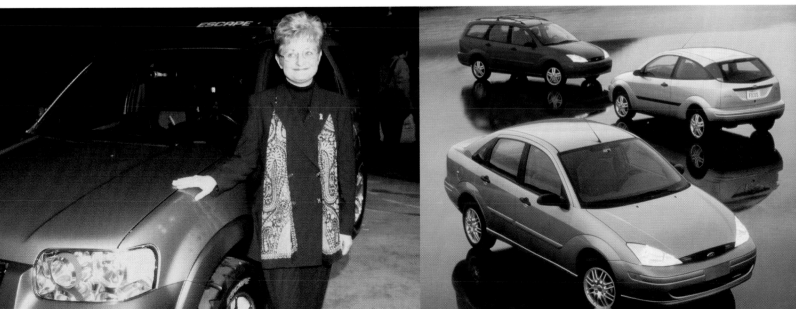

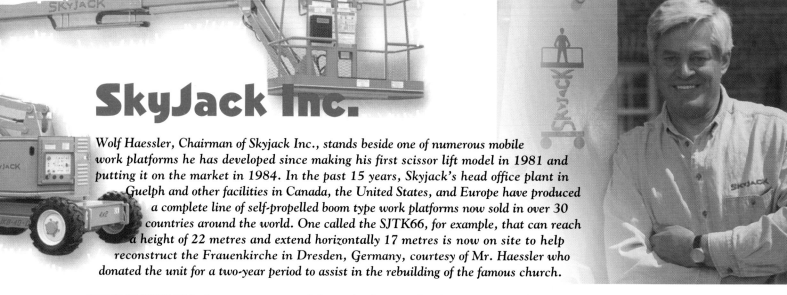

SkyJack Inc.

Wolf Haessler, Chairman of Skyjack Inc., stands beside one of numerous mobile work platforms he has developed since making his first scissor lift model in 1981 and putting it on the market in 1984. In the past 15 years, Skyjack's head office plant in Guelph and other facilities in Canada, the United States, and Europe have produced a complete line of self-propelled boom type work platforms now sold in over 30 countries around the world. One called the SJTK66, for example, that can reach a height of 22 metres and extend horizontally 17 metres is now on site to help reconstruct the Frauenkirche in Dresden, Germany, courtesy of Mr. Haessler who donated the unit for a two-year period to assist in the rebuilding of the famous church.

THE DESIGN of a scissor-type mobile work platform by Wolf Haessler early in the 1980s has lifted him and his company, Skyjack, into one of the world's largest suppliers of such units in less than 15 years.

The company, now established in Guelph, Ontario, with eight other facilities within Canada, the United States, and Europe, manufactures more than 12,000 units a year with gross sales for fiscal 1999 amounting to $262 million. For Wolf, who invested $5,000 to start his own machine shop with partner, Sid De Way, 1969, it's a success story. But 30 years later, Wolf admits "I get more kicks and more satisfaction taking the company to higher levels than I do taking money out of the bank every week."

A native of Germany, Wolf came to Canada with his parents and five siblings, settling in Richmond Hill, Ontario, in 1952. He graduated in engineering from the University of Guelph in 1966, adding a Master's degree from the University of Western Ontario before joining DuPont Canada. Soon he realized that he would rather run his own show and invested $5,000 to form a partnership with an older tradesman he had met on a summer job. Haessler & De Way opened in Brampton, Ontario, and over the next 15 years did repair work and made replacement parts for conveyor systems and bakery equipment.

A chance remark by the owner of an equipment rental firm prompted Wolf and his partner to develop their version of an aerial lift platform. They were ready to produce it by 1981, but the financial turndown of the early '80s made it impossible to find an interested

bank or investor. The prototype was hidden in a farmer's barn until the financial climate improved when they secured a distributor and sold 100 units in 1984.

Making a small profit by 1985, Haessler gambled that he was on to a good thing. He bought out his partner, promising to pay him with future profits. He expanded his product line by selling in Europe. When the contract with a distributor expired, Wolf decided to sell direct to North American clients. By 1989, more space was required. Employees were asked to invest with him in an existing Guelph building.

Since then several additions to both the office and plant areas have been made. In 1994, the company went public, with the $6.2 million raised used to consolidate ownership of both the Guelph plant and a smaller one opened earlier at Emmetsburg, Iowa. He also donated 300,000 shares to all employees with a minimum of two years service so they could participate in Skyjack's future.

Skyjack today employs more than 1,600 people in five countries and has produced more than 50,000 mobile scissor-type lift units now sold in over 30 countries around the world.

Mr Haessler is a recipient of several awards for his entrepreneurial skills and innovative programs, including the prestigious Canada Award for Excellence in Entrepreneurship in 1995. "Because a business is always alive and changing, there are always new goals to strive for. That's what gets me up in the morning." Wolf has no wish to be an overseer. He is a doer who gets results.

City of Cambridge

Civic Pride Inspires Business Growth

THE CITY OF CAMBRIDGE was created on January 1, 1973 when the municipalities of Galt, Hespeler, and Preston, including the hamlet of Blair, amalgamated with parts of the Townships of North Dumfries and Waterloo to form a thriving and diverse new community. While Cambridge dates only from 1973, the city's history is much older than that, starting in 1800 when Mennonite settlers from Pennsylvania arrived in the Blair area. These original settlers were soon followed by still other Mennonites, including John Erb, who built the area's first saw and flour mills in an area first called Cambridge Mills. The village that grew up around the mills was later to become the town of Preston.

The settlement of Galt had an origin somewhat different from that of Preston. Galt was founded in 1816 by William Dickson, a prominent businessman who had originally come to Canada from the lowlands of Scotland. With the assistance of his primary agent Absalom Shade, Mr. Dickson set out to populate his new townsite and the surrounding area with settlers from his home township of Dumfries. The initial efforts of Mr. Dickson and Mr. Shade achieved mixed results and it wasn't until the 1830s that the settlement began to develop into an economic power in the area. It was at this same time, about 1832, that the settlement of Hespeler got its start when Mennonite pioneer Michael Bergey built a house

and a saw mill along the Speed River. The hamlet was first known as Bergeytown, then New Hope, but was renamed Hespeler, in 1859, in honour of Jacob Hespeler, the village's most prominent and prosperous citizen.

While details of the origins of Cambridge's founding communities varied, the leaders in each of the settlements shared a positive belief in the importance of manufacturing to develop the local economies. Cambridge continues to recognize the importance of the region's manufacturing sector and encourages the growth of both traditional and high tech industries. At the same time the city's heritage takes a prominent place in any vision of the future. Cambridge celebrates the uniqueness of its founding communities and is united by its heritage, rivers, and common future. The city, as a community of opportunity, encourages business growth, entrepreneurial spirit, strong leadership, and civic pride.

This entrepreneurial spirit and civic pride have consistently attracted people from all parts of the world. Our earliest settlers came to Cambridge from the British Isles and Northern Europe, notably Germany and Switzerland. Beginning in the 1950s, Cambridge became home to a large Portuguese-speaking population and, more recently, to a number of immigrants fleeing the conflict in the former Yugoslavia. It is peace and prosperity they seek and find in abundance in Cambridge.

Cambridge straddles the Grand River, the first urban waterway designated a Canadian Heritage River.

St. Lawrence Cement Inc.

Leading By Building Value For You

CEMENT, one of the world's oldest and foremost construction materials for roads and buildings, both commercial and residential, is St. Lawrence Cement's core product. The company operates four cement plants and numerous other facilities to serve 15,000 customers in Canada and on the Eastern Seaboard of the United States.

The Mississauga cement plant, which began operations in 1956, remains the company's largest facility and marketing headquarters for Ontario. Its operations began with two wet process kilns producing a total capacity of 850 tonnes of cement per day (tpd). In 1968, a preheater kiln was added resulting in a total production capacity of 3,000 tpd. Since then, additions and improvements have included:

- a 3,500 hp mill moved from the company's Beauport, Quebec plant (1971);
- one of the largest cement mills in North America (1974);
- a storage hall to handle the raw materials such as coal and clinker (limestone and sand after processing through the kiln at temperatures reaching a high of 1450° C);

Chemical Lab

- a bag warehouse able to store some 150,000 bags of a variety of finished products, and
- a 1.6 km long enclosed reversible belt conveyor system, to bring raw materials from a ship loading dock on Lake Ontario to the plant, and clinker or cement from the plant to the loading dock.

St. Lawrence Cement is 61 percent owned by Holderbank Financière Glaris Ltd., a Swiss company, through its U.S. subsidiary Holnam Inc. Besides the Mississauga plant, the company's Canadian operations include a cement plant in Joliette, Quebec and 13 cement distribution terminals, one mineral components distribution terminal, 46 ready-mix concrete plants, 22 quarries and sand pits and two construction companies. These assets are located in Ontario, Quebec, and the Maritimes.

In the United States, the company operates two cement plants, one in Catskill, NY, and another in Hagerstown, MD. Its U.S. operations also include nine cement distribution terminals and sources and markets fly ash and ground slag, both mineral components.

In mid-1999, upgrades to the two Canadian plants have increased production capacity by 180,000 tonnes. As for the U.S. operations, plans are underway for the construction of a two million tonnes cement plant in Greenport, N.Y.

Throughout the years, St. Lawrence Cement has launched a number of marketing initiatives to meet the growing needs of customers. They include high silica fume cement (HSF) cementitious slag and a new line of masonry cements. Technical experts are available, both at the plant and in the field, to answer customer inquiries and to assist with innovative solutions while ensuring that all industry codes and standards are maintained. These specialists are part of the 2,500 people employed by St. Lawrence Cement, 1,400 in Ontario, 800 in Quebec and the Maritimes and 300 in the United States.

Kiln Rebricking

Club Meadowvale Corporate Fit & Fund Challenge. Proud champions 3 years in a row!

While St. Lawrence Cement's products and services make a positive contribution to society, the company recognizes the environmental implications of its activities as well as its responsibility to conserve clear air, pure water, and natural resources. Its commitment to address environmental concerns is carefully spelled out in the 1998 Report on Environmental Responsibility. St. Lawrence Cement's President and CEO, Patrick Dolberg, clearly states that the company's goal is to exceed environmental regulations "because it is the right thing to do."

Numerous steps have been or are being taken to exceed regulations. In 1998, an investment of $15 million on four new baghouses was made at the Joliette plant in Quebec. These are sophisticated filtering systems that capture particulates, reducing emissions to levels eight times lower than current provincial government norms. It also stepped up its use of alternative fuels, from 18.7 per cent in 1997 to 25.8 per cent in 1998. Another $100,000 investment was made in an environmental management database system, to track sites and archive information.

More recently, two environmentally significant expansion projects have been undertaken, one in Sault Ste. Marie, Ontario, and another in Camden, New Jersey. These new facilities will produce a performance enhancing cementitious material from a by-product of iron and steel manufacturing. In addition to recycling material, the new plants will save annually 1.6 million tonnes of limestone – a non-renewable resource.

St. Lawrence Cement is proud of its philanthropic contributions to local community organizations. The Mississauga Symphony, the Oakville Arts Council, Erindale College, and the Oakville Waterfront Festival are just a few examples of the many groups St. Lawrence Cement supports both through financial means and volunteers. St. Lawrence Cement is a proud, responsible corporate citizen of the Mississauga/ Oakville community.

Throughout the years, St. Lawrence Cement's Ontario group (Dufferin Construction, Dufferin Aggregates, Dufferin-Custom Concrete Group, and Boehmers) have participated in a number of high-profile projects in the Toronto market area. The most recent achievements include: the Pearson Airport, the Metro Convention Centre, the Windsor Casino, the Air Canada Centre, Highway 407, and the Queen Elizabeth Way.

Background: St. Lawrence Cement Plant

Xerox Canada Inc.

Embracing Cultural Diversity

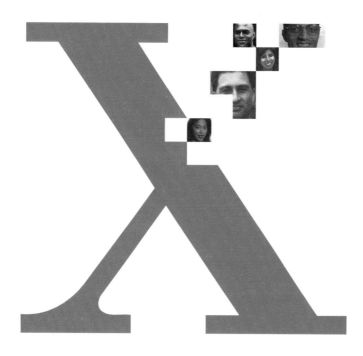

WE LIVE AND WORK in a society that is remarkable for the diversity of its make-up. Differences in ethnic background and culture, as well as in the way we think, add to both the complexity and richness of our lives.

Today Xerox Canada, known as the leader in document solutions and services, is not only bridging the gap between the paper and digital worlds, but is also bridging the gap between people. Employing people from over 30 different countries, Xerox Canada has demonstrated its commitment to the value of diversity in several ways including rigorous compliance with employment equity. Policies and awareness programs that foster inclusive behavior have helped us create a culture that is fair to people of all backgrounds. In fact, Xerox Canada has been consistently recognized as a leader in diversity initiatives.

Xerox Canada's aim in embracing diversity is two-fold: to have a workforce that reflects the Canadian population; to create an environment where diversity is valued and where all individuals can realize their full potential.

Violette Lareau, Director, Recruiting and Diversity, calls the culture "inclusive and empowering...one that respects and leverages people's differences to enrich our lives and the lives of our customers."

There are three trends that make creating an inclusive culture a business imperative: markets are becoming increasingly globalized, the pool of qualified candidates is shrinking, and the face of the Canadian population is changing.

In our eyes, however, creating an inclusive culture is not only a business imperative but also an opportunity. People from various backgrounds have different insights, thus offering more creative business solutions and approaches which are more in sync with our diverse customers.

Much of Xerox Canada's success is due to the fact that diversity has been integrated into the company's management systems. But creating an inclusive culture is an ongoing process, not a program with a beginning and an end.

An excellent starting point in implementing policies and awareness programs is for employees to try to identify and deconstruct misconceptions and stereotypes they might have about others. Xerox Canada provides cultural sensitivity training to address these misconceptions. Each employee has equal responsibility in creating a culture where individuals are treated the way they wish to be treated.

Xerox Canada also offers diversity-friendly employment practices such as flexible working arrangements and an employee assistance program that provides employees with guidance on issues such as elder and child care.

Today Xerox Canada's workforce is comprised of a variety of people in a variety of locations, including the leading edge Xerox Research Centre of Canada in Mississauga. Our workforce chose Xerox Canada because of its teamwork-oriented culture, respect for diversity and opportunities for advancement. We are committed to hiring the best people and to mirroring the communities in which we operate.

Xerox Canada is also committed to improving and promoting the full participation of Aboriginal people in the Canadian economy. This commitment is evident by our Aboriginal Education Support Program. It offers Aboriginal people the opportunity to acquire and improve technology skills, enabling their employment in the information technology industry so that they too can share in the economic prosperity of the knowledge age.

This program consists of two elements: scholarship awards and internship opportunities. Scholarships are awarded each year to up to eight Aboriginal students who are pursuing post-secondary education. The internships offered through the program provide short-term work experience and exposure to Xerox Canada's corporate culture.

Violette Lareau, Director, Recruiting and Diversity, calls the culture "Inclusive and empowering…one that respects and leverages people's differences to enrich our lives and the lives of our customers."

Xerox Canada believes its employees are a key element in realizing success in its new approach to its customers and markets, and to its vision of being the leader in providing document solutions. Crucial to our success will be harnessing the talent, energy and commitment of our present and future employees, so that they can anticipate and meet our customers' needs. In an era in which competitive success depends upon knowledge and the ability to leverage it, the biggest competitive advantage we have is our people – regardless of where they come from – and their ability to be the best that they can be.

THE DIGITAL DOCUMENT COMPANY

XEROX

McDermid Paper Converters

Making Good Impressions in Important Places

EARL AND LEONA MCDERMID have never abandoned the tenets of honesty and business integrity, twentieth-century values which have been the rock foundation of their company's mission statement for almost 30 years.

From its beginning "shoe-string" operation in 1971 to its role as Canada's leading paper converter, McDermid Paper Converters has consistently pursued innovation mainly as the result of the visionary foresight of Earl McDermid, company founder, and Leona Crouse McDermid, his wife of 48 years. Products of the Great Depression, Earl and Leona came from middle-class families who instilled in them the values of hard work, dedication, and commitment.

Lance and Michael McDermid, Earl and Leona's two sons, joined the company's management team in 1978 and 1980, respectively. Their collective contribution to the needs of the company has been of multiple significance both in new product development and corporate direction. As well, daughter Lori-Anne joined the firm in 1979 as a Sales Representative and Public Relations Officer. Today, an accomplished photographer, Lori-Anne's valuable lens and film skills have assisted the company in product promotion.

Long before he founded McDermid Paper Converters Inc., Earl, an avowed Canadian patriot, voiced his support for Canadian Confederation in numerous articles and many speeches. During the 1995 Quebec Referendum, he advised and received responses from senior Canadian officials. In a letter from Prime Minister Jean Chrétien, November, 1995, the Prime Minister expressed to Earl his "appreciation for the time you have taken to share your thoughts and feelings about the future of the nation. It is my strong desire that you will continue to lend your support, as we go about developing innovative response to the profound desire for change being felt among all Canadians."

Born in Kagawong, Manitoulin Island, Ontario, 1929, Earl found his way into the world at the hand of his compassionate Aunt Janet (Janetta) McDermid Palmer, who served as mid-wife/nurse in the absence of a doctor, often the case in remote areas. In 1951, he met Leona, of Ukrainian descent, born, 1933, on the Saskatchewan prairie in the tiny village of Goodeve. Married a year after they met while they were working for the Massey Harris Farm Machinery Company in Toronto, Earl and Leona instantly created a team which complimented each others skills, Earl, as salesman and innovator, Leona, as administrator and financial supervisor.

Earl and Leona McDermid, founders, 1971, McDermid Paper Converters. [Photo, courtesy Lori-Anne McDermid]

The function of paper converting is an accurate assessment of the core activities of McDermid Paper Converters since 1971. In the field of paper grade creation and improvement, this all-Canadian company has provided and is still providing economic opportunities for Canada worldwide.

The first and most notable of the company's innovations came to fruition in 1976 when Earl McDermid proposed the production of a non-existent paper grade, hopefully to save a northern Ontario paper mill from closing. The new paper became an almost overnight success and is today in demand by other paper converters and commercial printers, saving and creating thousands of jobs all across North America. Today this same but much improved paper is one of Canada's most valued exports.

A second company innovation was a successful attempt to overcome performance problems in cash registers and banking rolls, where existing paper grades could not perform. This was overcome by the addition of one simple finishing station inserted into the production line at mill level causing paper fibers to be redirected. The positive results created a new specification and perfect function in all dedicated applications. Several large mills in the United States today produce bond paper using McDermid's own form of this process.

The third and most significant contribution of McDermid Paper Converters to the world of communications came with the successful refinement of facsimile paper to an affordable semi-generic allowing all manufacturers and distributors to share in an opportunity of gigantic proportions. In 1982 very few people in North America knew what a facsimile or fax machine was, let alone how it worked or the kind of paper it used, that is, until Michael McDermid discovered one of only a handful of these seemingly magical machines in use. Driven by curiosity, the development of thermal paper for fax machines became a preoccupation of the McDermid company in order to bring this surprising but obvious pearl of paper futuristics to the worldwide multi-billion dollar industry that it had the potential to become.

The soon to be recognized problem was the complexity of the various types of thermal paper compliant with each make and model of fax machine which quickly was replacing teletype and telex machines. It was not until 1985 that McDermid's Research and Development Department broke through the variables of the image barrier to create an applied thermal generic that would reduce user cost and bring a high quality product to retail shelves all over the world.

McDermid marketing managers chose the stationery and business machine distribution lanes to launch their most important paper improvement idea in the company's history. To this day, original packaging and simplified marketing concept, created by Lance and Michael McDermid, has not been improved upon, making the trade name Telefax, an international standard for manufacturing specifications everywhere.

In between and since those years of implementation and change, McDermid Paper Converters, always concerned with protecting the environment, has introduced innumerable basic fundamentals that form an integral part of the industry as a whole.

The best example of this is soon to be revealed in a new applied to paper "host" invention. The value equivalent has not been seen in the paper industry over the last half century. This new inventive process carries a worldwide patent and will soon be recognized in offices large and small, wherever photocopiers and high-speed printing presses are in use.

The future of paper converting will continue to develop and expand. Products in demand, such as McDermid's specialty and digital printing paper, will change to meet the needs of the new Millennium. And McDermid Paper Converters is determined to lead the way.

The 1999 team at W.C. Wood Company Limited

IF W.C. WOOD were alive today he would be amazed that the small farm machinery business he founded in 1930 had grown and expanded to become Canada's largest freezer manufacturer and the largest Canadian owned appliance manufacturer in the world. Wilbert Copeland (Bert) Wood was born in 1896; a time when Ontarians like his grandfather John and his Uncle Charles were still clearing land for farming. Bert was raised on a farm in Luther Township until 1909 when (like many Ontarians) his family trekked to Saskatchewan where they took a homestead.

He graduated in the early 1920s from the University of Saskatchewan in Agricultural Engineering and joined Massey-Harris in Toronto. He worked as a research engineer on Massey's new farm machinery until the Great Depression forced Massey to lay him off in 1930.

Bert Wood saw the introduction of electrical power across rural Ontario as an opportunity for a new business and founded W.C. Wood Company Limited in February 1930. His first product was an electrically powered grain grinder, which would save farmers the necessity of having to transport grain from the farm to the feed mills and back to the farm for feed. He had parts for his grinder cast and tooled at a local machine shop and he assembled them on the back porch of his landlady's home. With the $150.00 he received from a Brampton area farmer for his first grinder, he established his new business.

Wood rented an empty candy shop on Howard Park Avenue in Toronto, bought a lathe, and machined his own castings for his electric grinders. In 1934 he moved to a larger factory on Dundas Street north of Bloor in Toronto, where he expanded his electrical farm equipment line to include an oat roller, a farm milking machine and a bulk milk cooler. It was the refrigeration system designed for the milk coolers that gave Wood a new idea and in 1938 the first electrically operated farm freezer was born. Little did he realize that this product would be the stepping stone on the path from farm equipment to appliance manufacturer.

In 1941, the company moved from Toronto to a 25,000 sq. ft. factory at 123 Woolwich Street in Guelph where, for the next 15 years, it grew, prospered, and expanded to a facility of 40,000 sq. ft. By 1956 another move was necessary. The company acquired the Taylor Forbes property and moved its manufacturing operation to an existing 90,000 sq. ft. plant at 5 Arthur Street South in Guelph where it continued to grow. By 1963, additional space was required and the first of many additions was undertaken.

During this time of immense growth another change took place. In 1974, Bert Wood, at the age of 78, stepped down as acting president and handed the reins over to his eldest son, John Frederick Wood. John had been working in the family business since he was a young boy and, after graduating in business from the University of Western Ontario, he naturally assumed the responsibility put before him and today remains the company's second president.

Young John F. Wood visits the family firm, 1944

John F. Wood, President, W.C. Wood Company Limited   **W.C. Wood, Founder, W.C. Wood Company Limited**

By 1985 the company had expanded its product line to include chest and upright freezers, compact refrigerators, compact kitchens, humidifiers and dehumidifiers. It was now operating two facilities totaling 600,000 sq. ft. and, although 95 percent of what was manufactured was for the domestic market, the company was shipping to the United States, Europe, Asia, and the Caribbean. With free trade becoming a very real possibility the company began to focus on a North American market strategy.

In the second half of the 1980s, as exports began to grow, it became apparent that a U.S. facility was necessary in order to keep operating costs in line and remain internationally competitive. In April 1990, W.C. Wood Company opened a 137,000 sq. ft. factory in Ottawa, Ohio, to manufacture upright freezers for the North American market.

This new plant has provided numerous benefits to the corporation, including significantly lower operating costs in serving the U.S. market, an expanding product line to meet North American needs, and significant additional capacity for its growing North American market. While most of the company's growth over the past decade has been outside Canada, and while the U.S. facility has expanded to over 370,000 sq. ft., the U.S. facility has given the company a broader product base which has resulted in a significant increase to Canadian-made exports.

Today, more than 50 percent of the company's

Canadian production is exported, and both Canadian and American facilities have seen employment growth. By 1995, a third plant was added to the Guelph-based operation, and it is managed today by W.C.'s grandson, David Wood.

Over the years, the company has received many awards from various sources for its products including the National Industrial Design Award, numerous customer recognition awards, the Province of Ontario "A" for Achievement Award, the California Energy Award, The Canadian Award of Business Excellence, and the Guelph Quality Award. This past year the company president, John Wood, received the HAIL (Home Appliance Industry Leader) Award. He is the first Canadian to receive such an honour.

In 1977, W.C. Wood produced its one-millionth freezer and by 1997 the company celebrated the production of its ten-millionth appliance.

W.C. Wood Company remains a privately owned Canadian Company that does not believe in absentee landlords and today there are eight family members working in various areas within the organization. The Company's objective is to see that at the end of every year its suppliers, customers, employees, and shareholders are each a little better off as a result of being in business. The company and its employees will continue to focus on productivity, quality, customer effectiveness, integrity, and organizational effectiveness as the cornerstones of its business.

ISECO

An Equal Opportunity Employer

A worker in El Salvador holds up an ISECO box containing a pair of safety boots donated by the company to help "needy people" in a number of countries. Through the years ISECO has sent boots and shoes to Columbia, Bolivia, Africa, Romania, Bosnia, as well as to native peoples in Canada.

SAFETY REGULATIONS were virtually non-existent in 1938 when George Munnings opened a business to sell safety equipment. More than six decades later, ISECO – letters to represent "Industrial Safety Equipment Co. Ltd." – is still family owned and the largest company of its kind in Canada. It has 20 stores and a fleet of more than 30 vehicles serving thousands of customers across the nation.

George's first shop in Etobicoke sold leggings, coats, first aid kits, and head, eye, and ear protective devices. Within a year, his father and two brothers joined the company which moved to Toronto in 1941, back to Etobicoke in 1945, and in 1990, settled in a new head office and modern plant in Mississauga.

Today's president Garry Munnings attributes ISECO's growth to listening to the needs of customers and being innovative in developing safety gear for workers in the steel, forestry, electrical, automotive, railway, lumber, and construction industries, and more recently for those in the hospital and hospitality services.

In 1947, for instance, ISECO added safety boots to their product line by signing a contract with the Tillsonburg Shoe Company. That year, brother Ted suggested ISECO's products be taken on the road. The first travelling unit was a trailer towed by his own car and, by 1959, six vehicles were in use.

ISECO continued to expand, establishing a boot and shoe company at Detroit in 1955, and by carrying on research that has resulted in making a number of specialized products such as static dissipating soled shoes for workers in the aircraft and computer industries where a static shock could purge valuable files, and puncture-proof metatarsalguard ballistic nylon boots for police force riot squads. ISECO also signed contracts with manufacturers of specialized equipment, such as non-slip footwear for the food service industry.

With the passing of numerous safety regulations in the mid-1960s, Bob Munnings, who became president in 1971, worked closely with the Canadian Standards Association in developing safety codes for footwear and other accessories.

Five years later, the company ventured into western Canada when Buchanan Safety in Edmonton was acquired and became its western headquarters. In 1979, Capital Safety at Regina was added and, in 1980, ISECO entered the Maritimes, acquiring the Palmer-McClellan Company at Fredericton, New Brunswick, which, in addition to selling and distributing safety shoes and clothing, also manufactured the highly regarded Moosehead brand name that has been retained. In 1986 ISECO also acquired Chaussures Sécurité Lamontagne in Montreal to make it a regional head office in Quebec.

To date, three generations of the Munnings family have been the driving force behind the success of ISECO. Following George as president was his younger brother Bob and now George's son, Garry. Randy (Bob's son) is the General Manager, Devin (Garry's son) is National Sales Manager/Director of Marketing, and Kim (Garry's daughter) is the Human Relations Manager. Garry is emphatic, however, that the dedication of employees coupled with listening to customer needs and meeting those needs with quality products at fair prices are the reasons, along with God's help, ISECO has continued to "thrive and grow for six decades."

An early innovation by ISECO was using vans to provide mobile stores, the first being a trailer in 1946. There are now 30 especially designed vans on the road across Canada, each carrying safety products such as gloves, safety glasses, ear plugs, and work clothing as well as up to 1,000 to 1,200 pairs of shoes in about 75 styles.

Canadian Auto Workers Union

CAW ✦ TCA
CANADA

THE CANADIAN AUTO WORKER'S Union approaches the new millennium with confidence, determination, and an increasingly diverse membership that reflects the changing face of Canada.

The CAW is Canada's largest private sector union. Its 238,000 members work from coast to coast to coast in virtually every sector of the economy. The union's membership is diverse with members from a rainbow of cultural backgrounds who have made major contributions to the growth of a strong, vibrant, and progressive workers movement.

The CAW is one of Canada's most active unions – constantly in the forefront of the fight for better working conditions for all workers. In 1985 the CAW left the U.S. based UAW with a strong desire to influence Canadian society. It began to forge its own distinct path in the struggle for workers' rights.

Since that time, the CAW has doubled the size of its membership through mergers with smaller unions and the effort to organize the unorganized.

Unions were born out of the struggle of working people to build better lives both in the workplace and in the broader society – struggles for greater equality, fairness, recognition, and security. They have fought for medicare, public pensions, and unemployment benefits. Reduced working time means more time with families and jobs for young people. Our gains in collective bargaining have led to higher standards for all workers in Canada.

As we enter a new century, one in three Canadian workers belong to unions. Yet every worker, every retiree and indeed every citizen enjoys the benefits of our collective struggle for a better society.

The CAW has built over the years a strong reputation of fighting for human rights and equality issues both within the workplace and across society. Simply put, racism, sexism, homophobia, and other prejudices had to be challenged in the workplace and beyond. The CAW was in the forefront of the international solidarity movement to bring about an end to apartheid in South Africa.

Within its ranks in Canada, the CAW has established workers of colour caucuses, women's conferences and women' s leadership courses, human rights committees, regional and national workers of colour and human rights conferences, to encourage the participation and the development of leadership skills among all its membership.

The union has also developed a worker's of colour Leadership program to encourage and to build strong participation and leadership from within its diverse membership ranks.

Over the years the CAW has continuously pushed to recognize and encourage the full participation of all its members. As the union enters a new millennium it, like the rest of society, faces greater and more complex challenges. The negative impact of globalization, free trade, the growing income gap, pollution, rapid technological change, continuing workplace inequalities, and so much more will test not only the union's leadership, but also its membership.

Much work remains to be done. But the challenges of this new millennium will be met by the CAW – a union that has built a solid foundation by tapping into the full potential of its increasingly diverse membership.

Buzz Hargrove, President, CAW

Imasco

In Step with Canada's Evolving Consumer Markets

IMASCO LIMITED, with headquarters in Montreal, was formed in 1970 to diversify Imperial Tobacco Company into other consumer markets. For 30 years, the company acquired and invested in other businesses, expanding the potential of each. Along the way it astutely adjusted its portfolio, retaining only those companies with the greatest promise.

In January 2000, shareholders accepted an acquisition proposal from UK-based British American Tobacco, and Imasco's operations will now carry on under new ownership. These companies have achieved outstanding success by keeping abreast of the evolving needs of Canada's diverse, ever-expanding family. Their continued success is a lasting legacy to Imasco, one of the most successful corporations in Canadian history.

Imperial Tobacco

Canada's largest tobacco enterprise, whose brand families Player's, du Maurier, and Matinée lead the domestic market.

Imperial Tobacco Company was incorporated in 1912 when the Canadian tobacco industry was still in its infancy. Begun as a consolidation of two Montreal companies, Imperial acquired many other Canadian tobacco businesses over its 88-year history. Its greatest growth spurt came following World War II when the company constructed additional plants in Ontario and Quebec, and Imperial engineers developed machinery for processing leaf tobacco that ultimately became licensed to manufacturers around the world. Imperial recently invested upwards of $230 million in state-of-the-art production facilities and information systems that will ensure the company's competitiveness far into the future.

The passing decades have wrought many changes in the tobacco industry, and Imperial's hallmark has been the capacity to adapt to market requirements. For instance, health concerns emerging in the 1960s led to greater regulation of tobacco products. By the early '70s Imperial voluntarily discontinued all TV and radio advertising and, in response to changing consumer preferences, developed lighter brands. These products were well received, and by 1980 Player's was Canada's most popular cigarette.

The company has long been a supporter of Canadian performing arts. du Maurier Arts Foundation was founded in 1971 to stimulate entertainment developed by Canadians and performed by Canadian artists from coast to coast. With total contributions of many millions of dollars, the Foundation is indelibly linked with some of Canada's finest artistic accomplishments.

Shoppers Drug Mart

Canada's leading drugstore group, with 824 stores, meeting health-care needs through personalized, convenient pharmacy services.

Shoppers Drug Mart traces its beginnings to the day a young Toronto man inherited two city drugstores. Scarcely 20 years old, Murray Koffler rose to the challenge presented by his pharmacist father's sudden death by enrolling in pharmacy school and learning the heart of the business. He then set about redefining the 20th century drugstore. First, Koffler ripped out his stores' soda fountains, determined to emphasize the pharmaceutical dispensaries. He required his pharmacists to wear starched white coats as a symbol of their professionalism. In the general merchandise sections, he developed groundbreaking, consumer-oriented approaches to displaying and promoting products.

In today's tobacco industry, being a cost-effective producer is a market imperative. Imperial Tobacco's new, high-speed cigarette makers are part of the company's $118-million investment in streamlining and modernizing manufacturing operations to increase productivity.

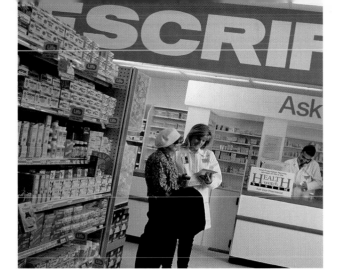

In the mid-'50s, Koffler began acquiring other drug-stores, instituting a franchising model in which pharmacist "associates" owned and operated their own stores. The concept became a cornerstone of the system's success. In 1962, Koffler's 17-store chain became known as Shoppers Drug Mart. The company went public, and major expansion occurred through acquisitions and mergers during the 1960s and '70s. Upon entering the chain, a store would typically double its profits from the previous year.

When it came time to sell his business in the late 1970s, Murray Koffler chose Imasco chiefly because of its strong financial position, but also because of the company's reputation for generous contributions to Canadian causes. Koffler had cultivated a strong tradition of community giving at Shoppers, carving out leadership roles for the company in public-health education and hospital support.

Shoppers Drug Mart has continued to grow and develop, in step with the evolving Canadian health-care system. Its pharmacists are important liaisons between physician and patient, counselling patients with chronic diseases such as diabetes and asthma to better manage their own care. It's a far cry from soda fountain days!

Canada Trust

A leader in Canadian personal banking services.

In 1986 Imasco acquired Canada Trust, one of the most respected financial institutions in Canada. The company started up in 1854 – Canada's frontier days – as the Huron & Erie Savings and Loan Society (H&E) in London, Ontario, then the country's western edge.

In pre-confederation days, Canadian banks handled commercial accounts only, and private citizens literally stashed their savings under mattresses. H&E was one of the earliest "building societies," innovative enterprises in which individuals pooled their savings to loan farmers the funds to buy land. Farmers paid back the money in monthly instalments of principal plus interest – another innovation. These loans remained H&E's dominant business until 1898, when the company acquired General Trust Corporation of Calgary. The subsidiary "Canada Trust" was formed, and the name eventually encompassed the corporate identity.

Business was difficult during the Depression years, particularly in the Prairies where drought led to the abandonment of both land and loans. The company helped its beleaguered customers by advancing money for seed, and sometimes by accepting harvested crops as payments on mortgages. Not surprisingly, profits dwindled and did not return to 1930 levels until 1950. Following World War II, the company launched a growth strategy of acquiring other trust companies.

During the '60s and '70s, Canada Trust continued to emphasize personal financial services, cultivating a reputation of friendliness and convenience. Innovations such as 8-to-8 service amazed a public used to traditional banking hours. The tradition of convenience evolved further in the '80s and '90s, thanks to technology, until, by now, Canada Trust customers have come to depend on a "comfortable banking experience" like no other.

Brothers Jeff and Malcolm Firkser, owners of
Newtonbrook Home Hardware in Toronto, Ontario.

Father-son team Ramzan and Rahim
Dadani own Nordel Home Hardware in
Delta, British Columbia.

Home Hardware Stores Ltd.

WITH 1,100 STORES in every province and territory in Canada, Home Hardware is a strong, contributing member of the communities it serves. And like those communities, the company has become more culturally diverse over the years. Ramzan and Rahim Dadani, a father-son team who own and operate Nordel Home Hardware in Delta, British Columbia, are examples of that cultural diversity in action.

After immigrating to Canada from Tanzania in 1971, Ramzan Dadani held jobs as a baker and janitor before purchasing a small corner hardware store in 1976. By the time the store became Home Hardware in 1983, it had grown from 75 to 650 square metres and had established a very loyal clientele, despite the large chain retailers going up around them. "We've built a successful business based on a reputation of integrity, value and service," said Rahim Dadani, who joined his father as a business partner in 1994. "My dad is very involved in the community. He places a lot of importance on building relationships with our customers, and we've been rewarded with the community's continued support."

Like the Dadanis, brothers Jeff and Malcolm Firkser have found a winning formula in the hardware business. They left South Africa in 1979 to escape political unrest, intending to distribute a line of housewares in Canada. A visit to a friend who owned a Home Hardware store gave them a better idea.

Today, they operate Newtonbrook and Sunnybrook Home Hardware stores in Toronto, Ontario. "Home Hardware has been very successful for us," said Jeff Firkser, who started the business with his father Bernie and was later joined by Malcolm. "We've adapted our business to better suit the diverse communities we serve, and Home Hardware's excellent buying power allows us the flexibility to bring in products our customers are looking for."

For the Frisker's, it was their first meeting with Walter Hachborn that inspired them to join Home Hardware's national dealer network. Walter Hachborn and two partners founded Home Hardware in 1964, creating a cooperative of dealer-owned and operated independent stores based on the traditional entrepreneurial spirit of vision and determination. In December 1999, Walter Hachborn was named Retailer of the Century by a leading hardware and building supply industry publication. In 2000, Mr. Hachborn received the Order of Canada for his commitment to small business and the well being of his community.

Since its inception, Home Hardware has been a community-based business, one that encourages its dealers to craft meaningful, long-term relationships with the communities they serve. It's a philosophy that has built one of the strongest retail forces in the country, and will contribute to its future success in this constantly changing Canadian retail landscape.

The Integral Group

Building Effective E-Commerce Solutions

WHILE the tools of a software integrator have changed dramatically over the past ten years, the basic goal remains the same: make sure disparate computer systems co-operate seamlessly to help people work more effectively. All organizations rely on a unique combination of hardware and software to meet their individual needs, and with the arrival of the new century it is becoming increasingly critical for all these components to be connected solidly together. Unfortunately this often requires connections where they were never anticipated, basically fitting proverbial square pegs into round holes where they were least expected. This is where Integral Consulting Inc. plays a key role.

In 1986, less than five years after arriving in Canada from her native Hungary, Emma Perlaky, having finished consulting to IBM on their upcoming AS/400 business computer platform, founded Integral Consulting in Toronto, to serve what would quickly become a healthy AS/400 mid-range market. Integral's broad experience and technical flexibility helped many of its first customers take advantage of constantly evolving techniques and practices.

Within a year Integral expanded its services to include a rapidly emerging practice called "electronic commerce," which referred to a number of separate but interconnected technologies allowing organizations to use their computers in more valuable ways. Electronic Data Interchange, for example, allowed documents and transactions to be communicated instantaneously between companies. The use of bar-code labels on merchandize allowed shipping, warehousing, and retail computers to track goods precisely. Electronic Funds Transfer made financial transactions faster and more reliable. Integral helped its customers take advantage of these new business tools.

In the new millennium, Integral has expanded its expertise to assist customers to take advantage of Internet-enabled electronic commerce. Using the latest technologies such as the World Wide Web, Java, and Lotus Domino, Integral builds effective e-commerce solutions by combining these technical tools with solid business experience. Integral's range of skills is broad enough to utilize the many different types of computer systems which need to work together in order to provide the greatest benefit. That is exactly the kind of service Integral Consulting Inc. continues to concentrate on, aided largely by two assets which Emma Perlaky brought with her from Hungary: her two sons, Tamas and Zoltan, both of whom play key roles in developing the implementation of these technologies seamlessly into the daily operations of customers despite a rapidly changing and sometimes confusing field.

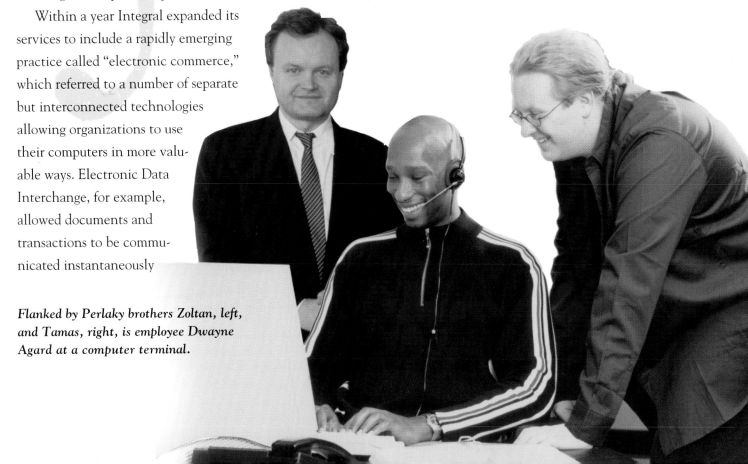

Flanked by Perlaky brothers Zoltan, left, and Tamas, right, is employee Dwayne Agard at a computer terminal.

DaimlerChrysler Canada

Building a Future for Canada

WHEN the Chrysler Corporation of Detroit, Michigan, experienced its first international expansion, it was a mere 11 days old: June 17, 1925, and Walter P. Chrysler couldn't wait any longer to expand his corporate enterprise. As a result, the Chrysler Corporation of Canada Ltd. was established across the Detroit River in Windsor, Ontario.

Proximity and a tradition of cross-border commerce between the two cities made the expansion to Windsor a logical step. Nonetheless, Chrysler's gambit was a bold and radical business manoeuvre, given the year and economic climate. The expansion established the Chrysler corporate identity early on: a world leader; a tireless, peerless innovator, a nation-builder.

As well, this first, early expansion established a precedent. Nearly three quarters of a century later, the Chrysler Corporation and Chrysler Canada Ltd. expanded their corporate borders through their dynamic groundbreaking merger with the German auto maker and transportation giant Daimler-Benz.

For Chrysler Canada Ltd., this meant a formal change in corporate identity, as the Chrysler Corporation was no longer just a North American auto maker, it was well on its way to realizing what had been a corporate goal for many years – becoming the world's foremost producer of transportation technology. In June 1999, Chrysler Canada Ltd. became DaimlerChrysler Canada Inc.

And with this change in corporate identity and an increased international presence came a renewed commitment to the many social and educational programs that Chrysler Canada had instituted and maintained over their first 73 years of existence. Now, DaimlerChrysler Canada is able to extend its corporate proactivity on not only a local (community-based) and national scale but on an international scale as well. And if you are planning on galvanizing the globe through transportation technology, you might as well be a global citizen.

Global corporate citizenry is an integral part of DaimlerChrysler's corporate identity for the new millennium.

Landry's Legacy: Forging the Global Link

But global citizenry begins at home. The late G. Yves Landry who served as Chairman, President, and Chief Executive Officer of Chrysler Canada Ltd. from 1990 to 1998, recognized this and incorporated it into his vision of Canadian industry working hand-in-hand with academia to create a curriculum that was more in tune with the needs of those same Canadian businesses and industries.

Perhaps Mr. Landry's most enduring corporate legacy is his founding of the University of Windsor-DaimlerChrysler Canada Automotive Research and Development Centre which was established in Windsor in 1996 with the support of all three levels of government – federal, provincial, and municipal.

The prestigious Synergy Award was presented to DaimlerChrysler Canada in 1998. It is presented annually by the National Council and the Conference Board of Canada to recognize the most outstanding collaborative partnerships between academia and industry.

Under this partnership, a culturally diverse group of students based in Canada's automotive capital, are given the opportunity to increase their employability (in Canada, one in seven jobs is related to the auto industry) by learning, first hand, the technological skills that are mandatory in Canada's multi-skilled workforce. Ranging from undergraduate to post-doctoral, the students are benefited by a facility that includes: a curriculum which allows them to work on research projects that have actual, practical applications in DaimlerChrysler products and the automotive industry at large; use of the most advanced vehicle testing equipment and facilities; and easy access to the tutelage and guidance of instructors who are the foremost automotive researchers in the world. Indeed, the University of Windsor-DaimlerChrysler Canada Automotive Research and Development Centre is the only facility of its kind – anywhere.

John Mann, who is the Director of Engineering at the Research and Development Centre, points to the uniqueness of the partnership formed between DaimlerChrysler Canada and the University of Windsor, saying that it "transcends the traditional concept of industrially funded academic research" because the partnership is truly collaborative and the facility's budget is "not intended to cover any internal manufacturing costs. There is no direct profit associated with what we do. It's strictly research and development with an education focus. It is investment in our futures. And it is here in Canada, for Canadians most notably here in Windsor, the automotive capital of Canada."

Strength through Diversity

Part of being a corporate-industrial/educational leader is recognizing that you need to be at the front of the pack. Yves Landry recognized, at a very high level, that what was being done as far as collaboration between academia and industry in Canada was not enough.

Interestingly, it was DaimlerBenz, based in Stuttgart, Germany, and their highly successful collaborative efforts with postsecondary institutions in their community, that provided a solid model upon which the Windsor experiment was launched.

Through the recent merger and through collaborative projects throughout North America and Europe, DaimlerChrysler has achieved the employee diversity – from cultural background to educational experiences and specializations – that leads to innovative and analytical thinking of the highest order, which in turn leads to the kinds of ideas and concepts that make DaimlerChrysler an industry leader from both community and global perspectives.

Mr. Landry referred to this union of industry, academia, and government as "Forging the Link," and his metaphor rings true five years later as what began as a local project has become an international success story. Indeed, the merger with DaimlerBenz can be seen as the ultimate "forging of the link."

And the results have been … stellar. National honours have been, and continue to be, bestowed. Recently the University of Windsor-DaimlerChrysler Canada Automotive Research and Development Centre was awarded The Conference Board of Canada – Royal Bank of Canada Post-Secondary Award for Excellence in Business – Educational Partnerships. And in 1998, the centre earned the prestigious NSERC and Conference Board of Canada sponsored National Synergy Award in the large industry category for the synergistic benefits that have resulted from this unique collaboration between academia and industry.

The award itself is a uniquely Canadian symbol of synergy. The bronze, hand-sculpted award depicts seven Canada geese flying in their distinctive "V" formation. "Geese," says Mann "are the perfect, naturally occurring symbol of synergy because geese flying together can fly higher, faster, and further than they ever could fly as individuals."

The added synergistic symbolism, given the Daimler-Chrysler merger, is hard to refute: like the flight of the Canada geese, DaimlerChrysler's journey towards diversification has global implications.

Hyd-Mech Group

World Leader in Band Saw Technology

THE DEVELOPMENT of highly technical band saw machines used to cut virtually every metal product used by industry in more than two dozen countries can be traced to a Polish-born engineer who came to Canada in 1966 and founded Hyd-Mech at Woodstock, in southwestern Ontario.

A university graduate in engineering from Germany with a postgraduate degree in science from his native land, Stanley K. Jasinski gave up a successful career in his own country in 1966 because he dreamed of one day having his own company. Since that was not possible in Poland, he and his wife and three children drove across the border into Germany and immigrated to Canada that year.

Settling in Woodstock, Ontario, Mr. Jasinski worked for other companies for a dozen years before leaving one manufacturing plant as chief design engineer to strike out on his own in 1978. Naming the company Hyd-Mech, at first Stan developed and produced hydraulic equipment, initially specializing in machines for the forest industry. He also designed a roll-forming machine for producing eavestroughing, a power steering system for heavy vehicles and a telescopic dump cylinder for the 300-ton General Motors trucks, before being faced with a need for a mitering band saw capable of cutting through metal.

Unable to find what he needed, he designed and built his own mitering band saw in 1980 and within months found business associates and machine dealers so interested in buying the unit that he decided Hyd-Mech would concentrate its efforts in band saw technology. The success of this decision was almost instant: from sales of just $80,000 in 1980, the company surpassed the $1 million mark in 1983. Nine years later it surpassed the $10 million mark and since then its manufacturing of three distinct families of metal cutting band saws are being used for virtually every production application, enabling Hyd-Mech to become a leading manufacturer of band saw machines worldwide.

In fact, today it has captured some 70 percent of the Canadian market, and its success in the United

States caused the establishment of a plant in Houston, Texas, in 1991 and at Pueblo, Colorado, in 1995, each plant specializing in manufacturing its own particular models.

In Houston, it is the H Series, described as horizontal guillotine style saws that are designed for straight heavy duty cut-offs and where the all-function control console allows an operator to program up to 99 different jobs including both piece length and piece count and with the ability to do five jobs consecutively.

In Colorado, the V-Series are vertical style saws that miter in both directions and are also capable of programming up to 99 jobs. Both models initially developed at the company's research and development centre in Woodstock which, besides its research facility, also produces the S series and M series of machines that have swing heads for cutting miters and straight cuts.

In total, some 20 different models are being produced and marketed in the three plants, with metal cutting applications ranging from 10 inches for the smaller units to 80 inches and a workload of 75,000 pounds for the larger band saws.

Headquarters for Hyd-Mech remains in Woodstock where Mr. Jasinski, in addition to being Chairman, continues taking a particular interest in the research aspect of the business now under the direction of his son-in-law, Pat Whitehead, who has been with the company since it began. Another member of the management team is Machine Shop Supervisor Mieczyslaw Jaszczur. As Machine Shop Supervisor, he has also played a major role in the company's success. Two

others who have been with the company since leaving school are Ian Tatham and Jim Hutchison, Vice Presidents respectively of Sales & Marketing and Customer Services which now has a dealer network encompassing nearly all the countries of Europe as well as Mexico, Argentina, Japan, Korea, Malaysia, New Zealand, and Australia.

The Woodstock plant employs roughly half the 200 employees in North America and retains the corporate offices. It also produces the S-Series and M-Series of band saws that together with the models produced in the United states, are being utilized by manufacturing plants, steel service centres, structural fabricators and such high-tech organizations as the auto and aerospace industries.

Mr. Jasinski attributes the success of Hyd-Mech to excellence in engineering "through our own research and development, followed by quality manufacturing to ensure longevity and productivity of all Hyd-Mech products." This point is backed up in the company brochure for each series that claims Hyd-Mech is dedicated to produce the most rugged and economical saws available, to provide innovative engineering to stay well ahead of competitors, and to produce the variety of products and options to fit any particular production requirements.

"The fact that our organization is oriented towards satisfying customer needs, and takes pride in meeting whatever those needs are is another reason for our success to date, and we intend remaining a world leader in band saw technology in the future," says Mr. Jasinski.

Hyd-Mech headquarters,
Woodstock, Ontario

Kaneff Group of Companies

Building Today for Tomorrow

IT WAS A RISKY venture in 1957, but Ignat Kaneff, with characteristic visionary zeal, built the very first apartment building in Mississauga, Ontario, a nine-suite unit that was immediately rented. Since then, there has been no looking back....

Strategic planning has led the company to diversify into such real estate specialization, as land development and property management of both residential and commercial properties. Landmark office buildings, along with retail commercial plazas, gas retail outlets, a car wash and several renowned golf courses are also an integral part of the Kaneff Group of Companies holdings.

Born in Gorno Ablanovo, Bulgaria, Ignat Kaneff immigrated to Toronto, Ontario, in 1951. By the end of his first year in Canada, he had purchased a building lot and subsequently built his own home. Borrowing against the home, he purchased two more lots and built two additional houses. He fondly remembers his friend Mariano Elia, who gave him a chance to sell homes on lots usually reserved for established builders. Mr. Kaneff attributes this generosity as one reason why, by 1956, as President of Kaneff Properties Limited, he had built nearly 50 homes.

The company's focus was on constructing customized single family homes in the Mississauga area, but shifted its attention in the 1960s to apartment buildings and hi-rise condominiums and the many commercial towers dominating Mississauga's landscape today. By year 2000, thousands of dwelling units had been constructed by the Kaneff Group of Companies, the majority of these homes appearing in Halton and Peel Regions, heeding Iggy's father's advice to build within proximity in order to service clients best.

The Kaneff Group of Companies has also developed five prominent golf courses. Kaneff's Lionhead Golf and Country Club, located in Brampton, Ontario, is one of the finest golf courses in North America. Over 70,000 golfers annually enjoy this world-class, 36-hole course.

In honour of Iggy Kaneff's 60th birthday, in 1986, the Ignat Kaneff Charitable Foundation was established to benefit education, health, social services and the arts throughout the Peel Region. A great many community organizations have enjoyed a long-standing relationship with the Foundation, including the University of Toronto, Erindale Campus; The Mississauga Symphony Orchestra; Community Living of Mississauga; several area hospitals, including Credit Valley Hospital; Erin Oak; United Way; Breakfast for Children; Living Arts Centre; and local sports teams.

Mr. Kaneff received the 1982 Mississauga Board of Trade Business Person of the Year Award and, in 2000, he received the Business Person of the Year Award from the Brampton Board of Trade.

Kaneff Group of Companies has an enviable reputation in the marketplace for superior quality and service. It is a reputation the company and its founder richly deserve.

Kaneff Mississauga Skyline

Legends, Lionhead Golf Course, Brampton

The Canadian Race Relations Foundation

"Aiming to help bring about a more harmonious Canada that acknowledges its racist past, recognizes the pervasiveness of racism today, and is committed to creating a future in which all Canadians are treated equitably and fairly."

Historical significance

In 1988, the Government of Canada and the National Association of Japanese Canadians signed the Japanese Canadian Redress Agreement, which acknowledged that the treatment of Japanese Canadians during and after World War II was unjust and violated principles of human rights. The federal government also promised to create a foundation that would "foster racial harmony and cross-cultural understanding and help to eliminate racism."

Opening the doors to fostering racial harmony

The federal government proclaimed the Canadian Race Relations Foundation Act into law on October 28, 1996. The Canadian Race Relations Foundation (CRRF) was officially opened in November 1997. It has registered charitable status and is governed by a national board of directors, with day-to-day operations managed by an executive director and CEO. Strategically located in Toronto, the Foundation's activities reach out in support of organizations across Canada.

In accordance with the Japanese Canadian Redress Agreement, the federal government provided the Foundation with a $24 million endowment fund. The Foundation's annual operational budget is generated from investments and donations.

Our Mission

The CRRF's commitment to building a national framework for the fight against racism in Canada encompasses all aspects of our programs by:
- Shedding light on the causes and manifestations of racism;
- Providing independent, outspoken national leadership;
- Pursuing equity, fairness and social justice.

Our work focus

We address different issues of importance to racialized minorities and Aboriginal peoples with an emphasis on eliminating racism in employment and education through our three program initiatives.

- Contract Research Program invites submission of research proposals to further knowledge about employment equity for racialized minorities and Aboriginal peoples; racism and Aboriginal peoples; and racism and youth. Proposals are requested every two years. The findings are subsequently announced.

- Initiatives Against Racism Sponsorship program supports public awareness projects across Canada developed by community and non-governmental organizations. Funding eligibility is based on their efforts to foster harmony and dispel popular misconceptions about racialized minorities and Aboriginal peoples.

- Award of Excellence program recognizes public, private and voluntary organizations whose efforts represent excellence and innovation in combating racism. Nominations are invited for this biennial event and assessed by an independent awards jury.

The Foundation speaks out on selected current issues and undertakes public speaking engagements; publishes a newsletter, CRRF Perspectives; and produces fact sheets on topical issues. A rich collection of resource materials forms the basis of our clearinghouse. This information is available through our website at www.crr.ca together with links to organizations, government departments and institutions that work towards the elimination of racism.

The Honourable Lincoln Alexander, founding Chair of the Canadian Race Relations Foundation.

The Foundation's "Unite Against Racism" Campaign is the largest and most diverse anti-racism campaign of its kind in Canadian history.

Nelson Mandela Children's Fund

"There can be no keener revelation of a society's soul than the way in which it treats its children." Nelson Rolihlahla Mandela

CANADIAN FRIENDS
of the
Nelson Mandela
CHILDREN'S FUND

NELSON MANDELA, former President of South Africa (1994-99) and Nobel Peace Prize Laureate (1993), brought his vision of a brighter future for children of all nations to Toronto's SkyDome on September 25, 1998.

A beloved world leader who had been imprisoned in his homeland for 27 years because of his relentless struggle against the system of racial segregation known as "apartheid," Mr. Mandela received a thunderous and emotional reception from 45,000 school children as he launched the Nelson Mandela Children's Fund (NMCF) in Canada.

The SkyDome event, "Mandela and the Children," was billed as "the largest classroom event in Canadian history." The students who were present and tens of thousands who watched on live television across the country listened intently as the President of South Africa spoke to them about the legacy of apartheid and the toll it had taken on the children of South Africa.

He thanked Canada for its unflinching opposition to apartheid and encouraged all Canadians to reach out to those less fortunate and to continue to fight against all forms of injustice. He spoke of "Ubuntu" the African concept of community that defines our human potential in terms of what we do for others.

"The spirit of Ubuntu – that profound African sense that we are human only through the humanity of other human beings – is not a parochial phenomenon, but has added globally to our common search for a better world."

Prime Minister Jean Chrétien, in his introductory remarks, reminded the young audience that they were participating in a truly historic event. "When you will be my age," said the Prime Minister, "you will tell your grandchildren I was there when Nelson Mandela came to Toronto and Canada."

The NMCF was established by Nelson Mandela when he was elected President of South Africa in 1994 and pledged one-third of his salary to the fund. The focus areas of the

NMCF are disadvantaged children and youth who fall in the following seven categories:

- Neglected, orphaned, abandoned and homeless
- Educationally deprived
- Disabled
- At risk of habitual delinquency
- Unemployed
- Sexually abused
- In crisis

Canadian Friends of the Nelson Mandela Children's F▮ (CFNMCF) was organized by Canadians who had been l▮ time supporters of the struggle against apartheid. The C▮ MCF raises money for the Children's Fund and also w▮ to raise awareness among Canadian school children and general public at large on the issues of discrimination, rac▮ and human rights.

Index